# Perspectives
# in American History

*Editors:* DONALD FLEMING *and* BERNARD BAILYN

VOLUME VII · 1973

## DISLOCATION AND EMIGRATION
The Social Background of
American Immigration

PUBLISHED BY THE

Charles Warren Center for Studies
in American History

HARVARD UNIVERSITY

*Perspectives in American History* is published annually by the Charles Warren Center for Studies in American History, Robinson Hall, Cambridge, Massachusetts, and is **sold by subscription only in advance of publication.** The Center does not assume responsibility for statements of fact or opinion made by the contributors. ¶ Yearly subscription, $7.50; five-year subscription, $35.00. ¶ All communications should be addressed to the Editors, Robinson Hall, Harvard University, Cambridge, Massachusetts 02138. ¶ Copyright © 1974 by the President and Fellows of Harvard College.

Printed at The Stinehour Press, Lunenburg, Vermont.

# DISLOCATION AND EMIGRATION

The Social Background of
American Immigration

## Contents

# INTRODUCTION

IN 'the age of white expansion' from 1450 to 1950," Leo Schelbert writes in his essay on the Swiss migration, "some seventy million are estimated to have left the European homeland for transoceanic areas (and Siberia) where they mingled with, pushed out, or destroyed the indigenous peoples. New Spains, New Englands, New Frances, New Hollands were created, even New Switzerlands or, more narrowly, New Berns and Nova Friburgos." It was a voluntary movement of such geographic range—to the east of Europe as well as to the west and south and north from the heartland of Europe and from its island fringes—involving such a mass of humanity over so long a period of time and with such permanent effect on the course of human history that it can be compared in importance only to the Romanization of the Mediterranean world after the Punic Wars or the invasion of the west by the Germanic peoples in the late Roman empire.

We shall never cease studying this massive movement of peoples and we shall never comprehend its totality, for its ramifications extend in one way or other to almost every aspect of the social history of the western world. Segments of this vast story must be brought into focus, however, if we are to understand the foundations of modern society. One small element of this history is the subject of the essays that follow.

For almost the whole of the past five hundred years the western hemisphere, and especially the United States, has been the chief magnet of these mass migrations. In all, close to fifty million people have migrated to the territory that now comprises the

United States, and the process still goes on, though in greatly reduced numbers. "If they could," Arthur Corwin writes in commenting on the Mexican *braceros*, "probably half the people of the world would walk to the United States," attracted by greater economic opportunity, or the hope of independence and personal fulfillment. But people in such numbers do not disrupt their lives and voyage to distant lands and to unknown futures merely because of the abstract prospect of betterment. They move because they feel they have to: because they are dislodged by immediate pressures set in motion by social and economic forces they cannot control. Such forces in the early modern era, and especially in the nineteenth century, swept through the European landmass touching almost every village, town, and city. "From Ireland to the Urals," Maldwyn Jones writes, "from the North Cape to Sicily, it was the pressure of rising population, coupled with the transformation of the old economic order, that dislodged people from their homes. But it would have been surprising if, in so vast and varied a continent, these forces had appeared everywhere simultaneously or if they had produced identical results in every country. In fact they did neither." They were as disparate, erratic, and as varied in their detailed character as the peoples they affected. Yet there are common characteristics in these dislocating pressures, and it was our hope, in assembling these essays on the migrations that helped people America, to consider some of these vital elements in the dislocating process.

For that purpose it was not necessary to concentrate on the numerically dominant sources of American immigration: Ireland, Italy, and Russia—though in subsequent issues we expect to publish essays on the dislocating pressures in those countries too. What was needed, we believe, were deep probes into the local springs of dislocation and emigration wherever such studies could be made— the deeper, the more intimate, the more concrete and personal, the better. Large-scale demographic analyses of overseas emigration, which have only recently begun to appear in any detail, will greatly advance our understanding of the overall history, but for our purposes the scale is not what matters: small-scale qualitative analyses are needed too, not only for conveying human realities in familiar form but for uncovering elements of the story that purely quantitative studies are not likely to reveal.

Thus Professor Schelbert, in his intense examination of the tiny community clustered in the Glarus Valley of Switzerland—a significant portion of whose population would ultimately migrate to southern Wisconsin—finds what no simple quantitative correlation would reveal: that there was no direct relation among the processes of economic modernization, human displacement, and overseas emigration. The mechanization of weaving in Glarus did displace the handicraft weavers, but it was not the weavers primarily who left the valley; it was, rather, a variety of others who felt the pressure indirectly and decided to leave. Similarly, probing the history of migrations in Wales, Professor Conway is able to illustrate the peculiar relationship among dislodgment of agricultural workers, industrialization, and eventual migration. For some, he writes, migration to industrial centers proved to be only "a knight's move" in their emigration to the United States; but for many more, relocation to the quickly developing South Wales industrial centers was a life experience similar to overseas emigration, for industrialization had created on the South Wales coalfield "a new Welsh nation, highly cohesive, Welsh-speaking, secure in its nonconformity, politically articulate, and potentially powerful as a nation within the United Kingdom." Without that target for its distressed and dislocated thousands, Wales might well have become a small-scale Ireland in the history of American immigration. So too in Germany industrialization drew off into short-range movements a mass population that was already dislodged from traditional roots and that otherwise might well have sought relocation overseas.

It is the *context* of dislocation and departure that we sought to examine. For nothing is more deceptive in historical study than explaining causes by analyzing effects: in this case explaining the sources and hence the character of American immigration by examining only those groups that ended up in America and their condition in the perspective of American society. In many cases their arrival in the United States was incidental to their desire to emigrate. Johann Chmelar's essay on the Austrian emigration makes clear that the tens of thousands of migrants propelled out from their original homes in the dense peasant concentrations of the Dual Monarchy could as well have ended in Argentina or Canada as in the United States, however attractive a choice America may have been. Wherever they resettled they bore the marks of their original dislodgment, marks that were shared with thousands who did not leave and with thousands more who left but only temporarily.

The appearance of a group in its original context can be quite different from its appearance in its new setting overseas. What was originally in the European context a group distinguished by its relative affluence, enterprise, and modernity appears in America to be part of an almost undifferentiated mass of a traditional-minded or regressive peasantry alien to the quasi-democratic norms of Anglo-American culture. What begins as success in surviving the pressures of poverty or oppression ends as a failure in adaptation. One must see the original setting to understand fully the ultimate resolution in America of the lives of the dislocated millions who account for so much of the peopling of the nation. The essays that follow—and others on other countries that will appear in subsequent issues—are contributions to the deepening of this perspective in the study of American history.

D.F.

B.B.

# THE BACKGROUND TO EMIGRATION FROM GREAT BRITAIN IN THE NINETEENTH CENTURY

Maldwyn A. Jones

# THE BACKGROUND TO EMIGRATION FROM GREAT BRITAIN IN THE NINETEENTH CENTURY

EMIGRATION from Europe in the century after 1815 owed its impetus to a single set of underlying forces. From Ireland to the Urals, from the North Cape to Sicily, it was the pressure of rising population, coupled with the transformation of the old economic order, that dislodged people from their homes. But it would have been surprising if, in so vast and varied a continent, these forces had appeared everywhere simultaneously or if they had produced identical results in every country. In fact they did neither. The social and economic changes which set people in motion occurred first in the extreme north and west of Europe and only spread to the south and east later in the century. The effect of these changes was, moreover, powerfully modified—even at times cancelled out—by special local conditions. European emigration did not, therefore, have a monolithic character or ebb and flow with uniformity. On the contrary there were significant variations between country and country in the volume, timing, and composition of the outflow. Each part of Europe had an emigration history of its own. Thus in order to comprehend fully the realities of European emigration the background to the movement in each part of the continent needs to be carefully studied. Nor will a country-by-country approach suffice. Emigrants should be seen as coming not from vaguely defined "countries of origin" but from particular provinces and regions, each with its own kind of response or lack of it to the forces shaping emigration.[1]

This last point is of particular relevance to an understanding of emigration from the country which first experienced the social and economic changes which were to produce a mass exodus. The political entity known as the United Kingdom did not have a common emigration history; emigration from Great Britain and emigration from Ireland were two quite separate phenomena. It is difficult enough for the historian of emigration to generalize about the larger of the two islands, for within it England, Wales, and Scotland each had distinct social and economic characteristics and responded in their own ways to the forces of change. But their economic and social history in the nineteenth century was sufficiently interconnected, overlapping, and similar to make it possible to treat them—though with due regard for local exceptionalism—as a unit. Moreover there was, as we shall see, a remarkable demographic similarity between English, Welsh, and Scottish emigration which provides a further justification for linking them together and for separating them from Irish emigration. Ireland, indeed, was a different case. Here was a society differently constituted from that of Great Britain, unaffected moreover by the forces of industrialization that were transforming the sister island, and with a different historical experience. Irish emigration may have been caused by the same basic forces as those operating in Great Britain, but it had a character and a rhythm all its own. To confuse the two is to risk distorting reality. If we confine ourselves to the aggregate flow from the United Kingdom the distinctive character of emigration from its component elements tends to be lost to view. For this reason as well as for reasons of length and emphasis this essay will deal with the Irish dimension only incidentally and for purposes of comparison. The focus will be upon the background to emigration from Great Britain, a subject which has too often been overshadowed by the more spectacular movement from Ireland.

1. Frank Thistlethwaite, "Migration from Europe Overseas in the Nineteenth and Twentieth Centuries," Comité International des Sciences Historiques, ed., *Rapports*, V (1960), 42–43.

The dramatic and possibly unprecedented rise in the population of Great Britain after 1750 has not yet been satisfactorily explained.[2] The prolonged scholarly controversy about the problem seems indeed to have done little more than demonstrate how little is known about population growth. Until recently it was believed that the main cause of the accelerating growth of Britain's population in the latter half of the eighteenth century was a fall in mortality, occasioned by such factors as the decline of gin drinking and improvements in diet, food supply, urban sanitation, and medical services. But in recent years previously accepted explanations for the fall in the death rate have been challenged and the search for causation has shifted to the pattern of mortality fluctuations and to the dynamics of endemic and epidemic disease. Moreover some scholars have suggested that the crucial factor in population growth was not a decline in mortality but a rise in fertility. But most of what has been written on fertility has been concerned with the short run, or based upon admittedly imperfect statistical materials, or has consisted merely of conjecture about the relationship between fertility and economic growth. There are still some grounds for believing that fertility rose and even better grounds for asserting that mortality fell. But we do not yet know much about long-term demographic trends in the late eighteenth and early nineteenth centuries, and we cannot therefore say with any certainty whether population growth in Britain, or for that matter elsewhere in Europe, was the consequence of a rise in fertility, a fall in mortality, or some combination of the two.

The date at which the increase in population began is not, however, in dispute; neither is the rate of growth nor the fact that it was general throughout Great Britain. There was no official count before 1801, but all the indications are that numbers began to grow about the middle of the eighteenth century and that the rate of growth accelerated to about ten percent per decade after 1780. In 1750 the British population may have numbered about seven mil-

2. Recent work on the problem is synthesized and assessed in M. W. Flinn, *British Population Growth, 1700–1850* (London, 1970), on which the following paragraphs are largely based.

lion, and the best estimates are that in the next half century a further four million were added to the total. After 1800 there was a further acceleration in the rate of growth, which averaged fifteen percent per decade between 1800 and 1880 and remained at well over ten percent until 1911. Thanks to the wider use of contraceptives there was a steady fall in the birth rate after 1880, but improved medical services, hygiene, and housing insured that the fall in the death rate more or less kept pace with it. Hence in little more than a century the population of Great Britain quadrupled. The first official census, taken in 1801, showed nearly 9 million for England and Wales and just over 1½ million for Scotland, a total for Great Britain as a whole of 10½ million. The census of 1851 showed that after 1801 the total had exactly doubled to 21 million, and that of 1911 that it had almost doubled again to nearly 41 million. Only then, in the second decade of the twentieth century, did the rate of growth begin to fall appreciably, and when it did, the fall was as dramatic as the rise had been a century and a half earlier —and, one might add, just as little understood.

Population growth was an essential, but not by itself a sufficient, precondition of large-scale emigration. Only when the rise in numbers interacted with other major economic changes did a mass exodus get under way. These changes, occurring between 1750 and 1850, altered the entire nature of the British economy, transforming a predominantly agricultural into a predominantly industrial society. Exactly what kind of stimulus was given to emigration by the industrial revolution is difficult to say. Historians have generally assumed technological unemployment to have been the main influence—the displacement, that is, of skilled handicraftsmen by machinery. But recent work on the handloom weavers,[3] long regarded as the classic victims of technological progress, appears to undermine this hypothesis. It has been shown that handloom weaving was neither a traditional nor a skilled occupation, nor for that matter a full-time one, and that the deterioration in the condition of the handloom weavers in the early decades of the nineteenth

3. Duncan Bythell, *The Handloom Weavers: A Study in the English Cotton Industry during the Industrial Revolution* (Cambridge, Eng., 1969).

century was only in part a consequence of the introduction of power looms. The power loom was not widely adopted until 1820, but the most catastrophic fall in handloom weaving wage rates had occurred before then. Moreover, even after the power loom had made its appearance the number of handloom weavers continued for a time to increase. But even if the power loom had had in fact the results attributed to it, that would still not have demonstrated a causal relationship between technological progress and emigration. For such was the depth of poverty to which the wretched handloom weavers had been reduced that all but a few must have lacked the means to emigrate.

While an emphasis on technological unemployment may have been misplaced, the rise of industry seems nevertheless to have given an impetus to emigration in a number of ways. First, industrialization created in Britain a unique pool of technological skill which, if rewards at home were deemed inadequate and sufficient inducements were offered, its possessors were prepared to transfer wherever there was need for it. Even before restrictions on the emigration of skilled artisans were removed in 1825 men with specialized knowledge of industrial techniques were beginning to leave Britain, and for long afterwards such individuals continued to be the carriers of the new technology to less developed countries anxious to emulate "the first industrial nation." Second, there was the expulsive pressure, not so much of technological as of cyclical unemployment. As industrialization gained momentum there developed a regular pattern of boom and slump, and the despair and discontent produced by recurrent industrial depression were reflected as much in increased emigration as in riot, disturbance, and demands for economic and political reform. Third, there was the indirect but no less real stimulus to emigration provided by internal migration. The wholesale movement from rural to urban areas which the new industrial system brought about weakened both social controls and traditional attachments, and predisposed many who had already moved once or more within Britain to contemplate venturing even further afield.

Comparable pressure would be exerted by the course of agricultural change. But, contrary to what is generally asserted, it cannot be argued that emigration owed much to the supposed combination in the late eighteenth century of an "agricultural revolution" and the enclosure movement. The view that there were dramatic and far-reaching changes in British agriculture during the reign of George III is no longer tenable.[4] The changes which made up the "agricultural revolution"—the improvement of farming methods, the introduction of new crops, the application of improved types of agricultural machinery, the enclosure of the open fields, the consolidation of small holdings into large farms better suited to the new husbandry—took place not over decades but over centuries. They can in some cases be traced back to the middle of the seventeenth century and in many instances they continued well into the nineteenth. They had had only a limited effect on British farming in 1815. Enclosure acts in particular did not have the destructive and dislocating effects which used to be attributed to them. They did not, as has sometimes been charged, significantly accelerate the process of amalgamation or lead to the disappearance of the small farmer. On the other hand enclosures undoubtedly injured those whose claim to the land rested not on legal ownership but on rights of common. Cottagers and others who had hitherto enjoyed rights over wasteland and commons found themselves squeezed out. Rather than sink into the ranks of paid laborers, many of the dispossessed dispersed to the towns but not yet in such numbers as to depopulate the villages. In fact the rural population continued to grow in the late eighteenth century.[5]

Nevertheless the cumulative effect of agricultural change should not be minimized. There was a slow but inexorable movement toward holdings large enough to make scientific farming practicable, and the combined long-term effect of consolidation and the adoption of the new husbandry was greatly to increase agricultural output without making corresponding demands upon the labor

4. For what follows see J. D. Chambers and G. E. Mingay, *The Agricultural Revolution, 1750–1880* (London, 1966), and, more especially, G. E. Mingay, "The Agricultural Revolution in English History: A Reconsideration," *Agricultural History*, 37 (1963), 123–133.

5. G. E. Mingay, *Enclosure and the Small Farmer in the Age of the Industrial Revolution* (London, 1968).

supply. These developments, together with the major changes in land use that were to occur in the course of the nineteenth century, brought about the collapse of the old agricultural order and with it the displacement and pauperization of a substantial part of a rural population.

Not until impediments to emigration were removed, however, could an increase in social and geographical mobility become more than an internal phenomenon. There had in particular to be an end to the official hostility to emigration which had been spawned by mercantilism. The mercantilists had equated population with wealth and saw emigration simply as a drain upon national strength. This doctrine, which won general acceptance about 1660, went unchallenged until the early nineteenth century, largely because it took several decades for the expansion of population to attract public attention. Thus for a century and a half after 1660 emigration was officially frowned upon. There was never a general prohibition, and even the laws forbidding skilled artificers to go abroad to practice their trades were not always very effective. But emigration was subject to official sanction, and all who wished to leave the king's dominions were obliged by law to obtain a certificate from the parson and churchwardens, countersigned by a resident magistrate, stating that the intending emigrant was not and had not been employed in any of the prohibited trades or manufactures. Moreover, government was quick to seize any opportunity to throw obstacles in the way of emigration. It was still prepared to do so as late as 1803, this time under the guise of humanitarianism. A committee of the Royal Highland Society, which had been appointed to consider remedies for the threatened depopulation of the Highlands, had produced a report drawing attention to abuses on ships carrying emigrants from Scotland.[6] These revelations appear to have suggested to the government a devious but effective method of restricting departures. The Passenger Act of 1803, which limited the number of passengers on vessels from the United King-

6. Kathleen A. Walpole, "Emigration to British North America under the Early Passenger Acts, 1803–1842," *Transactions of the Historic Society of Lancashire and Cheshire for 1929*, 81 (1930), 111.

dom to North America to a fixed proportion of the ship's registered tonnage, was ostensibly an attempt to safeguard the welfare
of emigrants. But its real purpose, as Castlereagh admitted to John
Quincy Adams some years later, was to check emigration.[7]

All this changed very rapidly after 1815. Within a decade the
belief that emigration was a national evil had given way to a conviction that it could be a remedy for overpopulation as well as a
safety valve for popular discontent. The spectre of overpopulation
had been conjured up in 1798 by Malthus, whose *Essay on the Principle of Population* argued that subsistence could not keep pace with
numbers. Malthus' gloomy diagnosis had caused controversy at
first but after the first census of 1801, and still more after the second
ten years later, there could be no disputing that the population was
rising at an unprecedented rate. The intensification of pauperism
and unemployment during and immediately after the Napoleonic
Wars seemed to confirm the Malthusian theory and facilitated acceptance of the concept of redundancy. As the scale and implications of these newly discovered problems were apprehended there
was a change in attitudes to emigration. Instead of hostility there
was a growing readiness to question the wisdom of restraint, and
some enthusiasts led by R. J. Wilmot Horton, under-secretary for
the colonies, 1822–1828, went so far as to champion extensive
schemes of state-aided emigration.[8]

Public willingness to entertain the notion of emigration did not,
however, stem from sympathy with the sufferings of the poor.
Rather was it a case of finding some means of reducing the burden
of the poor rates and averting the disorders which might arise from
domestic distress. It is true that not all of those who came to favor
emigration did so out of concern with Britain's domestic difficulties. The motives of the Colonial Office in assisting emigrants to
settle in Canada between 1815 and 1819 were first to strengthen a
colony whose vulnerability to attack had been painfully demon-

7. Worthington C. Ford, ed., *The Writings of John Quincy Adams* (New York, 1913–
1917), VI, 54.

8. H. J. M. Johnston, *British Emigration Policy, 1815–1830: 'Shovelling out Paupers'*
(Oxford, 1972), chap. iv.

strated during the War of 1812 and second to direct emigration away from the United States. Wilmot Horton, though accused by opponents of "shovelling out paupers," was in fact as much concerned to remedy the underpopulation of the colonies as he was the overpopulation of Great Britain. But he failed to persuade Lord Liverpool's government to adopt his ambitious schemes, and the small-scale experiments in state-aided emigration that were tried between 1819 and 1826 were prompted not by a desire to strengthen colonial defense but by the need to remedy domestic distress.[9]

Furthermore, although the Select Committee on Emigration over which Wilmot Horton presided in 1826–1827 endorsed his proposals for state-aided emigration to the colonies, the only tangible result of the committee's work arose from its anxiety to check the growing influx of impoverished Irishmen into England and Scotland. Such an influx, declared the committee, threatened "to deluge Great Britain with poverty and wretchedness and gradually but certainly to equalize the state of the English and Irish peasantry."[10] The need to find an alternative outlet for the Irish exodus led the committee to recommend the removal of all remaining obstacles to emigration. The laws prohibiting the emigration of artisans had already been repealed in 1825. Repeal had been decided upon partly out of deference to free trade ideas, partly because of a feeling that it was unjust to discriminate against one class of the population, but mainly because it was apparent that the laws were not being and could not be enforced, and that their only effect was to discourage artificers who had gone abroad from returning home lest they be prosecuted.[11] Hence the obstacles the emigration committee had in mind were those imposed by the Passenger Act of 1825, a relatively strict measure which was said by many witnesses to have raised the cost of passage to North America beyond the means of many would-be emigrants. So urgent did the need appear to divert the Irish elsewhere that the committee was prepared to

9. *Ibid.*, chaps. ii–v.

10. *Third Report from the Select Committee on Emigration from the United Kingdom, 1827, Parliamentary Papers* 1826–1827, V, 7.

11. *Sixth Report from the Select Committee on Artizans and Machinery*, P.P. 1824, V, 590–591.

deprive all emigrants, whether Irish or otherwise, of the admittedly slim protection afforded by the law. Parliament accepted this reasoning and early in 1827 repealed all regulations governing the emigrant traffic.[12] With this step the reaction against mercantilist attitudes to emigration was complete. A typhus outbreak on several vessels bound for Nova Scotia made it necessary to adopt a new passenger act in 1828, but from that date until the disasters of the Irish famine emigration compelled a new approach, care was taken to keep regulation below the point at which it would produce a prohibitive rise in fares.[13]

Not even the removal of legal restraints was enough, however, to generate a large-scale exodus, even when the desire to emigrate had become widespread. What was also needed was a massive expansion of cheap transportation facilities. The lack of such facilities had not in earlier periods been an absolute bar to the emigration of the poor for those who had lacked the means to travel to America could still emigrate by becoming indentured servants. But by the beginning of the nineteenth century this was no longer possible. The traffic in bound labor from Britain had died out or, more accurately, had been killed off by the 1785 act extending to the United States the ban on artisan emigration.[14] Now emigration was possible only for those individuals who could afford the passage or who had their fares paid for them. And while passage rates remained at the high level to which they had been raised by the Passenger Act of 1803, the numbers in either category would remain limited.

What changed the picture was the expansion of transatlantic commerce in the decades after 1815. Emigrants still had to depend for passage upon ordinary merchant vessels whose primary function was the carriage of freight: not until steam supplanted sail on the Atlantic in the 1860's did the specialized passenger ship make its

12. Johnston, *British Emigration Policy*, p. 124.

13. *Ibid.*, p. 126.

14. "An Act to prohibit the Exportation to foreign Parts of Tools and Utensils made use of in the Iron and Steel Manufactures . . . and to prevent the seducing of Artificers or Workmen, employed in those Manufactures, to go into Parts beyond the Seas." 25 Geo. III, c. 67.

appearance. Thus the sudden rise of the timber trade with the North American colonies and the steady growth of the cotton trade with the United States gave facilities to emigration after 1815 which it had never possessed at any former period. It was not merely that the number of vessels trading with North America increased sharply between 1815 and 1850, or even that the average size of sailing vessels doubled in the same period. It was a matter also of unused cargo space on the westward voyage. The manufactured goods exported to North America were much less bulky than commodities like timber and cotton, and space was thus available for the conveyance of emigrants. The relative scarcity of westbound cargoes was not the only reason for carrying emigrants; there were fat profits to be made from doing so. Until regulation became strict in the middle years of the century the outlay involved in fitting out a vessel for the emigrant traffic was slight. It was necessary only to throw up rough wooden berths in the between decks and, since emigrants brought their own provisions, to supply them with fuel and water. Returns could therefore be high, sometimes higher even than on the homeward voyage.

Admittedly many of the vessels which now entered the emigrant traffic were ill-suited to the purpose. This was particularly true of those whose main function was to carry timber from Canada and the Maritime Provinces. A Parliamentary committee inquiring into shipwrecks in 1839 was told that while there were some good ships in the colonial timber trade these were the exception. Those built in the North American colonies were as a rule "an inferior class of vessel even when newly built," while the British-built vessels employed in the trade were usually "the cast-off ships of other trades" and included "some of the worst kind of ships afloat."[15] An earlier committee had spoken highly, however, of the American vessels which predominated in the carrying trade between Britain and the United States. They were infinitely superior to their British counterparts, more soundly constructed, longer lasting, faster sailers,

15. *Report from the Select Committee on Shipwrecks of Timber Ships*, P.P. 1839, IX, Qns. 112, 139, 181–184, 403, 493–494.

and, in particular, more competently commanded and manned.[16] But apart from being more seaworthy and of better appearance than the squat and dirty British timber ships, American vessels were hardly better equipped in the 1830's for carrying emigrants in comfort. Most of them consisted of sturdy, bluff-bowed vessels sometimes known as "kettle-bottoms" because of a characteristic flatness of hull underwater which enabled them to traverse the shallow bars at the entrance to the cotton ports of the South. But this characteristic also made them roll in even the smoothest sea, and although cotton freighters were more roomy between decks than other vessels there was the same lack of ventilation and light in the steerage.

Nor were steerage conditions substantially different on the regular American packet ships. These turned increasingly to the emigrant traffic after 1840, when they lost to the steamships the monopoly they had formerly enjoyed of the fine freight and cabin passenger trades.[17] Emigrants tended to be impressed by the fact that the packet ships, always larger and faster than the cotton freighters, grew steadily in size. From an approximate average of 400 tons in 1820 they rose to 800 tons by 1840 and to 1,250 tons by 1854. Great numbers of these packet ships, as well as of vessels which, though not strictly packets, were of the same general type, were turned out by American shipyards in the late 1840's and early 1850's. Considered strictly as examples of marine architecture they were among the finest wooden sailing ships ever built. Fuller of line and consequently less graceful than the celebrated clippers, they were nevertheless splendidly constructed by famous American builders like Donald Mackay and William H. Webb; and in spite of the fact that they were not designed for great speed they were capable of making what were by sailing ship standards fast passages.[18] Though intended to be both freight and passenger carriers, these vessels had been designed with the emigrant traffic in mind—as

16. *Report from the Select Committee on the Causes of Shipwrecks*, P.P. 1836, XVII, xi.

17. Robert G. Albion, *Square-Riggers on Schedule* (Princeton, 1938), pp. 247–251.

18. John G. B. Hutchins, *The American Maritime Industries and Public Policy, 1789–1914* (Cambridge, 1941), pp. 283–284, 289–291.

well they might be, given the fact that the carriage of emigrants had become the greatest single source of revenue to packet ship owners. By the 1850's such vessels were usually equipped with iron ventilation tubes, glass portholes, and hinged iron bedsteads; they were also very lofty between decks, though this was due less to a desire to add to the comfort of emigrants than to the need to provide maximum storage space for cotton bales.[19]

But even on fine vessels such as these, steerage accommodations were still seriously deficient. This was clear from the Parliamentary investigations of the early 1850's as well as from that conducted by a United States Senate committee in 1854.[20] British and American law still permitted as many as five hundred people to be berthed together indiscriminately in a single compartment about one hundred fifty feet long by about thirty-five feet wide. Matters had in fact been made somewhat worse by the American Passenger Act of 1848 which, by making space rather than tonnage the measure of passenger capacity, had had the unintended effect of stimulating the construction of large three-decked vessels with two steerages, one above the other. Such an arrangement permitted vessels to carry more passengers—the largest could now take about one thousand—but it exacerbated overcrowding and increased the difficulties of ventilation, especially in bad weather when the hatches had to be closed. Moreover cooking and washing facilities, even on the best vessels, were hopelessly inadequate. Such disclosures, following on the cholera epidemics on emigrant vessels of 1853–1854, were the reason why both Parliament and Congress adopted new and more severe passenger acts in 1855.

It could hardly be claimed, therefore, that the commercial revolution of the first half of the nineteenth century had robbed the Atlantic crossing of its terrors. Even in the 1850's it could be a harrowing, even a traumatic, experience. The voyage was certainly in

19. *Report from the Select Committee on the Passengers' Act, 1851*, P.P. 1851, XIX, Qns. 2260–2262, 3387–3392.

20. For these investigations see *ibid.*; *First and Second Reports from the Select Committee on Emigrant Ships, 1854*, P.P. 1854, XII; U. S. Senate, *Report of the Select Committee of the Senate of the United States on Sickness and Mortality on Board Emigrant Ships*, 33 Cong., 1 Sess. (1854), Sen. Rep. no. 386.

some respects less hazardous than before, thanks to advances in marine architecture and navigational aids. But if the risk of ship-wreck had declined that of disease had not. The frightful 1847 epi-demic of ship fever on vessels carrying Irish emigrants may have been unparalleled in its severity; cholera outbreaks in 1832 and 1853–1854 were also exceptional. But even in normal years, when only a small minority of vessels were affected, and the overall mortality rate was well under one percent, deaths from typhus, smallpox, and measles could still run into hundreds.[21] In any case it did not require an epidemic to produce hardship and discomfort. They were the inevitable consequence of overcrowding and want of sanitation, as well as of the fact that the voyage by sailing ship was necessarily a long one. It rarely took less than a month and it might well be extended by bad weather to two or even three.

The continuing deficiencies of the steerage do not, however, alter the fact that the expansion of transatlantic commerce reduced the price of passage to a level that all but the poorest could afford. Hitherto passage rates had been high, after 1803 prohibitively so. Even as late as 1817 a steerage berth without provisions from Liver-pool to New York had cost anything from £7 to £12. But a de-cade later rates had fallen to around £5 and by 1832 to only £3. 10s. Fares to the North American colonies dropped more steeply still, rates to Quebec and St. John, New Brunswick, having fallen to between £2 and £3 as early as 1820. And despite the tendency of the passenger acts after 1827 to impose progressively higher standards, fares did not rise much above these levels for the rest of the sailing ship era.

This was because of the competition that developed as the emi-grant trade became an organized branch of commerce. By the 1820's the passenger broker had come into existence. One of the earliest was the Liverpool firm of Fitzhugh and Grimshaw which began the practice of chartering vessels for the conveyance of emi-grants, established a network of agents to attract business, and ad-

21. This paragraph and those immediately following are based upon Maldwyn A. Jones, "The Role of the United Kingdom in the Transatlantic Emigrant Trade, 1815–1875" (unpub. PhD diss., University of Oxford, 1956).

vertised extensively in both British and Irish newspapers. Fitzhugh and Grimshaw was a reputable firm but its imitators in the emigrant trade were with few exceptions unprincipled rogues who usually exploited and cheated emigrants. But although passenger brokers were on the whole an unsavory group, the competition between them at least kept fares low. And that there was a correlation between passage rates and the volume of emigration was universally acknowledged. The framers of the British passenger acts kept the fact constantly in mind, varying their provisions in accordance with changing official attitudes. Thus, after 1827, officials were concerned mainly to avoid excessive regulation lest, by raising fares, the passenger acts should act as a brake on emigration.

The significance of cheap fares was further demonstrated by the high proportion of emigrants sailing to the North American colonies. Between 1818 and 1834 emigration to those colonies generally exceeded that to the United States and remained relatively high until the late 1840's. It was no secret, however, that a large majority of those who embarked for colonial ports did so with every intention of settling ultimately in the United States. Their preference for the colonial route arose in part from the fact that vessels going out for colonial timber were to be found in practically every port in Great Britain and Ireland, whereas American-bound vessels tended to be heavily concentrated at Liverpool. Emigrants naturally wished wherever possible to embark at ports near their homes. As one emigrant guidebook pointed out, "the most expensive and the least profitable part of an emigrant's journey is that overland in the country which he is leaving."[22] Certainly the journey to Liverpool was a deterrent before the building of railways and an emigrant from, say, East Anglia or Cornwall would tend to be impressed by the advantages of the local timber ships going out from ports like Yarmouth or Padstow.

But the most important consideration was the expense of passage itself, and until the middle years of the century fares to Quebec and St. John remained appreciably lower than to American ports. The difference in rates was initially the result of the government's

22. Robert Mudie, *The Emigrant's Pocket Companion* (London, 1832), p. 199.

attempt just after 1815 to divert emigration from the United States to Canada. The Passenger Act of 1817 differentiated between vessels proceeding to the two countries, allowing those bound for the colonies to carry three or four times as many passengers as those going to the United States. This distinction was abandoned in 1823 when strategic considerations had ceased to influence emigration policy, but because the British passenger acts of 1823 and later years did not restrict numbers as severely as did the American Passenger Act of 1819, the difference in carrying capacity persisted. How that affected fares was described by a Belfast passenger broker in 1842 and, although his remarks related specifically to the Irish emigrant traffic, they could equally be applied to the British.

When sending a vessel with emigrants to the United States, we come under their laws which only allow two souls to every 5 tons of the vessel, . . . [whereas] to British America we come under our own laws which allow three adults to every 5 tons, . . . two children under 14 years or three children under 7 years being reckoned as one adult; and infants are not counted in the ship's complement. Consequently, the number of passengers to the tonnage of a ship to Quebec is almost double that to New York, and therefore we are enabled to make the passage to the former port proportionately lower.[23]

This was a special boon to emigrating families. A family consisting of a man, his wife and four children under seven years of age could all be provided with passages from Belfast to Quebec for the sum of £6, but "the lowest rate under which the same family could obtain a passage to New York would be £21."

In analyzing the causes of nineteenth-century emigration historians customarily emphasize the stimulus provided by the growth of popular knowledge of America. They point to the flood of travel accounts, emigrant guidebooks, and colonization journals, as well as to the widespread discussion of emigration in newspapers and magazines. It is generally accepted that such publications were an important factor in uprooting people from their homes.

But it is easier to assert such a causal relationship than to demonstrate it; so far as Britain is concerned, the connection is by no

23. *The Emigration Gazette and Colonial Settlers' Universal Guide* (London), April 23, 1842.

means established. There can be no doubt that popular interest in America increased after 1815; the two hundred or so American travel accounts published in Britain in the quarter century before the Civil War are proof enough of that. But many of these books were hostile to America and in any case they were not widely read, except by the educated classes, because of their cost. Nor do works written specifically to promote emigration appear to have had much effect. One of the best known of them, Morris Birkbeck's *Letters from Illinois*, published in 1818, was discussed at length in the expensive quarterlies but failed to persuade many people to join Birkbeck's English colony. There can be little doubt either that most emigrant guidebooks were devised not so much to stimulate emigration as to provide those already disposed to emigrate with the kind of information which would be helpful in deciding where precisely to settle. The typical guidebook, such as the pamphlets about the United States, Canada, Australia, and other fields of emigration which the Scottish publisher, William Chambers, brought out in the 1840's, simply provided factual information about wages, prices, topography, climate, crops, and natural resources, together with information about the journey. Sober compilations such as these were certainly widely read and their effect on those contemplating emigration is likely to have been encouraging rather than otherwise. But it is difficult to regard them as one of the major catalysts of emigration. Hardly more influential were emigration periodicals like *The Emigrant and Colonial Advocate, The Emigration Record and Colonial Journal*, and *The Emigrant and Colonial Gazette*. As their titles suggest the main object of such journals was to promote colonial settlement; for that reason they tended to discourage emigration to the United States. In this aim they certainly failed, and though they may have done something to publicize the colonies they seem to have reflected than generated interest in emigration.

Emigrant letters were a different matter. One must of course be careful not to exaggerate their influence. Of those which appeared in the newspapers not all were favorable to emigration, and many of those that were tended to be discounted by prospective emigrants as having been written to promote land sales or for some other ulterior purpose. It is no longer universally accepted, moreover, that private letters from emigrants to relatives back home had the stimulating effect generally ascribed to them. Analysis of a number of letters written by British emigrants has led Charlotte Erickson to challenge the whole notion of the widely circulated emigrant letter.[24] She asserts that most of those she examined seem to have been intended for private consumption and that the writers sometimes forbade their being shown outside the family. But such instructions were not necessarily followed: that they were given at all is surely suggestive. In any case there is positive evidence that emigrant letters were widely passed around and with results which were precisely those which Marcus Hansen and others have claimed. Thus the Poor Law Commissioners of 1834 were told by a Northumberland witness that "the generally prosperous accounts which are sent home by . . . individuals [in Upper Canada] were always circulated throughout the parish and neighbourhood, and after creating quite a commotion in a village, they act as a constant stimulus to the inhabitants."[25] The private letter was beyond question the most trusted source of information about emigration and may well have been for that reason the most effective stimulus. While the printed word undoubtedly projected a general image of America as a land of economic opportunity and free institutions, it seems likely that what lured Britons across the Atlantic more frequently was the specific vision conjured up by an emigrant letter of a good job or a cheap farm in a locality where relatives or friends had settled earlier.

The freedom of emigration enjoyed in Britain became in the course of the nineteenth century a cause for national pride. Together with exemption from cumpulsory military service it was regarded as one of the hallmarks of British liberty, one of the things

---

24. Charlotte Erickson, *Invisible Immigrants: The Adaptation of English and Scottish Immigrants in Nineteenth-Century America* (London, 1972), pp. 35–36.

25. *Report from His Majesty's Commissioners for inquiring into . . . the Poor Laws*, P.P. 1834, XXXVII, App. (C), 448–449.

distinguishing the subjects of Queen Victoria from those of despotic European monarchs. But for the historian this distinction must be a matter for wry regret. It goes far to account for the notorious inadequacy of the statistical evidence about British emigration. It is true that none of the countries of emigration began to pay proper attention to their statistical records until the era of mass migration was nearly over. But when governments were alarmed by emigration they were more likely to take steps to measure its extent. The sources available for the study of European emigration seem, indeed, to vary with the amount of governmental hostility emigration provoked. When emigration was hedged about with restriction careful and detailed records tended to be kept. Thus in the German states and in the cantons of Switzerland the need to obtain official permission to emigrate called forth a mass of individual applications whose survival provides the historian not only with basic demographic data but also with information about the economic and social status of the emigrants and their reasons for emigrating.[26] Moreover those governments which were fearful of the consequences of mass emigration for national well-being were more inclined, when they did not ban emigration absolutely, to make systematic and searching inquiries into its character. To such fears one owes the rich literature of Italian official emigration publications[27] and the exhaustive and scholarly study known as *Emigrationsutredningen*, commissioned by the Swedish government.[28]

But in Britain the motive for such inquiries largely disappeared with the rejection of the doctrine that emigration was a national evil. Even in the eighteenth century there had been no sustained attempt to record the outflow. Only at times of unusually heavy emigration, such as the early 1770's, had detailed returns been called

---

26. This material is listed in part in Marion D. Learned, *Guide to the Manuscript Materials relating to American History in the German State Archives* (Washington, 1912), and Albert B. Faust, *Guide to the Materials for American History in Swiss and Austrian Archives* (Washington, 1916).

27. See especially *Statistica della Emigrazione Italiana* (Rome, 1884–  ), *Bollettino dell' Emigrazione* (Rome, 1902–  ), and *Emigrazioni e Colonie: Raccolta di Rapporti dei R.R. Agenti Diplomatici e Consolari*, 3 vols. (Rome, 1903–1909).

28. *Emigrationsutredningen*, Bilaga I–XX (Stockholm, 1908–1912).

for.[29] Once government came to look upon emigration with equanimity there was little disposition to probe into what there was no longer any wish to prevent. After the last legal obstacles to departure had been removed in the 1820's the government concerned itself with emigration only in certain limited ways. It sought by means of the passenger acts to promote the safety and well-being of emigrants during the voyage. It provided intending emigrants with information about conditions and opportunities in the British colonies. And between 1840 and 1860 the Colonial Land and Emigration Commissioners selected and arranged for the transportation of those to whom the Australasian colonies were prepared to offer free or assisted passages.

Otherwise emigration attracted scant official notice. From time to time Parliament debated—and rejected—proposals for state aid to emigration as a remedy for distress. Parliamentary committees investigating other matters occasionally exhibited a mild interest in the exodus. But no extensive investigation was ever made. Nor, except in regard to Ireland, did the census takers show much curiosity. In 1851 the Census Commissioners instituted a separate series of returns of emigration from Ireland which provided information about age, sex, occupation, county of origin, destination abroad, and intended length of residence there. But nothing comparable was ever done for Britain. In 1841 the census enumerators were told to ascertain how many emigrants had left each county in England, Wales, and Scotland since the beginning of the calendar year. But on other occasions they were given no special instructions about emigration. The early censuses did in fact occasionally make brief references to emigration to explain the decline of population in some places; but there was nothing systematic or comprehensive about their inquiries. After 1861 even the meager comments cease.

The student is thus dependent upon the official statistics of "emi-

29. In 1774 and 1775 weekly returns of emigration were compiled in accordance with a Treasury instruction of December 9, 1773, to the Commissioners of Customs. Public Record Office, *Treasury Papers*, *T.* 11/30, f. 450. The returns themselves are in *T.* 47/9–12.

gration," compiled and published regularly from 1815 onwards.[30] They were not in fact statistics of emigration proper but of the total number of passengers who embarked at British and Irish ports for certain overseas destinations on vessels subject to the provisions of the passenger acts. These figures were purely a by-product of the passenger acts. In order to comply with the regulations and, more particularly, with those provisions which limited the numbers which emigrant vessels could carry, ship captains had to furnish lists of passengers, and it was from these lists that the customs officers compiled the emigration statistics. They are an unreliable guide to British emigration. For the first half of the nineteenth century they are too low and for the latter half much too high. Their incompleteness in the earlier period stemmed mainly from the narrowness of the legal definition of the terms "passenger" and "passenger ship." Before 1863 masters were not required to include cabin passengers in the muster rolls—though some in fact did so—and no account was taken of vessels carrying mails. Also omitted were "short ships," that is, vessels on which the proportion of passengers to tonnage was insufficient to bring them within the operation of the law. For other reasons, too, the number of passengers was underestimated. Masters carrying excessive numbers did not always include all the names on the passenger lists; other masters evaded inspection by sailing from out-of-the-way ports. Still more common was the practice of embarking additional passengers after obtaining clearance papers from the customs. And there was a not inconsiderable number of stowaways.

Another source of confusion, though one which tended to inflate rather than understate emigration, was the fact that no distinction was made between emigrants proper and passengers of other descriptions. Travel for reasons other than migration is unlikely to have been extensive during the sailing ship era, but from the 1860's, when steamship travel became general, passenger lists in-

30. These are most accessible in N. H. Carrier and J. R. Jeffery, *External Migration: A Study of the Available Statistics, 1815–1950* (London, 1953). The deficiencies of the statistics are discussed in Brinley Thomas, *Migration and Economic Growth: A Study of Great Britain and the Atlantic Economy* (Cambridge, Eng., 1954), pp. 36–41.

cluded substantial and growing numbers of transient visitors. "During the last twenty years especially," commented the Board of Trade in 1887, "it has become obvious that many passengers are dealt with [under the passenger acts] who do not go away from the United Kingdom to settle abroad."[31] Yet it was not until 1912 that an attempt was made to distinguish permanent emigrants from tourists, businessmen, and other temporary absentees.

Furthermore, because they were not concerned with emigration as such those who compiled the statistics were slow to do more than record the gross outflow of passengers. Until quite late in the century they did not attempt to calculate the net emigration by taking into account the return passenger movement from the United States and elsewhere. This had become sizable and indeed regular as early as the 1850's. Statistics of what was called "return emigration" were in fact kept for the period 1858–1861 and these show that arrivals from the United States averaged about twenty thousand a year, or about one-third of the annual emigration for that period.[32] Yet it was not until 1876, after the Merchant Shipping Act transferred to the Board of Trade the power and duties formerly vested in the Emigration Commissioners by the passenger acts, that statistics of passengers arriving at United Kingdom ports began to be regularly compiled. Only then did it become possible to estimate at all accurately the net outward movement.

The statistics have other shortcomings too. Until 1853 they did not distinguish between the different nationalities within the British Isles or between British subjects and aliens. That they then began to classify passengers as English, "Scotch," Irish, or foreigners seems to have been due to the Emigration Commissioners' anxiety to discover some general peculiarity common to the minority of vessels affected by the cholera epidemic of 1853—a peculiarity which might account for the heavy mortality they experienced. For some time after 1853, however, distinctions of nationality were not made

31. *Copy of Memorandum on the Immigration of Foreigners into the United Kingdom* . . . , P.P. 1887, LXXXIX.

32. *Twenty Second General Report of the Emigration Commissioners, 1862*, P.P. 1862, XXII.

in respect to all passengers. There remained a relatively large group under the designation "not distinguished"; these averaged about twenty thousand a year in the period 1853–1863 and made up about a fifth of the total in 1860. The size of this group dropped sharply after 1863, however, when details began to be required about cabin passengers as well as those in the steerage. After 1863 the only passengers listed as "not distinguished" by nationality were infants under one year old. But one further distinction remained to be made. Like English officialdom generally, the framers of the passenger acts refused to recognize that the Welsh constituted a separate nationality and insisted on counting them as English. Not until 1908 was this absurdity remedied. Only when the era of mass emigration was almost over did the statistics at last begin to distinguish properly, and even then with doubtful accuracy, between the four nationalities that made up the population of the United Kingdom.

For all their limitations the published statistics suffice to illustrate the main trends in British emigration since the end of the Napoleonic Wars. Perhaps the most striking things they reveal are how gradual was the rise in the volume of emigration from Britain and how long it took for the movement to reach its peak. From northwestern Europe as a whole emigration had a relatively limited span. It became sizable in the 1830's, reached mass proportions by mid-century, and, after soaring to unprecedented levels in the 1880's, dwindled to relative insignificance by the end of the century. Between one country and another there were admittedly variations within this pattern. Emigration from Ireland was concentrated into a much shorter period than the norm and decline set in earlier; as soon as the famine exodus was spent the rate of departure fell dramatically and not even a renewed spurt in the early 1880's reversed the general downward trend. In Sweden the movement began somewhat later than elsewhere and declined more gradually. Yet in most of the countries of emigration in northwestern Europe the movement had a basically similar configuration.

Britain, however, was an exception. Here the movement spanned the entire century of large-scale international migration. Emigration from Britain gathered momentum more slowly than that from other northwest European countries but retained its force much longer. For about one hundred years after 1815 emigration from England, Wales, and Scotland proceeded in a series of waves, each slightly more powerful than the last. The first substantial wave reached its crest about the middle of the century, though it was both relatively and absolutely much smaller than the mass movements going on simultaneously from Ireland and Germany. And in contrast to what happened in Ireland and Germany there was no irreversible decline in emigration at the end of the century. Instead the curve went on rising steadily from one bulge in emigration to another, even into the twentieth century. The absolute level of emigration from England reached its peak only in 1911; that from Scotland not until 1932. Rates of emigration, that is, the proportions of emigration to population size, followed a more complex pattern than the absolute level of departures. But contrary to what used often to be claimed they were generally higher in the latter half of the nineteenth century than in the first half, and did not drop appreciably in the early years of the twentieth century. In Scotland, indeed, the rate of emigration was never higher than in the 1920's. These facts require emphasis in view of the frequently made assertion that growing industrialization tends to check emigration. However much support that view derives from the precipitate fall in German emigration from the late 1880's onward, it is flatly contradicted by the contours of emigration from Britain.

Just how many British emigrants there were before 1853, when nationality began to be recorded, it is impossible to say. But reasonable estimates can nonetheless be made from 1825 onward because the returns provide details of the number of passengers sailing from the different ports of the United Kingdom. Not all of those who embarked at British ports, however, were Englishmen, Welshmen, or Scots. At most ports it may be safely assumed that they were, but at the larger ports, and especially at Liverpool, where the emigrant traffic became increasingly concentrated, it is certain that they were not. Contemporary observers are agreed that from the late 1820's a large majority of emigrants from Liverpool were Irish.[33] In the 1830's the Irish proportion of the Liverpool total was commonly put at two-thirds and some believed it to be as high as five-sixths. During the famine years emigration from Liverpool became almost exclusively Irish and after 1846 the Emigration Commissioners estimated that the Irish accounted for at least nine-tenths of the Liverpool totals. This may possibly have been a slight exaggeration, but the commissioners were certainly justified in claiming in 1852 that, in addition to the massive Hibernian out-flow from the Mersey, one-third of the departures from the Clyde were Irish and so too was perhaps one-fifth of the emigration to Australia from English ports like Plymouth and London.[34]

Not that the Irish were the only non-British element to be taken into account. The 1840's saw the beginning of an important transit traffic in emigrants from continental Europe that was to reach huge proportions later in the century. Facilities for reaching the United States from continental ports were not as good as from England, and Germans were apprized of the fact by an extensive advertising campaign conducted in the Rhineland by the agents for the American packet ships operating from London and Liverpool.[35] The 4,361 Germans who embarked at London for New York in 1846 constituted the first fruits of that campaign. Germans accounted for seventy-five percent of the emigration from London to North America in 1846, for nearly eighty percent the following year, and for over sixty percent well into the 1850's.[36] Liverpool soon at-tracted even greater numbers but the twenty thousand or so Germans who passed through the city in 1852 on their way to America made up less than ten percent of the port's total.

If the above estimates may be relied upon there could have been

33. *Appendix* [G] *to the Third Report of the Commissioners for the Inquiry into the Conditions of the Poorer Classes in Ireland,* P.P. 1836, XXXIV, 508–509; John Finch, Jr., *Statistics of Vauxhall Ward, Liverpool . . .* (Liverpool, 1842), p. 21.

34. *Twelfth General Report of the Colonial Land and Emigration Commissioners, 1852,* P.P. 1852, XVIII.

35. Jones, "United Kingdom," pp. 318ff.

36. *Ibid.,* pp. 331–338.

no sustained heavy outflow of English and Scottish emigrants before the 1840's. There was a sudden upsurge in the early 1830's, culminating in more than 49,000 departures in 1832.[37] A similar upsurge a decade later resulted in 54,000 emigrants leaving in 1841 and 51,000 in 1842. But in between the peaks of 1832 and 1841–1842 the average was below 30,000 and in 1838, 1843, and 1846 numbers fell below 20,000, which was not much higher than the level reached in the late 1820's. The sudden increase in departures in 1848, however, marked the beginning of the first really large wave of British emigration. The estimates suggest that emigration jumped to 54,000 in 1848, then to 72,000 in 1849 and remained around the 60,000 mark for the next three years. Thereafter the statistics of nationality enable us to be more precise. These show that emigration from Britain averaged more than 76,000 for the rest of the decade, with new peaks in 1853 of 85,520 and in 1854 of 116,838.

It would be wrong, however, to suggest that such levels, unprecedented though they were for Britain, implied that the movement had now attained mass proportions. In fact emigration from Britain as a whole never became a mass movement of the kind experienced in Ireland and parts of Germany, though Scotland, and more particularly the Highlands, did so in some decades. But in the 1850's overall emigration rates remained low. With a population of almost 18 million Great Britain suffered a net emigration loss between 1851 and 1860 of perhaps 700,000 people. By contrast, Ireland, with a population in 1841 of only 8 million, lost 1¾ million people in the eight years of the famine exodus. It is true that in the next half century gross emigration levels from Britain rose substantially: the peaks were 144,653 in 1873, 214,375 in 1883, 331,584 in 1907, and 387,148 in 1912.[38] But because of the size of the return movement the net outflow was perhaps as much as one-third less

37. *Thirteenth General Report of the Colonial Land and Emigration Commissioners, 1853*, P.P. 1852–1853, XL, App. 28; *Times* (London), April 14, 17, May 5, June 4, August 4, September 4, 1852.

38. Estimates of gross and net emigration from the different countries of Europe may be found in Gustav Sundbärg, *Aperçus Statistiques Internationaux*, 11e Année (Stockholm, 1908), p. 105.

and may have done no more between 1850 and 1914 than keep
pace with population growth.

No historian has yet attempted to analyze in detail the way in
which economic factors regulated the level of the British outflow.
But economists have long been probing the question, and have
sought in particular to clarify the relationship between variations
in emigration levels and fluctuations in the business cycle. The
"push-pull" controversy has not yet produced a consensus, and
discussion still tends to begin with the views of Harry Jerome. It
was Jerome's conclusion that in the latter half of the nineteenth
century the pull of American prosperity had a greater influence on
the timing of emigration to the United States than the push of depression in the home country.[39] But at least so far as the timing of
emigration from Britain is concerned, Jerome's analysis is not entirely convincing. He did not distinguish clearly enough between
the respective levels of British and Irish emigration, nor did he
make a thorough study of business cycles in all the countries which
attracted large numbers of British emigrants. Because of these and
other deficiencies it cannot be accepted as proved that cyclical fluctuations in emigration from Great Britain were determined primarily by American business conditions. All that Jerome succeeded
in demonstrating was that there was no clear correlation between
emigration and economic conditions in Britain itself. This, however, is merely another way of putting Clapham's view that emigration cannot "be treated always, or even usually, as a mere product of distress."

A more complex correlation between emigration and economic
activity has been suggested by Brinley Thomas.[40] In his *Migration
and Economic Growth* Thomas was concerned not with short-term
business cycle fluctuations but with long swings in rates of economic growth. He assumed the existence of an Atlantic economy
made up of interdependent countries and set out to show that the

39. Harry Jerome, *Migration and Business Cycles* (New York, 1926), chap. viii.
40. Brinley Thomas, *Migration and Economic Growth*, pp. 83–122.

rhythms of economic growth in Europe and America were closely related to the course of migration. He found an inverse relationship between the long swings in capital formation in the United Kingdom and the United States. When home investment was high in Britain the rate of growth in the United States slackened and the westward movement of men and money fell off; then when the United States in turn experienced an upsurge of economic activity there was a decline in home investment in Britain and large quantities of capital and labor were exported. Before about 1870 Thomas found that the upswing in American business activity tended to follow an upswing in immigration, suggesting that push factors were more influential than pull; but after 1870, when a structural change occurred in the American economy—the United States became for the first time more industrial than agricultural—a rise in immigration preceded the upswing, indicating that the pull of American prosperity was now dominant. Thomas suggested, moreover, that in countries exporting population there was an inverse relation between internal and external migration. When the American economy was expanding and that of Britain was relatively declining, surplus labor from the rural areas of Britain tended to emigrate to America rather than to urban areas at home; in the succeeding phase, when the rate of capital formation in Britain rose rapidly, displaced agriculturalists moved to the towns and emigration declined.

This sophisticated analysis represents a great advance upon earlier attempts to relate migration to economic activity. Particularly helpful to historians of emigration is Thomas' focus upon problems of timing. But his hypotheses leave much out of account. He does not investigate, for example, the nature of the expulsive forces which up to 1870 are said to have been primarily responsible for upswings in British emigration. What is more, he occasionally contradicts his own conclusion that push factors were more important than pull until after the Civil War. Although claiming that the British economy interacted with the Australian in much the same way as with the American economy, he goes on to assert that it was the discovery of gold that accounted for the heavy emigration to the Australian colonies in the 1850's.[41] Then again the alleged inverse relationship between internal and external migration rests upon an unproven and, as we shall see later, probably false, assumption, namely, that British emigrants to the United States in the late nineteenth century consisted mainly of displaced agriculturalists. Moreover, although Thomas rightly remarks that "some significant facts about emigration are lost from view when we confine ourselves to the aggregate flow," the American immigration statistics upon which he relies to separate the different streams of emigration from England, Wales, and Scotland cannot be used for such a purpose until 1875 and were not entirely reliable even then.

Quite apart from such objections of detail it may be doubted whether quantifiable economic factors such as railroad construction and coal output can ever wholly account for fluctuations in emigration levels. The timing of the movement could be powerfully affected by factors which cannot be measured in any quantifiable way. How is it possible to measure, for example, the extent to which emigration may have been affected in 1854 by reports of heavy loss of life from shipwreck, by the prevalence of cholera at the ports of embarkation and on many emigrant ships, and by the outbreak of the Crimean War which drew young men into the army and at the same time led to a reduction in transatlantic travel facilities? Or, to turn to a nonquantifiable American factor, how much heavier might emigration have been in 1854 but for the hostility then being displayed toward immigrants by the Know Nothing movement? The point is not of course that Thomas' theory fails to explain why emigration rose or fell in a particular year—his concern was with the long term—but that studies whether of business cycle fluctuations or of long swings can never hope to tell the whole story and may sometimes leave out the most important part of it. That the sharp increase in emigration to Australia in the decade before World War I coincided with an upswing in the Australian economy is both true and significant; but as an explanation of why emigration rose so dramatically this correlation is less revealing than the fact that assisted passages, which had been discon-

41. *Ibid.*, chap. xiii.

tinued for several decades, were renewed in 1905 as part of a "White Australia" policy which owed nothing to economics and everything to racism. In such a context economic theory is clearly no substitute for careful historical analysis based on nonquantifiable as well as on quantifiable data.

The problem of balancing push factors against pull is of course made more difficult where emigration proceeds not to one destination but to several. Unlike emigration from Ireland, which was almost wholly to the United States, that from Britain was directed to a variety of emigration fields. The relative attraction of these fields varied a good deal, moreover, in different periods. In the first half of the nineteenth century the problem was somewhat less complicated than it subsequently became because the overwhelming majority of emigrants went either to the United States or to British North America. Except between 1838 and 1842, when a sizable proportion went to Australia and New Zealand, over ninety percent of all English and Scottish emigrants before 1848 went to transatlantic destinations. In what proportions they were divided between the United States and the British colonies it is hard to tell before 1853. The respective number of passengers sailing to the two places is not a safe guide because, as we have seen, a large proportion of those who embarked for the North American colonies were attracted only by the cheapness of the route and went on immediately to the United States. Two-thirds of all the arrivals at Quebec between 1816 and 1828 were estimated to have gone to the United States[42] and, although greater efforts were then made to persuade those immigrants who arrived in Canada to stay there, the proportion passing through to the United States remained substantial. This meant that the United States was from the start the favored destination, at least of the English and Welsh, though even in their case the preference for the United States did not become really marked until the late 1830's. Of the Scots, however, a much larger proportion—a majority probably—seem to have gone to Canada and the Maritime Provinces right into the 1850's. Thereafter the picture becomes clearer. For the rest of the nineteenth

42. *Colonial Office Records*, C.O. 42/233, Buchanan to Aylmer, May 7, 1831.

century Canada was not a serious rival for the affections of either Englishmen or Scots. Between 1850 and 1900 roughly four times as many British emigrants sailed for the United States as for Canada. The disproportion may well have been much greater than the respective passenger returns indicate. Some of those who sailed to the United States settled finally in Canada, but these were only a fraction of the numbers who made use of the St. Lawrence route to reach the United States.[43] Even when the steamship had become the normal method of crossing the Atlantic the St. Lawrence route still offered advantages to emigrants bound for the Middle West; it meant a shorter sea voyage, and it was usually a little cheaper.

Despite the relative unpopularity of Canada the proportion of British emigrants going to the United States rarely matched that of the Irish. This was because of the size of the movement to Australia and New Zealand. Emigration to these places must have accounted for fully one-third of the British total between 1838 and 1842 and for more than one-half during the gold rush of 1852–1854. It was in fact the strength of the movement to Victoria, New South Wales, and other Australian colonies, rather than transatlantic emigration, that made the 1850's one of the peak periods of emigration from Britain. Even as late as 1862 departures for Australasia still exceeded the combined totals to the United States and British North America. Emigration to Australia and New Zealand then declined, both absolutely and relatively; it was not until the era of World War I that it again reached the absolute levels of the 1850's and then only for a few years. Nevertheless between 1860 and 1890 departures for the Antipodes were nearly always more numerous than those for British North America.

It was to the United States, however, that a substantial majority of British emigrants went in the last third of the nineteenth century. The proportion rose sharply after the Civil War, reaching seventy-four percent in 1869; and although in the 1870's it fell again, even dropping below fifty percent in 1878, it was generally between sixty and seventy percent. The heavy British emigration of the

43. Norman MacDonald, *Canada: Immigration and Colonization, 1841–1903* (Aberdeen, 1966), *passim*.

1880's was distributed in a way that could be regarded as characteristic of the late nineteenth century generally; out of a total of
1,380,564 emigrants between 1880 and 1889, 891,728 (sixty-four
percent) went to the United States, 271,468 (twenty percent) to
Australia and New Zealand, and 217,368 (sixteen percent) to Canada. Only after 1900 did the current of emigration turn toward
Britain's colonies, and when the swing occurred it was a dramatic one. In the decade 1890–1899, when British emigration had
amounted to just over one million, only twenty-eight percent had
stayed within the Empire; between 1900 and 1912 it was fifty-nine
percent of a total of more than 2½ million; and in 1913, when just
over 300,000 people left, it had become eighty percent. There was
no corresponding swing in the direction of Irish emigration; it
continued to flow to the United States in the same proportions as
before. But from 1905 onward the volume of British emigration
to the United States was always less, and sometimes substantially
less, than that to Canada; from 1911 it was also less than that to
Australia. The United States had now indeed become a poor third.
In 1913, which marks the all-time high in British emigration, the
51,595 emigrants who went to the United States were only seventeen percent of the total; Canada, with 182,482, took sixty percent;
and Australia, with 68,214 claimed twenty-three percent.

It would of course be easier to understand why people emigrated
from Britain if we knew more about the emigrants themselves.
But in fact we know practically nothing about them, especially
about those who emigrated in the earlier decades of the nineteenth
century. The difficulty lies once again with the statistics. Until 1876
the demographic information they contain relates only to emigrants in the aggregate. Particulars of the age, sex, and marital
condition of steerage passengers were included in the returns as
early as 1842, but because no record of nationality was yet kept we
can learn nothing about the demographic characteristics of the different nationalities. This difficulty remained even after nationality
began to be recorded in 1853 because the basic demographic data,
and indeed the particulars of occupation which were now also introduced, were still not presented in a form which disaggregated

the British from the rest. Only when the Board of Trade assumed responsibility for the collection of emigration statistics in the 1870's do the returns begin to provide us with particulars of age, sex, marital condition, and occupational distribution of each nationality. But that is all that the British records are able to tell us. They do not specify which parts of the country the emigrants came from or where they had been born.

Nor, except to a limited extent, can the deficiencies of the British statistics be remedied by turning to the records kept in the countries of immigration. Little help is to be obtained from American sources—at least from the immigration returns proper. It was not until after 1893, when Congress passed an immigration law providing for a set of questions to be answered on the ships' manifests, that an effort was made to obtain statistics relating to the social and economic characteristics of immigrants. Even then the statistics were for some time unreliable. In 1899 the assistant commissioner of immigration at New York told the Industrial Commission that before that date the statistics were of little or no value as sources of information about national origin, occupation, and destination.[44] However, the passenger lists which customs officials transmitted to Washington from 1820 onward in compliance with the United States passenger acts were occasionally more informative. Recent work on them, as well as on similar lists preserved in Australia, has demonstrated that they can be made to yield valuable clues about the geographical origins and occupational distribution of British immigrants.[45] Further investigations of this kind may be expected to remove some of the mystery that surrounds the English and Scottish emigrants of the nineteenth century. But they can never do so completely because of the fragmentary nature of the infor-

44. U.S. Industrial Commission, *Reports of the Industrial Commission . . . , Immigration* (Washington, 1901), XV, 82, evidence of Edward F. McSweeney, assistant commissioner of immigration at the Port of New York.

45. American and Australian passenger lists are analyzed respectively in Charlotte Erickson, "Who Were the English and Scots Emigrants to the United States in the Late Nineteenth Century?" in David V. Glass and Roger Revelle, eds., *Population and Social Change* (London, 1972), pp. 347–381, and Ross Duncan, "Case Studies in Emigration: Cornwall, Gloucestershire and New South Wales, 1877–1886," *Economic History Review*, 2d ser., 16 (1963), 272–289.

mation contained in the passenger lists which have survived. Only very occasionally do the American passenger lists, for example, contain the kind of detail that enables us to identify the economic and geographical origins of immigrants. In the vast majority of cases all that was recorded was the name, age, sex, and occupation of passengers and even that was done with less than complete accuracy.

Because of the limitations of the statistical material, historians of nineteenth-century British emigration—indeed of emigration generally—have relied heavily upon other types of evidence. This exists in plenty because emigration was one of the most discussed issues of the age. But the abundance of contemporary comment is a mixed blessing for much of what was said and written on the subject is either vague, superficial, or misleading. What the newspapers said was frequently all of these things. Newspaper reports commonly referred to the departure of "vast numbers of emigrants" without giving any indication of whether they were talking about scores or thousands. Nor were they always very precise about the kind of people who made up the departing throngs. Much depended upon the writer's point of view. One should not take literally therefore such descriptions of emigrants as "poor, deluded wretches" or, alternatively, "those whom the country can least afford to lose."[46] One might also derive from newspaper comment the totally false impression that most of those who emigrated were assisted in doing so by poor-law unions, charitable organizations, or individual philanthropists. This misconception was understandable because self-directed emigrants, even though they constituted the vast majority, were apt to be less visible than organized groups. It was understandable, too, that the press should devote a disproportionate amount of space to numerically insignificant but newsworthy groups of emigrants such as the Mormons. The reports of Parliamentary committees were free of this kind of distortion but most of what they contain about emigration was

---

46. For contrasting examples see *Times* (London), September 9, 1837, and December 9, 1852.

not the result of systematic investigation into the subject itself but a by-product of inquiries into other matters. All the same the Blue Books constitute an indispensable quarry for the study of emigration. They are unrivalled as a source of information about economic change and, together with impressionistic evidence from other sources, provide an invaluable complement to the emigration statistics.

Detailed inquiry into the circumstances in which emigration was apt to take place necessarily begins with the impact of agricultural change. Despite the rapid growth of industry England and Scotland were still essentially agricultural communities in the first half of the nineteenth century. More people worked on the land than in factories, mills, and mines and it was agriculture rather than industry that held the key to the national economy. The effects of the "agricultural revolution," and in particular of the trend toward large-scale scientific farming, were bound therefore to be considerable. In the long term they would bring about the displacement of a significant proportion of the agricultural population. But they had not done so to any great extent in 1815. As was noted earlier, the process of change was still far from complete. Besides, the effect on population movements of such changes as had occurred had been strongly counteracted by the agricultural boom of the French Revolution and Napoleonic Wars. Not only the new large-scale farmers but smaller men too had shared in the prosperity of wartime. Nor, while high prices for farm products persisted and additional plowland was brought under cultivation, had there been a falling off in the demand for agricultural labor.

But the bubble of prosperity was pricked even before the war ended. The excellent harvest of 1813 resulted in a drastic fall in the price of grain, and when peace brought a revival of foreign competition not even the new Corn Law of 1815 proved capable of stabilizing price levels. The fall in wheat prices went on virtually unchecked until 1835, causing widespread suffering and distress to the landed interest. It is true that distress was not the experience of all. The depression was confined to arable farming and even in that sector it was intermittent and far from universal.[47] Some arable farmers were able to contend with falling prices by adopting more productive techniques which brought higher yields at lower unit costs. Other branches of farming were hardly depressed at all. Livestock producers in the northern and western counties, for example, could still make a profit. So could dairy farmers in counties like Lancashire and Cheshire which were near to expanding urban markets. But arable farmers in southern and eastern England, especially those cultivating heavy clay soils, found it exceedingly difficult to do so. The result was that tenancies were abandoned, rent rolls dwindled, much land went out of cultivation, and, with the demand for agricultural labor falling far short of the supply, rural destitution became chronic.

Agricultural distress began to act as a stimulus to emigration the moment the Napoleonic Wars were over. George Flower, sailing from Liverpool to New York in April 1816 on his way to survey lands in Illinois Territory where he and Morris Birkbeck were shortly to establish an English Settlement, confided to his diary that foremost among the reasons for his emigration was "the disturbed condition of the farming interest."[48] Flower and Birkbeck were exceptionally wealthy farmers and untypical of those who emigrated. But contemporary newspaper reports claimed that quite a number of those who left England in the immediate postwar years did so because of the unprofitability of agriculture and were "respectable farmers" who possessed enough capital to buy farms of their own in America.[49] And even though the majority of emigrants from the agricultural districts were probably those whom contemporaries described as "small farmers and labourers in husbandry," there was probably a considerable sprinkling of men of capital.

The volume of agricultural emigration could hardly have been extensive until the late 1820's and early 1830's, when the first siz-

[47]. E. L. Jones, *The Development of English Agriculture, 1815–1873* (London, 1968), pp. 10–13.

[48]. Charles Boewe, ed., *Prairie Albion; An English Settlement in Pioneer Illinois* (Carbondale, Ill., 1962), p. 9.

[49]. *Liverpool Mercury*, June 14, 1816, May 18, 1821; *Times* (London), April 23, 1818.

able bulge in the movement from England occurred. This was the period when agricultural distress became so severe as to lead to the "village labourers' revolt," the spontaneous outbreak of rick burning and machine breaking that affected thirteen English counties from Kent to Dorset. It was promptly and ruthlessly suppressed, nine laborers being hanged, four hundred imprisoned, and about the same number transported for life to the Australian colonies. These events coincided with a sharp rise in emigration, but this took place equally from counties which did not experience outbreaks of violence and from those which did. In 1833 the Select Committee on Agriculture was told of a recent heavy emigration not only from "violent" counties like Kent, Sussex, Hampshire, and Surrey, but also from Yorkshire, Derbyshire, Cheshire, and Cumberland.[50] There was thus no correlation between emigration and discontent.

The economic pressures that induced people to leave were not necessarily those that drove half-starved laborers to violence. What the counties of heavy emigration had in common was not social unrest but an unprofitable agriculture. This was recognized by at least one of the witnesses who gave evidence before the select committee. In denying that emigration owed anything to political causes he asserted that it was due simply "to the want of a sufficient margin between the value of the produce of the soil and the cost of it."[51]

All the committee's witnesses were agreed that the emigrants were not drawn from any one class. Those who had emigrated from Hampshire and Sussex, for example, were said to have included "some of the best and some of the worst."[52] But the testimony suggests that the majority were small farmers and the better class of laborers. It was rare for really well-to-do farmers to emigrate and, except when they were assisted to do so, the very poorest were unable to go because they lacked the means. Those who

50. *Report from the Select Committee on Agriculture*, P.P. 1833, V, Qns. 2524, 2527, 2552, 5240–5252, 6178–6195, 6414–6420, 6899–6913, 9246–9255, 9613–9615, 10034–10055, 12557–12564, 12848–12854.

51. *Ibid.*, Qns. 4217–4221.

52. *Ibid.*, Qn. 10034.

did go from one part of England were described quite fully to the committee by a farmer from the North Riding of Yorkshire, where "there was not a township, or hardly a family but what have some of their inhabitants and some of their relatives gone to America." The character and motives of the North Riding emigrants was described as follows:

They were small freeholders that were in debt and compelled to sell the land, and they went away, saying that if they stopped here there was nothing but poverty for them; and they got away with the remainder of their property, under the fear of losing the whole; and also some of the farmers that were losing money went away. The labourers that have emigrated have been in general the best of the labourers that we had, saying that they were going to be ruined if they remained here; a labourer that had got his wife and child, and saved his £20 or £30 in service, got off before his money was gone. And then among the labourers that emigrated there was another proportion that had got further than that; the whole of their money was gone, and they were sent away in many cases at the expense of the parishes. . . .[53]

This picture, though based on first-hand knowledge of only one part of England, was identical with that drawn by witnesses from other farming regions. It suggests therefore that in social composition and motivation English agricultural emigration in the 1830's was very similar to that taking place in southwestern Germany at the same time. In both countries it was not the pressure of existing want that induced people to emigrate but uncertainty about the future. The emigrants consisted not of people who had already been engulfed by poverty but of those who feared a loss of status if they stayed where they were.[54]

This generalization does not of course apply in the case of the paupers whose emigration was subsidized by the ratepayers or by individual landowners. Emigration of this kind was never more than a fraction of the total volume but in some years it accounted for a not inconsiderable proportion of the departures from certain localities. The practice of shipping off the surplus poor at public

53. *Ibid.*, Qn. 2552.
54. For the social characteristics of German emigration between 1830 and 1845 see Mack Walker, *Germany and the Emigration, 1816–1855* (Cambridge, 1964), chap. ii, especially pp. 47, 51–52.

expense had its origin in the mounting pressure of poor rates. Expenditure on poor relief rose sharply from the late eighteenth century onward, reaching a peak of £7 million per annum in the early 1830's. Some counties were harder hit than others. Worst off were those rural counties, mainly in the south and east, where the population depended entirely on agriculture for its livelihood and which as arable regions were suffering most from falling prices.[55] That with few exceptions they were also Speenhamland counties, where the principle was followed of paying allowances in aid of wages, seems to have been coincidental. What mattered was not the method of paying relief but the per capita cost of supporting the unemployed poor.

Not until the Poor Law Amendment Act of 1834 were parishes given legal authority to mortgage the rates in order to subsidize emigration. But for at least a decade before then many parishes had been appropriating money for emigration, believing it to be cheaper in the long run to pay for the removal of the poor than to support them permanently at home. Parish-aided emigration was adopted over a wide area of southern and eastern England but appears to have been commonest in Kent, Sussex, Wiltshire, and East Anglia.[56] These were also the districts where landlords gave most assistance to emigration. One of the most widely publicized and most successful examples was the Petworth emigration of 1832–1837, when nearly five hundred paupers from the Earl of Egremont's estates in Sussex were sent to Canada. The Petworth emigrants were unusually well provided for; they received free passages on specially chartered ships, exceptionally generous supplies of food and water during the voyage, and outfit allowances of £5 each on arrival at Montreal.[57] Other assisted emigrants were not so fortunate; their landlords provided them sometimes only with free passages, sometimes only a contribution toward the fare.

55. Mark Blaug, "The Myth of the Old Poor Law and the Making of the New," *Journal of Economic History*, 23 (1963), 151–184.

56. Helen I. Cowan, *British Emigration to British North America: The First Hundred Years*, rev. ed. (Toronto, 1961), p. 206.

57. Edwin C. Guillet, *The Great Migration: The Atlantic Crossing by Sailing Ship since 1770* (Toronto, 1937), pp. 25–27.

It is not difficult to explain why the expedient of parish-aided emigration was not more widely adopted. Farmers on short leases were not always willing to incur the expense of subsidizing emigration when they could not hope to benefit from a future reduction in rates.[58] Parishes occasionally found too that some of those assisted to emigrate returned home after a short interval and once more became chargeable.[59] Nor did the Poor Law Amendment Act of 1834 help matters by insisting that paupers assisted to emigrate out of the rates could only be sent to a British colony. How this stipulation could operate in practice was demonstrated in 1835 in one Sussex parish. Finding that they were not permitted by law to go direct to New York to join their friends as they had intended, several paupers in Yapton who had agreed to emigrate changed their minds and refused to go.[60]

In most places paupers appear to have taken kindly to the idea of emigration. But there were instances where they did not; a few had even to be coerced into going. Some observers claimed that the relief that could be claimed under the old Poor Law made paupers reluctant to move. "The idle and profligate are never disposed to emigrate," declared a Kent landowner in 1832, "they are supported in idleness at home, and nearly as well as their industrious neighbours."[61] Others held that where popular antipathy to emigration existed this was because it was confused with the legal punishment of transportation.[62] Among other explanations was one that shed light on popular attitudes to emigration generally, not merely the assisted variety: rural folk, it was said, were afraid of the sea. "The sea voyage," asserted the rector of Hadleigh, Suffolk, in 1834, "is a universal object of dread with country people."[63] It was doubly so in parts of Oxfordshire at this time since several

58. *Report from His Majesty's Commissioners for Inquiry into the Poor Laws* . . . , P.P. 1834, XXVIII, App. (A), Part I, 15.

59. *Ibid.*, p. 757.

60. *Third Report from the Select Committee on the State of Agriculture*, P.P. 1836, VIII, Part II, Qn. 13168.

61. *Report from His Majesty's Commissioners for Inquiry into the Poor Laws*, P.P. 1834, XXXVII, App. (C), 450.

62. *Ibid.*, XXVIII, App. (A), Part I, 376.

63. *Ibid.*, XXXVII, App. (C), 452.

paupers had in 1832 died on board the *Brutus* from cholera while on their way to Canada.[64] Similar apprehensions were said to have discouraged emigration from such counties as Warwickshire and Worcestershire. Attitudes to emigration in such inland districts were in great contrast to what one of the Poor Law Commissioners found in North Devon in 1832.[65] Here the sea and its dangers were not a serious obstacle to emigration. Moreover the frequency with which the well-to-do emigrated had affected the attitude of the laboring population. "The example shown by so many men of capital and substantial farmers in emigrating," declared C. P. Villiers, "has greatly tended to remove prejudice against emigration among the poor."[66] His acknowledgment that prejudice had existed is of course very suggestive. It may have been a reason for the slow increase in emigration in the decades after 1815.

On the land social hardship was the result of a chronic condition, that of long-term underemployment. In the growing industrial cities on the other hand it took more acute forms, namely, short periods of intense cyclical unemployment and the displacement of skilled handicraftsmen by machines. Accepted notions about technological unemployment have in part had to be revised however in the light of recent research on the handloom weavers.[67] It has now been shown that handloom weaving was not a skilled occupation and that its difficulties were not wholly the result of technological advances. In any case the sufferings of the handloom weavers, uniquely intense though they were, are of little relevance to the history of emigration. The fact is that relatively few of them emigrated. Like the agricultural poor they lacked the means to do so without assistance, and this they were not given except to a very limited extent in Scotland. Wilmot Horton's emigration committee of 1826–1827 devoted much attention to the distress of the handloom weavers but only in an effort to show the necessity of government assistance.

64. *Ibid.*, XXVIII, App. (A), Part I, 2.
65. *Ibid.*, Part II, pp. 68–70.
66. *Ibid.*
67. Bythell, *The Handloom Weavers*, pp. 42–43, 65, 270–272.

That it was cyclical rather than technological unemployment that provided the main impetus to industrial emigration is suggested by the fact that the largest outflows of industrial workers seem to have coincided with the worst periods of urban unemployment—1816, 1819, 1826–1827, 1830–1831, and 1841–1842. It is evident, moreover, that during depressions at least industrial emigration was made up of skilled workers rather than handicraftsmen. William S. Fitzhugh, the leading Liverpool passenger broker, told Wilmot Horton's committee in March 1827 that emigration from Liverpool to the United States during the previous two years of slump "consisted chiefly of manufacturers from the different parts of Lancashire and Yorkshire."[68] A great many of them, he said, were cotton spinners, power loom weavers, and calico printers, some of whom had had their passages paid by the American employers by whom they had been engaged. How closely this kind of emigration was linked to the trade cycle is clear from a report by another well-informed observer in 1828 when the slump was over. A. C. Buchanan, the Londonderry merchant who had just been appointed resident emigration agent at Quebec, passed through Liverpool that spring on his way to take up his new appointment. He reported to the Colonial Office that most of the Liverpool emigrants were now farming laborers and their families, mainly from the southern counties. "Very few manufacturers have emigrated," he asserted, "but the families of those who went out in 1826 and 1827 are going in considerable numbers, their passages being paid for in the United States by their relatives out of the savings they have accumulated since then."[69]

Of course industrial emigration did not entirely cease in prosperous times. There was always a steady outflow of skilled men, attracted by American high wages. A businessman travelling on an emigrant ship from Liverpool to New York in 1829 noted that, while the majority of the steerage passengers were poor farm laborers and their families, "others were of a higher grade, being

68. *Third Report from the Select Committee on Emigration*, P.P. 1826–1827, V, Qn. 2241, evidence of W. S. Fitzhugh.
69. *Colonial Office Records*, C.O. 384/20, A. C. Buchanan to R. W. Hay, May 22, 1828.

mechanics who had nothing to complain of either on the score of work or pay, but who wished to visit this wonderful America, or El Dorado of the age."[70] Such presumably were the motives of the skilled technicians who crossed the Atlantic in increasing numbers during the mainly prosperous years of the 1830's. They included weavers and spinners from Lancashire, colliers and ironworkers from South Wales and Staffordshire, carpet weavers from Kidderminster, and Kilmarnock and Cornish miners.[71] But their numbers remained limited until depression returned in an unprecedentedly acute form in 1841–1842. During those gloomy years the Lancashire and Yorkshire papers were full of accounts of the way unemployment and distress were emptying the industrial towns of the North.[72] Emigration was said to be especially heavy among power loom weavers from Manchester and Oldham, woolen operatives from Huddersfield, miners from Barnsley, and mechanics from Sheffield and Leeds. Yet as soon as the economic outlook brightened, emigration from these places died away. In May 1843 a Liverpool paper called attention to "a remarkable change" in the class of emigrant. "Last year the bulk of the emigrants were of the manufacturing class; this year very few comparatively of that class are emigrating, while there is a marked increase in the numbers of the agricultural class."[73]

One should not make too much of impressionistic evidence but all of it suggests that, except in periods of extreme industrial depression, a majority of English emigrants in the first half of the nineteenth century was drawn from rural rather than urban areas. This conclusion would seem also to be supported by the statistics collected by the census takers in 1841.[74] Parishes were asked to state the number of emigrants during the period January 1 to June

70. *America and the Americans by a Citizen of the World* [James Boardman] (London, 1833), pp. 2–5.

71. Rowland T. Berthoff, *British Immigrants in Industrial America, 1790–1950* (Cambridge, 1953), pp. 31, 39, 48, 58, 63.

72. *Liverpool Mercury*, October 29, 1841, March 25, April 1, May 13, 27, 1842. *Sheffield Iris*, n.d., quoted in *Liverpool Mercury*, June 10, 1842.

73. *Liverpool Albion*, n.d., quoted in *Times* (London), May 23, 1843.

74. *Census of Great Britain, 1841: Abstract of the Answers and Returns . . .* , P.P. 1843, XXII.

5 of that year. As we have seen this was a period of unusually heavy emigration from the industrial areas. Even so urban emigrants do not seem to have outnumbered those from the countryside by very much, if they did so at all. Out of a total of 9,569 emigrants from the whole of England, only just over one quarter came from the most highly industrialized counties, namely, Lancashire, the West Riding of Yorkshire, Nottinghamshire, Warwickshire, and Staffordshire. One must assume that there must also have been a number of urban dwellers from counties which were industrial only in part; this applied particularly to Cheshire, Derbyshire, Leicestershire, Cornwall, Gloucestershire, Somerset, and Wiltshire. But even if one regards the whole of the emigration from these seven counties as having been industrial rather than agricultural, which was certainly not the case, industrial emigrants still could not have accounted for more than a bare majority. From the twelve counties named, emigration amounted to 5,004, or just over fifty-two percent of the total.

The emigration figures collected in 1841 can provide the basis for further generalizations. Well over one-half of the emigrants came from counties south of the Trent, and there were far more from the maritime counties than from those inland. Three groups of counties stand out as regions of relatively heavy emigration. The first consisted of the two most highly industrialized counties, Lancashire and the West Riding of Yorkshire; together they accounted for 2,306 emigrants. The second was made up of the four purely agricultural counties stretching along the south coast from Kent to Dorset; their total was 1,667. The third region was located in the West Country, and was made up of five counties where on the whole agriculture was the main source of employment but where there were significant mining and textile interests. These counties —Cornwall, Devon, Wiltshire, Somerset, and Gloucestershire— recorded the departure of 2,591 emigrants. Conversely there were regions where emigration was insignificant: the counties bordering London on the North, the Black Country, East Anglia, and indeed all the eastern counties between the Thames and the Scottish border.

Although the existence of well-defined regions of emigration is

evident enough there appears to be no obvious common characteristic that would explain their location. They were extremely
diverse in terms of economic activity, ranging from the purely
agricultural to the heavily industrial. Nor does it seem that the
centers of emigration were to be found in the least prosperous parts
of England. On the contrary there is no correlation between emigration and the level of average weekly wages. Departures were
numerous from a small minority of the low-wage agricultural
counties such as Dorset and Somerset and heavier still from a minority of high-wage agricultural counties like Kent and Sussex.[75]

Viewing England as a whole the annual emigration rate in 1841
was only 0.7 per thousand. This was low by any standard, and by
Irish standards insignificant. Even in the early 1830's the overall
Irish emigration rate had been 11.5 per thousand and during the
famine it was to be several times greater than that. No English
county, indeed, experienced anything like a mass exodus in 1841.
Emigration rates were highest in Sussex and Cornwall, where rates
of 2.5 and 2.3 persons per thousand respectively were recorded. At
the other extreme were the agricultural counties just north and
northeast of London and the industrial counties of the Midlands,
where rates never rose above 0.5 per thousand. Even in Lancashire
and Yorkshire, which sent the highest absolute numbers, the rate
was less than 1 per thousand.

The variations revealed by these returns are not readily explained.
It is not easy to see, for example, why emigration rates should have
been so much higher in Kent and Sussex than in East Anglia, though
a comparative study of agricultural conditions would doubtless
shed light on the matter. But some of the variations appear less
puzzling when viewed against the background of internal migration. It is of course important to remember that emigration was
only one strand in the large and complex pattern of population

---

75. The classification of counties used here is that adopted by Sir Arthur Lyon Bowley
in his *Wages in the United Kingdom in the Nineteenth Century* (London, 1900). For Bowley
an agricultural county was one in which at least one-third of the male labor force was
employed in agriculture; a low-wage agricultural county was one in which nominal
weekly wages in agriculture were ten shillings or less.

movements.[76] Another, and a more important one quantitatively, was the migration within England, more particularly the drift from the countryside to the rising industrial towns. The broad characteristics of the townward movement are now well enough known. It is no longer believed that the population of the North and the Midlands grew during the first half of the nineteenth century because of an influx of migrants from the rural South. On the contrary internal migration was for the most part a short distance affair.[77] The new industrial conurbations of Lancashire, Yorkshire, and the Black Country recruited their population locally; so did London, the greatest magnet of all. That being so one is not surprised to learn that emigration rates were low in the North, the Midlands, and in most of the counties around the capital. In these areas the availability of nearby urban employment made emigration less of a necessity for the rural poor. Equally it was the relative absence of industrial cities that helped account for the strength of the emigration impulse in such counties as Devon, Cornwall, Cumberland, Kent, and Sussex. Where short distance internal migration was less feasible people may have been more ready to consider the alternative of emigration, especially in maritime counties where facilities for emigration lay at hand.

Had the 1841 practice of asking parishes for details of emigration been followed in the next census a decade later the geographical origins of the great mid-century wave of British emigration would be easier to identify. In the event, however, no such request was made, and although the 1851 census returns contain numerous incidental references to emigration, these were extremely fragmentary and relate only to localities which had experienced an absolute loss of population. The returns do of course throw light upon special local conditions which stimulated emigration—the decline of the cloth industry in Gloucestershire and Wiltshire, the closing of manganese mines in parts of Cornwall, the depression in stocking

76. Thistlethwaite, "Migration from Europe," p. 42.
77. Arthur Redford, *Labour Migration in England, 1800–1850*, 2d ed. (Manchester, 1926), p. 186.

manufacture in some Leicestershire parishes[78]—but they are too selective to provide an adequate basis for a systematic analysis of the causes of emigration. Nor do the newspapers do much to remedy the deficiency; press comment on the mid-century emigration was understandably focused on the Irish exodus.

A clue to the character of the heavy mid-century emigration from Britain has however emerged from an examination of the American passenger lists for the period 1846–1854.[79] The sample is smaller than one would wish but if it is at all representative it would seem that the geographical origins of emigrants in this period were much as they had been in 1841. It suggests that relatively more people were leaving for America from the rural areas and that the inhabitants of the larger towns were underrepresented among the emigrants. It should be remembered of course that the data relate only to emigration to the United States, which received only a minority of those leaving Britain at this time. As no comparable analysis has yet been made of emigration to other destinations such as British North America and the Australasian colonies, it is not possible to draw firm conclusions about British emigration generally at this time.

Because of the inadequacy of the data, indeed, one remains largely in the dark until the 1870's. The official statistics enable us to chart the fluctuations in the outflow and to infer that the proportion of skilled workers among the emigrants increased during the 1850's and 1860's. The latter impression is strengthened by numerous newspaper references from the middle of the Civil War to the scale of the movement from industrial districts.[80] The reports agreed that throughout the 1860's emigration was brisk from the iron and coal districts of Staffordshire and South Wales, the Lancashire manufacturing towns, and the Cornish mining areas. In times of depression, such as the Lancashire cotton "famine" and the slump in the coal and textile trades in the late 1860's, editors tended to look

78. *Population, (Great Britain). England and Wales*, P.P. 1852–1853, LXXXV, Part I, Divisions I–VI.

79. Erickson, "English and Scots Emigrants."

80. *Times* (London), August 15, November 25, 1863, April 5, 26, May 23, October 2, 1866, June 4, 1867, May 21, 1868, May 3, 1869.

upon the exodus of skilled men as an understandable, if regrettable, response to hard times. But they were frequently puzzled at the fact that emigration did not always fall off when trade revived. Thus the stream of coal miners and ironworkers leaving South Wales for the United States in 1865, when wages were said to be fifteen to twenty percent higher than they had been three years earlier, prompted *The Times* to characterize the movement as the product of artificial stimulation. The "mania for emigration" in South Wales could only be attributed, it declared, to the "false representations and delusive hopes" raised by recruiters for American industry.[81]

The explanation was certainly plausible. Agents of the American Emigrant Company, a labor-recruiting agency organized in 1864 with the aim of supplying skilled immigrant labor to American industry, had indeed been active not only in South Wales but in the other regions from which heavy industrial emigration had been reported.[82] But their efforts had had very limited success. A few hundred miners, ironworkers, and textile operatives emigrated under contract to the company between 1864 and 1866, and others may have been persuaded to emigrate independently as a result of the company's propaganda. But its influence, such as it was, was short-lived. That the employers and the upper-class press were consistently unfriendly to the company was not perhaps a serious impediment to its activities. But the refusal of the trade unions to continue helping in the work of recruitment certainly was. Before the end of the decade the company's failure to import skilled industrial workers on any scale had led to its disappearance.

Whatever doubts they came to have about the wisdom of cooperating with American labor agencies, British trade unions actively encouraged emigration in the latter half of the nineteenth century.[83] As early as the 1840's, indeed, unions were turning to

81. *Ibid.*, August 7, 1865, April 5, 1866.

82. Charlotte Erickson, *American Industry and the European Immigrant, 1860–1885* (Cambridge, 1957), pp. 9–11, 17–28.

83. Charlotte Erickson, "Encouragement of Emigration by British Trade Unions," *Population Studies*, 3 (1949), 248–273; R. V. Clements, "Trade Unions and Emigration, 1840–80," *ibid.*, 9 (1955), 167–180.

emigration as a panacea for distress. Believing in the wage-fund theory union leaders argued that by diminishing the supply of labor they could improve the condition of those workers who stayed at home as well as of those who emigrated. Accordingly most of the leading unions operated emigration benefit schemes; especially active in this field were the textile workers, builders, engineers, metalworkers, and glassworkers. In some unions, like the Durham Miners' Association and the Cotton Spinners' Society, emigration benefit was limited to members who had become marked men in consequence of their prominence in union activities and who were unlikely therefore to find work in England again. Usually however any member who was willing to emigrate was eligible for benefit. In the event lack of funds severely limited the scale of assistance. According to trade union emigration theories the need to thin the ranks of labor was greatest in hard times; but these were precisely the times when funds for promoting emigration were at their lowest. In practice therefore the largest grants for emigration tended to be made in good times rather than bad. How much money unions spent on assisting emigration and how many skilled operatives were enabled to emigrate is impossible to say because of the incompleteness of most union records. But the indications are that the numbers were never very great. Thus the Iron Founders' Union, whose records are fairly complete and which was one of the more active in promoting emigration, spent less than £5,000 on emigration between 1854 and 1874. This sum could not have paid the emigration expenses of more than one thousand members; in eight years no assistance was given and even in the peak years of 1867 and 1873 the numbers assisted could not have exceeded two hundred fifty.[84]

Faith in the efficacy of emigration as a means of raising living standards died hard in some unions. The iron founders and some unions of cotton spinners, for example, were still paying emigration benefits on the eve of World War I. But the practice went largely out of favor after 1880. Some union leaders came to feel that the tide of voluntary emigration was flowing so rapidly as to

84. Erickson, "Encouragement of Emigration," pp. 268–269.

make assistance unnecessary. Others doubted whether, in view of the rapidity and ease of transatlantic travel, any permanent improvement in the situation of labor could result from emigration. With skilled workmen passing frequently between Britain and America there was felt to be no guarantee that members assisted to emigrate might not be back home again soon. The depression of the 1880's also brought into being a more militant unionism which placed less emphasis upon adjusting the labor supply to the needs of the market and more upon coercing employers by means of industrial action. Moreover as a sense of working class solidarity developed British labor leaders became increasingly sympathetic to the protests of American and Australian trade unionists at the practice of assisting emigration. The new mood was apparent at the annual conference of the Trade Union Congress in 1886. Strong hostility was expressed to emigration as a cure for social ills or as a substitute for social and economic reform. Delegates doubted whether emigration could relieve the labor market in times of great depression, and, in the course of a debate on state-aided emigration, adopted a resolution refusing support to any scheme of emigration, state-aided or otherwise, until a reform of the land laws had been achieved. This, it was hoped, would create a peasant proprietary and thus reduce the competition for work in the towns.[85]

A watershed in the history of emigration from the British Isles was reached in 1869. Until then the number of English emigrants had always been exceeded by the Irish. Now for the first time the reverse was true. It was to remain the case until the era of large-scale international emigration was over. Indeed the disparity in numbers between the English, Welsh, and Scots on the one hand and the Irish on the other grew steadily with time. By 1882 the ratio was 2 to 1; by 1905, 4 to 1; and by 1912 almost 8 to 1.

The replacement of the Irish by the English as the largest element in the outflow from the United Kingdom brought forth in 1877 some suggestive comments from Robert Giffen, the Board of

85. *Ibid.*; *Report from the Select Committee on Colonisation*, P.P. 1889, X, Qns. 1796–1803.

Trade official responsible for compiling the emigration returns.[86] "The change in the composition of the so-called emigration," he wrote, "is probably connected with the fact . . . that the returns include a larger amount and proportion than formerly of people who are not really emigrants." In becoming more English, he pointed out, the outward flow of population had also become more temporary. To illustrate the decline in genuine emigration Giffen called attention to the narrowing margin between the outward passenger movement and the inward. In 1876, so far as emigration to the United States was concerned, the two movements had been so nearly balanced that there had been virtually no net emigration at all. This suggested to Giffen that, for the moment at least, emigration to the United States in the sense of permanent settlement could almost be said to have ceased. The conclusion seemed to him to be confirmed by two contrasts he had discerned between the movement to the United States and that to Australia. One was a difference in age and sex distribution. In the case of emigrants to the United States there were relatively fewer children and a much larger proportion of single men and women. The other was the much larger proportion of agricultural laborers in the movement to Australasia; among emigrants to the United States, indeed, there were hardly any. All this confirmed Giffen in his belief that whereas emigration to Australasia was for the purpose of settlement, the "so-called emigration to the United States . . . [was] really of a very different character." Though he did not enlarge upon that remark the inference was clear: British emigrants to the United States were now largely temporary and transient.

Giffen's analysis was statistically faulty. By concentrating upon a single year, and an untypical one at that—1876 marked the deepest trough in British emigration in the whole of the century—he mistook a cyclical fluctuation for a trend. Within a year or two the outward balance of passengers to the United States had again become large enough to discount any possibility that emigration to that country had come permanently to an end or that the outward

---

86. *Statistical Tables relating to Emigration and Immigration from and into the United Kingdom in the Year 1876*, P.P. 1877, LXXXV, 7.

passenger movement now consisted only of tourists and other transient visitors. But Giffen was not altogether wide of the mark in suggesting that, by the 1870's, the impermanence that was later to be thought characteristic of the "new" immigration from southern and eastern Europe had to some extent become a feature of the movement from Britain. Whenever trade was slack in the United States, as it was in the middle of the decade, British immigrants tended to go home. But even in good times there was now a substantial transient movement. Considerable numbers of English and Scottish workmen went to the United States each spring with the fixed intention of returning home in the fall. Bricklayers, carpenters, house painters, stonecutters, and others whose trades shut down in America during the winter months became in effect transatlantic commuters.[87]

The increased numbers shuttling back and forth between Britain and the United States were largely a result of the expansion of transatlantic steamship services. Steam replaced sail in the North American emigrant traffic from Britain in the course of a single decade. Though regular transatlantic steamship services began as early as 1840 few steamships carried other than cabin passengers for the next twenty years. As late as 1862 over eighty percent of those emigrating to North America from British ports travelled by sail, mostly in American packet ships. But the threat posed by the *Alabama* and other Confederate commerce raiders during the Civil War drove insurance premiums so high as virtually to force American vessels off the Atlantic.[88] Their days were in any event numbered because the amount of mostly British-built steamship tonnage was rapidly increasing. But war conditions accelerated the process. By 1863 new steamship lines like the Guion and the National had appeared on the Liverpool–New York run; older lines like the Inman Line, which had pioneered emigrant travel by steamship in the early 1850's, expanded their fleets; and even the Cunard Line, which had tended hitherto to despise the emigrant traffic,

---

87. Berthoff, *British Immigrants*, pp. 52, 80–84.
88. George W. Dalzell, *The Flight from the Flag* (Chapel Hill, 1940).

now resolved to enter it.[89] The result was a rapid and progressive shift to steam. In 1863 nearly half of the emigrants to North America from Britain travelled by steamship; in 1865 nearly three-quarters; in 1867 over nine-tenths. A few years later the use of sailing ships for the conveyance of emigrants across the Atlantic had ceased altogether.[90]

The transition from sail to steam was as important an event in the history of emigration as the expansion of the cotton and timber trades had been half a century earlier. The emigrant steamship transformed conditions of travel and made the crossing less of a deterrent than it had been before. Fares were thirty to fifty percent higher than by sail but as against that the crossing became safer, somewhat more comfortable, and, above all, faster; the voyage now took ten days or so instead of between one and three months. Steerage conditions remained fairly primitive and there were still periodic complaints about food and overcrowding.[91] But unlike the sailing packets, the new steamships had been designed specifically for the emigrant traffic and were sufficiently well conducted for a Congressional investigating committee to report in 1873 that "the cruelty, ill-usage and general discomfort of the steerage belong to the history of the past."[92] The same could have been said of the frightful mortality produced by epidemics on board ship. An outbreak of cholera in 1866 carried off hundreds of victims on some National Line steamers from Liverpool.[93] This demonstrated that improved steerage conditions were no proof against cholera without corresponding advances in epidemiology. But once the cholera bacillus had been isolated methods of control steadily improved and the 1866 outbreak was the last to affect Britain or British vessels.

After remaining relatively low in the late 1870's the volume of British emigration rose appreciably in the following decade and

89. Jones, "United Kingdom," pp. 473–480.
90. *Ibid.*, p. 471.
91. *Ibid.*, pp. 498–503.
92. U. S. Senate, *Letter from the Secretary of the Treasury Communicating . . . Information in relation to the Space Allotted to each Steerage-immigrant on board Ship*, 43 Cong., 1 Sess. (1873), Sen. Ex. Doc. no. 23.
93. Jones, "United Kingdom," pp. 491–493.

remained high until a further decline set in during the last years of the century. Even during the 1880's, however, rates of emigration never even approached 1 per thousand. For the decade as a whole it was 0.50 for England and 0.73 for Scotland. Despite the disparity between emigration rates in England and Scotland, however, the age and sex characteristics of emigrants from the two countries were remarkably similar and, moreover, very different from those in Ireland. The distinguishing features of Irish emigration in this period were the relatively low proportions of married adults and children and the relatively high proportion of women. In the period 1877–1907 the proportion of married emigrants from Ireland to the United States never exceeded sixteen percent, and in most years the number of women exceeded the men. Among English and Scottish emigrants on the other hand, married people were generally about half as numerous as the single, and the proportion of children was generally not far short of twenty percent, or about double the Irish proportion. These variations reflected in part the relatively high age of marriage prevailing in Ireland. But they probably owed most to the fact that British emigrants were on average somewhat older than the Irish. Information about the ages of emigrants is lacking for this period, but we do have it for the period just before World War I. They show that about seventy percent of the people emigrating from England, Wales, and Scotland were under thirty years of age, while only seven percent were over forty-five. In Ireland emigrants were younger still; eighty-three percent were under thirty and only four percent were over forty-five. In addition, whereas about forty-five percent of those leaving England and Scotland were between eighteen and thirty-one, nearly seventy percent of the Irish were between those ages.

The differing demographic characteristics of British and Irish emigrants show the necessity of distinguishing between them in discussing occupational distribution. But until 1912 the official British statistics recorded occupations by destination rather than by country of origin. The separate series on the occupations of Irish emigrants, dating from 1877, might seem to offer a method of separating the British from the Irish by occupation; but since different systems of occupational classification were used in the two series, this cannot be done with any exactness. Thus the published British statistics enable us to draw only a few and unsurprising conclusions about occupation. They show, for example, that irrespective of destination the largest proportion of male emigrants from the United Kingdom in the late nineteenth century was drawn from the ranks of general laborers, and that the great majority of skilled emigrants went to the United States. Nor, as was indicated earlier, do the oft-quoted American statistics constitute a reliable guide to occupation before 1889.

The want of reliable data about occupations has been responsible, together with the absence of information about places of origin, for the conjectural and unsubstantiated character of much of what has been written about late nineteenth-century British emigration. Some historians have accounted for its volume by emphasizing the difficulties of specific groups of industrial workers. Others believe it to have been associated with the collapse of British agriculture during the "Great Depression." A recent article by Charlotte Erickson has, however, cast doubt upon both explanations, at least so far as they relate to emigration to the United States in the late 1880's. Her analysis of a group of New York passenger lists for the period 1885–1888 led her to suggest that English and Scottish emigrants came overwhelmingly from the towns, not from the countryside, and that they consisted predominantly of unskilled laborers rather than of skilled artisans.[94] The data upon which these conclusions rest are biased toward a narrow span of years and toward the first few months of those years. It may also be significant that the ship lists, like the American immigration statistics, record a lower percentage of agricultural laborers than do the British emigration records, even when the Irish are subtracted. But Dr. Erickson's conclusions have the rare merit of being based upon empirical investigation. Moreover, they are in line with the findings of Ross Duncan, who analyzed the composition of a group of assisted emigrants who went to New South Wales between 1879

94. Erickson, "English and Scots Emigrants," p. 373.

and 1886[95] and who turned out to be heavily urban in origin. At the very least, therefore, there is ground for reexamining the assumption that the heavy emigration of the 1880's was essentially the product of agricultural distress.

In its incidence, as in its severity, the agricultural depression of 1873–1896 closely resembled that of the twenty years after Waterloo.[96] That is to say, its worst effects were limited to the wheat-growing areas of southern and eastern England; the grazing counties of the north and west and those regions which were strategically placed to provide urban markets with fruit and vegetables remained relatively prosperous. There is no doubt, however, that the collapse of wheat prices in the 1870's brought severe distress to wheat producers, especially those in high-cost farming areas with less flexibility in switching to other forms of agriculture. The ruin of English farming which many had expected to follow the repeal of the Corn Laws in 1846 did not immediately occur. Overseas supplies of grain were not abundant enough in the 1840's to constitute a threat and in the era of sail could not have been shipped at competitive rates from Argentina, Australia, and the United States. In any case home demand for wheat increased steadily during the mid-Victorian industrial boom, and if wheat producers fared less well during the "Golden Age" than livestock producers or mixed farmers they had no particular reason to lament the loss of protection.

But once cheap American grain began to flood in during the 1870's wheat producers entered an era of adversity. Wheat prices fell suddenly and massively, went on falling for twenty years, and did not again rise substantially before World War I. The distress which resulted from foreign competition would not have been as great if British agriculture had been flexible enough to adjust quickly to a price structure which not only favored but dictated a switch to livestock rearing and market gardening. But some farmers were slow to see the necessity of conversion. A run of excep-

95. Duncan, "Case Studies in Emigration," pp. 272–289.

96. For what follows see T. W. Fletcher, "The Great Depression of British Agriculture, 1873–1896," *Economic History Review*, 2d ser., 13 (1961), 417–432.

tionally bad harvests in the late 1870's had the effect of masking the real causes of low grain prices and, even where the truth of the situation was appreciated, there was in places an economically irrational reluctance to abandon traditional ways. The continued downward spiral of prices forced even traditionalists, however, to recognize that some change in land use was imperative if bankruptcy were to be avoided. Accordingly plowland was increasingly laid down to grass with the result that between 1866 and 1911 two million acres of arable land were lost.

Accompanying this change was a sharp decline in the agricultural population. The number of farmers and graziers did not change a great deal but the number of agricultural laborers fell dramatically—from 962,000 in 1871 to 621,000 in 1901. Rural depopulation was not by any means caused solely by the depression. The decline in the agricultural population was as marked in the relatively prosperous north and west as it was elsewhere. Moreover, the largest absolute fall in numbers occurred in the 1860's, before the collapse of farm prices. It is clear that, quite apart from any dislocating effects that agricultural change might have had, the rural population was being drawn to the towns by the prospect of higher wages, more congenial hours of work, and superior social and cultural advantages. These attractions, observed a Parliamentary committee in 1906, had led in very many cases to "a deliberate and calculated abandonment of rural labour."[97] Nevertheless the drift to the cities was undoubtedly accelerated by the diminished demand for farm labor. The change from arable to pasture itself threw thousands out of work. So did the wider use of machinery which was attributable in large part to the new standards of commercial efficiency to which British farming had now to conform and, in particular, to the need to cut labor costs. Whereas in the 1880's labor-saving machinery had been adopted by relatively few, it became in the next twenty years almost universal on all holdings of sufficient size to make its use practicable. The greatly extended use of drills, horse hoes, mowers, binders, manure distributors, and so

97. *Report on the Decline of the Agricultural Population of Great Britain, 1881–1906*, P.P. 1906, XCVI, 15.

on involved a large-scale displacement of manual labor and was thought by some observers to be the main reason for the reduced demand for agricultural laborers.[98]

The state of British agriculture and the rural population generally were the subject of several full-scale official inquiries in the quarter century or so after 1880. There were royal commissions on agriculture (the Richmond Commission) in 1881–1882, on agricultural depression in 1894, on labor in 1891–1894, and on land in Wales and Monmouthshire in 1894–1896; in addition there were select committees on small holdings in 1889 and on the decline of the agricultural population of Great Britain in 1906. The massive and detailed reports that resulted constitute the historian's main source for the study of agricultural change and its social consequences in late nineteenth-century Britain. But while they provide us with a great deal of information about internal migration they contain little to suggest that overseas emigration was proceeding on any substantial scale from the rural districts.

Though rural depopulation was one of the many subjects investigated by the Richmond Commission in 1881–1882, its bulky report contains a mere handful of references to overseas emigration. One assistant commissioner who had visited the United States on behalf of the commission reported that, as a result of the agricultural depression of the past two or three years, "a great number" of young farmers and agricultural laborers had emigrated to that country.[99] But this view was not widely corroborated. Only one of the assistant commissioners who had toured the agricultural districts of England mentioned emigration at all,[100] and the only witness to discuss the subject in any detail was Joseph Arch who, as we shall see, subsequently retracted what he told the commission about emigration to Canada.[101] But there were innumerable reports of young men leaving their villages to seek employment in the towns, the railways, and the mines. This in fact is the recurrent theme of the

98. *Ibid.*, pp. 11–15.

99. *Minutes of Evidence Taken Before Her Majesty's Commissioners on Agriculture*, P.P. 1882, III, Qns. 65059–65061, 65134. Hereafter cited as *Minutes of Evidence*.

100. *Reports of the Assistant Commissioners*, P.P. 1882, XV, 21.

101. *Minutes of Evidence*, III, Qn. 58426.

reports of all the assistant commissioners sent out to investigate conditions in the countryside.[102]

Very similar were the reports on agricultural labor compiled a decade later for the Royal Commission on Labour. Out of hundreds of pages of testimony there are only three brief references to emigration. One witness told of young men emigrating, chiefly to Australia, from the Wetherby district of Yorkshire.[103] Another, referring to the agricultural districts around Truro, declared: "The constant emigration to America, which is thought nothing of by the miners, keeps up a spirit of restlessness in all other labourers, including the agricultural."[104] The third, significantly enough, used the term "emigration" to mean both internal and external migration, but placed greater emphasis on the former. Reporting from the south and southwest of England, one of the commission's investigators declared that the main reason for the decrease of the rural population was "the emigration of country labourers to the large towns . . . , or to the Colonies, or, as regards the West of England, to the South Wales mining districts, while a number of young men have also found employment on the railways, in the army or in the police service."[105] These examples apart, the report treated the drain of population from the countryside as though it were simply a matter of moving to the towns.

Not that internal migration invariably took that particular form or was restricted to farm laborers. There was also movement from one agricultural area to another, usually involving depressed farmers. In the 1880's there was, for example, a considerable movement of Scottish dairy farmers into Essex and Hertfordshire, where competition for farms was less keen than at home and where, as the Royal Commission on Agricultural Depression of 1894–1895 was to discover, they were to make a success of raising cattle in what had formerly been wheat country.[106] A parallel movement in the

102. *Reports of the Assistant Commissioners*, P.P. 1882, XV, 9, 30, 43, 54, 56, 67, 94.

103. *Royal Commission on Labour*, P.P. 1893–1894, XXXV, *The Agricultural Labourer*, I, *England*, Part VI, 79.

104. *Ibid.*, Part II, p. 107.

105. *Ibid.*, Part V, p. 7.

106. John H. Clapham, *An Economic History of Modern Britain* (Cambridge, Eng., 1938), III, 84–85.

West Country took dairy farmers from Cornwall and Devon into East Somerset, Gloucestershire, and Warwickshire.[107] Similarly Welsh farmers from Pembrokeshire and Carmarthenshire, smarting under what they considered unfair treatment at the hands of their landlords, migrated to more than a dozen English counties extending from Hereford to Hampshire.[108] That they did not venture further afield may well have been due to linguistic and religious factors: they were reluctant, it was said, to move even to England because of their ignorance of the English language and their attachment to religious services in their own tongue.

But this was by no means a universal Welsh characteristic, as the Royal Commission on Land in Wales discovered in the 1890's. It found that rural depopulation had been at least as marked in the Principality as in England and that, in the decade preceding 1891, no fewer than eight of the twelve Welsh counties—those which were predominantly agricultural—had suffered a loss of population.[109] A large but unknown number had gone to the coal and iron districts of South Wales, but considerable numbers had gone farther afield. The American census of 1890 showed that 100,079 Welsh-born people were living in the United States, but the British census of 1890 revealed that there were 228,616 natives of Wales in England and 2,309 more in Scotland. These statistics provide of course only a partial view of the location of natives of Wales. Welshmen were to be found also in Canada, Australia, Patagonia, and elsewhere—but since the United States took the vast majority of those who left the United Kingdom, the figures may nevertheless be seen as confirming the impression conveyed by contemporary reports, namely, that overseas emigration was quantitatively less important than internal migration. Precisely the same conclusion could be demonstrated in respect of the Scots,[110] and one would be unlikely to be wrong in suggesting that it was characteristic of British population movements generally.

107. *Ibid.*
108. *Report of the Royal Commission on Land in Wales and Monmouthshire*, P.P. 1896, XXXIV, 61–64. Hereafter cited as *Commission on Land in Wales.*
109. *Ibid.*, pp. 44–45.
110. *Ibid.*, p. 48.

Even so, one should avoid giving the impression that agricultural emigration was insignificant. The American census figures alone would refute such an assertion. The census of 1890, for instance, found more than ninety thousand British-born farmers in the United States and well over one hundred thousand British-born farm laborers. Not all may have worked on the land in the Old Country, but it may reasonably be assumed that most of them had. Only a small proportion appear to have emigrated, however, as a direct result of the propaganda put out by American states and railroads. This was widely disseminated in Britain in the 1870's, but the results were hardly proportionate to the scale of the advertising effort. The Northern Pacific Railroad and the Burlington, among others, employed hundreds of British agents, published emigration newspapers and flooded England and Scotland with posters and other advertising matter.[111] But the numbers they persuaded to settle on their lands in Minnesota, Kansas, Missouri, and elsewhere were never very great. None of the English, Welsh, and Scottish farming communities in the trans-Mississippi West which owed their existence to railroad colonization activities numbered more than a few hundred. The vast majority of British agricultural emigrants to the United States made their own way across the Atlantic and did not cluster together on railroad or other lands.

If the Australasian colonies were more successful in their efforts to attract British agriculturalists this was due not to superior propaganda but to generous assistance plans. Recognizing that high fares and the length of the voyage were serious deterrents to voluntary emigration to the Antipodes, colonial authorities had long used the proceeds of land sales to promote emigration from Britain.[112] As they became more autonomous some of the Australasian colonies grew less inclined to finance emigration. Assisted emigration nevertheless accounted for fifty-two percent of the emigration to Australia between 1877 and 1886. Ross Duncan's analysis of those assisted to emigrate during these years from Cornwall and

---

111. Philip Taylor, *The Distant Magnet: European Emigration to the U.S.A.* (London, 1971), pp. 78–79.
112. *Ibid.*, p. 82.

Gloucestershire to New South Wales shows that they were predominantly from mining and urban areas rather than from the countryside.[113] But this was hardly surprising in view of the somewhat unusual stipulation in the New South Wales scheme that assisted emigrants were to be selected "with a special view to the promotion of the industrial pursuits of the colony." Queensland was more typical in being interested in securing farm laborers, country artisans, and domestic servants. How far she succeeded is not known but contemporary reports of emigration to Queensland give the impression that agricultural laborers made up the largest group.[114]

The importance of assisted passages in the competition for emigrants was demonstrated by the comparative failure of nineteenth-century Canadian emigration propaganda. The aims of Canadian policy at this time were actively to promote the emigration of tenant farmers, agricultural laborers, domestic servants, and children under proper supervision, and to discourage mechanics, artisans, navvies, general laborers, and clerks from emigrating.[115] Time and again, however, the Canadian emigration agents in Britain complained of the disadvantage they were under in being unable to offer the same degree of assistance to prospective emigrants as the Australasian colonies.[116] Not even the passenger warrant system, which the Dominion government operated for a time in the 1870's and which enabled selected emigrants to obtain passages to Canada at about two-thirds the normal fare, sufficed to set in motion a really substantial movement to Canada. Canadian agents were unanimous that the explanation lay in the extreme poverty of the class it was hoped to attract. "Unlimited numbers" of English agricultural laborers were said to be both anxious and willing to emigrate to Canada, but were wholly without the means to do so. "The great difficulty . . . with agricultural laborers as a class," remarked a Canadian emigration agent in 1872, "is that they are

---

113. Duncan, "Case Studies in Emigration," pp. 277–278, 283.

114. *Times* (London), March 5, 25, 1873, July 31, 1874, April 30, 1875.

115. Taylor, *The Distant Magnet*, p. 82.

116. See for example Dominion of Canada, Sessional Papers 1885, no. 8, *Report of the Minister of Agriculture for the Calendar Year 1884*, App. 25, p. 199.

poor, living so to speak constantly from hand to mouth, and are almost all absolutely unable to pay even a part of the passage money for the short and comparatively unexpensive voyage to North America."[117]

Such comments, occurring almost annually in the reports of the Canadian agents during the 1870's and 1880's, go a long way toward explaining why relatively few agricultural laborers emigrated during the Great Depression. It was not that they were unwilling to leave England, but that they were too poor to do so. True though it was that the condition of agricultural laborers greatly improved in the last third of the nineteenth century, the improvement was not of a kind to leave them with a cash surplus.[118] Agricultural laborers, as the agents pointed out more than once, were nearly all married men and a wage of between twelve and sixteen shillings per week was not sufficient to enable them to do more than support themselves and their families at the most economical rate. They had no savings, and not even the sale of their household goods could realize enough to pay the cost of the voyage across the Atlantic.[119]

The most widely publicized group of rural emigrants in the last decades of the century was made up of those who left under the auspices of agricultural trade unions.[120] The main aim of the National Agricultural Labourers' Union and similar organizations was to secure better wages and working conditions for their members. Many of their leaders, however, shared the view of industrial unionists that one way of bringing this about was by eliminating local surpluses of labor through emigration. The local strikes and disputes in the midland and eastern counties that followed closely upon the birth of the agricultural unions in the early 1870's provided an opportunity to put this philosophy into practice. But the unions themselves lacked the resources to do more than offer nominal assistance to members who were prepared to emigrate, and it

117. *Ibid.*, 1873, no. 26, *Report of the Minister of Agriculture . . . 1872*, p. 101.
118. Clapham, *Economic History of Modern Britain*, III, 97–100.
119. Sessional Papers 1873, *Report of the Minister of Agriculture . . . 1872*, p. 6.
120. Pamela Horn, "Agricultural Trade Unionism and Emigration, 1872–1881," *The Historical Journal*, 15 (1972), 87–102.

was only because assistance was forthcoming from governments eager to recruit agricultural emigrants that the policy of union-sponsored emigration could be implemented at all. In the event groups of agricultural laborers were sent to Brazil, Queensland, and New Zealand, all of which offered free passages, and to Canada which, after Joseph Arch, the president of the National Agricultural Labourers' Union, had visited the Dominion in 1873 and reported favorably upon prospects for emigrants, arranged a specially low passage rate. So great was the poverty of the emigrants, however, that the unions had invariably to find the small sums needed to provide them with outfits for the voyage or pay the balance of their fares.

The first parties to leave were those sent to Brazil in 1872–1873 from Warwickshire and other counties in central and southwestern England. But the heaviest outflow was to come from the nine eastern counties, where emigration received a powerful boost from the long and bitter agricultural dispute of 1874–1875, in the course of which several thousand laborers, especially in Cambridgeshire and Suffolk, were locked out in an attempt to smash the union. The exodus was short-lived, however, for economic depression soon compelled Canada, New Zealand, and Queensland in turn to cut down sharply on assistance, and Brazil ceased to be a viable alternative after the 1872–1873 enterprise ended in failure. In any case the unions themselves suffered heavy losses of membership in the late 1870's. By the beginning of the following decade they were moribund and union-sponsored emigration had come to an end.

No firm evidence exists as to how many agricultural laborers received union assistance to emigrate. Joseph Arch told the Richmond Commission in 1881 that a total of seven hundred thousand union members and their families had been sent overseas, but on being closely questioned he withdrew what was obviously a grossly inflated estimate.[121] That the real figure was very much lower is suggested by the fact that even in the peak year of 1874 the total is unlikely to have reached ten thousand; we know that thirty-six hundred went to Canada, sixteen hundred to New Zealand, and

121. *Minutes of Evidence*, XIV, Qns. 58, 421–431, 60, 354.

"a considerable number" to Queensland. Perhaps the best estimate for the whole period 1872–1881 is that of Pamela Horn, who puts the total, including families, as between forty and forty-five thousand.[122]

Agricultural trade unions were thus able to help only relatively small numbers. It was not entirely a matter of resources, for their leaders came to feel that if Canada wanted agricultural immigrants she ought to be prepared to pay for them.[123] Repeated efforts were made to persuade the Canadian authorities to do just that. At an emigration conference in Ottawa in 1871, for example, Standish Haly, an official of the British and Colonial Emigration Society, reiterated what Canadian emigration agents in England had been saying for some time, namely, that English agricultural laborers with families were as a rule unable to emigrate without assistance, and that no assistance was forthcoming either from poor law guardians or from landlords.[124] Nor, as it turned out, were either the Dominion or the provincial authorities prepared to incur the heavy expenditure involved. In the United States, of course, there was no shortage of agricultural labor, and the question of assistance was never contemplated. In these circumstances one ought not to be surprised to find British agricultural laborers migrating to the towns rather than crossing the Atlantic.

Poverty was not, however, the reason—or at all events the main reason—why other elements in the agricultural population stayed at home. In the case of tenant farmers it was often a matter of conservatism, of hoping for better times, of a dogged refusal to contemplate leaving the land until disaster actually struck. The Canadian authorities made great efforts to woo tenant farmers, notably by inviting a group of them to visit the Dominion as delegates in 1879. It was hoped that their reports would carry greater conviction with other tenant farmers than the propaganda of emigration

122. Horn, "Agricultural Trade Unionism," p. 97.

123. *Ibid.*, pp. 100–101.

124. Sessional Papers 1872, no. 2A, *Report of the Minister of Agriculture . . . 1871*, pp. 11–13, 108.

agents. But results were disappointing if not, to at least one Canadian agent, a matter for surprise. "English agriculturalists," remarked John Dyke in 1879, "have always been a stay-at-home race. . . . In many instances they have farmed the same land for many generations and will not give it up without a most determined struggle."[125] Two years later Dyke reported that although the agricultural depression still persisted comparatively few farmers had emigrated. "In conversation with several of the leading agricultural authorities on the subject," he went on, "I was informed that a large number of tenant farmers, instead of emigrating, have migrated to the suburbs of the leading centers of population and engaged in dairy keeping, market gardening and other kindred pursuits. . . ."[126]

What had been true of Canadian promotional activities during the 1870's, when emigration had been comparatively light, was equally true during the heavy outflow of the 1880's. Though Canadian agents redoubled their efforts to persuade agriculturalists to emigrate, their reports to Ottawa were devoted chiefly to explaining their lack of success. There was the same emphasis as before on the attachment of farmers to the soil, on the immobilizing effects of poverty, and on the tendency of the displaced rural population to gravitate to the towns.[127] Taken in conjunction with the other evidence discussed above, notably the information collected by Parliamentary committees, these Canadian reports leave little room for doubt that Charlotte Erickson is correct in suggesting that the heavy emigration of the 1880's was drawn not from the British countryside but from the towns and cities.

Whether Dr. Erickson is equally correct in what she says about the occupations and origins of these urban emigrants is less certain. Her conclusion,[128] based upon an examination of a small sample of American passenger lists, is that, except for miners and building-trades workers, skilled craftsmen were not strongly represented

125. *Ibid.*, 1880, no. 10, *Report . . . for 1879*, p. 126.
126. *Ibid.*, 1882, no. 11, *Report . . . for 1881*, p. 193.
127. *Ibid.*, 1885, no. 8, *Report . . . for 1884*, p. 166; 1886, no. 10, *Report . . . for 1885*, p. 294.
128. Erickson, "English and Scots Emigrants," pp. 364–365.

among the emigrants of the eighties. The most numerous group in her sample was made up of general laborers without industrial skills, many of whom, she believes, had moved first from rural locations to towns. There they formed a marginal element in the labor force, the group most susceptible to the severe cyclical unemployment of the decade and the one most responsive therefore to the return of prosperity to America after 1879.

The first thing that needs to be said about this hypothesis is that none of the passenger lists Dr. Erickson examined contains any information about where emigrants came from originally; they merely record the place of last residence. The lists do not therefore support the argument that those emigrants classed as urban laborers had originally come from the countryside. It is moreover debatable whether unskilled laborers predominated among emigrants to the United States between 1885 and 1888. Despite the evidence of the passenger lists contemporary judges were less certain. It so happens that twice in this period, first in 1886 and again in 1888, the State Department instructed all American consuls in Europe to submit full reports on the extent and character of emigration to the United States from their respective consular districts. The reports submitted by the consuls in the United Kingdom were unusually full, and although in some cases the value of what they said was vitiated by a failure to recognize the limitations of the British emigration returns, most were the product of independent inquiry and made a genuine attempt to ascertain the causes of emigration and to estimate the proportion of emigrants drawn from different occupations.[129]

Though they did not say so in so many words the consuls appear to have assumed that British emigrants at this time were predominantly town dwellers. Certainly they were agreed that the main causes of emigration were the difficulty of finding work at a time of business depression in Britain and the attraction of high wages in the United States. But in 1886 at least opinions differed on the

129. U. S. House, *Emigration and Immigration. Reports of the Consular Officers of the United States*, 49 Cong., 2 Sess. (1887), House Ex. Doc. no. 157; U. S. House, *Reports of Diplomatic and Consular Officers concerning Emigration from Europe to the United States . . .*, 50 Cong., 1 Sess. (1888), House Misc. Doc. no. 572, Part 2.

question of whether emigrants were skilled workmen or ordinary laborers. Inquiries in the Manchester area seemed to indicate that, because their living standards had risen, Lancashire cotton operatives were no longer emigrating in such numbers as had been the case twenty years earlier.[130] Indeed one informant stated categorically that emigration from Lancashire now consisted largely of unskilled laborers.[131] But emigration from the southern and western counties was said to have an opposite character. "Emigration," reported Consul Lathrop from Bristol, "like flour made with rollers, has two classes, a very good and a very bad one. The cream of the industrial population—the provident, the ambitious—go; so also do the shiftless, the roving and the idlers; but most of the emigrants from this district belong in the first class. The second class may have the will, but they cannot obtain the means."[132]

The 1888 reports, on the other hand, were more nearly unanimous that emigration consisted largely of skilled men. Consul Wigfall in Leeds, though noting that opinions differed as to the proportion existing between skilled workers and common laborers, declared that most of the ticket agents he had consulted thought that tradesmen and skilled workers greatly outnumbered laborers.[133] A similar report came from Consul Grinnell in Bradford. Emigrants from that area to the United States, he wrote, "were almost wholly of the high artisan class—expert wool-sorters, machinists, foremen, managers and supervisors."[134] Similarly from Birmingham Consul Hughes reported that in the past twenty years many of the city's most skilled and intelligent workmen had been found in large numbers among those who had emigrated to the United States; jewelers, buttonmakers, gunmakers, and glass workers had been especially numerous.[135]

This kind of evidence is of course impressionistic, fragmentary, and uninformative as to numbers. It is not possible to draw from

130. U. S. House, *Emigration and Immigration*, pp. 422–426.
131. *Ibid.*, pp. 451–452.
132. *Ibid.*, p. 375.
133. U. S. House, *Reports of Diplomatic and Consular Officers*, p. 14.
134. *Ibid.*, pp. 32–33.
135. *Ibid.*, pp. 33–35.

it any firm conclusions about the characteristics of late nineteenth-century emigration. But it does at least appear to cast doubt upon the notion that the heavy urban emigration of the 1880's was made up largely of unskilled laborers. Similar doubts are suggested by the emphasis placed in contemporary public discussion upon the necessity of assistance if the urban unemployed were to be enabled to emigrate in large numbers. All were agreed that the least skilled members of the urban labor force were also, because of their poverty, the people least able to move. This view was widely expressed during the debate on state-aided emigration that occurred in the early 1870's. What had revived public interest in the matter was the growing problem of urban destitution. By 1870 over one million were supported out of the poor rates and another million lived at subsistence level. The distress of the unemployed in the large cities, especially London, produced a widespread feeling that some outlet must be provided for the surplus urban population. Numerous societies were organized for the purpose of promoting emigration, and in February 1870 a deputation from a confederation of such societies, the National Emigration League, waited upon Gladstone to urge the case for mass emigration at public expense. Later the same year the question of state-aided emigration was raised in Parliament for the first time since the Irish famine. The proposal was, however, heavily defeated. Gladstone's government was strongly opposed, mainly on the grounds that emigration should be a matter of individual choice. It was held not to be the state's function to decide which individuals should emigrate or where they should go; nor was it felt to be right to spend public money on a particular class of individuals.[136]

That was the end of the matter for more than a decade. But the severe trade depression of the 1880's brought it to the fore again. In 1886, when the slump was at its worst, respectable opinion was alarmed by the riots and demonstrations of the unemployed in London, Manchester, and other cities and was inclined to look more favorably upon state-aided emigration. It would be a safety

136. Sessional Papers 1871, no. 64, *Report of the Minister of Agriculture for 1870*, pp. 4, 66–67.

valve for discontent and a method of diminishing the problem of poor relief. To advocates of empire, moreover, emigration was seen as the best means of developing the immense material resources of the colonies. Once more, therefore, the question was aired in public and debated in Parliament. But the government, again led by Gladstone, was still unwilling to use public funds to promote emigration or colonization; all it would agree to was the setting up of an emigrants' information office whose purpose was the collection and dissemination of information about the prospects of emigrants to the British colonies.[137]

Salisbury's Conservative government, which took office later in 1886, seemed likely for a time to be more sympathetic. In the spring of 1888 it undertook a limited and experimental scheme of crofter colonization in Canada as a means of relieving distress in the western Highlands and the Hebrides.[138] The following year it appointed a select committee on colonization to look into various schemes for state-aided colonization from the congested districts of the United Kingdom. But by now the depression had given way to better times and by the time the select committee reported in 1891 it was able to claim that such was the general level of prosperity that no extensive scheme of state-aided emigration was necessary, except perhaps in the chronically congested areas of the Scottish Highlands. Moreover the committee took the view that, so long as the bulk of colonial opinion was strongly opposed to emigration directly assisted by the state, this was not an expedient which ought to be recommended to Parliament. In any case it was felt that the statutory powers already possessed by local authorities ought to be sufficient to enable them to provide for or assist the emigration of the poor from their own parishes. The committee went on to note, however, that these powers did not seem to have been widely used because the majority of those chargeable to the rates were unsuitable material for emigration. Those who had lived

137. *Report from the Select Committee on Colonisation*, P.P. 1890–1891, XI, iv; Stanley C. Johnson, *Emigration from the United Kingdom to North America, 1763–1912* (London, 1913), pp. 29–30.
138. *Ibid.*, pp. 240–243.

in congested districts in large towns, especially in London, had usually migrated there from the countryside some time earlier but after several years of urban living lacked the vigor or the fitness for rural pursuits. "They are," concluded the select committee, "the last species of population that foreign countries or colonies would want to receive. . . ."[139]

What the British government refused to undertake comprehensively, individual philanthropists, charitable organizations, and local emigration societies attempted piecemeal. Organized effort was directed especially to the problem of destitution in London, particularly in the crowded slums of the east end. One of the first organizations in the field was the East End Family Emigration Fund, founded in 1868 by a group of wealthy philanthropists of whom the moving spirit was the Honourable Mrs. Hobart. This body was particularly concerned to relieve the distress caused in the east end by the closure of two Thames-side dockyards; the 1,035 emigrants it assisted in 1869 came chiefly from Poplar, Bow, the Isle of Dogs, Limehouse, Stepney, Mile End, Whitechapel, Bethnal Green, Clerkenwell, Shadwell, St. George's East, and Spitalfields.[140] Other organizations confined their activities more narrowly. One was the Clerkenwell Emigration Society, founded by a local clergyman, the Reverend A. Styleman Herring, and organized along the lines of self-help. Between 1868 and 1872 it assisted over three thousand people to emigrate.[141] But the body which attracted the largest amount of public support was the British and Colonial Emigration Fund, presided over by the lord mayor of London and including on its committee such prominent philanthropists as Shaftesbury and Sir Thomas Fowell Buxton.[142] Though many of the local emigration societies disbanded when trade revived, most of the charitable organizations were still actively promoting emigration when the depression of the mid-1880's gave renewed point to their work. In fact the 1880's saw several newcomers to the field of assisted

---

139. *Report from the Select Committee on Colonisation*, P.P. 1890–1891, XI, xiv, xv.
140. Sessional Papers 1871, no. 64, *Report of the Minister of Agriculture for 1870*, p. 76.
141. *Ibid.*, p. 5.
142. *Ibid.*, p. 6.

emigration: the Charity Organization Society, the Self-Help Emigration Society, and the Church Emigration Society.

Very few of those assisted by these bodies were sent to the United States. "After . . . diligent inquiry . . . ," reported Consul General Waller from London in 1888, "I am not able to mention a single case of assisted emigration in pursuance of any English statute, local or municipal regulation occurring within the last two or three years, and I notice that none of my consular colleagues in this Kingdom in their reports on the subject have cited an instance."[143] The reason, he believed—and it applied equally to those assisted by private charity—was the attention paid in Britain to American state and federal laws prohibiting pauper immigration. Canada was equally anxious to exclude the indigent but, after assurances had been given that the completely destitute would no longer be sent, the Dominion Emigration Act of 1869 made an exception in favor of emigrants sponsored by approved charitable societies.[144] Hence it was to Canada that assisted emigration was principally directed, though some of those sent there may have found their way ultimately into the United States. The movement of assisted emigrants to Canada reached its peak between 1869 and 1871; in those three years a total of nearly twenty thousand reached Quebec. Thereafter the numbers dwindled and within a few years it amounted to only a few hundred annually. Even in the depressed years of the 1880's the numbers involved annually rarely exceeded more than two thousand, most of them children. Orphaned and abandoned children sent out by charitable bodies proved to be very acceptable in Canada and indeed were much in demand there. The pioneer of juvenile emigration was Maria S. Rye, secretary of the Church Emigration Society, who in 1867 began sending out children from among workhouse inmates. Other philanthropists followed suit, among them the founder of Dr. Barnardo's Homes for destitute children. At one time or another about sixty different agencies were engaged in the work of juvenile emigration and be-

143. U. S. House, *Reports of Diplomatic and Consular Officers*, p. 9.
144. MacDonald, *Canada*, pp. 95–96.

tween 1867 and 1908 a total of sixty thousand children was sent to Canada.[145]

In the decade immediately preceding World War I the current of British emigration turned decisively toward Canada. Contemporaries tended to attribute the shift to the growth of imperial sentiment and the success of Canadian recruiting efforts in Great Britain.[146] But neither of these explanations is convincing. That there was much popular enthusiasm for the Empire around the turn of the century is certainly true; its strength had been demonstrated particularly at the time of Queen Victoria's Diamond Jubilee celebrations in 1897. But there had been a similar wave of imperial patriotism at the time of her Golden Jubilee ten years earlier and that had had no effect upon emigrants' choice of destination. Two years later, in 1889, the official in charge of the Emigrants' Information Office told the select committee on colonization that the laboring classes "do not have any very strong feeling about remaining under the British flag; they go to the country where they think they can do best, or where they may have friends."[147] People did not for example look upon going to America as expatriation, he declared, whereas they did in the case of Australia on account of the distance. This was undoubtedly true and one may feel confident that it was not vague notions of imperial unity but individual self-interest that sent the British to Canada in such numbers in the first decade of the twentieth century.

There can be no doubt that Canada made unprecedented efforts at this time to attract British emigrants. The recruiting drive in Britain was part of the vigorous immigration campaign launched by Clifford Sifton, the dynamic minister of the interior in Laurier's cabinet between 1896 and 1906.[148] It was Sifton's aim to people the

145. Johnson, *Emigration from the United Kingdom*, pp. 257, 278, 285, 290; MacDonald, *Canada*, pp. 266–269; Sessional Papers 1909, no. 25, *Report of the Department of the Interior for the fiscal year ending 31 March, 1908*, p. xxxi.

146. *Report on the Decline of the Agricultural Population of Great Britain, 1881–1906*, P.P. 1906, XCVI, 44.

147. *Report from the Select Committee on Colonisation*, P.P. 1889, X, Qns. 1938–1939, 1944–1946.

148. Sifton's immigration policies are described in J. W. Dafoe, *Clifford Sifton in Relation to His Time* (Toronto, 1931).

Canadian west and he spent millions of dollars to publicize its attractions. Among other things he greatly expanded the amount of advertising in British newspapers and increased the number of agents on salary and commission. But the only thing new about this propaganda was its scale. Canadians had been trying for nearly half a century to attract British agriculturalists but, as we have seen, with scant success. That failure was the reason why Sifton had come to the conclusion that if the prairie provinces were to be filled up with farmers he must look for settlers not only to Britain but to all continental Europe and, more particularly, to the United States. Whether Sifton deserves the credit he is usually given for the ensuing increase in immigration into Canada from all these areas is debatable. Thus the large-scale movement of American farmers into Manitoba and the Canadian Northwest was due as much to the closing of the frontier in the United States as to the effects of Canadian propaganda.[149] Nor can it be automatically assumed that the great and growing flood of British immigrants into Canada after 1903 was a response to an advertising campaign which stressed the Dominion's fertile and unoccupied lands, its abundant wheat harvests, and its unrivalled farming opportunities.

The fact was that Canada was rapidly becoming urbanized.[150] It was still predominantly an agricultural country but manufacturing enjoyed a spectacular growth, especially in Ontario. By 1900 Toronto, Hamilton, and Kingston were major industrial centers; so was Montreal. Even Manitoba and the Northwest were far from being wholly rural; Winnipeg was the only really big city, but further west along the line of the Canadian Pacific Railway there was a string of expanding urban settlements.

Urban growth was the key to Canada's newfound popularity with British immigrants. Whatever may have been the motives of American farmers and Ukrainian peasants in emigrating to Canada, the British seem to have been drawn chiefly by the expanding opportunities for urban employment. Certainly it was not agriculturalists who predominated among those who arrived in Ca-

---

149. Marcus Lee Hansen, *The Mingling of the Canadian and American Peoples* (New Haven, 1940), pp. 220ff.

150. MacDonald, *Canada*, pp. 125–127, 270–271.

nada from Britain during these years. Thus in the twelve months ending March 31, 1908, a period which saw the heaviest immigration yet recorded in Canadian history, the number of farmers and farm laborers among English, Welsh, and Scottish immigrants was only 14,279 compared with 22,670 mechanics and 12,188 general laborers.[151] Quite obviously Canada was now attracting the British urban dwellers who in the 1880's had gone preponderantly to the United States. Why there was such a marked change of direction can only be surmised, but it may well have been connected with the increasing volume of the "new" immigration into the United States. Whether or not it is true that immigrants from southern and eastern Europe displaced those from the north and west of the continent, their presence in such numbers certainly limited the range of opportunities available to the British industrial immigrant in the United States. In this situation the appeal of Canadian cities was hardly surprising.

The factors which impelled or facilitated emigration were broadly the same in all three countries which made up Great Britain. Nevertheless there were special local conditions which imparted distinctive flavors to the outflow from the two Celtic countries. The emigration history of Wales and Scotland differed in certain respects from that of England and, indeed, from that of each other. Thus the rate of emigration from Scotland was always higher than that from England and Wales and the movement retained its momentum for a longer period. Wales, on the other hand, after having maintained an emigration rate second only to Scotland's for much of the century, virtually ceased to export population after about 1880.

The beginnings of Welsh emigration[152] date back to the late seventeenth century when groups of religious dissenters began to settle in Pennsylvania. But by 1700 or so the movement had run

151. Sessional Papers 1909, no. 25, *Report of the Department of Interior . . . 1908*, pp. 14–15.

152. See on this subject A. H. Dodd, *The Character of Early Welsh Emigration to the United States*, 2d ed. (Cardiff, 1957), and, more particularly, Thomas A. Glenn, *Welsh Founders of Pennsylvania*, 2 vols. (Oxford, 1911–1913).

its course and for almost a century Welsh emigration was virtually at a standstill. The revival of the outflow in the 1790's was the consequence of agricultural distress. Though the French Wars brought prosperity to the lowland farmers, many hill farmers experienced hard times. They benefited from the high price of dairy products but, growing little wheat, suffered acutely from the shortage and high price of corn. These depressed conditions led to the departure for the United States of many upland farmers like those from Llanbrynmair, Montgomeryshire, who set out in a body in 1795.[153]

The war years from 1793 to 1815 were a period of extensive enclosure in Wales but, as in the rest of Great Britain, enclosure did not result in widespread depopulation. But that was certainly the consequence of the tendency, first apparent during these years but continuing well into the nineteenth century, to consolidate farms into larger units. Another factor which in the long run would help to displace the agricultural population was a change in land tenure. In the hope of increasing rents at short notice landlords refused to renew long leases and began instead to let the land on a year-to-year basis. Insecurity of tenure became a bitter grievance after 1815 when the agricultural depression which affected British agriculture generally brought distress to Welsh uplands and lowlands alike.[154]

But even when the long agricultural depression lifted there was much in the state of Welsh agriculture to cause discontent. Throughout the nineteenth century the Welsh land system exhibited many of the characteristics of that of Ireland. There was the same land hunger, the same attachment to the soil and to antiquated farming methods. Welsh and Irish peasants shared many grievances: insecurity of tenure, the arbitrary fixing of rent, inadequacy of compensation at the conclusion of a tenancy. Above all there was a similar divergence in religion and social origin between the cultivators of the soil and those who owned it. There was the same hostility, though perhaps more veiled, to the agents of the landlord.[155]

153. Dodd, *Early Welsh Emigration*, p. 23.
154. David Williams, *A History of Modern Wales* (London, 1950), pp. 197ff.
155. *Commission on Land in Wales*, pp. 911–912.

If an iniquitous land system produced large-scale emigration from Ireland, why, one is impelled to ask, did a very similar system fail to generate a comparable movement from Wales?

Part of the answer is that the pressure of population on land was only half as intense in Wales as in Ireland. Wales, with an area of about eight thousand square miles, had a population in 1841 of little more than one million. Ireland at that date had to support over eight million people in an area of about thirty-two thousand square miles. Furthermore the Welsh peasant was not as dependent as his Irish counterpart upon the soil. Most smallholders and cottagers in Wales had some occupation other than that of farming—weaving or mining, for example. Nor were class lines as rigid in Wales as in Ireland—or in England for that matter. Welsh farmers were little removed in social position from the laborers they employed, and the latter was often a smallholder or could hope to become one.[156] Most important of all, however, was the fact that, unlike the Irish, most Welshmen displaced by agrarian change had no need to cross the sea in order to find alternative employment. Not only were the industrial regions of England within easy reach, but in Wales itself industrialization took place on such a scale as to absorb a sizable proportion of those uprooted from the countryside. The opening up of mines and mills in South Wales made it less necessary for the Welsh to emigrate.

Nevertheless there was an appreciable outflow of Welsh agriculturalists in the half century or so after 1815. The census of 1831 showed that although the population of the agricultural districts was generally on the increase many parishes had suffered a decline through departures for America. The census of 1841 drew a fuller picture.[157] It appeared that 1,149 people had emigrated from Wales and Monmouthshire in the period between January 1 and June 5, 1841—an annual emigration rate, that is, of about 1.6 per thousand, compared with an English rate of 0.7. The purely agricultural counties sent easily the largest numbers, with Cardigan and Carmarthen

156. *Appendices to the . . . Commission on Land in Wales*, P.P. 1896, XXXIII, App. (A), p. 72.
157. *Commission on Land in Wales*, p. 52n.

accounting for nearly one-half of the total and Montgomery for a further one-fifth. Agriculturalists probably continued to make up a substantial majority of Welsh emigrants until well into the 1860's, though the high proportion of urban dwellers among Mormon emigrants from Wales, as indeed from England, did something to redress the balance.[158]

Though there was a lessening of agricultural distress in Wales in the 1850's, it was now that the land question began to be aggressively agitated. The best-known advocate of land reform was the Reverend Samuel Roberts, a Montgomeryshire pastor and tenant of an upland farm.[159] In a number of impassioned pamphlets Roberts championed the cause of the Welsh peasant against the tyranny of landlords, heavy taxation, tithes, and church rates. In 1857, despairing of improving conditions in Wales, he came to the conclusion that emigration offered the only hope of emancipation. But few Welsh farmers could be persuaded to follow him when he established an exclusively Welsh settlement in eastern Tennessee. Nor would more than a few hundred join the Reverend Michael D. Jones when in 1865 he made a similar attempt to establish a New Wales, this time in Patagonia.[160] Yet agrarian discontent not only persisted but took on an increasingly political character. This was a result of the evictions which occurred after the 1859 election in Merionethshire and, more extensively, after the 1868 election in Carmarthenshire and Cardiganshire. Many tenants who abstained from voting or who voted contrary to the wishes of their landlords were punished with eviction notices; others had their rents increased or were told that attendance at Anglican church services would in future be a condition of tenancy.[161]

These events produced great and lasting indignation throughout Wales and are popularly believed to have resulted in heavy emi-

158. P. A. M. Taylor, *Expectations Westward: The Mormons and the Emigration of their British Converts in the Nineteenth Century* (Edinburgh, 1965), pp. 148–149.

159. Wilbur S. Shepperson, *Samuel Roberts: A Welsh Colonizer in Civil War Tennessee* (Knoxville, 1961).

160. The Welsh settlement of Patagonia is described in R. Bryn Williams, *Y Wladfa* (Cardiff, 1962).

161. Williams, *History of Modern Wales*, pp. 260–262.

gration. Some of the evicted tenants undoubtedly did emigrate as a consequence of the treatment they received, but neither then nor later does agrarian discontent, even of a political or religious nature, appear to have had a substantial effect on departures. Bitter relations between landlord and tenant persisted for decades, culminating in the so-called tithe war of 1886–1891, but they did not result in a massive rural exodus. The Welsh land commission declared in 1896 that, whereas earlier in the century there had been a substantial amount of agricultural emigration to America, there was reason to believe that "in more recent years, expecially within the last 20 years, the number of those who have emigrated to the [United] States from the agricultural districts of Wales has fallen very considerably."[162]

The commission went on to add that in the same period the number of emigrants from the industrial districts had "probably very largely increased." This was an impression which many contemporaries appear to have shared and, although there are no means of verifying it statistically, it was almost certainly a correct one. Even in the 1830's Welsh miners and ironworkers, attracted by the higher rewards their skills could command in the United States, were emigrating to Pennsylvania and other industrial states. But their numbers and those of other industrial workers do not seem to have become appreciable until the late 1860's, when a decline in the demand for coal coincided with a crisis in the iron industry. But, as Brinley Thomas has shown,[163] the popular belief in a massive industrial exodus from Wales in the last third of the nineteenth century cannot be substantiated. There was certainly a steady movement of coal miners and iron and steel workers to the United States throughout the period, especially in times of depression and wage reduction in Wales. Moreover, the widespread unemployment in the Welsh tinplate industry resulting from the McKinley tariff of 1890 led thousands to go to America. The ruin of the North Wales slate industry, arising from the protracted strikes of 1896–1897 and

162. *Commission on Land in Wales*, p. 54.
163. Brinley Thomas, *Migration and Urban Development: A Reappraisal of British and American Long Cycles* (London, 1972), pp. 177–178.

1900–1903, seems to have had a similar effect. But the numbers involved cannot have been great—even in 1900, when the number of Welsh-born in the United States reached its peak, the figure was under one hundred thousand. In the last decades of the nineteenth century industrial expansion proceeded on such a scale in Wales as to turn the country, on balance, into a country of immigration rather than of emigration. In the first decade of the twentieth century, in fact, Wales was absorbing immigrants—chiefly from England but also from Ireland—at a rate not much less than that of the United States.[164] And, as we have already seen, those Welshmen who did leave the Principality tended to go increasingly to England rather than across the Atlantic.

It has been claimed that no other European country has lost such a high proportion of its people through emigration as Scotland.[165] Whether or not this claim is justified it seems beyond dispute that throughout the nineteenth century and during the first third of the twentieth emigrants from Scotland were proportionately more numerous than those from other parts of Great Britain. Despite having a population only one-fifth that of England, Scotland in the early 1820's seems to have sent out a larger number of emigrants than her southern neighbor; at least the number of emigrants leaving Scottish ports was greater than that from English ports. Similarly in 1841, when the Scottish population was only one-sixth that of England, Scotland was losing almost as many poeple through emigration: compared with 9,569 emigrants from England there were 8,572 from Scotland. Later on, in each of the decennial periods between 1861 and 1931 Scotland's rate of emigration remained much greater than those of England and Wales, a climax being reached in the decade 1921–1931, when the rate from Scotland to all destinations was sixteen times greater than that from the two countries south of the border.[166]

164. *Ibid.*, p. 174.
165. James Gray Kyd, *Scottish Population Statistics, including Webster's Analysis of Population, 1755* (Edinburgh, 1952), p. xxii.
166. *Ibid.*, pp. xxi–xxiv.

Investigation of the background to Scottish emigration must begin with the fact that Scotland was not one country but two. Nature had divided Scotland into Highlands and Lowlands and, in the century after the defeat of the 'Forty-Five, the differences between the two sections were greatly accentuated.[167] While Lowland Scotland prospered, by and large, under the stimulus of the industrial and agricultural changes at work in Britain generally, the Highland half of the country stagnated, becoming increasingly a dependent and impoverished backwater. The gap which thus developed between the two regions was reflected in the character and timing of their respective contributions to the flow of population from Scotland. Though emigration from the Lowlands had certain features of its own, it was for the most part shaped and regulated by the level of economic activity in Britain as a whole. Highland emigration, on the other hand, had close affinities with the Irish exodus in that it was purely the product of local distress.

This had been the case even in the eighteenth century when Highland emigration first began.[168] Poverty had long been endemic in the mountainous mass of northern Scotland. It was a rocky, barren, but densely populated region, containing around 1750 about one quarter of the population of Scotland. Incapable even in normal times of supporting the numbers who sought a living from them the Highlands were plunged into crisis by the succession of crop failures and cattle blights that occurred in the early 1770's. This period of dearth saw the climax of an emigration movement which had been slowly gathering momentum since the 1730's and which had been especially vigorous since the 'Forty-Five. The urge to emigrate was not entirely the product of economic forces. It owed much to the disintegration of the traditional social structure, a pro-

167. For the Scottish background see George S. Pryde, *Scotland from 1603 to the Present Day* (London, 1962), and William Ferguson, *Scotland: 1689 to the Present* (Edinburgh, 1968). The most comprehensive survey of Scottish emigration is Gordon Donaldson, *The Scots Overseas* (London, 1966).

168. The background to eighteenth-century Highland emigration is examined in M. I. Adam, "The Highland Emigrations of 1770," *Scottish Historical Review*, 16, no. 64 (1919), 280–293; "The Causes of the Highland Emigrations, 1783–1803," *ibid.*, 17, no. 66 (1920), 73–89; and Ian C. C. Graham, *Colonists from Scotland: Emigration to North America, 1707–1783* (Ithaca, N.Y., 1956).

cess which had begun before 1745 but which was greatly accelerated by the destruction of the clan system after Culloden. Under
the new dispensation a pattern of social relationships emerged which
was based upon commercial rather than feudal values. The chief
became simply a landlord, his clansmen merely tenants who paid
rent instead of rendering military services and labor dues. The result was that the chiefs, as Dr. Johnson remarked during his Highland journey of 1773, "turned their thoughts to the improvement
of their revenues, . . . expect[ing] more rent as they [had] less
homage."[169] The sharp rise in rents that followed was more than
many tenants could afford or were prepared to pay. Worst affected
were the tacksmen, or superior tenants, for whom the end of the
clan system meant a shattering loss of prestige. The response of
many was to lead their undertenants across the Atlantic, thus giving to Highland emigration a distinctively communal character
which it was long to retain.

Estimates vary widely of the number of Highlanders emigrating
at this time. Most scholars, however, accept a figure of between
twenty and twenty-five thousand for the period 1763–1775, with
most of the departures taking place in the years immediately before
the American Revolution. Dr. Johnson was only one of many observers who were struck by the feverish urge to emigrate prevailing in the early 1770's both on the mainland and in the islands.
Great numbers left from the glens of Inverness-shire, but the really
sensational departures were from the Western Isles—Skye, Lewis,
North and South Uist, Jura, Islay, and Arran. Encouraged by reports sent home by disbanded Highland soldiers who had settled in
New York after the French and Indian War, many Highlanders
went to the Mohawk and upper Hudson valleys. Others sailed to
Nova Scotia, Cape Breton, and Prince Edward Island. But the
majority, numbering several thousand, settled in the Cape Fear
region of North Carolina.

The problem of Highland overpopulation, already acute by 1750,
was greatly exacerbated during the century that followed. En-

169. Samuel Johnson, *A Journey to the Western Islands of Scotland* (London, 1775),
pp. 216–217.

couraged by the introduction of the potato, now to become as much the standard diet of the Highland crofter as of the Irish peasant, the population of the region increased phenomenally. It is true that the proportion of Scots living in the Highlands steadily declined, but the absolute growth in the Highland population was nevertheless astonishing, especially in the more remote Highlands. In some parts of the Highlands and the west coast the population doubled and even trebled between 1755 and 1841, and the rate of increase was always greater than that of Scotland as a whole.[170] The other major component in the intractable Highland problem was the contraction of the already small area of arable land. This was the result of the spectacular growth of large-scale sheep raising, especially after 1800. The coming of the sheep was the occasion for the notorious Highland clearances, in the course of which thousands of crofters were evicted and whole glens denuded of their inhabitants.[171] There were sound economic reasons for the clearances. The minute subdivision of land which had come to characterize the Highlands was calculated to impoverish landlord and tenant alike. But, as in Ireland, the heartless treatment of the evicted tenants left long and bitter memories.

What made the situation worse was the absence of alternative employment. One after another the industries which might have revived the Highland economy went into decline. Highland fishing proved incapable of competing with the better-equipped fleets of the Clyde and the northeast coast, the linen industry succumbed to Baltic competition, even the long-established Highland cattle trade became less profitable. During the Revolutionary and Napoleonic Wars, when foreign supplies of barilla and potash were cut off, the kelp industry prospered. But the return of peace, followed shortly by the reduction of tariff duties and the discovery by the chemical industry of alternative sources of alkali, knocked the bottom out of the kelp market. In the long run kelping did more harm than good,

---

170. Pryde, *Scotland*, pp. 160–161.
171. The most recent account is that of John Prebble, *The Highland Clearances* (London, 1963).

especially by adding to the congestion of the Highland population.[172]

These conditions made the Scottish Highlands the most chronically depressed area in Britain and ensured the continuance well
into the nineteenth century of the heavy emigration of the 1770's.
There were numerous departures between 1785 and 1793 and so
many between 1801 and 1803 that, as we saw earlier, the Royal
Highland Society demanded government intervention to stop emigration. For a time the Passenger Act of 1803 dammed the stream
but it burst forth with renewed vigor after 1815 and by the 1820's
had again reached the level of half a century earlier. The Highland
tide now turned decisively toward Canada and the Maritime Provinces, and was distinguished by a tendency for emigrants from
different localities to concentrate in particular destinations. Thus
people from South Uist and Barra tended to go to Prince Edward
Island, those from Lewis and Skye to Nova Scotia, those from
other Hebridean isles to Cape Breton.

After 1815 the chronic poverty of the Highlands produced in
many landlords a change of heart toward emigration. Hitherto,
they had been convinced of the virtues of a teeming population
and had done everything in their power to check emigration. But
the inability of tenants to pay their rent and the heavy demands
made upon proprietors for charity encouraged the belief that emigration was the only remedy for the region's economic ills.[173] As
early as 1805 the earl of Selkirk had advocated a policy of government assistance to Highland emigration. It was a demand which
many proprietors were to endorse in the ensuing decades. So, too,
did Parliamentary committees which inquired into conditions in
the Highlands and Islands in 1837 and 1851.[174] But for a long time
the only response from the government was a half-hearted measure, the Emigration Advances Act of 1851, which provided limited financial assistance to private emigration societies and permit-

172. Pryde, *Scotland*, pp. 158–159; Ferguson, *Scotland: 1689 to the Present*, p. 177.
173. *Ibid.*, pp. 159–160.
174. *Report of the Agent-General for Emigration on the Applicability of Emigration to relieve
Distress in the Highlands, 1837*, P.P. 1841, XXVII; *Report on the Western Highlands and
Islands of Scotland*, P.P. 1851, XXVI.

ted landlords to borrow from public funds to assist tenants prepared to emigrate.[175] Nor did the Crofters' Colonisation Scheme, sponsored by the government in 1888, do more than scratch the surface of the problem; it enabled only a few hundred Highlanders to settle in Manitoba. This came after the "Crofters' War" of 1882, which was provoked by a fresh round of evictions whose purpose was the conversion of sheep walks into deer forests and grouse moors for the benefit of rich sportsmen from the south.

Long before this many proprietors, despairing of official assistance, undertook themselves to promote the emigration of their tenants. Emigration at landlord expense began in the 1830's, but was most widely practiced after the potato famine of 1846–1847, which produced in the Highlands suffering on the Irish scale. Between 1851 and 1863 Sir James Matheson spent the sum of £11,855 in sending to Canada a total of 2,231 tenants from his estates on the island of Lewis. In the 1850's the duke of Argyll sent almost as large a number from Tiree and Mull, Colonel Gordon dispatched several hundred from South Uist and Barra, and Lachlan Macdonald a similar number from North Uist.[176] But according to Sir John MacNeill, who reported to the government on conditions in the Highlands and Islands in 1851, there was considerable reluctance on the part of tenants to accept assistance to emigrate. They were confident they would be provided for at home, and were understandably suspicious that emigration was to the landlords simply a means of clearing more land to make way for sheep. As a consequence many proprietors found no takers when they offered free passages to Canada.[177]

Even when there was no question of enforced clearance the poorer class of Highlander was loath to emigrate. Rather than move elsewhere he preferred to lead a life of grinding poverty in familiar surroundings.[178] Generally speaking, therefore, it was not the most

175. Prebble, *Highland Clearances*, pp. 200–202; Cowan, *British Emigration to British North America*, pp. 104, 213.

176. *Ibid.*, pp. 212–213; William A. Carrothers, *Emigration from the British Isles* (London, 1929), p. 17.

177. *Report on the Western Highlands and Islands of Scotland*, P.P. 1851, XXVI, 61.

178. Prebble, *Highland Clearances*, p. 200.

poverty-stricken who emigrated but those who still possessed a modest capital and feared to lose it if they stayed where they were. Typical of mid-century Highland emigrants was a group of Mull crofters who obtained the means to travel to America by selling their stock. Of them Sir John MacNeill wrote in 1851:

These people did not emigrate from fear of destitution—at least of immediate destitution—but seeing the failure of the potatoes, the fall in the price of cattle, and that they were not, therefore, thriving in their crofts, wisely, in my opinion, resolved to emigrate before their means were exhausted.[179]

Until about 1830 Highlanders probably accounted for a majority of the emigrants from Scotland. Ten years later the statistics gathered by the census takers show that they still made up a substantial part of the outflow. Out of a total emigration from Scotland of 8,572 in the first half of 1841, no fewer than 3,861 came from the five Highland counties of Perth, Argyll, Inverness, Ross, and Sutherland, including the Western Isles from Islay to Lewis. Even this figure may not represent the full Highland contribution, for a further 1,967 emigrants came from Caithness and the five northeastern maritime counties from Kincardine to Nairn which, if not strictly part of the Highlands, at least lay north of the Highland line. In any case, no matter how one defines the Highlands, the figures show that nearly seventy percent of the emigrants from Scotland were drawn from the northern half of the country.

This was a situation which would not last much longer. In the second half of the century Scotland's emigrants were to be composed increasingly of industrial workers from the Lowlands. But in 1841 Lowland emigrants were not only a small minority but were drawn for the most part from mainly agricultural counties like Roxburgh, Berwick, and Dumfries, which together accounted for a total of 1,795. By contrast, the five Lowland industrial counties—Renfrew, Lanark, Edinburgh, Forfar, and Fife—which contained nearly all of Scotland's chief cities and where the textile trade and coal mining had taken firm root, sent between them a mere 612. This was an astonishingly low figure, especially at a time of severe industrial depression when, as we have seen, there was heavy emi-

179. *Report on the Western Highlands and Islands*, p. 66.

gration from the textile regions of England. It is not easy to account for the contrast but the explanation may be that, although there was serious unemployment in the Scottish textile areas in 1841, the raising of a national subscription to relieve destitution in Paisley served to restrain departures.

Certainly there was no reluctance to emigrate on the part of Scotland's industrial poor. This had been shown in earlier depressions, but so had the need for government assistance to emigration. Thus in the winter of 1819–1820 mass meetings of unemployed weavers in Glasgow had petitioned Parliament for assistance to enable them to emigrate. With some reluctance, and largely with a view to ending the violence that had erupted in Glasgow out of the agitation for radical reform, the government assisted some twenty-seven hundred paupers from Lanarkshire and Renfrewshire to settle in Canada. But when the demand for help was repeated during the depression of 1826–1827, the government turned a deaf ear with the result that no large-scale movement was possible.[180] Would-be emigrants thus had to pay their own fares or stay at home and wait for better times. To be sure, there was a certain amount of self-financed emigration from the Scottish textile regions at all times, but that it was limited in volume when the desire to emigrate was so manifest suggests that industrial poverty in Scotland, in this period at least, had a greater intensity than in the corresponding districts of England.

At all events Scottish emigration up to 1860 or so had a predominantly agricultural cast. This was to a large extent a reflection of the scale of Highland emigration, the reasons for which have already been discussed. As for the Lowland agricultural areas, the pressure to emigrate stemmed mainly from the same causes as in England: the excess of agricultural labor resulting from the consolidation of farms and the change from arable to pasture, and the declining profitability of farming in the decades after 1815.[181] These

180. Johnston, *British Emigration Policy*, pp. 102–103, 156–157.
181. These factors are stressed in Dallas L. Jones, "The Background and Motives of Scottish Emigration to the United States of America in the Period 1815 to 1861, with Special Reference to Emigrant Correspondence" (unpub. PhD diss., University of Edinburgh, 1970).

were the factors most commonly mentioned by the ministers to whom the compilers of the *New Statistical Account* turned for information in the late 1830's.[182] But some ministers referred to a further expulsive factor which, though not peculiar to Scotland, seems to have had a more profound effect there than elsewhere. This was the competition for work resulting from an influx of Irishmen. Wrote the minister of Whitehorn, Wigtownshire, in January 1839:

> The greatest grievance that is felt in this parish at present, and which is most detrimental to its respectability and improvement, is the extent of emigration, and the description of people who emigrate. Our native labourers and artisans, with their little property and many virtues, are drifting across the Atlantic, and Ireland, from her exhaustless store, is supplying their place. The number of Irish families that every year take up their abode in this place is almost incredible. They are possessed of nothing but a number of naked, starving children. The supply of labourers usually exceeds the demand, and wages are thereby reduced so low that Scottish labourers who wish to feed, clothe and educate their children have it not in their power and are compelled to seek in a foreign country what is denied them in their own.[183]

The minister's comparisons between Scot and Irishman may not have been free from prejudice, but his comments seem to confirm what other sources suggest about the character, social position, resources, and motives of the mass of emigrants from Scotland at this time. Poor but by no means destitute, these people were not the victims of oppression or want but the casualties of economic change and social disruption. They emigrated to better their condition but also because they were fearful of losing what they had of material things and of hope for the future.

This characterization has a wider application. It serves to describe not only emigrants from Lowland Scotland but those from Great Britain generally in the first two-thirds of the nineteenth century. But it will not serve to describe later departures. Analysis of the British background suggests a change in the character of emigration in the 1870's. Up to that date emigrants were mostly

182. *The New Statistical Account of Scotland*, 15 vols. (Edinburgh, 1845).
183. *Ibid.*, IV, 60.

people seeking escape from the maladjustments which population growth and economic change were inflicting upon their communities. In particular they were fleeing from an apprehended loss of social status, a fate with which they were threatened by the modernization of the British economy. After the 1870's, however, the scene changes. Thanks mainly to the increased mobility made possible by advances in ocean transportation the movement from Britain, to North America at least, becomes predominantly one of people following economic advantage and shuttling back and forth between countries in its pursuit. So far as the United States and Canada were concerned, late nineteenth-century emigrants from Britain were in many essentials "new" immigrants, indistinguishable in motive if not in function from those coming from southern and eastern Europe.

Yet generalizations about nineteenth-century British emigration can be no more than tentative in the present state of knowledge. No one who attempts to survey and synthesize what is known of the subject can fail to be aware of how much remains to be done. We still know little about the geographical origins, occupations, and demographic characteristics of those who left Britain; it may be that we shall never know as much as we should like. A host of other problems cries out for solution: why the rate of emigration from Scotland was consistently so much higher than that from the rest of Britain, what precisely was the relationship between internal and overseas migration, what were the relative strengths of "push" and "pull" factors, why the tide of emigration turned from the United States to the Empire in the early twentieth century.

Much basic research will be needed before these and similar problems can be solved and the movement can be fully comprehended. That research will have to examine the varying ways in which scores of local communities were influenced by and reacted to economic and social change. At the same time it will have to employ a broad canvas, recognizing that overseas emigration was only part of an extensive and intricate pattern of population movement. Above all it will have to probe the complex interrelationship between economic change and emigration. It will not be enough to list the new developments in agriculture and industry and the social disruption they caused. That would imply too simple, too automatic a causal relationship. The transformation of the economy might indeed lead to emigration, but it did not necessarily do so. Rather than seek new homes abroad the dispossessed might choose instead to move to nearby towns. Or they might choose not to move at all. Thus in order fully to grasp the true character of emigration it will be necessary to identify the circumstances in which men opted for the most drastic of the available alternatives.

# SCOTTISH EMIGRATION:
## THE SOCIAL IMPACT OF
## AGRARIAN CHANGE IN
## THE RURAL LOWLANDS, 1775–1875

Malcolm Gray

# SCOTTISH EMIGRATION: THE SOCIAL IMPACT OF AGRARIAN CHANGE IN THE RURAL LOWLANDS, 1775-1875

## Introduction

**M**IGRATION overseas in the late eighteenth and early nineteenth centuries was but one of the ways in which Scottish people were coming to seek new homes away from their places of birth. In fact migration within the country affected far more people than did movement to other lands. Such internal migration had, by 1851, reached a high level. By the census report of that year it is evident that, of native-born Scots resident within the country, one person in three had crossed from one county to the other or had moved into the major towns from county hinterlands.[1] The report, of course, does not indicate the numbers, presumably considerable, who had moved within their original counties, from parish to parish or from rural areas into the smaller towns of the same county. Nor does it even hint at the numbers who had left Scotland although it is clear that such emigrants must have numbered but a fraction of the local migrants. The interweaving of the different forms of migration is, however, so close that there can be no clear distinction made between the causes promoting them. People were becoming more willing to contemplate moving from their places of birth and changing attitudes might lead either to the search for a new home in a nearby

1. *1851 Census Great Britain, Parliamentary Papers*, 1852–1853, LXXXV–LXXXVII, *Birth Places of the People*.

town or to the more drastic decision to leave the country of birth entirely.

The pattern as well as the volume of internal migration can be seen from the census report. It was in the main a movement from the rural to the urban and industrial areas. It can be shown that nearly all rural parishes were losing population relative to the country as a whole and, even more so, relative to the urban areas, and it is fair to assume that such discrepancies were due in the main to net losses by migration in the rural parishes. Thus the propensity to migrate is connected with attitudes, economic opportunities, and material conditions within the rural communities that were providing the bulk of the migrants. It cannot be shown decisively that the emigrants were drawn from precisely the same areas as the people who would move only short distances. But it seems likely that the roots of the two movements lay together. Even if a disproportionate number of emigrants came from the towns, such populations as a base for further migrations had themselves been created by movements of the Scottish country people. Till nearly the close of the eighteenth century at least four-fifths of the population were rural and no broadly based movement could arise except from this rural sector either in first or in later moves.[2] In fact the period from 1775 onwards is one of drastic change in an agriculture which had been exceptionally resistant to change. It is the task, therefore, of this essay to trace the connections between agricultural, and consequently agrarian, changes and migration, mainly in the period between 1775 and 1875.

From time out of mind, the Scottish people have divided themselves into two very distinct groups—the Lowland and the Highland. Although it has become customary to discuss emigration and even internal migration as if they were mainly Highland phenom-

2. This estimate is based on Dr. Webster's Enumeration of 1755, and on the returns made for the *Old Statistical Account*. Highland parishes have been separated from Lowland and urban parishes from rural, in order to make the calculation, although in some cases the basis for making these distinctions—and particularly for deciding whether parishes were urban or rural—was necessarily somewhat rudimentary. See James G. Kyd, ed., *Scotland's Population Statistics* (Edinburgh, 1952); *Statistical Account of Scotland* (Edinburgh, 1791–1798), XX, 587–621. As this work is familiarly known as the *Old Statistical Account* it is hereafter cited as *O.S.A.*

ena, it is the Lowlands we will discuss.[3] In fact the population even of the purely rural Lowlands was at least twice that of the Highlands in the middle of the eighteenth century and the briefest reading of the census results a century later shows that, among the internal migrants, the Lowlanders were greatly in the majority; it is likely that they were so among the emigrants too.[4] Emigration from the rural Lowlands must often have gone unrecorded not because it was a rare event, but because Lowlanders tended to move as individuals or in small family groups rather than en masse. "Many [laborers] have gone to America. . . . But they retire peaceably, and indeed slip away, without their design being generally known in the vicinity."[5]

There is some direct evidence that emigrants were coming from wide areas of the Lowlands in the first half of the nineteenth century. In the report on the *1851 Census* notes were frequently appended to explain the population history of particular parishes and "emigration" is fairly often cited as a cause of population declines in particular decades between 1801 and 1851. The comments show emigration occurring not infrequently among the parishes of a wide belt of the eastern Lowlands, running from the English border to the North-East and also among the counties of the extreme South-West.[6] One fairly solid area of the countryside, however, seems not to have been much affected. All the counties of this area, running through the middle of the more southerly part of Scotland, had a large industrial component and there is no doubt that the rural parishes of these counties sent many migrants to the in-

3. An exception is Donald F. MacDonald who recognizes the importance of the Lowlands as a source for emigration; *Scotland's Shifting Population* (Glasgow, 1957), pp. 150–151.

4. The migrants from mainly Lowland outnumber those from mainly Highland counties, by a proportion of seventeen to one. There is a crudity in this calculation because several counties have sections with Highland as well as sections with Lowland characteristics.

5. "Agricultural Intelligence," *Farmer's Magazine*, 20 (1819), 358, hereafter cited as *Farm. Mag.*

6. *1851 Census, Numbers of the Inhabitants, 1801–1851*. See the map in MacDonald, *Scotland's Shifting Population*, p. 162.

dustrial towns. The lack of emigrants was due to the strong pull of growing industry nearby.

Some evidence for the strength of the emigration movement from the rural Lowlands is given by the lists of emigrants to Australia. Between 1815 and 1832 the Scottish applicants to settle in the Australian colonies came mainly from the southern and eastern part of the country and particularly from Fife, the Lothians, and Berwickshire; the Highlands contributed sporadically, rather than in a continuous flow, and not in very great total numbers.[7] Later in the century, when the scale of emigration was altogether larger, the North-East and the South-West come to play a predominant part. Judging by the places of birth of the bounty emigrants from 1838 to 1842 (brought out by private operators), Aberdeenshire, Ayrshire, and Dumfries-shire had now become leading contributors; the emigration from Glasgow, Lanarkshire, and Renfrewshire, also figuring largely, was probably mainly urban in origin. The more southerly Highlands also appear to provide many names.

In the earlier eighteenth century, the rural areas with which we are concerned were settled within limits rather rigidly determined by the harsh facts of geography. Rural life in all these areas was based on the cultivation of at least a small section of land as arable. But in no part of Scotland is cultivation possible much above the thousand-foot contour and in some parts, particularly around the wet western half of the country, the limit must be set a good deal lower. In a generally mountainous country this imposes a severe control on the position of settlements and sometimes on the amount of land available for the individual or the community. North of the narrow waist between the Firths of Clyde and of Forth, the greater part of the land surface is occupied by a single mass of hills. This mass tilts from the high ridges of the west, dropping slowly through many irregularities of surface to the smooth foothills of the east. In the west, too, the high peaks lie very close to the long indented coastline leaving only discontinuous patches and stretches of low-lying ground to be used for cultivation and settlement. Such restricted conditions are typical also of most of the islands, some of

7. David S. MacMillan, *Scotland and Australia, 1788–1850* (Oxford, 1967), pp. 94, 295.

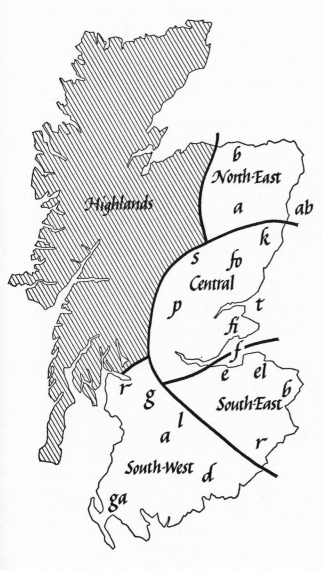

### North-East

a  Aberdeenshire
ab Aberdeen City
b  Banffshire

### Central

fi Fife
fo Forfarshire (Angus)
k  Kincardineshire
p  Perthshire
s  Strathmore
t  Firth of Tay

### South-East

b  Berwickshire
e  Edinburgh
el East Lothian
   (Haddingtonshire)
f  Firth of Forth
r  Roxburghshire

### South-West

a  Ayrshire
d  Dumfries-shire
g  Glasgow
ga Galloway
l  Lanarkshire
r  Renfrewshire

them large and well populated, which lie off the western coastline. Limited space, linked with a deeply felt land hunger and the propensity to cling to every tiniest base for settlement has helped to create in the west social conditions, indeed a form of society, very different from those prevailing both to the east and the south of the mountains, that is, in the Lowlands.

The Lowlands consist of the much more spacious plain which sweeps around the easterly and southerly edges of the main mountain mass, together with the lands lying on all sides of the less dramatic uplands set in the southern part of the country. The Lowland plains, between hill areas and the sea, are nowhere broad in extent and lie in complicated patterns of land, narrowing and widening between the opposing edges of coast and mountain. There are great variations, too, in climate, soil, and accessibility, making for differences from place to place in cropping and in social organization. The forces of development, then, can only be understood in terms of a division into distinct sections, each with its own characteristics of physical setting and of social tradition. The various sections of the Lowlands may be briefly listed.

The region of the *South-East* is girt along its northern edge by the arc of the lower part of the Firth of Forth. Across this block of land, on an axis lying parallel to the coast, runs a range of hills, moderate in altitude but heathy and uncultivated towards the summit plateaux. This elevated ridge divides two of the main agricultural areas of Scotland—to the north, East Lothian, consisting mainly of a plain some thirty miles in length and of an average breadth of ten miles, and to the south, Berwickshire and Roxburghshire, an area roughly similar in extent and shape, lying between the hills to the north and the River Tweed and the English border to the south. These fertile plains, with a climate favorable to growing wheat and a generally strong soil, give way on the westerly edges to higher country of some agricultural potential but of severer climate and thinner soil.

The *Central* area of the Lowlands extends northwards from a narrow base on the upper reaches of the Firth of Forth and the lower stretches of the river proper. A second side of the region is formed by the edge of the hills as they trend northeastwards and the third consists of the sea coast. At the narrow northerly apex, the line of the hills reaches almost to the seas just south of the city of Aberdeen. The eastern side of this plain is deeply indented by two great arms of the sea, the Firths of Forth and of Tay, and the surface is further broken up by the smaller hill masses of the Ochils and Sidlaws. Thus the region is divided into smaller subsections bounded by hill and sea. Within the area are to be found considerable variations of soil type. Around the estuaries of Forth and Tay lie solid areas of deep fertile alluvial soil—the "carse" lands. They occur on both sides of the inner reaches of the Firth of Forth and some distance inland along the river itself till they disappear under a blanket of peat; north of the Firth of Tay also there is a considerable stretch of this heavy soil (the Carse of Gowrie) and the valley of the Earn, flowing directly into the inner neck of the Firth of Tay, has much good heavy soil. The other coastal lands, around the Fife peninsula and northwards along the coast of Forfarshire and Kincardine, are of mixed soil type. Inland, running northeastwards along the edge of the main mountain mass but sheltered from the sea by the lesser bulk of the Sidlaws is the important area of Strathmore, fertile but of mainly light soils.

The *North-East* lies beyond the northerly apex of this Central area and in fact contains the most extensive single stretch of arable land in Scotland. The heart of the area is formed by the retreat to the northwest of the edge of the hill land just at the point where the coastline juts strongly towards the northeastern promontory. The land in this corner is very flat to some distance inland but towards the west rises in smoothly shaped hills to the agriculturally impenetrable barrier of the mountains. In general it is an area of light soils with some sections of clay. Much of it, being cool in summer, is unsuitable for wheat growing. In spite of the general severity of the climate, cultivation is effected at a height above sea level as great as anywhere in Scotland.

Finally there is the *South-West*, including the western part of the corridor between Forth and Clyde, with an arc of land which curves from the Clyde valley to the upper waters of the Forth. To the south of the Clyde estuary there are several distinct areas. On the western slopes of the southern hill mass is a region, somewhat elevated, of clay land, covering much of the interior of the great agricultural county of Ayr, but extending northwards towards the industrial regions of Lanark and Renfrew. This region of clay land falls towards the coastal plain of Ayrshire, which is fairly broad and has a mild winter climate, moderate rainfall, and lighter soils. On the southern edge of the whole complex the two main rivers of the Nith and the Annan, forming broad valleys of fine arable, flow southwards to the Solway plain which runs east and west on the rough line of the coast.

## The Process of Migration

THE parishes of the rural Lowlands were evidently losing population by migration in the later eighteenth century. The census taken by Dr. Webster in 1755 together with the enumerations found in the *Old Statistical Account* give an opportunity for a broad statistical view of the process (Table I). The population of Scotland as a whole increased by twenty percent between 1755 and the 1790's. With net emigration or immigration not yet of any great magnitude this rate would certainly not be less for the rural districts than for the country as a whole. Thus any rural parish which shows a population increase of less than the national average was probably experiencing net emigration. By this criterion the majority of, but by no means all, rural parishes were losing by migration, although usually at a fairly slow rate. The typical parish would show some increase of population but at somewhat less than the national rate of twenty percent. One area stands out as different. Aberdeenshire, covering a large part of the North-East, was showing considerably heavier losses, with nearly two-thirds of its rural parishes producing an actual decline of population. Berwickshire had the greatest increases. In this almost entirely rural county, over half the parishes were gaining population at a rate above the national average. In Ayrshire, in East Lothian, and over the Central district there was a fairly wide range of parish experiences with substantial numbers in each group (of moderate loss, heavy loss, or gain).

Table I

RURAL POPULATION, 1755 TO 1790–1798

*Percentage of Parishes*

| County | No. of Parishes | Decrease of 30% or more | Decrease of up to 29% | Increase of 1% to 29% | Increase of 30% or more | Total |
|---|---|---|---|---|---|---|
| Berwick | 33 | | 19 | 45 | 36 | 100 |
| East Lothian | 24 | 13 | 46 | 33 | 8 | 100 |
| Perth Fife | 23 | 13 | 30 | 48 | 9 | 100 |
| Aberdeen | 57 | 9 | 53 | 19 | 19 | 100 |
| Ayr | 15 | 7 | 40 | 20 | 33 | 100 |

SOURCES: J. G. Kyd, *Scottish Population Statistics; Statistical Account of Scotland*, 1790–1798, Vol. XX.

Between 1801 and 1851 migration evidently increased in volume with the great bulk of the parishes at least thirty points behind the national rate of increase of eighty percent (which was now, it is true, somewhat more affected by immigration) (Table II). There had also been a marked shift in the relative performances of the different districts. Notably the North-East as represented by Aberdeenshire was now holding its population better than any district to the south. Only one parish in the county showed a decline of population and just under a half had increases of more than fifty percent. The typical parish had an increase of between ten and forty percent. Berwickshire and East Lothian were also reasonably stable, with increases up to thirty percent being by far the commonest tale. By contrast Perthshire, in the Central district, was losing heavily with well over half the parishes in decline. Nearby Fife, on the other hand, more nearly approximated to the counties of the South-East in its experience.

Table II

RURAL POPULATION, 1801–1851

*Percentage of Parishes*

| County | No. of Parishes | Decrease of 30% or more | Decrease of up to 29% | Increase of 1% to 29% | Increase of 30% or more | Total |
|--------|-----------------|------------------------|----------------------|----------------------|------------------------|-------|
| Berwick | 29 | | 7 | 86 | 7 | 100 |
| East Lothian | 19 | | 16 | 68 | 16 | 100 |
| Perth | 44 | 7 | 50 | 30 | 13 | 100 |
| Fife | 26 | | 27 | 35 | 38 | 100 |
| Aberdeen | 60 | | 2 | 33 | 65 | 100 |
| Ayr | 16 | | | 19 | 81 | 100 |

SOURCE: *1851 Census, Numbers of the Inhabitants.*

After 1861, from census information, it is possible for the first time to determine natural rates of increase at the parish level and therefore to establish the net migration into, or out of, every particular parish (Table III). The results confirm the rough estimates of the period before 1851. Migration was proceeding fast, with the North-East still holding its population somewhat better than elsewhere, Perthshire much the greatest loser, and the counties of Ayr, Berwick, East Lothian, and Fife somewhere between the two extremes. On the whole, however, the regional differences seem somewhat less marked than they had been. In most cases the net migration rates spread between a loss by migration of less than ten percent to a loss of thirty percent. In Aberdeenshire and in East Lothian and Berwickshire most commonly the rates lay between ten and twenty percent but in Perth the greatest number of parishes lost between twenty and thirty percent of their inhabitants by net migration.

## Table III

### NET MIGRATION, 1861–1871

*Percentage of Parishes*

| County | No. of Parishes | Gain by Net Migration* | Loss by Migration of up to 19% | Loss by Migration of 20% or more | Total |
|---|---|---|---|---|---|
| Berwick | 27 | | 67 | 33 | 100 |
| East Lothian | 17 | | 65 | 35 | 100 |
| Perth | 48 | 2 | 38 | 60 | 100 |
| Fife | 23 | 2 | 49 | 49 | 100 |
| Aberdeen | 67 | 1 | 69 | 30 | 100 |
| Ayr | 20 | | 65 | 35 | 100 |

SOURCES: *1871 Census*, LIX, Table VIII; *1871 Census*, LXXIII, Table XV.

\* "Net Migration" in this table shows the net number of migrants (in or out) as a percentage of the average population of the decade, 1861–1871.

There is no simple explanation of the variations and changes in the regional pattern. The growth of towns and centers of concentrated industry would pull out the rural population with varying force from place to place. Yet the differences in the rate of migration do not seem to fall into a pattern determined by fields of force radiating from the industrial centers. There was certainly no nearby industrial presence that could explain the severity of the population decline of the North-East in the late eighteenth century. Even after 1801, while the stability of the North-East could be explained by the fact that the area was relatively shielded from the influence of the main growing centers of industry, no such reason can explain why East Lothian and Ayrshire also produced relatively low figures of migration. Industry, of course, could make itself felt as a presence within the basically rural areas themselves. The calculations have excluded parishes with towns of more than fifteen hundred inhabitants or concentrated groups of industrial workers, clearly distinguishable from the agricultural workers. But this left within the samples many parishes in which industrial incomes and activities were comparable to those deriving from agriculture. Because the industrial population was so intertwined with the agricultural it is impracticable to exclude such parishes; it would also be undesirable to do so because the greater part of the rural population was continually presented with alternatives in industrial and agricultural work. The family with no opportunity of industrial earnings was very much the exception in late eighteenth-century Scotland. Industrial opportunity worked in varying fashion from one part of the country to the other and growth, stagnation, or decline in this sector may well be one of the reasons for the variations in the demographic record.

Yet the agrarian influence must have been the main one. Nearly every family was to some degree involved in agriculture and alterations in the conditions of agricultural livelihood had the widest possible impact. In fact, agricultural workers were carried forward by the multiplying changes in farming methods and the social relations conditioned by the arrangement of land. From about 1780 onwards the whole agricultural population of the Lowlands was subjected to a broadly uniform and immensely powerful agrarian transformation terminating the very physical existence of the old form of settlement, to be replaced by new types of farming and of social grouping. Though the broad movement was everywhere the same, there were sufficient local differences to explain some of the discrepancies in the population record.

## The Old Order

THE agricultural improvement movement of the eighteenth century arose in settlements that were fairly uniform from one end of the Lowland plain to the other.[8] Characteristically, until at least the middle of the eighteenth century, the people lived in small groups. The individual's feeling of social position, his attachment to a particular location for his home, his understanding of how to work the land—in fact almost the whole range of social feeling and attitude—were defined by the relations between various members of the small community. The shift of attitudes and interests which lay behind the increasing mobility of the people must have been accompanied by a change in some of the elements, particularly the agricultural elements, in the traditional community. The agriculture was backward and when it began to be reformed the whole social structure was thrown out of balance, with inevitable questioning by the individual of his traditional position —a questioning which might be reinforced by the practical difficulties of finding familiar occupations within a newly organized system of production.

In the traditional agricultural communities of the Scottish Lowlands, each settlement, small in size, contained a huddled group of cottages and farm buildings. In these lived and worked a balanced grouping of tenants, cottagers, servants, and tradesmen, usually amounting in all to no more than ten or fifteen families. Sometimes there would be fewer than ten but seldom were there completely isolated dwellings. Nearly all the working farmers rented their

8. The most complete picture of the social structure over any considerable part of the Lowland countryside in the days before improvement is given in John Stuart, ed., *List of Pollable Persons within the Shire of Aberdeen, 1696* (Aberdeen, 1844), hereafter cited as *List of Pollable Persons, 1696*, which enumerates the whole adult population of the county, within settlements, and gives clear indications of social and agricultural positions. This northeastern county was not necessarily typical of the whole of Lowland Scotland, but more impressionistic and retrospective accounts from other parts seem to agree largely with the picture given in the Aberdeenshire account. In particular, see the many snatches of reminiscent account and of surviving archaic structure set down in the 1790's in the *O.S.A.* and in the various *General Views* of the agriculture in the particular counties.

land from a landowner, who was of the higher social strata, perhaps a member of the higher nobility with tens of thousands of
acres but more frequently a man of lesser standing, say a "laird"
with less than a thousand acres and a few dozen tenants. Only in
the South-West and in Fife was there any considerable number of
owner-occupiers.[9] Sometimes the land would be allocated to
groups of tenants who would live in the human association of the
"ferm toun" and would share in the common fields so that each
man had his section intermixed with the rest. These joint tenants
formed the upper rank of the working agricultural population and
would subdivide part of their land to be used by cottagers or subtenants, who would receive small allotments of land and rights of
grazing cattle, in return for helping the superior tenant with his
land; they had also landless servants, in full-time employ, who lived
either in cottages alongside the main farm house or in the masters'
houses. Finally through most settlements, there was a scattering of
tradesmen who plied their trades of weaving, tailoring, shoemak-
ing, carpentering, and similar occupations, generally working for
the market formed by their immediate fellows. Very frequently—
possibly in the majority of settlements—the land would be let to
one main tenant who ran the whole as his personal domain; but
such a man would always have his servants and cottagers to make
up the social group, to help him with their labor, and to occupy
some part of the land.[10]

9. William Fullarton, *General View of the Agriculture of the County of Ayr* (Edinburgh,
1793), p. 14; John Thomson, *General View of the Agriculture of the County of Fife* (Edinburgh, 1800), pp. 46, 54; George Robertson, *Rural Recollections* (Irvine, 1829), p. 551;
William Kirk Dickson, ed., "Memories of Ayrshire about 1780 by the Reverend John
Mitchell, D.D.," *Miscellany of the Scottish History Society*, 3rd ser., 6 (1939), 257.

10. The agrarian historians of Scotland have tended to assume that the settlement in
which several tenants shared the land was typical or even universal. This view is almost
certainly wrong for one part of the country—the North-East—for which there is solid
evidence from before 1700 of the layout of farms. On this evidence the settlements which
were under the control of one tenant were just as numerous as those in divided occupation.
See, *List of Pollable Persons, 1696*; "The Rentall of the Lordschipe of Huntlye," *The Miscellany of the Spaulding Club*, 4 (1849), 261–319. There is less solid evidence for other
parts of the country for this early period but it seems likely that at least in areas such as the
Lothians where the holdings were generally larger than in the North-East the single
holding would be no less common. For the period after 1750 there is much more information, particularly in the form of estate rentals. They tend to show that when in this

The features common to all settlements were the congestion of the buildings and the intricate social grading between the main tenants or employers and the subordinate grades of cottagers and servants, with the craftsmen in less easily identifiable social positions. Within particular settlements there might be considerable inequalities as between the sharing tenants, and in the agrarian community as a whole there were farms, held directly of the landlord, of all sizes, running from one hundred fifty acres downwards.

The tenants themselves fell into ranks and grades, with somewhat different standard holdings in different parts of the country. In the South-East, the greater men would have one hundred or even one hundred fifty acres, while in the North-East very few had more than one hundred acres although there was a definite group of men with more than fifty acres.[11] Alongside such relatively well-to-do tenants, who would have three or four subordinates in

---

general period a record is made of holdings there were already a considerable number of holdings separated from their neighbors. Whether this was because such holdings had always been present in numbers or because the movement towards separation was already gaining momentum is not clear. It is also striking how little direct memory there was of a functioning runrig system in the multitudinous reports of the 1790's. James E. Handley, *The Agricultural Revolution in Scotland* (Glasgow, 1963), pp. 19, 21, 24–26; Robertson, *Rural Recollections*, p. 259; Dickson, "Memories of Ayrshire," p. 276; B. M. W. Third, "The Significance of Scottish Estate Plans and Associated Documents," *Scottish Studies*, 1 (1957), 39–64; B. M. W. Third, "Changing Landscape and Social Structure in the Scottish Lowlands as revealed by Eighteenth-Century Estate Plans," *Scottish Geographical Magazine*, 71 (1955), 83–93, hereafter cited as *Scot. Geog. Mag.*; J. H. G. Lebon, "The Face of the Countryside in Central Ayrshire during the Eighteenth and Nineteenth Centuries," *Scot. Geog. Mag.*, 62 (1946), 7–15.

11. The *List of Pollable Persons, 1696* gives valuations based on the holdings of all tenants in Aberdeenshire, but no direct clue as to what these valuations may mean in terms of acreage or income. Some inferences, however, are possible. It is evident that there was a great range in the size of holdings with considerable numbers in the upper ranges of the scale. If the smallest type of holding is assumed to be of about five acres, then a substantial group is to be found in the fifty- to one-hundred-acre range, but very few—except those described as "gentlemen"—above that point in the scale. Another approach is to compare the valuations for parishes with the acreage figures given for some of the same units in the O.S.A. A rough equivalence emerges of about £1 (Scots) to each arable acre (including both infield and outfield). From this, the biggest holdings—of which there are a considerable number—would again appear to be somewhere around the one hundred-acre level. See also "Comparative View of East Lothian Husbandry in 1778 and 1810," *Farm. Mag.*, 12 (1811), 52; Robertson, *Rural Recollections*, pp. 259, 536; Dickson, "Memories of Ayrshire," p. 257; Fullarton, *County of Ayr*, p. 18.

the shape of servants or subtenants, there were large numbers of people with tiny holdings, although with the full standing of direct tenants, not being bound to work for anyone except the laird. Cottagers and servants were generally more numerous than the full tenants and their situation was much more precarious; cottagers had only fragments of land and an uncertain living derived from day labor. It was a system, then, in which even moderate-sized holdings were burdened with considerable numbers of dependents and in which the great majority either lived entirely by wages or had merest fragments of land.

The cultivated fields of the settlement normally took the shape of irregular patches of land. These sections were arranged in two main groups. In one, the land would be cropped, year after year, without intermission; in the other, each part would be only intermittently in crop. In the intensively worked area, which consisted of the best available land, a continous succession of cereal crops would be taken. Oats and barley would share such ground, or a slightly more elaborate sequence of peas, wheat, barley, and oats. Such punishing successions could only be pursued on ground of higher quality, helped by liberal use of manure. Thus the land under continuous crop—the "infield" or "croft-land"—could normally be sustained only by the much more extensive cropping of a wider area, too weak to be subjected to a similar regime, but indispensable in helping to produce the manure that went into the infield. This second section, the outfield, was cultivated so that a period of several years (generally three or four) of continuous unmanured cropping, in which yields would decline to barely two seeds from one, was followed by a longer period of rest in which the land would slowly recover to produce at best a rank natural growth; then the cycle would start again as the land was broken in for its first year of crop. To achieve this the outfield was divided into sections so that every year equal amounts would be falling out of, and coming into, cultivation and the cultivated acreage would be kept at the same level from year to year. As a consequence, not much more than half of the crop land would be under the plow each year. On the best infield land yields of four seeds from one might be attained and held, but on outfield land the average of all sections at their various stages of the cycle, which tended to steady weakening, would be well below three seeds from one.

The main implement, the "old Scots" plow, was a cumbersome instrument requiring the haulage power of a large team of animals, whether of horses or of oxen, and the attendance of at least two men. The operations of plowing, conducted on the same pattern for years or generations, had produced irregular and exaggerated ridges, in which the better soil was piled towards the summit, leaving intermediate furrows to act as drains but also serving to sterilize much of the land as wet and inferior in composition. No systematic method was used to clean the land of weeds.

Every farm also had its animals—oxen and horses (or ponies) for the plow, cows for the dairy, sheep for a subsistence supply of wool. In areas with considerable stretches of natural pasture, the rearing of cattle for sale as store animals provided the main form of income and in the South-West dairying was also a source of income.[12] Whatever their use, the animals subsisted on rough natural pasture interspersed in patches through the arable lands, or on the more extensive but generally poor pastures of the common muir (i.e., moor), or on the aftermath of the arable land and on the straw of the corn crops. It was poor feeding and there was a low (and largely wasted) conversion to dung—although the dung-heap in front of the farm door was a common offense to travellers from other countries.

12. Dickson, "Memories of Ayrshire," pp. 271–272; James Fulton, "On the Best Mode of Making Dunlop and Cheddar Cheese," *Transactions of the Highlands and Agricultural Society*, 9 (1859–1861), 46, hereafter cited as *T.H.A.S.*; John McMaster, "Scotch Cheese-making," *T.H.A.S.*, 17 (1885), 215.

## The Progress of Improvement

SCOTTISH agriculture which had seemed so unshakably backward in 1750 or even in 1770 had by 1830 the reputation of
outstanding efficiency. The wide and deep transformation of methods entailed a great number of small interlocking changes within
long-existing communities in which economic behavior and social grading were bound by an older form of agriculture. Thus it
was not merely a change in methods that occurred but also the
upset of a social order. Individuals lost the cross-bearings of a traditional system, as holdings were thrown together, new tenants
were settled, new conditions of labor imposed, and new working
routines devised. As their familiar world crumbled, the country
people would increasingly be drawn to look outwards.

The crescendo of change came between 1780 and 1830. At the
earlier date there were only small areas in which new forms of agriculture were solidly established and only select groups among
whom new ideas were accepted or practiced;[13] but by 1830 the
whole mass of the farming population were either practicing some
form of the "new agriculture" on land of their own or were employed as wage earners on improved farms. Yet the elements of
the new schemes applied so thoroughly in that period were put together in working systems only after a period of experiment lasting
at least sixty years and even then only in isolated units. The wide
application of new methods of cropping and working occurred on
a basis of tenure and farm layout that had slowly emerged by
piecemeal rearrangement.

Long before any new schemes of cropping had been devised—
much less generally accepted—new forms of tenure were being
offered to the farmer and the land was being laid out in units that
were more capable of economical management. Increasing numbers of tenants were being offered leases which would give them

---

13. The crop schemes even of the very advanced area of the East Lothian in 1778 would
have been far from satisfactory to the ordinary farmer of thirty years later. See "Comparative View of East Lothian Husbandry," pp. 204–209.

security for long periods and which often enjoined novel methods of working the land.[14] Another aspect of the process of change was the movement which began to separate from one another the tangled possessions in farms where groups of tenants held intermixed strips. Even in 1700 farms held by single tenants were fairly common but the task remained of separating the joint units into holdings each under undivided control. By 1750 or 1760 the process of disentangling the lands of the individual tenants from the mixture of strips in the common fields was complete in some areas. By the 1790's agriculture in which the lands of the different holders were intermixed was but a faint and occasional memory. As lands were separated to form neatly squared holdings each with the single farmstead at its convenient center, so also were the farms increased in size; the new farms were often much greater than the aggregates of the strips that had previously been held by each man. Subtenants, too, began to fall to the reforming zeal of the greater farmers, who now took over all the subsections of land into the main farms.[15] Many of the intermediate tiers in the agrarian scale were knocked away and the division between the holders of the land and the laborers became increasingly sharp.

These developments, striking at the older types of relationships between groups and between families, were evidently conceived

14. "The foundation of Scottish improvements was laid by granting long leases," "Memoirs of John Cockburn, Esq. of Ormiston," *Farm. Mag.*, 5 (1804), 135. Early in the century even in East Lothian leases were far from general; by the end of the century in Aberdeenshire where improvement had scarcely begun they were already universal. See "Comparative View of East Lothian Husbandry," p. 52; James Anderson, *General View of the Agriculture of the County of Aberdeen* (Edinburgh, 1794), p. 93.

15. The process of dispossession of subtenants and cottagers was reminiscently described for the parish of Moonzie in Fife. "It was also the practice of the farmers in these times to lease out to each of their cottars and to those who had houses on the farm, two or three acres of land at a moderate rent, and to give it the requisite cultivation. They also allowed them to keep cows, and provided them with grass in the summer and straw in the winter, for their maintenance. . . . But this practice has been discontinued, and none even of the farm servants enjoy the advantage of a cow except the Foreman. In consequence of this change the people of the country who were tradesmen, seeing that they enjoyed none of the comforts of the country, left the habitations of their fathers and established themselves in the towns from which their employment principally derived." *New Statistical Account of Scotland* (Edinburgh, 1845), IX, *Fife*, 793, hereafter cited as *N.S.A.* See also *O.S.A.*, IX, 199; X, 481; XII, 234, 242, 296, 340, 510; XIV, 109, 220, 497, 589.

as a basis for the more effective working of the land. Yet up to the last quarter of the century, the changes in method were very partial or piecemeal and scarcely entrenched on what seemed to later improvers to be the central and decisive weaknesses of the established agriculture. The elements of "good husbandry" as understood in the early nineteenth century began to appear by 1750 but they are not for many years, even in particular experiments, put together in fully articulated systems.

With unified control of particular patches of land it became possible to plow out the high ridges and abolish a long-standing waste of land. But the ridges did not completely disappear, and the furrow, the counterpart of the ridge, remained the chief means of drainage. Rather ridges were straightened and flattened, created fresh every year to the width that would suit the particular type of soil.[16] Deep draining did begin to make an impression on sodden areas created by the water welling up from underground springs; but it was not until the nineteenth century that surface drainage began to be tackled other than by the furrow created by the plowman. The straightening of the ridges usually went with the laying out of fields in regular formation, and ditches often acted as a form of enclosure. Yet the separation of holdings did not always result in physical enclosure even by a ring fence. Enclosures—of stone dike, hedge, or ditch—began to appear but, even when dispersed strips had completely disappeared, they were often partial and over wide areas completely lacking. Even so advanced an area as Fife still had land awaiting enclosure in 1830—land that had lain in big compact farms for at least fifty years.[17]

No element in the old husbandry was more subject to the derision of later farmers than its methods of plowing. The movement

16. Robert Kerr, *General View of the Agriculture of the County of Berwick* (London, 1809), pp. 192–193; Robertson, *Rural Recollections*, pp. 197–202; J. Buchan-Hepburn, *General View of the Agriculture of the County of East Lothian* (Edinburgh, 1794), p. 52; Sir John Sinclair, *An Account of the Systems of Husbandry adopted in the more improved Districts of Scotland* (Edinburgh, 1814), I, 156–170.

17. *N.S.A.*, IX, *Fife*, 108; "On Perthshire Husbandry," *Farm. Mag.*, 8 (1807), 444; *Third Report from the Select Committee Appointed to Inquire into the State of Agriculture*, *Parliamentary Papers*, 1836, VIII, Q. 13,619, 13,826; hereafter cited as *S.C. on Agric., 1836*.

towards using two-horse plows—which became virtually universal in Scotland—was slow and complicated. Various types of improved plows began to appear in the first half of the eighteenth
century. Improvements were so much a matter of minute adjustment in the shaping of the basic parts and particularly of the moldboard that the separation into sharply different types is perhaps un-
realistic. But it was the plow associated with the experimental and
designing skill, and even more with the capacity as a producer, of
James Small that was generally held to make possible the spread of
the two-horse team.[18] Even so, the use of new plows was not
merely a matter of invention, design, and production but also of
accompanying clearance of "sit-fast" stones, of the drainage of
stiff land, and of greater regularity of the shape of fields.[19] Plowing
had to be made easier before the economical two-horse team became the standard. Such changes took many years to accomplish.

The key to a true reform of agriculture lay in innovation and
rearrangement of crops within the general farm scheme. The first
change to be tried in the cropping sequence was the introduction of
a fallow year.[20] It had long been customary to allow portions of
the outfield to lie unplowed and uncropped for years at a time; but
this was not a true fallow, for which the ground had to be thoroughly cleaned, plowed, and dunged. Without fallow or cleaning
crop, any cultivation was unrelievedly choked with weeds. Fallow
also in some measure diminished the effect of the scourging successions of white (cereal) crops to which the infield was continuously,
and the outfield periodically, subjected. Any fallow break seemed
likely, then, to bring some immediate advantages. From early in
the century fallow breaks were being inserted on progressive farms
in which the ground would be repeatedly plowed, cross-plowed,
and dunged. But this was an isolated change which made but a
small break in a sequence that retained most of its old characteris-

18. Handley, *Agricultural Revolution*, pp. 46–51; Thomson, *County of Fife*, p. 125; J.
Naismith, *General View of Agriculture of the County of Clydesdale* (Glasgow, 1798), pp.
58–60; Kerr, *County of Berwick*, pp. 150–152; Sinclair, *Account of Husbandry*, II, App. 5.
19. Robertson, *Rural Recollections*, pp. 555–556.
20. "Account of the Introduction of Summer Fallow into Scotland," *Farm. Mag.*, 1
(1800), 163; "Comparative View of East Lothian Husbandry," p. 52.

tics. It was also inevitably unpopular with the conservative farmer who saw merely that much hard work went into ground that was being kept out of production for a year.

The second modification of the cropping scheme came with the innovation of sown grasses, although it was to be many years after the first introduction of a field of sown grass before this crop and fallow would be used in yearly alternation with white crops; it was another small interjection in long successions of white crops.[21] It was not only for their part in diversifying the crop sequence that grasses were of value. The increased the supply of fodder, allowed a greater carry of animals, and, just as important, allowed a production of dung half as much again as that arising from white crops even when both ear and straw were fed to the animals.[22] Grasses shifted the position of the old balance between arable land and available manure by which intensive cultivation had been limited to the relatively restricted area of the infield. Lime had already begun to bring outfield areas into more continuous use; artificial grass brought still more land under regular and continuous cropping schemes. Agriculture was, in fact, moving towards a regulated balance in which, at a time when farms were mainly self-supporting in the manure they created and used, the area under fodder crop was adjusted to the full manuring of a cereal crop area that covered most of the farm. When the grasses were used along with fallow there was a natural tendency to break up the sequence of crops so that white crops rarely followed in unbroken succession, thereby introducing almost by accident one of the great principles of nineteenth-century improved agriculture. It took some time to achieve the careful adjustment of grass to a proper and controlled position in a farm where the main object continued to be a heavy yield of grain. However, by the 1770's there were farms, mainly in the South-East, in which the vital purposes of cleaning, proper alternation of crops, and adjustment of animal feeding to the manurial needs of the soil were secured. The proper propor-

21. "The Rural Enquirer," *Farm. Mag.*, 1 (1800), 123.
22. Sinclair, *Account of Husbandry*, I, 295–299.

tions of the different elements were slowly being discovered.[23]

Another vital constituent of improved agriculture was the turnip —destined to play a part even more complicated and powerful than fallow or sown grasses. In fact it could combine the functions of both. Turnips could be used for field cleaning since, when they were sown in drills, weeding could be pursued through the growing season; and they provided a heavy feeding crop to be eaten on the fields—when the tramping of the sheep had a valuable mechanical effect on certain lighter types of soil—or carried back to the farmstead for use in feeding in the stalls or courts. The balance between animal and crop husbandry was again beneficially adjusted. Even on farms where the chief object was the production of grain, animals other than the plowing beasts and the milk cows—which were part of the complement of every farm—were brought in to eat the turnips and fertilize the arable acres. Another great principle was recognized: the whole growth of roots and of hay should be consumed on the farm.[24] Many nineteenth-century leases laid this down as a requirement. But again the proper balance took time to discover, for haphazard growing of turnips did not mean that turnip husbandry in its full implications was in operation. Turnips had been grown on some sections of particular farms since the early decades of the eighteenth century but it was not till the 1760's that they began to be sown in drills and to be carefully adjusted to a general farm economy in which the feeding of animals could be made to play a much bigger part. One of the first results of the improvement and enclosure of many arable farms in the South-East had been the banishment of the flocks of sheep that had existed on the small waste patches of undercultivated farms. The return of sheep, now to be fattened, and the importation of cattle for feeding

23. The cropping systems on advanced farms in all parts of the country are recounted many times over in Andrew Wight, *Present State of Husbandry in Scotland* (Edinburgh, 1778–1784). But notice that even in East Lothian the common mode of cropping was still far from that which would have been approved, say, in 1810. See "Comparative View of East Lothian Husbandry," pp. 204–215; Sinclair, *Account of Husbandry*, I, 311–342.

24. Wight was thoroughly contemptuous of farmers who were accustomed to selling hay from the product of their farms, thus showing both that this was in the 1770's a not uncommon practice and that it was abhorrent to advanced opinion about farming. Wight, *Husbandry in Scotland*, II, 92.

were a recognition of how the turnip could be fitted into an improved arable system. The center of this development seems to have been Berwickshire and Roxburghshire. Dawson of Frogden, from his first sowing of drilled turnips in 1762, by stages developed the feeding of animals on his farm and from there his practices spread.[25] The results are shown in the Berwickshire parish of Gordon. In 1775 in the parish only eleven cattle were being fed; by 1782 the number had risen to two hundred.[26] But even in the South-East, the home of turnip husbandry related to arable production, the turnip acreage was still small in 1790.[27] Its spread was limited not so much by an unthinking conservatism as by the fact that the stiffer soils could not carry the crop.

By the early 1790's there were considerable areas in which the farmers were applying the rules of good husbandry as they came to be understood in the nineteenth century—in which root and grass crops were kept in due relation to grain crops, in which the farm stock was adjusted so as to consume the whole fodder product, in which cereal crops were made to alternate with roots, grasses, or fallow, in which green crop or fallow was used at some point in the rotation to clean the soil. In the advanced areas of the time, the two-horse plow was generally used and the threshing machine was beginning to spread. The farms were generally extensive, with big farmhouses and new steadings, rationally planned to allow the orderly performance of farm functions, and centrally placed among

25. Dawson appears to have been the most influential innovator of turnip husbandry in Scotland. His achievement was greater than that of the experimental lairds who had preceded him in the use of turnips. As well as planting a large area of turnips and developing their use in the feeding of cattle and sheep, he pioneered the operation of the two-horse plow by one man, which allowed drills to be sown with a small interval between them. Further, he was instrumental in training plowmen who carried his techniques both to the surrounding areas of Roxburgh and Berwickshire, and also, slightly later, to East Lothian. It seems to have been this preparation that spurred the growth of turnip husbandry in the later seventies and eighties. See Kerr, *County of Berwick*, p. 267; *S.C. on Agric., 1836*, Q. 14,588; R. Douglas, *General View of the Agriculture of the Counties of Roxburgh and Selkirk* (Edinburgh, 1798), pp. 69–70; "On the Drilled Turnip Husbandry of Berwickshire," *Farm. Mag.*, 5 (1804), 466; "Memoir of the late William Dawson, Esq.," *Farm. Mag.*, 16 (1815), 165; "Comparative View of East Lothian Husbandry," pp. 219–220.

26. *O.S.A.*, V, 90.

27. The rapid development of turnip husbandry in the South-East seems to have begun about 1790. See Douglas, *Roxburgh and Selkirk*, p. 79.

fields which were now of rectangular shape, often enclosed and sometimes of twenty or more acres.

The greatest development occurred where wheat could easily be grown and the most complete systems of improvement were directed mainly to the production of wheat as a cash crop. There were in fact two main ways in which this might be done. The first system turned on the continuing use of the fallow year. It was applied on strong but stiff soils where turnips could not well be grown. A year of fallow—when in fact the soil was carefully cultivated—would be followed by three, five, or even seven years when cereals alternated with grass, and with beans; if possible two years of wheat would be taken in rotation but it was necessary to grow some oats and barley for subsistence purposes on the farm. It was an intensive, even a punishing, system in which the production of manure tended to be low for the cereal acreage and there was little rest for the land. It was only the strongest soils, low-lying and therefore adapted to the production of wheat, which would take it. Such soils, with an appropriate wheat-growing climate, were found on the floor of the Tweed valley, running inland along the border with England; in parts of the coastal plain of the Lothians, to the south of the Forth; in patches around the Fife peninsula; in the solid area north of the Tay (the Carse of Gowrie); and along the banks of the Earn, the river which flows mainly through lowland or rolling country into the Firth of Tay. There were also some coastal areas further north where intensive wheat growing was possible. In all these parts improved intensive cropping was common by 1790.

In the second type of improved farming, a cereal cash crop was again the object, but the turnip played a large part. The turnip break, in which the land was thoroughly plowed, weeded, and dunged, was followed, like the fallow in the clay lands, by years of grass or beans alternating with cereal and, if possible, two years of wheat before the cycle was complete. On the strong turnip soils only one year of grass would be taken at a time and the proportion of cereal years was kept high. Therefore, turnip husbandry could be used as an intensive system of unremitting cultivation but it was always linked with a large and carefully managed stock of farm animals. Cattle would be brought in for fattening, generally from further north, while sheep also would be fattened, being either taken from a breeding stock on the farm or brought from the flocks of separate hill farms which were often nearby—and which might, in fact, be in the same ownership as the Lowland arable and fattening farm. Such arable farming, in which turnips were used along with hard cereal cropping and feeding of animals, was of relatively restricted extent in 1790 but in selected areas it had been fully established as a workable and profitable form. It required a strong but not too stiff soil and a wheat-growing climate. It was in Berwickshire and the Lothians that such husbandry balanced with a general farm economy was developed. In these earliest days the sectors where turnips could be developed lay among acres where the fallow year had to be used to keep intensive crop schemes going.

The turnip was destined to play a much bigger part in advancing Scottish agriculture than could be discerned in 1790. But its greatest role would not be in the intensive methods designed to produce cereals as the main cash crop but in less demanding systems which would fully utilize the lighter soils, many of them above the wheat-growing limit, common in Scotland. It would find its greatest use in rotations which contained two, or even three, successive years of grass along with oats and barley as the main cereal crop. Such rotations would produce some grain for sale but the main product would be animals, particularly cattle, either bred and sold as stores, or fattened, or bred and fattened. In 1790, however, while grass was being widely introduced into traditional cereal sequences, the use of turnips in this way was still very limited and the proportioning of grass, turnips, and cereal had not settled down into a recognized system adapted to light soil. In fact, outside the areas of intensive cereal production and some nearby stretches where the less intensive five-shift system was being conscientiously applied, improvement in cropping took the form of random injections of new crops with turnips covering a very small extent—sown grasses much more.

The clay lands of Ayrshire became the great dairying region of Scotland. In the course of the eighteenth century commercial cheese making, using sweet milk, was developed, the product being sold to merchants from Glasgow.[28] Improvement, then, took the form of enclosures for the grazing of the dairy cattle with a crop system which gave a big part to grass. The common rotation came to consist of three or four years of oats, followed by a much longer period of sown grass.[29] At any time, then, on the typical Ayrshire dairy farm at the most one-third of the land would be under crop. Neither turnips nor fallow played much part in this region. Farms had their own breeding stock and whey, the by-product of cheese making, was used to feed pigs. Calves not required for the dairy stock were sold for slaughter. Thus the cheese farm had two important subsidiary products. In the northern part of this dairying belt, which ran into the counties of Lanark and Renfrew with their great urban markets, another form of dairying predominated owing to the proximity of the market rather than to the climate and soil.[30] Within a ten-mile radius of main urban markets it was more rewarding to convert milk into butter and sell the buttermilk in the towns as a by-product.[31] Nearer still to the town the sale of liquid milk became the major interest. By buying cows in milk and by drawing on the supply of manure which came from the towns, the milk farms were able to crowd a large stock on their intensively farmed acres. Glasgow and Paisley, the main towns of the western belt, were not alone in stimulating this type of farm-

28. Fullarton, *County of Ayr*, pp. 16, 60; Agricola, "On the Agriculture of Ayrshire," *Farm. Mag.*, 8 (1807), 318–320; McMaster, "Scotch Cheesemaking," p. 215; Archibald Sturrock, "On the Agriculture of Ayrshire," *T.H.A.S.*, 1 (1886–1867), 74–78; R. Belsches, *General View of the Agriculture of the County of Stirling* (Edinburgh, 1796), pp. 46–47; Robertson, *Rural Recollections*, pp. 565–568.

29. Fullarton, *County of Ayr*, pp. 20–21; Robertson, *Rural Recollections*, p. 614; *S.C. on Agric., 1836*, Q. 12,157, 12,357; Sturrock, "Ayrshire," p. 30; Sir John Sinclair, *General Report of the Agricultural State and Political Circumstances of Scotland* (Edinburgh, 1814), III, 55–71.

30. Sturrock, "Ayrshire," p. 81; Naismith, *County of Clydesdale*, pp. 66–67; Sinclair, *General Report*, III, 60–64.

31. Naismith, *County of Clydesdale*, pp. 66–67; A. Martin, *General View of the Agriculture of the County of Renfrew* (London, 1794), p. 14; Sinclair, *Account of Husbandry*, II, 120; Sinclair, *General Report*, III, 56–59.

ing. All the chief towns, and in particular Edinburgh, had their narrow surrounding belts of intensive dairying. Near to Glasgow and Edinburgh, farms were intensively worked with methods conditioned by the fact that manure could be bought in the towns, to provide a range of commodities saleable in an urban market.[32] Farmers sold turnips, potatoes, hay, and grain, grown on highly rented acres, without having to make a careful adjustment of grass and fodder acreage to the acres under cereal.

Thus, in 1790, possibly ten years after the general run of farmers had begun to change their ways, completely improved systems—in the sense of farming routines which obeyed the main precepts of good husbandry as understood throughout the following century —were in general use in certain well-defined areas of country, usually where wheat could be grown under an intensive system or towns were nearby.[33] Where the example of the great wheat farmers was remote—that is over the Uplands and interior in the south and over most of the arable areas north of the Tay—the new crops were capriciously used. Infield and outfield divisions were still observed even though very crude alterations had been made in the method of cultivating the outfield; and it was still common to find the white crops following in unbroken succession. The intermixture of the strips of different occupiers had almost disappeared but the exaggerated irregular ridges were still to be found and the physical enclosure of fields was uncommon. Grass had become more plentiful but turnips were still rare. Plowing was carried on by widely varying methods with some farms using new two-horse plows, others sticking to old-fashioned implements drawn by ten

32. Sinclair, *Account of Husbandry*, II, 126–133.

33. The agricultural practices of the different parts of the country in the 1790's are laid out in great detail in the parish accounts of the O.S.A. and the impressions that are conveyed by the inevitably varying accounts of the parish ministers are largely confirmed in the volumes devoted to the agriculture of the particular counties of which the first series appeared in the 1790's. The clear distinction emerges between the improved and backward regions with, in general, the higher ground and the interior in the south and the coastal lands as well as the interior in the north still showing antique practices. Descriptions abound of infield and outfield in full operation, of old-fashioned ridges, of scourging sequences of crops, of old plows with teams of many animals, of miserable and inadequate farm buildings.

or twelve oxen or by teams which combined oxen and horses in varying proportions.

The great agricultural development of the next thirty or forty years was the modernization of this sector to match in efficiency, although not in detailed method, the improved and intensively cultivated areas of 1790.[34] The answer to the problems of the lighter soils and the colder climates with their late crops was the application of the less intensive five- or six-shift system which had been pioneered in Berwickshire. This kept the emphasis on grass which had become evident in previous decades but brought turnips to a new central importance. The big supply of fodder meant a heavier carry of animals, which formed the main cash product, but also helped the production of grain on that minor proportion of the farm retained under white crop. Most of the improved areas had grain to sell.

In almost every part of the Lowlands by 1830, farming had come to be conducted as by the precepts of the improver, but there was no single pattern. The intensive cropping to produce wheat or barley for sale, whether by aid of fallow or of green crop and with more or less emphasis on the feeding of imported animals, continued as the main type of farming in those areas where improvement, so closely related to intensive wheat production, had been well established in 1790. But hard by these areas—in East Lothian, and in the counties of Berwick, Roxburgh, Fife, and Perth—there were considerable stretches which were brought into full improved operation by linking turnip husbandry with a strong emphasis on grass and by developing the arts of cattle breeding and feeding. In

34. For the 1830's the reports for the different parishes of the N.S.A. balance those of forty years before. They are, however, much more stereotyped than those of the first account. While there is some gain in eliminating the very poor reports that sometimes occur in the earlier record, there is also loss in that really sharp insights are less to be found. The main complementary evidence for this period is that contained in the Minutes of Evidence of the S.C. on Agric. 1836. In addition the second series of county accounts appearing between 1800 and 1815 show all parts of the country moving to the improved state. From these different sources it is evident that agriculture was much more uniform as between one part of the country than it had been forty years before. The differences, which are equally clear, are not those of the advanced as opposed to backward sections, but rather of adaptations necessarily different because of differences of situation, soil, and climate.

the Central region, north of the Tay, along the valley of Strathmore, and across the wide arable stretch of the North-East corner
this became the main system; cattle, still largely sold as store animals
for the drover, were the main product, while grain made a secondary addition to farm income. Essentially turnips were used as the
same mechanism in general farm improvement as had been pioneered in conjunction with heavy grain cropping in the South-
East. Five-shift cropping and the breeding and feeding of cattle
also took hold on the lighter soils of the South-West to the south
and east of the dairying district. But dairying itself continued with
little change on the clay districts of Ayrshire. North of the cheese
belt, butter making and the production of sweet milk were intensified by the growth of the urban population. Another form of
farming related to the urban market received a stimulus. This was
the cultivation of potatoes, a foodstuff much in demand among the
new urban population and difficult to transport for any distance, a
crop, too, which could make good use both of the manure supply
from the towns and of the laborers who were eager for the seasonal
earnings of work in the potato fields.[35]

Cutting across this wide range of farming adaptations there were
certain common features. Holdings were now entirely separate from
each other but, in fact, each farm was in itself a tiny settlement with
most of the farm staff living in, or close to, the farmstead rather
than in general villages. The land was now generally laid out in
rectangular fields. Such subdivisions varied in size according to the
overall size of the farm—of which the local average varied from
place to place—and to the contours of the land. In the areas of older
improvement the fields were well enclosed but in some parts where
improvement had come later, particularly the North-East, much
of the land still lay open. Lack of enclosure did not prevent the use
of rotations in which grass and turnip played a large part and across

35. Around the industrial towns of the South-West it was common for farmers to
make arrangements with the townspeople whereby plots (of four or five acres) were
plowed and prepared for planting by the farmers so that the townspeople, who paid a
rent, could plant and lift the roots themselves. The deathblow to this arrangement came
with the potato disease in the 1840's. Sturrock, "Ayrshire," p. 30; Sinclair, *General Report*, I, 572–573.

which animals had to be systematically moved. Every small croft in the North-East had its quota of turnips and its few beasts being bred and fed; without enclosure, control was maintained by herding.[36] Plowing was now carried on almost entirely by the two-horse team and it was only on the smallest croft holdings, where the holder could not afford to keep two horses, that oxen might be yoked. With new farm layouts the internal shifting of dung, building materials, and produce was facilitated by the rational placing of farm buildings and the cutting of connecting tracks. Farms were also better connected with the outside world by a general program of road building. Private roads, for which landowners were responsible, were linked with commutation roads, for which public funds were available, and commutation roads with turnpikes which by 1820 laced almost the entire country. The result was a transport revolution. Not only could all the necessary bulk movements about the farm be made on wheels but also the farm produce now moved easily and at relatively low cost to its immediate market while, just as important, stores could be cheaply brought into the farm. Great improvements were made in cart design. For example, the clumsy axle rigidly fixed to the wheel and rotating with it gave place to smoothly running bearings on which the wheel rotated around the axle fixed to the body of the cart.[37] Commonly carts came to be pulled by one horse and the prevalence of such vehicles was claimed to be an advantage almost as important for Scottish agriculture as the two-horse plow. The threshing machine, invented effectively in 1787, was rapidly and widely adopted, whether powered by water, wind, horse, or steam, and by 1830 it was only the smaller grade of farms in certain parts of the country that were without a machine of their own.[38] Thereby much labor was saved. Sowing and reaping were carried on much in the traditional man-

36. David Souter, *General View of the Agriculture of the County of Banff* (Edinburgh, 1812), p. 98.

37. George Robertson, *General View of the Agriculture of the County of Kincardineshire* (London, 1810), pp. 237–238; Robertson, *Rural Recollections*, p. 145; J. Erskine, *General View of the Agriculture of the County of Clackmannan* (Edinburgh, 1795), pp. 32–33; Sinclair, *Account of Husbandry*, I, 74–77.

38. Sinclair, *Account of Husbandry*, I, 79–104; Sinclair, *General Report*, I, 226–233.

ner—sowing by the hand-broadcast method and reaping usually by the sickle or hook (although the more economical scythe was used for hay and, in the North-East to some extent, for grain).[39] One of the main features of the traditional Scottish landscape was now gone—the old irregular heaped-up ridges were replaced by furrows, drawn in regular patterns, generally separated by a distance of eighteen feet. Another contrast between the landscape of 1830 and that of 1780, frequently visualized by those with long memories, was the obliteration of the ragged waste sections of poor rank growth by fields of colorful crops; much waste land had been reclaimed since the earlier period by draining, trenching, paring and burning, or simply removing stones.[40]

In one respect there was little uniformity about the country: the average size of farm varied a great deal.[41] In the South-East the large farm, of at least one hundred fifty acres, was completely dominant and the counties just to the north—Stirling, Perth, and Fife—also had examples of such units in every minor district. On the carse lands of the vale of Forth, both north and south of the river, the farms were generally smaller, averaging about one hundred acres, most being around that level and a few of more than two hundred. This area, however, had few genuine small holdings. Further north, in Fife and parts of Perth, large farms were again to

39. John Taylor, "On the Comparative Merits of Different Modes of Reaping," *T.H.S.A.*, 1 (1846–1847), 264, 268; *N.S.A.*, XII, *Aberdeenshire*, 336, 507.

40. It is common for the reporters in the *N.S.A.* to reflect on the changes since the previous Account, using either their own memories or the reports of their predecessors for comparison. Several vivid descriptions occur of the changes in the land over the years.

41. All the county reports have sections devoted to the "Size of Farms," but the account is usually given in very general terms with the range of size and, without any accurate quantification, the typical holding. Comparatively seldom is any breakdown given for the size of holdings for particular parishes in the *N.S.A.*, but it is more common to find a figure for the total number of farms in the parish. For 1830, however, it is probably legitimate to take the comprehensive statistics for size and number of holdings which become available from the 1850's; there seems to have been very little change between 1830 and 1850 and the later years of the century. Figures for size of holdings arranged by counties are available from the census report of 1851, but they seem to understate the number, particularly, of small holdings; they give, however, a clear indication of the great differences between the various counties. In 1866 official figures were made up for the size of holdings, but it was not till 1870 that a full record is given of all holdings down to the very smallest. Moreover this data is available for the parish units.

be found in numbers but surrounded by more small units than in the Lothians. The carse lands of the Tay, to the north of the estuary, like those of the Forth, were characterized by farms of medium rather than large size. From there northwards, the number of small holdings tended to increase although every county had examples of the larger type, the unit of three hundred acres or more. Across the plain of the North-East was found a vast predominance of holdings under the fifty-acre level—the minimum unit for efficient cultivation and indeed the minimum to provide full employment and livelihood for the holder. The North-East also had its big farms, although only occasionally of more than two hundred acres. Even among the holdings that could be called true farms, the average was very modest. Such farms were interspersed and outnumbered by the small croft holdings. In the main dairying districts of the west the family unit was typical, with few above the one hundred fifty-acre level but also relatively few below the level of independent subsistence. South of the main dairy district, the farms tended to be somewhat larger even when dairying was the main object.

The farms thus laid out by 1830 and the number of occupying tenants were to change little in the next hundred years and developments were relatively slow by comparison with the previous fifty years. The basic patterns of crop and of animal stock also changed only by slow adjustments of proportion and scale. Yet the expansion in many aspects of agriculture proceeded at an undiminished pace until the mid-seventies. The greatest advance was in cattle rearing on the more marginal soils. Until the 1820's, in those parts outside the immediate ambit of Glasgow and Edinburgh there was difficulty in finding a market for fat cattle; the further one went north the greater the proportion of stock that had to be sold, as store animals, to the drover. From the northern end of Strathmore some were sent off fattened to cover nearly a hundred miles on the hoof to the central markets but more were sold lean. The great arable stretch of the North-East, well adapted to feeding animals, was underutilized because, apart from the beasts for the smallish Aberdeen market, all stock had to be sold lean and underpriced. Then in the 1820's the steamships came and in 1850 the rail-way, by which stock could be carried quickly to the London mar-ket. The North-East farmer for the first time was able to get full price for fattened cattle on almost as many beasts as he could rear.[42] The turnip-based rotations with their good supply of provender were the source of increasing profit; and more land could profit-ably be taken into the standard five- or six-shift course. It was not only the hitherto isolated North-East that felt the pull of better markets; every part of Scotland now had an opening to the Lon-don market and everywhere the profits of stock fattening increased, with an impetus to the expansion of acreage.[43] Another factor en-couraged the growth of turnips. The efficacy of bone dust as a prep-aration for this crop, particularly on thin and unpromising lands, had been discovered in the 1820's.[44] Many acres were made pro-ductive, particularly among the foothill areas which are so com-mon in Scotland.

Turnip cultivation could also be extended because of the better drainage of the stiff soils.[45] The fallow break ceased to be a neces-sity on some of the clays as green crop was planted over at least part of the fallow fields. This crop extension was achieved by sur-face drainage. In the twenties, farmers began to cut below their lands to form grids of covered drains, running in parallel lines across the fields. This system of drainage, which was applied much more generally than any that had been previously tried, successfully re-moved the surface moisture from wide acres of land and altered the whole scope of cultivation. The growing season was lengthened,

42. George Skene Keith, *General View of the Agriculture of the County of Aberdeen* (Aber-deen, 1811), p. 353; Anderson, *County of Aberdeen*, p. 81; *N.S.A.*, X, *Perth*, 919; XI, *Forfar*, 202, 684; XI, *Kincardine*, 140; *S.C. on Agric.*, *1836*, Q. 10,651, 10,673–10,679, 13,610, 13,762, 14,083; Geoffrey Channon, "The Aberdeenshire Beef Trade and London: A Study in Steamship and Railway Competition, 1850–1869," *Transport History*, 2 (1969), 1–23.

43. *S.C. on Agric. 1836*, Q. 11,145, 11,926; John Gillespie, "The Agriculture of Dum-fries-shire," *T.H.A.S.*, 2 (1868–1869), 277–279.

44. *S.C. on Agric.*, *1836*, Q. 11,145, 11,926, 13,610, 13,762, 14,083; Gillespie, "Dum-fries-shire," pp. 279–280; Thomas MacLelland, "The Agriculture of Kirkcudbright and Wigtownshire," *T.H.A.S.*, 7 (1875), 17–18.

45. *S.C. on Agric.*, *1836*, Q. 10,246, 10,541, 11,869, 13,606, 13,678, 13,955; John Dick-son, "The Agriculture of Perthshire," *T.H.A.S.*, 2 (1868–1869), 179.

plowing was eased, turnips could be grown where they had previously been forbidden. With the invention of the cylindrical clay pipe to act as a drainage channel and the provision of government funds at low interest it became profitable to aim at the drainage of a large proportion of the arable land. The process could never be quick or cheap. Slowly, year by year, the farmer would trench a few more acres of his farm. All through the middle decades of the century, in all parts of Lowland Scotland, the work went on, bringing a slow but wonderful transformation to many stiff, cold acres.[46]

The spreading range of green crops sometimes took the form of increased planting of potatoes as a field crop. Potatoes might give high but rather uncertain profit according to the physical yield and the price which they could command from year to year. It was around the estuary of the Tay, in northern Fife and in lower Perthshire, that potatoes first became a major commercial crop.[47] By the 1820's they were being shipped from the parishes close to the river, mainly for the London market, but the "Perthshire reds" were particularly affected by the potato disease of the forties and thereafter this region gave up its interest in commercially grown potatoes.[48] The immediate loss of Perthshire was the gain of the Lothians. The dry free soil south of the Forth produced a root which proved resistant to the disease and potatoes, introduced often as a second green crop in the rotation, became a major export of the region. The opening of the railway line along the coast and leading to England further helped in the development of this crop.

Drainage promised to be of great importance also in the clay district of Ayrshire and attempts were made to increase the production of turnips in the dairying region but with less success than

46. *S.C. on Agric., 1836*, Q. 9,902, 9,965, 10,031, 10,331, 11,089–11,092; James Macdonald, "The Agriculture of Fife," *T.H.A.S.*, 8 (1876), 11–12; Robert Scott Skirving, "The Agriculture of East Lothian," *T.H.A.S.*, 5 (1873), 26; Dickson, "Perthshire," pp. 167–168, 179; Highland and Agricultural Society, *Report on the Present State of Agriculture in Scotland* (Edinburgh, 1878), pp. 26–27, 62–64, hereafter cited as *Report on Agriculture, 1878*; Gillespie, "Dumfries-shire," pp. 280–281, 320–321.

47. *N.S.A.*, X, Perth, 205, 244, 364, 820, 956.

48. Skirving, "East Lothian," pp. 22–23; Macdonald, "Fife," p. 15; *Report on Agriculture, 1878*, p. 29.

in many parts of the east.[49] Possibly more important for dairying was the opening before 1850 of railway communication, north to Glasgow and south to England, from the interior region which had built up its dairy stock on the basis of the sale of easily transportable cheese. The more perishable dairy products of milk and buttermilk could be brought into the cities which were growing both in population and in purchasing power.[50] The edge of the butter-producing sector tended to move southwards into the cheese-making area and, correspondingly, dairying for cheese making expanded over the stock-rearing districts of Dumfries-shire and Galloway. But the sending of milk by rail tended to be limited and seasonal with some winter traffic out of areas which depended more generally upon cheese making.[51] The areas of true specialized milk production were still confined largely to the outer-city rings from which daily distribution by cart was possible.

One change of great importance was the increasing use of feedingstuffs bought from outside the farm.[52] With these new supplies the old limit on farm stock had been removed and the balance between grain and fodder acreage was not now closely determined by calculation of how much was needed to feed animals that would fully manure the remaining arable acres. In fact, imported feedingstuffs were used to increase the farm stock without any substantial decrease, such as had been made theoretically possible, in the fodder or green crop acreage. Thereby the carry of animals was increased even though arable yields were being raised. Farming was everywhere intensified as more capital was injected for the purchase of feedingstuffs and fertilizers. By the 1870's it had become common to pay as much for these items as was due in rent. Capital was needed, too, for advanced forms of machinery. Steam power was

49. *Report on Agriculture, 1878*, p. 65.

50. James Tait, "The Agriculture of Stirling," *T.H.A.S.*, 16 (1884), 156; William H. Ralston, "The Agriculture of Wigtownshire," *T.H.A.S.*, 17 (1885), 122; Gillespie, "Dumfries-shire," pp. 307–312.

51. *Report on Agriculture, 1878*, pp. 45, 90; James Tait, "The Agriculture of Lanarkshire," *T.H.A.S.*, 17, (1885), 38–39, 58–59, 62–63; Gillespie, "Dumfries-shire," p. 311; Ralston, "Wigtownshire," p. 122.

52. Skirving, "East Lothian," p. 23.

more and more used for threshing; the steam engine gave a more efficient performance than the horse but meant a higher initial expenditure.[53] There was experimentation with the use of steam power for plowing, not without success, but the impact, except on the very largest farms, was slight.[54] The most important mechanical innovation was the reaper. As early as 1828 reapers were in use but only after 1850 were they at all common. From that time forward the adoption of machinery was rapid and by the seventies the greater part of the grain and hay crop was being mechanically cut.[55] Another innovation of some importance was the use of wire for fencing. This particularly affected the North-East where the cattle, on which the region depended, had on many farms continued to be herded.[56] By 1870, however, the last open stretches, used for rotation crops, were disappearing.

53. *Ibid.*, p. 24.

54. *Report on Agriculture, 1878*, pp. 38–39, 149–151; Dickson, "Perthshire," p. 189; Alexander Smith, ed., *A New History of Aberdeenshire* (Aberdeen, 1875), Part I, pp. 597, 622.

55. The county most suited to make good use of the mechanical reaper was East Lothian. It had 160 reapers in 1860, and at most one-half of the farms would be using the device. By 1873 the whole crop in the county was being cut mechanically. Other parts of the country were slower to use the new machines, but by the mid-seventies a high proportion everywhere was being cut mechanically. Even in Aberdeenshire, with its multitude of small farms, reapers were common, and in Ayrshire every farm of one hundred acres or more had its machine. Jacob Wilson, "Reaping Machines," *T.H.A.S.*, 11 (1863–1865), 143; Sturrock, "Ayrshire," p. 59; Skirving, "East Lothian," p. 25; Smith, *History of Aberdeenshire*, Pt. I, 241.

56. Dickson, "Perthshire," p. 170; James D. Young, "On Wire Fences," *T.H.A.S.*, 4 (1849–1851), 242–262; *Fourth Report on the Employment of Children, Young Persons and Women in Agriculture, Parliamentary Papers*, 1870, XIII, Appendix I, p. 34, hereafter cited as *Fourth Report on Women in Agric.*

## Social Consequences

BEYOND doubt the improvement of agriculture tended to generate, over the whole period from 1775 to 1875, an almost continually increasing income. The acreage under the plow was always being extended in some part of the country; the yield per acre of grain doubled at least and to this must be added the output of the new green crops and of sown grasses; the complement of animals increased several times over and from a given stock of animals a much larger proportion yielded net income for the farm as opposed to those which were used in the production process. Yet improvement was also inherently disturbing to the settled social order, to the old scheme in which everyone had a known place and in which the son graduated automatically, without conscious choice, to the position of the father. People were unsettled by rearrangements which blurred their social expectations. The nature of the work, the number of jobs, the social relations implicit in the job, the number of places on the land were all abruptly shaken up. The disturbance was made worse by an accelerating natural increase of population which itself disturbed the proportioning of the size of the potential work force to the number of openings. Youngsters could not now graduate to the secure traditional place that had been held by their fathers. Many already working found themselves in strange social surroundings, perhaps having lost their land, or having to shift from the old muddled sociability of the ferm toun to a lonely and grimly uniform string of cottages, or having to labor constantly at one agricultural operation where previously the year had passed in a succession of different tasks. Individuals, whose lives were to change anyway, were now more and more forced to a conscious choice between jobs. They began to have to compare the life and wages of the towndweller or even the distantly imagined prospects of the emigrant with the known facts of the life on the land.

The process of improvement was tending, at least from 1750 onwards, to narrow the opportunities to acquire land. Before the agrarian changes started there was everywhere in Scotland a sub-stantial class of main tenants—amounting roughly to one-third of the rural population—and to this has to be added the cottars, often still more numerous, who occupied portions as subtenants. In some parts the only truly landless people were the unmarried farm ser-vants, although in the South-East the importance of the "hind"—the married farm servant—does indicate already a substantial group of people who would remain landless throughout their lives. Im-provement was to wreak havoc both among the direct tenants and among the subtenants, reducing a much larger proportion of the population to the landless condition.

Consider first the direct tenants, the upper layer of peasant so-ciety. This group had contained individuals of varying substance from the man with one hundred or one hundred fifty acres to the holder of fewer than five. It included both holders of entire farms and members of joint communities of tenants. The latter would be affected by the movement to separate consolidated holdings from their joint (runrig) farms—a movement which we have seen was well advanced in the 1770's. This was not always the result of sud-den and systematic replanning by landlords, although they did have the nominal power to decide on a drawing board scheme and fit the tenants to it. Some at least of the joint farms moved slowly towards separation of the constituent parts by piecemeal exchange and consolidation; piece by piece the nineteenth-century map of farm boundaries takes shape.[57] The shocks involved in this slow redrawing can only be guessed. In any event, settlement on a sep-arate holding, in a farmhouse lying convenient to the fields if not to the neighbors, did not necessarily mean social isolation. The new farms gathered their considerable labor force around them, some-times in the shape of married men with families, sometimes of un-married lads who would eat in the farm kitchen. Where densities of population on the new farms are known, they appear scarcely less than must have been typical of the old order. In the intensively cultivated Lothians the large farms sometimes had populations of

57. Lebon. "Face of the Countryside in Central Ayrshire," pp. 7–15; Third, "Chang-ing Landscape," pp. 83–93; Third, "Scottish Estate Plans," pp. 39–64.

more than one hundred persons on them at a density of one person to every five or six acres.[58] In some cases there were more people living on the farms after they had been thrown together to form larger units than there had been on the multiple units of the old system. If there was isolation it was by social choice rather than physical compulsion. The farmers were tending to draw away from the men and the families who labored the land. There was a growing difference between the large farmers of Fife or the South-East and their laborers, who generally inhabited cottages around the steading; no sphere of sociability was left in which they ceased to behave as master and men. Even in the smaller family holdings of Aberdeenshire the farmers would begin to eat separately from the men. The dairy districts of Ayrshire and Lanarkshire, however, seem to have retained the customs of common sharing.[59]

Much more serious and much more likely to lead a person to flee the whole rural environment was the threat that tenants or their heirs might entirely lose their land. If even the oldest son of a tenant's family might fail to inherit the position of his father, still more parlous was the position of the younger sons as they reached maturity; with an increasing population, more and more would fall into this category. There can be no doubt of the general tendency to throw farms together to make larger units. The improvers regarded seventy acres as the very minimum for efficient working, the area in most districts that could be worked by a single plow-team. But such a "one-pair horse" farm was inevitably less efficient than larger units. Other workers were required besides the plowman and they would scarcely be fully employed on a farm of such a size. It was only with several plowteams that the full advantage of division of labor could be achieved. The larger farm had advantages in meeting the expenses of farm buildings and of fenc-

58. *S.C. on Agric., 1836*, Q. 14,541; Sinclair, *Account of Husbandry*, II, 143–146; James Robertson, *General View of the Agriculture in the Southern Districts of the County of Perth* (London, 1794), p. 83; Keith, *County of Aberdeen*, p. 513; *N.S.A.*, IX, *Fife*, 94–97.

59. *Fourth Report on Women in Agric.*, App. I, p. 97; "On the Husbandry of Buchan," *Farm. Mag.*, 8 (1807), 347. The custom of master and men eating at the same table did, however, survive in some parts notably the dairying districts of North Ayrshire and Lanarkshire, possibly because here the plowmen were frequently farmers' sons spending a period in service before they took over the farm. See *Fourth Report on Women in Agric.*, App. II, p. 234.

ing and could better sustain the overhead costs of the threshing machine. The maximum size of a farm that could be conveniently worked from the one set of farm buildings and domestic quarters was about six hundred acres and some argued that this was also the best size.[60] Such units were far greater than the usual type of farm in the earlier eighteenth century, when even in the most advanced districts the husbandmen would characteristically have about one hundred acres. In most areas the well-doing tenant would have had between fifty and one hundred acres and the average size of a farm would be below the fifty-acre mark. Thus improvers, and landlords following in their wake, had a strong desire to establish more economic units. They could not always move fast. Tenant resistance was generally strong and the capital and managerial skill to run the larger units might be hard to find. In the later eighteenth century the stocking of an up-to-date farm would cost at least £5 per acre not to mention the expense of the new buildings always essential to the success of a new scheme. Undoubtedly, however, there was a general movement in every part of Lowland Scotland to lay down larger farms and nearly always larger farms meant fewer tenants; dispossession and eviction became a common experience.

Such change had become a common folk memory by the 1790's and the plaints are frequent through the pages of the *Old Statistical Account*. The overwhelming tenor of the evidence, in every county, is of holdings thrown together to make larger farms and of tenants evicted. In some part, the process had by then reached its culmination with the number of holders down to levels that would remain steady throughout the nineteenth century. In East Lothian several of the parishes contained fewer than a dozen farms, and the average size could stand at over the two hundred-acre mark.[61] This

60. See, for example, Kerr, *County of Berwick*, p. 117; Sinclair, *Account of Husbandry*, II, 86.

61. The "usual" size of a farm in East Lothian is given in 1778 as being two hundred acres, possibly twice as great as it had been earlier in the century. Between 1778 and 1810, "on a cursory view of some parishes," the number of farms is seen to have further diminished by about one-fourth. Many by that time exceeded five hundred acres in extent, whereas in 1778 very few had been of more than three hundred acres. "Comparative View of East Lothian Husbandry," pp. 67–68.

was a big decrease from former numbers. In the parish of Athelstaneford, for example, there were in 1794 sixteen farms, mostly between one hundred fifty and two hundred acres; three were over three hundred acres but only one under two hundred.[62] In that of Spott, in sixty years the number of farms had shrunk by two-thirds.[63] In most other parts of the country, however, the large farms were less firmly established, partly because in 1790 the process of consolidation still had some way to go, and partly because no other part of the country would become so completely dominated by large farms as East Lothian or, to a lesser degree, Berwickshire. The carse areas both of the Forth and Tay, for example, were already well improved in 1790, but the usual type of farm was still about one hundred acres and in Ayrshire the family farm, where the farmer held the plow, was the standard type.[64] Even in this more mixed picture, however, the decline in the number of occupying tenants when it can be traced is seen to have been sharp. Ruthven, in Forfarshire, had forty tenants in 1742 and twelve in 1792, Clackmannan (parish) ninety-one in 1750 and, forty years later, fifty-one.[65] And in many parts there was still much consolidation to be done; evictions might carry on for at least twenty years.

In contrast to the movement elsewhere, the North-East never ceased to be a region of numerous small holdings and fairly infrequent large farms, themselves only of moderate extent. In the parish of Old Deer, for example, by 1840 there were 140 farms capable of fully using at least one plow, the great majority being of less than one hundred acres, but there were also 401 crofts or small holdings.[66] This structure of the mid-nineteenth century would seem largely to conform to the patterns of land tenure a century earlier. Yet in fact there had been a complicated reshuffling

62. O.S.A., X, 164–166.

63. Ibid., V, 453.

64. William Aiton, General View of the Agriculture of the County of Ayr (Glasgow, 1811), p. 138; James Donaldson, General View of the Agriculture of the Carse of Gowrie in the County of Perth (London, 1794), p. 11; Martin, County of Renfrew, p. 21.

65. O.S.A., XII, 304; XIV, 617, 629.

66. N.S.A., XII, Aberdeenshire, 152, 155–156.

both of tenants and their holdings. In the 1790's the parishes of the North-East were reporting the throwing together of farms and be-wailing the evictions with scarcely less fervor than in the large-farm areas. What was peculiar to the region was the extent to which new small holdings would be created even as the older ones were put into larger units.[67] In an area where there was much land await-ing reclamation, landlords might use smallholders as agents in the clearing of land. Tenants would be given tracts of moorland and allowed some years of minimal rent till the land began to bear fruit and earn money. The drive to clear land was extraordinarily suc-cessful and reached its peak in the first half of the nineteenth cen-tury. There are few parishes which do not in 1840 report consider-able additions to their arable acreage over the past thirty or forty years. Some of this was done by considerable farmers extending the bounds of cultivation across intractable land within the original nominal divisions of their farms, but much also was undoubtedly achieved by smallholders starting with only unimproved land.

The changes in the number of holdings laid out by the landlords give little indication of the complex shifts by which men were changing from one social position to another. The smallholders of the new order were not simply the transferred small tenants of the old. It is true that some, who had been evicted to make way for larger and more successful farmers, might be resettled in colonies of holders set down within notional lines of division drawn over the wastelands that were to be brought into use. But such new groupings also contained men who had been cottars and subtenants and had been evicted in the interest of more efficient farming. A subtenant might well become a direct tenant. Some tenants who had been evicted would leave the land entirely; some would find new small holdings; some might become landless laborers, settling

67. *Ibid.* See also, Smith, *History of Aberdeenshire*, Pt. I, pp. 187, 202, 232, etc.; Urquhart Fraser, "Improvement of Waste Land," *T.H.A.S.*, 7 (1855–1857), 441–445; Alexander Thomson, "Report on the Improvement of Waste Land," *T.H.A.S.*, 6 (1853–1855), 90–98; John Milne, "The Agriculture of Aberdeenshire and Banffshire," *T.H.A.S.*, 3 (1870–1871), 400. In a large number of the Aberdeenshire parishes, the *1851 Census* report indicates the clearance of waste land and the settlement of crofters.

in the villages that were growing at this time. Meanwhile the old subtenants were similarly having to find new positions.

In the more fertile and better cultivated portions of Buchan, a system has prevailed of augmenting the number of large farms; and in consequence diminishing that of the small. By the operation of this system, many of the small holders, deprived of their possessions, were forced to betake themselves to the improvement and cultivation of a piece of wasteland on the side of a hill, or on the margin of a moor or moss, given them by the proprietor at a nominal rent for a stipulated number of years, seldom exceeding seven, and afterwards to be paid for at value. At the same time the active spirit of improvement . . . led to the removal from their farms of the cottars and subtenants, whose families had hitherto supplied the best farm servants; and those also had no other resource left them but that of the crofters.[68]

The outcome seems to have been to increase the number of people who could describe themselves as holders of land, with the great majority holding directly of the landowner rather than adhering to the position of subtenants.[69] Yet it must be remembered that the need for new holdings was determined by the aggregate number of cottars and subtenants rather than simply by the size of the smaller group of evicted main tenants.

68. James Black, "Report on Cottage Accommodation in the District of Buchan, Aberdeenshire," *T.H.A.S.*, 5 (1851–1853), 93.

69. In a sample of fifteen parishes, drawn from different parts of Aberdeenshire, there were, according to the *List of Pollable Persons, 1696*, a total of 823 tenants and 681 subtenants and cottars; the same parishes, in 1870, had 2,054 holdings. Even when those classified as tradesmen are added to the 1696 total, increasing it thereby to 1,935, the number does not quite match the total of holders of land at the later date. Clearly there had been a considerable creation of new holdings, and a multiplication by more than two-fold of units of land held directly of the landlord. (The valuation rolls which were compiled for 1855 and for following years made it clear that there remained very little subtenure.) In each of the parishes taken individually, the number of direct tenants in 1696 is substantially below that of all holders in 1870 and in all but one very substantially so. In only three out of the fifteen parishes were there in 1870 fewer holdings than there were tenants, subtenants, and cottars in 1696. The creation of new holdings seems to have occurred mostly after 1800. In a few instances it is possible from the data in the *O.S.A.*, to make comparisons of the 1790's with 1696 and with 1870. It emerges that, in the five parishes where this is possible, between 1696 and the 1790's, in one there was substantial decline in the number of direct tenancies, in two there had been little change in this category, and in two there had been substantial increase of numbers; but in all five cases there was a large increase in the number of tenancies between the 1790's and 1870. *List of Pollable Persons, 1696*; *O.S.A.*; Scottish Record Office, A.F. 39/1/1.

## The Laborer under the New Order

MORE families were in fact affected by the changing position of the farm laborer than by the share-out of land among the main farmers. The reshaping of farms and the reform of farming methods meant considerable changes in the life of the farm worker as well as increase in the size of the farm laborer class. The new conditions formed the binding limits in the lives of the majority of the population and thence sprang the attitudes that helped to determine how many would stay in an agricultural life and how many would seek other jobs and move to other places.

The key to the farmer's policy of hiring was the need to use his work animals economically. One plowteam of two horses could deal with between forty and eighty acres of land in regular crop rotation, the exact ratio being determined by the efficiency of the farmer, the intensiveness of the rotation, and, most of all, the nature of the soil; it took twice as much horse labor to work a carse farm as it did one of thinner soil.[70] At the same time the produce of ten acres was needed to feed the team.[71] A horse, then, was an expensive item for which the cost remained virtually the same however intermittently it might be at work. Thus, within the limits of the seasonal demands, the whole work of the farm had to be arranged so that the work of the horse was equalized over the year. Fortunately, the new husbandry helped to spread the work more evenly between the seasons than in the past. Summer fallow meant plow work in that season as well as in the traditional heavy season of winter and spring; the culture of the green crops and particularly of turnips created summer work for the horse hoe and the light plow; carrying the roots back to the steading was another new task; the growing use of carts for moving dung and crops added to the intensity and the regularity of horse work;[72] threshing, a steady

70. Sinclair, *Account of Husbandry*, I, 139–143; *Fourth Report on Women in Agric.*, App. I, p. 32; *Report on Agriculture, 1878*, p. 32.

71. Sinclair, *Account of Husbandry*, II, 136–139; Sinclair, *General Report*, III, 193–195.

72. The importance of this factor may be understood when it is noted that on a moderate-sized farm, seven hundred loads of dung might have to be moved in the year.

year-round task, might well be performed by the horses; the mechanization of the processes of sowing, and later of reaping, produced a further call upon the labor of horses.

To secure the economical working of the horses it became the custom all over Scotland for each plowman to have charge of a particular pair of animals; he would use no others and no one else would interfere in his management.[73] The bond of horses and man was a recurring element in the folklore of the country, the subject of song and, beyond doubt, of personal pride. There arose a great craft skill in plowing, an expression of the continuing intricate cooperation of man and beast. A considerable aesthetic drive went into the decoration of these animals. It followed that the plowman, equally with the horses, had to be constantly available about the farm the whole year around and that he must as far as possible confine himself to work with his own team of horses, whether in plowing or in other horse work, such as carrying dung to the fields, bringing in grain or roots, working the threshing mill, or carrying produce from farm to market. His day's work consisted of an early morning preparation and yoking of the horses, a work period of five hours, a midday break of two hours when the horses were unyoked, an afternoon period of work, and an evening inspection and grooming of the animals.[74] Such a routine could not be carried on by anyone who lived off the farm nor could it be performed by one engaged by the day. Thus the plowman was a full-time ser-

73. *Fourth Report on Women in Agric.*, App. I, p. 46; Sinclair, *General Report*, III, 196–197; *Royal Commission on Labour, Parliamentary Papers*, 1893–1894, XXXVI, *The Agricultural Labourer*, III, *Scotland*, Part II, 95. The dexterity of the plowmen with their horses is illustrated by Robertson in *Kincardineshire*, pp. 424–425, and in *Rural Recollections*, pp. 162–163.

74. When the days were long enough the afternoon period of plowing would be five hours on the lighter soils, four on the heavier. Otherwise the daily routines were very similar from one part of the country to the other. The long midday break when the horses were unyoked and the custom of using the same pair for both morning and afternoon plowing were universal. The arrangements for the evening grooming were less rigid but always some evening work had to be undertaken. Also the morning start had always to be some time before the commencement of the five-hour stint in the fields. There seems to have been no change in the established customs of plowing from the time the two-horse team was adopted till the end of the century. See, for example, Sinclair, *General Report*, III, 196–197; *Fourth Report on Women in Agric.*, App. I, 46–47; *Royal Commission on Labour, The Agricultural Labourer*, III, *Scotland*, Pt. II, 54, 101.

vant, wholly at his master's call and housed in, or near, the steading. He might be engaged for periods of six months or a year at a time, but in either case he stayed in dependent employ through the whole year, so that the master constantly had plowmen to a given number at his call.

A man became a plowman after a number of years' training and when he was strong enough and old enough to hold the plow; thereafter he would do only the one type of work as he took his place in a hierarchy of first, second, and third plowmen, remunerated according to his position. Every farm also had a quota of work changing in form but occurring at all seasons of the year—jobs such as spreading dung, building stacks, sowing, feeding cattle in the courts and byres, herding. If the plowman was entirely specialized it was necessary to have some other laborers constantly on hand. Where there was only one plowman—who might be the farmer himself—and no room for specialization, the additional laborer would have to perform a variety of tasks. Boys were engaged as servants as young as twelve or thirteen years of age and while learning the trade of the plowman, as a "haflin," would also perform miscellaneous tasks about the farm. Sometimes an older man, the "orraman," would be hired for these tasks and it was not unusual to find female servants engaged even in such heavy work as spreading dung. Every small farm, then, had its two categories— the plowmen and general laborers—but on the bigger units further specialization became possible. Along with the plowmen there would be a somewhat less numerous band consisting of a grieve (foreman), cattlemen, sparemen, shepherd, and possibly one or two female servants.

Such, then, was the staff to be found on nearly every large farm. In Scotland a particularly high proportion of the farm work would be done by the steady toil of such full-time employees but there still remained a problem of meeting the seasonal variations in employment and it might also be convenient to have certain jobs performed by workers hired for short periods. The tendency with the new methods of husbandry was to fill in the empty gaps of the summer where previously there had been little to do around the farm. Plowing, we have seen, had become a steadier year-round task but in addition there was work on the potato fields, planting, weeding, and lifting. Turnips had to be weeded and singled and ultimately lifted so that the demand for labor had become heavier in summer than in winter. The hay harvest brought a heavy period of work into the summer months. Then there was the traditional corn harvest, which until the coming of the mechanical reaper, occasioned the use of many more laborers than at any other time of the year. Some of the summer tasks could be met by using the unspecialized laborers on the permanent staff but generally it was necessary also to hire some additional workers—who might be male or female—by the day or week; and at harvest, of course, the additional complement of temporary workers became very great. Thus every farm had to use both laborers who were hired full-time and stayed in cottages or other buildings which were part of the farm equipment, and outside laborers who were hired temporarily. The proportion between the two categories varied somewhat according to the local nature of the husbandry and the choice of the farmer; but, in general, the workers who were hired occasionally at some time in the year would outnumber the permanent staff on the farm.

The proportion between hired servants and day laborers varied within limits that were broadly determined by the need of agriculture, but there were big local differences as to the social groups from which the laborers were hired. On these differences depended the extent of the disturbance inflicted on the laboring population by applying the new methods of husbandry. Whether, for example, harvesters were hired from among itinerant bands, from a local small holding population, or from villages in the locality, greatly affected the circulation of incomes and might tend to the retention or to the dispersal of a given local population.

As the schedule of work on the farm became less sporadic, employers strove to enforce a more general and rigid discipline on their laborers. Cottagers who had worked part-time in return for the occupation of a cottage and a piece of land were dispossessed and full-time workers were hired on terms by which they were more easily subject to complete and continuing discipline. It seems likely that many of the men who found themselves without land—whether they had previously been tenants or subtenants—would now be engaged as full-time servants. There was nothing essentially new about the terms and duties imposed upon the new laborers. On the whole, traditional patterns of relationship between employer and employee were imported into the new order and were, very often, blown up in scale. The main social change was the shift in the balance of numbers among large farmers, smallholders, and hired laborers together with the virtual disappearance of most forms of subtenancy.

Traditionally there had been considerable differences in the type of engagement offered to the hired man in different parts of the country. In particular, the servants in some parts, and notably in the South-East, would be mostly married men, who would live in separate cottages provided by the farmer,[75] while in other parts they would be mostly unmarried and would live in quarters around the farmstead, receiving their food in the farm kitchen.[76] All received a high proportion of their wages in kind, whether full maintenance out of the farm kitchen, or an allowance of meal and milk, or perhaps the keep of a cow. But by custom there were considerable differences, even within the general categories, in the detailed allowances. As the number of dependent laborers increased and the new farming techniques created new requirements of discipline, changes occurred in some of these traditional local customs. The system of providing lodging around the farm buildings and offering food in the farm kitchen could not survive where large bodies of workers were collected on the large farm; in some areas farmers who had been accustomed to providing cottages found it cheaper to hire unmarried men and place them in dormitories; in other

75. Alexander Lowe, *General View of the Agriculture of the County of Berwick* (London 1794), p. 52; Robert Beatson, *General View of the Agriculture of the County of Fife* (Edinburgh, 1794), p. 16; Buchan-Hepburn, *County of East Lothian*, p. 91; Alexander Fenton, "Farm Servant Life in the 17th-19th Centuries," *Scottish Agriculture*, 44 (1965), 281.

76. The great number of unmarried servants who were attached even to smallish farms in Aberdeenshire in the late seventeenth century is made clear in the *List of Pollable Persons, 1696.*

cases an adequate supply of labor could be ensured only where married men were accommodated in cottages in replacement of the old farm-kitchen system.[77] But in the main the old regional distinctions were retained. Certainly the differences in the terms of the laborer as between different parts of the country were very marked and with the general increase of numbers in the position of the full-time wage earner these differences were critical in determining the attitudes that might lead to migration.[78] In general, the South-East retained its old custom of hiring married men and placing them in cottages; they received little or no money wage but fairly large allowances in kind. One change that came in the eighteenth century was to grant land for the planting of potatoes. Turnip husbandry also increased the importance of finding occasional workers for the fields in summer and under this hind system of the South-East the main occupier of the cottage would be held bound to provide for work in the fields one or two female workers at certain times of the year. The North-East also largely retained its traditional system of hiring unmarried men to be fed in the farm kitchen and to live in quarters that formed integral parts of the farmstead; the same system applied, at the other extreme of the country, in the South-West. Across the Central districts were to be found both these systems, of the cottage and farm kitchen, but in addition, where the services of women were less needed on the farm, dormitories or "bothies" would house a considerable proportion of the farm staffs, with the men responsible for their own cooking.

77. Erskine, *County of Clackmannan*, p. 72; "On Perthshire Husbandry," *Farm. Mag.*, 8 (1807), 448; *Fourth Report on Women in Agric.*, App. I, pp. 50–52; *Report on Agriculture, 1878*, pp. 138–139.

78. For a comparative view of the different systems of hiring servants in different parts of the country, see Sinclair, *General Report*, III, 226–235.

## The Demand for Labor

LOCAL traditions and differences in the system of hiring labor—somewhat reinforced as the labor force was placed under stronger discipline—were of some importance in determining attitudes among laborers but probably the overriding influence was *how many* laborers were likely to be hired as improvement took its course. There were several forces working to determine the numbers who would, in fact, find places whether as occupiers of land or as employees. Advances in agricultural technique sometimes meant that less labor would be required for given tasks. Plowing was performed by one man rather than two and the better design of the moldboard probably meant that the ground was covered more quickly; the rate of plowing would also be increased where stiff land was drained.[79] The scythe made some small gains on the sickle in the cutting of grain while all hay would be mowed by the former implement, but there was little substantial change in the manner of harvesting until the mechanical reaper began to be widely adopted after 1850.[80] The threshing machine, on the other hand, meant a sudden and large economy in the use of labor on farms generally. The use of carts, which were becoming widespread from 1750 onwards, was another source of general economy and the improvement in design continuing till well into the nineteenth century further diminished the time and therefore the labor required for particular tasks.[81] The economical use of farm labor stemmed also from developments outside the farm itself. When independently provided transportation came closer to the farm gate—as it did

79. Once the ground had been properly cleared the new two-horse plows were estimated to add up to fifty percent to the area covered in a days' plowing as compared with operations under the old system. See "On Perthshire Husbandry," p. 449; *O.S.A.*, II, 347.

80. Sturrock, "Ayrshire," p. 39; "Agricultural Intelligence," *Farm Mag.*, 14 (1813), 99.

81. Farm dairies indicate how great a cost was transport in the older farms. Whoever performed the carting, roads and wheeled vehicles cut to a fraction some of the older costs. See, for example, Thomas P. Soper, "Monymusk, 1770–1850" (unpub. PhD diss., University of Aberdeen, 1954), pp. 76–81; C. E. Sleigh, "Agriculture on Strichen Home Farm, 1793–1797," *Transactions of the Buchan Club*, 14 (1930), 72–76. See also *O.S.A.*, XIV, 506.

with the improvement in the roads and even more with the coming of the railways—there was less need to use farm labor and working stock in transporting grain or driving animals to the main market centers.[82] Enclosure, a long process which was carried to its virtual completion only with the use of wire in the sixties, meant less labor in the herding of animals. Thus in one or two major ways and many minor ones the farm tasks could be performed with less labor.

Another factor tending to the employment of fewer hands was the great specialization of labor. Much of the labor employed on the farm had in the past been only sporadically applied to true agricultural tasks.[83] Employment in a subordinate capacity on a large farm was often combined with working a tiny personal unit and often with earning in other ways to eke out a livelihood. The removal of subtenants—which was a general move—was in part an attempt by farmers to get more thorough control over the time of their laborers and to force them to concentrate on farm tasks. Although some agricultural labor remained inevitably seasonal and many hands came only as occasional laborers, a larger proportion of the work was coming to be done by full-time employees. This increased use of specialist laborers was helped not only by the changing nature of the farm routine but also by the decline in the nonagricultural tasks performed within the rural community.[84] In particular, the declining use of peat in favor of the imported commodity of coal diverted a great deal of labor from a heavy summer task. The tendency to use imported rather than locally made cloth also diminished an employment that had been combined with work in the fields. These are instances, of course, of the shifting in the place of work rather than its actual reduction, but very often that location was now outside the rural community. More specialized hands were coming to be employed on farms to exchange the

82. Sinclair, *Account of Husbandry*, I, 63; "On Perthshire Husbandry," p. 460.

83. For a description of the old system which intermingled industrial with agricultural work, see Keith, *County of Aberdeen*, p. 513.

84. Skirving, "East Lothian," p. 19; Robertson, *South Perthshire*, p. 65; *Report on Agriculture, 1878*, p. 146.

product of their labor for the output of specialized establishments elsewhere.

These economies in the use of labor for given tasks were counterbalanced by changes in the nature and volume of the tasks themselves in the developing systems of farm operation. Here it is convenient to designate two distinct periods. Up to 1830, at a pace which greatly accelerated after 1780, the old husbandry was being replaced by the new methods either of turnip husbandry or of fallow followed by an intensive succession of crops. There is no question that the new systems increased the intensity of work on each acre in full cultivation. Potatoes and turnips, which were taking over continually increasing acreages from 1780 onwards, and which by 1830 accounted for a major section of the farm acreage in the areas of lighter soil, demanded much labor. It was part of the function of the turnip crop to further the cleaning of the soil. Drill sowing, which was the usual practice in Scotland, allowed the use of a light plow or hoe to be drawn between the drills of growing plants; but the use of the horse was invariably accompanied by hand-weeding. Singling of turnips also had to be done by hand. Finally there came the lifting of the heavy crop, work for the plowman with his cart as well as for fieldworkers to collect the roots ready for transfer. Where turnips could not be grown the soil was cleaned by fallowing with the accompanying multiple plowings, cross-plowings, and harrowing that required more labor than the growing of a crop. On many of the up-to-date farms a key element was the use of roots and grasses for their big return in dung and part of this method was feeding in stalls or courts from which the dung could be collected. The heavy dunging of the fields, particularly at the turnip break, meant much work in the carting and spreading of manure. The heavier crops also implied more work for each person at the harvest, although it does not seem that the ratio of reapers to area of ground was increased. Altogether, then, it seems likely that as improvement proceeded the working of each acre would require more labor. Animal husbandry, closely linked with the working of the arable acres, also involved extra care and labor. Feeding of animals in courts or stalls created many tasks in the preparation of feed and the removal of soil and litter. Where sheep fed off the turnips in the fields the flocks had to be carefully shepherded to the appropriate sections of the fields and had to be prevented from straying by the erection of temporary hurdles. The larger carry of animals on the cultivated acreage—an increase which was one of the main objects of the change of method—created more work in general management of flocks and herds. Enclosure of the interior divisions of the farm, so that each crop area was physically separated from the other, diminished the effort of herding but such enclosure was by no means universal even in fully improved areas. The herd boy was still a common member of the farm complement.

After 1830 there was some tendency for less intensive forms of working the farm to spread. The increased emphasis on cattle rearing rather than on wheat growing meant that where the more intensive systems already prevailed grass might well be given a greater place in the rotation. On the other hand, the use of imported feedstuffs and of portable fertilizers allowed a greater carry of animals on a given crop base and more animals meant more labor. Potatoes, a crop requiring much labor, although vanishing after 1846 from the Perthshire acres, were taken up by the East Lothian farmers and spread across the coastal lands of Ayrshire and in the sixties there was a spurt in potato growing in Fife.[85] More general was the broadening of the turnip acreage as land was drained, or brought to more effective use by bone dust and guano. On the whole, then, changes in crops and in methods of using the land tended to use of more rather than less labor in the period after 1830.

Whatever the effect of changing systems of using land already in cultivation, there can be no doubt that until 1830 extension of acreage under crop was in all districts tending to increase the employment on the land. Deep drainage meant that many of the sodden areas within existing farm boundaries could be brought under the plow; stony areas were slowly cleared; the plow also encroached upon heathery moorland and peat moss as the ground was pared and burnt, deep-plowed, or trenched. In the period up to 1840 all

85. Macdonald, "Fife," p. 15.

parts were affected to some degree. In the parish of Dirleton, for example, at the heart of a fertile area which was among the earliest to be fully developed, the crop acreage increased from 4,020 to 5,325 between 1790 and 1836.[86] Even more notable was the increase in the northerly districts. In the county of Kincardine—which contains one section which is attached to the Central district and one which is more properly attached to the North-East—nearly all parishes show a considerable increase in crop land between 1809 and 1840. And it is notable that in Aberdeenshire, the county at the heart of the North-East, the great majority of parishes in 1840 were recording additions to their arable acreage over the previous thirty or forty years. The expansion continued in this region up to the mid-seventies. Kincardine gained thirty percent between 1807 and 1854, and seventeen percent between 1854 and 1876, while in the latter period Aberdeenshire and Banffshire grew by larger proportions. More southerly districts, however, seem to have reached the limits of their growth in acreage at an earlier stage. Perthshire records almost the same crop acreage in 1876 as in 1854, while Fife shows considerable, and Haddington very moderate, decline.[87]

In short, then, as husbandry everywhere swung into its new forms and, in some districts, continued to expand strongly until 1875, there was little slackening in agriculture's demand for labor. A norm of fifteen to twenty acres to each hand employed on the average through the year was established—as agriculture settled down after the great series of changes.[88] This includes women workers and unmarried servants and does not very accurately indicate the total population that would be mainly dependent on agricultural incomes. But in the Lothians system of employment—

86. *N.S.A.*, II, *Haddington*, 222.

87. The increase in the cultivated acreage of Kincardineshire is shown by comparing the figures given in Robertson, *Kincardineshire*, with the details of the various parish accounts in *N.S.A.* Statistics for acreages under crop as well as for other agricultural features in Scotland were first collected in 1854. After this experimental exercise there is a gap until 1866 when official statistics began to be issued on the basis of returns made by the farmers. See "Agricultural Statistics of Scotland," *T.H.A.S.*, 6 (1851–1855), 201–209, 457–493; "Agricultural Statistics of Scotland," *T.H.A.S.*, 9 (1877), 343–345.

88. *S.C. on Agric.*, *1836*, Q. 9,694, 11,846, 12,381; *N.S.A.*, IX, *Fife*, 94–97.

where most of the plowmen were married and most of the occasional labor came out of the farm cottages—it seems to have implied a density of one person to between five and ten acres.[89] Where the full-time labor force consisted largely of unmarried servants the density of the dependent population might be somewhat lower, although in the carse areas there was a compensating factor in the relatively small acreage that could be managed by each plowman. How these figures compare with those of the period before 1780 must be largely guesswork. It seems that in Aberdeenshire a farm of seventy acres would have had two servants and possibly three subtenants who helped in the working of the main farm.[90] Allowing the average family to be of five persons, the population to land would then be of one person to less than five acres. Probably more people were employed around the farm, intermittently, than would be the case after 1800.[91] But the difference is not very great and it should be remembered that the employment in agriculture at the earlier time was much more sporadic. It is by no means certain that on a given acreage more man-hours were used at the earlier time. Much of the apparently large employment in the old ferm toun was devoted to nonagricultural work.

The demand for labor, even in rural parishes, very often derived from industry as well as agriculture. Indeed, over many tracts of Scottish countryside, industry and agriculture were so closely interlocked that they had a joint effect upon the lives of communities and even of individuals. Mining and fishing often engaged small communities, but we leave them aside because they were essentially separate in terms of the participation of the laborer. The textile processes, however, cannot so easily be separated as an influence and here it is scarcely possible to distinguish industrial and agricultural families. The connection was closest, perhaps, when spinning was a common rural activity. In the eighteenth century spinning wheels, used to provide a saleable commodity, were to be

---

89. Sinclair, *Account of Husbandry*, II, 143–146.
90. *List of Pollable Persons, 1696.*
91. George Kay, "The Landscape of Improvement," *Scot. Geog. Mag.*, 78 (1962), 102.

found generally in the farmhouses and cottages of many parts of rural Scotland. Of the main regions, only the South-East did not have a well-developed and widely spread spinning industry. An activity similarly placed within the social scheme was the knitting of stockings in the North-East.[92] Spinning and knitting created work for women and added to the incomes of small holding and laboring families without altering their position on the agrarian scale. But they tended to make the position of the casual agricultural laborer easier and to sustain an organization in which holders of very little land could work intermittently on the larger farms, cultivate their own pieces, and work up industrial products. Such activities interlocked easily with an agriculture in which the need for labor was spasmodic. In Aberdeenshire:

... while meal and provisions were cheap, the knitting of stockings employed a cottager's wife and daughter, and he himself acted occasionally as a day-labourer to the land-holder, working at his mains or personal farm, or sometimes assisted the neighbouring farmers, when called upon by them, and received in return no wages in money, but the use of cattle in ploughing or harrowing his land, or in carting dung to his small possession. When this consisted only of two or three acres of arable land, exclusive of the pasture which maintained one or two cows ... by his own and his family's industry, he generally improved his situation.[93]

After 1800, however, the mechanization of linen spinning and the decline of stocking knitting restricted earnings in many cottages just at the time when, in any case, farmers were seeking to confine the use of their cottages to specialized agricultural laborers.

The influence of weaving was more sustained and complicated. Handloom weaving remained an important rural activity up to 1850. The cotton weavers of the South-West tended to collect more in towns and to separate themselves entirely from the agricultural population.[94] In the Central area, however, weaving remained an activity largely of villages or even of isolated cottages

92. Keith, *County of Aberdeen*, p. 149; "Sketch of a Tour through the Northern Parts of Scotland," *Farm. Mag.*, 2 (1801), 160.

93. Keith, *County of Aberdeen*, p. 149.

94. *Handloom Weavers, Reports from Assistant Commissioners, Parliamentary Papers*, 1839, XLII, 2–4.

on the farms.[95] The relation between such industry and agriculture was complex. Many of the weavers were men and heads of families but increasingly after 1800 weaving could also well be carried on by the family dependents—by the weaver's wife, his daughters, and unmarried sons. Many families were to be found with several members engaged in weaving or in the process of winding which supplied the weaver. There emerged an intricate cross-dependence between agriculture and the textile industry.[96] Even families which were normally fully involved as textile workers could, under the conditions of domestic production, turn a seasonal hand to meet the needs of agriculture at times of peak necessity.[97] Further, some of the members of the textile families became agricultural day laborers, living in the villages but sufficiently regular in their attendance at farm work to classify themselves as agricultural workers. In addition the daughters of agricultural laborers, living in farm cottages, might well engage in weaving. And there was a possibility of shifting from agricultural work into textiles—an important feature where the farmers wished to hire mainly unmarried men as laborers. The relationship between linen making and farming was a changing one, both year by year and over longer term. When the profits of weaving were high, it might be hard to get the necessary seasonal labor for farming, but depression in the textiles would promote a reflux to agriculture reflected in pressure to find day laboring jobs. "In harvest 1792, before the manufacturers met with any check, journeymen weavers who used formerly to reap in harvest refused to work under 2/- to 2/6d a day, which they could

95. Alexander J. Warden, *The Linen Trade Ancient and Modern* (London, 1864), pp. 483–537.

96. For example, in the parish of Collessie (Fife), in 1851 there were 275 textile workers, mostly engaged in handloom weaving or in winding pirns to supply the weavers. Of these 92 were heads of families; 9 were wives, 39 daughters, 37 sons, and 14 other relatives of weavers; 15 were sons and 13 were daughters of agricultural laborers; and 28 were sons and 28 were daughters in households where the head was of some other occupation than agriculture or weaving. *1851 Census, Enumerator's Books.*

97. In the parish of Cults (Fife), one-half of the weavers were under twenty years of age, one-fifth would be employed at weaving only in winter, taking to outdoor work in the summer, but all would take part in the harvest. In another parish in the same county, the young females were said to work at the loom in winter and take to outdoor pursuits in the summer. *N.S.A.*, IX, Fife, 226, 572.

make at the loom."[98] In the long run, however, the decline of textiles after 1850 brought a shortage of labor for agriculture by promoting the emigration of the labor force which had intermittently served both occupations. "The cause of this [scarcity of labor] may be found in men and women now having difficulty in finding a living, when not working on the farms, which they formerly obtained in handloom weaving or needlework of various kinds."[99]

The high natural rate of increase of population did not lead to persistent redundancy of laborers or of men disappointed in their expectations of taking land. The sufficiency of work was helped rather than hindered by changes in agriculture. Up to 1830 the tendency to adopt more intensive methods and the growth of the acreage under the plow probably increased the number of jobs. If after that time there were places where the grass husbandry took greater hold and the expansion had of necessity slowed down, there was at least no decline of employment. It is true that change in agriculture played a part by shaking people out of their accustomed manner of living and by making them more responsive to the dimly perceived lures of life in the towns or overseas. But it did not restrict their chances of finding work on the countryside. The low pressure on the labor market was also due to migration and to this agriculture made some contribution. The work of the farm laborer was always hard, exposed, and long, and the wages remained, by urban standards, low. To that extent the reactions of the agricultural employer might be said to contribute to migration and to the shortage of labor. "They find that the wages at the factories . . . are better and more certain than the hard labour and uncertain wages of outdoor work."[100] But this very comparison of rural and urban conditions shows how far the migration was generated by changes outside agriculture itself. An increasing population, which would have created a crisis even in a strictly static rural organization, a rising demand for labor in the towns, and publicized opportunity for overseas emigration tended to make for in-

98. *O.S.A.*, XIV, 220.
99. *Fourth Report on Women in Agric.*, App. I, p. 51.
100. *Ibid.*, App. I, p. 151. See also *O.S.A.*, VI, 497.

creasing movement out of the rural enclaves. In such a situation, agricultural development, with farmers tending to bid more highly to hold a labor force which probably did not decrease in numbers, was a factor tending to hold back the migration rather than a further propellant.

One sign that the labor market was far from congestion was rising wages.[101] There is persistent and uniform report in the *Old Statistical Account* that wages both of day laborers and servants—who were hired for six months or a year—had risen very steeply since mid-century.[102] For servants who were maintained by their masters or were paid to a large extent in kind, this appears mainly to have been a rise in the money component; the rise in remuneration was not at all proportionate to the rise in the money wages which were added to a basic subsistence, and for which movements are difficult to trace. But the rise must have been considerable. With the war and inflation after 1790 the increase in this money component becomes even less valid as a measure of true increase in real wages or of differential advance as compared with wages generally. But the peak seems to have been reached about 1809. In that year the top plowman's wage in the North-East touched £20 as compared with the £6 that had been paid in 1790 and £8 in the later nineties. There was a slight sag in the next year or two but complaints of scarcity and of high wages never ceased, and wages were once more on the increase by 1815, although they never again touched the level of 1809. Wages sank after the war but there was

101. Congestion or otherwise in the labor market is well indicated by the course of wages. Wages as arranged at the periodic hiring markets for six-month or year contracts were highly sensitive to the conditions of the market. If an excess of laborers offered themselves the rates agreed might drop sharply and conversely a shortage of laborers would show itself by a sharp rise. The path traced by the graph of wages was a very fluctuating one.

102. Valerie Morgan has brought together the very considerable amount of data that is available on agricultural wages in the 1790's, and to some extent for the preceding decades. Her conclusion about wage differences between the various regions are open to question, but there can be little doubt either about the rise of wages she charts between the earlier decades of the century and 1790, or about the continuation of the trend through the nineties. See Valerie Morgan, "Agricultural Wage Rates in Late Eighteenth-Century Scotland," *Economic History Review*, 2d ser., 24 (1971), 181–201; "Quarterly Intelligence Reports," in the *Farm. Mag.*

no serious collapse. Even in the years of bad trade and general un-employment before 1820, there was little sign of redundancy in the countryside. By 1819, it is true, plowmen were finding it some-what more difficult to place themselves at the hiring markets, but there was still work for all day laborers—a type of work to which the unemployed plowman might have recourse. From 1821 to 1823 there was unemployment among all grades of agricultural labor, and wages fell back to the level of the mid-nineties. This was but a short episode of difficulty when redundancy of labor replaced the more usual scarcity.

The level of employment remained fairly constant through the middle decades of the century but rising wages show farmers hav-ing to bid higher to retain their existing labor force.[103] It is true that until well into the thirties wages lay in a trough considerably below the level reached in the war years. But money payments formed a relatively small proportion of all remuneration. Allow-ances in kind, although not rigid, remained fairly constant. By the forties a fresh rise had started which was to continue, though not at a steady rate, almost without interruption till the mid-seventies. In the South-East, at current prices, increases of at least one-third occurred between the late thirties and the early fifties, while by 1868, on the same measure, there had been a further increase of

103. The valuations of wages given in the N.S.A. indicate "gains" worth £21 to £24 in East Lothian and slightly more in Berwickshire. For 1852 there is account of farmers paying wages, largely in kind, to the value of £33. There is a big crop of information for 1868 given in the *Fourth Report on Women in Agric.*, and it shows wages valued at between £40 and £45 in these counties. In 1881 a further collection of statistics appears for the *Royal Commission on Agriculture*. Wages were now reaching the £50 mark, but this was probably lower than the level of the mid-seventies. A detailed series is available for the North-East counties from 1870 to 1900 in R. Molland and G. Evans, "Scottish Farm Wages from 1870 to 1900," *Journal of the Royal Statistical Society*, Ser. A, 113 (1950), 220–227. It pinpoints the sharp peak of the mid-seventies and enables comparisons to be made for this area between the period of the thirties (and earlier) and the seventies. A first plow-man in this area was making £14 or £15 in the mid-thirties (which compared with over £20 in the war years) and at the peak of the seventies such a man would be engaged at up to £35. See, N.S.A.; *Fourth Report on Women in Agric.*, App. II, pp. 91–98, 118–120, 130–134, 143–147, 165–166, 176–178; *Royal Commission on Agriculture, Parliamentary Papers*, 1881, XVI, 583; *Royal Commission on Labour, The Agricultural Labourer*, III, Scot-land, Pt. II, 103–105; George Houston, "Farm Wages in Central Scotland from 1814 to 1870," *Journal of the Royal Statistical Society*, Ser. A, 118 (1955), 224–228.

one-quarter. By the seventies the current value of wages was at least twice as great as it had been forty years previously. The necessary adjustments for increase of prices over the same period are of small proportionate significance and it is clear that there had been a big gain in real wages. The same picture is displayed in the movement of the money wage paid to the unmarried man, fully maintained by his master. It is difficult to say what change there may have been in the standards as represented by the meals he received from his master, and the lodgings which he was allowed in the farmsteading. But clearly any tendency was one of improvement and to this must be added a considerable rise in the money component. The money earned by a first plowman in 1875 was nearly three times the amount earned by his like in the 1830's.

The picture, then, is of labor moving away from the countryside as farmers were forced to pay increased wages if they were to collect an adequate labor force. The movement, however, showed itself not only in the rise in wages, but also in difficulties in finding labor at any price. It was generally day laborers for fieldwork that were most difficult to find. In the Central district, as long as the rural textile industry was active and considerable populations lived in the villages, seasonal fieldworkers were reasonably plentiful; in the South-East the farm cottages maintained the supply; in the South-West near the mining towns colliers' wives and daughters were eager to supplement the family incomes by taking fieldwork; and in the North-East the crofts supplied the men who, more than women, would do fieldwork in the summer.[104] But these were temporary and partial alleviations in a situation of threatening scarcity. After 1850 the decline of handloom weaving led not to more men and women seeking agricultural work but to a faster rate of depopulation and to growing scarcity of laborers.[105] In the South-

104. *Fourth Report on Women in Agric.*, App. I, pp., 33, 50, 54, 95, 108.

105. In Collessie the number of textile workers had declined from 275 in 1851 to 160 in 1871. And of this last number 64 were daughters in households where the head was not engaged in textiles; they were mainly full-time workers at power looms. The number of heads of families declined from 92 to 56. It is perhaps significant also that sons of weavers were now no longer engaged in textile work. The decline in the parish of Abdie, also in Fife, was from 207 to 127. *1851 Census, Enumerators' Books; Fourth Report on Women in Agric.*, App. I, pp. 50–51; Dickson, "Perthshire," p. 174.

West, away from the towns, there was always difficulty in finding enough workers for the fields. And in the South-East there was growing revulsion from heavy agricultural work even among the families of agricultural workers.[106] Only in the North-East was the supply of labor reasonably maintained.[107] As a result it became common in all the southern areas to call upon the help of Irish immigrants for the work of midsummer as well as at the corn harvest.[108] Girls from the Highlands, also, would be housed in small bothies for the summer, while they earned day wages. Even with the use of temporary immigrants, the shortage might persist. "Emigration also has tended to thin the population and must do so the more it proceeds. . . . If threshing machines, reapers, horse rakes and various other agricultural implements had not been invented, farming operations would long ere this [i.e., 1868] have come to a dead lock."[109] The drain from the countryside was clearly not due to people being unable to find work, or to their wages falling below accustomed levels.

## Regional Summaries

SOME of the forces making for a considerable volume of migration were common to every rural area. Yet every district also had its peculiarities of industrial as well as of agrarian experience and rates of migration were the outcome of complicated forces uniquely balanced in each region. In this section we look at the interplay of the different forces as they focussed on the particular regions.

The South-East, we have seen, tended to hold its population relatively well both in the period from 1755 to 1790–1798 and in that from 1801 to 1851. Migration rates were of course accelerating

---

106. *Fourth Report on Women in Agric.*, App. I, pp. 84, 91; *Royal Commission on Labour, The Agricultural Labourer*, III, *Scotland*, Pt. II, 97, 196.

107. *Fourth Report on Women in Agric.*, App. II, p. 7–15.

108. *Ibid.*, App. I, pp. 51–52, 55, 104; Tait, "Stirling," p. 172.

109. *Fourth Report on Women in Agric.*, App. I, p. 51.

on a comparison of the two periods in the one district or county and between 1861 and 1871 the rate of net migration in the rural parishes of the counties of East Lothian and Berwick was typically between ten and thirty percent.

One reason for the comparative stability of the region must have been the intensive and early occurrence of improved farming that covered at least the lower parts. The soil did not generally demand as much plow work for given acreages as the carse areas further north, but the careful husbandry and the unfailing yearly cultivation of much of the land required much labor, particularly in East Lothian. Improvement was widely applied on the big farms that were already typical of the area in the 1790's but the growth in crop acreage had still some way to go; expansion as well as further improvement was to characterize the next thirty or forty years. More and more land was brought into a turnip system associated with intensive arable cropping and land continued to be reclaimed from the waste. The crisis of a falling price of wheat was met by placing even more emphasis on turnips and cattle and sheep fattening—sometimes with more grass in the rotation—by drainage of existing cultivated land, and by making a rotation crop of potatoes. By 1830 the increase in the area under crop had come to an end on the lower ground and between 1854 and 1876 the crop acreage was almost stationary. Yet on the whole the cultivation of the existing fields tended to require more rather than less labor.[110]

Another reason for the comparative stability of the labor force of this region was the manner of its hiring. The new farming made use of a labor force that was already settled in family units on the farms, with much of the seasonal as well as the full-time labor coming out of the cottages. To provide the base of the intensive system, it was only necessary to reinforce the existing employment of married laborers. As expansion proceeded more laborers were engaged as hinds under the terms that were traditional. The married plow-

110. On the whole, the number of hands engaged per one hundred acres seems to be somewhat less in the 1830's than it was to be in the 1870's. See *N.S.A.*, IX, *Fife*, 24–27; *S.C. on Agric.*, *1836*, Q. 14, 541; *Fourth Report on Women in Agric.*, App. II, pp. 64–65, 179–188.

men, who remained typical of the area, would be accommodated in cottages on the farm and, by the terms of the bondage system, would be held bound to provide an extra female worker at specific times of the year. Thus a good part of the necessary occasional labor of the farm came from the plowmen's cottages.[111] Sometimes the plowman, or hind, provided a second man who would perform the plowing along with him. This system was adapted and expanded as farming itself expanded and as subtenants were cleared from the land. The larger farm allowed a greater degree of specialization. Shepherds, cattlemen, and spademen were engaged, broadly under the same terms as the plowmen, and altogether the number of married servants continued to grow. It is probable, then, that some of the evicted subtenants—or their descendants—were assimilated to this newly expanded landless wage-earning class. Such servants would receive the use of a cottage, a supply of meal, fuel, rights of pasturing a cow and of planting a certain measure of potatoes, and if there was no cow they would have a fairly liberal allowance of milk. Until the nineteenth century no money was given in payment but they seem to have sold some of their allowance of meal to obtain the cash required, for example, for the new necessities of tobacco and tea. The wages of the female members would also contribute to the family income. By 1870, bondage was disappearing from the East Lothian farms, although it continued in the agriculturally similar county of Berwickshire at least until 1890.[112] But the decline of bondage did not substantially diminish the dependence of the farmers on the labor of the hinds' families.[113] Although wives did not often engage in work for

111. For example, on one farm in East Lothian, there were twenty-two cottages. Thirteen were occupied by men on the farm staff, most of them married, nine by single or widowed "cottar women," who would perform day labor. In addition, the families of the married men provided eight female workers. *Fourth Report on Women in Agric.*, App. II, p. 113.

112. *Ibid.*, App. I, pp. 53, 56–57; *Royal Commission on Labour, The Agricultural Labourer*, III, *Scotland*, Pt. II, 197.

113. For example, of seventy-five people helping on an East Lothian farm, four were supplied by families not mainly engaged on the farm and the remaining seventy-one came out of twenty-seven families most of them with multiple incomes derived from farm work. *Fourth Report on Women in Agric.*, App. II, p. 113.

wages, partly because they were occupied daily in the milking and tending of the cows which formed part of the laborer's appurtenances, most households had unmarried sisters and daughters who added to family income by day labor. In addition, some of the cottages accommodated widows who put in their quota of work on the farm. A family system in which just as many days were being worked for the farmer by the female dependents as by the full-time hired men still did not meet all the needs of the intensive farming characteristic of the county. The gap in summer labor left even after the efforts of the families settled in the farm cottages was filled by temporary immigrants from the Highlands. Girls from the west came to live, in groups of four or five, in bothies—cottages fitted out as lodgings.[114] Normally they stayed in the east for about six months, returning to their homes for the winter, but often they would return to the same farm in the following year or years. Finally, at harvest time, extra hands would be hired from the gangs of Irish immigrants, who arrived in the country to work their way through the country from the early to the late harvest districts.[115]

The custom of total but informal family engagement which formed the basis of the improved husbandry of the South-East seemed to make for great stability and for a secure but rather restricted livelihood. The plowman, once he was trained, was completely secure in his employment and remuneration for periods—for married men—of a year at a time; and he had substantial security for his working lifetime. There was a direct continuity between his earliest training as a lad and the work and position he would hold through his life, and the custom of employing the sons of laborers around the farm encouraged the succeeding generations to follow each other in exactly the same social positions. Further, a large proportion of the income going to labor from farming went to the families which were permanently settled as farm dependents, that is to local families of long farming tradition. Such families,

---

114. *Ibid.*, App. I, p. 53.

115. *Ibid.*, App. I, p. 104; Skirving, "East Lothian," p. 46; James E. Handley, *The Irish in Scotland* (Cork, 1943), pp. 34–54.

with a number of earners, made not inconsiderable incomes.[116] The aggregate incomes that were being earned were high by the working-class standards of the time; and they were almost wholly secure. Yet there were underlying tensions; such prospects could not fully have met the expectations of all born in the lower ranks of Lothian rural society. First, it should be remembered that this was a very unequal society. There was no farming ladder by which the wage earner or the boy from a wage-earning family could rise to independence. There were very few units of less than one hundred acres and the stocking of one hundred acres required anything from £500 to £1,000.[117] The limit of most laborers' ambitions must have been to become a grieve, a position of responsibility but not one which carried very much more pay. This was also a literate society and it would have been strange if there were no one to question their position of immutable dependence. Secondly, there was a high degree of geographical mobility and keen periodic bargaining between masters and men. The existence of hiring markets allowed men to test the demand for their services and to some extent to play one employer against another. An unmarried man could move every six months if he wished and some of them reputedly did so. Once married, a man tended to be more settled and to accept one employer for longer periods. But even among this group there was considerable movement if only over short distances.[118] Mobility of this sort could easily turn by a touch of local misfortune into a more permanent and distant move. Lastly, there is the question whether the places being offered to farm servants were sufficient to accommodate each generation of plowmen's families. If there was not sufficient employment as hinds, the re-

116. Incomes going to hinds and their families very often ran to between £75 and £100 per annum. See *Fourth Report on Women in Agric.*, App. II, pp. 119, 130–134.

117. East Lothian, in 1875, had 237 holdings of less than fifty acres and, in 1871, 3,184 male farm servants and laborers. *1871 Census, Occupations of the People;* "Agricultural Statistics of Scotland," *T.H.A.S.*, 8 (1876), 303.

118. It is clear from the *1851 Census, Enumerators' Books* that even married hinds would make frequent moves from one parish to another. Of those who had three or more children, more than half are found to have had at least one of their children in a parish other than that of domicile at the time of the census. For a considerable number there is evidence of moves even more frequent.

strictive structure of a stratified society dominated entirely by agriculture could offer little else. In the first generation after the general onset of agriculture improvement there were men of the old cottar class as well as the new generation out of the plowmen's families to be accommodated. Once society had settled into its simple mold of farmer and landless wage earner, the rising tendency of population brought always increasing numbers to the stage of seeking jobs. Yet, as we have seen, only very infrequently was there congestion of the labor market.

In the Central area there was great local variety both in population history and in the systems applied in hiring labor. In the eighteenth century, Perthshire held its population less firmly than the counties of the South-East although at this time the county was losing less than the North-East; in the nineteenth century, however, as the North-East begins to show a general tendency for a growth of population higher than that of any other rural area, Perthshire emerges as the biggest loser by migration and the losses in the decade 1861 to 1871 were heavy in most parishes of the county. In the rural north of Fife, conditions were more akin to those of the South-East, showing neither before 1800 the losses of the North-East nor after 1801 the losses of Perthshire.

The area had sections which were early in improving and where the cultivation was just as intensive as in the South-East. In the carse areas, indeed, not only was there an early development of intensive cropping systems but also the heavy work of plowing had to be applied to a soil in which the acreage covered by the plowteam was substantially less than that for even fairly heavy soils in the South-East. In these areas of early improvement there was little scope for expansion after 1840. The county of Fife had probably reached the limits of its arable by that date. Perth and Angus, however, still had foothill areas awaiting development when the conditions became favorable to cattle rearing and to turnip cultivation on lighter soils. Altogether the area under crop in Fife declined between 1854 and 1875 and remained almost stationary in Perthshire.[119]

119. "Agricultural Statistics of Scotland," pp. 201–209, 457–493; *ibid.*, pp. 343–345.

Soil type and crop system affected both the amount of labor required and the condition of its hiring. On the carse grounds the main demand was for labor for plowing, with a comparatively small need for female labor through the summer. Unmarried plowmen for the year-round work and immigrants for the harvest would meet most needs. A second type of agriculture, pursued on the "dry-field" near the carse, relied more on turnips, followed by intensive arable cropping, and needed therefore a mixed labor force of male and female. Then on the higher land of Strathmore and in the interior of Fife there were found types of turnip husbandry where grass played a big part in the rotation. The labor required on such a farm was less than on a carse farm but more balanced in composition as between male and female.

On the carse, then, unmarried labor met most needs; the farmer had little need of families in his cottages to provide field laborers in the summer.[120] On the clay lands around the Forth the servants, unmarried men, would be housed around the steading and would eat in the farm kitchen.[121] But in the Carse of Gowrie, north of the Tay, the farmers had another way of housing their unmarried men.[122] They would be lodged in bothies which were no more than small dormitories for the laborers. These quarters were barely furnished with the beds and chests in which the men would keep their possessions and, payment being made largely in the shape of an allowance of meal and milk, the hands had to do their own cooking. The materials of the diet were simple and the preparation given to the food by men who were generally out in the fields for twelve hours of the day was sketchy. The living standard of the bothyman was notoriously rough. Bothies were found all over the Central districts but they were generally intermixed with cottages in which married plowmen were accommodated; the labor force consisted in part of unmarried plowmen, in part of married men living in much the same way as the hinds of the South-East. In Fife, while there were bothies to be found, the bulk of the plow-

120. *Fouth Report on Women in Agric.*, App. I, p. 50.
121. Sinclair, *General Report*, III, 231.
122. *Fourth Report on Women in Agric.*, App. I, pp. 50–52.

men were married and accommodated in the farm cottages.[123]

Any undue local predominance of unmarried servants tended to create a social unbalance which could only be corrected by a good deal of movement of young men between jobs and places of residence, or by emigration. In districts where there were few others than employing farmers and unmarried servants, lads necessarily had to come from elsewhere at their first engagement and when they married might well have to move out again. Such a society could not exist in isolation and might well create critical breaking points in the lives of the laborers. The conditions of life for the young men tended to be uncertain and rootless. Thus the carse areas of Perthshire, with their heavy use of unmarried men, drew upon Fife where the cottages and the married laboring families were far more numerous;[124] it seems likely also that the villages would provide a quota of young men for agricultural service. When a man reached the age of marriage there was again a critical problem. The farmers in certain localities either did not have the cottages or were unwilling to provide for married men living on the farm. The married servant might live on the farm and keep his family in lodgings which he would visit on weekends. This was an arrangement both financially taxing and emotionally disturbing. Or he might find a cottage for himself and become a day laborer; but in this case he lost his status as a plowman. Or he might drop out of agriculture altogether, taking some alternative local occupation or perhaps emigrating from the region. Conceivably he might take a small holding of land, although there were few regions in Scotland where the holdings were sufficiently numerous for this to happen on any scale. Finally, he might move as a trained plowman to an area which had the cottages and the openings for married men. Difficulty in finding a cottage might well lead to migration from the home area. "On marrying, many of them go into towns and turn to other occupations."[125] In any case there is the picture of a shifting group of uncertain standing. The men come to

123. *Ibid.*, App. I, p. 52.
124. *Ibid.*, App. I, pp. 51–52.
125. *Ibid.*, App. I, p. 51.

their first job from a distance; when they are hired and live in the bothy they have only the narrow society of their fellows and they tend to move quickly from one job to the other; then they are forced into a longer and more decisive move in which they often leave the district or, if they stay, have to find a new occupation, lose status in their existing one, or continue as plowmen under harrowing conditions of personal life. It should be understood, however, that it was only a few sectors of the Central area, between the Tay and the North-East, which had this unbalanced excess of unmarried men in the labor force. Bothies might be found dotted about the region and it was often described as a bothy area, but for the most part they were balanced by cottages to which the bothymen might move when they married. The contemporary concern with the moral flavor of the bothies obscured this much more crucial question of whether the bothies were balanced by adequate places for married laborers. It is evident, however, that at least in Perthshire, the dependence on unmarried laborers was sufficiently marked to cause a drain from agricultural employment and possibly from the countryside of men reaching the age of marriage. Between a quarter and a third of the men in Perthshire who had been farm servants or agricultural laborers were likely to leave for some other occupation by the time they were thirty; in Fife less than one-sixth would change occupation in this way and in Angus less than a tenth.[126]

Married or unmarried, the plowmen met only part of the farmer's need for labor particularly where turnip or potato cultivation had a large place in the crop system. The supply of day laborers in the Central area was conditioned by a social feature which was absent from the South-East; villages were here more numerous

126. For this calculation I have used the number of agricultural laborers recorded in the cohort of the age-group 15 to 20 to establish the numbers which would be found in the 25 to 30 group if there were only the gain and wastage shown in the agricultural population as a whole. From this notional figure for the 25 to 30 group is subtracted the number actually recorded. The result is the supposed "loss" to the laboring ranks in agriculture. This calculation can be made both for the particular categories of "in-servant" and "out-servant," and for agricultural laborers as a whole. The result is normally some loss in the category of "in-servant" and some gain in "out-servant," but with the gain not quite sufficient to make up for the loss. Different counties give very different results.

and larger in population. The numerous villages of the counties of Perth, Fife, and Angus were the homes of textile workers—cotton in the southern part of Perthshire but linen over the rest of the region—and the textile economy when it flourished helped to sustain the rural population. It also kept up the supply of labor for agriculture, particularly where the main part of the full-time labor force consisted of unmarried men.[127] From the villages came recruits to be trained as plowmen and when they married they might well revert to textile work. Day laborers, too, and even harvesters were available for hire. The ebbing of textile work from the villages was a blow at this joint economy and the result was not to swing labor towards agricultural work but to hasten the movement from the countryside. Labor for agricultural work became more, rather than less, scarce. Agriculture in itself did not offer sufficiently attractive conditions or perhaps high enough wages to hold in the rural community those who had depended on day work as an occasional resource.

The conditions affecting migration from the North-East were distinctly different from those prevailing further south. Till the end of the eighteenth century this region was evidently losing more of its people than any other part of the country. But after 1800 when migration from rural areas generally was speeding up, most of the North-East rural parishes showed considerable increases of population although nearly all at a few points behind the national rate of increase. From 1861 to 1871 migration had evidently increased to approximate closely that of the more stable districts of the south.

In part, the differences evidently stem from the varying course of agricultural reform. By the 1790's there was no well-established area of improved agriculture in the North-East. Such general change as there had been was mainly in the direction of increasing the grass acreage. In the 1790's began a period of rapid change. Big increases of crop acreage were achieved by 1840 but there was still a sufficient reserve of unused but cultivable land for the expansion to continue till the 1870's. The new systems of cultivation were more intensive than the old, but, with great emphasis on turnips,

127. N.S.A., IX, Fife, 226, 572.

grass, and cattle rearing, there was somewhat less work for the plow, acre for acre, than where arable cropping was the main agricultural object.

There were striking differences, too, of agrarian structure in the North-East as compared with other parts of Lowland Scotland. And the differences gave the region a much greater social conservatism. The agricultural changes did not as completely as elsewhere obliterate social groupings as expressed in the division of the land. Farms were enlarged but so moderately that great numbers of farms of the one- or two-pair horse type were created; only a tiny handful of units could even approximate in size to the common farms of East Lothian. At the same time, the destruction of the old cottagers' holdings and subtenancies was at least partly matched by the creation of new small holdings held directly of the landowner. As a result a substantial majority of holdings in the North-East area were too small either to provide a full livelihood, or to occupy the holder continuously, or to keep a plowteam in continuous operation. They were worked sometimes by the greater farmers being paid to provide horses or plowing facilities, sometimes by sharing the use of the animals provided by different crofters.[128] These two groups—of independent, mainly family-sized, farms and of units too small for full livelihood—were to an extent dependent on each other. The larger farmers could use the labor of the crofters and their families, who in turn needed the additional earnings to keep going, and it is perhaps significant that the North-East, alone of all the districts of Lowland Scotland, was able to keep all farms served at all times of the year by local labor alone. In these two sectors there seemed to be a society of massive stability. A considerable proportion of the people were settled in small holdings living much as their ancestors had done. They had a firm stake in the land but they also had the chance of earning wages that raised them above the level of the poorest small-holding societies.[129] The system, too, allowed the whole growing income-stream from an ex-

128. *Fourth Report on Women in Agric.*, App. I, p. 33; *N.S.A.*, XII *Aberdeenshire*, 156.
129. The small-holding population of the North-East never suffered from such hardship and insecurity as did that of the Highlands and the North-West.

panding agriculture to percolate through local society without loss
to incoming migrants. Not only did the wide distribution of land
titles spread the sense of attachment to the land, but also the existence of holdings at all levels of size created a ladder by which the
more ambitious and successful of the crofters might climb to independence.

Yet there was at least one group which did not fit into this
picture of firmly settled families, with permanent positions that
matched their ambitions—the hired servants. Even the smallest
one-pair horse farms, where the farmer himself held the plow,
needed extra help to be constantly available; unless he had a son
of convenient age he would have to hire a servant. In fact, allowing
for the number of farms which were above this minimum size,
independent farming was supported by a large body of servants.
Aberdeenshire, for example, in 1851 had 15,601 servants on its
9,555 farms.[130] The servants were mainly housed around the steadings and fed in the farm kitchen. They were nearly all unmarried
and comparatively few were more than twenty-five years of age.[131]
Since this fairly large group covered a relatively small age span it
obviously interlocked with much wider sections of the population
in the origins of its members and in their ultimately finding new
positions for life. Its fortunes and frustrations reverberated through
a considerable area of society. Reputedly, many of the farm servants came from the crofts; one of the reasons for the approval of
the croft system was that they provided a nursery of good servants.
To this extent, to enter into farm service was a natural and easy step
for a lad who had been brought up in a nearby farming household.
Most of the servants were fee-ed (i.e., engaged) at some distance
from their place of birth but they still remained within a social
circle with which they were familiar. They had the reputation, too,
of being ever on the move.

130. *1851 Census, Occupations of the People.*
131. See the age-structure of the whole body of indoor servants as given in the census
reports. *1851 Census, Occupations of the People.* Even clearer is the picture that can be
drawn for particular parishes from the *Enumerators' Books.* In the parish of Old Deer, for
example, only 41 our of 246 in-servants were above twenty-five years of age. *1851 Census,
Enumerators' Books.*

It was when the time came to marry that the natural and sure progression might be halted. A few settled down as married men on the farm but there was a notorious lack of cottages and only a small minority took this step. Another possibility was to lodge wife and family in a nearby town or village and, while continuing to work on the farm through the week, to visit them on Sunday. Such severe arrangements were sufficiently in evidence to be discussed in articles and Parliamentary enquiries.[132] Like any abuse which comes to the surface of social inquiry its very enormity as an arrangement gave it an exaggerated place in the discussion. In fact, there is little warrant either in the age statistics or in the census record of married servants for believing that it affected any considerable number. In Aberdeenshire it was apparently much more common to leave the land entirely than to continue as servants under such strained conditions. Over two-thirds of the "in-servants" (i.e., housed within the steading) had left such positions by the time they were thirty; some became out-laborers but a considerable majority of those who started in agricultural service evidently ceased to be employed as agricultural laborers of any sort.[133]

Some would doubtless obtain crofts and to that extent agricultural service may be seen as an interlude in the lives of men who were basically smallholders, representatives of families which continued to hold a settled position in society. An interlude of restlessness did not necessarily unsettle the solid mass of the small-holding population. Yet the crofts were evidently too few to accommodate all those who left full-time employment on the farms when, in their mid-twenties, they married. In specimen parishes in various parts of Aberdeenshire the number of men employed in agriculture in their late twenties and early thirties shows a much greater drop from the number below the age of twenty-five than would be accounted for by normal attrition; and, of this abnormal drop, only a small part can be matched by men holding crofts, in the

132. *Fourth Report on Women in Agric.*, App. I, p. 38; App. II, pp. 9, 13.
133. Based on calculations from *1851 Census, Occupations of the People*.

appropriate age groups.[134] Considerable numbers, then, must have left the land when they reached the age of marriage. These conclusions are confirmed by an examination of age-structure. Even when indoor servants, outdoor servants, day laborers, and crofters are considered as one population, there appears to be a considerable difference in the age-distribution as compared with that of the occupied male population in rural Scotland as a whole. A higher proportion of the agricultural laboring and small-holding population is found to be below the age of twenty-five than is normal for the whole population; correspondingly there were fewer, proportionately, in the group of twenty-five years of age and upwards.

The South-West had considerable diversity in its farming. Around Glasgow and the associated industrial towns there was an area of intensive dairying. It stretched north and west to the upper waters of the Forth, eastwards to meet the carse belt and southwards till it merged with the cheese-making areas of the Ayrshire clays; cheese making in its turn gave way to cattle rearing, sheep rearing, or mixed corn-and-cattle in the uplands and in the valleys running southwards to the Solway coast. There was equally a diversity in the scale of farming, with holdings tending to be larger towards the south. But, in general, the farming of the area may be said to have been more clearly and simply of the family type than in any other main regions. There were comparatively few farms of the capitalist type found commonly in the South-East but few also of the very small holdings characteristic of the North-East. In the dairying parts of Ayrshire the standard type of holding would run to around one hundred acres on which would be kept fifteen to twenty milk cattle together with the young cows of the breeding stock;[135] nearer to the towns there would be no young cows and a greater carry of milk cows. In either case the farm could be run as a family unit. The farmer would be helped by his son in the plowing (since only one-third of the land would be under the plow); the womenfolk, wife and daughters, would look after the dairy, milk-

<hr>

134. *1861 Census, Enumerators' Books* for the parishes of Chapel of Garioch, Cluny, Cruden, Glenmuick, Huntly, Kinnellar, Leslie, Tarves, Turriff, Tyrie.

135. Sturrock, "Ayrshire," pp. 88–89; *Report on Agriculture, 1878*, pp. 87–88.

ing, cheese or butter making, and moving the cattle.[136] The simple order of this system was somewhat complicated by the use of "bowing," by which the dairy work was performed on contract by a separate business unit while the plowing, cropping, and provision of feed for the animals was done by the tenant of the land, but both the "farm" unit and the "bower" could still be organized by family principles with all the necessary labor from within the independently operating family.[137] Under the dairy system with its demands for a mix of male and female labor steadily employed, the family might well provide the bulk of the labor required on the farm; and with units of moderate size the families acquired a permanent interest in the land. Sons would work on the family farm till in due course they followed the father in occupying the farm. Indeed the interest might be almost unbroken in that here, exceptionally for Scotland, were to be found a considerable number of owner-occupiers; and even farms held under lease were normally handed on from father to son. Thus a considerable proportion of the population was endowed with a permanent interest which would tend to keep families on the same farm generation after generation. But, even in Ayrshire, not all farms conformed to this type and not all families were inevitably adjusted to providing at all times just the right amount of labor. For one thing, nearly every family would go through a cycle in its affairs in which it moved from having an inadequate labor force to superfluity and then back perhaps to scarcity. There were numbers of farms which were too large to be managed by unaided family labor. Along the coast different forms of farming, with wheat and potatoes as important products, upset the simple balanced demand for permanent male and female labor. And even the dairy farm needed extra workers at harvest. Thus servants were needed although not so widely distributed among the farms as in the North-East which also had its large complement of family units. In the South-West the kitchen

136. *Report on Agriculture, 1878*, pp. 88–89; *Fourth Report on Women in Agric.*, App. I, p. 106.

137. On all aspects of the labor supply to the dairying districts of the South-West and on the importance of the labor from the manufacturing and mining towns see *Fourth Report on Women in Agric.*, App. I, pp. 94–96, 104–109; App. II, 209–236.

system prevailed, with the bulk of the servants young and unmarried.

Farm servants as a group, being predominantly young and presumably unmarried, could not directly provide from their own
ranks the fresh recruits of each generation; nor in the South-West
were there the small holdings from which they might be drawn.
It seems likely then that they were drawn from the laboring classes
in the small towns, from the families of agricultural day laborers or
of other occupations. When they reached the age of marriage the
same questions about their future arose as in the North-East. Cottages were few and poor and the same range of choice offered itself. The textile industry was strong in the villages and nearby
there were greater towns offering a wide range of employments.
So it seems likely that many men who had been placed as agricultural servants at one time in their lives moved to other occupations
and that such occupations in their turn provided the men who
would, for a period, be the servants of the next generation. But
it should be noticed that fewer left agricultural employment than
in the North-East and a larger body of agricultural day laborers
remained to provide boys to be farm servants. It was not unusual
in this region for farmers' sons to engage as servants for a period
before returning to help on the parent's holding or to take over
completely from the father. The supply of occasional labor for harvest and general fieldwork was increased by the proximity of so
many industrial communities engaged in mining, ironworking,
and textiles. It was common for the farms close to the towns to
draw on the help of bands of men and women who came to the
fields for some extra seasonal earnings. Potato lifting particularly
depended on this type of labor. But there were many farms of the
region which were too remote to be served in this way. Then, as in
the Central region, the Irish migrant became essential.

The migrations of the people of the rural Lowlands of Scotland,
from the late eighteenth century onwards, were stirred, in part, by
forces that were general to the whole country. Everywhere an accelerating natural increase of population was associated with a
crumbling of the old rural order; everywhere a major agricultural

reorganization disturbed the expectations of old established communities. But the movements out of different rural areas were far from uniform in scale and there were many particular local influences which help to explain the variety of experience and suggest that the local and particular causes may have been as important as the more general ones. The new agricultural system took different shapes in different parts of the country, producing a varying ratio of labor to land and a varying average or typical size of holding. The opportunity of acquiring, or of holding on to, land and the likelihood of finding work on the reconstructed farms—major considerations for people as they decided to stay or move—consequently also varied from place to place. The South-East had much work to offer but few places as independent holders; the North-East hired fewer men for every hundred acres in cultivation but had some compensation in the speed at which the cultivated acreage was expanded at least up to 1875 and in the great number of new holdings that were being created; the Central districts contained areas of intensive and areas of extensive land use with more holdings than in the South-East but fewer than in the North-East; the South-West had its firmly rooted family system in which a large proportion of the holders would continue in possession generation after generation. Just as critical were the local customs that came to prevail in the hiring of labor. The South-East and many parts of the Central district offered a stable prospect to a number of men which probably increased when the agricultural system was being reorganized—say up to 1830—and then remained stable, and thus failed to employ the whole increasing population, through the middle decades to 1870. The Central districts also offered secure, lifelong employment in dependent positions to many who first engaged as servants as young men, but they also contained substantial blocks of men who would have little prospect in agriculture once they had married; and the further one moved north the greater became the proportion of servants in the predicament of having their positions terminated when they married. The South-West, too, had many of its wage earners in this position. Much depended, also, on the strength of the local and still rural industry that clung to certain parts of the country. In particular, first the increase and then, after 1850, the decrease of handloom weaving across the middle block of counties of Fife, Perth, and Forfar helped initially to stabilize and then to disperse the rural population.

These influences of local internal development took on meaning, as precipitants of migration, only within the context of the choices suggested by the conditions of life, or the images of the conditions of life, at the various possible destinations for the migrant. The attractiveness of emigration overseas as opposed to migration within the national boundaries seems to have varied with geographical position. In those parishes which were particularly close to the growing towns, overseas countries seem to have exerted little pull. From the more remote parts there was a strong movement, probably involving the majority of all migrants, towards the industrial towns but also a perceptible movement overseas. Emigration seems to have run at higher levels, therefore, because competing possibilities were relatively weak rather than because the attraction to overseas countries was particularly strong. The main determining influences seem to have been the developments within the rural community, with only the choice of destination settled by the forces of attraction.

# WELSH EMIGRATION TO THE UNITED STATES

Alan Conway

# WELSH EMIGRATION TO
# THE UNITED STATES

## 1. Introduction

We cannot refrain from representing to Your Majesty that the Welsh people form a specially interesting portion of Your Majesty's subjects. They possess marked and distinctive characteristics which separate them from the remainder of the people of the United Kingdom. They cherish an ancient language, they possess a valuable literature, they are imbued with traditions of an honourable past and they have aspirations which . . . are . . . in many respects national in the highest and best sense of the term.*

THE Royal Commissioners in the introduction to their report were writing at a time when Welsh emigration to the United States had reached its peak.[1] While listing the elements which distinguished the Welsh from the English, they also drew attention to the fact that within Wales severe divisions existed between the Welsh and the English. Politically the majority of Welsh supported the Liberal party; the minority of English supported the Conservative or Tory party. A similar major division could be found in religion. The mass of Welsh people belonged to one or other of the many nonconformist bodies; the English supported the Church of England. On the land, tenant farmers were mainly Welsh, the owners of the land either English or Anglicized Welshmen. A similar division existed in the coal mines and ironworks. Perhaps the most significant and distinct division between Welsh and English was the Welsh language—the greatest preserver of Welsh nationalism.

The estrangement of Welsh and English in every aspect of social,

---

* *Royal Commission on Land in Wales and Monmouthshire, Parliamentary Papers*, 1896, XXXIV, p. 12, hereafter cited as *Commission on Land in Wales*.

1. The census returns of 1890 show that in that year there were 100,079 "foreign born Welsh" in the United States. By 1930 their number had dropped to 60,205.

political, religious, and economic contact reached its apogee in the nineteenth century when, in common with most other European peoples, the Welsh emigrated in significant numbers to the United States, to the British colonies and dominions, and to Latin America. In comparison with the great battalions of Germans, Irish, Italians, and other nationalities who crossed the Atlantic, the Welsh represented little more than a corporal's guard. As we shall see, even if the known number of Welsh emigrants to the United States is doubled or trebled to allow for errors of accounting, they still remain a small if distinctive element in the total ethnic brew.

The very Welshness of the Welsh both encouraged and retarded emigration to the United States. For some it increased the desire to remove themselves from subordination to England, for others the devotion to Wales, the Welsh language, and the Welsh way of life hardened their determination to remain in the land of their fathers. Like other European peoples they were stimulated to emigration by land hunger, by poverty, by industrial distress, by the desire for a better life; they were no more proof than other emigrants against the attractions of free land, higher wages, and the promotional literature of American railroads and their agents. Indeed, the impulses that mainly account for the Welsh emigration were widely shared by the other, major groups of European emigrants, and one may see the character and development of these forces in microcosm, as it were, in the Welsh example. More important, however, is the opportunity the Welsh example affords of examining in the historical context of the society from which immigrants to America came one of the circumstances that impeded emigration and that biased the character of the groups that left. For not only was the native society of the Welsh immigrants distinguished by a peculiarly complex relationship to its dominant neighbor England, by the cohesiveness of a comparatively small nation, and by an almost mystical attachment to the few thousand square miles of Wales—all circumstances that tended to limit emigration—but in the economic history of Wales in the nineteenth century an alternative to emigration developed that allowed these centripetal forces to operate fully. Such an alternative to emigration was not unique to Wales, but its effect may be traced more fully there than elsewhere. The contrast with nearby Ireland is especially striking.

The Principality of Wales and Monmouthshire occupies an area of 8,017 square miles (approximately one-twelfth of the total area of Great Britain) with a population at the present day of some two and three-quarter million people.[2] Wales is thus almost the same size as Massachusetts with a population little more than that of the American state. It has, moreover, almost the same number of counties or shires as Massachusetts, namely Anglesey, Caernarvon, Flint, Denbigh, and Merioneth in North Wales, Montgomery, Cardigan, and Radnor in mid-Wales, and Pembroke, Carmarthen, Brecknock, Glamorgan, and Monmouth in South Wales. The greater portion of the population now lives in Glamorgan and Monmouth, the legacy of the movement of population away from the rural areas of Central and North Wales which began in the middle of the nineteenth century. This mobility of population within Wales in the nineteenth century was accompanied by the migration of people to the industrial and urban centers of England as well as overseas. Rural depopulation was certainly not unique to Wales. The rural areas, however, have always been the areas where Welsh has been spoken, hence rural depopulation has threatened the preservation of the Welsh language as the major symbol and vehicle of Welsh nationalism and threatened too the existence of Wales as a distinct entity within the United Kingdom.

The geographical position of Wales and its geological nature have had great political, social, and economic effects on the development of the country; both strongly influenced the displacements and emigrations of the nineteenth century.

Wales is roughly rectangular in shape with two westward-facing peninsulas, Lleyn in the north and Pembroke in the south. The heartland of Wales is a mountainous core surrounded by a low-

2. Estimates of population before the census are as follows: 1500: 250,000; 1600: 379,000; 1700: 419,000. After the census the figures are: 1801: 587,245; 1811: 673,340; 1821: 794,154; 1831: 894,400; 1841: 1,046,073.

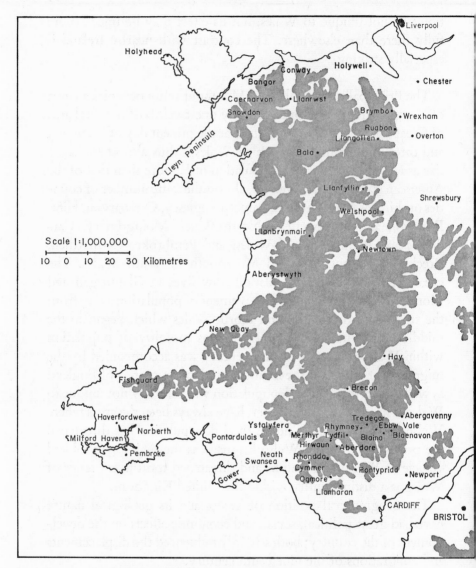

Wales: General, showing land over six hundred feet and major towns and cities (from *The University Atlas*, ed. Harold Fuller and H. C. Darby, 12th ed. [London, 1967], pl. 37).

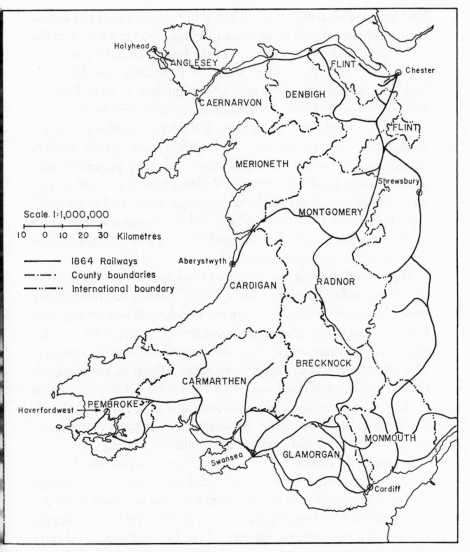

Scale 1:1,000,000

10   0  10  20  30  Kilometres

———— 1864 Railways
—·—·— County boundaries
—··—··— International boundary

Holyhead
ANGLESEY
CAERNARVON
FLINT
Chester
DENBIGH
FLINT
MERIONETH
Shrewsbury
MONTGOMERY
Aberystwyth
CARDIGAN
RADNOR
BRECKNOCK
CARMARTHEN
Haverfordwest
PEMBROKE
MONMOUTH
Swansea
GLAMORGAN
Cardiff

Wales: Political and historical (from *The University Atlas*, pl. 37; 1864 railway network from *Wales*, ed. E. G. Bowen [London, 1957], p. 224).

land fringe. This fringe is fairly broad in the northwest and southwest, very narrow on its western margins, and very broad in the
east where the English lowlands of the border counties join those
of Wales. The great upland massif of Palaeozoic and Mesozoic
rocks, most of it at an elevation of six hundred to two thousand
feet, runs irregularly from Snowdon in the northwest to the moorlands of the South Wales coal basin, and the rivers radiate from this
central core in deep narrow valleys. High relief, heavy rainfall,
strong westerly winds, and bleak moorlands have permitted only
pastoral farming for a large part of Wales, a type of economy, originally concentrated on cattle raising, that seems to have existed
from the days of the Iron Age Celts and that continued down into
the nineteenth century relatively unchanged, except that sheep rearing became increasingly important.

The coastal areas in the west and the lowlands on the English
border proved to be more suitable for an agrarian economy. They
were also more vulnerable to enemy invasion. It was on the lowlands, consequently, that estates were set up by Anglicized Welsh
gentry cut off increasingly from the mass of the Welsh peasantry.
The central heartland thus became more Welsh as the lowlands
became more Anglicized, and until the middle of the nineteenth
century when the industrial revolution came to full flower in South
Wales, the Welsh-speaking peasant, tenant farmer, and laborer
pursued the traditional pastoral life of upland Wales.

It would, of course, be erroneous to suggest that the pastoral
life of a large portion of Wales remained unchanged and unchanging until comparatively recent times. Changes occurred as the result of political settlements, the union with England in the sixteenth
century, the enclosure movements of the late eighteenth and early
nineteenth centuries, and the industrial revolution. But Wales remained a predominantly pastoral and peasant society until the nineteenth century, when the picture was altered completely by fundamental shifts in the economic basis of community life, resulting in
the migration of thousands of Welsh men and women to England,
to South Wales, and to the United States.

## II. Emigration to Colonial America

THERE had been little to attract the Welsh to the British
settlements in mainland America in the early and mid-seven-
teenth century, though one finds occasional Welsh names in the
early colonies and in the lists of emigrants leaving England for
America. There is evidence of an effort of the Welsh people to
settle in America in the seventeenth century associated with the
name of William Vaughan, a substantial landowner from Llan-
gyndeyrn in Carmarthenshire. Motivated by concern for the impoverished condition of the Carmarthenshire peasantry and the
possibility of profit in the establishment of a Welsh settlement on
the North American continent, he secured a patent in 1616 from
James I and attempted, and failed, to establish a community in
Newfoundland at the head of Tripaney Bay.[3] The Welsh who did
emigrate to America in the early years of colonial settlement went
as individuals and not as parts of any group settlement. Most commonly they appear in the records as indentured servants, frequently
under the headright system which secured fifty acres for anyone
paying the cost of passage for an able-bodied settler. The Act of
Union (1536) having brought the English and Welsh into much
closer contact, Welsh servants had been much in demand in large
English households and the same demand operated strongly in the
colonies as well.[4] Yet though Welsh names can be found in both
Virginia and Maryland in the first half of the seventeenth century[5]
the number of such emigrants is small. The more affluent gentry in
Wales were more attracted to Ireland, where cultivated land could
be obtained much more easily than in the American wilderness.[6]
New England attracted a few as a religious haven—as did Mary-

3. David Williams, *Cymru ac America* (Cardiff, 1946).
4. A. E. Smith, *Colonists in Bondage* (Chapel Hill, 1947), p. 289.
5. M. L. Hansen, *The Atlantic Migration, 1607–1860* (Cambridge, 1940), p. 30.
6. A. H. Dodd, *The Character of Early Welsh Emigration to the United States* (Cardiff, 1953), p. 6.

land for Catholic recusants—but the volatile religious situation in seventeenth-century England did not create permanent emigration of any size from Wales until late in the century. Then, the movement of substantial numbers of Quakers, Baptists, and Presbyterians from Wales to the New World was occasioned by reaction against persecution, often combined with a flight from poverty. Puritanism like the Reformation came to Wales from England. Its progress in the first half of the seventeenth century was tentative and slow and limited very much to the Welsh border counties. The situation changed significantly with the Roundhead victory after Naseby. In 1649, John Miles, a Baptist, established a separatist church at Ilston in Gower, followed by others at Llanharan, Carmarthen, Hay, and Abergavenny. Cromwell's interest in Wales as a mission field was given substance in February 1650 when an act for the Propagation of the Gospel in Wales was passed in Parliament.[7] Numbers of Anglican clergy were rooted out for, among other things, their inability to preach in Welsh, and authority was given to men like John Miles and Vavasor Powell to replace them with godly men of whom they approved. By the late fifties, the Quaker influence had appeared in the figure of John ap John of Ruabon who returned from a visit to John Fox as the first Quaker missionary in Wales. In 1657 Fox himself conducted a great missionary tour of Wales particularly in Radnorshire, Montgomeryshire, and Pembrokeshire. In the same years the Baptists too strengthened their position with the result that at the Restoration the Baptists and Quakers had become the dominant nonconformist groups, and the Independents were little more than a handful of obscure church gatherings.

The Restoration threatened the suppression of all of these nonconformist groups, and they turned to emigration as a possible form of survival. This was the policy adopted by the Baptist, John Miles, of Swansea, who with some of his congregation emigrated

7. The mysticism of the Propagation was in part reaction against the stiff orthodoxy of Puritan New England and was fostered by returned emigrants from America. The idea of an organized Puritan mission from New England to Wales is attributed to Hugh Peters who returned home in 1641. See *ibid.*, p. 11.

in 1663 to New England where, after a succession of moves to escape the pressures of the Plymouth authorities, they found a permanent home in Swanzey, about ten miles from the present-day Providence, Rhode Island, where relations with the Congregationalists were tolerable. The church at Swanzey became one of the major centers of the Baptist faith in America, and the settlers prospered as farmers.

This was the first important group of Welsh immigrants impelled by the religious pressures of the Restoration. Others followed quickly. The emigration of Welsh Quakers later in the century, followed by Baptists from Radnorshire and West Wales, furnished America, and particularly Pennsylvania, with its first significant numbers of Welsh settlers. The Quakers of Montgomeryshire and Merionethshire eagerly grasped at the opportunity to emigrate when William Penn received his charter from Charles II. Penn himself was, in fact, attracted to the idea of calling the area of his grant "New Wales" until the King bestowed the name of Pennsylvania upon it in honor of Penn's father. In May 1681 Penn met with a number of prominent Welsh Quakers whom he wished to interest in participating in his "Holy Experiment," and it was agreed that some forty to fifty thousand acres of the vast area of the grant should be set aside for a "Welsh Tract" which, with its emphasis on Welsh customs and the Welsh language, was intended to be virtually a Welsh dominion.

In August of that year Richard Davies purchased from Penn a patent for five thousand acres of land in the proposed Welsh tract and then commenced to find settlers for it from among his friends in Wales. The majority of the twenty-six subscribers who took up land at fivepence an acre were from Merionethshire and Radnorshire. They were men of no great wealth—carpenters, weavers, and glovers. They did not all take up their titles in America; some, like Richard Davies himself, sold them to later emigrants. The first Welsh party left for America in mid-1682, and found the hard Pennsylvania winters difficult to endure. Some had to survive in caves cut out from the banks of the Delaware and Schuylkill rivers.

By 1685 the lands nearest the site of Philadelphia had a population of some twenty-five hundred, and accounts sent back to Wales reported favorably on the prospects of the new settlement.[8] In January 1684 Penn ordered the Welsh tract surveyed and divided into townships. The first township on the Schuylkill River was named Merion, west of that was Haverford, and north of that was Radnor, all reflecting the areas from which the first Welsh emigrants had come. Later emigrants from Wales spread out from the original townships into Goshen, Tredyffrin, and Uwchlan townships.

The hopes of the Welsh that they would be able to maintain a separate, exclusive Welsh barony within Pennsylvania were dashed in 1691 when lands within the Welsh tract were opened to other settlers. Subsequently, the Welsh influence was further diminished when Merion was placed in Philadelphia County and Radnor and Haverford in Chester County. At the same time the economic advantages to be gained from this prospering colony were not lost upon the Welsh settlers or upon relatives and friends in Wales.[9]

Pennsylvania attracted not only Quakers from Wales but also Welsh Baptists and Welsh Anglicans. In 1686 a small group of Welsh Baptists from Radnorshire arrived and established the first Baptist church in Pennsylvania at Pennepek, on the outskirts of Philadelphia. In 1701 these original Arminian Baptists were joined by Calvinistic Baptists from West Wales. They organized themselves into a church before emigrating and initially were well received by their coreligionists at Pennepek. Very soon, however, the latter group, being stricter in their observances and entirely Welsh speaking, broke away from the later comers and in 1703 migrated to thirty thousand acres in the Welsh tract on the Delaware River and established there the Iron Hill Baptist Church. This in turn became the mother church of other congregations which were established far afield in the next forty years. One small group settled along the Black River in North Carolina in the

8. F. A. Nobel, "Radnorshire Settlers in the Foundation of Pennsylvania," *Radnorshire Society Transactions*, 29 (1959), 1–17. See also T. A. Glenn, *Welsh Founders of Pennsylvania* (Oxford, 1913).

9. The effect on the Quakers in Wales was one of decline and decay occasioned by the more vigorous elements of the Quaker communities emigrating to Pennsylvania.

1730's[10] and a larger group settled at Welsh Neck on the Peedee River in South Carolina in 1736. The Welsh settlement on the Peedee became exclusively Welsh and prosperous; it is one of the few instances in which the Welsh settled in a slave area.

Ministers for these Baptist churches for many years were brought out from Wales, thus firmly maintaining the links between the colonies and the homeland. Interest in America was kept very much alive in these nonconformist circles in Wales and the importance of the ministry in Welsh emigration movements was in this way established. Men such as Rev. Benjamin Chidlaw, Rev. Samuel Roberts, and Rev. Michael D. Jones, who would play such an important part in the emigration movement from Wales in the nineteenth century, were following very much in the steps of their eighteenth-century ministerial predecessors.

The Welsh Anglicans were also involved in the early emigrations to Pennsylvania. They settled principally in Gwynedd Township, in Montgomery County north of Philadelphia. Their interest in emigration to Pennsylvania had been stimulated by reports sent back from America by Welsh Quakers, reinforced by the return to Wales of Hugh Roberts, an influential Quaker, in 1697. Agents of the Anglicans who were sent over to America purchased nearly eight thousand acres in Montgomery County, and the main body of settlers arrived in 1698. As with the Baptists, ministers, such as Rev. Evan Evans, played a significant role in these Anglican settlements.[11]

In the mid-eighteenth century religion again had a significant influence upon Welsh emigration as a result of the Methodist revival. This time, however, the evangelical flavor was much stronger. Before the war of American Independence, students of the Methodist College at Trevecka in Wales went to a similar institution in Georgia which had been set up there by George Whitefield to train missionaries for the back-country settlements and the Indian territories. Close touch was maintained between the mis-

10. S. A. Ashe, *History of North Carolina* (Greensboro, 1908), I, 254 and note.
11. Some Presbyterians from West Wales also settled in Pennsylvania in the early eighteenth century at Pencader.

sionaries trained there and the leaders of the revival in Wales concerning the progress being made in the evangelization of Kentucky backwoodsmen. And with Independence another religious motive for migration appeared in the belief of many British Methodists that the United States was the "wilderness" of the Book of Revelation where God had prepared a place for his Church.

The number of Welsh in Pennsylvania in the early and mideighteenth century was sufficient to justify the publication of books in the Welsh language, mostly of a religious nature,[12] but inevitably the inability of the Welsh to remain in compact and exclusive settlements meant that the Welsh language and Welsh customs would be undermined by the prevalence of the English language. The process of assimilation, and with it the decline of the Welsh language, was accelerated by the fact that for three-quarters of the eighteenth century emigration from Wales declined until the numbers involved became insignificant. When the Welsh Society of Pennsylvania was founded in 1798 for the relief of emigrants from Wales, Welsh had not been in common use in Pennsylvania for half a century. Its members were clearly as much American as Welsh, and they had little command of the Welsh language.

The war of American Independence had a strong influence on Wales in stimulating a new political consciousness and in reshaping the attitudes of dissenters toward politics. Some of the first political pamphlets that examined the reasons for the dispute between the colonies and Great Britain were distributed in Wales in 1776. The best known of these tracts was written in 1776 by a leading dissenter, Richard Price, entitled *Observations on the Nature of Civil Liberty*. This pamphlet, which swung the issue away from the question of taxation to the basic principles of government, argued that sovereignty stemmed from the people who were the masters of the King and his ministers: their authority had been delegated to them by the people. Even more radical were the views of David

---

12. In 1721 Ellis Pugh, a stonemason from Dolgelley and a disciple of John ap John, wrote *Annerch i'r Cymry* for circulation among the poor people of Wales. In 1727 it was translated into English as *A Salutation to the Britains* for wider circulation in America by his patron Rowland Ellis who had left his family seat at Bryn Mawr to found another of the same name in Pennsylvania.

Williams, a Welsh dissenter and an acquaintance of Benjamin Franklin, who in 1782 defended the Americans in his *Letters on Political Liberty*, which called not only for freedom of the press, but also for manhood suffrage, the secret ballot, and annual parliaments.[13]

The identification of America with the best of radical democratic ideals did not immediately result in a fresh stream of emigration to America but it did deepen popular awareness of America in Wales. The same effect was intensified by the resurrection of the rather bizarre claim that America had been discovered in 1170 by Prince Madoc ap Owain Gwynnedd and that somewhere in the western parts of America there existed fair-skinned Welsh-Indians who spoke "yr hen iaith" and were the descendants of the Welsh settlers who had gone to America with Madoc.[14] The myth of the Welsh Indians appealed equally to the missionary zeal of the Methodists, to national pride in an era of the romantic literature of exploration, and to commercial interest in establishing trading affiliations with Indians of Welsh descent. Echoes of all these interests can be found in the writings of William Jones of Llangadfan in Montgomeryshire whose primary aim was to apply the principles of Voltaire to a settlement in New York state.

The hardships which the poor inhabitants of this barren country [Wales] suffer by the Insatiable Avarice of the Landowners, have affected my feelings so, that I had determined to write to London to get Intelligence of some proprietor of uncultivated land in America in order to offer my services to concert a Plan for removing such of my countrymen as have spirit enough to leave their Aegyptian Taskmasters and try their fortune on the other side of the Atlantic. . . . The chief object we should have in view is to gain a separate settlement for our countrymen on some of the Western Waters in order to keep up a friendly correspondence with our cousins the Padoucas [the Welsh Indians].[15]

13. David Williams, "David Williams," *Dictionary of Welsh Biography* (London, 1959), pp. 1031–1032.

14. A fine, scholarly examination of this subject is by David Williams, "John Evans' Strange Journey," *Transactions of the Honourable Society of Cymmrodorion* (1948), and also in *American Historical Review*, 54 (1949), 277–295, 508–529.

15. National Library of Wales, MS. 13221E, hereafter cited as N.L.W.

He had little success in his attempt to acquire a block of land owned by Sir William Pulteney in New York despite approaches for support to Thomas Pinckney, United States minister to Great Britain. Nevertheless, his urging of America upon his countrymen as the land of political and religious freedom had some effect in Wales. Some emigrants left Bala and east Denbighshire for New York between 1791 and 1794.[16] In the decade that followed, other individuals and small groups—motivated by a continuing interest in locating Welsh Indians, Methodist and Baptist zeal, and commercial enterprise—settled in the northeastern United States and in Ohio, strengthening the Welsh communities that were permanently established in Pennsylvania, New York, and Ohio by the end of the Napoleonic Wars.

It is tempting to ascribe this emigration of Welshmen in the last decade of the eighteenth century to rural distress consequent upon the succession of bad harvests which Wales experienced between 1789 and 1802. Undoubtedly, the war with France increased the cost of living and resulted in depressed conditions among small Welsh farmers. Contemporary writers spoke of a spirit of emigration infatuating a great part of Wales because of this rural distress.[17] But the groups that settled in America in these years were not without some means. The purchasing of thousands of acres in New York, Pennsylvania, and Ohio was not accomplished without quite substantial financial resources. The more well-to-do may well have supported those of their neighbors with more limited means, but the picture at that point was not one of poverty stricken Welsh emigrants fleeing from starvation. Freedom from religious discrimination, if not persecution, undoubtedly was a factor, as was the greater political freedom available in America. Concern for the preservation of the Welsh language and culture and for the continuing identity of Wales as a nation is also evident. The knowledge that cheap and fertile land was available in America to those who had the resources and initiative to take it was a further factor.

Emigration to America in the period before the end of the first

16. Dodd, *Early Welsh Emigration*, p. 21.
17. W. Davies, *General View of the Agriculture of North Wales* (London, 1810), p. 443.

third of the nineteenth century, impelled as it was by these impulses and limited to small groups from particular areas under the leadership of a few prominent men, was not large. Nothing that could be called a mass emigration took place until the mid-nineteenth century. Before then Welsh emigration was a carefully considered move of a few people to what seemed the greater attractions of America. This early emigration of Welsh people to America in the seventeenth and eighteenth centuries was a bridging movement to the emigration of the nineteenth century. Many of the motives for the earlier emigration would reappear in the nineteenth century, but economic, social, and political forces would predominate as expulsive forces in the nineteenth century.

## III. Welsh Emigration to the United States in the Nineteeth Century

WHAT were the numbers involved in the Welsh emigration to the United States in the nineteenth century? Fully reliable figures are impossible to find. Only from January 1 to June 7, 1841, do the British census returns give the number of emigrants from each county in Britain, and so it can be established that during that time some 1,149 emigrants from Wales and Monmouthshire left for the United States, the largest numbers being from Cardiganshire, Carmarthenshire, Monmouthshire, Merionethshire, and Montgomeryshire.[18] Comparable figures would not be available again until 1908 when the Board of Trade began to distinguish between Welsh and English passengers in its shipping returns. From British sources, therefore, the statistics of Welsh emigration in the nineteenth century are almost totally absent. United States returns are more helpful but far from conclusive. According to United States immigration figures, fewer than ninety thousand people emigrated from Wales between 1820 and 1950, the major portion of whom did so in the years between 1850 and 1930. After

18. *Commission on Land in Wales*, 1896, p. 53.

1930 the annual number entering the United States was negligible. As against this, the census figures for "Foreign-born Welsh" in the United States reveal that in 1850 there were 29,868; in 1860, 45,-763; in 1870, 74,533; in 1880, 83,302; in 1890, 100,079; in 1900, 93,586; in 1910, 82,488; in 1920, 67,066; and in 1930, 60,205.

Despite this seeming precision, little reliance can be placed upon these figures. Many Welsh sailing from Liverpool were undoubtedly classified as English. Monmouthshire, which provided so many Welsh emigrants from its industrial centers in the second half of the nineteenth century, was administratively part of England and thus Welsh immigrants from Monmouthshire were in many cases also classified as English. Perhaps the discrepancy between official returns and actual immigrants can best be illustrated by the fact that between 1847 and 1860 the New York Commissioners of Emigration reported that over seventeen thousand Welsh entered the United States through the port of New York. During the same period United States government figures show less than seven thousand Welsh entering the country.[19]

Thus the number of one hundred thousand Welsh immigrants entering the United States in the nineteenth century might well be doubled or even trebled, but even then it has to be recognized that the Welsh element in the United States has always been very small when compared to the German, Irish, Italians, and other ethnic groups that entered the United States during the same period.

Welsh emigration in the nineteenth century can be divided roughly into two phases. The first from 1815 to the middle of the century was predominantly a rural emigration set in motion by agrarian discontent. The second, from mid-century on, was predominantly but not exclusively an industrial emigration, primarily from the iron and steel and coalmining regions of South Wales, stimulated by industrial disputes, poor conditions, low wages, and unemployment. To a considerable extent, the latter phase of emigration was a continuation of the former because, as will be seen,

19. See Robert Ernst, *Immigrant Life in New York City, 1825–1863* (New York, 1949), p. 188.

the human resources for the great industrial growth of South Wales were largely supplied by the rural counties bordering the South Wales coalfield. The result was that in many cases the rural emigrant to the United States moved first to industrial South Wales and then, finding conditions there no more to his liking than they had been in the rural areas, moved once more and finally across the Atlantic. Intermingled with these basic forces of poverty and discontent, whether of a rural or industrial nature, were resurgences of religious motives for emigration, especially in the case of the Welsh Mormons, and the desire to preserve the Welsh nation from oblivion by re-creating a truly Welsh community in the United States. For, through most of the nineteenth century, Wales was a land of two nations. In the rural areas the division was between a Welsh-speaking, nonconformist, politically Liberal Welsh peasantry and an English-speaking, Anglican, politically Tory landowner class. In the industrial areas of the country the same linguistic, ethnic, religious, and political differences divided the foundrymen from the ironmasters.[20] The disputes and discontent arising from such explosive opposites, polarizing Welsh and English, intensified the basic discontents that impelled the main groups of Welsh emigrants across the Atlantic.

## A. EMIGRATION FROM RURAL WALES

The mid-eighteenth century Welshman whether peasant, fisherman, shepherd, or drover still lived much as he had done for cen-

---

20. A Commissioner reporting on the state of education in Wales in 1847 emphasized the division in the ironworks: "In the works the Welsh workman never finds his way into the office. He never becomes either clerk or agent. . . . Equally in his new, as in his old, home, his language keeps him under the hatches, being one in which he can neither acquire nor communicate the necessary information. It is a language of old-fashioned agriculture, of theology and of simple rustic life, while all the world about him is English." *Royal Commission on the State of Education in Wales, Parliamentary Papers*, 1847, XXVII, Part I, 2. This commission, composed of three young Englishmen who were Anglicans without any knowledge of Wales or the Welsh language, conducted investigations with incredible arrogance and moved beyond their brief to assert that Welsh country-women were "almost universally unchaste." Their report created intense indignation in Wales and animosity against the English. Henceforward, the 1847 report would be known as *Brad y Llyfrau Gleision* ("the treachery of the blue books"). This title was based on *Brad y Cyllyll Hirion* ("the treachery of the long knives"), a mythical incident in the ancient wars between Welsh and Saxons.

turies. Generally dressed in homespun woolens, he lived on a diet of oat cake, rye or barley bread, flummery, fish, and occasionally a little meat. Buttermilk and mead were the main beverages. It was rare to discover the Welsh peasant drinking tea. This poor diet resulted, for the most part, in poor health. Housing, even by the standards of the times, was primitive. Cottages or low cabins were built normally of timber and wattle although stone would sometimes be used if sufficiently near and available. Roofs were usually thatched, but in the more northern parts of Wales slate was also used. The floor was of dirt and windows were often lacking. Peat fires were used for cooking and warmth. The accommodation for living and sleeping was equally primitive. Families of a dozen or more children were brought up in rat-infested, one-room cottages on straw-covered board beds, or on the floor itself. Soap was a luxury and rarely used, while no sanitary facilities existed inside or outside the house. Pigs and poultry shared the family hearth. Women and children worked in the fields with the men, driving oxen, planting and digging potatoes, milking, and loading dung. The rent would be paid from the sale of butter and eggs. After the introduction of the potato in the first decades of the nineteenth century, the peasant diet was adequate to sustain larger families and with it increasing poverty. As one Welsh historian has pungently expressed it, "Poverty, potatoes, larger families, more potatoes and greater poverty represented the interaction of cause and effect in Wales as in Ireland."[21]

The English type of nucleated village was rare in the rural areas of North and mid-Wales. The pattern of settlement was that of scattered farmsteads with squatters erecting crude cabins on the upland wasteland. Roads as such were nonexistent; the best to be found were little more than cart tracks. In the more mountainous areas horses pulling sledges were the only way to move goods. The only social centers that existed were the larger farmhouses. Only along the lowlands of the English border were there village communities based on arable farming; subsistence farming predominated.

21. David Williams, *The Rebecca Riots* (Cardiff, 1955), p. 95.

Some wheat was grown in Wales but oats, barley, and rye were for long the staple crops. Cattle, sheep, and goats were, however, the mainstay of the Welsh rural economy. For with the growth of London and the large towns of the English Midlands, the cattle trade had become increasingly important. The Welsh cattle drover took thousands of animals each year across country to the English markets. Sheep too were driven as far as southeast England for fattening and sale, though not in great numbers, for the Welsh peasant could be said to have lived off the sheep's back. Every farmer spun some wool and wove it into coarse cloth on primitive looms. This cloth not only served a farmer's family needs but was sold for use in the army and exported by English middlemen in Liverpool, Bristol, and London to Europe, Africa, the West Indies, and the southern colonies of America, where it was used quite extensively on the slave plantations.

It is worth noting at this point that, despite the geographical isolation of Wales and its primitive ethnocentric rural population, population mobility had been a feature from time immemorial. Well before the beginning of the nineteenth century, Welsh laborers had moved at harvest time to the English border counties, and Welsh women and girls had found employment in eastern England in fruit picking and haymaking. Emigration to the United States in the nineteenth century would thus be an extension, albeit a permanent one, of a tradition that had long persisted on a temporary basis in the rural areas of Wales.

The agricultural revolution which was such a marked feature of eighteenth-century England, brought about in part by the necessity of feeding a rapidly growing population, was slow in coming to Wales. The reasons for this are numerous. Wales was remote from the large centers of population, and the absence of roads provided few means for the transportation of agricultural produce. The land owners who promoted agricultural improvements were, more often than not, nonresident and more concerned with their estates in England. The smaller resident gentry lacked the capital necessary for improvements on a large scale and the individual farm with holdings of little more than forty acres was even less able to afford the cost. A few local and county agricultural societies sprang up by the end of the eighteenth century, which encouraged the growing of potatoes, turnips, and clover and improvements in cattle breeding. Apart from that, however, the great mass of rural dwellers remained unaffected by the new ideas of crop rotation and animal husbandry. The perpetuation of these traditional practices rested on the small size of the population and its ability to survive on this very low standard of living. Once the great population increases began to take effect at the beginning of the nineteenth century, with mounting demands for food, innovations in agricultural practices would have to be tried.

There were two methods used to meet the increasing demand for food: enclosure, to ensure more production and efficient units, and the extension of agriculture to the less productive wasteland. Neither of these operations was entirely new to Wales, but they were used on an entirely new scale at the end of the eighteenth century. The great enclosure movement in Wales coincided precisely with the wars with France from 1793 to 1815. The rise in the price of corn consequent upon the wars made it attractive to farm at unprecedented heights on the hills. By the end of the war more than one hundred thousand acres of upland Wales had been enclosed, mostly in the counties of Montgomeryshire, Brecknockshire, and Cardiganshire.

This development did not take place without some opposition; but the Welsh peasantry was incapable of engaging in expensive litigation or, because of the cost of hedging and ditching, of enclosing the land themselves. Thus, claims to the open moorland were rarely sustained, particularly since the landowners, as members of Parliament, were most likely to be the official recipients of whatever petitions against enclosure were presented. Squatters, who were in a particularly precarious situation, were swiftly evicted. The superficial and temporary prosperity of the war years for some farmers dampened much of the protest which might have been forthcoming. Only with the postwar depression was the full extent of the changes that had taken place realized. Farmers ousted from their holdings had little choice but to become part of a growing army of landless farm laborers, to leave the land for the new industrial towns, or to emigrate overseas where abundant land was available.

At the same time as enclosure and encroachment expanded, a significant change in the nature of land tenure took place. Prior to the nineteenth century a large number of yeoman farmers were either freeholders, copyholders, or owners of leases for several lives ("three lives" being the most common). The freeholder, though he might have no more than twenty acres and might live only very little above the poverty line, was socially respectable. With the subdivision of his property on his death, the farmer's freehold became increasingly uneconomic and often disappeared altogether, along with any claims to the common land which might have been retained in the face of enclosure and encroachment. The ultimate result for the freeholder was a descent into the ranks of the farm laborers. For the small freeholder had independence but lacked capital. His life was often harder than that of tenant farmers and laborers in that they had some measure of security as long as they could hold their tenure of lease beyond one year or one life. But the tenant farmers too were in difficulties. Their short-term leases ran into the difficulty of higher rents for improvements which stultified whatever initiative they might have had to improve their farms. The system which took over from the long lease was a system of annual leases to the highest bidder which added to the bitterness and grievances of those attempting to secure land after the wars in a period of depression and general poverty.[22]

The long wars against France brought prosperity to the larger landowners in Wales and to the lowland farmers. Some of the upland farmers also benefited from higher prices for dairy produce while feeling the effects of the higher prices for corn which they

---

22. It was not uncommon for potential tenants to hasten from the graveside to the landowner to bid for the expired tenancy. This tremendous competition for tenancy of land enabled the landlords to keep the rents excessively high. W. Davies in his *Agriculture of North Wales*, p. 99, asserted that in 1799 some of the leaseholders on the Vaenol estate in Caernarvonshire, regardless of the remainder of their term, emigrated to America before their leases expired.

did not produce themselves. For the small farmer a series of wet and unproductive harvests brought much distress.

The bleakness of the war years for some was captured by one nineteenth-century writer drawing upon local records for Dinas Mawddwy at the beginning of the century:

It was a time of remarkable depression from 1745 to 1815. Thus 1795 was a year of great scarcity, the crops were poor and the winter hard, but by 1798 the depression had become still worse. Moreover, the summer turned out extremely dry so that the cattle died for want of water and the crops were consequently very scanty. In January 1799 there fell great quantities of snow which remained on the ground in many places until the month of May. Scarcely any sheep escaped death. Heavy floods followed in July and scarcely any peat or hay was harvested and that in poor condition. The following year also, 1800, was noted for great snow and frost. Provisions rose in price and were poor and unwholesome. It was known to the old people as "the year of the saddened bread." The wheat was 9s a measure (20 quarts) and it was almost impossible to obtain any even at that price. The Year of Waterloo is also one to be remembered. Nearly everything came to a standstill; the laborers could get no employment and the farmers too were in want. The poor rate for the parish was 6s 3d in the £. Tea was 1s 6d an ounce, sugar 1s 6d a pound, salt 5d a pound and the best flour 1s a half-pound. People would buy an occasional half pound of that at Bala or Shrewsbury so as to make pap for the infant children. This year 7s 6d a peck was paid for wheat and 15s 2d a peck for flour at Bala.[23]

With the coming of peace in 1815 depression overtook Wales as a whole, a depression which was felt intensely at first but which became part of the daily burden as it continued almost unchanged down to the middle of the century. Unemployment in small industrial centers saw workers from small villages returning home to compete in an already saturated labor market. To add to their troubles immigrants from Ireland who were prepared to work at any job at any price were moving into Wales in large numbers.

The immediate result of the end of the war was a sharp decline in prices which made farming even for the larger landowners less profitable. As a result, farm laborers were dismissed to add yet more to the number of those seeking employment. Even the weath-

23. Tecwyn, *Dinas Mawddwy a'i Hamgylchoed* (Machynlleth, 1893), quoted in *Commission on Land in Wales*, 1896, p. 626.

er seemed to be affected. Immediately after the war the harvests were disastrous. The winter of 1814 proved to be the coldest in memory and 1816 was cold and wet and became known as "the year without a summer." By 1817, with the failure of the harvest, Wales was in the grip of famine. Farmers sold livestock for whatever price they would fetch, and food shortages led to rioting in Carmarthenshire and Montgomeryshire. The landowner, by maintaining high rents for tenancy, became the focus of popular hatred. This was especially the case with those nonresident owners who put in English or Scottish land agents to run their estates. The depression also saw the collapse of many of the country banks which wiped out the savings of the many small depositors.

To add yet further to the bleakness of the postwar situation, Wales, like most of England and Europe, began to experience the effects of a population explosion which would double its population by the middle of the nineteenth century. When dealing with this population increase in Western Europe it is customary to attribute it to better sanitary conditions, improved medical care, a decline in infant mortality, and increased longevity. Few of these seem to fit the case for the rural areas of Wales. Sanitary conditions in 1850 were little better than they had been half a century earlier and medical attention in the remote areas was no better nor more easily available. In rural Wales the increase was the result of a higher birthrate and an increased number of children born outside of marriage as the result, particularly in West Wales, of an excess of females over males. Also earlier marriages in a state of poverty took place with the expectation that the children of such marriages would be assisted by the parish. To these factors must be added the importance of the introduction of the potato, which would grow on any patch of ground and provide an adequately sustained diet taken in conjunction with milk.

The pauperization of sections of the peasantry threw a great strain on the administration of the Poor Laws. Since the middle of the seventeenth century responsibility for the relief of the poor had fallen upon the parish. Prior to the outbreak of the American war the extent of poverty had been such as to place no great burden on an inefficient system. By 1815 the poor rate over the whole country had increased fourfold; the laws were tightened up considerably and the poor suffered severely. Parishes adopted a policy of ridding themselves of any who seemed likely to become a charge on the parish. However harsh the treatment of the impotent poor, the able-bodied laborer was a much greater problem. The increases in the poor rates were indicative of the fact that the laboring poor were sinking deeper into a state of abject poverty. Wages were so low as to make it impossible even for those in employment to survive without some assistance from the parish. To deal with these problems on a large scale was far beyond the abilities of the Poor Law officials and overseers who were unequipped to deal with widespread poverty on a large scale. One method devised was to set up workhouses where the inmates were employed spinning wool or picking oakum. These "bastilles" later became the focal points of discontent; attempts to destroy them were made at places like Narberth and Carmarthen. Although the Speenhamland System, developed by the Berkshire magistrates in 1795 for supplementing wages according to the price of corn, was not adopted in any systematic fashion in Wales, similar types of relief were employed. Single able-bodied men were denied parish relief but married men with more than three children were declared eligible. This encouraged earlier marriages and swift breeding to qualify for relief. Attempts to supplement the wages of farm laborers from parish funds resulted in the dismissal of independent farm laborers and the hiring of others subsidized by the parish.

After the Reform Act of 1832 outdoor relief was abandoned and parishes were grouped into unions for the construction of workhouses where the conditions were to be made so bad as to deter any but the most desperate from entering them.

Not all parishes were run by monsters, and some parish vestries found in emigration to America a partial solution to the difficulties of the poor. Money was found to send paupers and their families to the United States although the resources available for this purpose were very limited. More numerous than paupers in the ranks of emigrants were small farmers and those peasants and laborers who had not reached the stage of destitution but who feared they soon would if they did not move. Notices began to appear more frequently than before in the local newspapers offering passage to Liverpool from small coastal ports like Carmarthen, Fishguard, Cardigan, Newquay, and Aberystwyth. By the 1840's ships were going directly from Cardigan, Carmarthen, and Aberystwyth to Quebec and New York, many of them timber ships looking for profitable human ballast on their return voyages.[24] From North Wales slate ships were also used as early as 1817 to carry passengers who bedded down between the stacks of slate from Caernarvon to New York.[25]

The workhouses set up in Wales, as elsewhere, created a sense of outrage at the separation of husbands and wives and of parents and children. The nonconformist press widely condemned the system and Chartism in Wales followed suit in trying to ameliorate the system.

In the midst of these distresses the Whig government of 1836 made commutation of the tithes to money payments compulsory. In Wales a substantial portion of the tithes had fallen into lay hands and their payment was bitterly resented by a population which was moving rapidly to universal religious nonconformity. Prior to commutation, tithes had been objected to on the grounds that they penalized the efficient farmer, but so long as they could be paid for in kind there was always room for bargaining. Commutation in a time of economic distress and little ready money made the tithe system that much more obnoxious. The Church of England was singularly unable to adapt itself to the changing conditions of nineteenth-century Wales, particularly in the coalfields, and thus nonconformity was the only real link between the older rural Wales and the new urban, industrial centers. The class struggle between the gentry and their tenants already divided by class and language was exacerbated by religious differences. The result was that the

24. Williams, *The Rebecca Riots*, p. 114.
25. *The Cambrian* (Swansea), XXVI (July 1906). The *Oswestry Herald*, April 25, 1820, commented on the number of emigrants from Montgomeryshire passing through on their way to Liverpool. This newspaper also reported that further groups from Llangollen and Welshpool were preparing to leave in 1822.

Welsh peasantry which in normal circumstances would have been conservative was quite radical. Church rates and tithes were eventually borne by the tenant farmer who had them passed on to him by his landlord.

The confluence of these social grievances came to a head in the Rebecca riots which struck the Welsh countryside first in West Wales in 1839 and then, elsewhere, in 1842 and 1843.[26] These outbreaks, which began as attacks on tollgates on the borders of Carmarthenshire and Pembrokeshire and in the Teify Valley, and finally spread to south Carmarthenshire, were not simple uprisings of an oppressed peasantry against a specific burden but a violent reaction against more complex and deep social difficulties which arose from the pressure of population upon a backward economy within an obsolescent system of government and administration.[27]

The state of the roads in Wales was notoriously bad and until 1835 dependent upon rates levied by the parish for their maintenance. With the passage of the Highways Act of 1835 the turnpike system was introduced with the tolls charged for their use intended to provide better maintenance and better roads. Unfortunately, the road trusts that were set up were small, inefficient, and grossly mismanaged when not directly corrupt. The number of tollgates and competition among various trusts led to a situation where the farmer, when moving stock or transporting lime for fertilizer, found himself obliged to pay tolls every few miles. The number of tollgates belonging to competing trusts increased around the larger towns like Swansea and Carmarthen, with the result that the traveller or the farmer trying to bring produce for sale approached these communities through barriers more suitable for a beleaguered fortress. It was not so much the rates charged by the trusts that caused resentment as the frequency of the gates.

The summer and autumn of 1838 were bad for farmers, and in January 1839 rural discontent exploded with the burning of the newly erected workhouse at Narberth, indicative of the continuing

26. By far the best study of these aspects of social protest is Williams, *The Rebecca Riots.*

27. *Ibid.*, p. vii.

hatred of the Poor Law system. This was followed in May by the destruction of a tollgate on the Carmarthenshire-Pembrokeshire border. The tollgate was rebuilt and special constables sworn in to protect it. On the night of June 6 three or four hundred men, with their faces blackened and dressed in women's clothes for disguise, drove off the constables and once more destroyed the tollgate.[28] Later another gate was destroyed a few miles away. Within a month, however, the riots had subsided and the countryside returned to normal.

More than three years elapsed before a resurgence of the attacks on the gates occurred in the same area in the winter of 1842. This time destruction was more widespread; soon not a single gate of the Whitland trust was left standing in either Carmarthenshire or Pembrokeshire. The movement of Rebecca and her daughters spread into south Cardiganshire, and other trusts began to experience the attentions of the mobs. So effective were their efforts, despite the attempts of the military and police sent down from London to catch the rioters, that by the summer of 1843 the country was without any tollgates. The success enjoyed by Rebecca emboldened them to direct their attention to other grievances. Threatening letters were received by tithe-grasping Church of England clergymen, and barns and hayricks of unpopular magistrates were burned. In mid-June three hundred or so horsemen descended upon Carmarthen in broad daylight, where they were joined by the town mob, and sacked the workhouse there.

This incident brought the disturbance to national attention, and the London *Times* sent a reporter to Wales. His accounts of the grievances of Welsh farmers were written up sympathetically and at length, and they provide some of the best insights into the condition of Wales at this period.

In the late summer of 1843 the riots spread to east Carmarthenshire and west Glamorganshire. Attacks on gates at Pontardulais

28. The Rebecca rioters took the name from the Bible where it stated that the seed of Rebecca should possess the gates of her enemies. There were many Rebeccas, the best known were John Jones (Shoni Sguborfawr) and David Davies (Dai's Cantwr), both from Glamorgan.

and Hendy saw firearms being used for the first time and an old woman who was the toll-keeper at Hendy was killed. Rioting continued to spread as far as Radnorshire by early autumn, but then its fury subsided.

The authorities used police and troops to stamp out the disturbances. Leading Rebecca-ites like John Jones and David Davies were captured, sentenced, and transported for life. As the result of the *Times* reports, commissioners were appointed to investigate the riots. Eventually, reform of the turnpike trusts, the general Enclosure Act of 1845, the repeal of the Corn Law in 1846, and the establishment of a Poor Law Board in 1847 removed many of the grievances of the rural areas. Added to this the return of prosperity in the 1850's made the lot of the Welsh farmer much better.[29]

Although for the best part of twenty years after 1850 economic and social conditions in the rural areas of Wales improved considerably, one more element was injected into Welsh life in the second half of the century that added yet further insecurity to a situation which was far from stable. Beginning at mid-century the Welsh people became much more politically conscious, and under the influence of nonconformity became more radical in politics, taking up a position diametrically opposed to that of the landowners who remained loyal to Anglicanism and the Tory party in England. In part this was due to the resentment aroused by the Education Commissioners of 1847 with their sweeping indictments of the culture, religion, and morals of the Welsh people in addition to their more justified criticisms of the educational backwardness, ignorance, and illiteracy of the country. In the political life of Great Britain, Wales had played a very minor part since the days of the Tudors. The great debates over the American Revolution, the French Revolution, Catholic emancipation, Parliamentary reform, and such issues of importance had left Wales virtually untouched. The economic and social distress after 1815 gave rise to a nascent,

29. It is interesting to note that one Swansea Rebecca reminded his countrymen, "tied down to slavery and doomed to bondage by the insolence of the brutal English," that "man is born free and is endowed by his Creator with the inalienable right of life, liberty and the pursuit of happiness." Home Office Papers 45/254, July 25, 1843, quoted by Williams, *The Rebecca Riots*, p. 236.

politically radical movement but this was generally localized in the growing towns of South Wales like Merthyr Tydfil.[30]

Welsh politics and society, for the most part, remained dominated by the landowning gentry connected one to the other by family connections through marriage. Their control of the countryside was maintained through the offices they held; they were lord-lieutenants of the counties and justices of the peace. This control was made even firmer by their monopolization of Parliamentary representation, which in turn was made easier by the single-member representation of Welsh counties, unchanged until the Reform Act of 1832.

The great families of Wales were thus able to maintain continuity of control, free from challenge except by their peers. Unlike the Irish gentry, they were resident landlords with old Welsh names who were on reasonably good terms with their tenants until the nineteenth century and its problems increasingly drove a wedge between Welsh-speaking Welsh and Anglicized English-speaking Welsh. The remoteness of Wales and its denomination as something little more than a geographical expression by many in England produced the paradox of geographical remoteness begetting increasing political assimilation based on the traditional control by the gentry. Unlike Ireland or Scotland, Wales was in no position to struggle for political independence. The only reasonable course was to recognize the fact that England and Wales were closely bound together and to wrest political control from the hands of the gentry and restore it to Welsh Welshmen who would be more cognizant of the real needs of the Principality.

The twin bastions from which the attack on the political control of Wales by the gentry would be launched were the Welsh language and the nonconformist chapel pulpit. Despite official attempts to stamp out the Welsh language it remained the language of Wales until well into the 1870's. Welsh as a literary medium remained in a strong position and was stimulated by the holding of numerous local eisteddfodau for the assessing and rewarding of

30. See Gwyn A. Williams, "The Making of Radical Merthyr, 1800–1836," *Welsh History Review*, 1 (1961), 161–187.

written works in the Welsh language. The strong alliance of nonconformity with the Welsh language stimulated the use of the language for education, religious instruction, and general exhortation on matters concerning Wales. Moreover, nonconformist ministers became increasingly identified as the spokesmen for the people of Wales and were much respected. This was facilitated by the growth of a popular press for the expression of Welsh opinion, generally edited by ministers of the various denominations. The Baptists and the Independents were particularly active from the beginning of the nineteenth century. The Baptist *Seren Gomer* began in 1814 as a weekly newspaper in Welsh and was followed in 1821 by *Y Dysgedydd*, the organ of the Independents and Congregationalists, and by *Y Drysorfa*, a Calvinistic Methodist monthly magazine begun in 1819 and revived in 1831. After the repeal of the Stamp Acts in 1855, Welsh newspapers and periodicals expanded rapidly and became socially and politically more active. Until 1868, the Welsh language, religious nonconformity, and political radicalism supported each other and advanced together. As the Welsh gentry became less and less identifiable with the true interests of Wales, nonconformist ministers became the undisputed leaders of Welsh opinion whether in the pulpit or in the press.[31]

The great Reform Act of 1832 did not have much effect in Wales. The gentry and the great landowning families remained untouched. Only in the rising industrial towns of South Wales did the great industrialists like Sir John Guest begin to exert greater political influence. The treachery of the Blue Books in 1847 roused Wales from a state of political torpor and brought common cause between nonconformist disabilities and the status of Wales as a nation. Methodists joined Baptists and Independents in espousing new radical doctrines. By 1868 Welsh nonconformists had evolved into a political organization which did not lack for speakers or polemical literature.

Although the 1832 Act did not extend the franchise sufficiently

---

31. It should be noted, however, that although they spoke for Wales, they were lukewarm if not hostile to trade unionism and working-class movements which they associated with violence and disorder.

to pose any threat to the ruling political families, there was always the possibility of reprisals being taken by landlords against tenants who voted against them. One account given to the Royal Commission instanced an election in Carmarthenshire in 1837 when agents of the Earl of Cawdor sent out letters ordering tenants to give "a plumper for Colonel Trevor."[32] Four tenants who happened to be in arrears with their rent declined at first to vote for Trevor and were informed that "as they were so very independent and so very ungrateful for the indulgences and favours shown them by their landlord, he hoped to receive their rents by Lady Day . . . and then he should see what further was to be done in the matter."

This would seem to have been an early and isolated instance and there is no authenticated account of actual eviction for political disagreement before 1859. Comparatively few tenant farmers took an intelligent interest in politics beyond that of voluntarily supporting their landlords; most did not feel that what pressures were exerted necessarily encroached upon their rights as citizens.

In 1859, however, a violent political controversy erupted which coincided with a great religious revival which swept through Wales heightening the division between Anglicans and dissenters. The sitting member for Merionethshire was W. W. E. Wynne of Peniarth, an Anglo-Catholic, and he was opposed by a nonconformist Liberal landowner from Penrhyndeudraeth, David Williams. The landowners of Merionethshire sensing a threat to their position from the nonconformists instructed their tenants to vote for Wynne. Nineteen tenants on the Rhiwlas estate requested permission to abstain from voting and were interviewed by their landowner. Wynne was elected by three of the Rhiwlas tenants who persisted in abstaining from voting, and two others who voted for David Williams were evicted. Furthermore, Sir Watkin Williams Wynn on his Wynnstay estate raised the rents of eleven tenants who had abstained and evicted five others who voted for Williams. Although Sir Watkin denied bringing economic pressure to bear on his tenants for political purposes, it was clear to the Welsh peasantry that prompt payment of rent was no guarantee of continued

32. *Commission on Land in Wales*, 1896, p. 161.

tenancy. In fact, in 1860 one Cardiganshire landowner informed her tenants that they could either join the Church of England or leave her estate.[33] Among those evicted by Sir Watkin Williams Wynn was the widowed mother of Rev. Michael D. Jones, probably because of the son's opposition to landlordism in Wales. It was Michael D. Jones who would be responsible for the Welsh settlement in the Chubut Valley of Argentina in 1865. One pseudonymous writer at this time, "William Penn," gave it as his opinion that:

A small farmer who can hardly live in this country although he works day and night in wind and rain, ice and snow . . . learns that if he sells his stock and with the money pays for a passage for himself and his family to Wisconsin or Ohio . . . on arrival, he can buy a farm eight or ten times as large as the one he held in this country. . . . This has actually happened to several families who went to Northern America twenty years ago. The small farmer who would go across the Atlantic has the chance of seeing his children becoming princely freeholders instead of becoming slaves to some arch-Jesuit like Mr. Prince of Rhiwlas and his type. . . . A country where wages vary from 7s to 15s a day, or even higher, should have no fears for Welshmen.[34]

The election of 1865 saw a majority of Whigs or Liberals returned from Wales, but the real trial of strength came after the extension of the Reform Act of 1867, in the general election of 1868. The most resounding setback for the established Parliamentary interests was the election in Merthyr of the Reverend Henry Richard, the son of a Calvinistic Methodist minister, the most articulate nonconformist spokesman in Wales, and one of the strongest critics of the notorious Blue Books. For the rural areas, however, the most significant campaign occurred in Denbighshire. There the Liberal candidate was George Osborne Morgan, the son of a vicar of Conway but the great champion of Church disestablishment in Wales. Behind Morgan stood a Denbigh publisher, Thomas Gee, who became the leader of political nonconformity in North Wales. Denbighshire was a two-member constituency. Sir Watkin Williams Wynn had a firm hold on one seat, but for

33. *Baner Cymru* [Banner of Wales] (Denbigh), June 1, 1859.
34. *Ibid.*, August 24, 1859.

the second Morgan was elected over Colonel Biddulph of Chirk Castle on a platform which placed great stress on the tenurial uncertainties of the Welsh tenant farmer and upon his religious grievances. In the other rural counties, nonconformists were also successful. In Cardiganshire, the Vaughan family of Trawsgoed was defeated by a nonconformist Swansea shipbuilder. In Caernarvonshire, the wealthy Penrhyn interests were defeated by a socially unorthodox landowner, Thomas Love Jones-Parry, with strong support from nonconformist ministers. In Merionethshire, David Williams of Penrhyndeudraeth was finally returned to Parliament unopposed. It was not simply the rebuff to the old landed interests which made this election significant but the aftermath of the election when a policy of evicting tenants for disloyalty was resorted to. In the counties of Caernarvonshire, Cardiganshire, and Carmarthenshire an estimated seventy or more evictions took place.[35]

It was also alleged that Lord Penrhyn had dismissed some eighty quarrymen from his North Wales slate quarries. A typical pressure notice from a landlord was given to the Select Committee:

I have received a letter from Cardiganshire informing me that you are wavering in your opinion which side you will give your vote at the coming election. My opinion is that every man living on the property of the Church is bound to support it, otherwise he is a traitor to it. . . .[36]

The questions of persecution, pressure, and eviction were raised by Henry Richard in the House of Commons in July 1869. One letter from a man sent to make enquiries was quoted:

The expulsion of a large number of Liberal tenant farmers is a matter of scandal and notoriety. It is indeed heartrending to witness the agonizing emotions of families at the thought of having to leave the homes of their childhood. . . . Some of these families have lived upon their farms for centuries and are now like the Pilgrim Fathers about to seek a home in a foreign country where they may obtain the political and religious freedom which is denied them in their fatherland.[37]

35. *Report from the Select Committee on Parliamentary and Municipal Elections, Parliamentary Papers*, 1868–1869, VIII (1869), 244ff.

36. *Ibid.*, p. 244.

37. *Parliamentary Debates*, Series III, 197 (1869), 1295ff.

The furor over the 1868 election contributed in no small measure to the passing of the Ballot Act of 1872. The evictions, in addition to providing Wales with more martyrs, highlighted the divisions in rural and industrial Wales and contributed to the growth of Welsh political consciousness.[38]

One writer of the day summed up the position of the Welsh tenant farmers and advocated emigration to the United States as the only solution to their tribulations.

The temporal conditions of many poor farmers in this country is nothing better than "a ceaseless degradation, a daily martyrdom, a funeral procession to the grave" and to make it worse some of the Tory landlords are now about to advance the rents of their farms simply because their tenants at the last election refused their votes to the Tory candidates. It is useless to appeal to the landlords. I am afraid that their blindness to the condition of the people is of an incurable character.... The fact is we are too numerous here and there is no remedy save what comes from emigration. Emigration is the *only* relief for a country where labour, food and population bear such painful disproportion to each other. A few rich families possess the land of this kingdom and the rich and poor are becoming so much divided that they stand apart like two separate states or races and there is no hope for the poor but in emigration. Pauperism and crime are becoming every day more familiar as institutions among us. I believe the chief cause to be the overcrowded state of the country. Happily there is plenty of land in America and other countries for the whole population of Britain twenty times over. Let our poor farmers who are oppressed with heavy rates and taxes, let them go away and form a colony where their labour would make them independent and free and their children after them. Let them go together to some place where the poor, honest, industrious, noble-minded man should be honoured and respected.[39]

The importance of the part played by nonconformist ministers in Welsh politics was paralleled in the field of emigration. The leadership was taken by three outstanding ministers: Rev. Benjamin Chidlaw, Rev. Samuel Roberts, and Rev. Michael D. Jones.

Rev. Benjamin Chidlaw had emigrated as a child with his parents to Ohio. After attending university, he became the Congregational minister at Paddy's Run in 1835. He was much concerned

38. For the best study of Welsh politics in the nineteenth and early twentieth centuries see K. O. Morgan, *Wales in British Politics, 1868–1922* (Cardiff, 1963).

39. *Cambrian News* (Aberystwyth), April 10, 1869.

to maintain the Welsh language in the chapels of the Welsh settlements, and to improve his own knowledge of the language he returned to Wales in 1836. There, for the best part of two months he preached both the Gospel and the advantages and opportunities which America had to offer.[40] He returned to Wales once more in 1839 for eight months during which time he again urged his fellow countrymen to emigrate to the United States. In 1840, he published at Llanrwst a Welsh handbook for emigrants which contained good advice on where to settle, how to get to America, and what to take on the journey.[41] His pamphlet was given wide distribution in Wales and undoubtedly encouraged many of his countrymen to leave for the United States. On a much smaller scale Chidlaw did for the Welsh was Ole Rynning did for the Norwegians and Gottfried Duden did for the Germans.

Chidlaw was a close friend of the Reverend Samuel Roberts of Llanbrynmair in Montgomeryshire and his advocacy of the United States as the goal of Welsh emigration undoubtedly strengthened the latter's belief that only in the United States could the Welsh farmer escape his manifold disabilities and there establish Welsh settlements strong enough to maintain the Welsh language and Welsh culture. The other major influence upon Samuel Roberts was his cousin, William Bebb, governor of Ohio, whose parents had emigrated from Llanbrynmair in 1795.[42] Bebb was as keen as Chidlaw to foster large-scale Welsh emigration to the United States, and during the 1840's he and Roberts in Wales helped to plan the migration of numerous friends and relatives to farm sites in Illinois and later in Wisconsin. Bebb purchased a large tract of land in Winnebago County, Illinois, and although his plan for a large Welsh settlement there did not materialize, sufficient numbers of Welsh took up farms to create in Wales the impression that America was indeed a land of milk and honey.[43]

40. *Y Dysgedydd* [The Instructor], XV (July 1836).
41. B. W. Chidlaw, *Yr America . . . nodau ar daeth o Ddyffrin Ohio y Gymru . . . Hanes Sefydliadau Cymraeq yn America* (Llanrwst, 1840), reprinted in *Quarterly Publications of the Historical and Philosophical Society of Ohio*, 6 (1911), 1–41.
42. *Y Cronicl* [The Chronicle], VIII (July 1850).
43. N.L.W., MS. 14093C.

Roberts had been from his youth a fiercely independent and radical thinker and in 1843 brought out his own journal, *Y Cronicl*, which proved to be a most successful venture and made Roberts as its editor one of the most influential voices in Wales. In 1850 Roberts published a pamphlet entitled *Farmer Careful of Cil-Haul Uchaf* in which he lambasted landlords and their agents as robbers and oppressors of the Welsh farmer and advocated emigration to America as the only means by which Welsh farmers could escape the clutches of such thieves. He followed this up in 1852 with an article in *Y Cronicl* in which he returned to the subject of emigration and pointed out to the landlords that large numbers of people were leaving Llanbrynmair for the United States, were flourishing there, and were assisting others to follow them.[44] These emigrants, young and the flower of the Welsh people, were forced to leave Wales by the oppression of the landlords. Two years later *Diosg Farm: A Sketch of Its History during the Tenancy of John Roberts and His Widow* gave a moving account of the harsh treatment meted out to his family by their landlord. *Diosg Farm* set forth in personal terms the great dissatisfaction with their lot which so many Welsh farmers could understand.

During the years when Roberts had been pressing strongly for emigration, William Bebb's younger brother Evan had been making a successful career for himself in New York where he became known to a land and railroad promoter by the name of Edmund D. Saxton.[45] The younger Bebb, knowing that his brother was eager to establish an exclusive Welsh settlement in the United States, suggested that Saxton, and particularly an associate of his, Evan Bebb Jones, who was a distant relative of the Bebb family, could be useful for such a project. In 1855 Jones, who also was a native of Llanbrynmair, and ex-governor William Bebb arrived in Britain in search of financing for a local railroad enterprise but also much involved in planning settlements on lands in Kentucky and Tennessee that Jones had surveyed and now managed as agent for the

44. "Cofiant y Tri Brawd o Llanbrynmair a Conway," *Y Cronicl*, X (July 1852).
45. N.L.W., MS. 13195D.

eastern land companies, including Saxton's, that owned them.[46]

Bebb and Jones visited Llanbrynmair, and expressed astonishment that hardworking Welsh farmers should suffer such cruel exactions from their landlords when freehold farms could be obtained cheaply in America. To back up their claim to know the best lands for the Welsh in America they showed Samuel Roberts and his brother Richard a schedule of some forty thousand acres of land in Tennessee which Jones claimed he had surveyed. Roberts may have been misled by his American relatives or possibly the enthusiasm of Bebb and Roberts for founding a Welsh settlement in Tennessee warped their judgment. Whatever the reason, Samuel Roberts embarked upon a settlement venture in Tennessee with great optimism and little real understanding of what he was doing. As it seemed unlikely that potential emigrants would have sufficient finance to purchase large amounts of land, Roberts and a few associates decided to buy the land themselves and subsequently resell small sections to those of their fellow countrymen who wished to partake in the venture. By early 1856 Roberts and his associates had purchased something like seventy-five thousand acres in east Tennessee, in Scot, Anderson, Cumberland, Campbell, and Morgan counties, at fifty cents or less an acre.

Early in the spring of 1856 Roberts issued a two-page brochure announcing that he and his associates had one hundred thousand acres of land for sale comprising "hills and valleys springs and rivulets, well adapted for pasturage and the production of grains, grasses, vegetables, fruits and flowers in a climate justly celebrated for its salubrity and loveliness." They offered the land at half-a-crown per acre and pointed out that once developed the land would advance rapidly in value to that of one hundred dollars an acre which was the cost of land nearby. Once settled upon the land

---

46. Luther Thomas Deposit, Tennessee Papers, N.L.W., hereafter Tennessee Papers, N.L.W. These papers written in both Welsh and English are not easily worked. In many cases the quality of paper is poor, especially those written from Tennessee during the Civil War. In addition, Samuel Roberts used his own personal shorthand which defies interpretation. Nevertheless a rich source which forms the basis for the study of Roberts by Wilbur S. Shepperson, *Samuel Roberts: A Welsh Colonizer in Civil War Tennessee* (Knoxville, 1961).

they intended to "clear farms, erect habitations, and build up the churches, academies and schools . . . [for] flourishing neighbour-hoods of industrious, energetic and honest families, cultivating peace, charity and hospitality, loving the Bible and considering their latter end." The brochure concluded with the words, "In offering land so productive, in a place so healthful, within reach of so many advantages, under a government so liberal, on terms so *low as half-a-crown an acre*, they believe they are offering a rich boon to many whose burdens in this country are now heavy and growing heavier and heavier from year to year."[47]

The financing of the venture would seem to have come almost entirely from the Welshmen at Llanbrynmair. Bebb's contribution appears to have been mostly of an advisory nature and the super-vision of the first settlements in Tennessee.[48]

Despite widespread advertising, very few Welshmen came for-ward to participate in the scheme. Some thirty or forty tentatively forwarded small sums of money for land, and among them were purchasers from England and South Wales. The speed with which they subsequently withdrew was indicative of little confidence in Robert's plans and less enthusiasm for accompanying him to Ten-nessee. Roberts could hardly have chosen a less propitious time for his settlement. The economic upturn in rural Wales which had begun in the early 1850's had taken the edge off rural dissatisfaction and the outbreak of the Crimean War improved the economic situation in Britain as a whole. The increasingly disturbed situation in the United States between slave and free states was not conducive to emigration, particularly to a slave state. And, finally, Roberts' unrelenting attacks upon his landlord enemies seemed less appro-priate in the late fifties than a decade earlier.

Such misgivings as Roberts may have had were quickly dis-pelled by the enthusiastic reports which Bebb and Evan B. Jones

47. Tennessee Papers, N.L.W. The Welsh version of the prospectus differed only slightly from that in English but it would appear to have been drafted by the Welsh and the Americans in conjunction.

48. It remains something of a mystery how Roberts was able to raise the money to embark on a venture of this scale.

sent back from Tennessee. As a result, therefore, Roberts' younger brother Richard (Gruffydd Rhisiart) left with a small party for Philadelphia in June 1856. They travelled via Ohio and arrived in September 1856 at Nancy's Branch of Pine Creek near present-day Oneida to find two primitive log cabins constructed by Evan B. Jones as the nucleus of the settlement which late in September was officially named Brynyffynon.

Samuel Roberts, still in Wales, by furious letter writing and publicization of the Brynyffynon settlement pushed ahead with his plans to take out a larger contingent of settlers in 1857. The good offices of people like Richard Cobden and Henry Richard, M.P., were sought and Roberts sailed from Liverpool for America in May 1857 with a party of twenty to thirty Welshmen. By the end of May they had reached Cincinnati and stayed with friends and relatives at Paddy's Run in Ohio. This was as far as most of the party went. Originally they intended to follow Roberts to Tennessee, but reports from Brynyffynon did not encourage them to move further. By November the sum total of the Welsh settlement in Scott County, Tennessee, was the two Roberts brothers and Richard's wife and baby daughter.

To make the fiasco even worse, the Roberts brothers soon discovered that the titles to much of the land they had purchased were disputed, largely as the result of overlapping claims arising from imperfect surveying and inaccurate boundary markings. Law suits and court cases in Tennessee were accompanied by bitter and acrimonious correspondence with Welshmen who wanted their investments in the venture returned. John R. Jones, one of the original contributors to the venture, wrote to Samuel Roberts in March 1858 from Ohio and summed up much of the disillusionment of those involved:

I wish that I had never seen Mr. Bebb and E. B. Jones and that I had never heard of Tennessee. . . . It would be a blessing if it could be sold and if each one had his money back. . . . When I heard Mr. Bebb in Wales sighing and groaning that we were suffering such oppression, living on hopeless and sunless farms, boasting of the great fortune that he had made for us and the paradise that was to be had on this side of the Atlantic, who would not have expected something from him!! I have not seen him proving any of his claims and I judge he had nothing in view except his own pocket.[49]

The whole sorry business dragged on for years even after Samuel Roberts returned to Wales in 1867. The real hero of the Tennessee venture was Richard Roberts, who doggedly remained at Brynyf-fynon until 1870. Both before and during the Civil War, Samuel Roberts embarked on numerous and lucrative lecture tours through the northern states until his antipathetic views on war in general and on the Civil War in particular were published, which made him *persona non grata* in the North and a controversial figure in Wales where many believed that his failure to quit Tennessee showed him to be a southern and pro-slavery sympathizer.[50]

One can only guess at the effect which the Tennessee debacle had upon emigration from rural Wales. The times were clearly out of joint for a venture of this nature even if the gross mismanagement of the whole affair were ignored. Roberts' credibility in Wales would, henceforth, be suspect and as an advocate of emigration he was, after his return to Wales in 1867, singularly reticent.

The third of the trio of Welsh ministers who had great influence on emigration from rural Wales was Michael D. Jones, who like Samuel Roberts sought a solution to the problems of the Welsh tenant farmer in emigration to the United States. Once again William Bebb of Illinois seems to have been the stimulating influence. Writing to Jones at Bala, Merionethshire, in 1837 about Jones's sister, Mary Ann, who emigrated to Ohio in the 1830's, grew up in the Bebb household, and eventually married Evan B. Jones, he stated that he was eager to set in motion the emigration of Welshmen to America. His enthusiastic description of America and Ohio,

49. N.L.W., MS. 14093C.

50. Before the outbreak of the Civil War it is interesting to note that Roberts received an offer from Richard Cobden, an acquaintance of Anti–Corn Law days, of a square mile of land belonging to the Illinois Central Railroad. In 1859, Cobden went to the United States to investigate the landholdings of British stockholders. He was accompanied by his brother-in-law, Hugh Williams, a former Welsh Chartist who was in contact with Roberts in Tennessee. Cobden decided that more immigrants from Britain would have to be attracted to settle on the Illinois Central lands. The offer was made to Roberts to act as an emigration promotion agent in Wales and in the American Welsh communities for the railroad. Roberts declined the offer. N.L.W., MS. 13197C.

in particular with such phrases as "No man is a beggar here from necessity" and "You would bid a last farewell to tythes, lords and beggars," encouraged Jones to emigrate to America in 1847.[51] He was ordained a Congregational minister in Cincinnati and founded a "Cymdeithas y Brython," a Welsh society to deal with the problems of Welsh immigrants. Jones was fanatical about the need to preserve Welsh culture and the Welsh language as the core of the Welsh nation but came to the realization that in the United States, Americanization was too strong a force for this to be possible. He returned to Wales in 1853 to succeed his father as principal of Bala College. On a lecture tour of the United States a few years later he briefly considered the possibility of founding a settlement, similar to that of Samuel Roberts in Tennessee, in Wisconsin, a state eager to encourage the settlement of Welsh immigrants. His earlier belief that the Welsh could not survive as Welshmen in a sea of Americans was confirmed and he began to look elsewhere for a place for settlement that would be more remote and less populous. He therefore sent out two emissaries to Patagonia in South America who reported favorably on Argentina as a place for a Welsh settlement. Jones approached the Argentinian government for land in the Chubut Valley for an exclusive Welsh settlement. Finally in July 1865 a party of 153 emigrants (but without Jones) set sail from Liverpool on the *Mimosa* for the Chubut River. The project was ill-conceived and the terrain and climate difficult. The settlement survived only with help from the governments of Argentina and Great Britain. Although many Welsh-Americans were enthusiastic about the venture, few, if any, left the United States for Argentina, and those who had been burned in the Tennessee scheme had no inclination to try yet another uncertain venture.[52]

Thus the attempts made by Roberts and Jones to found exclusive Welsh settlements had very little success. Nevertheless, their advocacy of emigration and the knowledge of and interest in America

51. Herbert Bebb, *Bebb Genealogy: The Descendants of William Bebb and Martha Hughes of Llanbrynmair, Wales* (Chicago, 1944), pp. 54–58, quoted by Wilbur S. Shepperson, *British Emigration to North America* (Oxford, 1957), p. 70.

52. The definitive work on the Welsh settlement in Argentina is in Welsh, Byrn Williams, *Y Wladfa Patagonia* (Cardiff, 1963).

which they generated did result in individuals leaving for the United States, generally for the older established Welsh communities in New York, Pennsylvania, and Ohio which for long were used as staging posts by those who needed to find their feet before committing themselves to settling in other parts of America. The ease with which Welsh nonconformist ministers moved back and forth across the Atlantic is surprising, and the contacts which were maintained between Wales and America facilitated the flow of Welsh emigrants to the United States.

Although various arguments were put forward by advocates of emigration in Wales to persuade their countrymen to quit the country of their birth, the objective advantages of the New World over conditions in Wales were probably more effective than persuasion in uprooting a peasantry which clung with surprising tenacity to its few acres of soil in Wales. These advantages were set out with care in letters from America by those who had already taken the plunge, and their effect on stimulating further emigration should not be underestimated.

To this must be added the promotional advertisements of American railroad companies looking for immigrants to take up their lands. These appeared frequently in the Welsh press in both Welsh and English. The impact of one typical advertisement by the Union Pacific Railroad in 1873 can easily be imagined. The company offered for sale twelve million acres of the best agricultural, grazing, and mining land in America. Nebraska was described as a land where

the gentle Spring and wonderful Summer pour down their blessings from over-flowing coffers and only the playing of the red deer and the wonderful singing of the birds break the silence. Waggonroads which reveal the black earth, cross green and verdant slopes where the tall grass of the prairies waves in the breeze.[53]

Many were, doubtless, skeptical of such overblown rhetoric, but letters sent home by kinsmen and former neighbors were generally accepted as reliable. Many of these letters have survived in the orig-

53. *Baner ac Amserau Cymru* (Denbigh), 1873, *passim.*

inal, but a greater number are known from their publication in one or other of the many periodicals and newspapers which flourished in Wales during the nineteenth century in both the English and Welsh languages. Some of these periodicals lasted for only a few numbers before collapsing, to be revived at a later date; others like *Yr Eurgrawn Wesleyaidd*, which commenced publication in 1809, continue to the present day. These were largely denominational magazines, edited by ministers who devoted much space to theological argument. They were also, however, the main channels for publishing emigrants' letters, and advocated in some cases the advantages, in other the disadvantages, of emigration to the United States. The most important of the newspapers which carried emigrant letters and editorialized on emigration as a possible solution to the problems facing the Welsh farmer were *Baner ac Amserau Cymru*, *The Flintshire Observer*, *Seren Cymru*, *Y Gwladgarwr* (the most America-conscious of all Welsh newspapers), *Yr Herald Cymraeg*, and the *Merthyr Telegraph*.[54]

Letters from Welsh people in America were published in both English and Welsh but the great majority were written in Welsh, as might be expected, since they were directed at a predominantly Welsh-speaking peasantry. The letters written from the rural areas of the United States were overwhelmingly in favor of the Welsh farmer emigrating to America and of the advantages to be gained by leaving Wales. Much of their contents, aside from personal matters, referred to the availability of land, the prices of crops and food, freedom from the control of landlords, the absence of tithes and taxes, the wages that could be secured by those unable to take up land immediately, political freedom, the state of religion in the new country, and details on the best way to cross the Atlantic. In short, most emigrant letters were mini-manuals for intending emigrants. The only despondent note struck by some on occasion was the inability of the emigrants to retain the Welsh language. This is particularly reflected in manuscript letters where difficulty in writing in Welsh is often apparent. Some letters, in fact, were in

54. For a fuller and more detailed analysis see Alan Conway, *The Welsh in America* (Minneapolis, 1961), pp. 330–332.

themselves indices of assimilation in that they were written in a mixture of Welsh and English.

A brief selection of typical emigrant letters which were given wide circulation in Wales will indicate the part played in Welsh emigration to the United States by those who from example and experience were in a position to exert leverage upon those of their compatriots who were trying to decide whether to emigrate and what the best places were for settlement.

Typical of the sort of advice about crossing the Atlantic was that given by the Reverend Benjamin Chidlaw writing to a friend in 1836:

From Liverpool you can get passage in American ships for £2 to £3. It is best to prepare oatbread, butter, cheese and meat in Wales. Everything else you can get in Liverpool like tea, treacle, flour, and potatoes. It is not necessary to bring any drink, particularly intoxicating liquor. Drinking at sea is bad for you. . . . Some are more liable to sea-sickness than others. Many get it because they are careless about taking salts, castor oil etc. before and after going on the ship. Change in living and idleness affect the body a great deal. The best treatment is to take physic and be on deck with your fellow-travellers. Loneliness of spirit is half the illness. A plaster of saffron on the stomach while at sea will keep the illness away.[55]

Twenty years later when steamships were making the emigrants' lot more bearable on the Atlantic crossing, the Reverend Samuel Roberts wrote:

Every emigrant should get well-bound boxes to carry his luggage. . . . The hinges and locks of about half of our boxes were broken. Many were ruined completely and much of their contents spoiled. The easiest way to carry linen, eiderdowns, clothes, etc. is to roll them up tightly, stitch them up and bind them with sacking instead of putting them in boxes. . . . There is more food to be had on the steamships than on the sailing ships. There is plenty of food aboard and that of the best kind. Their flour pudding was most tasty and quite as good as any porridge and sugar in Wales.[56]

A decade later, "Morddal" gave the following advice to his countrymen:

55. *Y Dysgedydd*, XV (July 1836).
56. *Y Cronicl*, XV (October 1857).

Once aboard it is like being in Paddington station at excursion time. Men are moving around like wild bees and this is the place for busybodies to learn to mind their own business. . . . It is better not to try to eat for three or four days but to stay hungry. . . . The food is pretty coarse and emigrants should try to lay in something for the voyage, things which will keep for two or three weeks without going off. The best things to prepare are a few of the best biscuits because the biscuits on the ship are like bones . . . a little currant bread, pickles, cheese and uncooked bacon, etc. . . . There is plenty of drink on sale but no food except that obtained by cunning and the kindness of the cooks. It is worth remembering that you get sixpence worth for every shilling. . . . Watch over your things on the last day aboard because there is every kind of creature here. Consider every man a thief until he proves the opposite. . . .[57]

Initial reactions to America on landing were generally favorable. Typical was a letter from Robert Williams written from New York soon after his arrival there in 1844.[58] He was clearly impressed by the prosperity around him.

The houses are excellent, mostly of brick and the meeting houses are like temples so that we in Wales would not believe that Nonconformists had such houses for worshiping God. Independence is seen on every face, not scared and frightened of bishop or priest. The people dress and live well. The farmers of Wales would be amazed to see the tables of the poor spread with five or ten course dishes at every meal.

For the small farmer of Wales, whether laborer, leaseholder, or freeholder, the information which could prove decisive for emigration concerned land and crops. Almost without exception, letters received throughout the nineteenth century in Wales were enthusiastic about the opportunities for Welsh emigrants in the rural areas of the United States.

As early as October 1817, David Jones, writing from Albany, New York, maintained:

Whoever has the heart and the resolution to come here will never be sorry after he once sets foot on the land. . . . In Steuben where all the old Welsh are collected together the earth is black and full of trees, the finest your eyes ever beheld. . . . I live better here now than I have ever lived before. . . . There is room for every man to get his stomach full of porridge without having to go begging from house to house. . . . If any of you are coming here take care not

---

57. *Y Gwladgarwr* [The Patriot] (Aberdare), August 17, 25, 1866.
58. *Y Bedyddiwr*, III (August 1844).

to come by the slate ships from Caernarvon. Walk to Liverpool for that will be cheaper in the long run. . . .[59]

David Jones's views were confirmed by John Richards, writing in November 1817 from Warren County, New York.

Millions of people can have land to work on in this country and they will be able to make it their own for ever after a few years of hard work. . . . The land here is not so fertile as in some of the western parts of the State but our land generally bears twenty to thirty bushels of rye or oats on each acre. I had 350 bushels of potatoes from one acre. . . . The price of land is from four to five dollars an acre and ten years or more to pay for it. . . . One can have land in parts of Ohio, Michigan and Indiana, very good land too, for two dollars an acre. . . .[60]

One of the few who were clearly opposed to the Welsh emigrating to the United States was William Thomas, who wrote from Utica, New York, in August 1818:

If it were not for the canal many of the Welsh would be without work. I beg all of my old neighbors not to think of coming here. . . . My advice to them is to love their district and stay there. I am thinking of coming home myself this Spring if I have support from the Lord. . . . The land is a desolate wilderness of uncleared timber and not worth the Welsh buying it. . . . I would rather work in the Old Country for eight guineas than get £20 here.[61]

Through the 1820's and 1830's, Pennsylvania and Ohio also had their advocates, but one of the best summaries of the advantages of emigration was that provided by Lewis Howell writing from New York in August 1844.

I have allowed myself a couple of hours to afford as far as I am able the wavering, hard-pressed, half-starved laborers of Wales an opportunity of judging which country is the best and of deciding the very important question "Which is best, to go or not to go?" and to advise as to the preparation for the voyage and above all to give particular warning to avoid the Liverpool and New York lodginghouse keepers . . . emigrant plunders—a set of lazy, ravenous scamps. . . .

To a stranger just landed from Europe, the first objects which attract his attention are its people, all so neatly and comfortably clad—the expression of

59. N.L.W., MS. 2722E. Jones was semiliterate in both Welsh and English.
60. *Ibid.*
61. *Ibid.*

happiness depicted upon every countenance. The stranger is involuntarily led to enquire where are the working-classes—the tattered and half-fed, miserable-looking starvelings . . . of his native land. . . . Even amidst the rudeness and wildness that surrounds the *poor* American farmer, he is perfectly happy and in a fair way of realizing a happy independence—whereas the poor Welsh farmer is continually *poor* and has no hope but the grave to extricate him from his miserable poverty.[62]

In the 1840's as settlement moved westward, Wisconsin received its share of praise as a place to obtain land. John H. Evans writing home in February 1842 reported:

In Ohio . . . one can get good farms from eighteen to twenty five dollars [an acre] but Wisconsin Territory is the place for the Welsh . . . it is said that the country is extremely healthy, the water clean, the air pure and the climate temperate . . . and land is to be had for one dollar to one dollar and a quarter an acre.[63]

His views were confirmed by Richard and Margaret Pugh, who wrote in November 1846 from Prairie Ville.

I found the country better than I had expected and I have bought an improved farm of 160 acres—two yoke of oxen, four cows, six yearlings and a lot of pigs and sheep with every kind of poultry . . . I would not for a considerable sum return to Wales again. The tax-gatherer only calls once a year in this country and then it is only a trifle. . . . There is not half the trouble to farm in this country as in England or Wales. We can raise five or six crops of wheat on the same ground without paying so much as a lime bill or manure of any kind. . . . We can eat our beefsteaks or ham every morning with our breakfast.[64]

John and Isaac Cheshire, writing to their parents on New Year's Day 1847 from Racine, Wisconsin, contrasted the situation in America with that in Wales where the "hungry forties" were having their effect.

We are very glad that we have come here. It would be better for you to do the same and that soon. We have plenty of reasons for this. One is that there is so much poverty there and likely to become worse all the time. According to what we hear in this country, we understand that the potatoes are rotting

62. *The Cambrian*, October 12, 1844, original in English.
63. N.L.W., Cwrtmawr MS. 1044E.
64. *The Welshman* (Carmarthen), January 8, 1847, original in English.

in the ground and that you have had a very poor harvest in addition, with many in great distress and some fresh trouble afflicting the country all the time. . . . The potatoes here are quite healthy and plenty to be had for eighteen cents a measure and a barrel of flour for about three dollars. Beef from about one to three cents a pound. . . . This is a good place to get a farm: you can get one within five miles of the town of 120 acres with a house and buildings on it with about twenty-five acres already cultivated for $800. They are cheaper further away from the town. . . .[65]

By the 1850's, Iowa was being pressed upon the Welsh farmer as the ideal place for settlement. One unidentified Welsh settler in Llewellyn, Iowa, wrote to his family in March 1856:

I am sure there is no more fertile land in creation than in the state of Iowa. It produces crops without any need of manure—from five to twenty feet of rich black earth. One can see miles of it as flat as a board without a single stone. . . . After plowing it once it is like a garden. . . . It is a healthy county and it is cheap. The price of land from the government is about 5s 3d in your money. Here you get it for less than a year's rent in Wales. . . . I have talked with men who have been here three or four years and they had but little or nothing to start with and now some of them are worth their thousands of dollars. . . .[66]

After the Civil War, Kansas and Nebraska in their turn were pictured as the New Canaan for the Welsh people. The son of a Welsh farmer wrote from Emporia, Kansas, in July 1870:

Emporia is a Welsh town. They are all Welsh people who live here. There is not a public-house on her body. Kansas is a splendid place for a man who has got £200 to come out and buy a farm. He can get land at $1.50 an acre and as good as there is in the valley of Towey. . . . Some men I know here keep three or four hundred head of cattle and they have not a yard of land of their own and don't pay a cent for grass. They keep their cattle on the prairies, land which has not been enclosed. . . .[67]

That settlement in Nebraska was not entirely haphazard and left to individual initiative is evident from a letter written by John N. Lewis of Carmarthen to his countrymen in April 1873 from Platte County, Nebraska.

65. Original in private possession. Copy in N.L.W.
66. *Seren Cymru* [Star of Wales] (Carmarthen), April 4, 1857.
67. *South Wales Press* (Llanelly), August 18, 1870, original in English.

In the State of Nebraska in Platte County there is a piece of land put by for the Welsh by that fine Welshman, Mr. D. Jones of Carmarthen, an agent of the Union Pacific Railroad . . . who has succeeded in persuading the railroad company to deed it to him for those who have been evicted from their farms in Wales. . . . It is unusually fertile and I can say that I have never seen such crops before. . . . There would not be an inch unsold had not Mr. Jones made sure of it and Welshmen owe him a great debt. . . . He comes out two or three times a year with emigrants.[68]

David Davies, writing from Platte County, Nebraska, in June 1874 expressed astonishment that his fellow countrymen were so reluctant to emigrate.

What a pity that the farmers of Wales care so little about emigrating to this fertile land. They are missing a chance that they will never get again. I often wonder why the farmers of Wales prefer to stay there, ploughing up trees and stones and paying such high rents for improvements. If they only came here they would have a farm of their own extremely cheaply. I think that this country is rather like Canaan which the Lord chose of the Israelites.[69]

The paean of praise for America continued throughout the nineteenth century and across the continent. In January 1886 John Lewis wrote to his friends from Big Bend Settlement, Washington Territory:

We consider that coming here was one of the wisest moves in our lives. We have 320 acres of land—one mile long by half a mile wide—and the land is generally as flat as from Dolfawr to Pontrhydfendigaid without one stone larger than a bird's egg. The land is much more fertile even than in Dolfawr. Within two months we will have 450 acres of land for ever. This is more than we could have hoped to have owned around Pontrhydfendigaid in two hundred years. We are amazed that anyone knowing the wonderful advantages of this country can stay in Wales.[70]

It is impossible to assess how much influence such letters had upon emigration from rural Wales. The indications are that they were very significant in inducing emigration by relatives or friends. The little success enjoyed by such organized ventures as the Ten-

---

68. *Baner ac Amserau Cymru*, April 23, 1873.
69. *Seren Cymru*, August 14, 1874.
70. *Baner ac Amserau Cymru*, March 17, 1886. For further and more extensive examples of such letters from emigrants see Conway, *The Welsh in America*.

nessee settlement strengthens the argument that the Welsh farmer emigrated individually or in small family groups relying on family connections to facilitate his initial settlement in the United States. At the same time, it must be recognized that emigration from the industrial parts of Wales, primarily in the second half of the nineteenth century, flowed more strongly than from the rural areas even though the tone of emigrant letters became increasingly hostile to emigration from Wales as the century progressed. The basic economic forces which stimulated emigration from South Wales in particular overrode the adverse comments of those already settled in the industrial centers of the United States.

### B. EMIGRATION FROM INDUSTRIAL WALES

Emigration to the United States from the industrial centers of South Wales was to a considerable degree an extension of emigration from the rural areas of Wales. The prosperity which marked the decades of the 1850's and 1860's declined rapidly in the 1870's until the fall of 1879 when Wales once more entered upon a quarter of a century of severe rural depression. As a result rural migration to South Wales and emigration to the United States became intertwined.

By 1880, the population pattern of Wales had changed dramatically as the result of the great migration of Welshmen from the rural areas to the South Wales coalfield. The phenomenal increase in the population of Monmouthshire and Glamorganshire testified to the attractive powers of the iron and steel and coal mining towns of South Wales. Rural depopulation and urban growth which became such a marked feature of Wales in the second half of the nineteenth century were but the two faces of the same population coin.

For some Welshmen in the rural areas migration to the industrial centers of South Wales was only a knight's move in their emigration to the United States. For the majority it was a final rejection of rural life for the higher wages and greater amenities which industry could provide even though urban slums showed little improvement over rural squalor. Employment in the ironworks and in the

mines offered them no more security than their precarious existence as tenant farmers or laborers on the land had done. Strikes,
lockouts, and violence, the inevitable concomitants of industrialization in the nineteenth century, hardly made for a comfortable
or settled life. Yet, in good times, wages were relatively high and
the rewards for hard and dangerous work greater than those which
could be obtained as a landless laborer. Had South Wales not developed into one of the world's industrial centers there can be little
doubt that the exodus of Welsh men and women to the United
States would have been far greater—in fact, Wales could well have
become another Ireland on a smaller scale.

The full impact of industrialization on Wales was not felt until
after 1850, but the iron industry which had existed in both North
and South Wales from medieval times was of major importance
from the beginning of the nineteenth century.[71] The early iron
industry of Wales was quite haphazard in its development. It depended very much upon the availability of wood for charcoal and
water for power. The result was that in the middle of the eighteenth century there were less than three dozen small ironworks
scattered throughout the Principality. The only two centers wor-
thy of the name were Pontypool in South Wales and Bersham near
Wrexham in North Wales. As long as the making of iron was
linked to wood and water no substantial progress could be expected.
In the second half of the eighteenth century, however, attention
was given to the use of coal for iron smelting with the result that
by the beginning of the nineteenth century some two thousand
men were working in six furnaces at Cyfarthfa, near Merthyr.
A decade later fifty furnaces were in operation employing from
twelve to fifteen thousand men.

The ironworks of South Wales were initially established in a
highly restricted area less than twenty miles long and little more
than a mile wide, from Hirwaun to Blaenavon. The steep, narrow
valleys of the area topped by ranges of high hills made housing for

71. The two standard works on the industrialization of Wales are A. H. Dodd, *The
Industrial Revolution in North Wales* (Cardiff, 1933), a work of immense scholarship,
and A. H. John, *The Industrial Development of South Wales, 1750–1850* (Cardiff, 1950).

the workmen and communication between the works very difficult. The great advantages of the area were that in addition to iron ore, coal was easily and amply available near to the surface, limestone for use in the smelting furnaces was within close reach, and millstone grit for lining the furnaces was in plentiful supply. The great natural advantages of the area were seized upon by capitalists from outside of Wales who brought to bear not only their knowledge of new techniques in the manufacturing of iron but also outstanding business ability.[72]

The future of the industry, however, would turn very much upon new inventions and processes such as the steam engine, "puddling" or the "Welsh method" whereby carbon impurities were removed from the molten iron, and the "hot blast" which raised furnace heats significantly and improved the quality of the iron. The use of anthracite for smelting was pioneered by David Thomas, the superintendent of the Ynyscedwyn ironworks near Ystalyfera. In 1839 he emigrated to Pennsylvania to set up furnaces there using local anthracite, and in the next fifty years thousands of Welsh ironworkers and miners followed him there to settle at Scranton and Wilkes Barre. Subsequent developments such as the Bessemer "converter" and the Siemens "open hearth" systems, the latter pioneered at Landore in 1867, increased immensely the production of steel in South Wales. Primacy in steelmaking and tinplating was maintained well down into the nineteenth century, but by the closing decades of the century European countries and the United States had developed their own industries and had cut severely into former Welsh markets.

The growth of the iron and steel industry in South Wales saw an increase also in coalmining which eventually superseded iron and steel in economic importance. Until the middle of the nineteenth

72. The iron industry was not, of course, limited to South Wales. The Bersham works in North Wales was one of the first to use coke for iron smelting. Ironworks were set up at Brymbo in 1795 to be followed by others in the Flintshire and Denbighshire areas of the North Wales coalfield with the main centers at Wrexham and Holywell. But the great population movements of the nineteenth century were to South Wales and, while industry in North Wales remained almost static, iron and steel subsequently followed by coal mining in South Wales became increasingly dominant in the economy.

century coal was mined in levels or drifts: very few shafts were sunk to any great depths. In 1865, however, the Rhondda valleys were opened up. Two tremendously deep shafts were sunk at Cwmparc and Ton in the Rhondda Fawr to get at the coal seam which reached its greatest depth there. The growth of the coal industry was due in part to the changeover from sail to steam. Welsh steam coal was superior to all others, and production grew to meet the demand. Thus coalmining moved from being simply a service industry to iron and steel to becoming a major industry in its own right, producing by World War I some sixty million tons of coal annually in South Wales.

The spectacular growth of the iron and steel industry and later that of the sale-coal industry was due in part to the fortunate coincidence of raw materials on the South Wales coalfield, in part to the managerial and business abilities of English and Welsh entrepreneurs, and in part to technological inventions and processes.[73] Two further elements were, however, essential for full development: greatly improved transportation systems and a large reservoir of cheap manpower.

As has been seen in the discussion of rural Wales, communications have always been difficult because of the physiography of the country. Little road building had ever been done, and travel between North and South Wales was easier by sea than by land. The turnpike companies of the eighteenth century brought about some improvements, especially after they adopted the new surfaces developed by Telford and Macadam. Such roads, however, were of little help in the transportation of iron and coal in great quantities. Recourse was had to canal construction which, although seriously limited by the mountainous nature of much of Wales, did provide the means whereby heavy loads of iron, coal, and limestone could be moved relatively cheaply and easily from the works to the ports.

Railroads in Wales evolved from horse-drawn tram roads which were used to link the more inaccessible parts of the country with

73. It is worth noting that whereas the iron industry was controlled almost entirely by Englishmen, the coal industry owed its growth to the efforts of Welshmen. In both industries, however, the great majority of workmen were Welsh-speaking Welshmen.

the canals. Until 1848 railroad construction was limited to short lines closely associated with the coalfields. In South Wales the lines ran between Cardiff, Merthyr, and Aberdare, and between Swansea and Pontardulais. In North Wales, Chester, Ruabon, and Shrewsbury were linked. From 1849 major through routes were constructed. In North Wales the railroad was completed between Chester and Holyhead. In South Wales, Newport was linked to Cardiff, Swansea, Carmarthen, Haverfordwest, and Milford by 1856. By 1864 the railroad through central Wales from Shrewsbury had reached Aberystwyth on the west coast. The construction of railroads was primarily concerned with the needs of industry and east-west trunk lines, and did not conform to any national plan. Yet the railroads did provide one tortuous link between North and South Wales which proved very beneficial to Welsh emigrants making their way to the United States.

In the early years of the nineteenth century, emigrants such as George Roberts, the uncle of Samuel Roberts of Llanbrynmair, had had to walk from Montgomeryshire to Bristol. Others had secured passage on the infrequent slate ships from Caernarvon or the equally infrequent timber ships from west coast ports like Aberystwyth and Newquay. A few made their way as best they could to London. With the growth of Liverpool as the primary port of emigration to the United States, most emigrants were forced to make their way thither. Without the railroad through mid-Wales and along the border counties this would have been most difficult and would have had an adverse effect on emigration from both rural and industrial Wales. As it was Liverpool became the focal point of Welsh emigration, with dozens of agents operating from that city and advertising widely in both the English and Welsh languages in the Welsh newspapers and denominational periodicals. They also employed subagents in most of the major towns whose task it was to encourage emigration locally and see that intending emigrants were channelled through the main agents in Liverpool. There, Welsh-speaking Welshmen with names like Eleazar Jones and Noah M. Jones (Cymro Gwyllt) provided them with lodgings in which a strict adherence to temperance was maintained, secured passage for them on selected vessels which were sound and seaworthy, assisted in the purchase of supplies and equipment for the voyage, transported the emigrants to the docks, found the best places for them in steerage aboard ship, and sent them away with recommendations to Welsh-speaking lodging-house keepers in New York and Philadelphia who would look after them on their arrival.[74] Without the railroad, it would have been very much more difficult for the Liverpool emigration agents to tap the lucrative South Wales emigration market.

As has already been mentioned, labor in large amounts and at cheap rates was also essential for the development of industry on the South Wales coalfield. It was fortunate for ironmasters and coal owners that the need for labor coincided with an upsurge in population accompanied by depression in the rural areas. It was also fortunate for many in the rural areas that they were able to find in the industrial regions an escape from rural poverty, even though this economic safety valve produced its own peculiar problems.

Early industry was concentrated around Neath and Swansea and along the northeastern rim of the coalfield where the iron industry was dominant. The result was a number of settlements running from Aberdare to Pontypool around the rim of the coalfield. In part, the labor force built up there was a short-distance movement of population from local sources, skilled labor especially being drawn from the early metallurgical centers. In part, however, the labor force came to be drawn from further afield, from southwest Wales and from Cardiganshire in mid-Wales. This labor was for the most part unskilled, travelling relatively long distances to seek employment in the ironworks and collieries. In this way much agricultural labor was drained off from Carmarthenshire to Merthyr where it adapted fairly rapidly to industrial conditions.[75] Welsh peasants were traditionally more mobile than their English coun-

74. None of the records of the day-to-day activities of emigration agents at Liverpool or within the Principality seem to have survived. Should such records come to light, they would be invaluable in revealing a great deal about the mechanics of emigration and the motives of those Welshmen who decided to leave Wales for the United States.

75. *Royal Commission on Education in Wales*, pp. 309–310.

terparts and accustomed to moving over very long distances. Thus the age-old summer migrations to English counties such as Herefordshire and Gloucestershire were replaced or added to by winter migration to the ironworks.[76] This mobility was also evident within the industrial areas, young men, particularly, moving frequently from valley to valley and from works to works in search of higher wages. The labor force thus remained undisciplined, unstable, and constantly restless.

Even by 1850 labor was still not sufficient to meet the needs of industry, but after that date a much heavier movement of population took place with the coal mines absorbing by far the greater number. This period saw the rapid growth of the Rhondda valleys which had a scattered rural population of little more than 1,600 in 1831, a population of 11,735 in 1861 largely dependent upon coal mining at Pontypridd, and a population of 163,000 in 1921. By 1861 South Wales also had a population of nearly 18,000 Irish living in colonies at the ports and in the iron-making districts. Fleeing from the appalling conditions of post-famine Ireland on ships plying between Wales and Ireland, they were regarded with great hostility by the Welsh as a source of cheap, unskilled labor which could be used by the ironmasters and coal owners to undermine the bargaining position of Welshmen out on strike. This hostility between Welsh and Irish, exacerbated by their religious differences, was transferred with the emigrants to the United States. The emigrant ships, where Welsh and Irish demonstrated their enmity toward each other in the cramped confines of the steerage, were a microcosm of their relationships in Wales and in the United States.[77]

In the first half of the nineteenth century the influx of labor into coal mining was not great. Professor Brinley Thomas suggests that the labor required for the expansion of the industry came from

76. *Ibid.* There is no evidence of the "padrone" system operating between the rural and industrial areas although undoubtedly informal family or village connections were maintained.

77. For examples of Welsh-Irish hostility aboard emigrant ships see Conway, *The Welsh in America*, pp. 14–50.

"the natural increase of a notoriously prolific section of the population."[78] Even between 1861 and 1871 migration to Glamorganshire was still of moderate proportions, but between 1871 and 1914 the number of coalminers in Glamorganshire rose almost fourfold from thirty-four to one hundred fifty thousand.[79] In the decade between 1861 and 1871 the bulk of the migrants came from the neighboring counties of Cardigan, Pembroke, Carmarthen, Brecknock, and Monmouth; but as the century progressed and the volume of migration increased the labor force came from greater distances within Wales and also from counties outside of Wales such as Gloucester, Somerset, Devon, and Cornwall. By the end of the century, a great mass of people had come together on the coalfield with population density in some areas being as high as four thousand and more to the square mile. On a much smaller scale, similar aggregations of population had taken place on the North Wales coalfield and in the slate-quarrying areas of Caernarvonshire and Merionethshire.

The increase of population in the South Wales coalfield was not, however, constant. In boom periods such as that of 1872–1874 when wages for all those involved in the mining of coal were phenomenally high, the drawing power on population was abnormally strong. On the other hand, the depression years of 1875–1879, when wages fell fifty percent and more, saw the exodus of over fifteen thousand people from Glamorganshire either back to the rural areas or to England or to the United States and especially to Pennsylvania.[80] Professor Thomas again suggests, however, that wage fluctuations in themselves were not necessarily decisive in causing permanent migration away from the coalfield.[81] The cycles

78. Brinley Thomas, "The Migration of Labour into the Glamorganshire Coalfield, 1801–1911," *Economica*, 10 (1930), 276.

79. *Ibid.* The total population of Monmouthshire and Glamorganshire had increased dramatically between 1801 and 1851, that of Monmouthshire from 45,568 to 157,418; that of Glamorganshire from 70,897 to 231,849.

80. In the last decade of the nineteenth century a further 35,000 left Glamorganshire as a result of recession.

81. Thomas, "The Migration of Labour into the Glamorganshire Coalfield," p. 291.

of boom and depression, he explains, taught the miner that in the nature of things a period of low wages would be followed by a period of prosperity. Thus a temporary tightening of the belt, the dispatch of daughters to be servants in English households, and an increase in output per man-hour were used as temporary stopgaps until a period of high wages returned. It was mainly when these periods of high wages seemed unnaturally long in reappearing that emigration to the United States became more attractive. There is much validity in Professor Thomas' argument, particularly when placed in the geographical context of the isolation of the South Wales coalfield from other heavily urbanized areas. Nevertheless, significant numbers of South Wales miners did emigrate to the United States, which may well have been the result of the lack of immediate urbanized areas to provide a short-distance, if temporary, alternative to staying in Wales.

The rapid industrialization of Wales contrasted strongly with the slower pace of industrialization in England. As a result there was little time for an industrial tradition or a real working-class movement to develop in Wales. The social impact of this rapid industrialization in a relatively constricted area was also much more dramatic. Although a large proportion of the population of the South Wales coalfield (and an even greater proportion in North Wales) was Welsh-speaking Welshmen, the influx of English from the western counties added to that of the Irish gave rise to social problems along ethnic lines. To this must be added the significant division between English management and a Welsh labor force in the ironworks. In the coal mines the ethnic division did not exist to the same extent since many of the coal owners were themselves Welsh. Here, however, industrial strife between owners and colliers was sufficiently intense to make the mines no more harmonious than were the ironworks.

The bleakness of the industrial scene was not improved by the fact that industrialization took place in areas of open moorland and steep, narrow valleys. When the pressure of population began to build up, serious problems of accommodating the labor force presented themselves. Houses were hastily and shoddily constructed around the ironworks and coal mines.[82] The responsibility for providing housing lay with the employers, who quickly realized that the control of company houses was a useful bludgeon when industrial disputes and strikes took place.

The geophysical nature of the mining valleys posed further problems. Their very narrowness and the steepness of the hills rising immediately behind them meant that there was no alternative to building the miners' cottages end-to-end in strips along the valley floor and along the narrow terraces immediately above. Dank and drab, with only the most primitive forms of sewage and sanitation, the miners' homes huddled below the mountainous slag-heaps of waste from the mines which towered dead and black above them. The narrowness of the valleys with their ribbon villages also precluded the growth of any real urban centers as the nuclei of communal life, although intense loyalty to individual valleys did develop.

Housing even with poor sanitation was always in short supply, and the problem of overcrowding was rarely solved except by the miners themselves. Several families lived together and took in lodgers from the superfluity of single, male workers. It was not uncommon for beds, like their occupants, to be on a shift system. Poor sanitation and overcrowding resulted, as elsewhere, in poor health and vulnerability to diseases in addition to those brought on by the harsh conditions of work. The cholera epidemic of 1849 was not lacking for victims in South Wales. The isolation of the coalfield forced a concentration upon two basic industries, iron and coal, which precluded the development of other industries on the coalfield. Thus the life of the ironworker and collier was controlled completely by the fluctuations of two industries with no opportunity to find other employment nearby when wage reductions, depression, and unemployment took place.

Isolation from any main center also made it essential for the employers to set up company shops or "truck" shops which for many years would prove to be among the more prominent of the

---

82. The Clydach ironworks as early as 1813 owned 150 houses which were rented to the workers. E. W. Evans, *The South Wales Miners* (Cardiff, 1961), p. 9.

workmen's grievances. When the "long pay" system became linked with the truck shop system, grievances multiplied. Under the "long pay" system workmen were paid once a month or at even longer intervals and advances or "draws" were common and made in the form of "truck" notes or vouchers which could only be used at the company shop. The inevitable result was that most workmen were constantly in debt to the company. This made it difficult for them to leave or to take strike action against the employers. It was, perhaps, unavoidable that the company shops enjoying a virtual monopoly would use this position to profit excessively at the expense of the workmen.

Conditions of work in the ironworks were bad. The men worked long hours, often 6 a.m. to 6 p.m., and the work itself was back-breaking and dangerous. Wages constantly fluctuated, but eighteen to twenty-one shillings a week were considered normal. These wages compared favorably with those of the agricultural laborer, but work at these rates was not necessarily constant and short-time working could quickly affect the amount of wages earned.

Conditions in the mines were worse than those in the ironworks. The coal seams of the South Wales coalfield were thin in comparison with those in the United States. The result was that the colliers worked hard for long hours in a cramped sitting or kneeling position or even lying on their sides, more often than not in the water which could not be kept out of the mines. The normal working hours were like those in the ironworks, 6 a.m. to 6 p.m., with the result that during the winter months the collier lived in perpetual darkness, never seeing the sun except on Sundays and holidays. Most collieries were closed overnight but this tended to increase the accumulation of gas which was by far the greatest threat to the safety of the miners. The explosion of firedamp or marsh gas was a constant hazard, especially as the methods employed to ventilate the mines were inadequate. The number of disasters from explosions and fires earned South Wales an unenviable notoriety in the nineteenth century.[83] Part of the blame for

83. For an account of one such colliery disaster at Cymmer when 114 lives were lost, see the *Merthyr Guardian*, July 19, 1856.

such disasters lay with the coal owners who were unable or unwilling to install the machinery that was needed to ventilate the
mines and clear the gas from the workings; part lay with the men
who persisted in using naked flames even after the invention of the
safety lamp. A writer in the *Merthyr Guardian* summed up the situation of the South Wales miner as "one of extreme toil, suffering
and fate."[84]

Women and children as elsewhere in Great Britain were employed in the mines, the women working seven or eight hours a
day for four shillings a week drawing up baskets of coal from the
stalls to the main headings, and when trams were introduced drag-
ging or pushing them out, bent double. Children were employed
opening and shutting doors below ground and occasionally helping fill the trams. Children were kept with their families, and there
is little evidence of harsh treatment.

The life of the collier was nasty, brutish, and often short. His
only solace was drink,[85] and the beerhouses were more than adequate in number to provide this relief from the harsh realities of
living and working in the mines and ironworks. The provision of
so many beerhouses suggests that they were looked upon with favor by the owners, as drink could effectively blunt the raw edges of
the miners' discontent.

The South Wales coalfield for much of its nineteenth-century
history exhibited many of the characteristics of a frontier town.
There were no resident magistrates and few police. A restless, floating population of hard-drinking, unmarried men contributed to
the turbulence and violence which conditions on the coalfield generated. The mines and foundries brutalized the workmen by the
conditions under which they were forced to live and work. It
would have been a miracle if relations between master and men
had been other than that of constant friction and enmity. Hardly a
year passed without a strike taking place to prevent the masters

84. *Ibid.*, December 7, 1844, quoted by A. H. John, *Industrial Development of South
Wales*, p. 149.
85. The similarity to Oscar Handlin's poor immigrant in the United States in *The
Uprooted* (Boston, 1951) is striking.

from imposing a reduction in wages.[86] Violence hovered over every strike, and it was only a short step from orderly protest to mob violence as hungry and discontented men struck out at the sources, real or imagined, of their discontent.

Industrial unrest, violence, and enmity between masters and men characterized the whole of the nineteenth and early twentieth centuries in South Wales as fumbling and mostly unsuccessful attempts were made to bring cohesion to working-class movements. In the first half of the nineteenth century, emigration to the United States or to other parts of the world does not appear to have been considered as the solution to industrial problems. Undoubtedly individuals and small groups did leave Wales to take up land in America or to take jobs, similar to those they were leaving, in the growing industrial centers of the United States. For the majority, however, strikes and political action seemed the best way to improve their situation. It was not difficult to organize a strike and intimidate nonstrikers, but if the masters stood firm they had at their disposal an impressive arsenal of weapons to break the strike: they could close the truck shops, call in troops to maintain order, evict workers from company houses, use "blackleg" labor, and threaten "blacklisting."[87] It was only when strikes proved fruitless and the pressure of population began to build up that emigration was given serious consideration.

It is against a background of appallingly bad living and working conditions, of turbulence and violence when strike action took place and failed, and of constant uncertainty in employment and wages that emigration to the United States has to be placed. The population concentrated on the South Wales coalfield was highly cohesive ethnically and also very mobile. It had tenacious Welsh roots but roots which could be severed if conditions in Wales went beyond endurance and those in the United States looked sufficiently

86. It is estimated that between 1800 and 1831 there were some fifty strikes and riots in South Wales, the majority of which were defensive actions against a reduction in wages.

87. The use of "blacklisting" in the late 1860's left some active trade unionists little alternative but to emigrate to the United States, their passage sometimes being paid from union funds.

attractive. Many of those who made up this industrial population were recent or latent agriculturalists who were equally capable of returning to the land or of going directly into American industry. The time when many seriously considered emigration was, however, also the time when good cheap or free land was becoming more scarce in the United States, when the rewards of farming were less attractive, and the migrations from the rural areas to the urban centers had already commenced. Successful farming even on free government land required some capital, but the fluctuating wage pattern in industrial Wales was not one which made for capital accumulation beyond that necessary to pay for passage to the United States. In contrast, the particular skills of the Welsh iron-worker or collier which were for many years highly prized in the United States did not need to wait upon some future harvest to be transformed into immediate hard cash. It is not surprising, therefore, that the majority of industrial workers followed along craft corridors to the urban centers of the United States, settling among their own countrymen in such places as Pittsburgh, Carbondale, Scranton, and Wilkes Barre. The welcome they received was often barely lukewarm because American labor, too, was engaged in a struggle with powerful business interests and viewed any increase in the labor force, wherever it came from, with no enthusiasm. The Welsh emigrant found himself involved in strikes and lockouts which were very similar to those he had left behind in Wales. Thus, at the time when emigration from Europe came to full flood, the movement out of Wales began to subside, not because conditions in Wales had necessarily improved but because the relative attractiveness of the United States to the Welsh had declined.

Paradoxically, one of the earlier and more significant movements of Welshmen from the industrial areas to the United States had little to do with wages, strikes, or industrial strife. The emigration of Welsh Mormons from the mid-nineteenth century on was very much a reemergence of the eighteenth-century search for a spiritual Zion in the wilderness.

The first converts in Wales to the Church of Jesus Christ of the Latter Day Saints were made by Liverpool missionaries who crossed over into the Principality and in the fall of 1840 organized the Overton branch in Flintshire. Elder James Burnham, writing from Wrexham in December 1840, was able to report that fifty-six baptisms had taken place there despite considerable opposition from the local clergy.[88] At the end of 1840, Elder John Needham was sent to labor in Monmouthshire but progress was slow until 1843 when Elder William Henshaw organized the Penydarren branch and ordained William Rees Davies who was able to preach in the Welsh language. While establishing the branch, Henshaw supported himself by working in the mines.[89]

It was not until the arrival of "Captain" Dan Jones in Wales in 1845, however, that Mormonism really took hold in South Wales. Jones described himself as "an unvarnished sailor, a tar of the five oceans."[90] He was born in Flintshire in 1811 and had first come into contact with Joseph Smith when transporting Mormons on the Mississippi River in his vessel, *The Maid of Iowa*.[91] He was with Joseph Smith the night before Smith and his brother Hyrum were lynched. Smith had prophesied that Jones would return to Wales and preach to the Welsh in their own language. The energy which Dan Jones put into his mission and the success of the Mormon periodical *Udgorn Seion* (The Trumpet of Zion) resulted in more than five thousand converts to the Church in Wales by 1850. The great majority of these belonged to the East Glamorganshire Conference which at that time was the largest in the whole of Great Britain.[92] This did not take into account the fact that in February 1849 Jones took out to the Great Salt Lake 249 Saints on the *Buena Vista*. Part of this group he left at Council Bluffs to form a Welsh staging-post for monoglot Welsh speakers who would be following from Wales.

One contemporary account described the scene of departure:

88. *Millennial Star*, XXV (1863), 775.

89. *Journal History of Joseph Smith* (Church Historian's Office, Salt Lake City), March 25, 1843.

90. *Times and Seasons*, London, Library of the British Mission, 6 (1845), 988.

91. Smith became half-owner of the *Maid of Iowa* in return for two notes for $1,375. *Journal History of Joseph Smith*, June 2, 1843.

92. This was a marked increase on the 687 members in twenty-eight branches when he arrived. The major branches were those at Penydarren, Beaufort, Rhymney, Tredegar, Merthyr, and Aberdare.

On Tuesday last Swansea was quite enlivened in consequence of the arrival of several waggons loaded with luggage, attended by some scores of the "bold peasantry" of Carmarthenshire and also an equal number of the inhabitants of Merthyr and the surrounding districts with their families. The formidable party were nearly all Latter Day Saints and came to this town for the purpose of proceeding to Liverpool in the "Troubadour" steamer where a ship is in readiness to transport them next week to the glittering regions of California. This goodly company is in command of a popular Saint, known as Capt. Dan Jones, a hardy traveller and a brother of the wellknown John Jones, Llandollen, the able disputant on the subject of baptism. On Wednesday morning, after being addressed by their leader, all repaired on board in admirable order and with extraordinary resignation. Their departure was witnessed by hundreds of spectators and while the steamer gaily passed down the river the Saints commenced singing a favorite hymn.[93]

The Mormons encountered strong opposition from the nonconformist chapels, and dire warnings were given as to the fate that awaited those sufficiently misguided to emigrate with the Mormons. Letters from America were published in denominational periodicals urging the Welsh not to be "blinded by such a system of roguery and plunder as Mormonism."[94] As in the United States, it was the practice of polygamy which aroused the strongest feelings in Wales. Evan Howell, writing from St. Louis in 1851, maintained: "They take everything from you at home and they starve you after coming here if they get the chance and they take your wives from you. Their leader, Brigham Young, has twenty-four wives and nineteen of them have babies."[95] Such startling allegations may have had some effect in stemming the tide of Mormon emigration from Wales but the question of polygamy was put into better perspective by two Welsh women, the first writing home in 1855, the second in 1862.

We have got plenty of everything except wheat. James is getting very good wages all the summer. I wish you were getting on as well as what we are. James has no other woman than myself yet; and when we have got more property—that is, when we are in a way to maintain her without injuring

93. *British Banner* (London), February 21, 1849.
94. *Y Diwygiwr*, XVII (April 1852).
95. *Ibid.*

ourselves—then it will be my duty to look out for another woman for him—that is my duty and not his.[96]

In contrast:

As to polygamy, *you* are without a dread of anyone claiming a share with you; this dread has made me so miserable in past times that I almost wished myself at the bottom of the sea instead of in Utah, but so far I have been spared trial. You cannot conceive what women have to suffer here with a view to obtain some great glory hereafter, which I for one am willing to forego, if I can escape the purgatory they think necessary.[97]

Despite such letters and ministerial exhortations against emigrating to a new Sodom and Gomorrah, the prospects of a new Zion which would free them from their economic troubles in Wales appealed to many Welsh men and women, and further Mormon companies left for America in the 1850's. Dan Jones himself returned to Wales in 1852 and despite poor health continued his work. In 1856 he finally returned to Utah aboard the *Samuel Curling* with seven hundred more Saints.[98] This brought the total of Welsh emigrants to nearly two thousand in less than eight years, many of whom were enabled to emigrate through the Perpetual Emigration Fund run by the Mormon Church. The need for the Saints to develop ironworks at Salt Lake made the skills of many of these Welsh emigrants very welcome.[99]

Emigration continued until the end of the century but the branches in Wales became smaller and the number of emigrants fewer. In April 1878 Joseph H. Parry reporting on meetings at Rhymney and Blaenavon uttered a *cri de coeur* not only for the Welsh but also for the Church.

The poverty that exists here is appalling, many of the poor Saints often suffering for want of bread and no hope for the future unless it comes from

96. *Merthyr Guardian*, February 23, 1856, original in English.

97. *Flintshire Observer* (Holywell), December 5, 1862, original in English.

98. Until the mid-fifties, most of the Mormon ships sailed for New Orleans from where passage up the Mississippi River could be obtained very cheaply. Numerous deaths from cholera and yellow fever and the growth of east-to-west railroad communication saw subsequent ships sailing mainly to Philadelphia and Boston.

99. *British Mission History* (Church Historian's Office), February 24, December 12, 1852.

Zion to gather them in. We have whole branches out of work and everything is going backward.[100]

The reference to Welsh Mormons going to "the glittering regions of California" introduces one further event which affected
Welsh emigration—the discovery of gold in California in 1848.
One suspects that some of those who emigrated from Wales with
the Mormons were motivated more by a lust for gold than for sal-
vation on the shores of the Great Salt Lake. Others who saw gold
mining as no more difficult and much more profitable than coalmining were attracted, if not in great numbers, to the Californian
goldfields. The "forty-niners" came from all over the world and
among them were Welshmen from Wales as well as from the
older settlements in the United States. From the California letters
still extant, the indications are that they were for the most part
young men without families. The cost of passage to New York and
from there to San Francisco by way of the Isthmus of Panama (at
least £25) made it impossible for the ordinary miner with a wife
and family to leave for the goldfields. Even if he were to go overland from New York to California, the distance, the time involved,
and the cost were again deterrents to all but the most irresponsible
and foolhardy.

Nevertheless, it is possible to find a scattering of Welshmen in
most of the gold-mining areas from California in the 1850's to
British Columbia in the 1860's[101] and Colorado in the 1870's. Few
of them in their letters to relatives in Wales were optimistic about
either their prospecting or their future prospects and gave no great
encouragement to others to follow them from Wales.[102] Although
news of the gold rushes was given wide coverage in the Welsh
press,[103] the inducement of very uncertain fortunes in gold mining

100. *Millennial Star*, XL (1878), 220. The standard work on the Mormons in Great
Britain is Richard L. Evans, *A Century of "Mormonism" in Great Britain* (Salt Lake City,
1937). A scholarly work on Mormon emigration is P. A. M. Taylor, *Expectations Westward* (Edinburgh, 1965).

101. See Alan Conway, "Welsh Goldminers in British Columbia in the 1860's," *British
Columbia Historical Quarterly*, 21 (1957–1958), 51–74.

102. See Conway, *The Welsh in America*, pp. 233–282.

103. See, for example, *Seren Cymru*, August 30, September 18, 1851.

attracted comparatively few emigrants from Wales. The mining frontiers were possibly more attractive to young, unmarried Welsh girls than to their parents because, as John Davies wrote from California in 1862:

This is an excellent place for girls. They can get as much as £6 to £8 a month, as much as they get there in a year. They would not have to be maids for long because a girl can get a husband here any time she wishes. Hundreds of wise girls have been maids for a few years and now have maids themselves.[104]

Gold mining and the frontier were put into good perspective where emigration was concerned by a well-known bard, Thomas Gwallter Price (Cuhelyn), who had emigrated to Pennsylvania in 1856, moved to California in 1859, and then continued on to British Columbia in 1862. He wrote in that year:

Would I advise you to come out? I must pause ere I answer. Are you healthy? Can your system sustain hardships? Are you fond of adventure? Can you brave danger? If so—come! I would rather brave all the wrath of the elements of creation and dare all the torments of human invention to acquire an independency than crawl like a worm through the mire of poverty. There are thousands who will, perhaps, curse the day that brought them here in search of gold, while thousands will bless the spirit of enterprise that led them hither.[105]

It is more than likely than not many were moved to emigrate in search of gold either by Price's purple prose or by his challenge to their spirit of adventure. Emigration from Wales was brought about by much more mundane economic and social factors.

Although there were reports as early as 1800 that Richard Crawshay, the ironmaster, was working out a scheme for settling Welsh ironworkers in Pennsylvania, little seems to have come of it. Apart from the Mormons and the California gold rush, the first half of the nineteenth century saw little in the way of organized or even significant emigration from the industrial parts of Wales. The *Salopian Journal* of August 25, 1841 reported that with the depressed state of the iron trade at Merthyr and a wage reduction of ten per-

104. *Ibid.*, December 5, 1862.
105. *Merthyr Telegraph*, May 31, 1852, original in English.

cent at Dowlais and neighboring ironworks some eighty or so had left for America, but this was an isolated report.

It was not until the late 1850's that emigration emerged as a matter for serious consideration. Undoubtedly in the previous decades there were those who had left inconspicuously for the United States, but not in numbers sufficient to warrant extended comment. Emigration agents were active but not specifically concerned with the United States; Australia, New Zealand, and South Africa figured just as prominently among countries suitable for Welsh emigrants.

In 1857 the *Merthyr Telegraph* drew the attention of its readers to the Wellington Emigration Fund set up with contributions from the Duke of Wellington, Sidney Herbert, Lord Stanley, the Lord Mayor of London, and others with a view to relieving the distress of the laboring classes by emigration.[106] This would seem, however, to have been little more than a snippet of information for its readers and not a serious attempt to encourage participation. At the same time, the United States clearly remained a country of much interest to Welsh people. Lectures on the United States by nonconformist ministers at such places as Abersychan and Bryn Mawr were well attended and the speakers roundly applauded.[107] Harriet Beecher Stowe's *Uncle Tom's Cabin* was translated into Welsh and serialized in the Welsh press and much attention was given to the events which led up to the outbreak of the Civil War.

In November 1858 an early emigration society was established at Aberdare.[108] Its lack of organization immediately brought it under attack but the Reverend Gwesyn Jones of Merthyr, in a lecture on the advantages of emigration, strongly urged upon his audience the desirability of forming emigration societies which could accumulate funds substantial enough to send out of the country large numbers of working people.[109]

By the end of the decade it was clear that emigration was be-

106. *Ibid.*, April 4, 1857.
107. *Monmouthshire Merlin*, September 11, 1858.
108. *Y Gwladgarwr*, November 6, 1858.
109. *Merthyr Telegraph*, November 6, 1858.

coming increasingly a matter of controversy. One writer in March 1859 maintained that Wales was overpopulated "in spite of continuous emigration" and for those who found themselves getting poorer every day, it was far better to emigrate.[110] Three months later another writer, under the somewhat inappropriate nom de plume of "John Bull," maintained that only the weak-minded embarked on such a foolhardy venture as emigrating to other parts of the world—"emigrating to America or to any other country only means a change of tribulation rather than its removal." His comments on the political situation in the United States were, however, very cogent arguments against emigrating at that time.

In the U.S.A., 3,000,000 people are slaves—they are the beasts of the field, possessions to be bought and sold. This is something we should think about because controversy over this monstrous thing convulses all the states and threatens, before long, to tear them apart.[111]

A rejoinder a month later in the same newspaper brought the question nearer home. "Slavery in America does not appear to be any less praiseworthy than the eviction of tenants from their farms by landlords in an attempt to coerce the farmers into following the religious beliefs and political ideas of the squirearchy."[112] Such verbal jousting did not alter the fact that in South Wales depression was bringing about a great deal of poverty, which at Hirwaun, for instance, was described as "gnawing out the life of this once busy little community."[113] Yet the outbreak of the Civil War in America, which was followed in Wales with close attention, made the United States a less attractive destination for the intending emigrant. One writer on emigration in 1861 put the situation into clear perspective.

There can be no doubt that we are in the midst of bad times. Trade is suffering from the pressure of depression and the workmen suffer from the scarcity of employment. Their earnings barely suffice to keep body and soul together. In days gone by there was always a great rush for emigration and those who

---

110. *Baner Cymru*, March 9, 1859.
111. *Ibid.*, July 13, 1859.
112. *Ibid.*, August 10, 1859.
113. *Merthyr Telegraph*, July 16, 1859.

had saved a little could go to Pennsylvania or other states in America. But, unfortunately, there are no such alluring attractions to emigrants to day. The Civil War is rampant but some workers still think there is a better chance for them in America and this opinion gains ground among the better class of workmen—the very ones the ironmasters should try to keep at home. But hundreds of the best workmen would gladly risk emigration rather than a reduction of their wages. It seems sheer madness to emigrate at such a time.[114]

With the uncertainties created in many minds by the outbreak of hostilities in America, not least the fear that on arrival an emigrant would be drafted into the armies, attention turned increasingly to Australia and New Zealand, with Queensland being considered as one of the most suitable places for resettlement.

In 1862 the departure of a considerable number of emigrants from Aberdare en route for Liverpool, where they were to take ship for Halifax, Nova Scotia, provided the *Baner ac Amserau Cymru* with the opportunity of asking the question why the Welsh were leaving the land of their birth. The editor concluded that with the coal mines idle and work in short supply, even those fortunate enough to have a job were getting wages insufficient to maintain a wife and family and certainly not enough to justify the dangers they encountered each day in the mines. "They know that if they stay here for very much longer they must surely sink into a state which would make it impossible to leave this country and must spend the rest of their days in poverty and distress."[115] The Civil War in America (Y Rhyfel yn America) was the lead article in every edition of *Y Gwladgarwr* throughout the war and although other newspapers in Wales did not devote as much space to the subject, interest in Wales in the outcome of the war remained high. This was not solely because of the war's effect upon future emigration but also because opinion in Wales was extremely strong in support of the Union. Lincoln was taken to task occasionally for failing to press ahead with the emancipation of the slaves.[116] Meetings to

114. *Merthyr Guardian*, May 18, 1861.

115. *Baner ac Amserau Cymru*, April 30, 1862.

116. Welshmen in the United States were found almost invariably in the Northern armies partly because of the abhorrence of slavery, partly because the great majority of Welsh had settled in New York, Pennsylvania, Ohio, Illinois, and Wisconsin. See Alan Conway, "Welshmen in the Union Armies," *Civil War History*, 4(1958), 143–174.

demonstrate support for the Union were held frequently and the visit of a Negro called Jackson who was, reputedly, one of Jefferson Davis' slaves, saw overflowing audiences in the Temperance Halls of Merthyr and Aberdare.[117]

It was also at this time that the advocates of emigration to Patagonia became vocal once more; but those who had doubts about the wisdom of settling in Argentina felt obliged to defend, if obliquely, the United States as the country to which the Welsh should emigrate, Civil War or no Civil War.

Once again, the old idea was resurrected of establishing an exclusive Welsh colony which would be capable of preserving the Welsh language and customs. Now, however, Texas was promoted as the state where this dream could be achieved.[118] A correspondent of the *Baner ac Amserau Cymru* in the United States reported that he had been to see Secretary of State William H. Seward to ask whether it was possible for a Welsh colony to be established in the United States on western lands as a constitutional part of the Union. Seward promised to look into the matter, and eventually a reply was received stating that the government could not favor such a colony as the Welsh had in mind. Nevertheless there was no reason why groups of Welsh people like other national groups should not take advantage of the Homestead Act and settle on land in Kansas, Nebraska, or the Dakotas.[119] Much of this was little more than idle speculation and wishful thinking which had little direct bearing on actual emigration.

Despite the uncertainties of emigrating to the United States in time of war, numbers of Welsh were reported to be on the move in the early months of 1863. Some left from Aberdare, Dowlais, and Merthyr while others were making last-minute preparations for departure from Swansea, Llansamlet, and Llanelly.[120] The de-

---

117. *Baner ac Amserau Cymru*, February 11, 25, 1863. Another Negro named Francis Frederick lectured on his escape from slavery at Bethany Chaple, Cardiff, *Monmouthshire Merlin*, August 22, 1863.

118. *Baner ac Amserau Cymru*, March 11, 1863. There would seem to have been some confusion as to whether Texas was in the Union or the Confederacy.

119. *Ibid.*, April 15, 1863.

120. *Ibid.*, May 27, 1863.

parture of one such group was reported from Merthyr on Easter Monday of that year. Some forty emigrants congregated at the Taff Vale railroad station described by the *Merthyr Telegraph* as "not the lees of humanity but the cream of the working classes, men who had put by their savings carefully week by week, with the sole object of being able to pay for their passage to another country."[121] The majority of those leaving were puddlers from the ironworks and colliers whose departure left at least one ironworks short of hands.[122]

This emigration led the *Merthyr Telegraph* to editorialize on the question of emigration and the effect it was having upon the ironworks in South Wales. The editor asked the simple question, what induced working men to emigrate in such numbers at this time? He was not prepared to accept the explanation that it was simply a desire for a change or that the emigration mania was some sort of contagion spreading from district to district. His view was that the Welsh workingman was too deeply attached to his homeland to leave without some really adequate reasons. The causes of emigration, he suggested, were first, the low wages which workingmen had been receiving for the previous six years and their having suffered much more than many realized. Although the iron trade had been depressed in the past, never before had it brought such hardship. Normally, the men could look forward to an improvement in their circumstances, but no such improvement seemed now to be in sight. Therefore, they were determined to see what rewards their skills might secure for them in the United States. Second, he ascribed the contemporary emigration to the crowded labor market in the ironworks and the coal industry. This labor glut had been evident for more than a year resulting in a desperate search for some sort of employment. By a combination of reduced production in the ironworks, stoppages, and a surplus of labor, wages were screwed down to the lowest possible point even when work could be secured. Third, the desire to emigrate could be attributed to the relationships between employers and workmen. These were

121. *Merthyr Telegraph*, April 11, 1863.
122. *Cardiff Times*, August 21, 1863.

far from good largely because the workmen were treated not as human beings but as machines designed to make iron or dig coal. Moreover, the master by using the truck system to his own advantage robbed the worker of what wages he did receive. Most masters—there were, of course, exceptions—were "hard, selfish and tyrannical," and the workmen were leaving without any regrets. Finally, the editor, while regretting the loss to Wales of some of its best and most industrious workmen, considered that emigration was preferable to remaining "to drag out a miserable existence."[123]

By September 1863 the same paper was more optimistic. There were rumors that wages were to be increased owing to the shortage of labor brought about by emigration. Should the Civil War end quickly, the volume of emigration would increase, labor would be in even shorter supply, and the ironworkers would be in a position to command wages such as they had not enjoyed for years.[124]

A week later the newspaper noticed the continued emigration from Dowlais of the best and most thrifty workmen, who were the ones who had put by sufficient to make emigration possible. It also stated that it was receiving many letters from America all describing "the wealth to be realised there by horny-handed, honest sons of labour."[125] This happy situation was attributed to the fact that American labor was being drained off to the armies and substantial wages were being offered to superior workmen to replace them.[126]

Emigration remained very much unorganized, and in April 1864 a meeting was held at Pontypridd to devise the best means of forming an Emigration Society. It was decided that representatives from each of the twenty-nine mines in the area should be appointed. After some discussion fifty-three representatives signified their willingness to participate in the formation of a society which would encourage emigration as a better way of raising

123. *Merthyr Telegraph*, August 29, 1863.
124. *Ibid.*, September 5, 1863.
125. This assertion is not borne out by the majority of letters received from the United States at this time.
126. *Merthyr Telegraph*, September 12, 19, 1863. See also *Baner ac Amserau Cymru*, September 2, 1863.

wages than taking part in strikes. Subscriptions would be sought of one shilling for the first month and sixpence a month thereafter. When sufficient money had been subscribed, a ballot would be held to decide whom to send to America.[127]

What success, if any, this society had in providing passage to America for those lucky enough to win the ballot has gone unrecorded but it did mark a new approach to emigration. It recognized the fact that those wishing to emigrate were not necessarily those who had the financial resources to do so and, therefore, in the interest of everyone it was worth the effort of regular subscriptions to a society followed by a lottery to keep up the pace of emigration and continue the reduction in the available supply of labor.

Later in 1864, J. W. Jones, the editor of *Y Drych* (*The Mirror*), the best-known Welsh language newspaper in the United States, returned to Wales and lectured widely on the subject of "America —A Free Home for All." He urged his audiences to emigrate to America, where they would be welcomed, where trade was flourishing, and where there was plenty of land and plenty of work. He also spoke at length on the contributions which had been made by famous Welshmen to the progress of the United States.[128]

The last stages of the Civil War were followed with close attention in the expectation that with the peace the United States would be looking for manpower from Europe, including the Welsh. In April and May 1865 emigrants began leaving Aberdare in large numbers not only for the United States but also for Patagonia. Some of those leaving for America were going "under the guidance and protection of the American Emigrant Co.'s local agent."[129]

The recruitment of workmen by the American Emigrant Company of Bowling Green, New York, injected a new element of controversy into the question of emigrating to the United States. Some of the local agents of the company maintained that the pro-

127. *Merthyr Guardian*, April 22, 29, 1864; *Y Gwladgarwr*, May 7, 1864.

128. *Merthyr Telegraph*, November 19, 1864; *Caernarvon and Denbigh Herald*, February 25, 1865.

129. *Merthyr Guardian*, April 28, May 12, 1865.

posed system was one which helped bring together the American employer who needed labor and the European workman who needed employment. They firmly denied allegations that the company was no more than a recruiting agency for the Union armies, and with the war virtually over their denials had much validity. Critics of the company, however, saw the contract labor scheme as one designed by the employers to secure cheap immigrant labor which would be forced to work until the passage money had been repaid, thus seriously undermining the position of American labor. They maintained that:

The articles of apprenticeship of these redemptioners create a species of servitude resembling that of Mexican peonage. A lien is held on the redemptioner's wages, land and property until the debt is liquidated; meanwhile his condition is menial, dependent and degraded.[130]

The *Merthyr Telegraph*, quoting the *American Workman's Advocate*, stated, "For the first year the immigrant is exactly in the position of a nigger coolie, bound to work for the master the Company has sold his labor to and until that period expires, he cannot make any move to better his position."[131]

First-hand information on this topic came from John J. Powell, late of Aberaman, from Pittston, Pennsylvania. He wrote in May 1865:

I have not been here very long but long enough to decide that I wish that I had stayed at home for at least another year. I knew before I left Aberdare that N. M. Jones, Cymro Gwyllt, had been raised to be an agent in some emigration society and that he is transporting men to the western world almost for nothing. One day I called at his office at Cross Inn, Trecynon—God save us all!—it was full of men who had come from every part of the valley to get their names on the list. As near as I can remember, the chief agent in Britain at Liverpool received passage certificates from the Company . . . and after they reached the other side, the men would work a year for the Company which deducted a quarter of their earnings every month until all the passage money was paid. I can show you that there is evil in this. A company from Aberdare who had come at the expense of the masters found that the works were on strike when they arrived and they were bound to go to work

130. *Seren Cymru*, April 7, 1865; *Y Gwladgarwr*, April 22, 1865.
131. *Merthyr Telegraph*, June 24, 1865.

at the expense of their fellow workers. . . . It must be remembered that turn-coats are more in danger working here than they are in Wales. Revolvers are ready weapons here with the ordinary people.[132]

Emigration continued strongly during 1865 despite reports from America that the labor market was glutted in such states as Ohio, Pennsylvania, and Illinois, three of the states most favored by Welsh miners and ironworkers. *Rylands Iron Trade Circular* warned those emigrating that almost every mill in Pittsburgh was at a standstill and that the prices of food and provisions were almost double what they were before the war.[133] Such warnings seemed to be of no avail, and emigration continued apace even though an upturn in trade indicated a rise in wages. At one pit alone, one hundred miners gave in their notices on deciding to leave for America.[134] The movement continued into 1866 with men leaving Blaenau, Nantyglo, and Glyn Ebbw in large numbers. Some felt that unless the owners raised wages at least by four shillings in the pound, they would find themselves with insufficient labor to keep their works going. To some extent this was wishful thinking, and it is significant that despite the numbers leaving, accommodation in such places as the Aberdare Valley was unaffected. No empty cottages became available and most continued to house two fam-ilies apiece as well as lodgers.[135] By the middle of April 1866 the emigration flow, which had been strongest in the districts around Merthyr and Aberdare, spread to Pontypridd despite continued warnings of a full labor market and frequent strikes in the United States.[136]

The upturn in trade which lasted until the middle of 1866 did not survive the end of hostilities on the continent of Europe. Wages were reduced once more by the ironmasters at Rhymney, Aber-dare, and Ebbw Vale.[137] At the same time, it became increasingly evident that the favorable picture of America painted by interested

132. *Y Byd Cymreig* [The Welsh World] (Newcastle Emlyn), June 22, 1865.
133. *Merthyr Telegraph*, May 20, 1865.
134. *Baner ac Amserau Cymru*, May 17, 31, 1865.
135. *Ibid.*, March 14, 21, 1866.
136. *Merthyr Telegraph*, April 14, 1866.
137. *Ibid.*, July 7, 1866.

emigration agents was far from the truth. A number of emigrants returning to Wales from the United States gave a totally different account of conditions there. They confirmed that wages in the United States were, on average, twenty percent higher than in Wales but that the cost of living was also very much higher and, on balance, the workman was better off in Wales.[138]

In 1868 there was a return once more to the idea of establishing cooperative emigration societies. In May of that year a large gathering of miners at Merthyr passed a number of resolutions asserting that emigration was essential if any improvements in working conditions were to be secured and that Missouri was the best state for the Welsh. It was unanimously agreed that it was the duty of them all to form a society to aid each other to emigrate.[139] The miners were convinced that if a number of emigration societies could be formed and whole families sent out to America, the labor supply would be reduced and wages would rise. Missouri was chosen as the state where a Welsh colony might be established because it had both agricultural and mining opportunities particularly suited to the agricultural-industrial ambidexterity of many Welshmen.[140] In an editorial two weeks later the *Merthyr Telegraph* commented on this fortunate aspect of Welsh emigration.

It appears singular that a large percentage of the immigrants who leave the industrial regions should take up agricultural pursuits in America. This is not so strange as first appears. Many Glamorgan colliers and miners are men from Cardiganshire, Carmarthenshire, Pembrokeshire and other agricultural areas of Wales and they obviously prefer to go back to more pleasant pursuits than mining.[141]

A number of families left Dowlais and Aberdare where emigration societies were also set up, but some emigrants were not above the moonlight flit, leaving a great deal of money owing to local tradesmen.[142]

Throughout the summer of 1868 meetings were held in most of

138. *Caernarvon and Denbigh Herald*, November 17, 1866.
139. *Y Gwladgarwr*, May 16, 1868.
140. *Merthyr Telegraph*, May 16, 1868.
141. *Ibid.*, May 30, 1868.
142. *Ibid.*, June 6, 1868.

the larger towns of South Wales to examine the possibilities of setting up emigration societies. The emphasis upon emigration siphoning off excess labor was drearily familiar. The only new note in the argument was the advantages that the United States had to offer for education. No mention was made of the possibility that although the emigration of skilled men from the foundries and mines might create a labor shortage, this shortage might be only of short duration as migrants from other parts of Great Britain moved in to fill the gaps.[143] Moreover, the question of emigration was debated almost entirely in terms of wages and the availability of labor. There seems to have been little appreciation of the fact that wages were governed as much by the demand for and the price of coal and iron as by the amount of labor on the market.

Nor did the enthusiastic advocates of emigration seem to have taken much notice of the letters appearing in the Welsh press from Welshmen in America, such as that of Charles Evans from Merthyr, who wrote from Elston, Missouri, in October 1868:

Trade has been very stagnant throughout the summer and tyranny has been found everywhere. The yoke became too heavy to bear any longer with many families suffering want for those things needed to keep body and soul together because goods were so expensive. On 1 May we came out as one man for our rights. I feel sure the young men of Aberdare would feel hard done by if they had to live on corn bread, smoked ham and coffee without sugar. The houses are so poor I can count the stars when lying in bed and know what the weather is like without opening the door.[144]

Similar adverse comment was made about the iron trade by D. Tydvil Davies from Trumbull County, Ohio.

It is very full here at the moment and it is almost impossible for puddlers to get work because so many mills have stopped throughout the country. It is true that there is plenty of work for colliers here now after a strike of nearly six months but their wages are so small they are not worth having. Many tell me they only earn two dollars a day after much hard work. I think it would be wise for those who intend emigrating to wait until the Spring.[145]

143. In 1871 it was, however, reported that Irish were being recruited to work in South Wales. *Ibid.*, May 12, 1871.
144. *Y Gwladgarwr*, October 31, 1868.
145. *Ibid.*, November 7, 14, 1868.

Numbers continued to emigrate in 1868 and 1869 but by April 1869 the *Merthyr Telegraph*, which had long been a strong advocate of emigration, struck a warning note in a lengthy editorial which indicated that the editor had begun to appreciate the wider economic implications of skilled emigration for the future. He pointed out that, although emigrants to America would provide a larger market for British goods while reducing competition for employment at home, they could also become competitors. The skilled workman going to the United States would carry on his trade there to the benefit of American industry. If the time came when Americans produced goods equal in quality to those in Wales, not only would they cease to be customers but they would drive such British products as iron out of the American market. Pressure upon Congress to place tariffs on British goods might not succeed but a better solution than emigration would be to induce skilled workmen to stay at home for higher wages.[146]

That there was some substance to this argument can be seen from an account of the growth of the iron and steel industry near Cleveland, Ohio, which one writer described as being like Merthyr or Dowlais with "ironworks and blast furnaces in every direction." One town, Coalburgh, had a population of six thousand, two-thirds of whom were Welshmen from Blainau, Dowlais, Merthyr, and Aberdare.[147]

In 1870, an attempt was made to set up a National Emigration Society[148] but this had little success. Interest in emigration over the next few years waned perceptibly as trade unionism notched up some successes and the development of the Rhondda valleys provided a much nearer source of employment than the United States, where the panic of 1873 was having serious effects.

The industrial recession in Wales after 1873 coupled with that in America left the workmen of South Wales with little choice except to endure what could not be changed. Suggestions made in 1875 that the quarrymen of North Wales and the miners of South

146. *Merthyr Telegraph*, April 24, 1869.
147. *Seren Cymru*, April 30, 1869.
148. *Baner ac Amserau Cymru*, February 2, 1870.

Wales form a joint emigration society received very little support. The suggested subscription rate of one shilling a month from some two hundred thousand quarrymen and colliers would have brought in £120,000, which would have been sufficient to pay the passage money and a little to spare for six thousand emigrants each year. On paper it seemed to be a reasonable scheme but as one critic pointed out, even if twenty thousand Welsh left for America, twenty thousand English and Irish would rush in to take their places. Moreover, conditions in America were such that many Welshmen would give anything to return to Wales.[149]

Severe depression particularly in the iron industry marked the period after 1876 and reports from America of some two million unemployed there did not present an encouraging picture for those contemplating emigration. Late in 1878, however, one more attempt was made to form an emigration society, this time in the Rhondda Valley.[150] An initial meeting made it clear that the sponsors of this new society were not thinking in terms of emigration to the industrial regions of the United States but to agricultural land in Texas where it was hoped that a Welsh settlement could be established as the nucleus for other emigrants who would follow. It was agreed that meetings of the men should be held in every coal-pit in the valley and a working committee was set up to gather more information about Texas. The prospects of success for this society were better than for most of its predecessors because the miners' leader, William Abraham (Mabon), was firmly behind it. In an address to the miners of the Rhondda Valley in January 1879 he returned to the theme that, when there was plenty of work but only a few workmen, wages remained high, but when work was scarce and workmen plentiful, wages remained low. Large-scale emigration was, therefore, the safety valve necessary to redress the imbalance between an abundance of labor and a scarcity of work.[151]

A Workmen's Emigration Society was founded, and with Ma-

149. *Y Gwladgarwr*, April 2, 1875.
150. *Ibid.*, August 23, 1878.
151. *Tarian y Gweithiwr* [Shield of the Workers] (Aberdare), January 17, 1879. This was the nearest approach to a socialist newspaper in Wales.

bon's eloquent support further meetings were held which resulted in the formation of some half-dozen branches in the Rhondda Valley. Members of the society would initially contribute £5 each with a guaranteed seven percent interest on their money. Their intention was to invite workingmen throughout the country to contribute two shillings and sixpence a month and as soon as enough money was available, a drawing would be held and six to eight families would be sent out to Texas. In addition to their passage, they would receive eighty acres of land freehold, a house, a pair of oxen, two cows, twelve fowls, two pigs, a set of farm implements, cooking utensils, a stove, and £10 for food until they could support themselves. Already there were three to four thousand acres available for purchase at twelve shillings an acre along the Galveston, Harrisburg, and San Antonio railroad. The company's agents would be on hand to meet the emigrants on their arrival and they would have five years to pay off the original investment at seven percent.

Mabon was optimistic that within a few months there would be one hundred thousand subscribers and some fifty families could be sent out every month. Once the interest repayments began to come in, the Fund would swell rapidly and in less than five years over a thousand people could be sent out each month.[152] The actual financial arrangements of the company seemed somewhat confused. By May it was being suggested that an initial membership fee of one shilling should be paid and those lucky enough in the ballot should be sent out with £150, to be repaid in ten years at seven percent interest.[153]

In August 1879 the *Merthyr Telegraph* was reporting the departure of large numbers of emigrants from the Rhondda and the Rhymney valleys but did not specify Texas as their destination.[154] Some Welsh did, however, reach Texas under the auspices of the Workmen's Emigration Society. They landed at New Orleans early in November 1879 and then travelled by steamship to Gal-

---

152. *Ibid.*, January 24, 1879.
153. *Ibid.*, May 9, 1879.
154. *Merthyr Telegraph*, August 22, 1879.

veston and from there to New Philadelphia by train. Houses and stock were ready for them as promised and food was supplied by the company on credit. This promising start was not maintained, however. Credit for food was stopped because no funds were received from Wales, and the whole sorry business ended in January 1880 with the departure of the would-be settlers to coal mining in the Indian territory.[155]

Word of this fiasco, spread across the pages of the miners' journal, brought emigration to Texas to an abrupt halt, signalled the demise of the Workmen's Emigration Society, and saw Mabon thenceforth singularly silent on the subject of emigration as a solution to the problem of labor surpluses in South Wales. This was the last serious attempt to promote large-scale emigration by organized societies in Wales.[156]

Throughout the seventies and eighties, letters from emigrants who had gone to the foundries and coal mines of the United States were positive deterrents to emigration. Invariably they were filled with accounts of strikes and lockouts and the conflicts between unions and owners which were stories only too familiar to the Welsh miner and foundryman. The particular skills of the Welsh had for long enabled them to obtain work in America, but with the increasing number of immigrants from southern and eastern Europe entering the country and the development of new techniques, the Welsh were less sought after. Some rose up the ladder into managerial positions, but the bulk of the Welsh labor force increasingly became identified in the minds of American employers with active unionism and strike action. Particularly was this the case in the coalfields, where, as one Welshman saw the situation in 1880 when writing home from Ohio: "There are strikes nearly every week in one place or another. The complaint is that the Welsh are foremost in these and many of the masters, because of this, are prejudiced against them and choose other nationalities who take the best paying jobs from them."[157] Welsh emigrants who hitherto

155. *Tarian y Gweithiwr*, December 19, 1879; January 9, 16, 1880; May 7, 1880.
156. As late as 1894 there were still those putting forward schemes for emigration societies to be formed on a subscription basis but with no response. *Ibid.*, April 5, 1894.
157. *Baner ac Amserau Cymru*, September 15, 1880.

had enjoyed something of a privileged position in the industrial centers of the United States could no longer expect the same treatment, a fact which was not lost upon those weighing the pros and cons of emigration in the last two decades of the nineteenth century. This trend toward the employment of other nationalities was confirmed in 1895 by John R. Williams, a native of Aberdare, who wrote home about the situation in Pennsylvania:

The coal trade in the anthracite districts has been extremely dull all through the year, the production overwhelmingly over balancing the demand. Labor is so plentiful that operators can do just what they please. Pennsylvania is swarming with foreigners—Poles, Hungarians, Slavish, Swedes and Italians etc. who are fast driving the English, Welsh, and Scotch miners out of competition. Noticeably, the Poles and Hungarians are harder-working people and physically stronger than the English and Welsh. They live much harder and at about half the cost and can stand much harder work than our countrymen.

Before the influx of the foreigners, the Welsh had the best show in the mines here, but in consequence of their foolhardy and unreasonable impositions, they became at length perfectly unmanageable and the operators had no alternative but to send and get whole cargoes of the foreigners who now practically monopolize the business.[158]

The gloomy picture thus presented for the Welsh coupled with the constant exhortations from fellow Welshmen in American industry to stay where they were blunted what enthusiasm still remained for emigration. It is no coincidence that 1890 was the high-water mark of Welsh emigration to the United States. Thereafter, when the immigration of southern and eastern Europeans was reaching unprecedented heights, the relative contribution of the Welsh to the immigrant flow began to diminish until it became almost inconspicuous among the many millions of other nationalities entering the United States.

The last significant and clearly identifiable emigration of Welshmen from the industrial areas to the United States was that of tinplate workers in the 1890's after the McKinley tariff of 1890 had

158. N.L.W., MS. 3293E, original in English.

given the *coup de grâce* to the monopoly in tinplating which Wales had enjoyed for many years.

A pioneer attempt to set up tinplate works in the United States had been made without success in the 1820's but nothing further had been done in this respect until after the Civil War. Then, the Cambria Iron Company sent representatives to Europe to examine the possibility of setting up competitive tinplate works in the United States. They came to the conclusion that worthwhile competition was not possible as long as European labor was so much cheaper.[159] In the early 1870's, however, a substantial rise in the price of imported tinplate made it worthwhile to set up tinplate works in America. Using Welsh tinplate workers, the American Tinplate Company built a plant at Wellsville, Ohio, and the United States Iron and Tinplate Manufacturing Company built others at Demmler, Pennsylvania.[160] There is some evidence to suggest that the owners were Welshmen from Glamorgan but this did not prevent strife developing with the men, who hastily advised their compatriots in Wales to ignore any offers of employment they might receive.[161] Falling prices and a reduced tariff soon made these works uneconomic and tinplating was abandoned completely by 1877.

In 1883, it was reported that the Pioneer Tin and Terne Plate Company of America had opened works at Hubbard, Ohio, with tinplate workers brought over from Wales. Once again letters were received in Wales warning against emigrating to America to work at lower wages.[162]

In the latter part of the decade pressure built up for placing a high tariff on foreign tinplate, which achieved success with the McKinley tariff of 1890, effective in July 1891. The result of this was that in the next five years there was a reduction of tinplate production in Wales of twenty percent and a fall in exports of over forty percent.

159. W. E. Minchinton, *The British Tinplate Industry* (Oxford, 1957), p. 62.

160. *Industrial World* (Swansea), September 20, 1895. See also R. T. Berthoff, *British Immigrants in Industrial America, 1790–1950* (Cambridge, 1953), p. 68.

161. *Y Gwladgarwr*, November 8, 1873; April 18, 1874.

162. *South Wales Press*, June 7, November 22, 1883.

One beneficiary of the tariff, the St. Louis Stamping Company, expanded its operations and sent agents to Llanelly to recruit skilled Welsh tinplate workers.[163] The *South Wales Press* saw this as an attempt to use Welsh labor for strikebreaking purposes while admitting that the wages offered to tinplate workers prepared to emigrate were six to eight dollars a day. The possibility that manufacturers of tinplate in Wales were preparing to export black plates for tinning in America also gave cause for concern.[164] By 1892, this possibility became a reality when the firm of Morewood & Company at Llanelly was reported to be looking for a site near New York where black plates shipped on a lower tariff would be tinned.[165] Those of its workmen who were sent out to America found on arrival in Indianapolis four excellent mills and wages double those in Wales.

In July 1893 the *South Wales Daily News* carried an advertisement of Hughes and Patterson's tinplate works in Philadelphia seeking "reliable, sober, industrious tin-men and washmen who would find ready employment." The *Industrial World* replied:

Reliable, sober, industrious tin-men and washmen are not likely to leave their present employment to take service in Philadelphia. It was force of circumstances and not choice that induced many to leave during the depression caused by the dislocation of trade by the McKinley tariff. Welsh tin-plate men are not likely to help American employers by their presence in America to lower the wage-rates there.[166]

By 1895 reports were being published that the American market was surfeited with tinplaters and they were advised to think twice before leaving employment in South Wales for America.[167] Increasingly, Welsh tinplaters who emigrated to America became involved in strikes, although some were prepared to act as strikebreakers.[168]

---

163. V. S. Clarke, *History of Manufactures in the United States* (New York, 1929), II, 374.
164. *South Wales Press*, August 27, October 8, 1891.
165. *Ibid.*, August 25, November 17, 1892; February 2, 1893. Works were set up at Port Elizabeth, New Jersey, and others at Indianapolis.
166. *Industrial World*, July 8, 1893.
167. *Ibid.*, August 9, 1895.
168. *Ibid.*, September 17, 1897.

By the end of the century Welsh workmen were no longer considered essential, their output per man was less than that of their American counterparts, and it is not without significance that the law against contract labor was used to keep Welsh tinplaters out of the United States.[169]

With the beginning of the twentieth century the emigration of Welsh to the United States, like that of the English, was engulfed by that of other nationalities.[170] Industrial strife in Wales showed no signs of disappearing. In fact, miners' organizations became more radical in their demands, rejecting older trade-union ideas of cooperation between management and labor. Some success was achieved by the Eight Hours Act of 1909 and the Minimum Wage Act of 1912, but on the eve of World War I the coalfield was the center of mounting discontent. Escape to the United States remained a possibility but became less attractive in the face of increasing competition for employment from millions of unskilled European immigrants. Moreover, as the result of technological developments in American industry the particular skills of the Welsh were no longer at a premium. The depressed state of agriculture was no more attractive or even seriously considered by a generation which had grown up in industrial Wales.

World War I and its aftermath saw short-lived prosperity for both rural and industrial Wales, but after 1923 the country as a whole and South Wales in particular entered upon a period of depression which lasted until World War II and which in its intensity was greater than anything previously experienced.

Unemployment reached a peak in 1932 when one-tenth of the total population of Wales was out of work. Wales was by no means unique in the worldwide depression of the 1930's but her problems were intensified by the fact that such a large proportion of the population was totally dependent upon coal, iron, steel, and tinplate. The result was the movement out of Wales of over a quarter of a million people, nine-tenths of whom were from South Wales. Of

169. Berthoff, *British Immigrants*, p. 69.

170. For an excellent analysis of both the statistics of emigration and the decline of British emigration in the twentieth century see *ibid.*, pp. 1–11.

this number, only a few emigrated to the United States, where unemployment matched the dimensions of that in Wales. The great majority moved to the English Midlands and to the growing light industries of the southeast of England around London. Only with World War II and the postwar years would a renaissance take place in South Wales when the domination of coal, iron, and steel was broken by the introduction of new light industries.

The penultimate word on emigration from industrial Wales must go to Professor Brinley Thomas with the significant arguments he puts forward in "Wales and the Atlantic Economy."[171] His thesis is that the migration pattern of Wales was far different from that of other parts of Great Britain in the second half of the nineteenth century. If it had not been for the rapid industrialization of South Wales in a very short period, the whole of the surplus rural population which was Welsh to the core would have left Wales for England or for overseas countries such as the United States. Caught in the cumulative, downward spiral of mass emigration, which in the case of Ireland reduced her population by half, Wales would have been reduced to an aging population of about half a million, exporting her younger and more vigorous people to England and the United States. Thus, the opportunity for employment provided by the iron and steel industry, and even more by the coal industry, became an effective dam which prevented all but a comparatively small number of Welsh people from emigrating to the United States.

The statistics provided by Brinley Thomas go far to substantiate his argument. Between 1881 and 1931, Wales lost to the United States on average less than seven per ten thousand of her population, whereas England lost fourteen, Scotland thirty-five, and Ireland eighty-nine. Throughout this period, Welsh emigration to the United States was not only small but relatively steady with skilled workers in the majority and the proportion of farmers very low. Perhaps most significantly, in the decade from 1901 to 1911 Wales was absorbing population at a rate not much less than that of the United States.

171. Brinley Thomas, ed., *The Welsh Economy* (Cardiff, 1962), pp. 1–29.

It is difficult to dispute this thesis but one caveat needs to be entered to Professor Thomas' persuasive arguments. Although the South Wales coalfield may well have absorbed a high proportion of potential emigrants who might otherwise have gone to the United States, it also provided the means whereby the money necessary to pay for passage to the United States could be accumulated. Contemporary accounts referred frequently to the emigration of miners and foundrymen who had carefully put aside money for the purpose of emigrating to the United States. This indicates also that emigration was no spur-of-the-moment decision, particularly for those with families, but one taken after much consideration and made possible by steady saving from the wages earned in the mines and foundries.

The cost of passage to the United States in the latter part of the nineteenth century varied from about £3 10s to £4. By twentieth-century standards this may seem very cheap, but £4 represented approximately four weeks' wages for the foundryman or coal-miner and as much as six weeks' wages for the agricultural laborer. This is the equivalent of £80 at the present day and points to the fact that it was more expensive to emigrate to the United States a century ago than it is today. Prepaid passages by those already in the United States were one solution, but failing this, industrial South Wales provided the best chance for earning the wages that could make emigration possible.

This indication that industrial South Wales could be both a dam and a springboard to Welsh emigration is but a minor modification of Professor Thomas' argument. It does not substantially weaken the claim that the Welsh were less likely to emigrate to the United States than English, Scottish, or Irish. The fact that Wales had the smallest population base of any part of Great Britain simply meant that the number of Welsh emigrating overseas was correspondingly small.[172]

172. If Professor Thomas' more controversial thesis is accepted that the concentration in industry of Welsh-speaking rural Welshmen preserved the Welsh language, customs, and nation from extinction by Anglicization, the case is made even stronger. Part of the motivation for Welsh emigration had always been an attempt to preserve the language and culture from obliteration. This is what lay behind the abortive attempts to establish

## IV. Conclusion

THE reasons why the Welsh emigrated to North America were clearly different in the colonial period from what they became in the nineteenth century. Also, reasons for emigration from the rural areas were different from those in industrial areas. The time factor is also important: the availability of large amounts of cheap or free land in the United States for three quarters of the nineteenth century was as strong an inducement to emigration for the Welsh tenant farmer or rural laborer as it was for the peasantry of other countries. The growth of American industry also for a while attracted those with skills in iron making or mining to seek higher rewards for their labor in America. Rural depression and an overcrowded labor market at the end of the century, conversely, acted as a deterrent to those contemplating emigration.

Yet at no time did the motives for emigration remain in watertight compartments. Religious, political, social, and economic motives, all operative at one time or another, often acted in conjunction one with the other. The predominance of any one varied only with time and locality.

One can virtually ignore William Vaughn's pioneer attempt to found a Welsh colony in Newfoundland as basically ill-planned paternalism, and also the early indentured Welsh servants who were as much part of the English settlement as of Welsh. The first significant Welsh communities on the other side of the Atlantic, those of Welsh Quakers and Baptists in seventeenth-century Pennsylvania, were primarily the result of religious motivation. This emigration was in part a flight from religious persecution and in part, as A. H. Dodd argues convincingly, the result of evangelical zeal. Moreover, the opportunity to secure substantial amounts of land

---

exclusive Welsh settlements in the United States. If, instead, this need for preservation was met by industrial South Wales, then a more identifiable Welsh nation was recreated on the coalfield. This very Welshness of industrial Wales could, therefore, have acted as one further barrier to emigration. How much weight can be placed on this as against the expulsive forces of poverty and depression is a matter of conjecture.

was also an important force at work in this phase of the emigration. Religious fervor and land hunger were not necessarily antipathetic. Combined in the hope of establishing a separate and exclusive Welsh "barony" in Pennsylvania, they reflected personal, material ambition as much as religious interests and concern for the preservation of Welsh culture and the Welsh language.

The economic situation in Wales during the seventeenth and early eighteenth centuries does not appear to have had a significant effect on emigration. Those who left for America were not poverty-stricken peasants at the end of their tether but relatively well-to-do farmers who had enough capital to acquire land, who were attracted by the greater opportunities offered to them by a new country, and who were willing to help some of their neighbors to emigrate with them.

Political motivation would also seem to have played little part in emigration from Wales during the colonial period. The political stability of England, particularly after the accession of William and Mary, saw similar stability in Wales. The new ideas of political and social democracy which came with the American and French revolutions struck responsive chords with a few educated Welshmen, but the effect on the Welsh peasantry in general was negligible. There was little political persecution to cause Welshmen to seek a sanctuary in the new American republic. The absence of any sizeable emigration from Wales to America for most of the eighteenth century was indicative of all quiet on the religious, political, and economic fronts.

Although the French Revolution did not have major political effects on Wales, the wars which followed brought about economic changes which would bear directly upon Welsh emigration to the United States in the nineteenth century. The pauperization of the Welsh peasantry consequent upon the destruction of the traditional structure of land tenure at a time when the rural population was rapidly increasing made emigration to the United States, with its abundant land, a much more attractive proposition. The prospect of independence, cheap land, and prosperity proved difficult for some to resist.

In this context, the importance of the constant stream of letters from America to Wales urging friends and relatives to seize these opportunities should not be underestimated. Together with the promotional efforts of American railroads later in the century to attract settlers, these letters were probably the most decisive factor in rural emigration. In addition, men like Benjamin Chidlaw, Samuel Roberts, and Michael D. Jones were influential advocates of emigration in rural Wales and their advice carried considerable weight with the Welsh peasantry. The dream shared by Roberts and Jones of establishing a Welsh settlement where the language and culture could be preserved was never realized. The fiasco of the Tennessee venture and Jones's fragile Argentina settlement are sufficient testimony to the primacy of more practical considerations over idealism.

Emigration from industrial South Wales, particularly in the second half of the nineteenth century, presents a totally different picture. Letters from America, while admitting that the western states could still provide a living for potential emigrants, were adamant in their opposition to their fellow countrymen joining them in the industrial centers. The skills which had stood the earlier emigrants to American industry in good stead were of value for only a relatively short time. American technology quickly rendered many of these skills redundant and the Welsh were in no position—or of no mind—to compete with the hordes of unskilled European immigrants who flooded to America at the turn of the century.

Nevertheless, the foundries and coal mines gave rise to conditions which many thought could be bettered in the United States. They also provided the means whereby sufficient money could be saved to pay for passage across the Atlantic. Strikes which almost invariably failed and trade unions which were too weak to sustain strikes offered little hope for the amelioration of working conditions or for the raising of wages above the subsistence level. The grass in the American garden, whatever Welsh-Americans might say, looked appreciably greener.

Political and religious factors in the promotion of emigration in the nineteenth century are more difficult to assess. The Mormon emigration of mid-century was atypical, but political nonconformity, where religion, politics, and Welsh nationalism intersected, became increasingly important in the second half of the century and was not limited to the industrial areas of Wales. Evictions from farms in the rural areas on the grounds of political and religious nonconformity had their counterparts in the industrial centers, but the active promotion of trade unionism was the more common reason for dismissals which contributed to dissatisfaction and subsequent emigration.

Despite the enumeration of the major factors which helped to spur the movement of Welsh people to the United States, it has to be recognized that the numerical contribution of the Welsh to the population of the United States was a very small one. As the population of Wales did not exceed two million until the twentieth century, this is not altogether surprising. What is more difficult to explain, however, is the fact that in terms of percentage of population, the number of Welsh emigrants was much smaller when compared with those leaving Ireland, a country whose population was not overwhelmingly larger than that of Wales. This suggests either that the Welsh were much more difficult to uproot from their homeland or that the factors which brought about emigration from Ireland were significantly stronger than those in Wales. There can be little doubt that the bulk of the Irish peasantry in the middle of the nineteenth century experienced conditions of poverty much worse than those in Wales, a fact reflected in the great number of Irish who left in the Famine years.[173] Apart from this, however, a higher percentage of Welsh than of Irish should have emigrated to the United States. Unlike the Irish, they were eager to take up cheap or free land. Moreover, Welsh tenant farmers or farm laborers who were not at the same distress level as the Irish were probably better able to pay for their passage and to settle easily in the United States. The peasants turned foundrymen or miners also developed tech-

---

173. One intriguing question is how so many Irish peasants who were on or over the brink of starvation at the time of the Famine found the money needed to pay for passage to America. Either the extent of the poverty in Ireland was exaggerated or disguised, or the amount of assistance coming from Irish-Americans was extraordinarily large.

nical skills which were in demand in the United States. These skills enabled them to earn their passage money to America and assured them of an immediate pay packet once they had arrived. Emigration ports such as Liverpool were more accessible to the Welsh than the Irish although less scrupulous masters were happy to overload their ships by taking aboard Irish emigrants off the coast of southern Ireland. Yet despite these advantages, the Welsh emigrated only in their tens of thousands whereas the Irish emigrated in their millions. The simplest explanation is that the Irish emigrated from utter despair and catastrophe whereas the Welsh emigrated by design and not from disaster.

It was not that the Welsh were uninterested in the United States or oblivious of the opportunities there offered. From colonial times there was much interest in Wales concerning America and this interest was maintained during the nineteenth century, the most important period of emigration. Wales as a country politically subordinated to England found the democratic institutions of the United States attractive: religious nonconformity in Wales approved strongly of religious freedom and the absence of a state church in America; economically, the United States appealed as strongly to the Welsh as to other nationalities; and the social egalitarianism of the American people sat well with the basic egalitarianism of the majority of Welshmen. There can be no doubt of the attractiveness of America to the Welsh, yet only a relative few chose to seize the opportunity to emigrate. This can conceivably be explained in terms of negative factors which counterbalance the inducements to emigrate, yet such negative factors on examination were curiously weak.

It is tempting to ascribe the Welsh reluctance to emigrate to an attachment to Wales almost mystical in its intensity. "Hiraeth"—a longing for Wales—was frequently mentioned by those who had emigrated to the United States, but it is very much open to question whether this was stronger with the Welsh than with other nationalities. The fear, which proved correct, that the Welsh language and Welsh culture would disappear if transplanted from Wales to America was one likely to discourage only a few, for everyday problems of making a living were those that most concerned the average Welshman. Welsh nationalism could have been a factor inhibiting emigration, but the rural areas where its strength traditionally lay were the ones which suffered the heaviest depopulation after 1850. There is the possibility that Wales was never sufficiently depressed economically to bring about large-scale emigration in the nineteenth century. When the real depths of economic depression were reached in the twentieth century, the Welsh moved to England and not to the United States.

The motives for emigration from Wales appear to have been less strong than those in other parts of Great Britain, yet at the same time the factors inhibiting emigration were correspondingly weak. The answer to this paradox does, therefore, appear to be the thesis put forward by Brinley Thomas, that industrialization in Wales itself impeded a significant emigration movement from that country by providing an alternative to the United States much closer at hand. It created on the South Wales coalfield a new Welsh nation, highly cohesive, Welsh-speaking, secure in its nonconformity, politically articulate, and potentially powerful as a nation within the United Kingdom.

# THE AUSTRIAN EMIGRATION
## 1900–1914

Johann Chmelar

Translated by Thomas C. Childers

# THE AUSTRIAN EMIGRATION
# 1900–1914

## A. The Scope and Course of Emigration from Austria
## 1900–1914, with a Review of its Development to 1900

FOR Austria-Hungary emigration was of profound political, social, economic, and, not least, military importance, especially in the last peaceful decade of the Danubian Monarchy's existence. While the number of emigrants at the beginning of the second half of the nineteenth century lay within the range of a few thousand yearly, it soon climbed into the tens of thousands, and in 1903 exceeded the 100,000 mark in the Austrian half of the Empire alone. In the record year 1907, the number of emigrants from the entire Monarchy reached over 350,000, a figure surpassing the population of Graz, Austria's second largest city in 1971.

Two principal types of emigrants can be distinguished in the Austrian setting:[1] (a) those who traveled overseas, the overwhelming majority of whom turned their backs forever on their old homeland—they are the true emigrants—and (b) continental mi-

---

NOTE: The term "Austria" refers to the kingdoms and provinces represented in the *Reichsrat*, the parliament in Vienna. They are: Kingdom of Galicia; Kingdom of Bohemia; Kingdom of Dalmatia; Archduchy of Lower Austria; Archduchy of Upper Austria; Duchies of Bukovina, Silesia, Styria, Salzburg, Carinthia, and Carniola; Margraviate of Moravia; Earldom of Tirol and Küstenland (Görz, Gradisca, Istria, and Trieste).

1. Johann Chmelar, "Die Auswanderung aus den im Reichsrat vetretenen Königreichen und Ländern in den Jahren 1905–1914" (unpub. PhD diss., University of Vienna, 1972), p. 6.

grants who found temporary employment in non-Austrian Europe.[2]

The continental migration was more uniform, for it almost always remained a seasonal phenomenon.[3] By modern notions, however, this form of migration at the beginning of the twentieth century cannot properly be considered emigration in the strict sense.[4]

In Austria emigration had become a "permanent social category," and since it assumed various forms, it therefore also drew diverse social and economic consequences in its wake.[5]

### 1. A REVIEW OF THE EMIGRATION TO 1900

Around 1820 the great waves of emigration from Europe began. The disparity between the rapid increase of population and the relatively slower pace of industrialization with the concomitant scarcity of jobs throws the economic motives of emigration into sharp relief. However, the revolutionary years 1848–1849 in Europe were followed by a wave of politically motivated emigration to America. Thereafter, the number of emigrants receded again.[1]

In Austria the Constitution of 1867 contained the principle of freedom of emigration.[2] Several years later, in a treatise on the emigration and its causes, it was stated that,

one can, in general, accept the following as the chief causes of the emigration: the density of the population and the progressive increase of the latter due to the surplus of births over deaths; the barrenness or the slight productive capacity of the land; the unemployment resulting from the lack of sufficient commercial and industrial enterprises; the excessive competition; the poor pay; the disproportionate tax burden carried by the working class; great world-

2. In the contemporary literature they were referred to as "seasonal workers." Many workers from the northeastern crownlands earned their living in Germany. See Franz Markitan, *Die österreichischen Saisonwanderer* (Vienna, 1913).

3. Sigismund Gargas, *Zur Regelung des Auswanderungswesens in Österreich* (Vienna, 1913), p. 5.

4. Chmelar, "Die Auswanderung," pp. 3ff.

5. Gargas, *Zur Regelung des Auswanderungswesens*, p. 3.

1. Chmelar, "Die Auswanderung," p. 18.

2. Erich Zöllner, *Geschichte Österreichs von den Anfängen bis zur Gegenwart*, 4th ed. (Vienna, 1970), p. 444.

Names of crownland and one-time capitals of historico-political units within Hungary and Bosnia-Hercegovina are italicized.

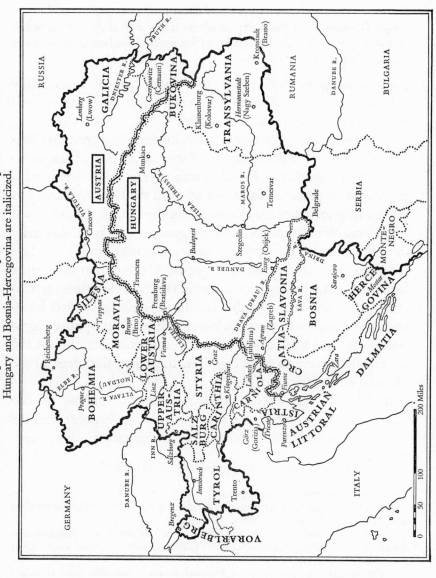

SOURCE: Robert A. Kann, *The Multinational Empire. Nationalism and National Reform in the Habsburg Monarchy 1848–1918* (New York: Columbia University Press, 1950), I, 20–21.

historical events such as wars, political discontent, and religious strife; even simple *Wanderlust* and the desire for adventure; as well as the current public education which provides knowledge of foreign lands and customs easier and quicker than before.[3]

Austria-Hungary, according to the writer, had, of course, only 0.25 emigrants per thousand inhabitants and thus, in the author's opinion, had "little cause for concern."[4]

Emigration, however, rose steadily, and an ever-increasing number of Austrians, representing a substantial portion of the country's surplus population, found its way overseas.[5] Emigration led more than 90 percent of all those who left the Dual Monarchy to build a new existence for themselves in the United States.[6]

The statistical definition of the emigrants is very poor, especially so at the outset of the period of mass emigration, and it is at best unsatisfactory for the following years. The Austrian authorities kept no emigration statistics, and until 1875 reliable figures on Austrian emigration are altogether lacking. Beginning in 1876, however, more exact statistics were kept in the large European emigration ports,[7] and these as well as the immigration statistics of the continental American states constitute the principal sources for the essential quantitative material.[8]

In the years 1821–1890 roughly 296,000 Austrians and 138,000 Hungarians immigrated into the United States.[9] Altogether, the Monarchy provided 2.8 percent of the immigrants in this period,

3. Friedrich Robert, *Zur Auswanderungsfrage* (Vienna, 1879), p. 7.

4. *Ibid.*, pp. 10–11.

5. Zöllner, *Geschichte Österreichs*, p. 444.

6. *Ibid.* Zöllner cites 1903, a year in which 206,000 of the 220,000 emigrants from the Monarchy settled in the United States.

7. Karl von Englisch, "Die österreichische Auswanderungsstatistik," *Statistische Monatsschrift*, edited by the Austrian Statistical Central Commission, new series, XVIII Jahrgang (Brünn, 1913), 72–73.

8. The immigration statistics of the American countries, especially those regarding nationality, must be treated with caution. The *Annual Report of the Commissioner General of Immigration* of the United States, which was published at the close of each fiscal year, classified immigrants by ethnic group but often not by citizenship. Thus, Polish immigrants were classified simply as Poles, regardless of whether they emigrated from Germany, Russia, or Galicia.

9. The United States received 90 percent of the Monarchy's emigrants. The figures are from the *Annual Report of the Commissioner General of Immigration*.

AUSTRIA-HUNGARY

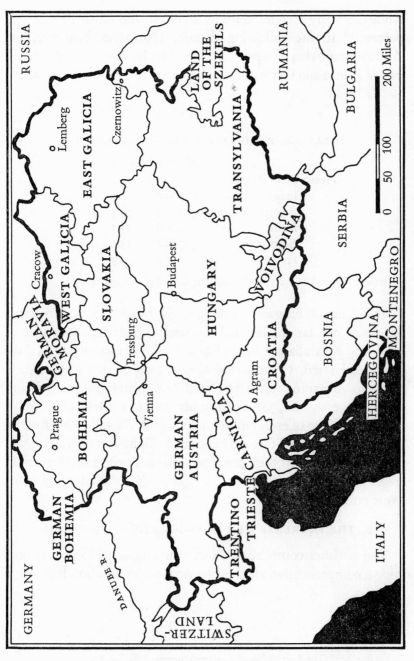

SOURCE: Robert A. Kann, *The Multinational Empire. Nationalism and National Reform in the Habsburg Monarchy 1848–1918* (New York: Columbia University Press, 1950), II, 199.

while Germany accounted for 29.2 percent and Great Britain 40.4 percent.[10] In the following decade, 1891–1900, however, the Austro-Hungarian emigration rose sharply, and the Monarchy passed France and Germany as a source for American immigration.

Table 1.1

TOTAL U.S. IMMIGRATION 1891–1900: 3,844,359

|  | Number | Percent |
|---|---|---|
| From: Great Britain | 745,853 | 19.4 |
| Italy | 655,668 | 17.1 |
| Austria-Hungary | 597,047 | 15.5 |
| Russia | 588,866 | 15.3 |
| Germany | 543,922 | 14.1 |
| France | 36,006 | 0.9 |

SOURCE: *Annual Report of the Commissioner General of Immigration.*

The Austro-Hungarian immigration to the other American countries was far smaller and to Asian and African countries as well as to Australia was insignificant. In 1900 a total of 62,605 Austrians emigrated, 53,930 to the United States, 5,122 to Canada,[11] 1,734 to Argentina, 1,361 to Brazil, 108 to the remaining South American countries, 388 to Australia, and 12 to Africa.[12]

The steep rise of emigration can be seen in the following figures. In 1876 only 7,809 Austrians emigrated. Eight years later, in 1884, 21,558 Austrians left their country, while after eight more years, in 1892, the figure reached 50,273. In 1900, 62,605 Austrian emigrants were counted.[13]

## 2. THE INCREASE OF THE EMIGRATION, 1901–1910

The statistics compiled by Karl von Englisch (Table 2.1) provide a comprehensive view of the Austrian emigration from 1876 to 1910.

10. *Ibid.*
11. Compared to other years, the number is relatively high.
12. Englisch, "Die österreichische Auswanderungsstatistik," p. 73.
13. *Ibid.*

From the figures it is clear that the United States absorbed the mainstream, indeed, 83 percent, of the Austrian emigrants. Their distribution among the four major centers of immigration appears in Table 2.II.

Table 2.II

DISTRIBUTION OF EMIGRANTS

|  | Number | Percent |
|---|---|---|
| U.S.A. | 1,531,382 | 83.0 |
| Canada | 151,913 | 8.2 |
| Argentina | 94,047 | 5.1 |
| Brazil | 55,860 | 3.0 |

From 1876 to 1910 emigration from the kingdoms and lands represented in the *Reichsrat* increased eighteenfold, and the share of several countries in the Austrian emigration increased substantially in this period. In 1876 Canada received only .08 percent of the Austrian emigrants; in 1910, 14.69 percent. For the same years Argentina's share rose from .05 to 4.42 percent.[1]

By the turn of the century the Dual Monarchy had become, along with Italy and tsarist Russia, the main source of emigration from continental Europe. The number of emigrants from the kingdoms and lands represented in the *Reichsrat* and from the lands of the Hungarian Holy Crown remained approximately even until 1914. Although the Austrians held a slight advantage, the ratio fluctuated substantially from year to year. The year of heaviest emigration from Hungary was 1907. Of the roughly 386,000 emigrants who left the Monarchy in that year,[2] 209,169 came from the Hungarian half.[3]

If, in surveying the statistics for the entire period, shown in Table 2.I, one focuses on the decade 1901–1910 an enormous increase in emigration is at once obvious. In ten years more people emigrated from Austria than in the previous twenty-five. The period 1906–

1. Englisch, "Die österreichische Auswanderungsstatistik," p. 74.
2. Heinrich Benedikt, "Die wirtschaftliche Entwicklung in der Franz-Joseph Zeit," *Wiener historische Studien*, 4 (1958), 165.
3. R. Riedl, *Die Organisation der Auswanderung in Österreich. Bericht über die vorläufigen Ergebnisse der im k.k. Handelsministerium durchgeführten Untersuchung* (Vienna, 1913), p. 12.

Table 2.1

EMIGRATION FROM AUSTRIA TO:

| Year | U.S.A. | Canada | Argentina | Brazil | S. America | Africa | Australia | Asia | Unknown | Total |
|---|---|---|---|---|---|---|---|---|---|---|
| 1876 | 6,173 | 6 | 4 | 1,433 | 4 | 5 | — | 1 | 183 | 7,809 |
| 1877 | 4,717 | — | — | 1,506 | 142 | — | — | — | — | 6,365 |
| 1878 | 4,605 | — | — | 66 | 34 | 112 | — | — | — | 4,817 |
| 1879 | 7,387 | — | 8 | — | — | — | — | — | — | 7,395 |
| 1880 | 19,302 | — | 400 | — | 171 | — | — | — | — | 19,873 |
| 1881 | 21,462 | — | 2,615 | — | 182 | — | — | — | — | 24,259 |
| 1882 | 17,071 | — | — | — | — | — | — | — | — | 17,071 |
| 1883 | 18,460 | 31 | — | 325 | 19 | — | 16 | — | — | 18,851 |
| 1884 | 20,115 | 56 | — | 333 | 1,032 | 3 | 19 | — | — | 21,558 |
| 1885 | 17,523 | 17 | 4,243 | 291 | 238 | 5 | 8 | — | — | 22,325 |
| 1886 | 19,330 | 61 | 73 | 273 | 50 | 3 | 12 | 1 | — | 19,803 |
| 1887 | 24,830 | 33 | 1,273 | 144 | 62 | 2 | 14 | — | — | 26,358 |
| 1888 | 27,751 | 78 | 1,347 | 1,705 | 57 | 11 | 10 | 10 | — | 30,969 |
| 1889 | 23,399 | 246 | 5,424 | 395 | 95 | 54 | 17 | 5 | — | 29,635 |
| 1890 | 32,848 | 261 | 1,801 | 2,889 | 62 | 197 | 11 | — | — | 38,069 |
| 1891 | 41,643 | 2,490 | 1,315 | 2,856 | 68 | 1 | 94 | 3 | — | 48,470 |
| 1892 | 46,203 | 824 | 707 | 1,754 | 732 | 2 | 51 | — | — | 50,273 |
| 1893 | 44,115 | 967 | 1,056 | 1,975 | 663 | 6 | 52 | 5 | — | 48,839 |
| 1894 | 16,252 | 379 | 512 | 1,380 | 239 | 27 | 16 | — | — | 18,805 |
| 1895 | 33,661 | 39 | 948 | 11,459 | 148 | — | 89 | — | — | 46,344 |
| 1896 | 32,697 | 1,124 | 1,368 | 11,549 | 424 | 36 | 457 | — | — | 47,655 |

| Year | U.S.A. | Canada | Argentina | Brazil | S. America | Africa | Australia | Asia | Unknown | Total |
|---|---|---|---|---|---|---|---|---|---|---|
| 1897 | 18,047 | 4,220 | 1,478 | 2,097 | 508 | 48 | 324 | — | — | 26,722 |
| 1898 | 27,653 | 4,126 | 441 | 856 | 119 | 18 | 729 | 3 | — | 33,945 |
| 1899 | 47,277 | 5,708 | 583 | 1,912 | 23 | 31 | 30 | 4 | — | 55,598 |
| 1900 | 53,930 | 5,122 | 1,734 | 1,361 | 108 | 12 | 338 | — | — | 62,605 |
| 1901 | 59,581 | 2,561 | 2,312 | 445 | 60 | 72 | 41 | 11 | — | 65,083 |
| 1902 | 80,908 | 10,629 | 1,753 | 262 | 66 | 18 | 51 | — | — | 93,687 |
| 1903 | 85,572 | 15,035 | 1,113 | 320 | 14 | 71 | 6 | — | 503 | 102,634 |
| 1904 | 60,893 | 12,649 | 4,622 | 265 | 110 | 7 | 464 | 7 | — | 79,017 |
| 1905 | 98,670 | 11,489 | 12,772 | 293 | 157 | 68 | 285 | 22 | — | 123,756 |
| 1906 | 110,599 | 9,924 | 15,013 | 297 | 154 | 87 | 330 | 10 | — | 136,414 |
| 1907 | 139,756 | 23,494 | 13,601 | 408 | 103 | 42 | 241 | 8 | — | 177,653 |
| 1908 | 42,943 | 7,704 | 3,423 | 3,919 | 85 | 62 | 178 | 9 | — | 58,323 |
| 1909 | 112,791 | 11,801 | 5,835 | 2,020 | 41 | 34 | 13 | 2 | — | 132,537 |
| 1910 | 113,218 | 20,839 | 6,273 | 1,042 | 315 | 151 | 23 | 4 | — | 141,865 |

Total Austrian Emigrants:

| | | | | | | | | | | |
|---|---|---|---|---|---|---|---|---|---|---|
| | 1,531,382 | 151,913 | 94,047 | 55,860 | 6,285 | 1,185 | 3,919 | 105 | 686 | 1,845,382 |

Total Austrian and Hungarian Emigrants:

| | | | | | | | | | | |
|---|---|---|---|---|---|---|---|---|---|---|
| | 2,953,587 | 157,969 | 358,507 | 64,360 | 6,544 | 1,771 | 4,097 | 109 | 686 | 3,517,630 |

SOURCE: Englisch, "Die österreichische Auswanderungsstatistik," p. 73.
NOTE: Englisch relies on the oldest sources, the harbor statistics. Contrary to his opinion, these figures do not represent a "complete and errorless compilation." Nevertheless, no better sources are available for the early years. Still a number of differences appear if one compares the harbor figures from 1900 onward with other statistics..

1910 was, in turn, more prolific than the preceding five years. In fact, the years 1901–1905 account for 25.2 percent and the following five years for 35.1 percent of the total emigration after 1876.[4]

Viewed broadly, the main territorial sources of European emigration gradually shifted from west to east.

In Germany, France, and England, the desire to emigrate had subsided as a result of the feeling that the opportunities for the easy successes achieved abroad in the first decades were waning, while at home expanding industrial development held labor back. On the other hand, enterprises of American capital sought out cheaper labor instead of masses of skilled workers who would demand higher wages.[5]

For the United States, this epoch brought the fourth wave of immigration.

The fourth wave of immigration was produced by a huge demand for cheap, unskilled labor resulting from extensive changes in the production process. It began at the close of the century and, although interrupted by minor setbacks after the panic of 1870 and slight disturbances in 1911, it lasted until the World War. In this period, as the economic expansion of the United States assumed its present character and industrialization achieved a maturity and a more or less stable form, immigration reached a new high point. In this surge the lead was taken not by the immigrants from the "old" West European nations but by the immigrants from Italy, Austria-Hungary, and Russia.[6]

### 3. EMIGRATION, 1911–1914

This period is characterized by the increased interest which governmental authorities and the general public, represented by the press, brought to the emigration movement. In Austria, two different fundamental attitudes toward emigration were discernible.[1] One side saw it as a safety valve for social-revolutionary pressure, an evil to be sure, but a necessary one. This view was essentially

---

4. Englisch, "Die österreichische Auswanderungsstatistik," p. 75.

5. "Auswanderung und Rückwanderung der Länder der ungarischen heiligen Krone in den Jahren 1899–1913," *Ungarische Statistische Mitteilungen*, edited by the Royal Hungarian Statistical Office, German edition, new series, 67 (Budapest, 1918), pt. I, p. 6.

6. V. Nikša, "Geschichtliche Analyse der Einwanderung in die Vereinigten Staaten unter Berücksichtigung der wirtschaftlichten, sozialen, politischen und allgemein kulturellen Faktoren" (unpub. PhD diss., University of Vienna, 1949), p. 100.

1. Chmelar, "Die Auswanderung," p. 63.

held by the Social Democrats who saw a potential improvement of the remaining proletariat's position as one consequence of emigration. Within the Austrian government this interpretation was supported by the Ministry of Trade. The other side, represented by the so-called "state-preserving" forces, stood for a rigorous limitation of emigration. The principle of freedom of emigration was limited by the obligation for military service, and this seemed to provide a possible legal basis for restriction. Belonging to these forces were the great estate owners, who feared the loss of their cheap labor, and various industrial circles, both in league with the *Reichspost*[2] and many *Christlich Soziale* who wanted to solve a social problem with police methods. The military establishment of the Danubian Monarchy also belonged to this group. It was not only concerned with raising the necessary recruits but also warned that the emigrants from Austria-Hungary might possibly serve, in the future, in "enemy armies."

The interest of the military establishment in an extensive suppression of emigration resulted from the fact that the emigrants were, for the most part, men between the ages of twenty and forty, thus men liable for military service.[3] The imperial minister of war, Krobatin, was alarmed to discover that in the disposition of troops, in 1913, 111,678 men in the Austrian half of the Empire alone were missing, of whom 81,179 were listed in the three Galician corps.[4] The high emigration figures also aroused the interest of the successor to the throne, Archduke Franz Ferdinand.[5] Through his aide-de-camp Colonel Karl Bardolff he declared his interest in the question and expressed the desire to hold down emigration as much as possible.[6]

2. See numerous articles in the *Reichspost*, newspaper of the conservative "Christlich-Soziale Partei," August, September, October, and November 1913.

3. Chmelar, "Die Auswanderung," pp. 63ff.

4. Allgemeines Verwaltungsarchiv (hereafter cited as AVA), Ministerium des Innern (hereafter cited as MdI), Auswanderungsakten 8/4 file 320, no. 28 044/13. Krobatin to the Austrian minister of defense, General Friederich von Georgi, July 14, 1913.

5. See Chmelar, "Die Auswanderung," pp. 65ff.

6. AVA, Handelsministerium Auswanderung (hereafter cited as AW) file 1882, no. 18 952/13. Communication of the aide-de-camp of Archduke Franz Ferdinand, Colonel Bardolff, to Stürgkh, Austrian prime minister, June 2, 1913.

The attention won by emigration in the last years of peace was not, however, restricted to official circles. By then the general public had also become interested. Entrepreneurs and the great estate owners, fearing for their cheap labor supply, demanded a curtailment for "patriotic reasons."[7] While industrial and agricultural entrepreneurial interests demanded a restriction of the emigration for capitalist motives—specifically, in order to have the largest possible number of cheap laborers and thus to keep the wage level low —the transportation companies, railroad and shipping lines, along with the Ministry of Trade, maintained that emigration could not be restricted by the state. Although liberal motives were advanced, the transportation companies in fact had a financial interest. These groups were, however, not averse to a regulation of emigration which would benefit the native port of Trieste and the national "United Austrian Shipping Corporation" (formerly the Austro-Americana and Fratelli Cosulich).[8] The Austrian shipping line could hardly compete with the powerful foreign companies, but it wanted to secure its share of the emigration business by legislative means.

In the period 1911–1914 Austrian emigration continued to grow and in 1913 reached a new record. The rise was especially reflected in the immigration to North America, to the United States as well as Canada, while the migration to South America stagnated and even declined somewhat.

The outbreak of World War I put a stop to the emigration; with the beginning of the war, it declined almost to the zero point.[9] Yet, even before then, in the first half of 1914, repressive measures and chicanery on the part of the authorities had reduced emigration.

---

7. In the foreword to his work on the "harmful sides of emigration," Alexander Fischel wrote: "The danger which threatens our army and therefore our power position, our agriculture, industry, and in the end the prosperity of the Austrian people, as opposed to the statements from various quarters that the size of the emigration has been exaggerated and that it is necessary because of overpopulation, has induced me to enter into the following hastily sketched discussion. May it achieve the desired patriotic success!" *Die schädlichen Seiten der Auswanderung und deren Bekämpfung. Einige Worte zu einer brennenden Frage* (Vienna, 1914).

8. The line was usually referred to as the "Austro-Americana."

9. Chmelar, "Die Auswanderung," p. 127.

Table 3.1

| Destination | 1909 | 1910 | 1911 | 1912 | 1913 | Total |
|---|---|---|---|---|---|---|
| *U.S.A.* | | | | | | |
| Dual Monarchy | 170,191 | 258,737 | 159,057 | 178,882 | 254,825 | 1,021,692 |
| Austrians | 80,853 | 153,793 | 82,129 | 85,854 | 137,245 | 521,874 |
| *Canada* | | | | | | |
| Dual Monarchy | 20,123 | 10,240 | 17,420 | 24,394 | 29,460 | 101,637 |
| Austrians | 8,709 | 9,402† | 16,751 | 23,472 | 27,846 | 86,180 |
| *Argentina* | | | | | | |
| Dual Monarchy | 4,552 | 4,542 | 4,703 | 6,545 | 24,085‡ | 44,427 |
| Austrians | 3,803 | 4,031† | 4,398 | 5,832 | 3,202 | 21,266 |
| *Brazil* | | | | | | |
| Dual Monarchy | 4,065 | 2,920 | 3,352 | 3,045 | 1,560 | 14,942 |
| Austrians | 4,008 | 3,517 | 3,158 | — | — | 10,683§ |
| *Uruguay and Paraguay* | | | | | | |
| Dual Monarchy | 93 | 42 | 13 | 79 | 78 | 305 |
| *Australia and New Zealand* | | | | | | |
| Dual Monarchy | 254 | 306 | 218 | 29 | 3 | 810 |
| *Africa* | | | | | | |
| Dual Monarchy | — | 21 | 114 | 4 | 5 | 144 |
| TOTALS | | | | | | |
| Dual Monarchy | 199,278 | 276,808 | 184,877 | 212,978 | 310,016 | 1,183,957 |
| Austrians | 97,373 | 152,743 | 106,436 | 115,158 | 168,293 | 640,003 |

SOURCE: *Österreichisches Statistisches Handbuch*, ed. by the Austrian Statistical Central Commission, 32 Jahrgang, 1913 (Vienna, 1914), 60. Source for all figures unless otherwise noted.

* Fiscal year.

† This figure was listed as "unknown" in the *Statistisches Handbuch*, thus recourse to Riedl, *Die Organisation der Auswanderung*, pp. 90–91, was taken.

‡ This number is extremely dubious, since Hungary, on the average, provided 400–600 immigrants to Argentina annually and then suddenly the figure is given at around 21,000.

§ Total up to 1911.

## Table 4.1

### IMMIGRATION TO THE UNITED STATES 1901–1911

| Country of origin | 1901 | 1902 | 1903 | 1904 | 1905 | 1906 | 1907 | 1908 | 1909 | 1910 | 1901–1910 Total in absolute numbers | Percent of total immigration | 1911 |
|---|---|---|---|---|---|---|---|---|---|---|---|---|---|
| Austria-Hungary | 113,300 | 172,532 | 206,009 | 177,158 | 275,723 | 265,291 | 338,507 | 168,529 | 170,191 | 258,737 | 2,145,977 | 24.39 | 159,057 |
| Italy | 135,996 | 178,375 | 230,622 | 193,296 | 221,479 | 273,120 | 285,731 | 128,503 | 183,218 | 215,537 | 2,045,877 | 23.26 | 182,882 |
| Russia | 85,257 | 107,347 | 136,093 | 145,141 | 184,897 | 215,665 | 258,943 | 156,711 | 120,460 | 186,792 | 1,597,306 | 18.16 | 158,721 |
| Great Britain | 45,546 | 46,036 | 68,947 | 87,733 | 137,147 | 102,241 | 113,674 | 93,477 | 71,866 | 98,947 | 865,614 | 9.84 | 102,873 |
| Germany | 21,651 | 28,304 | 40,086 | 46,380 | 40,574 | 37,564 | 37,807 | 32,309 | 25,540 | 31,283 | 341,498 | 3.88 | 32,061 |
| France | 3,150 | 3,117 | 5,578 | 9,406 | 10,168 | 9,386 | 9,731 | 8,788 | 6,672 | 7,383 | 73,379 | 0.84 | 8,022 |
| Spain and Portugal | 4,757 | 6,282 | 11,397 | 10,711 | 7,628 | 10,438 | 15,392 | 11,206 | 7,572 | 11,701 | 97,084 | 1.10 | 13,448 |
| Sweden and Norway | 35,579 | 48,378 | 70,489 | 51,571 | 51,655 | 45,040 | 42,722 | 25,221 | 28,101 | 41,283 | 440,039 | 5.00 | 34,730 |
| TOTAL | 445,236 | 590,371 | 769,221 | 721,396 | 929,271 | 958,745 | 1,102,507 | 624,744 | 613,620 | 851,663 | 7,606,774 | 86.47 | 691,794 |
| All immigration to the U.S. | 487,828 | 649,286 | 857,044 | 812,872 | 1,026,529 | 1,100,888 | 1,285,404 | 782,890 | 751,786 | 1,041,570 | 8,796,097 | 100.00 | 878,587 |

SOURCE: Englisch, "Die österreichische Auswanderungsstatistik," p. 89.

## 4. AUSTRIAN EMIGRATION TO THE UNITED STATES

As already mentioned, the United States received the major contingent of the Austrian emigrants. From 1901 to 1910 Austria-Hungary supplied the largest number of immigrants to the United States, as shown in Table 4.I. Its 2,145,977 represented 24.39 percent of the total in that period.[1] In 1905, 1907, 1908, and 1910, the Dual Monarchy provided the largest contingent of Austrian immigrants. From 1901 to 1904 as well as in 1906, 1909, and 1911, most of the immigrants came from Italy. It is noteworthy that the number of immigrants from Germany remained relatively modest and did not increase even in the record year 1907, while the number of immigrants from other countries rose more or less sharply. In 1907, for example, only 37,807 Germans emigrated to the United States, while nine times as many, 338,507, left the Dual Monarchy.

On the basis of the figures provided by the *Annual Report of the Commissioner General of Immigration*, it is possible to compute the overall immigration to the United States from 1821 to 1911, as shown in Table 4.II.

The years 1906 to 1910 brought an additional increase of immigration to the United States from the Habsburg Monarchy. The

Table 4.II

TOTAL IMMIGRATION FROM 1821 TO 1911: 28,946,761

| From: England | 7,949,617 |
|---|---|
| Germany | 5,421,609 |
| Austria-Hungary | 3,336,569 |
| Italy | 3,272,985 |
| Russia | 2,669,785 |
| France | 483,753 |

NOTE: The remainder was distributed among other countries.
SOURCE: Englisch, "Die österreichische Auswanderungsstatistik," p. 87.

1. Englisch, "Die österreichische Auswanderungsstatistik," p. 89.

Table 4.III

IMMIGRATION FROM THE HABSBURG MONARCHY
TO THE UNITED STATES

| Year | Austrians | Hungarians | Total |
|------|-----------|------------|-------|
| 1906 | 59,674 | 70,047 | 129,721 |
| 1907 | 85,318 | 123,413 | 208,731 |
| 1908 | 82,983 | 85,526 | 168,509 |
| 1909 | 80,853 | 89,338 | 170,191 |
| 1910 | 135,793 | 122,944 | 258,737 |

SOURCE: Riedl, *Die Organisation der Auswanderung*, pp. 90–91.

total number of immigrants reached about 1,200,000, an increase of roughly 33 percent over the period 1901–1905. In this decade, the majority of immigrants came from Hungary. In 1906 and 1907, the preponderance of the Hungarian immigrants was clear, while in 1908 and 1909 they held only a slight advantage. In 1910 the largest contingent again came from the Austrian half of the Empire, but between 1906 and 1910 emigration to the United States from Hungary exceeded that from Austria by approximately 90,000. In 1912–1913, the wave of immigration to the United States reached a new peak, the total of 1,197,892 almost equalling the record 1,285,349 of 1906–1907.[2]

Table 4.IV

IMMIGRATION FROM THE HABSBURG MONARCHY
TO THE UNITED STATES

| Year | Austrians | Hungarians | Total |
|------|-----------|------------|-------|
| 1911 | 82,129 | 76,928 | 159,057 |
| 1912 | 85,854 | 93,028 | 178,882 |
| 1913 | 137,245 | 117,580 | 254,825 |

SOURCE: Chmelar, "Die Auswanderung," p. 76.

2. AVA, MdI Auswanderungsakten 8/4 file 323, no. 17 843/14. Austro-Hungarian Ambassador Dumba to the Foreign Ministry, March 19, 1914.

Table 4.v

GRAPH OF THE AUSTRIAN IMMIGRATION
TO THE UNITED STATES 1908–1913

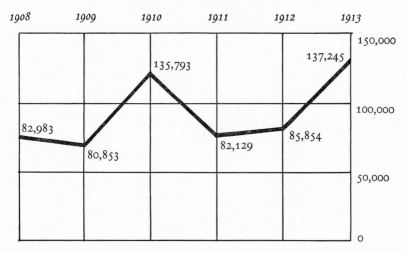

SOURCE: AVA, MdI Auswanderungsakten 8/4 file 323, no. 17 843/14.

To distinguish between the emigrants from the Monarchy on
the basis of Austrian or Hungarian citizenship is quite difficult,
since much of the statistical data is based only on ethnic identification without considering citizenship (*Staatsangehörigkeit*).[3] The categorization of Poles and Jews is especially difficult in this respect.
The Slavs represented the dominant element in the emigration.
Each year they composed around 60 percent of the Austro-Hungarian emigrants.[4] In 1912 they comprised 64.3 percent.[5] The Poles
and Ruthenians were the largest groups in the Austrian half of the
Empire; the Slovaks and South Slavs played the leading role in the
Hungarian. Of the Monarchy's German emigrants, two thirds

3. AVA, Handelsministerium AW, file 1924, no. 31 769/14. Report of the Austro-
Hungarian General Consulate in New York, May 29, 1914.
4. Chmelar, "Die Auswanderung," p. 73.
5. AVA, Justizministerium I B I, 2 carton 49, no. 31 825/13. Gesetzentwurf 1913,
Motivenbericht, p. 32.

sprang from the Hungarian half of the Empire and only one third from Austria.[6]

Table 4.VI

ETHNIC GROUPS EMIGRATING FROM THE
MONARCHY IN FISCAL YEAR 1912–1913

|  | Austria | Hungary |
|---|---|---|
| Poles | 54,997 | 336 |
| Ruthenians | 24,700 | 3,879 |
| Magyars | 399 | 29,422 |
| Croats and Slovenes | 17,797 | |
| Croats and Slavonians | | 22,970 |
| Slovaks | 911 | 25,923 |
| Germans | 8,113 | 16,002 |
| Jews | 11,831 | 3,371 |
| Bohemians and Moravians | 10,362 | 179 |
| Dalmatians (including Bosnia-Herzegovina) | 4,120 | 144 |
| Italians | 1,962 | 70 |

SOURCE: AVA, Handelsministerium AW, file 1924, no. 31 769/14. Report of the Austro-Hungarian General Consulate in New York, May 29, 1914.

Confronted with the new mass proletarian migration, the attitude of the United States toward immigration had however changed. The immigration of Britons and other western Europeans, including Germans, was welcome, but a strong opposition developed against immigration from southern and eastern Europe.

The most heavily represented occupational groups among the emigrants from Austria-Hungary were agricultural workers, day laborers, and servants. A large segment of them was illiterate. Among the immigrants in 1913, 3,208 Ruthenians, 3,160 Poles, 417 Rumanians, 407 Croatians, 225 Slovaks, and an equal number of Magyars were illiterate.[7] Among Russian immigrants illiteracy was even higher. Of the 174,365 Poles immigrating from the states of

6. Chmelar, "Die Auswanderung," p. 77.
7. AVA, MdI Auswanderungsakten 8/4 file 323, no. 17 843/14 (based on Embassy reports).

Central and Eastern Europe in 1913, 51,636 were illiterate.[8] Relatively few Galician Poles (the above mentioned 3,160) were among them, the rest being almost exclusively from Russian Poland. Legal measures by the United States government to curb immigration or to bar the immigration of illiterates were, therefore, of great importance to the East European migrants. However, only these immigrants could satisfy America's great need for unskilled workers.[9]

Among the Austrian immigrants, more men were to be found than women. For every 100 Austrian women, there were 155 men. With 161 men for every 100 women the ratio was even more one-sided among the Hungarians. Comparing these ratios to those of the two other important emigration countries, one finds 191 Italian and 137 Russian men for every 100 women from those states respectively.[10]

The return of Austrians from the United States, which occurred with varying degrees of frequency, was not viewed with great favor in Austria. The reservations expressed by Ambassador Dumba in Washington were widely held. He believed that many of the returning emigrants were no longer fit to work and were "worn out by hard labor."

From the social, political, and military points of view, this returning stream only exerts a directly pernicious influence. These people are usually saturated with radical, democratic, and for the most part republican maxims, and, as naturalized American citizens, they are hostilely disposed toward the authority of the native administration. . . . They lure other fellows to illegal emigration . . . and, therefore, they are not only undesirable, they are clearly dangerous members of the state whose continued stay in America would certainly have been preferable.[11]

Dumba saw the expanded awareness of the agrarian proletariat after its confrontation with the relatively democratic society in the

---

8. *Ibid.*, file 326, no. 36 234/14. The Austro-Hungarian General Consulate in New York to the Foreign Office, May 29, 1914.

9. Arthur Salz, "Auswanderung und Schiffahrt (mit besonderer Berücksichtigung der österreichischen Verhältnisse)," Edgar Jaffé, ed., *Archiv für Sozialwissenschaft und Sozialpolitik*, 39 (1915), 110.

10. S. Altmann, *Geschichte der Wanderungen* (Vienna, 1922), p. 162.

11. AVA, MdI Auswanderungsakten 8/4 file 321, no. 44 869/13. Report of Austro-Hungarian Ambassador Dumba to the Foreign Office, August 16, 1913, and forwarded to the Ministry of Interior, November 13, 1913.

United States as a potential threat to the existing order in Austria.[12] As long as the emigrant stayed in America, no acute danger to existing conditions was present. The function of emigration, Benedikt maintains, was the perpetuation of the established order by reducing or completely excluding the possibility of change.

As long as the freedom of emigration, which was anchored in the Constitution of December 21, 1867, and the freedom of immigration to the United States remained untouched, there existed a safety valve for overpopulation and unemployment which reduced the social-revolutionary pressure and made possible the peaceful coexistence of the peoples.[13]

### 5. AUSTRIAN EMIGRATION TO CANADA

Austrian emigration to Canada was, on the average, about one-tenth of the emigration to the United States annually. This was, in part, a result of Canada's anglophile settlement policy.[1]

By 1896 only about 6,000 Austrians had immigrated to Canada, but in the next year alone 4,220 arrived.[2] The number rose quickly here, as in the United States. The preponderance of the Austrian over the Hungarian immigration is clearly reflected in Table 5.1.

Table 5.1

THE CANADIAN IMMIGRATION 1906–1910

| Year | Total Canadian Immigration | From Austria-Hungary | From Austria | From Hungary |
|---|---|---|---|---|
| 1906 | 189,064 | 10,326 | 8,501 | 1,825 |
| 1907 | 124,667 | 4,420 | 2,370 | 2,050 |
| 1908 | 262,469 | 21,962 | 21,361 | 601 |
| 1909 | 146,908 | 10,840 | 10,057 | 783 |
| 1910 | 208,794 | 10,240 | 9,402 | 838 |
| TOTAL | 931,902 | 57,788 | 51,691 | 6,097 |

SOURCE: Riedl, *Die Organisation der Auswanderung*, pp. 90–91.

12. Chmelar, "Die Auswanderung," p. 90.
13. Benedikt, "Die wirtschaftliche Entwicklung in der Franz-Joseph Zeit," p. 166.

1. Riedl, *Die Organisation der Auswanderung*, p. 1.
2. Englisch, "Die österreichische Auswanderungsstatistik," p. 73.

In the composite picture of the Canadian immigration from 1901 to 1910, the Dual Monarchy occupies third place behind Great Britain and the United States, as shown in Table 5.II. Thus, Austria-Hungary stands ahead of all continental European states.

Table 5.II

THE IMMIGRATION TO CANADA 1901–1910

Total:   1,453,391

| From: | |
|---|---|
| Great Britain | 562,054 |
| United States | 497,751 |
| Austria-Hungary | 105,544 |
| Russia | 74,720 |
| Italy | 46,919 |
| Germany | 18,612 |
| Others | 147,791 |

SOURCE: Englisch, "Die österreichische Auswanderungsstatistik," p. 104.

The *Canada Year Book*, published by the Census and Statistics Office in Ottawa, records a total of 128,724 immigrants from the Monarchy between 1902 and 1911. The largest single group was formed by the 81,514 immigrants from Galicia, approximately 63 percent of the Monarchy's total. There were 11,730 from Bukovina and only 10,961 from Hungary. The other nationalities found in the crownland were only slightly represented.[3]

Characteristic of Canadian immigration was the fact that far more than one third of the immigrants were supplied by Great Britain and the United States, many of whom had earlier come to America from Europe and only later decided to travel on into Canada. In 1912 around 80,000 immigrants arrived from continental Europe.[4]

Occupationally, the immigrants were people with agricultural backgrounds hoping to acquire their own property (*Grundbesitz*).[5]

3. AVA, Justizministerium I B I, 2 carton 49. Gesetzentwurf 1913, Motivenbericht, p. 35.

4. Chmelar, "Die Auswanderung," p. 93.

5. AVA, MdI Auswanderungsakten 8/4 file 320, no. 28.044/13. Foreign Ministry to Ministry of War, June 26, 1913.

The statistics concerning the ethnic identity of the immigrants are not very precise. Approximately 95 percent of the Austrian and Hungarian immigrants were Slavs, primarily Poles and Ruthenians from Galicia as well as some Ruthenians from Bukovina.[6]

### 6. AUSTRIAN EMIGRATION TO SOUTH AMERICA AND OTHER COUNTRIES

The role played by South America in Austrian emigration is clearly subordinate to that of the continent to the north. The South American states recruited their immigrants primarily from the Latin countries of the Mediterranean. Austria-Hungary remained permanently in fifth place behind Spain, Italy, Russia, and Turkey. The small number of returning emigrants was a prominent feature of immigration to South America. Immigrants to Brazil and Argentina only seldom returned home because most had acquired agrarian property there[1] and had thus established a firm bond with their new homeland.

If the United States was interested only in the quality of its immigrants, the quantity of immigrant labor was most important to the South American states. For Argentina, short-term transient workers offered only an expedient. A permanent labor force was desired.[2]

Of the South American countries, Argentina was the one most frequently selected by emigrating Austrians. In fact, Argentina occupied third place behind the United States and Canada as a destination of Austrian emigrants. According to consular reports, a total of 36,575 emigrants from Austria-Hungary arrived in Argentina between 1857 and 1902,[3] the greatest influx coming between 1883 and 1890.

---

6. Chmelar, "Die Auswanderung," p. 95.

1. Leopold Caro, "Auswanderung und Auswanderungspolitik in Österreich," *Schriften des Vereins für Sozialpolitik*, 131 (1909), 42.

2. Staatsarchiv, Auswanderungsakten F 15, carton 8, folio I/80. Freiherr von Hoenning to the Foreign Ministry, Buenos Aires, March 6, 1912.

3. Caro, "Auswanderung und Auswanderungspolitik," p. 35.

Table 6.I

IMMIGRATION TO ARGENTINA

| Year | Total Immigration | From Austria-Hungary | From Austria | From Hungary |
|---|---|---|---|---|
| 1906 | 252,536 | 6,120 | 5,491 | 629 |
| 1907 | 209,103 | 4,659 | 4,152 | 507 |
| 1908 | 255,710 | 3,485 | 3,008 | 477 |
| 1909 | 213,172 | 4,552 | 4,060 | 492 |
| 1910 | 289,640 | 4,542 | 4,031 | 511 |
| 1911 | 225,772 | 4,703 | 4,054 | 649 |
| 1912 | 323,403 | 6,550 | 5,832 | 718 |
| TOTAL | 1,769,336 | 34,611 | 30,628 | 3,983 |

SOURCE: Riedl, *Die Organisation der Auswanderung*, pp. 38–39.

Although it is true that immigration to Argentina began earlier and was initially greater in scope than that to Canada, it did not, compared to immigration to the United States or Canada, continue to rise significantly in the period before the outbreak of World War I. Even in the record year 1907 the number of Austrian and Hungarian emigrants remained relatively constant at less than five thousand. The percentage of emigrants from the lands of the Hungarian Crown also remained very low.

From 1857 to 1910, 67,774 persons immigrated to Argentina from Austria-Hungary.[4] The predominant portion of the immigrants were people who had worked in agriculture and their dependents. Their goal was to procure land and establish their own farms. These emigrants did not return to the Monarchy, remaining instead, almost without exception, on their newly acquired property. The Argentine statistics in Table 6.II indicate the occupational groups among the Austro-Hungarian immigrants from 1905 to 1910.

4. Chmelar, "Die Auswanderung," p. 47.

Table 6.II

| | Percent |
|---|---|
| Independent farmers | 37.9 |
| Agricultural day laborers | 9.4 |
| Dependents without occupation | 10.2 |
| Tradesmen | 11.3 |
| Employed in commerce and trade | 7.4 |
| Free professions | 0.7 |
| Other occupations | 23.1 |

SOURCE: Englisch, "Die österreichische Auswanderungsstatistik," p. 113.

Among the South American states which were important in the Monarchy's emigration, Brazil ranked second to Argentina, although the extent of the Austro-Hungarian immigration to Brazil was just a little more than half as large as to the latter state. The first great influx came with 11,459 Austrians landing in Brazil in 1895 and 11,549 a year later.[5] Emigration to Brazil was publicized extensively by private persons and groups that had an interest in cheap labor and by so-called "Colonization Societies." Abuses, which became known in various ways, led to a rapid decline in the number of emigrants. Not until 1908 did emigration rise again slightly.

The Brazilian government supported immigration by paying the cost of the transatlantic passage. The Austrian national shipping line, the V.Ö.S.A.G.,[6] or simply the Austro-Americana, was also involved in this arrangement.

Although it draws a government subsidy for its South American line and, as a result of the differential tariff on coffee, can count on a permanent and lucrative cargo in its Brazilian business, it has assumed the transport of emigrants on the basis of arrangements made with the Brazilian government, which pays for the emigrant's passage. In its prospectus, overt propaganda for the migration to Brazil is conducted.[7]

This migration to South America was promoted by the Austro-

5. Englisch, "Die österreichische Auswanderungsstatistik," pp. 73, 25.
6. The official name was the United Austrian Shipping Company (Vereinigte österreichische Schiffahrts Aktien-Gesellschaft), formerly, as mentioned above, the Austro-Americana and Fratelli Cosulich.
7. Riedl, *Die Organisation der Auswanderung*, p. 73.

Americana in collaboration with the Polish Emigration Society in Cracow.[8]

In his book, Riedl presents the figures shown in Table 6.iii on Brazilian immigration from 1906 to 1911. The great increase in 1908 is striking. In that same year, the Austro-Americana initiated its service to South America. Thereafter, however, a slow retrograde movement set in which was further intensified in 1912–1913. This tendency was confirmed by figures from the Imperial General Consulate in Rio de Janeiro. In 1911 there were 3,327 Austrian immigrants; in 1912, 3,045.[9]

Table 6.iii

| Year | Total Immigration | From Austria-Hungary | From Austria | From Hungary |
|---|---|---|---|---|
| 1906 | 72,380 | 1,012 | 879 | 133 |
| 1907 | 57,556 | 522 | 505 | 17 |
| 1908 | 86,190 | 5,317 | 5,106 | 211 |
| 1909 | 74,213 | 4,065 | 4,008 | 57 |
| 1910 | 81,040 | 3,801 | 3,517 | 284 |
| 1911 | 153,203 | 3,327 | 3,158 | 169 |
| TOTAL | 524,582 | 18,044 | 17,173 | 871 |

SOURCE: Riedl, *Die Organisation der Auswanderung*, pp. 90–91.

The major part of the Brazilian immigration consisted of citizens from the Latin countries of the Mediterranean. According to Brazilian figures, Austrians occupied sixth place in the total Brazilian immigration from 1855 to 1910, only about 2 percent of the total. The largest group of Austrian emigrants came from Galicia, while the German-speaking crownlands were occasionally heavily represented. Between 1908 and 1912, the Austro-Americana carried 6,150 passengers from Austria to Brazil, but only 170 Hungarians and 553 Croats.[10]

8. *Ibid.*, p. 75.

9. AVA, Handelsministerium, file 1924 AW, no. 42 144/14. Report of the Imperial General Consulate to the Foreign Office, October 30, 1913, forwarded to the Ministry of Trade, December 2, 1914; or, Staatsarchiv, Auswanderungsakten F 15, carton 16, Statistische Auswanderungsberichte Rio de Janeiro. Report of the Imperial Diplomatic Mission Concerning Immigration to Brazil, 1911.

10. AVA, Handelsministerium file 1924 AW, no. 30 018/14. Distinta dei colonisti partiti negli anni 1908, 1909, 1910, 1911, e 1912 per il Brasile.

Table 6.IV

AUSTRIAN IMMIGRATION TO BRAZIL FROM 1908 TO 1912

Total: 6,150

| From: Galicia | 3,540 |
|---|---|
| Küstenland | 1,526 |
| Tirol | 377 |
| Lower Austria | 197 |
| Carinthia | 103 |
| Carniola | 91 |
| Bohemia | 87 |
| Moravia | 79 |
| Styria | 78 |
| Dalmatia | 26 |
| Salzburg | 8 |
| Bukovina | 8 |

NOTE: In the Italian list, 103 colonists are reported for Carniola and 91 for Carinthia.
SOURCE: AVA, Handelsministerium file 1924 AW, no. 30 018/14, Destinta dei Colonisti partiti negli anni 1908, 1909, 1910, 1911, and 1912 per il Brasile.

Austrian immigration to other countries was completely insignificant. While in regard to the four states already treated, it took the form of a mass movement, immigration to other countries remained scant and irregular. Chile, Uruguay, Paraguay, Mexico, and other South and Central American countries attracted emigrants from Austria, but the number remained below one hundred per year in each.[11]

Australia and New Zealand stood in the British sphere of influence, and a substantial immigration by continental Europeans was impeded by stringent immigration regulations. Illiterates, for example, were not admitted at all.[12] Before 1910, 3,919 Austrians are said to have immigrated to Australia,[13] though not all actually re-

11. Chmelar, "Die Auswanderung," pp. 57ff.
12. Staatsarchiv, Auswanderungsakten F 15, carton 15, Sydney. Supplements to the report of the Imperial General Consulate in Sydney, May 26, 1914, "Information regarding the emigrants from the Austro-Hungarian Monarchy who took the literacy exam, mandatory for all immigrants to New Zealand, at the Imperial General Consulate in Sydney, Australia, during 1913."
13. Englisch, "Die österreichische Auswanderungsstatistik," pp. 73, 25.

mained there. Some migrated further to New Zealand, which ultimately received about 200 to 300 Austrians annually.[14] The Dalmatians constituted the leading group of Austrian immigrants in Australia and New Zealand.[15]

While larger or smaller groups of emigrants from the Dual Monarchy were always present in the already mentioned South American countries or in Australia and New Zealand, only a few individuals left the Empire for Asia or Africa. They rarely found their way into official statistics, and diplomatic missions of the Austro-Hungarian Monarchy did not report on them.[16]

### 7. THE SIGNIFICANCE OF AUSTRIAN EMIGRATION IN THE EUROPEAN SEAPORTS AND THE ROLE OF TRIESTE AS AN EMIGRATION PORT

The statistics from the ports make possible a relatively close examination of the emigration movement. The two major north German ports Hamburg and Bremen, which were the most important for the Austrian emigration, kept detailed statistics on the citizenship and destination of embarking emigrants. Toward the close of 1910, however, the German authorities gave up their detailed reports and restricted themselves to general summaries. This change was said to have taken place in the interest of secrecy.[1]

From 1876 to 1910 emigrants from Austria-Hungary passed through ports of embarkation in the countries shown in Table 7.1. The important ports of emigration were: Hamburg and Bremen in Germany, Antwerp in Belgium, Rotterdam in Holland, Le Havre but also several smaller harbors in France, Genoa along with other scattered ports in Italy, Trieste in Austria, and Fiume in Hungary.

14. *Ibid.*, p. 125.

15. Staatsarchiv, Auswanderungsakten F 15, carton 15, Sydney—Bericht Neuseeland. Report of the Imperial Austro-Hungarian Consulate Auckland to the Foreign Ministry, November 6, 1905. Also see, *ibid.*, Sydney. Supplements to the report of the Imperial General Consulate in Sydney, May 26, 1914.

16. Chmelar, "Die Auswanderung," p. 61.

1. Staatsarchiv, Auswanderungsakten F 15, carton 16, Statistische Auswanderungsberichte—Hamburg. Ritter v. Frankeneck to the Foreign Ministry, June 16, 1911.

The greatest benefits from our emigration accrued to Germany, which transported 69.49 percent of our emigrants. The Low Lands (Belgium and Holland), Italy, and France, carrying 19.91 percent, 4.47 percent, and 2.81 percent respectively, profited to a much smaller degree and yet surpassed Austria, from whose ports barely 2.86 percent or 0.46 percent, of the Austrian emigrants embarked.[2]

Table 7.1

|  | Austrians | Hungarians | Total |
|---|---|---|---|
| Germany | 1,282,329 | 1,106,996 | 2,389,325 |
| Belgium and Holland | 367,409 | 286,204 | 653,613 |
| France | 51,814 | 37,521 | 89,335 |
| Italy | 82,487 | 13,551 | 96,038 |
| Austria | 52,726 | 24,123 | 76,849 |
| Hungary | 8,617 | 233,853 | 242,470 |
| TOTAL | 1,845,382 | 1,702,248 | 3,547,630 |

SOURCE: Englisch, "Die österreichische Auswanderungsstatistik," p. 77.

In each of the North Sea ports a single shipping line usually dominated the scene. In Bremen North German Lloyd held this position, in Hamburg the Hamburg-America Line,[3] in Rotterdam the Holland-America Line, and in Antwerp the Belgian Red Star Line. In the Mediterranean ports, however, several companies were active. The British Cunard Line also sailed from Trieste and Fiume.

From the table the dominance of the northwestern European and especially the German ports can clearly be seen. The number of Austrians emigrating via French and Italian ports was not substantial. Only in Le Havre and Genoa were significant numbers of Austrians registered: in Le Havre around three thousand to five thousand and in Genoa around one thousand to two thousand annually.[4]

Despite extensive publicity and promotion by the state, Trieste, Austria's only port, could attract only a small portion of the emigrants. The long train ride from Galicia and Bukovina, the major areas of emigration, and the much longer voyage from the port

2. Englisch, "Die österreichische Auswanderungsstatistik," p. 79.
3. Also called the Hamburg-Amerika Packetfahrt A.G., or HAPAG.
4. Österreichisches Statistisches Handbuch, 33 Jahrgang, 1914 (Vienna, 1916), 62.

Table 7.II

TABLE OF AUSTRIAN OVERSEAS EMIGRATION FROM 1906 TO 1913

| *Austrian Emigration* | 1906 | 1907 | 1908 | 1909 | 1910 | 1911 | 1912 | 1913 | *Total* |
|---|---|---|---|---|---|---|---|---|---|
| via Trieste | 8,265 | 8,893 | 3,085 | 7,773 | 7,531 | 8,415 | 9,062 | 13,394 | 66,418 |
| via Fiume | 2,643 | 1,975 | 186 | 328 | 417 | 286* | 494† | 587‡ | 6,916 |
| Austrian-Hungarian Ports | 10,908 | 10,868 | 3,271 | 8,101 | 7,948 | 8,701 | 9,556 | 13,981 | 73,334 |
| via Bremen | 52,549 | 61,389 | 17,469 | 45,788 | 45,258 | 22,381§ | 40,955§ | 70,622§ | 356,411 |
| via Hamburg | 36,647 | 51,890 | 18,251 | 40,497 | 42,637 | 25,382** | 32,983** | 51,319** | 299,606 |
| German Ports | 89,196 | 113,279 | 35,720 | 86,285 | 87,895 | 47,763 | 73,938 | 121,941 | 656,017 |
| via Antwerp | 22,005 | 36,721 | 12,408 | 23,012 | 25,115 | 20,013 | 28,653 | 32,354 | 200,281 |
| via Rotterdam[a] | 4,797 | 8,083 | 2,584 | 6,463 | 9,994 | 9,295 | 11,669 | 17,356 | 70,241 |
| via French Ports[b] | 5,669 | 5,932 | 2,335 | 3,844 | 5,567 | 4,983 | 6,495 | 8,065 | 42,890 |
| via Italian Ports[c] | 3,779 | 2,471 | 1,416 | 2,103 | 2,396 | 1,113 | 916 | 765 | 14,959 |
| Austrian Total | 136,354 | 177,354 | 57,734 | 129,808 | 138,915 | 91,868 | 131,227 | 194,462 | 1,057,722 |
| The Monarchy as a whole | 313,167 | 386,528 | 102,795 | 250,530 | 270,060 | 163,962 | 247,466 | 309,950 | 2,044,458 |

\* Including 52 emigrants via Kantrida.
† Including 242 emigrants via Kantrida.
‡ Including 305 emigrants via Kantrida.
§ With North German Lloyd.
\*\* According to the yearly report of the Hamburg Emigration Authority.
[a] Occasionally via Amsterdam; 1910, 18; 1911, 65; 1912, 338; 1913, 106.
[b] Primarily Le Havre.
[c] Almost exclusively via Genoa. No Austrian emigrants via Naples from 1909 to 1913.

SOURCES: Österreichisches Statistisches Handbuch, 29 Jahrgang, 1910 (Vienna, 1911), 38–39, for figures to 1908; ibid., 33 Jahrgang, 1914 (Vienna, 1916), 62, for figures to 1909. Reports of the Austrian Statthalterei, the Austrian sea authorities in Trieste, the imperial consulates, and records of port officials.

itself, worked to Trieste's disadvantage, as did the tighter police regulation. Such strict control was not possible for the state apparatus in the North Sea and Atlantic ports. Furthermore, the North Sea ports had the added advantage of greater accessibility and, above all, a shorter and faster voyage to America. Trieste, however, was able to draw a greater share of the emigration to South America. Beginning in 1911, the number of foreign emigrants bound for South America rose sharply in Trieste.

In a span of only eight years, 1,057,722 people from the kingdoms and lands represented in the *Reichsrat* and 986,736 from the lands of the Hungarian Crown had emigrated, thus bringing the total from the Dual Monarchy to 2,044,458. In addition to these figures, one must not forget the unknown number of emigrants who found their way illegally to America in order to escape military service and were obviously not recorded in the official statistics. Finally, there are the nonregistered emigrants who sailed from English ports.[5]

The ebb and flow of the emigration movement can also be distinguished in the table. The record year 1907 was followed by a rapid contraction in the next year and then in 1909 by a strong rise in all port cities.[6] An additional increase and then a decline followed 1910, but in 1912 former levels were again reached. A substantial increase in the last full year of emigration brought the highest figures for a single year, making 1913 along with 1907 the most active years of emigration from the Monarchy. Between 1910 and 1912, Austrian emigrants held a majority over their Hungarian counterparts in all ports except Fiume.[7] Bremen was the port most often used by both groups for emigration to the United States.

Data concerning English ports do not appear in the Austrian

---

5. Emigrants sailing via British ports were often already registered on the continent before leaving for England. Their number in these years was, however, quite small.

6. "An indication of the apparently planless impulse to emigrate can be found in the uniformly high rise of emigration observed in all ports which regularly represented an increase of about 150 to 200 percent above the level of the previous year." "Österreichisch-Ungarische Auswanderung in den Jahren 1908 und 1909," *Statistische Mitteilungen*, IV Jahrgang (Vienna, 1910), 32.

7. Englisch, "Die österreichische Auswanderungsstatistik," p. 86.

statistics or in the consular reports, and with the exception of the Cunard Line in Trieste and in Hungarian Fiume, English shipping companies did not have concessions in Austria-Hungary. Emigrants traveling via Great Britain were often already registered in the first continental port of emigration.[8] For the emigrants, the British route was the most troublesome. Nevertheless, in 1910, 18,444 Austro-Hungarian emigrants bound for lands overseas are said to have traveled via English ports. Of these, 11,834 were Austrians, accounting for 7.85 percent of that year's total Austrian emigration.[9]

In spite of government patronage and for reasons of an essentially geographic nature, the port of Trieste was unable to play a significant role in the Austrian emigration. Although already stated in absolute numbers, the situation is made even clearer by the overview in Table 7.III.

Table 7.III

EMIGRATION FROM AUSTRIA IN 1910 VIA:

| Northwest Europe | Southern Europe | |
|---|---|---|
| 91.5 percent | 8.5 percent | |
| (of which 80 | Trieste | Genoa |
| percent traveled | 6.79 | 1.71 |
| via Hamburg, | percent | percent |
| Bremen, Rotterdam, | | |
| and Antwerp) | | |

SOURCE: Markitan, *Auswandererverkehrswege in Österreich*, p. 10.

Emigration from Trieste began later than in most port cities and did not grow significantly until 1904. Begininng in the following year, an average of about 7 percent of Austria's emigrants passed through the port. In 1908 a reversal conditioned by the American economic crisis and felt in all European ports ensued. However, by increasing the transport of foreigners, a substantial recovery was

8. Chmelar, "Die Auswanderung," p. 116.
9. Franz Markitan, *Auswandererverkehrswege in Österreich* (speech given before the General Assembly of the Austrian St. Raphael Association, March 19, 1912 [Vienna, 1912]), p. 10.

achieved, and in 1913 the opening of new transport connections with Canada brought a record number of emigrants to Trieste, a number comparable to that recorded in the other large port cities.

Table 7.IV

OVERSEAS EMIGRATION VIA TRIESTE

| Years | Total via Trieste | Austrians | Austrians via European ports |
|---|---|---|---|
| 1903–1908 | 70,015 | 32,669 | 678,119 |
| 1909–1913 | 126,153 | 46,175 | 686,280 |
| TOTAL | 196,168 | 78,844 | 1,364,339 |

SOURCES: *Österreichisches Statistisches Handbuch*, 27 Jahrgang, 1908 (Vienna, 1909), 50; *ibid.*, 33 Jahrgang, 1914 (Vienna, 1916), 63.

THE COMPOSITION OF THE EMIGRATION VIA TRIESTE 1906–1913

| Year | Austrians | Hungarians | Foreigners* | Total |
|---|---|---|---|---|
| 1906 | 8,265 | 3,621 | 5,904 | 17,790 |
| 1907 | 8,893 | 5,517 | 7,138 | 21,548 |
| 1908 | 3,085 | 1,863 | 2,940 | 7,888 |
| 1909 | 7,773 | 5,351 | 2,990 | 16,114 |
| 1910 | 7,531 | 4,299 | 3,626 | 15,456 |
| 1911 | 8,415 | 2,887 | 11,165 | 22,467 |
| 1912 | 9,062 | 3,856 | 13,415 | 26,333 |
| 1913 | 13,394 | 4,666 | 27,723 | 45,783 |
| 1906–1913 | 66,418 | 32,060 | 74,901 | 173,379 |

NOTE: Particularly noteworthy is the high proportion of foreigners in the last three years. Hungarians were represented much more in Trieste than Austrians were in Fiume.
*A division of the foreigners is not provided. Most, however, were Russians.
SOURCES: *Österreichisches Statistisches Handbuch*, 29 Jahrgang, 1910 (Vienna, 1911), 38; *ibid.*, 33 Jahrgang, 1914 (Vienna, 1916), 62.

In these years three shipping companies offered service from Trieste to America: The United Austrian Shipping Company to the United States, Canada (from 1913), and South America (from 1908); the British Cunard Line to North America; and from 1913, the Canadian Pacific Railway Company (C.P.R.) to Canada.[10]

As indicated in Table 7.IV, the great increase of foreign emigrants

10. AVA, Handelsministerium AW, file 1883, no. 23 058/13. Camera di Commercio e d'Industria, Trieste on May 14, 1913.

through Trieste beginning in 1911 can be traced to Russian emigration.[11] The Austrians traveling through Trieste came primarily from Galicia, but also from Dalmatia, Küstenland, and Carniola. Thus, two major centers of emigration are discernible: Galicia and the lands of the South Slavs.[12] The emigration traffic to South America was always very heavy in Trieste, and in 1911 it even exceeded the emigration to North America.[13]

In 1913, Trieste witnessed a considerable increase of emigration, especially in the traffic to the United States and Canada. Compared to 1912, emigration almost doubled in volume.[14] Top position among the carriers was held by the Austro-Americana, while the other lines played subordinate roles.[15]

The increase of emigration produced a number of problems for Trieste. Emigrants who arrived by train had to be housed until the departure of their vessels, and only the Austro-Americana had its own lodging house. The two other companies resorted to quartering their passengers in private homes and in lodgings "of the lowest order," particularly in the old inner city. Then, in 1913, Cunard and C.P.R. were called upon to provide a lodging house for their emigrant passengers, in order to put an end to the terribly unsanitary conditions which made the danger of epidemic quite real.[16]

The demands of the Trieste Chamber of Commerce concerning emigration policy naturally emanated from a desire to strengthen the port's competitive position. Demands were made for a progressive nationalization of the emigration business, a new emigrant lodging house, and a subsidy of shipping in order to be able to meet the rising Hungarian and Italian competition.[17]

11. Statements of the Austrian Sea authorities in the Acts of the Ministries of Trade and Interior.

12. Chmelar, "Die Auswanderung," p. 122.

13. *Ibid.*, p. 124.

14. AVA, MdI Auswanderungsakten 8/4 file 322, no. 6 418/14. Sea authorities to MdI on February 14, 1914; *ibid.*, file 323, no. 18 987/14. Sea authorities to MdI on April 2, 1914.

15. *Ibid.*, file 322, no. 6 418/14.

16. AVA, Handelsministerium AW, file 1883, no. 23 058/13. Camera di Commercio e d'Industria to Ministerium des Handels (hereafter cited as MdH), Trieste, May 14, 1913.

17. *Ibid.*, file 1920, no. 8 118/14. Camera di Commercio e d'Industria to MdH, Trieste, March 6, 1914.

With the outbreak of World War I the flow of emigration via Trieste came to a complete standstill.

## 8. MAJOR CURRENTS IN THE FLOW OF EMIGRATION WITHIN AUSTRIA–HUNGARY

The emigration traffic within Austria was composed of two major currents, the first being the flow of emigrants from the crownlands to their ports of embarkation, particularly to the German or Swiss borders, and the second, the through-transit of foreign, primarily Russian, emigrants, as well as those from the Empire's Hungarian half.

The Austrian High Commissar of Police Franz Markitan[1] discerned these currents in 1910, but his observations apply to other years between approximately 1905 and 1913 as well.[2] Although beginning in 1913 the Austrian authorities regionally hindered the flow of emigration with various checks at the borders and in the large train stations, no basic structural shift occurred in the inner-Austrian emigration.

The flow of emigration from the crownlands followed different courses. The Poles and Ruthenians from Galicia fell into two groups: those who traveled via Szczakowa, Oswiecim, and Oderberg to Prussia, and, second, those who went to Trieste or via Vienna and Buchs into Switzerland. German-speaking Austrians emigrated primarily via Germany, with only about two hundred going to Trieste. Almost all Czechs from Bohemia and Moravia also passed through Germany, as did two thirds of the Slovenes, the remainder traveling through Trieste. The bulk of Rumanian emigrants from Bukovina likewise traveled through Germany, while the Dalmatians journied chiefly through Trieste and, to a lesser extent, Fiume. The Italians of South Tirol, preferring English and French lines, reached their destinations via Innsbruck and Buchs.[3]

Hungarians and Russians formed the two largest groups of transient emigrants. The Hungarians who did not emigrate via Fiume,

---

1. Markitan was attached to the Ministry of Interior.
2. Markitan, *Auswandererverkehrswege in Österreich.*
3. *Ibid.*, pp. 6–10.

on the average about 75 percent of the annual Hungarian emigration, were divided along three alternate routes: the route to the German border, to Buchs and Switzerland, and to Trieste.[4] The Russians arrived in Galicia, most of the influx centering in the Szczakowan corner of the Austrian, Russian, and German empires. "In 1910 the border police in Szczakowa recorded no fewer than 61,813 transient Russian emigrants. They entered from the neighboring Russian frontier station at Granica and exited to the adjacent German frontier post at Myslowitz."[5] Others traveled via Cracow on to Vienna where they split into two streams, one flowing to Trieste, the other via Innsbruck to Buchs. Smaller processions came from the Balkan lands. A considerable portion of these emigrants came via Agram-Steinbrück to Laibach. From there they journeyed either via Villach to Buchs or via Selzthal to Eger. For some Balkan emigrants, Trieste served as an embarkation port, for others it was merely an intermediate station on the path to a port in northwestern Europe. Still others traveled via Budapest and Oderberg to Germany.[6]

Although the public railway and, in part, also Trieste profited from the transients, these travelers, and especially the Russians, were not considered desirable. In the "Instruction for Imperial Tariff Officials, entrusted with the operation of the Border Police," section eighteen read:

Emigrants and colonists, especially of the Jewish religion, who intend to cross the border even if only for transit must not only prove their identity with legal travel documents, but also possess sufficient travel funds. Otherwise entry is to be denied. For persons who wish to continue their emigration to America via Germany, the funds to be shown have been set at 100 marks for persons below and 400 marks for persons above ten years of age.[7]

The implementation of this directive by Austrian authorities led to numerous complaints from the Cunard Line and the C.P.R. as well

4. *Ibid.*, p. 16.
5. *Ibid.*, p. 17.
6. *Ibid.*, pp. 17ff.
7. Staatsarchiv, Auswanderungsakten F 15, carton 23, Beschwerden. Information of the Ministry of Interior, no. 36 332/13, concerning Instruction no. 931/1889.

as the Russian legation, because of abusive treatment of Russians at the border.[8]

In the return of emigrants, only Austrians and Hungarians played major roles. Foreigners returned to their homeland through Austria only in small numbers. The return of Austrians and Hungarians took place at two focal points, the Silesian frontier stations and the harbor at Trieste.[9]

In 1910, the number of people in transit was approximately 410,000.[10] One may assume that the figure was correspondingly higher in 1913, when not only the Austrian but the Russian emigration was larger and the structure was basically unchanged.

Vienna was an important junction. In 1910, 47,000 emigrants and 20,000 returnees passed through the city on the way from the north to Trieste and from the southeast to the northwest, and so on.[11] Among the inland cities significant in the flow of emigration, Vienna ranked fourth behind Szczakowa, Oswiecim, and Oder-

---

8. AVA, MdI Auswanderungsakten 8/4 file 320, no. 30 084/13. Complaints in July and August 1913. One such case may be noted here. On March 29, 1913, the Russian legation in Vienna complained to the Foreign Office because two Russian emigrants had been denied entry. Stefan and Jakob Kobylanski had arrived in Nowosielitza on November 16, 1912, and, giving Bremen as their destination, wanted to cross the border. Each had proper passports and 80 rubles (about 220 crowns) but no ship ticket. They were denied entry. In the opinion expressed by the Ministry of the Interior on August 8, 1913, with regard to this matter, the action taken by the Austrian border officials was justified on the basis of the Instruction cited above, note 7. Staatsarchiv, Auswanderungsakten F 15, carton 23, Beschwerden. Complaint of the Russian Embassy, March 29; position of the Ministry of Interior, August 8, 1913. The interpretation given was that no proletariat was to be allowed to develop in frontier areas. Aside from this concern, the entry of criminals was also to be prevented. Actually, however, the authorities were primarily afraid of Russian spies. AVA, MdI Auswanderungsakten 8/4 file 320, no. 16 367/13. Report of the Imperial District Captaincy in Sokal to the Presidium of the Austrian Statthalterei in Lemberg, February 12, 1913, and forwarded to the Ministry of Interior, April 25, 1913; ibid., file 322, no. 4598/14. Ministry of War demanded closer inspection of Russian transients, since many were in Austria for purposes of espionage (January 8, 1914).

9. Markitan, Auswandererverkehrswege in Österreich, p. 19.

10. Ibid., 314,000 emigrants (140,800 Austrians, 83,300 Hungarians, 90,000 foreigners) and 96,000 returning emigrants (37,000 Austrians, 54,000 Hungarians, and 5,000 foreigners).

11. Ibid.

berg.[12] In 1912, 118,000 persons passed through Oderberg, on the German border: 49,924 emigrants, 53,922 returnees, and 14,200 seasonal migrants. In 1913, 44,100 emigrants, 43,600 returnees, and 13,700 seasonal migrants were counted.[13] The total, 101,000, was thus somewhat smaller than in 1912, a result primarily related to the decline of Hungarian emigration, since Hungarians accounted for about 80 percent of the border traffic in Oderberg. Of the Austrians passing through the frontier station in 1913, 5,136 came from Galicia and Bukovina and 1,663 from other Austrian crown-lands.[14]

Most Austrians migrated via Oswiecim,[15] although, aside from the already mentioned border stations, Bodenbach and Tetschen on the German frontier claimed a high number of emigrants. If they were not booked on one of the two large German lines, the emigrants encountered difficulties at the German registration stations.[16] These stations were established on the German border for purposes of health inspection, but there the emigrants were also steered to one of the two German lines or to an allied pool line.[17] The competition was, thus, put at the greatest possible disadvantage.[18]

Because of these measures, many emigrants took the detour via Innsbruck and Feldkirch to Buchs and Switzerland. No similar governmental inspection took place there.[19] Moreover, the train route stretched across the territory of the Duchy of Liechtenstein,

12. *Ibid.*, p. 20. "In Vienna, too, the emigrants, who constitute a welcome object of exploitation for conscienceless people, do not always remain shielded from material harm. Unfortunately, there are also among us enough unscrupulous people whose conscience does not trouble them about their occasional or customary exploitation of emigrants no matter how vigorously the authorities pursue these unsavory elements." However, also according to Markitan, the emigrants were also to blame for their misfortune because they were distrustful of the police.

13. AVA, MdI Auswanderungsakten 8/4 file 322, no. 2570/14. Austrian border police, Oderberg-Railway station, to the Presidium of the Silesian Diet, January 8, 1914.

14. *Ibid.*

15. Caro, "Auswanderung und Auswanderungspolitik," p. 45.

16. Riedl, *Die Organisation der Auswanderung*, p. 81.

17. Caro, "Auswanderung und Auswanderungspolitik," p. 71.

18. Riedl, *Die Organisation der Auswanderung*, p. 81.

19. Markitan, *Auswandererverkehrswege in Österreich*, p. 11.

and because of special agreements with the Duchy no really effective border patrol could be undertaken from the Austrian side.[20] The trains halted in Schaan for only a few minutes, and if an emigrant arrived in Buchs he could no longer be detained by Austrian customs officials on grounds of unauthorized emigration.[21] Relief could only be gained by the erection of a border inspection station in Feldkirch, and this did not take place until 1914.[22]

In Buchs the emigrant was confronted with all kinds of advertisements, some in Slavic languages.[23] The branches of the Swiss agents Johann Isidor Büchsel and Victor Klaus employed Hungarian- and Slavic-speaking agents.[24] The lodging houses were clean, but the emigration trains, it was said, were not. The district captaincy in Feldkirch reported that the cars were fouled in the grossest way by the smell of garlic and a lack of cleanliness in the lavatories.[25] The attendants[26] attempted to escape this atmosphere as quickly as possible.[27] Difficulties also arose with the control of Russian transients, that is, those who wore "Russian caps,"[28] carried papers in Cyrillic script, and spoke no German.[29]

At the time of the Balkan crisis an especially large number of

20. AVA, MdI Auswanderungsakten 8/4 file 326, no. 42 797/14. Austrian Statthalterei of Tirol and Vorarlberg to the Ministry of Interior, Innsbruck, November 2, 1914.

21. *Ibid.*, special instructions for the Buchs Customs Office, November 14, 1892, Landesgesetzblatt (hereafter cited as L.G.Bl.) no. 40. "Given the openness of the Austrian-Liechtenstein border, these circumstances have rendered the organization of an effective supervision of emigration impossible and many have contributed substantially to the development of a flourishing center for emigration agencies in Buchs." *Ibid.*, Statthalterei in Innsbruck to the Ministry of Interior, November 2, 1914.

22. *Ibid.*

23. Markitan, *Auswandererverkehrswege in Österreich*, p. 12.

24. AVA, Handelsministerium AW, file 1884, no. 35 814/13. Report of Chancellery Secretary Houda of the Imperial Basel Consulate about the emigration via Buchs, Basel, May 17, 1913.

25. AVA, MdI Auswanderungsakten 8/4 file 320, no. 30 042/13. District Captaincy of Feldkirch, July 12, 1913.

26. The train attendants conducted various police inspections. The Ministry of Interior noted that inspection by railway personnel was incompetent and the Feldkirch police supervision apparently deficient.

27. AVA, MdI Auswanderungsakten 8/4 file 320, no. 30 042/13.

28. It was feared and often publicized that Austrian Poles and Ruthenians dressed as Russians crossed the border illegally.

29. Nevertheless, it was determined that persons with Russian caps also always had Russian papers. AVA, MdI Auswanderungsakten 8/4 file 320, no. 30 042/13.

individual travelers from the south already possessing ship tickets was observed.[30] In 1913, groups of thirty to two hundred, sometimes even five hundred, passed almost daily.[31]

In Buchs the emigrants came into the hands of the agents. "The employees of the emigration agencies are almost always subjects of our Monarchy—Poles, Croats, Hungarians, and Jews whose chief task consists of scrupulously directing the emigrants to their employers. They attack each other in the most bitter fashion and their hunger for commissions knows no bounds."[32] From Buchs the journey continued via Basel—an important transfer point for emigrants with its cheap hotels, in which the emigrants were exploited to the utmost—onward either through Delle into France or St. Ludwig into Germany.[33] Passengers of the English lines, of the Compagnie Générale Transatlantique, and of other companies not allowed in Germany[34] traveled via Delle, while passengers of the N.D.L.V. lines[35] went via St. Ludwig.[36]

The Chancellery Secretary Houda of the Imperial Consulate in Basel described the railway situation vividly:

> Director Möhr[37] and I accompanied one such emigration train from Feldkirch to Basel. There were around 700 persons on board. Although the passengers were assigned enough space in the Austrian and Swiss cars, many cars were, nevertheless, overcrowded because the travelers, who were grouped by nationality, did not want to be separated from their group.
>
> Of these 700 emigrants, approximately 500 were Poles from Russia and Little Russia. The rest were mostly Slovenes from Carniola, Carinthia, and Styria with an admixture of Hungarians from the counties of Pozsony, Sopron, Liptó, and Nyitra as well as from Bács-Bodrog and Croatia. Their destination was the United States and Canada.

30. *Ibid.*

31. AVA, Handelsministerium AW, file 1883, no. 27 950/13. Report of August 12, 1913.

32. Markitan, *Auswandererverkehrswege in Österreich*, p. 12.

33. *Ibid.*, p. 15.

34. *Ibid.* Among others, the Uranium Steam Ship Company and Royal Dutch Lloyd were not permitted in Germany.

35. Nordatlantischer Dampferlinienverband (Association of North Atlantic Steamship lines). Membership in this international cartel was held by the Hamburg-America Line, the North German Lloyd, the Belgian Red Star Line, and the Holland-America Line.

36. Markitan, *Auswandererverkehrswege in Österreich*, p. 15.

37. J. Möhr was the director of the Swiss (Federal) Emigration Office.

I spoke with many of these people, and almost all only hesitantly answered my questions. As to the cause of their emigration, the Russians indicated the great misery prevailing in their homeland.

Our countrymen proved to be very uncommunicative. From the Hungarians I tried to find out at which agency they had purchased their ship tickets, but it was in vain. I was able to ascertain only that those from northern Hungary had been directed to an agency in Vienna and, in order to avoid the border inspection, some had crossed the Austrian frontier on foot.

The emigrants from the western counties and from Northern Croatia turn, as a rule, to an agency in Laibach. The emigration agency "Putnik," located in Agram is used less and less frequently. The formalities associated with clearance and also the required procurement of a passport, etc., make the people uneasy.

The most effective propaganda is conducted by those people who have already been in America once. They usually collect a number of emigrants at home and deliver them either to Laibach or to Buchs, where they receive a commission for each passenger.

Because of the widespread urge to emigrate, the agents don't find it particularly necessary to advertise continuously. Only in the summer, when the flow of migration subsides, do they send by means of the Imperial customs office in Buchs, printed propaganda material into the Monarchy.[38]

Passage occurred only after a medical examination, and fares were not uniform. Sometimes different prices were demanded for the same route and the same class ticket.

The emigrants booked by the domestic agencies usually bring their money in American currency. Those whom I asked about the value of crowns and dollars proved to be very well informed. The agencies in Buchs convert crowns to Swiss francs at the rate of 1:1.02 and exchange dollars according to the daily rate. The mounting of appropriate charts in the emigration cars of the domestic railways would be advisable as a means of orienting the emigrants on the value of the crown in relation to foreign currencies and also on the location of the Imperial consulates in Basel and the ports of embarkation to which they can turn for protection and help.[39]

The importance of the foreign emigration for Switzerland can be measured by its volume. According to the figures of the Swiss Emigration Office, 128,064 persons were carried in 1913. Only

---

38. AVA, Handelsministerium AW, file 1884, no. 35 814/13. Report of Consulate Cabinet Secretary Houda, Imperial Consulate Basel, concerning emigration via Buchs, Basel, May 17, 1913.

39. *Ibid.* The Ministry of Railways declared itself ready to provide such charts.

6,191 were Swiss, while 68,825 were foreigners in transit, 48,562 were foreigners carried by Swiss agencies, and 4,486 were not emigrant travelers. In 1912 the total had been 93,881.[40]

The transit of Italians through Tirol was also of interest to the Austrian state railways, but posed a considerable traffic problem for the railways and the port of Trieste.[41]

The beginning of the First World War, indeed events prior to the actual outbreak of hostilities, first brought the emigration along the Russian border to a halt. On July 30, 1914, the Husiatyn border station reported that the emigration there had come to a complete standstill. Only a few returning migrants were arriving. There was no longer contact with Russian border officials, who had been replaced by the military.[42] Thereafter, emigration was paralyzed at all points.[43]

## B. Structural Analysis of the Austrian Emigration

### 1. THE MAJOR AREAS OF EMIGRATION AND ITS CAUSES

AUSTRIA did not keep statistics on its emigrants, and America distinguished at best according to nationality, and that often quite arbitrarily. Nevertheless, since the United States absorbed the major flow of Austrian and Hungarian emigrants and kept statistics on them, the American records are the best we have and serve as the main source for the following numerical analysis.

Table 1.III provides a rough breakdown of the Austro-Hungarian immigration into the United States from 1901 to 1910,

40. AVA, MdI Auswanderungsakten 8/4 file 324, no. 20 433/14. Report of the Imperial General Consulate, Zurich, concerning Swiss emigration in 1913.

41. Markitan, *Auswandererverkehrswege in Österreich*, pp. 21ff.

42. AVA, MdI Auswanderungsakten 8/4 file 325, no. 33 649/14. Report of the Border Inspection Station in Husiatyn, July 30, 1914.

43. *Ibid.*, file 326, no. 42 797/14. Austrian Statthalterei for Tirol and Vorarlberg to the Ministry of Interior, Innsbruck, November 2, 1914. Report concerning the cessation of emigration via Feldkirch, as well as reports from other border stations.

classification being based on nationality or ethnic group. Together with these figures are the results of the censuses of 1900 and 1910. In relation to the population, emigration was highest among Slavs and Jews and lowest among Germans and the Latin peoples. Of the different ethnic groups, the Poles and South Slavs were most heavily represented.

Table 1.I

PERCENTAGE OF IMMIGRANTS FROM THE
MONARCHY BY ETHNIC GROUP

| | | | |
|---|---|---|---|
| 18.6 | Poles | 6.6 | Ruthenians |
| 16.1 | Serbo-Croatians, Slovenes | 4.3 | Czechs |
| 15.4 | Slovaks | 3.6 | Rumanians |
| 14.7 | Magyars | 0.8 | Italians |
| 11.8 | Germans | 1.0 | Others |
| 7.1 | Jews | | |

SOURCE: Englisch, "Die österreichische Auswanderungsstatistik," p. 91.

Table 1.II

THE PERCENTAGE OF SLAVS IN THE
EMIGRATION FROM 1901 TO 1912

| | | | |
|---|---|---|---|
| 1901 | 69.0 | 1907 | 58.9 |
| 1902 | 66.4 | 1908 | 54.4 |
| 1903 | 63.1 | 1909 | 61.0 |
| 1904 | 59.0 | 1910 | 68.0 |
| 1905 | 61.3 | 1911 | 62.2 |
| 1906 | 60.2 | 1912 | 64.3 |

SOURCES: *Beilagen zu den Stenographischen Protokollen des Abgeordnetenhauses* 2027, XXI Session (1913), 33, all figures except 1901. For that year see Englisch, "Die österreichische Auswanderungsstatistik," p. 91.

Two major centers of emigration are discernible in the kingdoms and lands represented in the *Reichsrat*: the prodigious Polish, Ruthenian, and Jewish mass emigration from the agrarian regions of Galicia, Lodomerien, and Bukovina on the one hand; and the relatively extensive South Slav emigration from Dalmatia and Carniola on the other. In absolute figures, the number of "Bohemian"[1]

1.Czechs in American terminology.

## Table 1.III

### AUSTRO-HUNGARIAN IMMIGRATION TO THE UNITED STATES

| Immigrants: Nationalities, i.e., Ethnic groups | 1901 | 1902 | 1903 | 1904 | 1905 | 1906 | 1907 | 1908 | 1909 | 1910 | Total 1901–1910 Absolute | Percent |
|---|---|---|---|---|---|---|---|---|---|---|---|---|
| Germans | 7,816 | 16,249 | 23,597 | 22,507 | 33,642 | 34,848 | 40,497 | 27,576 | 21,096 | 26,324 | 254,152 | 11.84 |
| Slavs | 77,105 | 113,709 | 125,920 | 102,519 | 166,394 | 156,449 | 193,036 | 91,825 | 104,035 | 177,046 | 1,308,038 | 60.96 |
| Latins | 2,020 | 3,449 | 6,343 | 5,835 | 9,616 | 12,773 | 19,935 | 9,912 | 8,635 | 15,317 | 93,835 | 4.37 |
| Magyars | 13,310 | 23,609 | 27,113 | 23,851 | 45,871 | 42,848 | 59,593 | 23,826 | 27,941 | 26,818 | 314,780 | 14.67 |
| Jews | 13,006 | 12,848 | 18,759 | 20,211 | 17,352 | 14,884 | 18,885 | 15,293 | 8,431 | 13,142 | 152,811 | 7.12 |
| Others | 43 | 2,668 | 4,277 | 2,235 | 2,848 | 3,489 | 6,561 | 97 | 53 | 90 | 22,361 | 1.04 |
| TOTAL | 113,300 | 172,532 | 206,009 | 177,158 | 275,723 | 265,291 | 338,507 | 168,529 | 170,191 | 258,737 | 2,145,977 | 100.00 |

### THE POPULATION OF AUSTRIA-HUNGARY

| According to the Census | State | Germans | Slavs | Latins | Magyars | Jews | Other | Total |
|---|---|---|---|---|---|---|---|---|
| 1900 | Austria | 8,752,404 | 14,771,514 | 954,750 | 9,351 | 1,224,711 | 437,978 | 26,150,708 |
| | Hungary | 1,918,483 | 5,151,589 | 2,795,272 | 8,143,604 | 851,378 | 394,233 | 19,254,559 |
| | Austria-Hungary | 10,670,887 | 19,923,103 | 3,750,022 | 8,152,955 | 2,076,089 | 832,211 | 45,405,267 |
| 1910 | Austria | 9,500,600 | 16,184,538 | 1,039,981 | 10,797 | 1,313,687 | 522,331 | 28,571,934 |
| | Hungary | 2,081,085 | 5,588,214 | 3,032,186 | 8,833,819 | 923,537 | 427,646 | 20,886,487 |
| | Austria-Hungary | 11,581,685 | 21,772,752 | 4,072,167 | 8,844,616 | 2,237,224 | 949,977 | 49,458,421 |

SOURCE: Englisch, "Die österreichische Auswanderungsstatistik," p. 90 (Immigration to the United States according to the *Annual Report of the Commissioner General of Immigration*).

and German emigrants was certainly also high, but these figures must be evaluated in relation to the high level of population in Bohemia and Moravia. Moreover, the categorization of German-speaking emigrants according to geographic area is most difficult, since they were dispersed throughout the various lands. The absolute preponderance of the emigrants from the eastern crownlands is expressed also in the Canadian immigration shown in Table 1.IV.

Table 1.IV

AUSTRO-HUNGARIAN IMMIGRANTS TO CANADA 1898–1909

| | | | |
|---|---|---|---|
| 73.19% | Galicians* | 0.53% | Slovaks |
| 8.42% | Bukovinians | 0.50% | Croats |
| 8.42% | Germans | 0.44% | Czechs |
| 8.41% | Hungarians | 0.09% | Serbs |

SOURCE: Englisch, "Die österreichische Auswanderungsstatistik," p. 106.
*Poles, Ruthenians, and Jews in the Canadian statistics.

(a) *Galicia*

Galicia, the most heavily populated crownland, had the highest emigration both in absolute and relative terms. According to the census of 1910, Galicia possessed 8,026,000 inhabitants, of whom 58.6 percent were Poles, 40.2 percent Ruthenians, and 1.1 percent Germans.[1] Poles and Ruthenians were, therefore, important groups in the emigration as were the unregistered Jews.

Of relatively greater statistical significance was the Jewish question, since in 1910 the Jews formed nearly 11 percent of the Galician population and nearly 13 percent of the population of Bukovina. The Austrian census did not recognize Yiddish as a national language in the terms of Article XIX of the Constitution of 1867. Neither did Hungary recognize any special Yiddish language rights. Thus, the large majority of Jews in Galicia registered as Poles in the Galician census, and, after 1900, they also registered in ever increas-

1. Robert A. Kann, "Das Nationalitätenproblem der Habsburgermonarchie, Geschichte und Ideengehalt der nationalen Bestrebungen vom Vormärz bis zur Auflösung des Reiches im Jahre 1918," *Veröffentlichungen der Arbeitsgemeinschaft Ost*, 2d ed. (Graz-Cologne, 1964), II, 388–389.

ing numbers as Ruthenians. In Bukovina, they registered uniformly as Germans. . . .[2]

Also in the early American statistics, Jews were counted as Slavs.[3]

In the Austrian census of 1910, a population loss of 683,430 was registered. This amounted to 2.61 percent of the total Austrian population and was attributable to the migratory movement of the previous nine years.[4] Galicia alone suffered a loss of 488,416 inhabitants or 6.67 percent of its population.[5]

Galicia's losses due to emigration were the greatest in the Monarchy. From 1881 to 1910 a total of 858,579 inhabitants, more than 10 percent of the population, emigrated.[6] Of these, 467,752 were from wholly Polish Western Galicia, while ethnically mixed Eastern Galicia contributed the remaining 137,384 Poles and 251,615 Ruthenians. Thus, about three times as many Poles emigrated as Ruthenians, which also corresponds with American statistics. Galicia's losses were attributed to overseas emigration and not seasonal migration.[7] Poles were more likely to emigrate the lower their income, while this does not apply to the same extent to Ruthenians.

2. Robert A. Kann, *The Multinational Empire. Nationalism and National Reform in the Habsburg Monarchy 1848–1918* (New York, 1950), II, 299ff.

3. Caro, "Auswanderung und Auswanderungspolitik," p. 17.

4. "Ergebnisse der Volkszählung vom 31. Dezember 1910 in den im Reichsrate vertretenen Königreichen und Ländern," *Österreichische Statistik*, edited by the Austrian Statistical Central Commission, new series, I (1), 29. See also, Englisch, "Die österreichische Auswanderungsstatistik," p. 155; or Leopold Caro, *Emigracya i polityka Emigracyjne* (Posen, 1914), p. 21. The number is ascertained by the relationship of births and deaths to departures and arrivals of emigrants.

5. *Ibid*.

6. Englisch, "Die österreichische Auswanderungsstatistik," p. 163.

7. *Ibid*. The East Galician statistics are computed in three groups according to the average ratio of Poles to total population. Group 1: 75 percent Poles; Group 2: 37.5 percent; Group 3: 12.5 percent.

Table 1.v

EMIGRATION FROM GALICIA

| | Average per capita income in crowns | Emigration | Percent of population |
|---|---|---|---|
| Western Galicia (wholly Polish) | 54.8 | 467,752 | 17.56 |
| Eastern Galicia | | | |
| a. Group I with over 50% Poles | 102.31 | 14,023 | 1.19 |
| b. Group II with 25–50% Poles | 36.51 | 319,973 | 9.61 |
| c. Group III with 10–25% Poles | 19.58 | 55,003 | 6.78 |

SOURCE: Englisch, "Die österreichische Auswanderungsstatistik," p. 167.

Poles were not always accurately classified by nationality in America, since a great many Poles from the regions of western Russia also immigrated to America. The number of Poles from Austria-Hungary and Russia remained approximately even, while the Polish emigration from Germany was always small. In 1904–1905, for example, 50,785 Poles from Austria-Hungary, 47,224 from Russia, and 4,428 from Prussia emigrated to America.[8]

The regional distribution of the Jewish emigration is difficult to ascertain. After the turn of the century, 13,000 to 20,000 Jews left Austria-Hungary annually for America,[9] most coming from the eastern crownlands. Far more, however, emigrated from neighboring Russia, on the average 70,000 to 120,000 annually. In 1905–1906, the number even reached 125,234.[10]

Altogether between 1880 and the beginning of the First World War almost two million Jews arrived in the United States.[11] In 1923, Trietsch wrote:

8. Leopold Caro, "Die Statistik der österreichische-ungarischen und polnischen Auswanderung nach den Vereinigten Staaten von Nordamerika," *Zeitschrift für Volkswirtschaft, Sozialpolitik und Verwaltung*, 16 (1907), 74.

9. See Table 2.III.

10. Caro, "Auswanderung und Auswanderungspolitik," pp. 15ff.

11. H. A. Citroen, *European Emigration Overseas Past and Future*, (*Publications of the Research Group for European Migration Problems*, II [The Hague, 1915]), 15.

Far more than two and a half million Jews from Eastern Europe have gone overseas in the last forty years, while the simultaneous Jewish migration within the European continent and in the different countries has escaped numerical registration. For the most part, the greater portion of this emigration falls on the Western countries, primarily the United States and England, though to a lesser extent on Argentina, Canada, and France as well. However, in these areas, the increasing immigration of Jews since the middle of the nineteenth century has already evoked feelings which led to growing immigration difficulties of various kinds.[12]

Aside from the overseas emigration, the so-called "seasonal migration"[13] was also of considerable importance to Galicia. According to the figures of the German Field Labor Center, beginning in 1908, two hundred fifty thousand to three hundred thousand subjects of the Monarchy arrived in Germany annually for short-term employment.[14] Only about twenty thousand annually were Hungarians, the large remainder coming from Austria, most of whom were Poles and Ruthenians.[15] (See Table 1.vi.) While these were included in the statistics, the true number of migrant workers may be higher. They left Austria-Hungary in March and April and returned in November and December.[16]

Table 1.vi

|           | Poles  | Ruthenians |
|-----------|--------|------------|
| 1908–1909 | 86,050 | 75,102     |
| 1909–1910 | 83,447 | 81,956     |
| 1910–1911 | 77,567 | 82,718     |
| 1911–1912 | 75,851 | 77,911     |
| 1912–1913 | 75,079 | 91,395     |

SOURCE: *Österreichisches Statistisches Handbuch*, 32 Jahrgang, 1913 (Vienna, 1914), 61.

12. David Trietsch, *Jüdische Emigration und Kolonisation*, 2nd ed. (Berlin, 1923), p. 1.
13. On the question of the Galician seasonal migration, see Franz Markitan, *Die österreichische Saisonwanderung* (speech given in Vienna, November 21, 1912 [Vienna, 1913]); K. L. Kumaniecki, *Die galizische Saisonauswanderung im Lichte ausländischer Arbeitsverträge* (Brünn, 1909.)
14. *Österreichisches Statistisches Handbuch*, 29 Jahrgang, 1910 (Vienna, 1911), 39; *ibid.*, 32 Jahrgang, 1913 (Vienna, 1914), 61; *ibid.*, 33 Jahrgang, 1914 (Vienna, 1916), 63.
15. *Ibid.*, 32 Jahrgang, 1913 (Vienna, 1914), 61.
16. Markitan, *Auswandererverkehrswege in Österreich*, p. 21.

In Germany seasonal workers were often taken advantage of, enduring swindles with currency exchange and intolerable working conditions because most of them did not understand German.[17] The Cracow lawyer Caro, therefore, demanded: (a) legal protection associations abroad for the protection of migrants, somewhat like the "Opera di assistenza degli operai italiani," founded by Bishop Bonomelli, (b) public ownership of labor procurement agencies, and (c) equality with native labor for Austro-Hungarian workers abroad.[18]

Widely ranging theories concerning the causes of and reasons for emigration were advanced. Although almost all contemporaries demanded economic measures for the solution of the problem,[19] many of them lacked a far-reaching understanding of its implications.[20] Religious motives or fear of political persecution were not factors in the emigration from Galicia.[21] Migration from Galicia was not a politically conditioned emigration of ethnic minorities, such as occurred in Russia. In Russia, the Poles and Jews provided the chief contingent of emigrants, a situation which the Russian government did not view as inopportune.[22] In Galicia the poor economic situation remained the primary factor motivating the inhabitants to emigrate. Overpopulation and the continued subdivision of landed property into the smallest possible holdings were also cited as causes.[23]

It will be necessary, at another point, to examine the factors ap-

17. Leopold Caro, "Unsere Abwanderer," *Österreichische Rundschau*, 14, no. 5 (1908), 327ff.

18. *Ibid.*, p. 339.

19. In numerous contemporary publications.

20. B. Balla, "Auswanderung und Gesellschaftsstruktur. Hundert Jahre ungarische Emigration aus soziologischer Sicht," in G. Stadtmüller, ed., *Ungarnjahrbuch—Zeitschrift für die Kunde Ungarns und verwandte Gebiete*, Jahrgang 1969 (Mainz, 1969), I, 174.

21. See also Karl von Englisch, "Zu unserer Auswanderungsfrage," *Statistische Monatsschrift*, new series, XVII Jahrgang (1912), 89ff.

22. Staatsarchiv, Auswanderungsakten F 15, carton 34, Gesetze 2/41. Study of the [Austro-Hungarian] Imperial Consulate in St. Petersburg concerning the draft of a Russian emigration law presented to the Council of Ministers at the end of 1913, St. Petersburg, April 6, 1914.

23. F. Hey, *Die Auswanderung und ihre eminente Bedeutung für unser Wirtschaftsleben* (Vienna, 1913), p. 7.

plicable to Austria in general, but here the special conditions in Galicia which led to the emigration of the agrarian proletariat should be analyzed.

In 1910, Galicia had 8 million inhabitants, in 1900 around 7.3 million. Seventy-five percent of the population made their living in agriculture. The industrial development of the other crownlands had not penetrated Galicia, for, in 1900, 83.31 percent of the population was employed in agriculture, while in Austria as a whole the figure was only 58.16 percent. Furthermore, whereas in the entire Austrian half of the Empire the decline in agricultural activity from 1890 to 1900 was 4.25 percent, in Galicia it amounted to only .57 percent.[24] Industry and commerce exhibited either no or, at most, only slight signs of improvement.

Finally, it must be emphasized that the entire Galician economy is short of capital and its agriculture, under the pressure of a conservative economic tradition, is conducted almost everywhere with very dated technology. At best, it adapts with utter passivity, sluggishness, and dullness to the growing demands of its few industrial establishments.[25]

The area devoted to agriculture composed 70.5 percent of the total Galician land, and if that land were divided equally among all those engaged in agriculture, each person would receive only 1.5 to 1.6 hectares.[26] For Blumenfeld, the unjust distribution of land is the essential cause of emigration,[27] and Caro also places the existence of the latifundia at the apex of his investigation of the causes of the emigration.[28]

Although an agricultural operation demanded at least five hectares to be economically viable, 81 percent of the enterprises in Galicia lay below that level.[29] Table 1.VII shows the distribution

---

24. L. Blumenfeld, "Grossgrundbesitz und Auswanderung in Galizien," *Der österreichische Volkswirt*, 6 Jahrgang (Vienna, 1914), part I, no. 33, p. 608. Blumenfeld himself explains that he wants to prove that emigration from Galicia resulted from purely economic causes.

25. *Ibid.*

26. *Ibid.*, p. 609.

27. *Ibid.*

28. Caro, "Auswanderung und Auswanderungspolitik," p. 52.

29. Blumenfeld, "Grossgrundbesitz und Auswanderung in Galizien," p. 609.

of enterprises in Galicia according to the general agricultural census of 1902.

Table 1.VII

|  | Percent of all enterprises | Percent of land area covered |
|---|---|---|
| Enterprises with up to 2 hectares | 42.6 | 5.97 |
| Enterprises with 2–5 hectares | 37.5 | 17.0 |
| Enterprises with 5–20 hectares | 18.35 | 20.0 |
| Enterprises with 20–100 hectares | 1.05 | 6.3 |
| Great Estates, over 100 hectares | 0.52 | 37.0 |

SOURCE: Blumenfeld, "Grossgrundbesitz und Auswanderung in Galizien," p. 609.

"Thus 81 percent of all enterprises—that is, the parcelled-out, dwarf, and small farming operations not possessing the minimum land for existence—covered 23 percent of the land area, whereas the other 19 percent covered 65.3 percent of the land."[30] This produced a proletarization of the peasants and a subnormal agricultural productivity in Galicia (two or three times lower than in other comparable lands). Russia also had a higher output.[31]

The production of grain, etc., both per capita and in relation to national consumption, is also strikingly below normal, and this is clear from the following official data: in the decade from 1896 to 1905, the population of Galicia produced 48 kilograms of wheat per capita, Russia (before the famine years) 130 kilograms per capita, France 240, and England 190.[32]

Moreover, the smallest holdings were repeatedly subdivided and parcelled out. The proprietors could feed themselves from their own soil for only a few months, and for the rest of the year they worked as hired labor for "others." Along with all the landless

30. *Ibid.*
31. *Ibid.*
32. *Ibid.*

agrarian workers, they could find employment on the larger farms during only part of the year, usually at harvest time, and at extremely low pay.[33] In addition, the absence of industry capable of easing the economic burden was significant, since, after Dalmatia, Galicia had less industry than any crownland. Most Galician urban workers, therefore, remained unemployed.

Table 1.VIII

THE NUMBER OF COMMERCIAL ENTERPRISES
PER 100 AGRARIAN ENTERPRISES

Austrian average: 61.8

| Lower Austria | 170 | | Bukovina | 14.6 |
| Silesia | 88.5 | as opposed to | Galicia | 14.2 |
| Bohemia | 84.7 | | Dalmatia | 8.2 |
| Salzburg | 56.9 | | | |

SOURCE: Blumenfeld, "Grossgrundbesitz und Auswanderung in Galizien," part II, no. 34, p. 632.

These factors resulted in mass emigration. "The causes of the emigration cited here for Galicia could, in much the same way, be applied to all Austria-Hungary. The parts of the Empire with a poor distribution of land and an absence of industrialization supply the largest contingents of emigrants."[34] Caro, while including deficient public education as an additional factor, is of the same opinion regarding economic conditions: "the great latifundia, the lack of profitable job opportunities in the homeland, the dearth or scant development of native industry, and the low level of public education seem to form the chief causes of emigration in all Austria."[35]

Overpopulation together with subdivision of property holdings[36] was often mentioned as a cause, without, however, being proven.

33. *Ibid.*, pt. II, no. 34, p. 632.
34. *Ibid.*, p. 633.
35. Caro, "Auswanderung und Auswanderungspolitik," p. 52.
36. Through hereditary division of agrarian holdings.

This overpopulation is given its special stamp by the breakdown of independent farms into dwarf holdings, thus creating the proletarization of the peasantry, a phenomenon which, in the interest of tranquil political and economic development, cannot be regretted enough. Aside from periodic emigration of the greatest magnitude, the general flight from the land, i.e., an excessive growth of cities and towns supposedly offering easier and more profitable employment, goes hand in hand with this development.[37]

The hypothesis, developed when overpopulation is correlated with emigration, is presented by Englisch:

Statistically, I would prefer to see this expressed thus: in areas where overpopulation should be discussed as a cause of emigration, the population's constant and high surplus of birth must exceed the rate of agricultural and industrial development, whereby one must keep in mind, that as a result of the crises which afflict the economy from time to time, the economy may have become temporarily less capable of absorbing this surplus.[38]

As an additional unique reason for the emigration from Galicia, Caro cites lack of education.[39] The uneducated man was easiest led astray, falling victim "more easily than the educated man to the usurious doings of the village banker, the corner pawn shops, and the money lenders."[40] According to the census of December 31, 1900, 52 percent of all males and 59.99 percent of all females over six years of age in Galicia were illiterate.[41] Drunkenness and usury, according to Caro, also belong among the causes of the emigration.[42] A passion for litigation also played a role. In Galicia, petty lawsuits with the sum in dispute less than one hundred crowns were frequently filed. In 1904, for every 10,000 inhabitants, 721 people in Galicia, 366 in Lower Austria and Vienna, and 158 in Bohemia were involved in minor lawsuits.[43] In the same year, there were 25 to 26 property damage lawsuits for every 10,000 in-

37. Hey, *Die Auswanderung und ihre eminente Bedeutung*, p. 7.
38. Englisch, "Zu unserer Auswanderungsfrage," p. 91.
39. Caro, "Auswanderung und Auswanderungspolitik," pp. 52ff. The number of illiterates among the Ruthenian emigrants was quite high.
40. *Ibid.*, p. 53.
41. *Ibid.*
42. *Ibid.* In the period from 1890 to 1901 an annual average of 18,319 persons were found guilty of violating the drunkenness statute.
43. *Ibid.*, p. 54.

habitants in Galicia, while in the other lands only 2 to 5 were recorded per 10,000 inhabitants.[44]

The chances to earn money in Galicia were extraordinarily few, though by way of exception opportunities did exist in a few factories and in large and medium scale farming, but there, often only during the harvest. Pay had increased since emigration had begun.[45] In a report to the governor's office, the district captaincy in Trembowla specified the starvation wages being paid in the district at the time as one of the causes of the extensive emigration in 1896. Only 8, 10, 12, or, at most, 15 to 20 kreuzers a day were paid.[46]

The numerous holidays may also have contributed to the poor economic situation.[47] In Eastern Galicia the double calendar was in effect, and thus Roman Catholic and Russian Orthodox holidays as well as numerous Corpus Christi and church consecration festivals were observed. "According to an inquiry conducted by the Lemberg Statistical Office in the seventies, 100 to 120 nonworking days were counted in 34 Galician districts, 120 to 150 in 22 other districts, and 150 to 200 in 16 more."[48]

---

44. *Ibid.* "In spite of all this there is a sharp increase in population, which is probably attributable to the few necessities of life demanded by the three peoples inhabiting Galicia (Poles, Ruthenians, and Jews). While in 1890 there were still only 84 inhabitants per square kilometer, in 1900 the number was already 93.2."

45. *Ibid.*

46. *Ibid.*, p. 55. "At the present time [around 1907] the estate owner in the Brzesko district pays 60 to 80 hellers, in midsummer 1 to 1.20 crowns, 2 to 3.60 crowns to mowers, 1.40 to 1.70 crowns to women and boys, 1.40 to 1.60 crowns to threshers, and in winter 40 hellers, though to be sure including board. In the Mielec district 80 hellers along with board or 1.20 crowns are paid in the spring and 1.20 to 2 crowns during the harvest."

47. *Ibid.*

48. "The blame for these conditions is shared partly by misguided piety which understands too little the blessings of work and the demands of modern culture, and partly by conservatism, especially in the eastern part of the land." *Ibid.*, p. 56. The fact that the per capita income was higher in many areas of ethnically mixed eastern Galicia than in wholly Polish western Galicia speaks against this hypothesis. See Table 1.v.

Blumenfeld complains that the existence of the large estates (*Grossgrundbesitz*) is cited either as a secondary factor or is not even mentioned at all. Instead—and here he refers to Caro, "Auswanderung und Auswanderungspolitik," and *Emigracya i polityka Emigracyjn* —the right of partition of the land, the agency business, illiteracy, alcoholism, the passion for litigation, overpopulation, usury, and land hunger are enumerated. These, however, are not analyzed observations. "Land mergers will not bring an increase of the small holders' property, but would instead transform a large part of these remaining farmers

Agriculture, which is to say the great agrarian landowners, complained the most about emigration,[49] claiming that agriculture suffered most from the shortage of people.[50] The blame was placed on the emigration agents.

Austrian agriculture and, indeed, one can say the Austrian economy in general, opposes every artificial enticement to emigration and its increase beyond the degree dictated by the situation of the domestic labor market alone. It is appalled by the fact that because of artificial agitation and only for the sake of the growing profits of the agitators and their backers, people who would never think of emigrating and who could find profitable employment at home are induced to turn their backs on their fatherland. Agriculture is, furthermore, of the opinion that the soliciting for permanent settlement abroad and the commending of foreign lands for the purpose of attracting colonists (for themselves) is not to be permitted.[51]

The effects of emigration were also revealed in the weak Galician industry. "Within three years a Galician chemical plant lost 50 percent of its workers to the emigration to America."[52] The loss of industrial workers in Galicia was, nevertheless, only a marginal phenomenon. One can conclude the examination of emigration in Galicia with Blumenfeld's comment: "The estates of above-average size produced the emigration."[53]

## (b) Bukovina

The second crownland which was a focal point of the emigration in the northeast was Bukovina. Although here the basic prob-

---

into landless proletarians." The term "land hunger" was commonly treated as the land hunger of small holders with pressure to parcellize in order to conceal the real land hunger of the great estate owners. Blumenfeld, "Grossgrundbesitz und Auswanderung in Galizien," pp. 633ff.

49. AVA, Justizministerium VI in genere Verzeichnis 18, no. 6921 ex 1914. Complaint of Viktor Rozwadowski, Imperial Reserve Captain and *Grossgrundbesitzer* in Glinna bei Zborów, to the Corps Command in Lemberg about the great number of emigrants from his district, February 8, 1914.

50. H. Mitscha von Märheim, *Die Auswanderungsfrage im Lichte der jüngsten Ereignisse* (address presented before the Agrarian and Forestry Club in Vienna on November 7, 1913 [Vienna, 1913]), p. 12.

51. *Ibid.*, and *Wiener landwirtschaftliche Zeitung*, August 27, 1913.

52. A. Friedmann, *Arbeitermangel und Auswanderung* (Vienna, 1907), p. 27.

53. Blumenfeld, "Grossgrundbesitz und Auswanderung in Galizien," p. 634.

lematic features of emigration and the conditions which produced it were in many ways similar to those in Galicia, a number of special regional characteristics were naturally also in evidence.

The census of 1910 recorded around 800,000 inhabitants in Bukovina. The Ruthenians formed 38.4 percent of the Bukovinian population, Rumanians 34.4 percent, Germans 21.4 percent, Poles 4.6 percent, and Magyars 1.3 percent.[1] Jews were registered as Germans.[2] The polarization of the population into two national groups, typical of Galicia, is absent in Bukovina; the composition of the population, at least according to nationality, was much more diverse. In absolute numbers the estimated population loss due to emigration in the period from 1901 to 1910 was 35,194 higher than in Carniola and Dalmatia, but at 4.82 percent was somewhat lower in relative terms. The loss was, however, higher than the Austrian average of 2.61 percent.[3]

Based on a report of the commander of the state police, of August 23, 1913, a total of 31,690 persons from Bukovina, according to the count on May 15, 1913, were classified as dwelling abroad.[4] The report is, however, questionable because 22,000 of the people were said to be living in Canada and only 585 in the United States, which contradicts the yearly ratio of Austro-Hungarian immigration to these countries. The Ministry of Interior also labeled these figures erroneous in a postscriptory note.[5] These statistics are arranged in the categories shown in Table 1.IX.

1. Kann, "Das Nationalitätenproblem der Habsburgermonarchie," pp. 389ff.
2. Concerning the statistical classification of Jews in Austria, see p. 61 above.
3. "Ergebnisse der Volkszählung vom 31. Dezember 1910," pp. 29–30; also in Englisch, "Die österreichische Auswanderungsstatistik," p. 155, or Caro, *Emigracya i polityka Emigracyjne*, p. 21.
4. AVA, MdI Präsidiale 15/15 Montreal, no. 40 034/13.
5. *Ibid.*, Zusatzvermerk des MdI.

## Table 1.IX

CATEGORIES OF EMIGRANTS

| Sex | Travel documents used | Districts with highest emigration | |
|---|---|---|---|
| 22,458 men* | 21,109 passports | Czernowitz | 4,526 |
| 3,337 women | 2,882 work books | Kotzman | 3,283 |
| 5,901 children | 5,824 without documents | Zastavna | 4,935 |
| | | Sereth | 2,820 |

SOURCE: AVA, Md I Präsidiale 15/15 Montreal, no. 40 034/13. Supplement.
*Among whom 4,875 were in the age group liable for military service.

Jacques Jaeger, the secretary of the Austro-Hungarian Colonial Society, described the emigrants from Bukovina as very poor, and for that reason they were often turned back by the American immigration authorities. The emigration was composed of three groups: the Swabians, descendents of those colonists who, in the time of the Emperor Joseph had moved into Buchenland; the Ruthenians, many of whom traveled to Winnipeg in Canada; and the Jews.[6]

The center of the emigration movement was Czernowitz, where the numerous agents and travel bureaus made it the meeting place and point of departure for the trip.[7] As a cause of the emigration, the unequal distribution of land was even more pronounced than in Galicia. Ninety percent of the landowners possessed less than the five hectares minimum for existence, while 75 percent had only the very smallest holding of less than two hectares. Fifteen percent of the holdings comprised only two to five hectares each. On the other hand, 7 percent of the enterprises had an area of five to twenty hectares, and a little more than 1 percent of the operations covered twenty to one hundred hectares.[8]

6. Der Weltverkehr—Zeitschrift für Ex- und Import, Handel, Verkehrs- und Auswanderungswesen—Offizielles Organ der Österr. Ungar. Kolonial Gesellschaft, 1 Jahrgang, no. 11 (November 1905), 10. See, AVA, Justizministerium I B I, 2 carton 49, no. 25 392/05.
7. Ibid.
8. Otto Neurath, "Zum österreichischen Auswanderungsgesetzentwurf," Zeitschrift für Volkswirtschaft, Sozialpolitik und Verwaltung. Organ der Gesellschaft österreichischer Volkswirte, 23 (1914), 370. Neurath investigated conditions in Bukovina on the basis of Blumenfeld's examination of Galicia, which he chose as his model. He also believes that the excessively large Grossgrundbesitz is the cause of emigration.

Not even one half of 1 percent are classified as great estates (*Grossgrundbesitz*) of more than one hundred hectares, and yet this group contains 60 percent of the land. In contrast, approximately 60 percent of the land in Styria is divided into lots of under five hectares and 25 percent by holdings of between five and twenty hectares. These figures make the seasonal migration and also the permanent emigration thoroughly comprehensible.[9]

On March 16, 1912, Dr. Benno Straucher, a deputy in the *Reichsrat* from Czernowitz, ascertained, in responding to an inquiry concerning emigration prepared by the Ministry of Trade, that in Buchenland 51 percent of the land was owned by state and private corporations, while 170 great estate owners possessed 0.5 million hectares of land, only 0.6 million hectares were owned by all the small holders. Of the total land, 26 percent belonged to the Greek Orthodox Church.[10] "How can one speak of a healthy peasantry there? Up to 83 percent of the small holdings are nothing but lots of three hectares or less. A similar case is not to be found in any Austrian province. For that very reason, Bukovina is a land short of capital. . . . That these people emigrate is not surprising."[11] Straucher was, however, pointedly rebuked by *Ministerialrat* Kautzky of the Ministry of Trade, who maintained that his statements "had gone too far," and the subject was quickly closed at that point.[12]

The decisive importance of the conditions of land ownership in agrarian areas for emigration is also illustrated by the comparison of two districts with different degrees of emigration. In the Gurahumora district, which had a high level of emigration, 14,000 of a total of 17,000 land owners possessed less than two hectares. In the Kimpolung district, with lower emigration, only about 7,100 of the 13,300 landowners had less than two hectares.[13]

The existence of large estates and the continued uneconomic parcellation of small holdings into smaller and smaller parcels of land

9. *Ibid.*, p. 371.

10. "Protokoll der im k.k. Handelsministerium durchgeführten Vernehmung von Auskunftspersonen über die Auswanderung aus Österreich" (Vienna, 1912) column 256.

11. *Ibid.*, column 257.

12. *Ibid.*, Kautzky, column 257.

13. Neurath, "Zum österreichischen Auswanderungsgesetzentwurf," p. 370.

remained the open question.[14] Many Ruthenian peasants were of the opinion that things were better for the peasant in Russia, because they paid fewer taxes and steps were taken there against the Jews.[15] The Jews controlled village banking also in Bukovina.

The authorities in Bukovina did not want to recognize the true causes of emigration. In a Bukovinian investigation held in Czernowitz in 1900 and 1901, usury and alcoholism were denoted as causes of emigration, and the blame was placed on village innkeepers and moneylenders.[16] Of course, these observations were not proven and the phenomena which they described were not understood for what they really were, namely, consequences of the existing social conditions.

Emigration due to the unfavorable business conditions, especially in the rural areas of northern and eastern Bukovina, led to a labor shortage, particularly in agricultural operations. To compensate, Galician workers were drawn upon, but they, so the complaints went, were more expensive. Many peasants, therefore, had to let part of their land lie fallow because they simply could not afford the new help.[17] The estate owners raised the greatest lament, but the substance of their complaints did not always conform exactly with the realities of the situation.[18]

14. The parcelling out of holdings often led to conflicts between Poles and Ruthenians in Galicia, for example, since neither wanted to relinquish land to the other. The Ruthenians especially feared that they would be gradually driven back. See *ibid.*

15. *Ibid.*, p. 373.

16. Caro, "Auswanderung und Auswanderungspolitik," p. 57.

17. AVA, MdI Präsidiale 15/15 Montreal, no. 40 034/13. Report of the State Police Command, no. 13 of August 23, 1913.

18. Estate owner Alexander-Freiherr von Styrcea sent a letter of complaint to Arthur Grünhut on August 2, 1913. Grünhut kindled his campaign against the Canadian Pacific through articles that primarily appeared in the *Danzers Armee Zeitung* (Vienna), and his petitions on the emigration issue which, as a reservist, he usually directed to the Ministry of War as he did Styrcea's letter. Finally landing in the appropriate Ministry of Interior, the letter of the estate owner from Krasna-Ilsky complained about the damages suffered by the landed gentry at the hands of the Canadian company. "All my peasants, old and young, have emigrated and [therefore] we sit here completely without workers and must spend a lot of money to bring in people from Russia and Rumania, since otherwise we would be here with no labor at all. . . . My cousin, one of the most prominent land owners here, said to me that he had almost no peasants at all, since everybody had emigrated to Canada." He had visited the C.P.R. office in Czernowitz himself and noted how "unscrupulous agents turn the heads of the poor stupid peasants." He also complained

## (c) *Dalmatia and Carniola*

A second focal point of emigration was located in the south. Of the Austrian crownlands, Dalmatia and Carniola were most greatly affected. However, due to the small number of people, the Croatian-Slovene emigration from these two lands and, marginally, South Carniola, South Carinthia, Görz, and Gradisca, did not reach the same magnitude as the two northeastern crownlands.

In 1910, Dalmatia had 646,000 inhabitants, of whom 92 percent were Serbo-Croatians, 5 percent Germans, and 2.8 percent Italians, while Carniola had 526,000 inhabitants, of whom 94.4 percent were Slovenes and 5.3 percent were Germans. Carinthia was less affected. In 1910, it had 396,000 inhabitants, 78.6 percent of whom were German and 21.2 percent were Slovenes.[1]

As already mentioned, Dalmatia and Carniola had the heaviest emigration. For the period from 1900 to 1910, 33,965 people emigrated from Carniola, amounting to a population loss of 6.68 percent.[2] The relative figure was just as high as in Galicia. The equivalent figures for Dalmatia were a loss of 31,814 people, or 5.36 per-

---

that even his own servant wanted to go over in September, although he still had to participate in a military exercise. AVA, MdI Präsidiale 15/15 Montreal, no. 32 140/13. Letter of Styrcea to Grünhut, August 2, 1913. Styrcea, like Grünhut a member of the Imperial Volunteer Motor Corps and the Jockey Club, apparently wanted to provide some auxiliary support for Grünhut in his campaign against the C.P.R., for his statements finally proved to be completely fallacious. Based on the results of inquiries carried out in the matter, the commander of the state police in Czernowitz informed the state government on September 7, 1913, that only eight persons from Styrcea's estate (a woodland estate with lumber and cement industry) had emigrated. All were of the Jewish faith, as was cited, and three of them were old enough to be liable for military service. From the nearby communities, Krasna-Ilsky and Althütten, twenty-eight had emigrated, of whom fifteen were liable for military service. Styrcea's statements probably were based on "rumors." Besides, no Russian workers were located and a great many native peasants went to Rumania to work. To replace them Galician workers were used exclusively. AVA, MdI Präsidiale 15/15 Montreal, no. 37 742/13. State Government of Bukovina to MdI, Czernowitz, October 3, 1913, report on emigration agitation. Styrcea's letter, which Grünhut appended with his own commentary and forwarded to the Ministry of War, induced War Minister Krobatin, without any substantiation of the assertions made in it, to inform the Interior Minister that "an emigration from Bukovina in such volume as is actually occurring now lies neither in the interest of the populace nor in the interest of the economy." *Ibid.*, Krobatin to MdI, August 21, 1913.

1. Kann, "Das Nationalitätenproblem der Habsburgermonarchie," pp. 389ff.
2. "Ergebnisse der Volkszählung vom 31. Dezember 1910," pp. 29–30.

cent of the population.[3] In comparison, Carinthia's loss was .54 percent; Styria's, 1.18 percent; Görz's and Gradisca's, 1.61 percent.[4]

The magnitude of the South Slav emigration is reflected in the annual American statistics. In the fiscal year 1911–1912, for example, 8,849 Croats and Slovenes from the Austrian half of the Empire immigrated to the United States, forming the third largest contingent behind the Poles, with 30,459, and the Ruthenians, with 17,284, and still ahead of the 8,535 Jews, the 7,840 Bohemians, and the 6,265 Germans. After them, a small number of Italians, Slovaks, Rumanians, and Serbs followed. The number of Croats from Hungary who emigrated was, however, significantly higher.[5]

Table 1.x

For every 100,000 members of the major ethnic groups, the following number emigrated to the United States in 1912:

| | |
|---|---|
| 711 Poles | 252 Magyars |
| 604 Serbs, Croats, and Slovenes | 225 Rumanians |
| 542 Ruthenians | 182 Germans |
| 480 Jews | 130 Italians |
| 386 Bohemians and Slovaks | |

SOURCE: Neurath, "Zum österreichischen Auswanderungsgesetzentwurf," p. 342.

In Dalmatia, the sterile soil and the minimial industrialization were the chief reasons for emigration.[6] The Dalmatians also showed the greatest individualism in selecting their destinations. The Monarchy's emigrants to Australia and New Zealand were almost exclusively Dalmatians.[7]

The rate of return emigration was relatively high among the

---

3. *Ibid.*; see also Blumenfeld, "Grossgrundbesitz und Auswanderung in Galizien," p. 633.

4. *Ibid.*

5. AVA, MdI Auswanderungsakten 8/4 file 320, no. 21 345/13. Report of the Imperial Embassy in Washington.

6. See Table 1.VIII in this section.

7. See p. 297 above.

South Slavs. In 1908, they provided the largest group of returning emigrants with 23.7 percent.[8]

The situation of the agrarian populace had hardly changed in preceding decades. New, liberal ideas had not penetrated into the villages.

The agrarian masses of Galicia, Bukovina, Dalmatia, Carinthia, etc. were actually only grazed by the liberal creed, which in Central Europe developed mainly in an urban setting. Getting along for decades primarily by farming, they experienced hardly a trace of liberal political life. They had, of course, been freed from many old pressures, but they lived, on the whole, much as they always had. They rarely made use of their various freedoms or of the rights of free citizens. They often did not know what was their legal due. This changed when international turmoil seized these areas and especially when the traditional village order was destroyed by emigration. The wage-labor relationship and the money economy made a neighbor of the stranger and a stranger of the neighbor.[9]

(d) *The Other Crownlands*

Emigration also shook other crownlands, but only partially. It never appeared as a mass movement, and its intensity varied from region to region. More people emigrated from Bohemia and Moravia than from the German Austrian lands. The ethnic structure of these lands, according to the census of 1910, is shown in Table 1.XI.

Table 1.XI

| Bohemia: 6,770,000 inhabitants | Moravia: 2,622,000 inhabitants |
|---|---|
| 63.2%  Czechs* | 71.8%  Czechs* |
| 36.8%  Germans | 27.6%  Germans |
|  | 0.6%  Poles |

SOURCE: Kann, "Das Nationalitäten problem der Habsburgermonarchie," p. 389.
* Including Slovaks.

The loss of population brought about by the emigration between 1900 and 1910 amounted to 171,513, or 2.71 percent of the popu-

8. *Beilagen zu den stenographischen Protokollen des Abgeordnetenhauses*, 2027, XXI Session (1913), 34.

9. Neurath, "Zum österreichischen Auswanderungsgesetzentwurf." p. 300.

lation in Bohemia and 93,928 or 3.85 percent in Moravia.[1] At first glance, these figures seem high, but they are results of circumstances which played either no role or a totally subordinate one in the lands already treated. The decline in population in Bohemia is primarily traceable to the domestic migration.[2] The increase in population in Lower Austria and especially in Vienna in the same period attributable to the migration amounted to 158,872 or 5.12 percent.[3] Vienna, above all, attracted a great number of Czechs, so that by 1910 the Czechs in Lower Austria accounted for 3.75 percent of its 3,532,000 inhabitants.[4] Aside from the domestic migration, the seasonal migration in Bohemia also played a significant role not only in the Czech but in the German part of the population. According to the reports of the German Labor Center, an annual average of 18,000 to 28,000 Bohemians and 40,000 to 59,000 Germans migrated on a seasonal basis from Austrian lands into neighboring Germany between 1908–1909 and 1912–1913.[5]

The Czech overseas emigration, which before 1900 had played a relatively important role—at the turn of the century 157,000 "Bohemians" already resided in the United States[6]—no longer developed as strongly thereafter, and its percentage of the Austrian emigration declined. From 1902 to 1911 not quite 100,000 "Bohemians" emigrated to the United States,[7] its most active years being 1904 and 1907. The Czechs usually emigrated with their families and preferred permanent emigration.[8] Their rate of return was thus quite small.[9]

1. "Ergebnisse der Volkszählung vom 31. Dezember 1910," pp. 29–30. See also Blumenfeld, "Grossgrundbesitz und Auswanderung in Galizien," p. 633, and Englisch, "Die österreichische Auswanderungsstatistik," p. 155.

2. *Ibid.*

3. "Ergebnisse der Volkszählung vom 31. Dezember 1910," pp. 29–30.

4. Kann, "Das Nationalitätenproblem der Habsburgermonarchie," p. 389.

5. *Österreichisches Statistisches Handbuch*, 32 Jahrgang, 1913 (Vienna, 1914), 61.

6. Zöllner, *Geschichte Österreichs*, p. 444.

7. AVA, Justizministerium I B I, 2 carton 49, no. 31 825/13. Gesetzentwurf 1913, Motivenbericht, p. 32.

8. J. S. Roucek, "Die Tschechen und Slowaken in den Vereinigten Staaten," *Schriftendienst Übersee*, no. 9 (1943), 4.

9. *Beilagen zu den stenographischen Protokollen des Abgeordnetenhauses*, 2027, XXI Session (1913), 34.

The Czech emigrants from Bohemia came chiefly from the southern part of the land, then from the regions around Tabor, Pisek, Kuttenberg, and Časlav, while the Moravian Czechs emigrated primarily from the southeast of the country.[10] The occupational structure of the Czechs was clearly different from that of the other Austrian emigrants. While among the Poles, Ruthenians, Croats, Slovenes, and Hungarian Slovaks, unskilled workers and agrarian day laborers were the largest groups, skilled workers from industry and business formed the dominant faction in Bohemian emigration.[11] In Bohemia it was no longer a matter of the emigration of an uneducated agrarian proletariat but of skilled workers from industry and business who decided to emigrate primarily because of the greater chances to earn money overseas.

The extent of the industrial-capitalist emigration is no longer conditioned by harvest failures, but by fluctuations of the industrial cycle. The emigration, therefore, runs parallel to the line reflecting the extent of unemployment and contrary to the lines indicating the change of commodity prices and the interest rate. Although the migrations to America, which long ago took on the character of a peaceful mass exodus, are larger than any in world history, they are nothing more than great balancing movements.[12]

The emigrants possessed knowledge of conditions overseas, since friends and relatives often already resided in America.[13]

As a result, industrialists in Prague and Brünn complained of labor shortages.[14] The Association of North Bohemian Industrialists wrote: "Most firms, especially the larger ones, suffer constantly from a shortage of labor which has been making itself felt for several years."[15] The Bohemian workers' search for employ-

10. Markitan, *Auswandererverkehrswege in Österreich*, p. 7.

11. AVA, Justizministerium I B I, 2 carton 49, no. 31 825/13. Gesetzentwurf 1913, Motivenbericht, p. 33.

12. O. Bauer, "Proletarische Wanderungen," *Neue Zeit* (1907), cited in Englisch, "Zu unserer Auswanderungsfrage," pp. 92ff., and in Friedmann, *Arbeitermangel und Auswanderung*, p. 34.

13. Englisch, "Zu unserer Auswanderungsfrage," pp. 92ff.

14. Friedmann, *Arbeitermangel und Auswanderung*, pp. 13ff.

15. *Ibid.*, p. 20.

ment in the industrial districts of Saxony also contributed to the labor shortage.[16]

In the other crownlands, above all in the areas populated by Germans, emigration was only a peripheral development. To be sure, significant population losses from 1900 to 1910 resulting from departures can be established in several lands, primarily in Upper Austria with 17,668 or 2.18 percent and in Silesia with 17,003 or 2.5 percent;[17] but these were chiefly traceable to domestic migration.[18] Several lands even registered a heavy influx; Lower Austria with Vienna gained 158,872 (or 5.12 percent), Küstenland as a whole gained 37,920 (or 5.01 percent), Tirol with Vorarlberg and Salzburg a 2.38 percent increase resulting from this influx.[19]

Of the ethnic German emigrants from the Dual Monarchy, averaging about twenty-eight thousand annually after 1903, approximately two thirds came from the Hungarian half of the Empire. The rest were scattered among the Austrian lands. Thus Germans clearly tended to emigrate from those lands in which they represented an ethnic minority, as the German emigration from Bukovina or the extensive emigration from Gotschee, the German-speaking enclave in Carniola, shows.

In individual cases, the desire for adventure may also have contributed to the decision to emigrate. The emigration agents of the shipping companies knew, for example, how to use the effects of Indian stories on students, and they approached students of the upper grades of the Vienna secondary schools in order to stimulate interest in emigration. Some of the students could be easily led astray, especially those with poor academic records who were met part way with regard to the cost of the trip.[20] A mass emigration from the German-speaking lands for social reasons did not take place.

---

16. *Ibid.*, p. 21.
17. Blumenfeld, "Grossgrundbesitz und Auswanderung in Galizien," p. 633.
18. Englisch, "Die österreichische Auswanderungsstatistik," p. 155.
19. Blumenfeld, "Grossgrundbesitz und Auswanderung in Galizien," p. 633.
20. AVA,MdI Auswanderungsakten 8/4 file 323, no. 13 474/14. Viennese Parents' Assembly to the Police Directory, Vienna, March 27, 1914.

## 2. GENERAL REASONS FOR EMIGRATION AND THE EMIGRANTS ACCORDING TO AGE, SEX, EDUCATION, AND OCCUPATION

In a private inquiry, conducted as early as 1897, of 142 people, including 103 Hungarians, concerning their motives for emigrating, many declared that they left because of better wages in America.[1] Improvement of one's economic position was the principal driving force of the mass emigration. Hürlimann distinguishes between the emigrant's objective and subjective motives. Everything between an extravagant desire for adventure and bitter unemployment belongs to subjective motivation. "We must divide the objective motives into three groups: (a) conditions in the homeland which drive or induce one to emigrate, (b) points of attraction in the immigration countries, and (c) international big capital interested in the emigration." While until the middle of the nineteenth century, thousands were able to escape religious and political oppression only by emigrating, since then the economic factor has become the driving force of the emigration.[2]

It is absolutely impossible to classify precisely the Austrian emigrants according to the categories of age, sex, education, and occupation. These features were recorded only in the rarest cases and for only a fraction of the emigrants.[3] The only possibility is to make comparisons based on the American statistics, which are the only useful sources on the subject.

The emigrants were predominantly men. From 1876 to 1910, a total of 1,845,382 Austrians emigrated, but the sex of the migrants was recorded for only 1,031,652, revealing 670,473 men and only 361,179 women.[4] The more precise Hungarian statistics indicate that for the lands of the Hungarian Crown, including Croatia-

1. G. Pacher, *Die Arbeiterwanderungen zwischen Österreich-Ungarn und Nord-Amerika* (Vienna, 1897), pp. 11ff.

2. W. Hürlimann, "Die schweizerische Auswanderung und ihre Gesetzgebung" (unpub. Juristic diss., University of Zürich, 1918), pp. 16–17.

3. Englisch, "Die österreichische Auswanderungsstatistik," p. 79.

4. *Ibid.*, p. 81.

Slovonia, from 1899 to 1913 there were 947,988 men and 442,537 women. Thus, 68.2 percent of the emigrants were men, and 31.8 percent were women.[5] In later years, however, the number of women emigrating rose even in Austria, often because already departed husbands had their families follow later.

As for age, the group between fifteen and forty years predominated. (See Table 2.1.) People over forty seldom emigrated, and the number of children under fifteen was also not very high. The emigration of men in the age group liable for military service provoked the intensely anti-emigration attitude of the military, which was concerned about the mustering of recruits. Englisch confirmed a decline in the number of marriages as one consequence of the emigration.[6]

Table 2.1

EMIGRANTS BY AGE GROUP

1876–1910  Below 15: 212,045 = 14.8%
15–40:  1,086,399 = 76%
Over 40:  131,424 = 9.2%

SOURCE: Englisch, "Die österreichische Auswanderungsstatistik," p. 81.

The American statistics are again the most dependable for occupational classification. However, all immigrants of a particular ethnic group were recorded without consideration of their citizenship. This must be kept in mind especially with regard to Poles, Jews, Germans, etc. (See Table 2.II.)

The greatest number of immigrants in almost every ethnic group came from the agrarian sector of the economy, being either independent farmers or day laborers. Only the Bohemians and Jews, among whom skilled tradesmen were most heavily represented, formed exceptions. Of the total amount, agrarian day laborers constituted 24 percent, the independent farmers 18.9 percent, the skilled tradesmen 16.2 percent, and domestic servants 10.5

---

5. "Auswanderung und Rückwanderung der Länder der ungarischen heiligen Krone," pt. II, p. 9.

6. Englisch, "Die österreichische Auswanderungsstatistik," p. 155.

Table 2.II

| | Free Professions | Skilled Tradesmen | Independent Farmers | Agrarian Day Laborers | Servants | Others | Dependents (Women and children without occupations) | Total |
|---|---|---|---|---|---|---|---|---|
| Bohemians | 829 | 25,534 | 10,519 | 8,372 | 15,832 | 981 | 38,063 | 100,130 |
| Croats | 260 | 13,148 | 96,279 | 144,490 | 21,191 | 549 | 34,864 | 310,781 |
| Serbs | 52 | 2,646 | 10,742 | 16,461 | 1,047 | 115 | 3,259 | 34,322 |
| Germans | 14,213 | 136,483 | 89,570 | 87,281 | 93,039 | 30,241 | 276,722 | 726,549 |
| Jews | 7,447 | 383,240 | 12,774 | 62,174 | 68,034 | 35,909 | 441,024 | 1,010,602 |
| Italians | 3,465 | 53,960 | 55,796 | 136,930 | 23,708 | 5,279 | 71,052 | 350,190 |
| Magyars | 1,447 | 22,302 | 104,426 | 91,791 | 33,461 | 1,509 | 75,416 | 330,352 |
| Poles | 1,412 | 47,858 | 239,183 | 313,363 | 127,538 | 1,870 | 173,719 | 904,943 |
| Rumanians | 176 | 2,203 | 45,099 | 25,851 | 2,150 | 273 | 8,571 | 84,323 |
| Ruthenians | 129 | 2,916 | 55,399 | 52,946 | 25,900 | 92 | 18,097 | 155,479 |
| Slovaks | 168 | 11,144 | 97,743 | 101,617 | 44,037 | 331 | 69,466 | 324,506 |
| TOTAL | 29,598 | 701,434 | 817,530 | 1,041,276 | 455,937 | 77,149 | 1,209,253 | 4,332,177 |

SOURCES: *Beilagen zu den stenographischen Protokollen des Abgeordnetenhauses*, 2027, XXI Session
913), p. 33, and AVA, Justizministerium IBI, 2, carton 49, no. 31 825/13. Gesetzentwurf 1913, Mo-
venbericht, p. 33.

percent. The free professions were most highly represented among the German immigrants, forming 2 percent of the German total, followed by the Italians with 1 percent, the Bohemians with .8 percent, and the Jews with .7 percent. Skilled tradesmen were also more in evidence in these ethnic groups than in the others, although in almost perfectly reversed order (Jews 37.9 percent, Bohemians 25.5 percent, Germans 18.8 percent, and Italians 15.4 percent).[7]

Table 2.III

THE AUSTRIAN EMIGRATION 1876–1910 BY OCCUPATION

| Agriculture and Forestry | 628,215 |
|---|---|
| Commerce and Industry | 122,790 |
| Trade and Transportation | 37,845 |
| Free Professions | 6,115 |
| Workers | 300,988 |
| Other Occupations | 95,833 |

SOURCE: Englisch, "Die österreichische Auswanderungsstatistik," p. 79.

From 1901 to 1910, 23.75 percent of all emigrants were day laborers and 19.45 percent independent farmers, these being the most significant groups. Tradesmen accounted for 15.86 percent, domestic servants 10.17 percent, and unemployed dependents 28.28 percent. The free professions accounted for only .72 percent, with Germans, Jews, and Italians most heavily represented.[8] The percentage of skilled workers and artisans varied from one ethnic group to another, being highest among Jews and lowest among Ruthenians. In 1905, according to Caro, they composed 46 percent of the Jewish emigration, 20 percent of the German, 4 percent each of the Croatian and Polish, and only 1 percent of the Ruthenian.[9]

Perhaps the most unfortunate aspect, however, is indicated by the occupational structure of our emigrants, in that, for example, 19.45% of all the Monarchy's emigrants to the United States belong to the class of independent farmers. The breaking up and mortgaging of native small holdings, whose

7. *Beilagen zu den stenographischen Protokollen des Abgeordnetenhauses*, 2027, p. 33.
8. Englisch, "Die österreichische Auswanderungsstatistik," pp. 97, 99.
9. Caro, "Auswanderung und Auswanderungspolitik," p. 87.

interest payments often exceed their profits; the speculation on parcelled-out lots which drives the price of land too high for returning emigrants to meet; the many premature retirement portions in Moravian Slovakia, in addition to the cash outlays for extremely numerous brothers and sisters; as well as the ravages caused by the liquor trade—all these and the promotional agents may all be held responsible for the prevailing conditions.[10]

Englisch did not, however, hold the great estate owners responsible.

For Hungary, exact occupational statistics are available for the periods 1905–1907 and 1911–1913,[11] making possible a comparison between the emigration and the society as a whole, shown in Table 2.IV.

With the aid of this table, the occupational structure of the emigration emerges clearly. Despite the fact that the number of people involved in agriculture is high in all of Hungary, the agrarian occupations are overrepresented in the total emigration. On the other hand, the groups which form the intelligentsia are strikingly underpresented, once again underscoring the agrarian-proletarian character of the emigrant society.[12]

The essence of this formulation also applies to the Austrian emigration.

A report of the Monarchy's General Consulate in Boston concerning the Austro-Hungarian immigrants who landed in four east coast states (Massachusetts, Maine, New Hampshire, and Vermont) in 1913–1914 makes an interesting disclosure about the particular occupations of the immigrants. Of 278,152 immigrants from the Monarchy, the occupations of about 209,500 are shown in Table 2.V. The rest were divided among various other occupations.

10. Englisch, "Die österreichische Auswanderungsstatistik," p. 156.
11. "Auswanderung und Rückwanderung der Länder der ungarischen heiligen Krone," pt. II, pp. 66–69.
12. Balla, "Auswanderung und Gesellschaftsstruktur," p. 167.

Table 2.IV

| Occupational sector | Emigration 1905–07 and 1911–13 (in percentage) | Percentage of population 1910 |
|---|---|---|
| Independent farmers | 19 | 41 |
| Agricultural workers and day laborers | 50 | 20.5 |
| Day laborers in different and unknown sectors of the economy | 10 | 3 |
| Household persons and servants | 5 | 4.5 |
| Independent artisans and merchants | 2.5 | 7 |
| Industrial and mining workers | 11 | 15 |
| Intelligentsia | 0.5 | 4.5 |
| Others | 2 | 5 |

SOURCE: Balla, "Auswanderung und Gesellschaftsstruktur," p. 167.

Table 2.V

| | |
|---|---|
| Farm workers | 65,731 |
| Employees | 35,936 |
| Day laborers | 31,580 |
| Without occupation (including women and children) | 60,849 |
| Total unskilled workers and dependents | 194,096 |
| Total skilled artisans and industrial workers | 12,410* |
| Farmers | 1,279 |
| Salesmen and merchants | 521 |
| Manufacturers and bankers | 13 |
| Intelligentsia | 504† |

* Including 1,130 shoemakers, 1,267 tailors, 768 masons, 877 locksmiths, 864 dressmakers, 1,007 blacksmiths, 446 bakers, 801 seamstresses, 493 butchers, but only 261 metal workers.

† Including 67 teachers, 64 engineers, 47 clerics, 26 literati and scholars, 14 doctors, 10 lawyers, but also 112 "musicians," 61 "electricians," and 11 officials.

SOURCE: Staatsarchiv, Auswanderungsakten F 15 carton 16, Statistische Auswanderungsberichte—Washington. Imperial General Consulate, Boston, April 15, 1915.

The educational level of the Austro-Hungarian emigrants was quite low. Of the Austro-Hungarian immigrants to the United States between 1901 and 1910, an average of 24.3 percent annually were illiterate. In these years Austria-Hungary provided almost half of the total number of illiterates immigrating to the United States. There were, however, radical differences among the various ethnic groups. The Czechs showed up best with only 1.3 percent illiterate, while 50 percent of the Ruthenians were illiterate.[13] In general, the Czechs and Germans possessed the best educational background, whereas the Jews had the highest percentage of qualified workers and the greatest number of dependents without a trade. The data indicate that the Jews who immigrated to the United States rarely returned.[14]

Table 2.vi

ILLITERATES PER 100 IMMIGRANTS
TO THE UNITED STATES 1902–1911

| Germans | 4.4 | Serbo-Croats and Slovaks | 34.5 |
|---|---|---|---|
| Bohemians | 1.3 | Italians | 9.8 |
| Slovaks | 20.6 | Rumanians | 35.0 |
| Poles | 32.3 | Magyars | 10.1 |
| Ruthenians | 50.6 | Jews | 19.8 |

SOURCE: *Beilagen zu den Stenographischen Protokollen des Abgeordnetenhauses*, 2027, XXI Session (1913), 34 (according to the annual report); and in AVA, Justizministerium I B I, 2 carton 49, no. 31 825/13. Gesetzentwurf 1913, Motivenbericht, p. 34.

Aside from the level of education, the financial basis of the emigrant was also a measure of his desirability or undesirability in the United States.[15] The Germans and Czechs were the most desirable ethnic groups from the Monarchy. Poles, Ruthenians, and Jews, which were the largest groups in the immigration, were also the

13. Englisch, "Die österreichische Auswanderungsstatistik," p. 100.
14. Caro, "Auswanderung und Auswanderungspolitik," p. 20.
15. See also, "Die Auswanderung aus Österreich-Ungarn in die Vereinigten Staaten von Nordamerika nach Nationalitäten und nach dem Grade ihrer Erwünschtheit für die Union," *Statistische Mitteilungen*, IV Jahrgang, no. 6 (1910), 30–31.

least well-to-do, and a high percentage of them were denied admission by the American immigration authorities.[16]

Table 2.VII

AVERAGE PER CAPITA AMOUNT OF MONEY
BROUGHT BY IMMIGRANTS 1902–1911

| | | | |
|---|---|---|---|
| Germans | $41.00 | Magyars | $15.80 |
| Czechs | $28.10 | Slovaks | $15.10 |
| Italians | $26.40 | Jews | $14.30 |
| Rumanians | $16.90 | Ruthenians | $14.10 |
| South Slavs | $16.00 | Poles | $12.80 |

SOURCE: *Beilagen zu den stenographischen Protokollen des Abgeordnetenhauses*, 2027, XXI Session (1913), 34.

### 3. THE COMMERCIAL ORGANIZATION OF THE EMIGRATION

Since it had assumed such great dimensions, emigration was one of shipping's most important sources of business, and Austria was a profitable field of activity for international shipping capital.[1] The natural emigration did not satisfy the companies, and they attempted to augment it artificially by recruitment.[2] In Austria, different groups profited by the emigration business: the domestic and foreign shipping companies; the large emigration agencies, usually associated with one of these shipping lines;[3] the domestic travel bureaus; and their emigration agents.[4] Besides these, so-called "emigrants' protection associations" sprang up and were organized on a national or religious basis, proclaiming their humanitarian motives. Most of them, however, also had financial gain in mind.

Emigration, shipping, the agency system, and also the export industry were so intertwined that clear lines of separation are almost

---

16. Englisch, "Die österreichische Auswanderungsstatistik," p. 103.

1. Chmelar, "Die Auswanderung," p. 183.
2. Salz, "Auswanderung und Schiffahrt," p. 123.
3. Missler in Bremen with North German Lloyd, Falck in Hamburg with the HAPAG.
4. Village notables were preferred for this position, especially the village innkeeper, teacher, and even the priest.

impossible to draw.[5] "The great shipping companies had to keep their capital employed. For both the two large German lines and the major English companies it was of extraordinary importance that the decline of the German and in part of the northwest European emigration was followed by an enormous increase in the east European wave."[6]

The large shipping companies had divided the emigration business among them. The great international shipping cartel, the "Atlantic Steerage Pool," was the foundation of the business. The Pool guaranteed the East European emigration business for the continental lines united under the leadership of the major German shipping companies in the "Association of North Atlantic Steamship Lines" (N.D.L.V.). The English and Scandinavian business was left to the British competition. The Austrian and Russian national lines with transatlantic service, which were bound together by pooling arrangements and financial interests, were also conceded a small share of the business, primarily in order to satisfy "national vanity." But their dependence on the larger firms was so great that they found it impossible to steer a more substantial portion of the East European emigrants to their Adriatic or Baltic ports. At the same time, they served as a control against independent competition.[7]

The unity of the shipping lines served to eliminate the competition which had temporarily led to very low transportation prices.[8] The Association of North Atlantic Steamship Lines, which was founded in 1891, counted as members: North German Lloyd in Bremen, the Hamburg-America line in Hamburg, the Holland-America Line (Neederlandsch-Amerikaansche Stoomvaart Maatschappij) in Rotterdam, and the Red Star Line (Société Anonyme de Navigation Belge-Américaine) in Antwerp. Each company had a certain percentage of the steerage business. Surpluses and def-

5. E. F. Weisl, *Auswanderung, Schiffahrt und Gewerbe* (speech delivered to the Lower Austrian Commercial Association, Vienna, January 2, 1902 [Vienna, 1902]), pp. 15ff. At that time Weisl was vice-president of the Austro-Hungarian Colonial Society.

6. Caro, "Auswanderung und Auswanderungspolitik," p. 28.

7. Riedl, *Die Organisation der Auswanderung*, p. III.

8. Chmelar, "Die Auswanderung," p. 185.

icits were evened out.[9] In 1903, the French line "Compagnie Générale Transatlantique" also became practically affiliated with the
Association.[10]

In 1903 the United Austrian Shipping Company (V.Ö.S.A.G.),
formerly the Austro-Americana and Fratelli Cosulich, was founded
in Trieste, and on June 9, 1904, its first steamer departed from that
port. Prior to that date negotiations with the German Hamburg-
America Line had begun. In July 1904 the Germans possessed 5
million of the V.Ö.S.A.G.'s total capital of 16 million crowns and
held an option on additional shares amounting to 3.15 million
crowns. With each increase of the company's capital, the German
holdings were proportionately supplemented so that, of the company's total capital of 24 million crowns in 1913, the Germans held
shares with a face value of 7.5 million crowns and had an option on
an additional 4.65 million crowns. Thus, by exercising this option,
the Germans could acquire the majority of shares at any time.
From the very start, the "national" Austrian shipping company
was under German control. On November 13, 1904, the company's
formal accession to the N.D.L.V. took place with an allotment of
4 percent in the North Atlantic business, but this contract did
not make the Austro-Americana a member.[11] This allotment meant
around 12,000 to 16,000 emigrants from Trieste per year.[12] "That
is ridiculously few compared to the 80,000 to 130,000 annual emigrants going to the United States and Canada from Austria alone,
and the disparity becomes even more glaring when one takes into
account the whole Monarchy and its doubly large emigration figures."[13] The transport of Greek, Italian, and Spanish emigrants
was not included in the 4 percent share.

Here the intention of the North Atlantic lines is to reserve for themselves the
emigrants from the Monarchy, and especially those from the northern areas,

---

9. Riedl, *Die Organisation der Auswanderung*, pp. 4ff.

10. *Ibid.*, pp. 6ff.

11. *Ibid.*, pp. 13–14.

12. This depended on the intensity of the emigration movement and was valid only
for immigration to North America. Immigration to South America was not affected.

13. Riedl, *Die Organisation der Auswanderung*, p. 15.

while satisfying Trieste with a trivial percentage. The Austro-Americana may carry Syrians and Greeks who in any case would never have come into question as passengers for the northern lines.[14]

The Near Eastern business, was, moreover, uncertain since Greece had established a line of its own and wanted to bind its emigrants to it by legislation.[15] One must, however, also remember that the Galician emigrants preferred the shorter trip via the North Sea ports.[16]

The Austrian government attempted to put pressure on the Pool by reaching an agreement with the Canadian railway and colonization organization, the Canadian Pacific Railway Company (C.P.R.), which had also founded a shipping line.[17] The Canadians were irritated because they had not been included in the Pool's distribution plan for the division of the emigration business. On the basis of the arrangements with the Austrian government, the Canadian Pacific opened a new line from Trieste to Canada in 1913. Along with other advantages for Austria, director of the shipping section in the Ministry of Trade and the initiator of the agreement, Section Chief Riedl, expected the new competing line to pressure the Pool into awarding the Austro-Americana a greater share of the emigration business.[18] Aside from these goals, a reduction of the German stock ownership was desired.

Besides the Austro-Americana, seven foreign shipping lines were permitted to operate in Austria: from 1885 the Holland-America Line,[19] from 1887 the Belgian Red Star Line,[20] from 1894 the North German Lloyd,[21] from 1899 the Hamburg-America Line,[22] from 1900 the French Compagnie Générale Transatlantique,[23]

14. *Ibid.*, p. 16.
15. *Ibid.*
16. Chmelar, "Die Auswanderung," p. 188.
17. *Ibid.*, pp. 189ff.
18. See Riedl, *Die Organisation der Auswanderung*, pp. 24ff.
19. By the edict of the Ministry of Interior, April 14, 1885, no. 4247.
20. By the edict of the Ministry of Interior, March 28, 1887, no. 2272.
21. By the edict of the Ministry of Interior, May 7, 1894, no. 5373.
22. Riedl, *Die Organisation der Auswanderung*, p. 28.
23. *Ibid.*

from 1903 the Cunard Line,[24] and from 1908 the Canadian Pacific Railway Company.[25]

The Austro-Americana maintained the most widespread network of agencies. Its affiliates also worked for the other Pool companies, which were themselves represented only in Vienna, Trieste, and occasionally in the most important provincial capitals. In 1913, the C.P.R. was granted more extensive concessions, including the right to open offices in the smaller towns of Galicia and Bukovina.[26] Almost all local offices made use of village agents who did not adhere to the regulations in the least.[27] Following the "Canadian scandal" in the fall of 1913,[28] negotiations were at last conducted with the shipping cartel. Minister of Trade Schuster wanted to reach an agreement with the German companies, and on April 24, 1914, the Austrian government, the Hamburg-America Line, and the North German Lloyd came to terms.[29] The Austro-Americana became the central booking office for all steerage passage, and its pool quota was to be raised from 4 to 7 percent sometime between January 1915 and the end of 1919 and to 10 percent at some point between 1920 and 1929. Furthermore, the German shares were transferred to an Austrian group.[30] The agreement did not, however, have significant effect, since several weeks later the flow of emigration was suddenly interrupted.[31]

Only a small portion of the emigration business was carried out in the officially approved affiliates which the shipping firms operated in Austria. The greatest part was conducted by the many

24. By the edict of the Ministry of Interior, December 5, 1903, no. 53 056.

25. AVA, MdI Präsidiale 15/15 Montreal, no. 49 031/10; Riedl, *Die Organisation der Auswanderung*, p. 28.

26. Chmelar, "Die Auswanderung," p. 193.

27. *Ibid.*

28. *Ibid.*, pp. 232ff.

29. AVA, MdI Auswanderungsakten 8/4 file 323, no. 13 281/14. Protocol of the discussion held in the Ministry of Trade, March 3, 1914, about regulation of the emigration business in Austria. *Ibid.*, file 326, no. 32 769/14.

30. "Die Bilanzen," *Beilage zum österreichischen Volkswirt*, 6 Jahrgang, no. 32 (May 9, 1914).

31. Chmelar, "Die Auswanderung," p. 196. In order to prevent illegal emigration of persons with military obligations, inspections by the Austrian consulates in Hamburg and Bremen were provided for in the agreement.

branches of the agent organizations. "The backers and directors of these organizations are the large emigration firms in the ports, such as Falck and Scharlach in Hamburg, Missler and Ischon in Bremen, and Freudberg and Canon in Antwerp. All Galicia down to the smallest village is full of their agents and subagents."[32] When tight police controls were set up on the German border, the route via Liechtenstein into Switzerland increased in importance for the emigrants with military obligations. Thus, the business of the Swiss agencies, especially the Staehli firm, grew.[33] All these agencies consciously disregarded the Austrian laws, since the seat of their business was abroad and their central offices were, thus, beyond the reach of the Austrian government.[34] Carrying emigrants with military obligation and without papers had become a branch of the business, operating with proven methods and well-established rules.[35] The regulations concerning documents necessary to cross the border were hardly observed, so that the authorities repeatedly protested against the emigration of persons with military obligations and without adequate papers.[36]

The importance of the agents is clearly illustrated when one considers that in 1912 only 20 percent of the Austrian emigrants traveling with the Hamburg-America Line and only 10 to 20 percent of those using North German Lloyd had purchased their tickets in the affiliates of these companies. The rest had acquired them in ways contrary to the stipulations of the concession agreement.[37] The activity of the emigration agents consisted of: propaganda, agitation, subjugation of competition, attraction of passengers, transport to the embarkation port, and elimination of all difficulties including the legal obstacles. Currency exchange also formed a lucrative side business. F. Missler in Bremen, acting exclusively for North German Lloyd, contracted approximately sixty thousand to eighty thousand Austrian and Hungarian citizens an-

32. Riedl, *Die Organisation der Auswanderung*, p. IV.
33. Staatsarchiv, Auswanderungsakten F 15, carton 21—agents. Agent Staehli.
34. Chmelar, "Die Auswanderung," p. 198.
35. Riedl, *Die Organisation der Auswanderung*, p. IV.
36. *Ibid.*, p. 34.
37. *Ibid.*

nually, while Falck and Company in Hamburg, acting primarily for the Hamburg-America Line, handled about forty thousand emigrants from the Monarchy annually. Aside from these agencies, smaller organizations such as Karesch and Stotzky (formerly in Prague, but located in this period in Bremen), with an average of twenty thousand emigrants per year, or Ischon, Freudberg, and Canon were also active in the business.[38]

Common to all was the practice of supplying the emigrants with tips on how to evade police controls, which routes to take, and how to cross the border unhindered.[39] The practice of giving the individual emigrant the chance to reduce the price of his own ship ticket if he could recruit friends or relatives was also not unusual.

In keeping with Marx's thesis that the exploited must always produce anew their exploitation, the emigration concerns create in every emigrant a recruiting agent by paying him a commission of varying amounts, which he can deduct from the price of his ship ticket, for every person whom he induces to emigrate, recruits for the company, and for whom he produces a deposit.[40]

The travel bureaus connected with the emigration business worked in part directly for the shipping companies and in part with the large emigration agencies in the port cities. The means used for the acquisition of passengers were the usual ones. The conclusion of the transaction was the collection of a deposit, from which any commission was deducted, and the drawing of an interim ship ticket or passage voucher with which the enlisted passenger was transferred to the emigration agent or shipping company.[41] In a formal sense, the travel bureaus operated legally.

The shipping company receives the emigrant from the Hamburg or Bremen bureau, the latter from a travel bureau in Galicia or Bukovina. Should any irregularity or illegality appear, it is always easy, with such cooperation, to push the blame from one to the other and thus obfuscate the facts of the case to such an extent that the intervention of the authorities ultimately remains fruitless.[42]

38. *Ibid.*, p. 35.
39. Chmelar, "Die Auswanderung," p. 199.
40. Salz, "Auswanderung und Schiffahrt," 42, pt. II, p. 881.
41. Riedl, *Die Organisation der Auswanderung*, p. 72.
42. *Ibid.*, p. 77.

The largest and most notorious travel bureaus which profited from the emigrants were located in Czernowitz, Lemberg, Cracow, and Vienna.[43] In Vienna the travel bureaus engaged in the emigration business were found primarily in Leopoldstadt.[44] In 1913–1914, legal action against almost each of these bureaus was initiated by the authorities and criminal proceedings were completed.[45] The guide line of the bureaus' work, however, remained:

> To adhere strictly to the statutory regulations in the emigration business at the present time is to renounce a good deal of the business. For it is clear that a large part of the legitimate business goes with the illegitimate and that the reputation of a travel bureau and a shipping line with the public is established better by transporting unauthorized emigrants successfully than by voluntarily serving the border police.[46]

The lowest rung in the hierarchy of the emigration business was occupied by local agents, who, without exception, operated on an illegal basis. The agents, spread everywhere across the country, were in part people without any other occupation. Most, however, were local notables, "respectable" men of solid reputation and influence whose close contact and familiarity with the populace predestined them to this advantageous position. They received ten to eighteen crowns for each emigrant recruited.[47] Village innkeepers and bankers as well as teachers and priests supplemented their incomes with these extra earnings.[48]

Another means of covering abuses was the establishment of associations, the so-called "associations for the protection of emigrants," which, in the guise of welfare organizations, stood in the service of the emigration firms.[49]

43. Chmelar, "Die Auswanderung," p. 200.
44. "Wiener Schlupfwinkel des Menschenhandels—die Reisebureaus in der Leopoldstadt," *Reichspost*, October 3, 1913. The *Reichspost* vehemently demanded disbandment of the largely Jewish bureaus. "Die Schlupfwinkel des Menschenhandels in Wien," *ibid.*, October 4, 1913.
45. AVA, Justizministerium VI in genere VZ 18. Extensive documentary material about agencies, travel bureaus, and agents.
46. Riedl, *Die Organisation der Auswanderung*, p. 78.
47. Salz, "Auswanderung und Schiffahrt," 42, pt. II, p. 881.
48. Chmelar, "Die Auswanderung," p. 203.
49. Riedl, *Die Organisation der Auswanderung*, pp. IV, 50.

The Catholic St. Raphael Association was spread over the entire Monarchy.[50] Founded in Germany (Trier) on Catholics' Day, 1865,[51] it spread to many Catholic countries. This large organization stood least in contact with the emigration firms. Instead of giving the emigrants effective humanitarian assistance, however, the Association concerned itself more with their religion and morals.[52] The standpoint taken by the Association concerning emigration, which was articulated in its monthly magazine, aimed at suppressing emigration.[53]

Also founded on a religious basis was the Jewish organization "Machsike Hadath" in Vienna.[54] The welfare associations "Unitas" and "Columbus,"[55] the protection club "Patria,"[56] and the Austro-Hungarian Colonial Society[57] were also active in Vienna. Columbus was founded in 1910 by the "merchant" Jakob Feldmann, who, as it later turned out, had previously been an agent of the Austro-Americana.[58] He immediately established contacts with emigration firms, especially with Falck and Company in Hamburg. In the decision of a civil suit between several persons involved in the association, it was determined that Columbus was by no means a welfare organization but a business operation.[59]

The Austro-Hungarian Colonial Society was very influential. It was, as it described itself, an "exclusively humanitarian and patriotic association," which stood for "the establishment of regulated

---

50. AVA, MdI Auswanderungsakten 8/4 file 321, no. 40.189/13. Auswanderervereine.

51. F. Schröder, *Der Mensch zwischen Heimat und Fremde. Das Verhältnis von Staat und Kirche zum wandernden Menschen in der europäischen Geschichte* (Stuttgart, 1960), p. 143.

52. Edict of the Ministry of Interior, October 11, 1906, no. 45.028. *Statuten des österreichischen St. Raphael Vereines zum Schutze der Auswanderer.* See especially § 1a.

53. *Der Auswanderer. Monatsschrift für Auswanderung, Abwanderung, Saisonwanderung und Mädchenschutz und für das Osterreichtum im Auslande. Mitteilungen des österreichischen St. Raphael Vereines zum Schutze der Auswanderer.*

54. AVA, MdI Auswanderungsakten 8/4 file 321, no. 40.189/13. Auswanderervereine.

55. *Ibid.*

56. *Stenographisches Protokoll der Sitzungen des Subkomitees des Budgetausschusses für Schiffahrtsangelegenheiten* (Vienna, 1913), p. 14.

57. AVA, MdI Auswanderungsakten 8/4 file 321, no. 40.189/13.

58. Riedl, *Die Organisation der Auswanderung*, p. 52.

59. *Ibid.*, p. 54.

emigration conditions."[60] Officially the society pursued the advancement of the export ecomony and also offered the emigrants information and protection.[61] Its tendency to direct as many emigrants as possible to South America, specifically to Brazil, was noted and not viewed with favor by the Ministry of Trade.[62] The society's leading members made several concrete proposals to the government concerning the regulation of the emigration,[63] and during World War I several of them called for the creation of Austrian colonies overseas as an aspect of population policy.[64]

The Polish Emigration Society (*Polskiego Towarzystwa Emigracyjnego*) was built upon an ethnic basis and was the most important emigration association in Austria. It was founded in Lemberg in 1908 and shifted to Cracow in 1909. The stated purpose of the society was to provide assistance to people intending to move either temporarily or permanently beyond the Monarchy's frontiers.[65] Unexplained financial transactions and the transport abroad of persons with military obligations discredited the society in 1913.[66]

#### 4. THE ECONOMIC CONSEQUENCES OF EMIGRATION

Mass emigration is a means of capital loss abroad. The emigration carries the stigma of an economic emergency action, of a forced sale and a squandering of "productive forces," indeed, of the only productive force that exists— human beings. Austria, therefore, is paying with people, in "natura" instead of with industrial products.[1]

From 1907 on, Austria-Hungary had a steadily growing negative balance of trade, which was improved by the money sent home by

60. AVA, MdI Auswanderungsakten 8/4 file 322, no. 2111/14. Austro-Hungarian Colonial Society to the Presidium of the Ministerial Council, January 17, 1914, Vienna.
61. *Ibid.*, file 321, no. 49.558/13. Document of December 22/26, 1913.
62. Staatsarchiv, Auswanderungsakten F 15, carton 40, *Publikationen Österreich-Ungarn. Österr. Ung. Kolonialgesellschaft.* Ministry of Trade to the Foreign Ministry, August 29, 1912.
63. Chmelar, "Die Auswanderung," p. 208.
64. Staatsarchiv, Auswanderungsakten F 15, carton 10, folio I/81. Ministry of War to the Foreign Ministry, July 27, 1918. Memorandum on emigration and colonial policy.
65. AVA, Justizministerium VI in genere VZ 18, no. 2081/14. *Polnische Emigrationsgesellschaft.*
66. Chmelar, "Die Auswanderung," pp. 209ff.

1. Salz, "Auswanderung und Schiffahrt," 39, pt. I, p. 100.

emigrants and brought back by those who returned.[2] "The emigration has an important place in the balance of payments. While the trade deficit amounted to 500 million crowns in 1908, an active balance of payments was maintained, to which the 300 million crowns sent to the homeland by emigrants contributed."[3] The exact amount of funds sent to Austria-Hungary by its emigrants can be ascertained only with considerable difficulty.[4] The records of innumerable banking institutions[5] would have to be consulted, for the money was sent not only by postal money orders and the great banking houses, but also by many small banks, the so-called "immigrant banks."[6] These banks took care of many things for the immigrants—mailed letters, sent telegrams, gave information, etc.— and were at the same time agencies of the shipping lines. These small banks were of considerable significance. In 1907, for example, approximately 55.3 million dollars were sent to Austria-Hungary from the "immigrant banks" and only about 6 million dollars via postal money orders.[7]

In 1914, the Austrian government also wanted to resolve the banking question, and, in May, a discussion with representatives of the Viennese banks took place. The Vienna Banking Association suggested turning to an American institution such as the American Express Company.[8]

Despite the money sent home, the emigrants proved damaging to the economy of the state from which they sprang and brought economic benefits to the state in which they settled. Especially Germany, whose ships carried the largest part of Austrian emigration, profited from the Monarchy's emigration.

2. *Ibid.*, p. 99.
3. Benedikt, "Die wirtschaftliche Entwicklung in der Franz-Joseph-Zeit," p. 165.
4. Caro, "Auswanderung und Auswanderungspolitik," p. 50.
5. Staatsarchiv, Auswanderungsakten F 15, carton 8, folio I/80. Imperial General Consulate New York to the Austro-Hungarian ambassador in Washington, March 4, 1912.
6. *Ibid.*, carton 32 Amerika. Imperial General Consulate New York to the Foreign Ministry, January 6, 1911; U. S. Senate, Immigration Commission, *Immigrant Banks*, 61 Cong., 2 Sess. (1910), Senate doc. 381.
7. *Ibid.*, pp. 69, 75.
8. AVA, MdI Auswanderungsakten 8/4 file 321, no. 45 794/13. Protocol of the Session of the Emigration Affairs Subcommittee of the Austrian Commission for Export Affairs, held on May 28, 1914, in the Ministry of Trade.

A statement of the Empire's gains and losses for the period from 1876 to 1910 has been drawn up by Englisch. See Table 4.1. The figures are, however, to be considered with the necessary caution. The deficit amounted to approximately 1.5 billion crowns for the kingdoms and lands represented in the Imperial Council and 2.33 billion crowns for the entire Monarchy.[9]

Table 4.1

ECONOMIC SUMMARY 1876–1910

| Losses 1876–1910 (given in crowns) | Austria | Monarchy |
|---|---|---|
| Transportation at 160 crowns per person | 294,416,960 | 566,760,640 |
| Money taken with emigrant (about $20 per person) | 184,010,600 | 354,225,400 |
| Loss due to population decline (estimate per person 2000 crowns) | 2,400,000,000 | 4,000,000,000 |
| TOTAL | 2,878,427,560 | 4,920,986,040 |
| Gains 1876–1900 (given in crowns) | | |
| Approximate total of money sent home | 265,000 000 | 500,000,000 |
| Gains 1901–1910 (given in crowns) | | |
| Bank drafts | 939,113,000 | 1,724,018,000 |
| Postal money orders | 169,812,000 | 370,394,000 |
| TOTAL | 1,108,925,000 | 2,094,412,000 |

SOURCE: Englisch, "Die österreichische Auswanderungsstatistik," p. 126.

Emigration also had ill effects on the Austrian domestic labor market, since a labor shortage prevailed in Bohemia, Moravia, Upper and Lower Austria, Styria, and other provinces.[10] Because most emigrants came from the agrarian sector, the agrarian pro-

9. Englisch, "Die österreichische Auswanderungsstatistik," p. 127.
10. Fischel, Die schädlichen Seiten der Auswanderung und deren Bekämpfung, p. 3.

ducers demanded that a future emigration law should not only protect emigrants but also regulate emigration.[11] Thus, restricting emigration from Galicia and Hungarian Slovakia in Moravia was considered.[12] In 1912, agrarian interests claimed to have suffered a production loss of roughly 65.5 million crowns, a loss affected by the emigration.[13] It was, moreover, these very agrarian circles which took part in the campaign against the C.P.R. and received praise from the *Reichspost* for their action. The grant of the concession to the C.P.R. was characterized as an "atrocity."[14] The magnitude of the emigration from Austria was especially "damaging" to agriculture and particularly to the great estate owners.[15]

Because it was less affected, Austrian industry reacted less vehemently. Yet, curtailment of the emigration was also demanded from this sector of the economy. Industrial interests hoped to offset the loss of workers by increasing the introduction of machines, and the state, they felt, should help with tax credits for industry.[16] However, the benefits of temporary emigration were recognized.

The benefits of the emigration reveal themselves most distinctly when we consider the utilization of savings. They serve to set new work forces into operation, to liquidate debts and tax liabilities, to replenish livestock and fixtures, to regulate family claims to inheritance, to create the possibility of taking over businesses, etc. Finally, I come to the most important consequence: the improvement of the standard of living. Aside from the changes in thinking and views of life, new needs have arisen and satisfaction of these needs is also being sought in the homeland. The returning emigrants are even bigger consumers, and this again is of benefit to industry. Agricultural knowledge is expanding and being put to use on our own soil. Additional technical skills are being acquired and developed. But most important is the acclimatization to intensive work.[17]

Curbing emigration was possible only by the initiation of extensive political-economic measures. The industrialization of the

---

11. Märheim, *Die Auswanderungsfrage im Lichte der jüngsten Ereignisse*, p. 23.
12. *Österreichische Agrarzeitung*, April 19, 1913.
13. Märheim, *Die Auswanderungsfrage im Lichte der jüngsten Ereignisse*, p. 15.
14. *Ibid.*, p. 5.
15. Fischel, *Die schädlichen Seiten der Auswanderung und deren Bekämpfung*, p. 7.
16. Friedmann, *Arbeitermangel und Auswanderung*, p. 41.
17. *Ibid.*, pp. 38ff.

lands of emigration, a better domestic colonization, the introduction of an emergency building program on the most elaborate scale, and similar projects were proposed.[18]

Emigration is an evil for the lands of emigration, and especially so for Austria, but under the existing economic conditions it is a necessary one. Furthermore, it is being encouraged by the radical-democratic parties of the nations affected. Its very nature and scope are conditioned by and dependent on the economic (and, to a lesser degree, social) conditions in the emigration countries as well as the state of business in the countries of immigration at any given time.[19]

For the affected regions, prohibiting emigration would draw unforeseeable consequences in its wake.[20] An increase in the labor supply would have resulted in pressure on pay and an intensified proletarization of the masses. At the same time, it was felt, money would not be sent home and the influx of capital would drop.[21]

### 5. REPORTS FROM EMIGRANTS

For shipping companies, travel bureaus, and agents, the emigrant represented an object of exploitation. If, because of his poor economic situation, an Austrian subject decided to emigrate, he had to be on guard not only against agents but also against the authorities. While the agents attempted to extract as much money as possible from him, the authorities, by all sorts of chicanery, endeavored to spoil emigration for anyone desirous of leaving the country. Furthermore, if the prospective emigrant was male and between the ages of seventeen and thirty years old, there was often no other alternative for him but to evade all inspections and cross the border illegally. This, as far as the authorities were concerned, constituted "unauthorized emigration." The police and customs officials entrusted with police duties were only occasionally successful, since the emigrants were usually led over the border or at least received tips from experienced agents who were acquainted with the official

18. Hey, *Die Auswanderung und ihre eminente Bedeutung für unser Wirtschaftsleben*, p. 10.
19. Salz, "Auswanderung und Schiffahrt," 39, pt. I, p. 96.
20. *Ibid.*, p. 97.
21. AVA, MdI Auswanderungsakten 8/4 file 323, no. 15 786/14. Memorandum of the Imperial League of Austrian General Labor Procurement Agencies to the Ministry of Interior, April 10, 1914.

procedures. In such cases the agent received commissions for his "efforts." One popular practice was to simulate a pilgrimage. Pilgrimages to Lourdes were commercially devised for illegal emigration.[1] However, inspections were conducted not only on the borders but also in the major transportation centers.

Now the poor people are constantly subjected to inspections throughout their entire journey in the empire. In almost every large station someone is "closely examined" by earnest officials, and even the lowest level functionaries torment them in a way that far exceeds the limits of their official authority. One cannot, therefore, hold it against the people when they attempt to get across the border by the shortest route in order to escape these annoyances as quickly as possible.[2]

Reporting on his emigration to officials of the Ministry of Trade in 1912, Wojciech Adamczyk, a Polish peasant, related the following experiences:

From Skowieczem in the Tarnobrzeg district, I traveled with the Austro-Americana via Trieste to New York, the journey from my home town to New York taking one month. The trip from my home town to Trieste lasted five days. In Trieste I waited five more days, since I arrived at seven in the evening and my ship had sailed at eleven that morning. The voyage lasted eighteen days. In New York the ship had to lie at anchor for a day because the arrival of an English emigration ship was expected. But the English emigrants were allowed to land before us.

I had traveled with a work book. In my home town I had received a train ticket to Cracow from a small Jewish agent who was sent to the village from the Cracow agency for recruitment. In Cracow I was received by the agents and my ship ticket was bought. The train and ship tickets from my home community to New York cost 200 crowns and 30 hellers. In Vienna the emigrants were again received by an agent, who demanded one crown per person from the roughly thirty emigrants for the "tramway." Since we had been

1. AVA, MdI Auswanderungsakten 8/4 file 322, no. 8810/14. Report of the Salzburg Railway station police, February 25, 1914. Four Hungarians came as far as Tetschen, each carrying a prayerbook and a rosary, which attracted attention at the border station there. In order to be admitted to Austria without papers, they had pretended to be pilgrms, traveled to Mariazell and from there to Prague, where they bought tickets to Leipzig. *Ibid.*, file 325, no. 31 288/14. Report of the Border Control Station, Tetschen, May 16, 1914, forwarded from the Governorship of Bohemia to the Ministry of Interior, June 6, 1914.

2. AVA, Handelsministerium AW, file 1885, no. 41 318/13. "Promemoria" by Dr. Richard Seyfert, October 8, 1913.

told in Cracow that nothing more remained to be paid, we refused and were transported anyway. The railway trip from Vienna to Trieste lasted twenty hours, and all the cars were completely occupied. In Trieste, the pieces of luggage were collected in a large hall in the railway station and submitted to a disinfection, which made all food unfit to eat. The sleeping accommodations were inadequate. For supper we received lamb and for the other meals also mostly lamb. Two hundred to three hundred people slept in the large hall, in a few cases two people to a bed. The journey then began with the steamer *Francesca*. The quarters and especially the mattresses were quite inadequate. After getting up, all emigrants, including women and children, were driven onto the deck, where they had to remain until four in the afternoon. In the meantime the sleeping quarters were straightened up in the morning, but returning to them was not permitted. Since it was February the people suffered terribly from the cold. The preparation of the food was bad, mostly meal dishes, at midday always meat or fish. One emigrant had to fetch food for six from the kitchen, and the dishes had to be washed by the emigrants themselves. The meals were taken on the deck and not in a particular room. Each sat where he could find a place. Tables and chairs were available but not sufficient. When buying their ship tickets the people had not been informed at all about what to expect in the way of food . . . which meals they would receive or of what they would consist or in what quantities. Treatment from the officers' side was good, but their supervision of the sailors was lax.

Grumblings and complaints were not listened to at all by the officers. (In response to the rebuke that experts had just said that the treatment had been good, he replied: "Yes, they didn't hit us!") The sailors were very unfriendly, rough and crude.

I remember the stay in Naples which lasted two days and a night. About two hundred emigrants were taken on board in Naples. They were probably Italians, since nobody could make himself understood. The Poles and Ruthenians took care of themselves and the Italians did the same, so during the voyage there was little contact but no friction either. There was no doctor among the emigrants and I don't remember having seen the ship's doctor until shortly before New York, when he examined the emigrants' eyes. Yet, I do recall that in Trieste another eye examination and a vaccination took place. Whether it was the same doctor who conducted the eye examination at sea, I no longer know. Two days before putting ashore, a doctor came aboard in a small boat, but only undertook a very superficial and by no means individual examination.[3]

3. Adamczyk then reported about the arrival in New York, the medical examination at the habor, and his employment in the Singer Sewing Machine factory where he

The emigrants were frequently swindled in the exchange of money. Some of these money changers made distinctions according to nationality, as the report of an information official in the Ministry of Trade illustrates:

There is, for example, a certain Mr. Jan Nemeth in New York, Washington Street, a banker by trade. Here I have an advertisement of his, composed in three languages, Ruthenian, Polish, and German. Suppose a Ruthenian peasant comes to him. When he puts down $3.00 he receives only ten crowns, and thus he is swindled out of five crowns. The Ruthenian peasant must pay the most. In contrast, the German—that is printed here—must pay only $2.75 for ten crowns. The Pole pays just as much, but also receives a finely printed letter as a present.[4]

The agents had no difficulty with the emigrants due to the latters' poor education and their complete mistrust of the authorities.

---

ultimately remained for three years until he suffered a job accident. Then he worked as a stoker for the Standard Oil Company. In the course of five years he sent four thousand crowns to his wife and four children. "Now I work in a brickyard and earn two crowns a day, from which four hellers are withheld for health insurance."

Another emigrant, Jan Szeser from Baranow, stated among other things that at forty he had proceeded via Rotterdam to England with the intention of earning more money in America. He then sailed from Liverpool to Philadelphia in an English ship. In steerage the ship had cabins with six beds in each. It was clean, and the food was good. "For breakfast there was coffee, rolls, butter, and meat, and for lunch, soup, meat with vegetables, bread and a glass of wine." Meals were taken on covered tables, where everyone had a place. The waitress served the meals.

Andrzej Lotz reported that he had found little work in Galicia and decided to emigrate via Bremen, where he arrived via Oświecim. He was examined at the border, but was not detained. He returned on an English ship. English ships, in his opinion, were better than German ones. "In the mornings there was no coffee, only soup, at lunch meat which one could eat sometimes and sometimes not. I didn't eat anything at all for four days. I had my own food." He found the unsanitary conditions caused by seasick passengers bad. He returned on an English ship with which he was satisfied. During his five year stay in America, he saved over four thousand gilders.

Another emigrant, Bernhard Zdamowski, a Russian citizen from Warsaw, proceeded via Bremen to Rio de Janeiro. In answer to a question concerning the length of the trip, he responded: "thirty-one days and nights, uninterrupted. We made a stop in Antwerp, then again in Lisbon, were we stayed for 48 hours, and then without halting until Rio." Eight hundred people, not separated by sex, were quartered in a single room.

"Protocol of the interrogation of informants concerning the emigration from Austria," conducted in the Austrian Ministry of Trade, Vienna, 1912, columns 225–441.

4. *Ibid.*, column 284.

## C. Austrian Emigration Policy

NO particular zeal can be attributed to the Austrian government in its treatment of the emigration question.[1] For a long time the government accepted the realities of the situation without exhibiting much concern. Of course, the speeches of the emperor in 1897, 1901, and 1907 held out the prospect of a statutory regulation of emigration, but everything remained as it was.[2] In 1904, a draft of such a law was introduced in the *Reichsrat*, but was not passed.[3] The government's proposal was based on German and Italian models[4] and provided for statutory protection of the emigrants.[5] In contrast to Austria, legal regulation of emigration had already been instituted in the most important European countries.[6] Hungary, too, had already promulgated a law for this purpose on March 14, 1903.[7] Then, in 1909, a new Hungarian law was enacted which, by establishing harsher penalties and expanding governmental competencies,[8] placed tremendous obstacles in the path of Hungarian emigrants. This law offered the Hungarian government more extensive powers for suppressing emigration than were possessed by any other European state. Of the major emigration countries, only Austria and Russia had no emigration law.

In Austria, the discussion of emigration legislation only slowly got underway. The principle of freedom of emigration stood in opposition to the desire for its restriction.[9] The state, it was felt,

1. Chmelar, "Die Auswanderung," p. 224.

2. Friedmann, *Arbeitermangel und Auswanderung*, p. 4.

3. *Beilagen zu den stenographischen Protokollen des Abgeordnetenhauses*, 2097, XVII Session (1904).

4. Friedmann, *Arbeitermangel und Auswanderung*, p. 4.

5. *Beilagen zu den stenographischen Protokollen des Abgeordnetenhauses*, 2097, XVII Session (1904).

6. Chmelar, "Die Auswanderung," pp. 224ff. Concerning emigration laws, see also vol. II: "Die wichtigsten Europäischen Auswanderungsgesetze (mit Berücksichtigung der beiden österreichischen Entwürfe) und ihre wichtigsten Vollzugsvorschriften," in F. von Srbik, *Die Auswanderungsgesetzgebung* (Vienna, 1911).

7. Friedmann, *Arbietermangel und Auswanderung*, p. 64.

8. L. Schneider, *Die ungarische Auswanderung* (Poszony, 1915), p. 143.

9. Chmelar, "Die Auswanderung," p. 226.

should conduct itself as passively as possible with regard to emigration. "If, on the one hand, the state should not place any artificial barriers in the way of emigration, then it must not, on the other, encourage it with artificial means."[10] Legally, the situation was managed on a provisional basis in Austria. Since 1897, aside from the obsolete emigration patent of 1832, a law concerning the operation of emigration businesses was on the books.[11] This law had proved a failure, and, in 1902, an emigration law was proposed in the *Reichsrat*.[12] On December 6, 1904, the government introduced the draft of a law for the protection of emigrants, which was basically an imitation of existing laws abroad.[13] Execution of the law was to be entrusted to the Ministry of Interior.[14] On February 6, 1905, the draft was sent to the Economic Committee without a first reading,[15] and from June 26 to June 28 a hearing was conducted in which representatives of shipping lines, chambers of commerce, the railway, as well as professors, parliamentary deputies, and journalists took part.[16] Interest in the emigrants was displayed chiefly by two groups. On one side were the domestic employers, industrial and agricultural, who stood for prevention of emigration and used "patriotic arguments" in doing so, while on the other were

10. Josef Buzek, "Das Auswanderungsproblem und die Regelung des Auswanderungswesens in Österreich," *Zeitschrift für Volkswirtschaft, Sozialpolitik und Verwaltung*, 10 (1901), 505.

11. Law of January 21, 1897, Reichsgesetzblatt (hereafter cited as R.G.Bl.), no. 27.

12. Caro, "Auswanderung und Auswanderungspolitik," p. 179; *Beilagen zu den stenographischen Protokollen des Abgeordnetenhauses*, 1575, XVII Session (1902). Motion of deputies Dr. Licht, Tambosi, Nowak, Dr. Silený, Dr. Stojan, Barwinski, Šustersič, Ritter v. Vukovič, and colleagues concerning expedition of the proposal of an emigration law and other measures relating to emigration policy and protection.

13. *Stenographische Protokolle über die Sitzungen des Hauses der Abgeordneten des österreichischen Reichsrates*, XVII Session, 290 (December 6, 1904), 26,003; *Beilagen zu den stenographischen Protokollen des Abgeordnetenhauses*, 2097, XVII Session (1904); Caro, "Auswanderung und Auswanderungspolitik," p. 180.

14. *Beilagen zu den stenographischen Protokollen des Abgeordnetenhauses*, 2097, XVII Session, § 78 of the law.

15. Parlamentsarchiv, Economic Committee, XVII Session, listed under no. 44 (February 6, 1905); *Stenographische Protokolle über die Sitzungen des Hauses der Abgeordneten des österreichischen Reichsrates*, XVII Session, 299 (February 6, 1905), 26,832.

16. "Stenographische Protokoll der Expertise über das Auswanderungswesen veranstaltet vom Subkomitee des volkswirtschaftlichen Ausschusses des Abgeordnetenhauses" (Vienna, 1905).

the shipping entrepreneurs and travel bureaus. The latter group wanted complete freedom of emigration in order to emancipate itself from burdensome governmental supervision. "That, in both cases the particular business interests of the party involved are glossed over, is evident."[17] Another point of view appeared in the demand for the "nationalization of the emigration business,"[18] but "the results of the inquiry were so contradictory that this subject was no longer put on the agenda of the House of Representatives."[19] A government draft, completed in 1908 and modeled in many ways on the earlier version, did not even succeed in being introduced in the *Reichsrat*.[20] On the province level, ordinances regulating the recruitment of workers for employment abroad were still in effect in Galicia and Bukovina.[21]

The emigration question was also the focal point of a conflict concerning the jurisdictions of the Ministries of Interior and Trade. The draft laws of 1904 and 1908 were prepared in the Ministry of Interior, but at the end of 1910 the general jurisdiction of emigration affairs and thus also the duty of preparing a law for the protection of emigrants was transferred to the Ministry of Trade. Trade Minister Roessler held a new inquiry, March 16–30, 1912, which was to contribute to the preparation of a new law. Sixty-nine people, among them nineteen deputies of the *Reichsrat*, were questioned. Forty people came from Galicia and Bukovina. Five estate owners, four bank directors, eight lawyers, eight journalists, four priests, and twenty officials also participated. Only four peasants, however, were questioned. The extent of the law's applicability was to be delineated and possible restrictions of emigration

17. Caro, "Unsere überseeische Auswanderer und die Enquete vom Jahre 1905," p. 529.

18. A. Wagner, *Schutz den Auswanderern! Eine Studie zur österreichischen Auswanderungsfrage nebst Randglossen zur parlamentarischen Enquete über dasselbe Thema* (Berlin, 1905), p. 2.

19. Caro, "Auswanderung und Auswanderungspolitik," p. 181.

20. *Beilagen zu den stenographischen Protokollen des Abgeordnetenhauses*, 2027, XXI Session (1913), 51.

21. *Ibid.*, pp. 50ff. Ordinance of the Bukovina state government, April 10, 1904, L.G.u.V.Bl., no. 22; Ordinance of the Lemberg Statthalterei, November 23, 1909, L.G.u.V.Bl., no. 152.

clarified by the inquiry. Transport regulations were also discussed, as were currency questions and enforcement of the law.[22] The causes of emigration were not researched, and economic counter-measures were not debated.

The Ministry of Trade, led by Section Chief Riedl, set about re-solving the emigration question not in the emigrants' interest but rather in that of the shipping and commercial circles.[23] The goal was to free domestic shipping from its position of dependence on the international cartel. A growing percentage of the Eastern European emigration was to be assured for the native shippers and the port of Trieste.[24] Riedl was certainly aware that the increase of emigration via Trieste could only be achieved gradually and that monopolization was impossible.[25] At the same time, domestic colonization was to be intensified.[26]

Most opposed to a liberal emigration policy was the Monarchy's military establishment. The high emigration figures were consid-ered menacing to the existence of the Imperial army. The right to emigrate had already been limited in the constitution by the obli-gation for military service, and the military, emphasizing national defense regulations,[27] repeatedly demanded an extensive suppres-sion of emigration, especially from 1913 on. In the mustering of troops in Austria in 1913, a shortage of over one hundred thousand men, eighty-one thousand of whom were to have held positions in the three Galician corps, was reported. The total number of unau-thorized absentees was even far greater. The increase of absenteeism occurred primarily in 1907, and thereafter the number barely rose. Yet, the call for a remedy was not raised at that time.[28] Along the

22. "Protocol of the interrogation of informants concerning emigration from Aus-tria," conducted in the Austrian Ministry of Trade, Vienna, 1912, pp. V, VI, XV, XVI.

23. Chmelar, "Die Auswanderung," p. 229.

24. Riedl, *Die Organisation der Auswanderung*, p. v.

25. *Ibid.*, p. VIII.

26. *Ibid.*

27. In Austria the following military laws were in effect: Wehrgesetz of July 5, 1912, R.G.Bl., no. 128/1912; Landwehrgesetz of July 5, 1912, R.G.Bl., no. 129/1912; Lands-turmgesetz of June 6, 1886, R.G.Bl., no. 90/1886.

28. Riedl, *Die Organisation der Auswanderung*, p. 2.

extended frontier with Germany an absolute supervision of the border could not be implemented.

The collision of opposing aspirations came in the Canadian Pacific Railway Company affair. The affair began when the Canadian company came into conflict with the international shipping cartel because it was not given proper consideration in the distribution of passage quotas.[29] Therefore, on October 7, 1912, the C.P.R. offered to the Austrian government the establishment of a direct line from Trieste to Canada. Emigration of people with military obligations was to be prevented by a regulation which provided the authorities numerous possibilities for intervention. In return, the C.P.R. demanded permission to establish branch offices in all provincial capitals and in several other towns in Galicia and Bukovina.[30] The other foreign companies, in contrast, did not have such an extensive network of affiliates. Minister of Trade Schuster supported the proposal, and the Ministry of Interior finally approved the establishment of Canadian Pacific affiliates in the desired towns.[31] Shortly thereafter, the C.P.R. began regular service between Trieste and Canada.

Soon a German commercial journal and Austrian army newspapers began to accuse the C.P.R. of illegal activities,[32] and although the company carried only a fraction of the Austrian emigrants,[33] a massive campaign was initiated against it. The central figure in these actions was a certain Artur Grünhut, an obscure man with a bad reputation,[34] who was, as Minister of Trade Schuster surmised, probably in the service of the shipping pool.[35] Grünhut directed his accusations to the Ministry of War, with which he had

29. See p. 349 above.
30. AVA, MdI Präsidiale 15/15 Montreal, no. 38.750/12. Petition of the Canadian Pacific to the Ministry of Trade.

31. *Ibid.*, recommendation of the C.P.R. petition by Trade Minister Schuster, October 23, 1913; *ibid.*, edict of the Ministry of Interior, January 3, 1913.

32. *Berliner Börsen-Courier*, April 25, 1913; *Danzer's Armee Zeitung*, XVIII Jahrgang, June 5, 1913.

33. AVA, MdI Auswanderungsakten 8/4 file 321, no. 44.872/13. Schuster to the minister of war, November 20, 1913.

34. AVA, MdI Präsidiale 15/15 Montreal, no. 32.858/13. Character report on Artur Grünhut by the Viennese Directory of Police.

35. *Ibid.*, no. 32.468/13. Schuster on Grünhut, August 9, 1913.

good connections.[36] The most vigorous polemic, however, was conducted by the *Reichspost*, and since most agents were Jews, the attacks had a strongly antisemitic character.[37]

Abuses were naturally present in the C.P.R. operation. Persons with military obligations were carried,[38] emigration agents of ill repute employed, and business ties to questionable travel bureaus established.[39] Yet, these practices could also be found to a greater or lesser degree in all other firms involved in the emigration business.[40] The most striking feature of the campaign was its onesidedness, and behind that stood the German competition.[41]

Yet, on the basis of Grünhut's reports, the police proceeded against the C.P.R. On October 16, 1913, the suspension of the Canadian Pacific's business operations in the kingdoms and lands represented in the *Reichsrat* was decreed, and the directors and leading officials of the company were arrested.[42]

The arrests and the prohibition of business activity for the C.P.R. greatly excited the public.[43] While the *Reichspost* triumphed, other newspapers demanded an extension of the investigation to other companies.[44] The authorities moved hesitantly against the others. Being forewarned, however, the action had little success.[45] The affair was also passionately debated in parliament.[46]

The case did not, however, remain a purely domestic question,

36. See Chmelar, "Die Auswanderung," p. 234.

37. *Reichspost*, August 30, 1913, see especially "Das Unwesen der Menschenfrächter," September 7, 10, 1913.

38. AVA, MdI Präsidiale 15/15 Montreal, no. 31.080/13. According to results of the Austrian police investigation, July 4, 1913, Vienna, and subsequent reports.

39. *Ibid.*, see also no. 37.741/13. Report of the Austrian state government of Bukovina concerning emigration intrigues, October 3, 1913, Czernowitz.

40. AVA, Justizministerium VI in genere VZ 18. Numerous criminal cases in Austria.

41. Chmelar, "Die Auswanderung," p. 235.

42. AVA, MdI Präsidiale 15/15 Montreal, no. 39.192/13. Edict of the Austrian Ministry of Interior, October 16, 1913; AVA, Justizministerium VI in genere VZ 18, no. 32.535/13. Report of the Austrian Public Prosecutor, Vienna, October 22, 1913.

43. *Neue Freie Presse*, October 16 and 17, 1913.

44. *Reichspost*, October 17 and 19, 1913. Among others, the *Arbeiter Zeitung*, which, in late October and early November, delved into the background of the affair in detail.

45. AVA, MdI Präsidiale 15/15 Montreal, no. 42.060/13. Report of the Directory of Police, Vienna, October 29, 1913.

46. "Stenographisches Protokoll der Sitzungen des Subkomitees des Budgetausschusses für Schiffahrtsangelegenheiten" (Vienna, 1913).

but led to tension with the Foreign Office. The action was discussed not only in Canada, where the matter produced a great sensation, but in England as well.[47] British embassy officials in Vienna sided with the C.P.R.[48] The Austrian authorities were ultimately forced to pull back, conceding that the proven transgressions of the Canadian Pacific did not warrant the precautionary measures taken.[49] Yet, not until the beginning of July 1914 was the complete exercise of the Canadian Pacific's concession rights, under the limitations of the new situation, again permitted.[50]

"The Canadian Pacific affair," according to Professor Zaloziecki, a deputy in the Galician diet, "at least had one good result: it directed attention to the extraordinary importance of the emigration and carried this conviction to wide segments of the population." Austrian emigration policy was awakened "from the lethargy of laissez faire."[51]

The Canadian Pacific was not the only firm against which legal steps were taken, but no other case was pursued with such vigor or developed into such a political issue.[52] Up to May 20, 1914, 2,072 emigration-related criminal proceedings with 3,097 defendants were recorded in Austria. In only a portion of the 2,072 reported cases could links to a shipping company be established. Of these cases, North German Lloyd was involved in 416 cases, the Hamburg-America Line in 286, the Belgian Red Star Line in 260, the Austro-Americana in 175, and the Canadian Pacific in 111. Thus, according to the number of cases, the C.P.R. stood only in fifth place.[53]

47. Staatsarchiv, Auswanderungsakten F 15, carton 21 Agenten-Agenturen—CPR/56. Imperial consul in Montreal, Hann, to the Foreign Ministry, November 27, 1913.

48. In this period three ambassadors served in Vienna: Fairfax Cartwright, Theo Russel, and finally Maurice de Bunsen.

49. AVA, MdI Präsidiale 15/15 Montreal, no. 5345/14. Minister of Justice Hochenburger to the Ministry of Interior, February 8, 1914.

50. *Ibid.*, no. 29.636/14. Letter of Heinolds to de Bunsen.

51. *Reichspost*, October 22, 1913, morning edition; *Der Auswanderer, Mitteilungen des österreichischen St. Raphael Vereines zum Schutze der Auswanderer*, V Jahrgang (March 1914).

52. Chmelar, "Die Auswanderung," p. 244.

53. AVA, Justizministerium VI in genere VZ 18. Report on the condition of emigration affairs, May 20, 1914.

Work on the draft of an emigration law ran parallel to the events concerning the C.P.R. Statutory regulation had become an absolute necessity, and pressure mounted for such action in the parliament, in the Ministry of Trade, and in the Ministry of War.[54] Ecclesiastical figures, especially Cardinal Leo von Skrbensky, prince-archbishop of Prague, speaking for the bishops, also advocated the most expeditious introduction of an emigration law in the *Reichsrat.* The Church feared that the emigrants would become alienated from the state, the Church, and their religion. In regard to the question of protection for emigrants, the Church referred to the action initiated by Pius X's "Motu proprio" of August 15, 1912. The most important of the bishop's demands were the restriction of overseas emigration and the subsidizing of ministers on the ships and overseas.[55] Free roundtrip passage for priests and the permission to hold services on the ships were generally the main concerns of the Church in the emigration question.[56]

It was most difficult to bring the opposing views of the Ministry of Trade and the army onto common ground. The Ministry of War inclined to overestimate the exclusively military aspects of the problem and displayed a complete ignorance of the actual situation. Instead of informing itself adequately, the military relied on Grünhut's "reports." In taking a position on the recruitment practices of the shipping companies, Krobatin commented: "The possibility that Russian influence is at work, aiming to damage the military of the Monarchy by secretly fomenting agitation, is by no means out of the question."[57] The Chief of the Imperial General Staff, Conrad, believed that as a result of Austria's falling behind in

54. *Beilagen zu den stenographischen Protokollen des Abgeordnetenhauses,* 1325, XXI Session (1912). Motion by Dr. Krek and colleagues on the proposal of an emigration law, April 24, 1912. AVA, Handelsministerium AW, file 1880, no. 6581/13. Krobatin to the Austrian Ministry of Defense, February 17, 1913.

55. *Ibid.,* file 1881, no. 9320/13. Cardinal Skrbensky to the Presidium of the Ministerial Council, November 6, 1912.

56. *Ibid.,* file 1920, no. 7648/14. Prince Bishop Dr. Franz Sedej von Görz to Schuster, March 4, 1914. The prince bishop was an advisor to the Episcopal Committee for Emigration Affairs.

57. Staatsarchiv, Auswanderungsakten F 15, carton 21 Agenten-Agenturen—CPR/26. Imperial War Minister Krobatin to the Foreign Ministry, June 25, 1913.

other areas of military capacity, "the preservation and full utilization of the available human resources" must be given special consideration. Each emigrant, therefore, represented a blow to military effectiveness, and the goal of the military was to restrict the right of emigration.[58] A model for this was provided by the Hungarian statute of 1909, the second article of which proscribed the emigration of certain groups. By means of a decree on December 6, 1912, the emigration of Austro-Hungarians with military obligations was completely forbidden for one year.[59] The first legislative proposal of the Ministry of Trade was rejected by Krobatin, because it gave first priority to economic interests and interests of the worker while showing insufficient regard for the military.[60] "The experiences of the crises of 1908–1909 and 1912–1919 have proven conclusively that emigration is a means to the end of evading one's primary obligation to the state in a threatening situation."[61] In March, common questions in emigration affairs were discussed with Hungary and the Imperial Ministry of Finance (matters concerning Bosnia and Herzegovina) in the Ministry of War.[62] The Ministry of Trade was accused of "partiality" by Krobatin. He also demanded that in the future all emigration matters be placed under the Ministry of Interior, as in Hungary.[63]

As a result, a jurisdictional struggle ensued between the Ministries of Interior and Trade, during which several different legislative drafts were simultaneously prepared.[64] On September 20, an

58. AVA, Handelsministerium AW, file 1881, no. 11.231/13. Letter of Chief of the General Staff Conrad to the Ministry of War, March 8, 1913; *ibid.*, file 1881, no. 11.963/13. Minister of War Krobatin to Minister of Trade Schuster, March 11, 1913.

59. *Ibid.*, file 1881, no. 11.231/13. Circular of the Imperial Foreign Ministry, March 18, 1913.

60. *Ibid.*, file 1881, no. 11.963/13. Krobatin to Schuster, March 11, 1913.

61. *Ibid.*, statements of the representative of the Ministry of War concerning the draft of the emigration law.

62. AVA, MdI Auswanderungsakten 8/4 file 320, no. 10.423/13. Protocol of the interministerial conference, held in the Ministry of War, for clarification of questions relating to emigration affairs.

63. Staatsarchiv, Auswanderungsakten F 15, carton 21 Agenten-Agenturen—CPR/26. Minister of war to foreign minister, June 25, 1913.

64. AVA, Justizministerium I B I, 2 carton 49. Minister of Trade Schuster to minister of justice, May 19, 1913.

agreement was reached in the Council of Ministers which stipulated that all further preliminary work on regulation of emigration was to be conducted in the Ministry of Interior.[65] Thus, the wishes of the military were fulfilled. On October 16 the draft was ready, and five days later the government's emigration proposal was introduced in the *Reichsrat* by Minister of Interior Heinold.[66] However, no further attention was devoted to the government's bill.

The legislative draft had two main provisions. First, the economically necessary emigration had to be accepted as a fact. In this case, the emigrant should be protected on his journey and in his country of destination. Second, the loss for "fatherland and military" should be prevented by curbing "unnatural" emigration.[67] Various aspects of Article Two violated the freedom of emigration guaranteed in the constitution.

In the preamble of the draft, better coordination of work procurement was demanded in order to win workers from the areas of emigration for the lands with labor shortages, such as Bohemia, Moravia, and Lower Austria.[68] The draft encountered very strong criticism. Otto Neurath's well-founded objections should be mentioned here as should Alexander Löffler's conservative criticism.[69] Neurath leveled his attack primarily at Article Two, which provided the government with the option of forbidding immigration to particular countries and, thus, represented a revision of the Constitution, which, as he said, required a two-thirds majority in the *Reichsrat*. "The transferal of emigration affairs to the Ministry of Interior from the Ministry of Trade means a turn towards police-state methods." The uneducated citizen was to receive "a type of guardian," since local mayors and police officials were to be given

65. *Ibid.*, Minister of Interior Heinold to Ministry of Justice, October 7, 1913.

66. *Stenographische Protokolle über die Sitzungen des Hauses der Abgeordneten des österreichischen Reichsrates*, XXI Session, 162 (October 21, 1913), 8088.

67. *Beilagen zu den stenographischen Protokollen des Abgeordnetenhauses*, 2027, XXI Session (1913), 29, 51.

68. *Ibid.*, p. 44.

69. Neurath, "Zum österreichischen Auswanderungsgesetzentwurf," pp. 297–378; Alexander Löffler, *Der Entwurf eines Gesetzes betreffend die Auswanderung. Eine Kritik (Sonderabdruck aus der österreichischen Zeitschrift für Strafrecht)*, 4 vols. (Vienna, 1913).

a dominant position.[70] Löffler contended that "the intention is to bind native labor as a type of serf if not to the soil then certainly to the territory of the state." Löffler demanded social, political, and economic measures. "It simply will not work for the state, according to the famous example, to stand behind its children with a police club thundering: 'You should love me! You should love me!'"[71]

The Austrian emigration bill gives the impression of an only partially successful compromise. It contains socio-political measures, partly for the protection of the emigrants and partly for the encouragement of those who want to emigrate but who must be dissuaded from doing so. On the other hand, the draft provides for police measures of a far-reaching nature aimed at repression. Of the groups which contributed to the formulation of the bill, one wanted to hold back as many people under a certain age as possible. In the front ranks of this faction were the military and many entrepreneurial circles who were concerned about the supply of cheap labor. The other faction advanced the extreme opinion that the state should not concern itself with emigration restrictions but should be content to protect its emigrants abroad. The proposals of the draft are certainly important, constituting in fact an alteration of the constitution, but they are by no means sufficiently grounded in principle. In particular, no conformity is established between the state's welfare activities for citizens remaining at home and those for emigrants. Police and socio-political views alternate with one another and provide room for all sorts of administrative chicanery. The reference and subsequent elaborations in the bill's text concerning the causes of the emigration are inadequate, lacking in particular any mention of the great estates or the problem of land subdivision. The most widespread approval will probably be found by its regulations intended to protect emigrants by subjecting agents and transportation concerns to extensive state supervision.[72]

The *Reichspost* was among the very few who viewed the bill positively.[73] The legislative initiative of Representative Friedmann[74] was also unsuccessful.

Archduke Franz Ferdinand saw the solution to the emigration

70. Neurath, "Zum österreichischen Auswanderungsgesetzentwurf," pp. 305, 310, 313, 321ff.

71. Löffler, *Der Entwurf eines Gesetzes betreffend die Auswanderung*, pp. 5, 19.

72. Neurath, "Zum österreichischen Auswanderungsgesetzentwurf," pp. 377ff.

73. *Reichspost*, October 22, 1913.

74. AVA, MdI Auswanderungsakten 8/4 file 322, no. 2942/14.

problem in two courses of action. The underlying causes were to be fought on a politico-economic plane, but the artificial increase of emigration was to be restrained.[75] Prime Minister Stürgkh demanded clear and definite principles from Heinold,[76] and the government's basic emigration program was then drawn up in the Ministry of Interior.[77] The result, however, conformed only to the wishes of the Ministry of Interior and the bureaucracy. Indeed, the goal was to place the emigration movement as completely as possible under governmental control. Since its economic advantages were recognized, seasonal migration was judged more favorably than overseas emigration. Measures to eliminate the economic conditions which precipitated the mass emigration were only marginally considered. Property relationships were not discussed at all. "The politically undesirable influences" to which the emigrant was exposed overseas were to be counteracted by intensifying contacts with the homeland. Returning emigrants with "extreme political and national views" were not wanted. Most of all, Heinold hoped to solve the burning military problem, but he saw that in the long run economic consolidation was absolutely necessary.[78]

Even before the government's emigration bill was introduced in parliament, the Ministry of Interior wanted to hinder the emigration of young men by a prohibitive ordinance,[79] but instead of the ordinance the Council of Ministers, on September 20, 1913, decided to issue only internal directives in which the frontier authorities would be ordered to tighten border inspection.[80] The control in railway stations was to be especially intensified, and train personnel were now obligated to report to the police probable

75. *Ibid.*, 8/4 in genere, no. 9954/14. Colonel Karl Bardolff (aide-de-camp of Archduke Franz Ferdinand) to the Imperial minister president, February 12, 1914.

76. *Ibid.*, 8/4 file 322, no. 6517/14. Stürgkh's letters of December 24, 1913, and January 26, 1914.

77. *Ibid.*, 8/4 in genere, no. 9954/14. "Voraussetzungen für das Programm staatlicher Auswanderungspolitik, Grundlagen der Auswanderungspolitik" (memorandum).

78. *Ibid.*, 8/4 file 324, no. 13.876/14. Answer of the Ministry of Interior to the inquiry of Colonel Bardolff, May 8, 1914.

79. *Ibid.*, 8/4 in genere, no. 32.824/13.

80. *Ibid.*, 8/4 in genere, no. 35.763/13. Ministry of Interior document, September 22, 1913.

draft evaders traveling toward the border.[81] The *Arbeiter Zeitung* protested vigorously against this program of railway spying.[82]

To prevent evasion of these strict regulations, an extensive control service was created for the entire state. The headquarters for this supervision of the emigration movement was established in the Austrian Police Directory in Vienna. Border control and surveillance stations were set up throughout the country and mobile control forces watched over the most important railway lines.

With regard to the existing migrant situation, all areas of the frontier which come into question as mass exit points for native emigrants, especially the Galician-Bukovinian border with Rumania, Russia, and Germany, as well as the Silesian and South Tirolian borders, must be lined with a thickly meshed net of stations. For the remaining parts of the frontier, the occupation of the most important railway stations, the already mentioned surveillance stations, and the establishment of mobile inspection units will be sufficient.[83]

The task of these stations, which were manned by local police forces, consisted of preventing people with military obligations from crossing the border as well as generally observing and supervising emigration. The Control Service became operative on March 1, 1914, and in the last months before the war, numerous activities were developed and many would-be emigrants were detained.[84]

Protest against the restriction of civil liberties and against this "solution" to the emigration problem was conducted primarily by Social Democratic parliamentary deputies.[85] Even the state legislature of Tirol passed a resolution calling on the Austrian government to take the economic needs of the people into consideration also.[86]

81. *Ibid.*, 8/4 in genere, no. 11.634/13. Instructions of the Railway Minister Forster to the Board of Directors of the Austrian (Private) Southern Railway Company, October 25, 1913, and the State Railway Board, Innsbruck, October 31, 1913.

82. *Arbeiter Zeitung*, March 29, 1914.

83. AVA, Handelsministerium AW, file 1920, no. 4602/14. Ministry of Interior to the Ministry of Trade, February 6, 1914. Establishment of an inspection service.

84. *Ibid.*; AVA, MdI Auswanderungsakten 8/4 file 324, no. 20.196/14. According to the reports of the inspections stations.

85. Including, among others, Sever, K. Seitz, Seliger, Dr. Adler, Glöckel, Dr. C. Battisti, Pernersdorfer, Ellenbogen, K. Renner, Bretschneider, Skaret, and Dr. Wróbel.

86. AVA, MdI Auswanderungsakten 8/4 file 326, no. 41.844/14. Landtag resolution, June 5, 1914. Governor to the Statthalterei, Innsbruck, June 9, 1914.

Aside from the police actions taken, the Austrian government could not contribute to the solution of the emigration problem. Economic reforms, which in Germany contributed to reduce emigration remarkably,[87] in Austria, though demanded by many groups, were never initiated. The freedom of emigration, "one of the most important subjective civil rights,"[88] was severely curtailed by the Austrian government's measures.

## D. Conclusion

THE Austro-Hungarian emigration to non-European countries in the years before the First World War can be characterized as a mass movement of the agrarian proletariat from certain provinces in the Austrian half of the Empire. The centers of migration were Galicia and Bukovina in the east and southern lands inhabited by Slovenes and Croats. From 1905 to 1914, over 1.2 million people emigrated from the Kingdoms and provinces represented in the *Reichsrat*, while 2.3 million left the Monarchy as a whole in the same period. An overwhelming majority of the emigrants from Austria moved to the United States, while far fewer went to Canada, Argentina, and Brazil. Immigration to other countries was insignificant. An even higher percentage of Hungarians preferred the United States, the other countries playing almost no role in the Hungarian emigration. Most of the Monarchy's emigrants sailed from the north German ports of Hamburg and Bremen. This enabled the shipping companies to reap gigantic profits, since the expense of carrying the emigrants was very small. Because of its less favorable geographical location, Trieste could attract only a small percentage of the emigrants, many of whom sailed for South America.

The cause of the emigration was the poor economic situation in the eastern and southern regions of Austria. The major lands of

87. Caro, "Auswanderung und Auswanderungspolitik," p. 6.
88. Hürlimann, "Die schweizerische Auswanderung und ihre Gesetzgebung," p. 21.

emigration, Galicia, Bukovina, and Dalmatia, were scarcely industrialized, and agriculture did not provide enough work for the population. In the east, conditions resulting from an unjust distribution of property also contributed to the emigration, since in Galicia and Bukovina, a few great landed proprietors owned the largest part of the agriculturally usable land. In contrast, the many small farms were simply not capable of providing a living for their owners. Thus, America seemed to many to offer the only way out of this social misery. In parliament, the situation was described in particularly drastic terms by the Polish deputy Stapinski, who had himself lived for a time in America. Only emigration brought a certain alleviation from these conditions for the peasant population. Stapinski explained that, as a Pole, he naturally preferred to keep his conationals at home, but he could not let the people starve.[1]

Occupationally, the emigrants came, for the most part, from the agricultural sector of the economy, those from industry and commerce representing a minority. Especially underrepresented were the professional people and intellectuals. Educational levels varied greatly from nationality to nationality. While only 1.3 percent of the Czech emigrants were illiterate, the figure was 50.6 percent for the Ruthenians. Illiterates were known to be undesirable in America.

Aside from the shipping lines, a large, hierarchically ordered agent apparatus, standing, from bottom to top, in contact with the shipping companies, profited from emigration. The whole of Galicia was flooded with full- and part-time agents who engaged in bitter competition with one another.

Money sent by emigrants to their families in the Monarchy played a significant role in the Empire's balance of payments. Under the prevailing economic conditions, the emigration was a necessity, for it reduced the excess supply of labor. Thus, it ultimately benefited those who remained at home, since they could press their wage demands more forcefully

Despite numerous attempts, statutory regulation of emigration was, in contrast with other European countries, not achieved in

1. *Parlamentarische Chronik* (November 1913), p. 643. Meetings of the Budget Committee, November 6-25, 1913.

Austria-Hungary. For years the reaction to emigration had been a passive one. Economic measures were not introduced in the regions affected by emigration. Beginning in the fall of 1913, many imped-iments were placed in the way of emigrants in order to prevent the departure of people with military obligations. In these months, the views of the Ministry of Interior and the military establishment prevailed. For reasons of military strength they sought to make more difficult, indeed to halt, the emigration of people liable for military service by enacting far-reaching control measures. The military standpoint received excessive consideration, while the economic necessity of the emigration was all but ignored. More-over, the military establishment was astonishingly ill-informed about the emigration, as became quite evident in the Canadian Pacific affair.

Once abroad, the emigrants often rejected the Monarchy and avoided contact with its consular officials. On the other hand, the Austro-Hungarian consulates in America showed little understand-ing of the emigrants. In their national associations, immigrants were often confronted with pan-Slav ideas, but anti-Austrian po-litical activity really got underway only during the war. This ap-plies particularly to the South Slavs, after many of their leading political figures had emigrated. In America, Dr. Ante Biankini, a Dalmatian, and Niko Grskovič, chairmen of the Croatian League in Cleveland, were especially active, but representatives of the ear-lier emigration also contributed to the South Slav movement.[2] For America, the Austrian immigrants unquestionably represented a great gain, playing an important role in many areas.[3] An end to this peaceful *Völkerwanderung* came in 1914. "World War I marked the end of an era in American immigration history as well as in Austria's history."[4]

2. Zbynek A. Zeman, *Der Zusammenbruch des Habsburgerreiches 1914–1918* (Vienna, 1963), p. 78.
3. See Wilhelm Schlag, "A Survey of Austrian Emigration to the United States," in Otto von Hietsch, ed., *Österreich und die angelsächsische Welt. Kulturbegegnungen und Ver-gleiche* (Stuttgart, 1916), pp. 139–196.
4. Ernest Wilder Spaulding, *The Quiet Invaders. The Story of the Austrian Impact upon America* (Vienna, 1968), p. 77.

# CAUSES AND PATTERNS OF GREEK EMIGRATION TO THE UNITED STATES

Theodore Saloutos

# CAUSES AND PATTERNS OF GREEK EMIGRATION TO THE UNITED STATES

## Introduction

GREECE ranks as one of the smallest of the European nations to contribute to the population of the United States. Her immigrants, who were among the last and least numerous of the "newer immigrants" to arrive, came from a nation which at the peak period of emigration had a population ranging from 2,632,000 people in 1909 to more than 5,000,000 in 1921. The pull of America was almost irresistible for those who chose to emigrate at all. Although the more immediate causes for the emigration of Greeks may have varied from period to period, the basic underlying causes were more or less constant. Of the 588,160 Greeks who arrived officially in the United States from 1820 through 1971, the overwhelming majority came during the twentieth century as a reaction to unfavorable conditions at home and the more favorable ones in America.[1]

Those Greeks living in their historic homeland were a conquered people until they unfurled the banner of revolt in 1821. The few who reached the New World during the voyages of exploration and discovery, the colonial period, or the early years of the Amer-

[1]. Percy F. Martin, *Greece of the Twentieth Century* (London, 1913), p. 25; Eliot Grinnell Mears, *Greece Today* (Stanford, 1929), pp. 24–25; U. S. Department of Justice, Immigration and Naturalization Service, *Annual Report of the Immigration and Naturalization Service, 1971* (Washington, 1971), p. 53.

ican republic either were in the employ of foreign powers or had managed to escape from the Turkish yoke. During the nineteenth century Greeks lived in Italy, the German states and later the German Empire, France, England, Russia, Turkey, and various countries of Asia and Africa.[2]

The dimensions of Greek emigration may be attributed in part to the venturesome and pioneering qualities of the people, likened by some to those of Odysseus. "Their roving spirit induces them to journey to far-distant lands in search of El-Dorado; for every Greek dreams of becoming rich either in America or elsewhere, and he is usually willing to submit to any amount of physical hardship and privation in order to realize this ideal."[3] Or as someone else wrote, ". . . Greece has always been a splendid place to go away from to make a fortune."[4]

The emigration of Greeks to the United States falls into several distinct epochs: (a) the era of explorations and discoveries, the colonial, the preindustrial, and the early industrial period that came to an end during the late 1870's, with relatively few arrivals; (b) accompanying the period of rapid industrial expansion in the United States, an era of mass emigration beginning in the 1880's, reaching a peak in the decade prior to 1914, and resuming in the years immediately after the war;[5] (c) the era of restricted emigration, beginning in the 1920's, when the quota system went into effect and the emigration of Greeks was reduced to a mere trickle;[6] (d) the

2. Michael A. Dendia, *Greek Communities Around the World* (Athens, 1919), in Greek; Andreas M. Andreadou, *Greek Immigration* (Athens, 1917), in Greek; "Greeks of the Diaspora," *Great Hellenic Encyclopaedia* (Athens, 1930), X, 729–770, in Greek; Athanase G. Politis, *L'Hellenisme et L'Égypte Moderne* (Paris, 1928–1930).

3. Martin, *Greece of the Twentieth Century*, p. 164; *To Kratos* [The Nation] (Athens), July 15, 1912.

4. Michael Choukas, "Greek-Americans," in Francis J. Brown and Joseph S. Roucek, eds., *Our Racial and National Minorities* (New York, 1937), p. 341.

5. Seraphim G. Canoutas, *Hellenism in America* (New York, 1918), pp. 19–32; U. S. Senate, *Reports of the Immigration Commission*, IV, *Emigration Conditions in Europe*, 61 Cong., 3 Sess., Sen. Doc. No. 748 (Washington, 1911), 391, hereafter cited as *Emigration Conditions in Europe*; U. S. Department of Labor, Bureau of Immigration, *Annual Report of the Commissioner General of Immigration, 1920* (Washington, 1920), pp. 188–189.

6. *Annual Report of the Commissioner General of Immigration, 1930* (Washington, 1930), pp. 26, 212–214; *Statistical Abstract of the United States, 1933* (Washington, 1933), p. 95; *ibid., 1936*, p. 99; *ibid., 1940*, p. 110.

refugee years of the 1950's and 1960's when permission was extended to certain Greeks to enter the country, in numbers exceeding those granted entry under the quota laws;[7] and (e) the period commencing with the Immigration and Nationality Act of 1965 that brought an end to the old quota system and increased the number of Greeks who could come to the United States.[8]

The United States was the choice of most Greeks emigrating to distant overseas countries during the twentieth century. More Greeks have wanted to come to this country than the American authorities were willing to admit, and most were of rural origins or not far removed from them. Beginning with the era of mass emigration, their movements began to assume discernible patterns that have continued to the present. No period in Greek emigration exceeded in volume that of the era of mass emigration, especially in the decade prior to World War I and the immediate postwar years.

## Colonial, Preindustrial, and Early Industrial Years

THE Greeks, like other ethnic groups generally classified as "newer immigrants," have insisted that their arrival is traceable to the earliest days of our history, and that these earlier arrivals were men of higher caliber and loftier purpose than those who came during the years of mass emigration. Their numbers were relatively small, only 398 according to the immigration authorities over the years 1820 through 1879, and their motives, diverse; but their social status was higher.[9]

Filiopietists have made much of the New Smyrna colony founded in Florida in 1768 by Dr. Andrew Turnbull.[10] Although Greeks

7. Abba P. Schwartz, *The Open Society* (New York, 1968), pp. 226–227.
8. *Immigration and Nationality Act, with Amendments and Notes on Related Decisions*, 6th ed., revised through May 1, 1969 (Washington, 1969), pp. 175–186.
9. *Annual Report of the Immigration and Naturalization Service, 1971*, p. 51.
10. "The 200th Anniversary of the First Greeks in America," *Orthodox Observer*, 34 (August 1968), 26–27; Bambi Malafouris, *Greeks in America, 1528–1948* (New York, 1948), p. 26, in Greek; *Hellenic Chronicle* (Boston), April 20, 1972.

played a significant part in New Smyrna, the colony belonged to Turnbull, who was married to a beautiful Greek woman and knew something about Greece, Greeks, and the Levant. The Greeks, he believed, were an ideal people to bring to Florida because they were accustomed to a hot climate, were familiar with the culture of vines, olives, cotton, tobacco, silk, and other products, and could help supply the British with goods they must otherwise obtain from Turkey and elsewhere. Moreover, the Greeks were a sober and industrious people eager for an opportunity to flee from their oppressors. "The Greeks of the islands would be the most useful, and the easiest to bring away, and they are more oppressed than any others, having the same taxes to pay as the Greeks of the Continent . . . they are excellent rowers, and might be of greatest service to the inland navigation of America."[11] Turnbull planned to bring about five hundred Greeks to the New World, but his plans went astray and only a fraction of this number came.[12] The New Smyrna colony collapsed almost immediately, but some of the Greek survivors managed to reach St. Augustine and established themselves there. There is no evidence, however, that this initial effort had any influence on Greeks who arrived during the late nineteenth century.

In 1860 a total of 328 Greeks were reported as living in the continental United States, yet the records show a total of only 116 Greeks having entered the country as immigrants in the preceding forty years.[13] How the other 212 entered the picture is a matter of conjecture. Conceivably some could have been Greek sailors; after all the Greeks were a maritime people, and some probably jumped ship once they reached port. Then, too, many who considered themselves Greeks were classified as nationals of other countries, such as Turkey, Romania, Bulgaria, and Egypt, because they were born in these countries instead of Greece. The practice of the im-

11. Epaminondas G. Panagopoulos, *New Smyrna, An Eighteenth Century Greek Colony* (Gainesville, Fla., 1966), pp. 11–12.

12. *Ibid.*, p. 17

13. *Emigration Conditions in Europe*, pp. 391–394.

migration authorities has been to count such people as nationals of their countries of birth.

The distribution of the Greeks in 1860 may furnish some clue to their reasons for coming. They were not concentrated on the East Coast as one would expect. The largest number, ninety-three, was found in California; the second largest number, sixty-five, in Arkansas; and the third largest, thirty-five, in New York. Massachusetts with twenty-five ranked fourth.[14] The attraction to California probably can be attributed to the accessibility of San Francisco by ship and the quest for gold; but the appeal of Arkansas, unless it was to labor in the cotton fields, defies explanation. The presence of Greeks in New York and Massachusetts, on the other hand, probably can be attributed to the proximity of these states to the ports of arrival, the prevalence of the large cities, and the availability of greater employment opportunities.

Among those arriving during this period were those who came of their own accord or were imported for purposes loftier than finding better jobs or making fortunes. We also have specific evidence of why they came to the United States, and whether they came with the intention of remaining permanently.

Unlike the arrival of most Greek immigrants, the arrival of some of the earlier ones was influenced by the religious humanitarianism of the period. During the 1820's missionaries of the American Board of Commissioners for Foreign Missions sent a number of Greek boys to the United States to be educated in American schools with the expectation that once their education had been completed they would go to the Greek mainland or return to one of the Greek islands to impart some of their newly gained knowledge to their compatriots. The first two, Photius Kavassales, thirteen or fourteen years of age, and Anastasius Karavalles, eleven, arrived in February 1823 during the early stages of the Greek Revolution. The parents of Kavassales and four of their children died in the Smyrna plague, and he, Photius, was the only one to survive the disaster. Another brother was in the Peloponnesus at the time. An uncle in Malta committed young Photius to the care of one of the missionaries

14. *Ibid.,* p. 394.

with the intention of sending him to America where he was to receive an education that "should fit him for extensive usefulness among his countrymen." An American ship captain who had heard of the plight of the youth provided him with free passage. Anastasius, the second boy, a native of Zante and the son of a Greek priest at Malta, had the cost of his passage paid for by his father, who was unable, however, to contribute anything toward the expense of his education.

The missionaries clearly had in mind the advantages to be gained from having "a considerable number of promising Greek boys" become acquainted with "the plain and powerful preachings of the Gospel." If any of them should return with "enlarged and cultivated minds, and especially with pious and devoted hearts, the good which they might communicate to their countrymen is beyond all human powers of calculation." The missionaries were going to select and send forth other youths, as circumstances permitted, "to enjoy the same means of intellectual and moral improvement, which are enjoyed by the most highly favored young men of our own country. . . ."[15]

Shortly thereafter, six other boys who had received instruction from the missionaries at Malta came to the United States to enjoy "the literary and religious advantages with which a kind Providence had so abundantly favored us." The names of these boys were Stephano and Pantoleon Galati, Constantine and Pandias Ralli, Nicola Petrokokino, and Allessandro Paspati. None of the parents of the young men were able to bear the expense of having their children educated in the United States, a responsibility that was born by "friends of the cause."[16] In 1827 the ABCFM reported that of the remaining eight young Greeks receiving their education in the United States under the care of the Board, four were attending Yale College and four Amherst. One of the first two young men to

15. *Report of the American Board of Commissioners for Foreign Missions Compiled From Documents Laid Before the Board at the Fourteenth Annual Meeting* (Boston, 1823), pp. 127–128.

16. *Ibid., Fifteenth Annual Meeting* (Boston, 1824), pp. 112–113.

come to the United States, Kavassales, after more than four years in
the country, left for Malta in the same year.[17]

The lofty purposes for which these young men were being sent
to the United States did not bear fruit. Petrokokino, a junior at
Amherst College believed to possess "fine talents" and a "pious
mind," returned to Malta during the winter of 1827–1828, presumably because his father was ill with consumption. Although the
missionaries knew that this was not true, they professed to believe
that after a residence of nearly four years in the United States he
had acquired principles and habits that would render him useful to
his people. Gregory Perdicari, on the other hand, had an offer to
become an assistant teacher at the Mt. Pleasant Classical Institute,
which he was advised to accept as a means of financing his education. Paspati was a member of the same school. Another young
man, Evangelos Sophocles, aged about twenty-one, described as a
person who "possessed uncommon advantages for getting a knowledge of the Greek classics, and who had showed himself capable of
rapid intellectual improvement," was placed in Monson Academy.[18]

In 1831 the ABCFM reported that twelve Greek youths had received their education in the United States, "more or less complete
at the expense of the Board." Two of them, Perdicari and Sophocles, were still in the United States; Paspati and Karavalles were
in the process of returning home; Nicholas Petrokokino, Pantoleon
Galaty, and Pandias Ralli were in Malta; Stephano Galaty and
Constantine Ralli were in Paris; Nicholas Prassus was in Smyrna;
and Photius Kavassales was in the Morea.[19] The Board itself regarded the whole program as ineffective. Writing a number of
years later about the education of the Greek youth in the United
States, Rufus B. Anderson said: "The experience proved so unsatisfactory in the end that all thought of educating foreign youth in
this country, whether from heathen or from Oriental churches was

---

17. *Ibid., Eighteenth Annual Meeting* (Boston, 1827), p. 72.
18. *Ibid., Nineteenth Annual Meeting* (Boston, 1828), p. 48.
19. *Ibid., Twenty-Second Annual Meeting* (Boston, 1831), p. 43.

abandoned; and it became a settled policy of the Board to do all its educational work in countries where it had its missions."[20]

The most important student from an American point of view was Sophocles, who chose not to return to Epirus but remained in the United States and become a distinguished scholar. In 1842 he became a tutor at Harvard after teaching at the Mt. Pleasant Classical Institute. As a result of his scholarship he demolished the theory that modern Greek was of Aeolic and Doric origins and traced it back to the Byzantine. His work "presented new and correct theories of morphology and syntax" and shed light on "the remoteness of America" from the learned centers of Europe. In 1860 Sophocles was appointed professor of Ancient, Byzantine, and Modern Greek at Harvard. His greatest contribution to scholarship was his *Greek Lexicon of the Roman and Byzantine Periods* (1870).[21]

The former student who gained most prominence among Greeks abroad, but not exactly along the lines that the ABCFM had envisioned, was Paspati, who, after graduating from Amherst in 1831, returned to Europe, studied medicine, and for years was "one of the most distinguished practitioners in Constantinople." After retiring from his practice in 1879 he lived in Athens until his death. The Amherst obituary record describes him as "a profound and accurate student, . . . an almost unrivalled authority on Byzantine history and archaeology, and an eminent glossologist." In Athens and Constantinople he was a member and sometimes founder of societies and other institutions dedicated to things Greek. He and other scholars were responsible for organizing the Greek Philological Society, which enrolled thousands of members and was credited with planting nearly two hundred schools in the Ottoman Empire.[22]

Another phase of Greek emigration revolved about the estab-

20. Rufus B. Anderson, ed., *Memorial Volume of the First Fifty Years of the ABCFM* (Boston, 1861), p. 332.

21. Charles Burton Gulick, "Sophocles," *Dictionary of American Biography*, XVII (1935), 397–398. See *Boston Transcript, Boston Daily Advertiser*, and *New York Times*, December 18, 1883, for obituaries; *The Nation*, 34 (January 3, 1884), for an account of his scholarly attainments.

22. Thomas Burgess, *Greeks in America* (Boston, 1913), p. 193.

lishment of branch offices by Greek-owned commercial firms in the years prior to the Civil War. About 1846 the Brothers Rhalli, the owners of the London-based firm bearing their name, decided to extend their operations to the United States by opening an agency in New York City. Their first manager, Leonidas Prassakis, also served as the consul of Greece until his return to Europe in 1856. His successor as branch manager and consul of Greece was Demetrios N. Botassis. Botassis' twofold career reached well into the twentieth century.[23]

The actions of the Rhalli brothers inspired the owners of other Greek-owned commercial firms to follow in their footsteps. These included the firms of Rodocanaki and Frankoudis, Argentis Sekiari and Sons, and Phakeres and Sons. The New York–based firms were engaged primarily in the export of farm products, flour, and cotton. Eventually they opened other branch offices in New Orleans that specialized in the exportation of cotton to Liverpool and the importation of coffee from Brazil. These houses, besides doing a thriving business, inspired still more Greek-owned companies to establish branches in New York and New Orleans until they totalled about twenty. These businesses continued to operate until the end of the Civil War, when they began to close their doors because they found it difficult to function without Negro labor; and the export trade in cotton and profits had declined. After 1870 most of the New York branches ceased their operations, with the exception of Rhalli Brothers, the first established, which thereafter confined itself to the import of products from India.

In short, the first Greeks in America were relatively few in number, widely scattered geographically, better educated, more cosmopolitan in their outlook, and for the most part committed, at least in theory, to returning to the place from which they came. In many respects they were unrepresentative of the rank and file who came during the years of mass emigration.

23. *New York Times*, September 28, 1924.

## Era of Mass Emigration

THE years from 1882 to 1930, but especially from 1903 to 1921, were the years of mass emigration for the Greeks. The bulk of these people came from Greece, but, as seen in Table I, a study of emigrant statistics differentiating immigrant aliens admitted by country of last residence from aliens admitted by "race or people" demonstrates that in some years the number of Greeks who came to the United States from countries other than Greece, as in 1907, 1910, 1911, 1912, 1913, 1914, and 1921, was impressive.

Table I

GREEK EMIGRANTS ADMITTED TO THE UNITED STATES, 1899–1930

| Year | From Greece | By "Race or People" |
|------|-------------|---------------------|
| 1899 | 2,333 | 2,395 |
| 1900 | 3,771 | 3,773 |
| 1901 | 5,910 | 5,919 |
| 1902 | 8,104 | 8,115 |
| 1903 | 14,090 | 14,376 |
| 1904 | 11,343 | 12,625 |
| 1905 | 10,515 | 12,144 |
| 1906 | 19,489 | 23,127 |
| 1907 | 36,580 | 46,283 |
| 1908 | 21,489 | 28,808 |
| 1909 | 14,111 | 20,262 |
| 1910 | 25,888 | 39,135 |
| 1911 | 26,226 | 37,021 |
| 1912 | 21,449 | 31,566 |
| 1913 | 22,817 | 38,644 |
| 1914 | 35,832 | 45,881 |
| 1915 | 12,592 | 15,187 |
| 1916 | 27,034 | 26,792 |
| 1917 | 23,974 | 25,919 |
| 1918 | 1,910 | 2,602 |
| 1919 | 386 | 813 |
| 1920 | 11,981 | 13,998 |
| 1921 | 28,502 | 31,828 |

| Year | From Greece | By "Race or People" |
|------|-------------|---------------------|
| 1922 | 3,457 | 3,821 |
| 1923 | 3,333 | 4,177 |
| 1924 | 4,871 | 5,252 |
| 1925 | 826 | 1,068 |
| 1926 | 1,121 | 1,385 |
| 1927 | 2,089 | 2,557 |
| 1928 | 2,328 | 2,848 |
| 1929 | 2,266 | 3,025 |
| 1930 | 2,291 | 3,793 |

SOURCES: *Annual Report of the Commissioner General of Immigration, 1920*, pp. 183–185; *ibid., 1930*, pp. 204, 206, 212–214.

The Greeks who arrived in the United States from countries other than Greece itself came in all likelihood from Turkey and other Balkan countries, Crete, Cyprus, and Egypt. The migration of Greeks from these countries, especially Turkey, which was relatively heavy from 1910 to 1914, coincided with the growing tensions between the Greeks and the Turks and the Balkan Wars of 1912–1913.

The Greeks who came to the United States from the 1870's through the 1930's were of a different breed, primarily of lower middle-class origins, and devoid of the worldliness of the earlier arrivals. Most of them had not previously travelled far beyond their native villages. The most conspicuous among these newer arrivals were the Spartans and then the Arcadians, who eventually outnumbered them.[24]

Apart from their peasant backgrounds, these Greeks had several things in common; they emigrated from a retarded agricultural economy; they were optimistic about the prospects of improving their lot in Greece itself, by first working, living, and saving in some other country that offered them better initial opportunities than their own; they had a minimum of education; and they were communicants of the Greek Orthodox Church. Other countries to which they could have emigrated included Turkey, Egypt, Romania, Russia, and Italy; but they chose to come to the United

24. Emmanuel Repouli, *A Study of Immigration with Suggested Legislation* (Athens, 1912), in Greek.

States despite the fact that fewer Greeks were established here than in the other lands.[25]

The magnitude of this new Greek emigration distinguished it from the "gradual, natural movement" of earlier years. "Within the last fifteen years," wrote Henry Pratt Fairchild in 1911,

. . . there has sprung up a new emigration—the emigration to America—which is no longer a gradual withdrawal of those who cannot find elbow room in the country, nor a natural departure of the more adventurous and enterprising, to seek more fertile fields of fortune. It is a radical violent exodus of all the strong young men, which has already devastated whole villages, and threatens to leave the entire kingdom depleted of its natural working force. . . .[26]

The reasons the Greeks came to the United States between 1880 and 1930 varied according to the region from which they came and when. By and large males from Greece itself came because of the backward state of the economy that had been left virtually untouched by the industrial revolution and reduced them to eking out a minimal existence. Some came to make a fortune and escape from military service. Greek females, if they did not come to join their spouses, came to find husbands because Greek women in the United States were in short supply and the demand for them was great; and because many parents were unable to provide suitable dowries for them in Greece while in the United States a woman could marry without a dowry. Many came because of the encouragement they received from relatives and friends already in America, and to a lesser extent as a result of the recruiting activities of padrones, steamship-company agents, and others. Greeks from Turkey (in both Europe and Asia) came because of religious discrimination, patriotism, the desire to escape from service in the Turkish army, and economic reasons.[27] Many left Greece because

25. Dendia, *Greek Communities Around the World; Great Hellenic Encyclopaedia*, X, *Greece* (Athens, 1934), 729–757, in Greek.

26. Henry Pratt Fairchild, *Greek Immigration to the United States* (New Haven, 1911), p. 58.

27. The causes of Greek emigration are discussed in Repouli, *A Study of Immigration*, pp. 34–48; Andreadou, *Greek Immigration*, p. 7; Fairchild, *Greek Immigration to the United States*, pp. 58–82; *Kratos*, July 15 and 19, 1912.

of the indifference of her political leaders to the problems of the peasant classes who comprised the bulk of the population; and also to escape from the endless crises, physical and social, that plagued the country.[28] In 1894, an observer wrote:

Within the twelve months past, or little more, she [Greece] has rounded a full cycle of calamity—earthquake well-nigh destroying Zante, constitutional crisis, national insolvency or the next thing to it. And now, in the very throes of her economic distress, she is prostrated by a fresh visitation of Heaven which is without parallel in her modern history. . . . It has shaken the solid core of Greece from the Isthmus to Thermopylae, as well as the great island of Euboea—rocked it like a ship upon an angry sea. . . .[29]

Greece was primarily a retarded agricultural and pastoral country. In the late 1880's the United States consul in Athens observed:

Agriculture is . . . in the most undeveloped condition, and even in the immediate neighborhood of Athens it is common to find wooden ploughs and the rude methods which were in use over 2,000 years ago. Fields are ploughed up, or scratched over, and crops replanted season after season until the exhausted soil will bear no more. Fertilizers are not used to any appreciable extent. . . . Irrigation is in use in some districts, and, so far as I can ascertain, the methods in use can be readily learned by a study of the practices of the ancient Egyptians. Greece has olives and grapes in abundance, and of a quality not excelled, but Greek olive oil and Greek wine will not bear transportation.[30]

Similar observations came from later American consular representatives. As Daniel F. McGinley remarked in 1903, "the principal cause for emigration from Greece is the desire to better their financial condition, as employment is not plentiful or steady, except on the farms, where the profits are usually very small and the wages very low. There is much poverty in Greece, even among the rural population."[31] Most of the land was in the hands of peasant proprietors and farmers who cultivated the land for a share of the yield. The currant was the most favored crop; wheat, olives, figs,

28. *Atlantis* (New York), March 31, 1909.

29. *Nation*, 58 (May 10, 1894), 346.

30. "Consular Reports," Despatch No. 211, Athens 5, Dept. of State Files (National Archives).

31. U. S. Department of Commerce and Labor, Bureau of Statistics, *Special Consular Reports, Emigration to the United States* (Washington, 1911), pp. 401–403.

corn, hashish, tobacco, and a wide variety of garden vegetables were also produced. The wages of the agricultural laborers, according to the fragmentary evidence available, were low. George W. Horton, the American consul-general in Athens, found that in 1895 male farm laborers received from 29 to 44 cents a day, and in 1908 from 58 to 72 cents. Unfortunately, these statistics are of little value because it was impossible to determine the yearly or monthly income of the farm laborers. Wages were paid only when the laborers worked, while "the numerous religious holidays observed in Greece detract[ed] considerably from the income of the working classes. . . ." Horton reported that there were "no less than 180 fast days in the Greek religious year" that were observed by the working classes.[32]

Industry in Greece was highly individualistic. There were few manufacturing establishments of any consequence, except in one or two cities; they had little machinery in them and were managed in antiquated ways. In fact Greece was a nation of small shopkeepers. The most numerous of all the shops in Athens, Piraeus, Patras, Volos, Syra, and Corfu in 1905 were those of the shoemakers, totalling 564 in number. They were followed by 91 tanneries; 76 marble yards; 50 chair factories; 44 macaroni factories; 42 straw hat factories; 39 machine shops and foundries.

Industrial wages in Greece were low. The daily wage for brick and stone layers ranged from 33 to 55 cents in 1895, and from 96 cents to $1.35 in 1908; for common laborers, 33 to 50 cents in 1895 and 68 to 77 cents in 1908; for carpenters, 44 to 65 cents in 1895 and $1.16 to $1.35 in 1908; for painters, 33 to 55 cents in 1895 and 77 cents to $1.35 in 1908; for plumbers, 55 cents in 1895 and $1.25 to $1.35 in 1908; for machinists, 44 to 88 cents in 1895 to $1.54 in 1908. These wages, according to the Immigration Commission, were higher than those paid in other countries of southern and eastern Europe. Where available data provided a comparison between wages paid in 1895 and 1908 a remarkable increase was usually apparent; and in many cases the wages in 1908 were more than

32. *Emigration Conditions in Europe*, pp. 401–403.

double those of 1895. This increase was due largely to emigration.[33]

The first to emigrate in sizable numbers during the nineteenth century were the Spartans, of whom American missionaries observed that "a Spartan . . . is commonly industrious and active" when he discovered it was in his own interest to work.[34] The first Spartan to emigrate to the United States was Christos Tsakonas, a native of the village of Zoupaina. Born in 1848 of parents of poor peasant stock, Tsakonas completed about two years in the elementary school, and held various jobs in Piraeus at a very early age. Failing to make much progress there he decided to go to Alexandria in search of employment to help his family. After meeting the same fate in Alexandria as in Piraeus, Tsakonas finally decided in 1873 to emigrate to the United States, a move which in those days required great courage for a Greek of peasant background. Tsakonas apparently found things more to his liking in the United States. He returned to Greece in 1875, but shortly thereafter left for the United States again, this time in the company of five others who together more or less pioneered the way for the thousands of other Greeks who were to follow.[35] Many, if not most, of the early arrivals were from Sparta.

In 1885 DeWitt T. Riley of the United States Consulate in Athens wrote to Washington, "In the present depressed condition of trade and industry here the emigration to the United States may increase."[36] In 1885, some 172 Greeks emigrated to the United States, which was the largest on record for any single year as of that date.[37] In May 1887 William H. Moffett, the United States consul in Athens wrote to Washington:

. . . within the past few weeks many applications have been made to me for transportation to the United States by intending Greek immigrants. The per-

33. *Ibid.*, pp. 403–404.

34. *Report of the American Board of Commissioners for Foreign Missions, Presented at the Thirtieth Annual Meeting* (Boston, 1839), p. 60.

35. Nick I. Rozakos, "The First Lacaidemonian Immigrants in The United States," *New Home*, 48 (August 15, 1950), 1080–1084, in Greek.

36. DeWitt T. Riley to Alvey A. Adee, March 1, 1885, "Consular Letters," Athens 4, Dept. of State Files (National Archives).

37. *Emigration Conditions in Europe*, p. 391.

sons applying for aid or information are young men, not mechanics, nor agriculturalists, and all tell the same thing, viz, "they have been told of a great demand in America for Greek laborers, that money is to be had in abundance, and that the American Government will furnish transportation." . . . many had gone to the United States with such views, having obtained the necessary fund by borrowing, or by selling or mortgaging what few possessions they may have had. I have tried in vain to discover the source of their delusion. The Greek Consul General in New York has given timely warning, and the Greek newspapers have given publicity to his words, but still the emigration goes on, and is likely to increase.

I do all I can to undeceive these people, and to let them know the truth, but I see only one here and there, and, speaking to them through an interpreter, find it difficult to get them to understand. Then, I am told, that the runners of the emigration lines, knowing that no encouragement will be given, try to keep their victims from applying at the Consulate.

As a class, there could hardly be more undesirable emigrants. They go without means, or barely with enough to land them in New York. They are not skilled workmen, and have no purpose whatever to settle down and become citizens. For the most part they are dirty, and ready to live like dogs, and their hope is to save up in a few years what to them will seem a fortune, and then return to their homes, and live on the interest of their money.[38]

Moffett further reported that emigration had been increasing of late, and that the emigrants passing through Piraeus were principally Laconians. From March to May 1887, he estimated that three hundred persons, all males, left Piraeus by French and Italian steamers for the central ports of Marseilles and Palermo whence they sailed to the United States. The Greek government gave no encouragement to this exodus from one of the most sparsely populated provinces in the country, and actually tried to discourage it even though placing no obstacles in the way of those who wanted to leave. Despite reports from the Greek consul in New York on the destitute conditions of the immigrants in New York City, and the wail sent up by the Greek press every time a new batch departed, the stream of emigration continued.[39]

38. William H. Moffett to James D. Porter, May 24, 1887, "Consular Letters," Athens 5.

39. A. C. McDowell, "Emigration From this District [Piraeus] to the United States of America," May 10, 1887, "Consular Letters," Athens 5.

Proposals to control the outflow from Greece, or from any other country for that matter, to the United States or to prepare a circular on emigration brought a negative response. Worthington C. Ford observed:

The attitude of this government has always been passive and it has never sought actively to encourage or to discourage immigration, except in certain cases where the police power demanded [e.g., paupers, criminals, contract labor, and Mormons]. Apart from such interference the course of emigration has been left to itself, and in the absence of any strong popular feeling or a definitive law on the subject I do not see how a consul can be instructed to actively exert himself in the matter. . . .[40]

During the 1890's the volume of emigration from Greece, still relatively small when compared with that of other countries, kept increasing. In 1891 for the first time in any single year more than one thousand Greeks emigrated to the United States, and in excess of two thousand in 1896.[41] By this time Greeks were leaving from all parts of the country, but the Peloponnesians were still the most numerous and conspicuous among the departees. Arcadians began arriving in impressive numbers between 1892 and 1894 till they eventually exceeded the Spartans. Greeks emigrated from the provinces of Argolidos and Corinthias, Achaea and Elidos, Messinia, Attica and Boeotia, Phtiotidos and Phokidos, Aetolia and Akarananias; from the area around Larissa, Trikkala, and Artis; from the Cyclades, the islands of the eastern Aegean, the Dodecanese, Crete, Cephalonia, and Zakynthos.[42]

The economic fortunes of many Peloponnesians were tied to currants, the principal commercial and export crop of Greece. But currants, like other commercial crops, suffered from overproduction; and by the mid-1890's the currant vineyards of the Peloponnesus, which a few years earlier brought immense profits to their owners, barely netted enough to cover the costs of cultiva-

40. Worthington C. Ford to Dr. St. Clair, May 8, 1888, "Consular Letters," Athens 5.
41. *Emigration Conditions in Europe*, p. 391.
42. Andreadou, *Greek Immigration*, pp. 77–79, 93; Repouli, *A Study of Immigration*, pp. 18–21; *Atlantis*, January 14, 1909.

tion.[43] "Scores of the oldest and of the most important currant houses of Greece came down like houses of cards; and the whole commercial class of the Peloponnesus, and almost of the whole kingdom, reeled under the terrible blow."[44] To aggravate matters the Peloponnesus, relatively speaking, was overcrowded when compared with other portions of Greece. It had a greater density of population than central Greece, and central Greece had a greater density than Thessaly.[45] The effects of this overcrowding were reflected in the departure of larger numbers of Greeks for the United States, as the statistics in Table II indicate.

Table II

EMIGRATION OF GREEKS TO THE UNITED STATES, 1890–1899

| Year | Males | Females | Total |
|------|-------|---------|-------|
| 1890 | 464   | 60      | 524   |
| 1891 | 1,040 | 65      | 1,105 |
| 1892 | 591   | 24      | 615   |
| 1893 | 1,099 | 32      | 1,131 |
| 1894 | 1,312 | 39      | 1,351 |
| 1895 | 574   | 31      | 605   |
| 1896 | 2,124 | 51      | 2,175 |
| 1897 | 546   | 25      | 571   |
| 1898 | 2,246 | 93      | 2,339 |
| 1899 |       |         | 2,333 |

SOURCE: *Special Consular Reports, Emigration to the United States*, p. 78.

Greece was capable of producing large quantities of olives, lemons, figs, and oranges; and there was room for the cultivation of tobacco, a product in universal demand and potentially of great

43. U. S. Bureau of Foreign Commerce, *United States Consular Reports*, 1897 (Washington, 1897), II, 456–457, title varies for the years 1880–1903; Martin, *Greece in the Twentieth Century*, p. 272; Rennel Rodd, *Customs and Lore of Modern Greece* (London, 1892), pp. 52–53.

44. Theodore A. Burlami, "The Overproduction of Currants," *Economic Journal*, 9 (1899), 638.

45. Rodd, *Customs and Lore of Modern Greece*, p. 55.

importance to a nation in need of income.[46] Wheat was the principal crop after currants, but the statistics on the acreage under cultivation are unavailable, and the prospect was that the country would continue importing wheat and flour for many years.[47] The small growers were still unconvinced that the cultivation of currants was a gamble, and that it would be to their advantage to put their land to uses that would net them a steadier yield though a smaller return. A bumper crop, such as that of 1901–1902, following a year of disaster, instilled new life into the Peloponnesus and the contiguous islands, encouraged the excessive cultivation of currants, and thwarted all efforts to prevent overproduction and low prices.[48]

In 1900 and 1901 the United States consul in Athens reported marked increases in the shipment of olives, olive oil, cheese, wine, figs, and other products of the southern Peloponnesus. The black olives, white cheese, and other products which had found favor with the Greeks at home had found even greater favor among those in the United States; and many Greek merchants, especially those in New York City, were energetic in pressing these articles on immigrants from other countries, especially those of Italy.[49]

The steady growth in the immigrant traffic and the shipment of currants and other products to foreign ports revived efforts to establish direct steamship connections between Greece and the United States. By 1908 nearly all the principal towns of the Peloponnesus had become accessible by railway; and the Anchor Line and the Phelps Brothers Company, whose ships plied the waters between New York and the Mediterranean ports, called regularly between August and December—the currant-shipping season—and carried the bulk of the currants destined for the United States.[50] The United States Consulate in Athens, after having made severa

46. U. S. Bureau of Manufacturers, *United States Commercial Relations, 1907* (Washington, 1908), II, 464. This publication was issued by the Bureau of Foreign Commerce, 1855/56–1902; the Bureau of Statistics in 1903; the Bureau of Manufactures, 1904–1910.

47. *Ibid.*, II, 406.

48. *Ibid.*, *1902*, p. 379.

49. *Ibid.*, p. 382.

50. *Ibid.*, *1898*, II, 377.

unsuccessful attempts to persuade different steamship companies to establish a direct line between Greek and American ports as a means of encouraging trade between the two countries, finally reported in March 1902 that the Deutsche Levant Line, which ran four steamships carrying passengers and freight, touched Greek ports once a month.[51] The Hamburg-American Line also entered the picture and guaranteed monthly departures that could be increased if business warranted. In addition to freight each steamship could accommodate from four hundred to five hundred passengers in steerage, make the trip between New York and Piraeus in eighteen days, and charge each passenger $40 for meals and berth.[52] Prior to 1911 Greeks came to the United States by direct lines from Patras and Piraeus, by way of Naples, or across France, or through Switzerland and Italy, or even by way of Germany.[53]

A number of other interrelated influences promoted the departure of an increasing number of Greeks for the New World. These included the continuing belief that the demand for unskilled labor in the United States was insatiable; the appearance of books and newspaper articles in the Greek press and newsstands extolling the virtues of America; the persistence of prospective emigrants in believing the favorable, and discounting the unfavorable, accounts of life and work in the United States; the emergence of the labor contractor or padrone system which, although operating in violation of the law, actually succeeded in persuading an undetermined number of young males to leave for the United States; the mounting social and economic pressures at home; the receipt of remittances in Greece that whetted the appetites of those who did not receive them and persuaded them to emigrate in turn; and finally a permissive policy on the part of the Greek authorities, who did not impose curbs on emigration, except in periods of military crisis. Especially in earlier years, the Greek government's premise seems to have been that the Greek emigrants were different from

51. *Ibid.*, *1900*, II, 388; *ibid.*, *1902*, p. 368.
52. Charles S. Francis to John Jay, February 12, 1902, Greece xiv, Dept. of State Files (National Archives).
53. Fairchild, *Greek Immigration to the United States*, p. 110.

those of Ireland, Germany, France, and other countries—more closely attached to their families, more patriotic, and more likely to return to the land of their birth.

For Greeks the margin of economic improvement to be gained through emigration was considerable.[54] The difference in wages between the United States and the countries of southern and eastern Europe was great. In parts of Italy, Austria-Hungary, Greece, Turkey, Russia, and the Balkan States, the United States Immigration Commission found that the average wage of men engaged in common and agricultural labor was less than 50 cents per day, while in some sections it was even much lower.[55] Of the 216,962 Greeks arriving in the United States from 1899 to 1910 only 678 and 15,289 were listed respectively as members of the professional classes and as skilled laborers; 132,059 were common laborers; farm laborers ranked second at 38,305. Women and children totalled 19,244.[56] Unfortunately, the fragmentary nature of the available data on wages in Greece, as in the United States, makes a meaningful comparison in wages between the two countries difficult.[57] The average weekly hours and hourly earning in the United States in 1899 were 59.1 hours and almost 21 cents compared with 56.6 hours and 26 cents in 1910.[58]

The cost of living in the United States was higher than in Greece, emigrants suffered from unemployment, and this ate into their earnings and savings, but the prospects of a brighter tomorrow were always there. Those anxious to expedite their return to Greece, and gainfully employed, often maintained a standard of living not far removed from what they had known at home. A thrifty-minded person living under such conditions obviously could amass greater savings than the one who chose to enjoy a higher standard im-

---

54. Isaac A. Hourwich, *Immigration and Labor* (New York, 1912), pp. 177–220.

55. U. S. Immigration Commission, *Abstracts of Reports of the Immigration Commission, 1907–1910* (Washington, 1911), I, 186.

56. *Ibid.*, I, 100.

57. *Ibid.*; Hourwich, *Immigration and Labor*, p. 293.

58. U. S. Department of Commerce, Bureau of the Census, *Historical Statistics of the United States, Colonial Times to 1957* (Washington, 1961), p. 91. The authoritative account on the subject is Paul H. Douglas, *Real Wages in the United States, 1890–1926* (New York, 1930).

mediately.[59] Reports of the difficulties that emigrants encountered in the United States in the form of exploitation, unemployment, starvation, and discrimination were not enough to deter fresh waves of emigrants from arriving.[60]

The success of many emigrants and the steady flow of remittances to the old country inspired some of the more ambitious and enterprising to want to profit still more from the labor of compatriots and relatives in Greece who could be persuaded to come and work for them. This was especially true of a few of the more successful Greeks in shoeshining, railroad construction work, flower vending, and fruit and vegetable peddling. Such persons sought to recruit young men first from their home provinces and, after these sources dried up, from elsewhere, under some prearranged plan, usually in violation of the contract labor laws of the United States.

The recruitment of bootblacks, especially in the Tripolis area, was begun by successful shoeshine parlor operators who came to America from this region. The shoeshining business had formerly been in the hands of Italians and Negroes and largely confined to booths, stands, or chairs inside or just outside of saloons and hotels. Greeks in New Jersey, Maryland, New York, Louisiana, Alabama, Illinois, and elsewhere quickly discovered that shoeshining was a profitable business; and they branched out by establishing shops in the leading cities of the United States. The more enterprising Greeks sought to dignify their places of business by establishing ornate shops in high rental areas. Most of them became financially independent, and one of the more ambitious reputedly "started and operated over 100 establishments in the United States." Success in this line of work triggered an influx of Greek youths who might previously have drifted to New England to find employment in the cotton mills.

The capital needed to enter the shoeshine business was small, fixtures and supplies were available on credit, and the big require-

59. Theodore Saloutos, *They Remember America* (Berkeley, 1956), pp. 88–89, 101–102.

60. Frank W. Jackson to David Hill, June 29, 1901, Greece xv, Dept. of State Files (National Archives); *Atlantis*, November 10 and 24, 1908; December 26, 1908; January 23, 1909.

ment was for labor that could be provided by young boys. This often could be arranged by writing letters to relatives and friends in Greece; and as a consequence, many youthful relatives and sons of friends, who regarded their padrones as guardians, came to the United States.[61] The relationships that the padrones capitalized upon in Greece were extensive, sometimes embracing entire villages and involving several hundred people. Relatives of theirs in Greece became godfathers at baptisms or best men at weddings for the sole purpose of contracting family alliances. The padrones themselves took trips to Greece and there became godparents to many children in many families. This enabled them to secure boys from these families for the shoeshining business.[62]

Some of the more ambitious padrones were inspired by the growth of trusts in the United States, and thought that they could organize a shoeshining trust. They believed that they could accomplish this if they controlled the labor supply; and a step in that direction would be taken if the parents of prospective shoeshine boys in Greece gave mortgages on their property to some agent of the padrone as a guarantee of the length of time that their sons would labor for the padrone in the United States. This was negotiated successfully in individual cases, but legislation in 1907 made it possible to institute criminal proceedings against padrones for the importation of labor under such conditions. This had the effect of discouraging some and making others more cautious. Labor imported thereafter was brought in through relatives in Greece in a manner that placed the boys beyond the reach of the law. Some of the shoeshine bosses refrained from importing boys but paid higher wages as a means of recruiting boys who entered the country with their parents.

The legislation enacted in 1907 also enabled the secretary of commerce and labor to exclude from the country all children under sixteen unless they were accompanied by one or both parents. That boys were in great demand in the shoeshine parlors of the

61. *Abstracts of Reports of the Immigration Commission*, II, 398–399.
62. *Ibid.*, II, 404–405.

United States was a well-advertised fact in Greece.[63] The predictable dodges followed. Many of the boys who arrived in the country after 1907 were accompanied by men who either claimed they were the fathers or said that they were heading for some interior point where they would meet the father. These "pseudo-fathers," as they were called, were adult immigrants bearing some distant or no relationship whatever to the boys in question. Usually they acted for compensation or as a favor to the father or to a padrone. Many boys, however, were accompanied by their real fathers, who found it less expensive and safer to come to the United States with their sons than to run the risk of having them deported.[64]

That such activities aroused the wrath of some authorities can be gleaned from a letter of Charles A. Bookwalter, mayor of Indianapolis, who wrote Secretary of State Elihu Root that he believed that "there exists in New York City an organization which secures these boys from their homes in Greece, and after bringing them to this country, sells them to branch organizations which in turn control hundreds of shoe shining parlors throughout the United States." The mayor continued:

I have made repeated efforts to secure evidence here, but the boys are completely terrorized, and even though we get them separated, they refuse to tell our interpreters, who in all instances must of necessity be a local Greek, anything whatever about their history. A striking similarity exists in their stories. In almost every instance they will say that their uncle brought them to this country; then sent them to their brother or their cousins, and this brother or cousin, when we examine the boy, is always located in St. Louis or Chicago or Kansas City or some other place hundreds of miles away, and they can never tell us the address of this mythical uncle, cousin or brother. These boys are coached in telling a uniform story, and through terror and fear of the interpreter telling what they say, always hold strictly to their manufactured tale.[65]

A shoeshine parlor operator in St. Louis who once had thirty-five boys under his control is said to have recruited them through

63. *Ibid.*, II, 399–400.
64. *Ibid.*, II, 400–401.
65. Charles A. Bookwalter to Elihu Root, January 15, 1907, Dept. of State Files (National Archives).

an agent who paid the parents of each $150 that was used in most cases to form a dowry for the sister.[66]

Padrones also persuaded Greeks to come to the western states to work on railroad construction gangs. In some instances the padrones were employed as interpreters or assistant foremen in charge of gangs of laborers. Agents of the padrones in Greece induced laborers to come under the promise that they would find work at wages ranging from $1.75 to $2.00 per day.

They tell the immigrants that their brothers or relatives are bosses on railroads in the United States, and that they have secured contracts insuring work for all those who wish to migrate for a period of over three years; that any immigrant who is willing to migrate will be furnished with his steamship ticket and "show money" [between $12 and $15] . . . that by emigrating as proposed by these agents the immigrants will be enabled within three or four months to pay from the proceeds of their labor their mortgage indebtedness at home.

In return for a mortgage or a promissory note, the Greek laborer would be given from $130 to $250 for his steamship passage in addition to "show money." After arriving at his destination, the emigrant was charged a labor agent's fee of $10 for being found employment, and an interpreter's fee of a dollar per month by the interpreter for the railroad gang despite the fact that he was a salaried employee of the railroad. Periodically the laborer was asked to contribute to purchase a present for the foreman or roadmaster to keep from being fired.[67]

One of the better-known Greek labor czars in the West was Leonidas G. Skliris, who worked out of Salt Lake City and was the labor agent of the Utah Copper Company, Western Pacific Railroad, Denver and Rio Grande Western Railroad, and the Carbon County coal mines. A shrewd and merciless operator, Skliris with the assistance of his three brothers and other associates managed to collect tribute from each immigrant who sought work on railroad gangs and in the smelters and mills. Skliris, in close communication with labor agents in the surrounding states, could recruit whatever

66. R. Crawford, *The Immigrant in St. Louis* (St. Louis, 1916), p. 42.
67. *Abstracts of Reports of the Immigration Commission*, II, 405–406.

number of men he desired. The men whom he hired, frequently as strikebreakers, had often suffered from months of unemployment and idleness and had been accustomed to making payments of money in the old country to petty officials for the smallest favors. Consequently, they acquiesced in making initial payments for their jobs and usually paid a dollar a month thereafter.[68]

The extent to which such practices prevailed is unknown, but it was sufficient to arouse the American authorities. The acting secretary of commerce and labor wrote to the secretary of state in midsummer 1909 that his department had been investigating the manner in which Greek emigrants had come to this country under the promise or offer of employment, and found that "the contract labor laws have been violated on a most extensive scale." Two Greek railroad foremen, Polychronopoulos and Kaplanis, reportedly "brought over some hundreds of laborers within the past few years" in return for twelve percent mortgages. The United States attorney in Kansas City in charge of prosecuting these padrones informed the Department of Commerce and Labor that it was essential to have authenticated copies of some of these mortgages as evidence in the trials. The Greek minister to the United States, Lambros A. Coromilas, unofficially expressed the desire to secure a list of the names of those Greeks who were induced to come to the United States fraudulently.[69] The hope was that as a result of such action the Greek government would be able to set aside the "excessive and usurious mortgages" and punish the responsible parties.

In general United States attorneys were less successful than they would have liked to be in prosecuting violators of the contract labor laws. The boys working in the shoeshine parlors might be peons for all practical purposes, but since "the elements of indebtedness and physical compulsion to work out the indebtedness" were missing, peonage laws could not apply. Boys under sixteen who came to the United States in the company of parents, or had

68. Helen Zeese Papanikolas, "Toil and Rage in a New Land, The Greek Immigrants in Utah," *Utah Historical Quarterly*, 38 (Spring, 1970), 115–116.

69. Ormsby McHarg to Secretary of State, July 27, 1909; Huntington Wilson to Secretary of Commerce and Labor, August 3, 1909; Wilson to Lambros A. Coromilas, August 3, 1909, Dept. of State Files (National Archives).

parents in the country to whom they were going, or deceived the authorities by coming with "pseudo-fathers" could not readily be excluded. "Once landed, it becomes a hard matter to trace them and almost impossible to secure evidence in the majority of cases, for the boys understand that they will be punished by deportation. This knowledge makes them persistent in withholding any information as to the manner of their entry into the United States."[70]

Emigration as a means of escaping from military service was another factor in the movement to the United States. The famous Repouli Report of 1912, named after Emmanuel Repouli, the minister of foreign affairs, confirmed what many Greek officials and American immigration authorities knew: that emigration from Greece was mainly a movement of the young, and that among them were many who were anxious to avoid serving with the Greek Army. This was especially true in the period immediately prior to the Balkan Wars of 1912–1913, as the statistics in Table III bear out.

## Table III

GREEK EMIGRANTS ACCORDING TO AGE, 1909–1911

| Year | Total | Under 14 | From 14 to 45 | Above 45 |
|------|-------|----------|---------------|----------|
| 1909 | 20,262 | 788 | 19,155 | 329 |
| 1910 | 39,135 | 1,041 | 37,589 | 502 |
| 1911 | 27,021 | 1,006 | 35,485 | 430 |

NOTE: Totals appear as printed in the source.
SOURCE: Repouli, *A Study of Immigration*, pp. 80–81.

Among those in the 14- to 45-years category were many between the ages of 18 and 30, and especially between 18 and 25. Many of the men who were far away from home were under obligation to serve in the Greek armed forces; and they were absent, it was charged, not merely because of economic reasons but from a belief on their part that in the long run their military obligations would become less burdensome, and that they would be able to pay a fine instead of rendering the actual service.

70. *Abstracts of Reports of the Immigration Commission*, II 406.

A study of the Greek military rolls confirmed the charges of the Greek authorities. Of the 29,266 listed for the classes of 1911, 11,913 failed to appear when they were called and were classified as delinquents. The delinquents in the class of 1910 numbered 11,816; those for 1908, 9,680; for 1907, 8,972; for 1906, 7,427; and for 1905, 7,093.[71]

In some communities as many as two-thirds of those whose names were called for service had emigrated. In the district of Thisvis, of the seventy-five names listed on the military rolls only fifteen presented themselves before the authorities; the remainder had emigrated. When the chief of the military council of Attica-Boeotia asked the mayor of Tanagra why eighteen of those whose names appeared on the rolls had departed for the United States, the mayor replied "in search of their fortunes," but primarily to escape from military service. They left for the United States without passports because it was then possible for them to enter the country if they were physically fit.[72]

Many Greeks, who were a fiercely proud and nationalistic people, resented the charge that they or many of their compatriots came to the United States with the intention of avoiding military service in Greece. They could, and often did, point to the volunteer units that were organized soon after word was received in the United States of the new difficulties brewing between the Greeks and the Turks, the formation of the Panhellenic Union designed to advance the national interests of Greece among Greeks living in the United States and other nations, the appearance in the country of "national apostles" who kept reminding the emigrants of their obligations to their families and the Mother Country, and finally the formation of the various local and provincial societies that sought to make improvements in their villages.[73] All this indicated that the professed intentions of the Greeks were not to remain in

---

71. Repouli, *A Study of Immigration*, pp. 80–81.

72. *Ibid.*, pp. 82–83; *Atlantis*, March 24, 1909, May 13, 1913, May 24, 1914; *Kratos*, August 26, 1912.

73. *Monthly Illustrated Atlantis*, 1 (July 1910), 16–17; *Kratos*, July 18, 1910, October 21, 1907, March 23, 1914; *Sphaira* (Athens), October 19, 1907, November 23, 1914; *Atlantis*, January 13, 1908, July 7, 1908; Saloutos, *They Remember America*, pp. 37–40.

the United States permanently but to return to Greece as soon as they had achieved their limited goals in the United States. The organizations, societies, churches, schools, and other groups formed in this country prior to World War I were designed to meet the needs of a people who were here temporarily and had some intentions of returning to Greece.[74] The fact that forty-two thousand Greeks, mostly from the United States, returned to Greece to serve in the Balkan Wars of 1912–1913 is proof that all Greeks did not emigrate to escape from military service.[75]

That emigration to the United States was nevertheless a problem for Greece, especially at a time when she had major military obligations to fulfill, is apparent. The Greek authorities struck back with the only weapon at their command, restriction of emigration and payment of heavy fines by all who violated the decree. In the spring of 1914 the minister of the interior issued a circular to prefects and other local administrative authorities of the Kingdom declaring that in conformance with the recent legislation governing military service no male subject of Greece between the ages of 14 and 40 could leave the country without a permit from the prefect of the province of which he was a resident. If he was between the ages of 14 and 20 years, such a subject in addition to obtaining a permit from the prefect had to post a bond ranging from 200 to 2,000 drachmas, or from $38.60 to $386, to be forfeited in case of failure to return and perform the required military service. Those who left the country without having complied with these requirements had to pay fines depending on their age.[76]

The Greek Legation in Washington advised the secretary of state of the law that forbade every male Hellenic subject between the ages of 14 and 40 from leaving the country for foreign parts without a special permit from the prefect. The same law provided that boys under 14 and men over 40 did not need such a travelling

---

74. *California* (San Francisco), February 3, November 17, December 1, 1917, May 3 and 11, 1918; *Hellinikos Astir* [Greek Star] (Chicago), March 16, 1917; *Saloniki* (Chicago), November 24, 1917, March 30, 1918.

75. *Kratos*, January 20, May 26, September 1, 1913.

76. Statement signed by William Cole, American Consul General, Athens, April 15, 1914, Dept. of State Files (National Archives).

permit, but they had to carry a certificate of their registration in the Kingdom's rolls with a visa from the Mayor declaring there was no objection to their leaving. The State Department also was asked whether it would lend its assistance to the Greek government by not permitting any Greek subject to land in the United States unless he carried these specific documents with him.[77]

The State Department in response drafted a letter, whose contents were approved by the secretary of labor, saying that the United States government, of course, was desirous of taking such steps as were practicable and proper to exclude criminal aliens from the United States, from whatever country they came, if the offense of which they had been proved guilty was not of a political nature. But there was no authority of law under which aliens seeking admission to the United States could be excluded merely because they had not been provided with permits or certificates of registration as described. The principal objective of the Greek law was the prevention of the emigration of Greeks whose continued presence in Greece was considered expedient for political reasons, i.e., military service under Greek law. Apart from the legal aspects, such proposed action would be contrary to the well-established policy of the United States of permitting an individual to expatriate himself if he so desired.[78]

An even more stringent decree was issued in 1915 as a means of curbing emigration and strengthening the military and naval manpower of Greece. Garrett Droppers of the American Legation in Athens wrote in late 1914, ". . . no Greek citizen is permitted to emigrate [except temporarily] unless he has completed his active military service; and he is not permitted to become a citizen of a foreign power except by Royal Decree." The result was that Greeks who became naturalized American citizens and returned to Greece for any purpose were constantly getting into trouble with the Greek military authorities and appealing to the American Legation

---

77. A. Vouros to William J. Bryan, June 11/24, 1914, Dept. of State Files.
78. Secretary of Labor in response to Secretary of State, July 17, 1914, Dept. of State Files.

in Athens for protection, which the Legation was powerless to give.[79]

Females were often attracted to the United States by matrimonial opportunities. In Greece, where it was common for a husband to lament the fact that his wife had given birth to another girl, where the number of daughters in a family was a source of great worry, where a girl in order to marry usually had to have a dowry, and where marriage was a matter of arrangement and contract, it was hardly surprising that the families of these girls, and sometimes the girls themselves, looked to countries such as the United States for husbands.[80]

This "barbarous system" was a cause of emigration because some fathers and brothers were unable to provide dowries for their daughters and sisters for a suitable marriage.[81] The United States had a surplus of Greek males of marriageable age, who had a preference for spouses of their own ethnic background and faith; and the American philosophy of marriage did not require dowries. The bulk of the financial burdens of matrimony in the United States, even among the immigrants, was assumed by the males.[82]

The statistical evidence on the preponderance of males over females is abundant. Over the period of 1899 to 1910 out of a total of 216,962 Greeks who emigrated to this country, some 206,306 or 95.1 percent were males, and only 10,656 or 4.9 percent were females.[83] In effect this put the husband-seeking female in a more favorable marriage position than in Greece. Although some Greeks continued to demand dowries, even in the United States, the system more or less crumbled because of the preponderance of males over females.[84]

79. Garrett Droppers to secretary of state, December 14, 1915, Dept. of State Files.

80. Rodd, *Customs and Lore of Modern Greece*, pp. 91–92; Lucy M. J. Gernett, *Greece of the Hellenes* (New York, 1914), pp. 197–198; John M. Hall, ed., *Greek Life* (Detroit, 1908), pp. 225–226; *Hellinikos Astir*, March 15, 1934.

81. *Abstracts of Reports of the Immigration Commission*, II, 402–403.

82. Interview with Alexandros Zouzoulas, Athens, Greece, December 4, 1952, in *They Remember America* collection.

83. U. S. Senate, *Reports of the Immigration Commission, Statistical Review of Immigration, 1870–1910*, 61 Cong., 3 Sess., Senate Doc. No. 756 (Washington, 1911), 47.

84. *Saloniki*, September 6, 1917.

A Greek female came to the United States in one of several ways: in the company of brothers, parents, close relatives, or friends; sometimes on her own, but almost always with a predetermined destination in mind and frequent warnings of what to avoid;[85] after an exchange of pictures between a would-be bride and a would-be groom usually arranged for by a close relative, a friend, or some other intermediary;[86] or after some Greek who was comfortably established in a business, a job, or otherwise felt he was eligible for marriage journeyed back to Greece, married, and brought his bride with him to the United States. The arrival of wives, brides, and young women in search of husbands increased immediately after the Balkan Wars of 1912–1913, and especially during the 1920's when the decision to remain in the United States became final for many.[87]

After the Balkan Wars a number of veterans, after discharging their military obligations in Greece, returned to the United States with their families or brides to remain permanently, and more single women recognized the matrimonial opportunities that the United States offered. At the end of the fiscal year of 1916, of the 26,792 Greeks arriving, 5,699 were females as against 21,093 males, or an average of one woman for almost every four men. This showed a narrowing in the disparity between the sexes that prevailed among arrivals in the years before the Balkan Wars.[88]

The statistics in Table IV show that, except for the years 1920 and 1921, the number of Greek female emigrants admitted into the country during the 1920's exceeded the number of males. Women were coming primarily to join husbands who had preceded them or as single women with hopes of acquiring husbands.

85. *Ibid.*, May 20, 1916; *Hellinikos Astir*, October 4, 1907.
86. *New York Times*, June 3, 1923.
87. *Ibid.*
88. *Annual Report of the Commissioner General of Immigration, 1916* (Washington, 1916).

Table IV

GREEKS ADMITTED INTO THE UNITED STATES BY SEX, 1920–1932

| Year | Total | Male | Female |
|------|-------|------|--------|
| 1920 | 13,998 | 11,167 | 2,831 |
| 1921 | 31,828 | 21,551 | 10,277 |
| 1922 | 3,821 | 1,679 | 2,142 |
| 1923 | 4,177 | 1,474 | 2,703 |
| 1924 | 5,252 | 2,256 | 2,996 |
| 1925 | 1,068 | 307 | 761 |
| 1926 | 1,385 | 344 | 1,041 |
| 1927 | 2,557 | 864 | 1,693 |
| 1928 | 2,848 | 696 | 2,152 |
| 1929 | 3,025 | 854 | 2,171 |
| 1930 | 3,793 | 1,570 | 2,223 |
| 1931 | 2,663 | 982 | 1,681 |
| 1932 | 1,105 | 208 | 897 |

SOURCES: *Annual Report of the Commissioner General of Immigration, 1920*, p. 95; *1921*, p. 34; *1922*, p. 32; *1923*, p. 48; *1924*, p. 42; *1925*, pp. 42–44; *1928*, pp. 44–45, 218; *1929*, pp. 45–46; *1930*, pp. 60–61; *1931*, pp. 80–81, 226; *1932*, pp. 66–67.

During the 1920's the American press devoted much space to Greek girls who came to the United States to be married. Representatives of the Traveler's Aid Society said that these girls were reared with the idea of becoming wives and mothers, and they did not consider it odd to marry someone they had not seen before. To them marriage was a serious business, more important than even the husband. On one day thirty civil weddings between Greeks were performed in New York City.[89] On another occasion sixteen girls, who arrived on the Greek liner Constantinople, were married in the New York City Hall, the selection of the husband in some cases having been made by the parents; and another one hundred fifty young women were still under the care of the Traveler's Aid Society until they were married or headed for their final destination.[90] The end result for some would-be brides was not always happy. As one reporter observed:

89. *National Herald* (New York), August 11, 1922.
90. *Ibid.*, August 5, 1922.

Several prospective bridegrooms were at the pier yesterday when the Greek lines docked and called out the names of their chosen ones. Apparently some of the young women did not measure up to their photographs, for they were left unclaimed at Ellis Island. Their eyes filled with tears as they told their stories . . . and they were set aside and telegrams sent to their men to make good.[91]

Census figures for 1920 and 1930 indicate that the disparity between male and female arrivals began to narrow still more. Of the 175,976 Greeks in the United States in 1920, some 32,370 or 18.4 percent were females.[92] Of the 189,066 who gave Greek as their mother-tongue in 1930, some 138,780 were males as against 50,286 females, which indicates that the disparity between males and females had continued to lessen.[93]

Letters to relatives and friends at home from persons who had emigrated to the United States figured prominently among the proximate causes of the exodus from Greece. Many, if not most, Greeks tended to retain a keen interest in the family in the Mother Country, and as a consequence a great deal of correspondence was exchanged. The Immigration Commission found that letters from emigrants in the United States "passed from hand to hand until most of the emigrant's friends and neighbors were acquainted with the contents." In periods of industrial activity these letters contained optimistic accounts of the wages and opportunities for employment in the United States, and when comparisons were drawn with conditions at home it was "inevitable that whole communities should be inoculated with a desire to emigrate." The reverse, however, was true in periods of depression. In such crises prospective emigrants were informed by their friends and relatives in the United States about the prevailing adverse conditions, and a noticeable drop in the emigration would set in.[94]

The letter of an emigrant to his former employer in Greece re-

91. *New York Times*, June 3, 1923.

92. U. S. Department of Commerce, Bureau of the Census, *Abstract of the Fourteenth Census of the United States, 1920* (Washington, 1923), p. 299.

93. *Abstract of the Fifteenth Census of the United States* (Washington, 1933), pp. 152–153.

94. *Abstracts of Reports of the Immigration Commission*, I, 187–188.

flects a highly optimistic tone that was probably representative of many other letters sent.

Here [in the United States] the people work much and regularly, and rest only on Sundays, but we fare well. This day that I am writing you is Sunday; I took my bath, had my milk, and the day will pass satisfactorily. Where did I know this life there [in Greece] with this order.

If you wish, master, you will also do well to come, and I will send you the cost of the fare.[95]

The former emigrant who returned to Greece for a visit or re-mained permanently was an immediate stimulus to emigration. Often those who returned spoke of the brighter side of life in the United States, how they worked and saved, the educational oppor-tunities, the freedom to move about unmolested, the success that many Greeks enjoyed, and the vast open spaces. Such persons as a rule were ostentatious in their personal behavior and spending habits. Generally the stay in the United States made these returned immigrants more enterprising and ambitious, and instilled in them a desire to improve things. The homes of the returned immigrants were usually better than those of the neighbors who had not been to the United States, and their economic status was generally higher. Often villagers were persuaded to come to the United States to obtain for themselves and their families some of the riches that the repatriates spoke about.[96]

Steamship companies and their agents, who were very active in distributing highly colored posters and other advertising materials, were another factor in the situation. The Repouli Report observed in 1912 that the most popular, if not the only decoration of the small coffee house, the public meeting hall, and the grocery store of every village in Greece was posters of transoceanic liners and literature promoting emigration to the United States.[97] The degree to which such advertisements influenced emigration is open to speculation. The Immigration Commission felt that because Greece in relation to her population furnished more emigrants than any

95. Repouli, *A Study of Immigration*, p. 57.
96. Saloutos, *They Remember America*, pp. 117–131.
97. Repouli, *A Study of Immigration*, p. 57.

other country, the likelihood was that the solicitation by steamship companies probably played only a minor role.[98]

Newspaper accounts and books that glamorized and popularized the United States also contributed to the flow of emigration. In September 1899 Constantine N. Maniakes, the acting attorney-general of the Supreme Court of Greece (Areopagus) wrote President William McKinley that "The benefits which the Greeks derived from the noble and benevolent exertions of the Great American Nation of the United States are innumerable. . . . Greece has discovered in the United States a great Patron, who pitied her her misfortunes and succored her needs."[99] In the fall of 1898 he wrote two articles that appeared in the *Acropolis* of Athens, a daily newspaper, which praised the United States, American institutions, the way the Americans celebrated Thanksgiving Day, and the prosperity of the average man. Thanksgiving Day was "the festival . . . of all classes of society. . . . every household in all the large territory of the forty-five states of America . . . was praying and fasting." In commenting on the opportunities in the United States, Maniakes wrote:

. . . citizens find themselves in the agreeable situation of acquiring by their labors, easily, all that is necessary for a comfortable life. Their exercises . . . have lucrative and useful results. . . . Prosperity in America, is not the exclusive privilege of certain classes. Every diligent man, helped by the state, is able to acquire easily what is necessary for the support and comfort of himself and family; thus all, by their combined efforts and mutual aid, succeed in furthering the progress of science and the cultivation of the fine arts.[100]

In his eulogistic and uncritical account Maniakes emphasized how it was possible for the small man to rise to a higher social and economic level, how it was possible for a small number of men to raise enough wheat on virgin soil to feed thousands of people, how the Americans understood it was impossible for agriculture to advance without encouragement to industries, how education was for the many and not the few, and how advancement, progress, and power came in proportion to the cares and toil of each member

98. *Abstracts of Reports of the Immigration Commission*, I, 191–192.
99. Constantine N. Maniakes, *America and Greece* (Athens, 1899), pp. i–ii.
100. *Ibid.*, pp. 3–4.

of the state.[101] Although the better-informed Greeks realized that this was a highly exaggerated portrayal of conditions in the United States at the time, and probably did not accept the observations of the attorney-general at face value, his comments are an indication that Greeks had become alerted to the opportunities offered by the United States.

Books circulating in Greece—such as *The Immigrants*, by Emmanuel Lekoude, which besides decrying the outflow of Greeks to the United States, gave a fair account of the causes of emigration at the start of the twentieth century—probably stimulated the curiosity of many. So did *The Nation of Wealth*, by G. M. Marinou, inspired by the work and writings of Andrew Carnegie.[102] A comparable small volume, *America and the Americans*, by N. Gortsi, which furnished a brief survey of the United States, its people and institutions, must also have been read by an appreciable number of people.[103]

In effect, the overriding factor that motivated Greeks to emigrate, especially during the years 1880–1939, was an insatiable drive to better their social and economic status by making it possible for them to lead fuller and more meaningful lives in Greece once they had accomplished their objective in the United States. In 1903 Daniel E. McGinley, the United States consul in Athens, wrote: "A very small percentage of the Greek emigrants go to foreign countries with the intention of remaining there. They all go abroad with the intention of bettering their financial conditions and nearly all intend to return to their native land sooner or later. . . ." In the same report McGinley said that some Greek villages were sending nearly all of their able-bodied men, "the women remaining to till the soil and care for the herds and flocks until the men return."[104]

In 1906 a special commission of the Greek Chamber of Deputies, while recommending that restrictions be placed on emigration from Greece, argued at the same time that emigration was also

---

101. *Ibid.*, pp. 4–7.
102. Emmanuel Lekoude, *The Immigrants* (Athens, 1903), in Greek; G. E. Marinou, *The Land of Wealth*, 6th printing (Athens, 1930), in Greek.
103. N. Gortsi, *America and the Americans* (Athens, 1907), in Greek.
104. *Special Consular Reports, Emigration to the United States*, p. 76.

beneficial to the Mother Country in that the emigrating Greeks, unlike the emigrants from the countries of northern and western Europe, had no intention of establishing new homes in a foreign country.

The Greek in departing from Greece to better his fortune not only has a firm determination to return home as soon as he shall have achieved his objective, but he intends to maintain a close relation with the fatherland during his absence. In emigrating the Greek relies for success upon his individual efforts, and therefore retains all his property in his own country with the exception of what may be necessary to take him to his destination. Moreover, he utilizes his savings in foreign lands in the improvement and development of his property at home. Conscious of the fact that the less hampered his movements are abroad the more certain he will be to succeed, he leaves the members of his family in the home village, and thanks to the close bonds which hold Greek families together, these constitute another link with the fatherland. Not only does he not forget his obligations to them, but when fortune smiles upon him he considers it his first duty to send them means for their own support and also for the maintenance and improvement of the family property. By nature ambitious and above all else, anxious for the good opinion of the people of his village, he attends to the settlement of his debts, and, having a firm determination to return and live in his own country he sends there all the savings of his labor abroad to be deposited in the usual manner, or for the purpose of purchasing real estate or making loans to his fellow villagers. The beneficial consequences of such intercommunication between the emigrant Greek and the mother country are admitted by all to-day.[105]

The statement of the special commission of the Greek Chamber of Deputies was a statement of the ideal rather than the actual situation. The bulk of those who emigrated were youths without families of their own and not family heads. Many among the emigrants who had families of their own remembered them with money remittances, and eventually returned home often with some kind of a fortune. Others remembered their families only temporarily, then forgot them, and did not return to Greece.

Several facts substantiate the argument that most Greeks came to the United States to work and live on a temporary basis: the single, unattached marital status of most of the male emigrants; the temporary character of many of the organizations and Greek-language schools established in the United States, especially in the

105. *Emigration Conditions in Europe*, p. 397.

years prior to World War I, and even the parish churches which remained under the jurisdiction of the Church of Greece until the early 1920's; the keen interest maintained in the politics of the old country, an interest that in many instances exceeded the interest displayed in the politics of the United States; and finally, the sizable number of Greeks who repatriated themselves over the years 1908–1923. The hold of the Mother Country was still strong among the emigrants in the United States.

The single, unattached male was the hope of many parents whose sons had emigrated. This single male was expected to toil in the United States and bring the fruits of his labors home to be shared by the other members of the family. He was more mobile than the family man and in theory less impeded in his efforts, and the hope always prevailed that he would not only labor to help his parents, sisters, and brothers, but also return to Greece to stay and eventually marry a Greek girl.[106]

The character and structure of the Greek-language schools, the courses they offered, and the emphasis they placed on Greek customs and traditions were such as to acquaint the children in the United States with the noble Greek heritage of which their parents were proud, and also to condition them for the day when they would return to Greece and be reabsorbed into Greek society. Although this turned out to be wishful thinking for the majority, the fact that such thoughts dominated the minds of some of the more patriotic, if not fanatical, Greeks cannot be ignored. In the earlier years these schools, with all their shortcomings, were geared to prepare children more for life in Greek than American society. Or as one well-drilled Greek youngster put it: "If you want Greeks give us Greek schools."[107]

Much the same can be said about the orientation of the local societies, of which many were formed in the United States. Membership in these societies, comprised almost entirely of men, at first was based on "former village connections in Greece." Every

106. *Abstracts of Reports of the Immigration Commission*, I, pp. 66–96, for data on the preponderance of male emigrants for the years 1869–1910.

107. *Hellinikos Astir*, March 15 and 22, 1907. See also Theodore Saloutos, *The Greeks in the United States* (Cambridge, 1964), pp. 72–75.

group of ten or twelve people from the same village could launch a society here as a branch of the parent society at home or as a matter of local pride. The principal object was to raise money to send to the village for a school, a church, a road, a water-supply system, or some other public improvement. In the earlier years, the chief interests of these groups lay in the Old World, not in the New.[108]

The Greek always had been a political animal, unbridled in many instances. If at first the Greeks were more concerned with the politics of the local scene at home, their interests in the Mother Country were broadened considerably by the clash between the forces of parliamentary liberalism as best exemplified by Eleutherios Venizelos, the most gifted Greek statesman of the twentieth century, and the royal dynasty headed by King Constantine I. This developed into a civil war of the first magnitude, exceeded in intensity and ferocity only by the civil war that broke out after World War II. Greek community after Greek community in the United States became embroiled in the bitter political dispute that raged at home. Parish churches, Greek-language schools, societies, organizations, and business, family, and social groups were sharply, sometimes permanently, divided. An uninformed outsider, judging from the way the Greeks bruised and mauled each other in their political quarrels, could easily have gained the impression that Venizelos and Constantine were candidates for local political office in the United States.[109] This was probably inevitable in view of the fact that most Greek emigrants had been in the country only a few years, and many still planned to return home as soon as conditions warranted.

Although most of those engaged in the battles between Royalists and Venizelists eventually remained in the United States, peace was restored on the domestic scene by the return to Greece of many who had planned to repatriate themselves, and the growing incli-

108. Vasileos I. Chebithes, *Ahepa and the Progress of Hellenism in America* (New York, 1935), pp. 7–8; M. M. Davis, *Immigrant Health and the Community* (New York, 1921), pp. 101–102.
109. Saloutos, *The Greeks in the United States*, ch. 10, "Royalists Versus Venizelists," pp. 184–209.

nation among American Greeks to forget the politics of the Mother Country and to accept the fact that they were here to stay and become citizens of the United States.[110]

Additional substance is lent to the argument that the overwhelming majority of Greeks originally emigrated to the United States with the intention of remaining only a few years by the statistics of Greek immigrants admitted and Greek emigrant aliens departed. Of the 517,802 Greeks who arrived as immigrants between 1899 and 1931, some 197,088 departed between the years 1908 and 1931.[111] Official statistics on emigrant departures became available for the first time in 1908.[112]

The number of Greek emigrant aliens leaving the United States during the earlier years was less than the average for all nationalities. As against 88,205 admitted from 1908 to 1910, some 21,852 or roughly twenty-five percent left. Of the eastern Mediterranean and Asian peoples, the Greeks at first were the least inclined to leave. More than half as many Koreans, Chinese, Turks, Magyars, Croatians, and South Italians left the United States during these years as entered it, and a relatively smaller number of the Irish, Jews, Welsh, Scots, Armenians, Bohemians, Flemish, Dutch, Portuguese, Ruthenians, English, Lithuanians, and Scandinavians.[113] Later, the picture for the Greeks changed. Of the 4,077,263 emigrant aliens who departed from the United States from 1908 to 1931, the Greeks were exceeded in numbers only by Italians (1,074,-404), Poles (339,428), and English (208,081). Greek departures reached 197,088. This was a relatively high total for a people whose numbers in the United States had not reached half a million prior to World War II, and whose own country's population ranged between five and six millions.[114] See Table V.

110. Chebithes, *Ahepa and the Progress of Hellenism in America*, pp. 24, 26–28.

111. *Annual Report of the Commissioner General of Immigration, 1931* (Washington, 1931), pp. 226–227.

112. *Annual Report of the Commissioner General of Immigration, 1907* (Washington, 1907), p. 45. This was made possible by the insertion of a provision into the law of 1907 requiring shipmasters of departing vessels to file accurate and detailed lists of alien passengers.

113. U. S. Senate, *Reports of the Immigration Commission, Statistical Review of Immigration, 1870–1910*, pp. 372, 383–384.

114. *Annual Report of the Commissioner General of Immigration, 1931*, p. 227.

Table V

GREEK EMIGRANT ALIENS DEPARTED, 1908–1940

| Year | Number Giving Greece as Country of Intended Permanent Residence | By "Race or People" |
|---|---|---|
| 1908 | 6,131 | 6,763 |
| 1909 | 5,606 | 6,275 |
| 1910 | 8,144 | 8,814 |
| 1911 | 9,376 | 11,134 |
| 1912 | 11,461 | 13,323 |
| 1913 | 30,603 | 31,556 |
| 1914 | 11,124 | 11,266 |
| 1915 | 9,775 | 9,767 |
| 1916 | 4,829 | 4,855 |
| 1917 | 2,034 | 2,082 |
| 1918 | 2,986 | 2,952 |
| 1919 | 15,482 | 15,562 |
| 1920 | 20,314 | 20,319 |
| 1921 | 13,423 | 13,470 |
| 1922 | 7,506 | 7,649 |
| 1923 | 2,988 | 3,060 |
| 1924 | 7,250 | 7,335 |
| 1925 | 6,574 | 6,659 |
| 1926 | 5,164 | 5,188 |
| 1927 | 3,130 | 3,140 |
| 1928 | 2,461 | 2,525 |
| 1929 | 1,736 | 1,793 |
| 1930 | 733 | 785 |
| 1931 | 753 | 816 |
| 1932 | 1,406 | 1,607 |
| 1933 | 1,277 | 1,402 |
| 1934 | 644 | 721 |
| 1935 | 402 | 450 |
| 1936 | 807 | 842 |
| 1937 | 374 | 406 |
| 1938 | 460 | 477 |
| 1939 | 470 | 493 |
| 1940 | 261 | 280 |

SOURCES: *Annual Report of the Commissioner General of Immigration, 1920*, pp. 188–189; *1930*, pp. 215–216; *1931*, p. 227; *Statistical Abstract of the United States, 1933*, pp. 95, 97; *1936*, pp. 99, 101; *1938*, pp. 100–101; *1941*, pp. 110–111.

The reasons the Greeks repatriated themselves varied. Some returned because they had made money in the United States and preferred the more leisurely and congenial life of Greece; some because they found life in the United States unsatisfying; some allegedly because of poor health and their wives' wishing to be closer to their families; some because of their desire to die in the land of their birth; and some because they believed Greece was a better country to live and raise a family in.[115]

Since the decision to remain in the United States permanently, at least for those who arrived during the period of mass emigration, came as an afterthought and was not a part of the original design, one may ask when the decision was reached to remain here permanently. When one well-established and financially secure former immigrant was asked this question he replied: "It came gradually. I got married, began to raise a family and was immobilized."[116] Another, who came to the United States in 1901, filed his declaration of intention to become an American citizen in 1910.[117]

World War I was the great period of decision for many. The war years gave many Greeks a sense of belonging which they had not possessed before. Greece had been an ally of the United States, which gave many a feeling of kinship, and the American influence in Greece was rising. Thousands of Greeks had joined the armed forces of the United States and the gaining of citizenship had been facilitated by this. Greek-American veterans returned from France with a healthier and more confident outlook on life in the United States. Prior to this they had been unable to boast of kin who had fought for the United States. Now, one Greek-American put it: "We have given our all for this country. We feel we are a part and parcel of it, and we are here to stay. . . ." Still more contributed to the war effort by investing their money in government bonds and working in war industries, and many Greek-Americans emerged

115. Saloutos, *They Remember America*, pp. 29–56.
116. Interview with Mr. G. S., May 11, 1972.
117. Interview with Mr. C. B., May 11, 1972.

financially stronger and psychologically more secure as a result of the lush war years.[118]

Conditions in Greece were not very inviting for a number of years after the war. Political turmoil and instability in Greece, economic hardship, a disastrous military campaign by the Greeks in Asia Minor and the destruction of Smyrna in 1922, political executions that followed in the wake of this disaster and the horror expressed by the world, forced government loans in 1922 and again in 1926, the emergence of a republican form of government followed by a dictatorship and then by the return of Venizelos—all this within the span of a few short years was more than many potential Greek-American repatriates were willing to accept.[119] Hence, the decision to remain in the United States.

## Era of Restricted Immigration

BEGINNING with the 1920's, and especially with 1924, the emigration of Greeks to the United States dropped drastically for a variety of reasons: the immigration restriction acts of 1921 and 1924, the coming of the Great Depression, the spread of totalitarianism that made it especially difficult for young Greeks to leave the country, the outbreak of World War II, and finally the occupation of the country by the Nazis. By far the greatest of these obstacles to the entry of Greeks into the United States was the quota system that kept down admissions from the countries of southern and eastern Europe.

Under the Act of May 19, 1921 the number of aliens of any nationality admissible in any fiscal year was limited to three percent of the number of that nationality residing in the United States in 1910, which made the annual Greek quota 3,063. But because the Act of 1921 was not severe enough, in the eyes of many re-

118. Nicholas G. Kyriakides, "America and Hellenism," *Outlook*, 35 (June 9, 1920), 284–285; *The Ahepa: Pre-Convocation Number* (Washington, September 1926), p. 6.

119. For a brief sketch of the turmoil that besieged Greece during the 1920's see Edward S. Forster, *A Short History of Modern Greece, 1821–1945* (London, 1946), pp. 141–168.

strictionists, the Immigration Act of 1924 limited the number of admissions to two percent of the population of each nationality living in the United States in 1890. The annual quota of Greeks to be admitted fell to 100.[120] The Immigration Act of 1924 became the subject of considerable debate after its enactment, and the quotas, as proclaimed by the President, did not become effective till July 1, 1929. The Greek quota was raised from the 100 stipulated in the Act of 1924 to 307.[121]

Far more than the number of Greeks permitted under the quota system entered the United States because of a provision in the law enabling American citizens to petition for visas for certain relatives. Naturally many Greeks took advantage of this. From 1925 to 1929, only 737 Greeks were admitted under the quota laws, but a total of 10,883 Greeks entered the country.[122] This trend persisted through the 1930's as shown in Table VI.

Table VI

GREEKS ADMITTED INTO THE UNITED STATES, 1930–1940

| Year | Under Quota | Non-Quota Entries By "Race or People" |
|------|-------------|----------------------------------------|
| 1930 | 362 | 3,793 |
| 1931 | 308 | 2,663 |
| 1932 | 141 | 1,105 |
| 1933 | 108 | 687 |
| 1934 | 200 | 696 |
| 1935 | 324 | 1,029 |
| 1936 | 347 | 1,002 |
| 1937 | 370 | 1,004 |
| 1938 | 351 | 1,130 |
| 1939 | 381 | 992 |
| 1940 | 346 | 1,049 |

SOURCES: *Annual Report of the Secretary of Labor, 1934*, p. 58; *1935*, p. 84; *1936*, p. 94; *1937*, p. 87; *1938*, p. 99; *1940*, p. 106; *Annual Report of the Commissioner General of Immigration, 1931*, p. 226; *1932*, p. 62; *Statistical Abstract of the United States, 1936*, p. 101; *1938*, p. 101; *1940*, p. 103; *1943*, p. 105.

120. *Annual Report of the Commissioner General of Immigration 1924* (Washington, 1924), pp. 24–25, 27.
121. *Ibid.*, *1929*, p. 3; *ibid.*, *1930*, p. 11.
122. *Statistical Abstract of the United States, 1938*, p. 102; *Annual Report of the Commissioner General of Immigration, 1931*, p. 226.

The effects that restriction had on Greek emigration can be studied by comparing admissions for the decades 1921–1930 and 1931–1940. The number decreased from 51,084 over the period 1921–1930 to 9,119 for the decade 1931–1940.[123]

A breakdown of the number of immigrant aliens admitted in 1940 by occupation, sex, age groups, and marital status shows some of the changes in the social and economic status of the Greeks arriving then as contrasted with the earlier years. Of the 1,049 admitted in 1940, the largest group, numbering 668 and including women, children, and men of advanced age, was listed with "no occupation." The next largest group, 140, consisted of skilled laborers. Thirty-nine were merchants and dealers, 35 farmers, 34 laborers. The overwhelming majority of the arrivals in 1940 were over 21; the most numerous group fell into the 21- to 30-year age bracket. The females continued to exceed the males in number, 601 to 448.[124]

The number of Greeks arriving from 1941 to 1950 was the lowest on record since the 1880's: only 2,308.[125] Apart from quota restrictions, other reasons for this are obvious: the outbreak of World War II, the invasion of Greece in 1940 by the forces of Benito Mussolini and the beginning of actual warfare between the two countries, followed by the Nazi occupation, the bloody civil war of 1947–1949, and the death and destruction that followed. During most of these years direct communication between the United States and Greece was almost cut off. It was impossible for civilians to travel between the two countries.[126]

123. *Annual Report of the Immigration and Naturalization Service, 1971*, p. 52.

124. U. S. Department of Labor, *Annual Report of the Secretary of Labor, 1940* (Washington, 1941), pp. 104–105.

125. *Annual Report of the Immigration and Naturalization Service, 1971*, p. 52.

126. William H. McNeill, *Greece: American Aid in Action, 1947–1956* (New York, 1957); Betty Wason, *Miracle in Hellas* (New York, 1943); W. Byford-Jones, *The Greek Trilogy* (London, 1945); Compton Mackenzie, *Wind of Freedom* (London, 1943).

## The Refugee Years

THOUGH the quota laws were in effect for two decades after World War II, slightly more than 141,000 Greeks emigrated to the United States from 1946 to 1970.[127] Refugees arrived as a result of specially enacted legislation from which many nationalities profited. The period also witnessed a persistent attack on the quota system, a relaxation in 1965, and finally the complete abandonment of it in 1968.[128]

The death and destruction that Greece endured from the war, which for her began in 1940 and ended in 1949, left her in need of help from the outside to rehabilitate herself and also to drain off the excessive population that emerged shortly after the fighting ceased. As a means of gaining relief from population pressures and unemployment, she tried to encourage some of her people to emigrate to other countries.[129] But these efforts encountered obstacles. In the first decade after World War II, when most of Europe was still recovering from the war, many refugees were relocated on the continent, and there was little in the way of strictly economic migration within Europe.[130] Large-scale entry into the United States had been sealed off by the inflexible quota system. Of the 8,973 Greeks admitted to the United States between 1941 and 1950 more than half arrived during 1947–1948.[131]

Greek emigrants benefited slightly from the refugee legislation enacted by the United States during the postwar decades. Under President Harry S Truman's directive of December 22, 1945, some twenty-eight thousand displaced persons were given visas to the United States by December 1947, but only seven Greeks were

127. *Statistical Abstract of the United States, 1949*, p. 96; *ibid., 1951*, p. 94; *ibid., 1955*, pp. 89–90, 94; *Annual Report of the Commissioner of Immigration and Naturalization, 1960*, p. 43; *ibid., 1970*, p. 54.

128. *New York Times*, March 18, 1963; December 2, 1965.

129. Bank of Athens, *Greece Today* (September 1951), p. 304, a leaflet.

130. Arnold M. Rose, *Migrants in Europe* (Minneapolis, 1969), p. 20.

131. *Statistical Abstract of the United States, 1949*, p. 96; *ibid., 1951*, p. 94.

among them.[132] Legislation to admit four hundred thousand refugees and displaced persons into the United States beyond the existing quotas was debated heatedly during 1947 in Congress and publicized widely by the press.[133] Prospects of such legislation being enacted raised more hope for the displaced persons of Central Europe than for Greeks, who were still locked in a bloody civil war. The Displaced Persons Act of 1948, as amended, provided for the admission of almost four hundred thousand persons from Poland, Germany, Latvia, the Soviet Union, Lithuania, Yugoslavia, and other countries besides Greece. All these "refugee-immigrants" were charged against the future quotas of their countries' birth, if the quotas of these countries had already been oversubscribed. The result was that the quotas of many countries, including Greece, were mortgaged well into the future.[134] Nevertheless, 10,272 Greeks were admitted into the country under the terms of the act.[135]

The Immigration and Nationality Act of 1952, better known as the McCarran-Walter Act, became law on June 27, 1952, despite a vigorous veto message by President Truman, and effective on December 24. Unfortunately, this act offered no relief to the Greeks, whose annual quota was raised from 307 to 308 by its provisions.[136]

Meanwhile Greek-Americans, especially members of the American Hellenic Educational Progressive Association (Ahepa), who believed that their compatriots had fought valiantly on the side of the Allies and were being treated as "second-class citizens," began to marshal their forces, and in cooperation with representatives of other nationality groups who felt discriminated against, continued their assault on the quota system. In the hearings before the President's Commission on Immigration and Naturalization, one of the principal spokesmen of the Ahepa charged that:

132. *Annual Report of the Immigration and Naturalization Service, 1971*, p. 35; *Britannica Book of the Year, 1948* (Chicago, 1948), p. 640.

133. *Britannica Book of the Year, 1948*, p. 640.

134. Schwartz, *The Open Society*, p. 107.

135. *Annual Report of the Immigration and Naturalization Service, 1971*, p. 35.

136. Schwartz, *The Open Society*, p. 108; "President Truman's Veto Message to the House on the Veto of Immigration Bill," in Benjamin M. Ziegler, ed., *Immigration, An American Dilemma* (Boston, 1953), pp. 97–103.

The American consulates, everywhere, are required to presume that anyone applying for an immigration visa has some evil design for the destruction of the Government, industry, and morality of the American people. Every applicant is immediately shouldered with the burden of proving—to the satisfaction of the consul, to the Attorney-General, to the Secretary of State, to the Secretary of Labor, and to the President of the United States—that he does not plan any harm to the American people and Government, and that he is not likely to acquire any habits or notions, or to make any mistakes which may reduce him to a state of poverty and want.

After the prospective immigrant complies with these requirements and is admitted, his conduct here is not judged by the regularly established system of determining justice before the open courts of the Republic, but he is subject to the rules, regulations, and discriminatory sensibilities of the Attorney General. This does not mean that the Attorney General, or the Secretaries of State, Labor, or Commerce, are personally cognizant of how the alien's case is handled and decided. The alien's accusers, prosecutors, judges, juries, and executors of the sentence passed against him are the agents and employees of the Immigration and Naturalization Service. It often happens that all these functions are performed by one and the same person.[137]

Many Greek-Americans viewed the McCarran-Walter Act as an anticlimax to the Displaced Persons Act of 1948 that had given a ray of hope to thousands of Greeks as well as Europeans. Those unfortunate Greeks who were unable to qualify in time to come under the Displaced Persons Act hoped that Congress would pass a liberal immigration act so they, too, would be able to qualify later; but the McCarran-Walter Act "shut the door tightly and extinguished that hope." Consequently, Greek-Americans joined with others who began pressing for a revision of the quota system and the adoption of a more equitable one, and who wanted Congress to pass a new act that would permit more displaced persons to come to the United States.[138]

Even for those whose prospects of coming to the United States appeared good, on paper at least, and those Greeks offering to adopt orphans, the obstacles were formidable. The American sponsor of a prospective emigrant had to prepare various papers to send

---

137. U. S. Congress, *Hearings Before the President's Commission on Naturalization and Immigration*, 82 Cong., 2 Sess. (Washington, 1952), pp. 216–217.

138. *Ibid.*, p. 349.

to the American consulate in Greece, which in turn notified the local persons involved to appear before one of its officers to answer certain questions regarding the petition to enter the country. This was further complicated by the fact that the consulate often was a great distance from the home of the potential emigré. The sponsor and the would-be immigrant had to be blood relatives, which made it difficult, if not impossible, for many to come to the United States because they did not have qualified relatives to invite them. For those who wanted to adopt orphans, it was expensive to go to Greece to adopt them at the probate court. The adoption papers when forwarded by the American consulate in Greece to the United States were often rejected under the discretionary powers of some officer in the State Department.[139]

The extent to which Greeks were pressing for admission into the United States may be gleaned from a study of the oversubscribed quotas and the number of Greek registrations. As of August 1, 1952, when the Greek quota happened to be 310 instead of 308, the Greek quota was mortgaged under the Displaced Persons Act of 1948 to the year 2014, and Greek registrants who wanted to enter the United States numbered 24,227. The estimated time a registrant would have had to wait, on the basis of these estimates, before a quota number would become available for him to enter the United States was placed at seventy-eight years.[140]

Although the basic immigration policy of the Immigration Act of 1924 remained in force until 1965, the quota system was severely eroded by special legislative enactments. The most important of these was the Refugee Relief Act of 1953, which made possible the admission of more than two hundred thousand refugees, mostly from Europe. Almost seventeen thousand Greeks were admitted under this act.[141]

The next important measure was the Act of September 11, 1957 that liberalized a number of provisions in the Act of 1953 and permitted the entry of another fifty-seven thousand non-quota im-

139. *Ibid.*, p. 536.
140. *Ibid.*, p. 1900.
141. *Annual Report of the Immigration and Naturalization Service, 1971*, p. 35.

migrants. This measure also "repealed the mortgaging of quotas provided for in the Displaced Persons Act of 1948," and represented another "assault on the spirit and letter of the national origins system."[142] Another 1,504 Greeks were admitted under its provisions.[143]

Beginning in the early 1960's the volume of emigration from Greece began to increase as shown in Table VII. This revived exodus of Greeks for foreign lands was attributable to familiar reasons. Greece lacked jobs for her people, despite energetic efforts to increase the productivity of the nation, the rise in the per capita income of the people, the creation of new employment opportunities, and the maintenance of a satisfactory annual rate of growth. In early 1960, the number of unemployed in Greece was in excess of 275,000, in a nation of 8,200,000 whose per capita income ranged between $200 and $299 annually.[144]

Table VII

EMIGRATION FROM GREECE, 1956–1969

| Year | Number | Year | Number |
|------|--------|------|--------|
| 1956 | 35,349 | 1963 | 100,072 |
| 1957 | 30,428 | 1964 | 105,072 |
| 1958 | 24,521 | 1965 | 117,167 |
| 1959 | 23,684 | 1966 | 86,896 |
| 1960 | 47,768 | 1967 | 42,730 |
| 1961 | 58,837 | 1968 | 50,866 |
| 1962 | 84,054 | 1969 | 91,552 |

SOURCES: For 1956–1963 see National Bank of Greece, *Greece Today* (April 1964), diagram 1, p. 28; *ibid.* (April 1966), p. 38; *ibid.* (May 1966), p. 58. See also the Bank of Greece, *The Greek Economy in 1968* (Athens, 1969), p. 48; *Report of the Governor of the Bank of Greece, 1969* (Athens, 1969), p. 47; in Greek.

From 1961 to 1965 emigration to the United States fluctuated between 3,002 and 4,825 annually, which indicated that no drastic increase in numbers had occurred, although this figure was well

142. Schwartz, *The Open Society*, pp. 109–111.
143. *Annual Report of the Immigration and Naturalization Service, 1971*, p. 35.
144. *New York Times*, January 10, 1960.

above the 308 quota limit.[145] Meanwhile, Greek-Americans, particularly the members of the Ahepa, kept agitating and hoping "for a more just and equitable quota for Greece and liberalized Refugee and Orphan legislation."[146]

As in the earlier years, draft evasion continued to harass the Greek authorities, especially during the 1960's when a sizable number left Greece permanently or temporarily in search of jobs abroad. According to the Greek authorities, some used their sojourn abroad as a means of avoiding the draft, which called for twenty-four months of service for all able-bodied men between the ages of 21 and 50. Estimates of the number abroad who were avoiding the draft varied. Some claimed that as many as fifty thousand Greek males living abroad had evaded the draft unwittingly or deliberately. In mid-August 1963, the chief of the draft section of the Greek General Staff said: "There are about twenty thousand Greeks living abroad who are listed as draft evaders." The Greek government, as a consequence, enforced a regulation effective July 1, 1963, providing that all native-Greek males who had acquired foreign citizenship without serving in the Greek armed forces had to do their service or pay a penalty.[147]

In applying the new code the Greek authorities apparently cast their net too wide and all visiting Americans of Greek origin were compelled to prove they were not draft evaders before they were permitted to leave the country.[148] Among those detained and harassed for some weeks were Greeks who had acquired foreign nationality on immigrant visas, naturalized Greek-Americans who already had served twenty-four months in the armed forces of either the United States or Greece, naturalized Greek-Americans who had done less than the required twenty-four months of service, and naturalized Greek-Americans who had never done service. Estimates of the number of Greek-Americans who would be subject to this law if they went to Greece came to seven hundred.[149]

145. *Annual Report of the Commissioner of Immigration and Naturalization, 1970*, p. 64.
146. Order of Ahepa, *1958 Year Book* (Washington, 1958), A26–27.
147. *New York Times*, August 11, 15, and 18, 1963.
148. *Ibid.*, August 18, 1963.
149. *Ibid.*, August 11, 1963.

The reaction against this law was vigorous not only on the part of those affected or likely to be affected, but also on the part of the Greek press and the Greek tourist trade which depended greatly on the Greek-American tourists. About half of the 120,000 Americans who visited Greece each year were of Greek descent.[150] Only after Henry L. Labouisse, the United States ambassador to Greece, informed the premier of Greece that the State Department was going to release a statement warning Greek-born Americans of the risks involved in visiting Greece did the authorities agree to suspend the draft rule.[151]

The domestic uproar against the draft rule as a threat to the tourist trade focused attention upon the actual number of persons born in Greece living abroad. Official statistics in August 1963 showed that nearly 2,500,000 persons of Greek birth were living in foreign countries. Greece, herself, at the time had a population of about 9,000,000. Of those living abroad, according to this source, by far the largest number lived in the United States. They lived in 384 communities, had 357 churches, 500 schools with 22,519 pupils, 595 Greek Orthodox Sunday schools, 670 organizations, and 58 Greek newspapers and periodicals.[152]

Nineteen sixty-five was a turning point in Greek emigration to the United States. The Immigration Act of 1965, by putting an end to the national-origins system in the allocation of immigrant quotas and expanding the non-quota and quota preference status that favored the entry of relatives, refugees, and persons with certain qualifications, gave new hope to Greeks, who were expected to arrive in larger numbers.[153] The old quota system was abandoned by stages, and ended completely in mid-1968. Between the time the Immigration Act of 1965 went into partial effect and July 1, 1968, when it went into full effect, those portions of the quotas that remained unused by the nations to which they were assigned were

150. *Ibid.*
151. *Ibid.*, September 7, 1963.
152. *Ibid.*, August 25, 1963.
153. Edward P. Hutchinson, "The New Immigration: An Introductory Comment," *The Annals*, 367 (September 1966), 1–2; "A New Mix For America's Melting Pot," *United States News and World Report*, 59 (October 11, 1965), 55–57.

divided among the countries that had been overfilling their quotas. The unfilled quotas had been running at about sixty thousand a year. Greece, along with Italy, Poland, and Portugal, were the nations with the largest number of people awaiting admittance. When the Immigration Act of 1965 became law some 98,385 Greeks were waiting for admission into the United States. They were exceeded in number only by the Italians, who had roughly two hundred fifty thousand on the waiting list.[154]

The provisions of the Immigration Act of 1965 had much to say about who could and who could not come to the United States as immigrants. Those with relatives in the country were to find it easier to gain admission than those without them; and preference was to be given to those who had skills the United States Department of Labor said were needed. An annual limit of twenty thousand admissions was placed on each country, "a 170,000 overall limit for Asia, Africa and Europe, and the 120,000 limit for the Western Hemisphere." In addition, outside the overall limitations, members of the "immediate families" of United States residents, estimated at about fifty thousand a year, were to be admitted. The total number of immigrants to be admitted into the country was about three hundred forty thousand a year, with the possibility of temporary annual bulges as proved to be the case each year from 1967 through 1971.[155]

The influx was substantial. From 1966 through 1971 a total of 86,344 Greeks entered the country, as Table VIII shows. The largest number to be admitted in any single year was in 1969, with 17,724, the largest number of Greeks to have entered the country since 1921, when more than thirty-one thousand arrived. More than ten thousand came during five of these six years, and more than fifteen thousand during three of these years.[156] This period ranks almost, but not quite, with the immediate pre- and post–World War I years in the number of arrivals.

154. "A New Mix For America's Melting Pot," p. 57.
155. *Ibid.*, p. 55; *Annual Report of the Immigration and Naturalization Service, 1971*, p. 54.
156. *Ibid.*, p. 14; *Annual Report of the Commissioner General of Immigration, 1930*, p. 214.

Table VIII

GREEKS ADMITTED INTO THE UNITED STATES, 1966–1971

| Year | Number | Year | Number |
|------|--------|------|--------|
| 1966 | 8,265 | 1969 | 17,724 |
| 1967 | 14,905 | 1970 | 16,464 |
| 1968 | 13,047 | 1971 | 15,939 |
| | | Total | 86,344 |

SOURCE: *Annual Report of Immigration and Naturalization Service, 1971*, p. 54.

It is difficult to determine how much the military coup of April 21, 1967, influenced the departure of Greeks for the United States. More than ninety-eight thousand Greeks were waiting to come to the United States when the Immigration Act of 1965 went into effect. These people had preference over those whose departure would be caused primarily by the military coup. Emigration to the United States was not merely a matter of picking up one's belongings and leaving. It cost money and much preparation. Long periods of time elapsed between making the decision to emigrate and the actual departure itself. In the long run those who were dissatisfied enough with the political turn of events to want to leave would show up in the immigration statistics. Many emigrants who were unhappy at the junta's seizure of power probably had planned to leave well in advance of the coup. The seizure of power by the junta cannot be listed as the prime cause of their departure.

## Conclusion

EMIGRATION of Greeks to the United States was primarily a twentieth-century phenomenon, even though evidence of their arrival can be traced back to colonial and precolonial times. The United States, once it became widely advertised and known in Greece, was the most popular country with those who chose to emigrate overseas temporarily or permanently. The reasons were best summed up in 1912 by a committee of the Greek Chamber of Deputies:

It is the strength of a new nation, strong, energetic, drastic, tireless, taking giant strides forward, building large cities, creating excellent opportunities, advancing civilization vigorously and happily. It is the strength [of a nation] with colossal capital in circulation, and capable of providing means of transportation on the ocean and into the interior which beckons the myriads of working hands.[157]

The bulk of the Greeks originally came with the thought of working for a few years, amassing savings, discharging obligations, providing for the marriage of their sisters, and returning to Greece to lead economically more secure lives. The decision to remain in the United States permanently came as an afterthought. Factors that influenced this decision included: a better understanding of the language, customs, and traditions of the new country to which they had emigrated; the establishment of businesses, permanency of employment, and families; and a comparison of conditions that prevailed in the United States and those at home, usually to the disadvantage of the latter.

In later years, especially in the late 1950's, the 1960's, and the early 1970's thousands of Greeks emigrated to the Federal Republic of Germany, Canada, and Australia. Many would have preferred to come to the United States but till late in this period they were barred by the quota restrictions. The passage of the Immigration Act of 1965 facilitated the entry of more Greeks during the late 1960's and early 1970's. The big waves of Greek immigration came from 1900 to 1914, in the immediate wake of World War I, and after 1965, periods which for the most part were relatively prosperous.

Significant differences were noticeable in the social and economic status of the arrivals before and after World War II. Before World War II most of the emigrants were of peasant origin, limited in education and occupational skills. The need in the United States

157. Repouli, *A Study of Immigration*, p. 34.

had been primarily for immigrants with strong backs and strong arms, capable of doing the heavy work required in an industrial nation. After World War II more members of the professional classes, the skilled occupations, and the educated groups came to the United States. The majority, however, were still of peasant origins or not far removed from them, despite claims that they came directly from Athens, Piraeus, Salonika, and other cities.

The reasons for coming in the later years resembled those in earlier years: the desire to escape from the ravages of war, famine, or death, to lead better and more secure lives in the United States, and to escape from military service. The presence of Greek relatives and friends already established in the United States, and the satisfaction of living in a strong and wealthy country friendly to Greece facilitated the process. There is no demonstrable evidence that sizable numbers of Greeks emigrated because of the military coup of 1967. The United States will probably continue to be the country to which most Greeks will prefer to emigrate as long as remittances from this country to Greece remain high, and stories of economic success continue to filter back into Greece.[158]

158. Bank of Greece, *Monthly Statistical Bulletin*, 37 (September 1972), 61.

# ON BECOMING AN EMIGRANT: A STRUCTURAL VIEW OF EIGHTEENTH- AND NINETEENTH-CENTURY SWISS DATA

Leo Schelbert

# ON BECOMING AN EMIGRANT: A STRUCTURAL VIEW OF EIGHTEENTH- AND NINETEENTH-CENTURY SWISS DATA

## Introduction

The search for gain encourages the Swiss to emigration; it is furthermore stimulated by a variety of notices published in newspapers. It is true that the spirit of emigration has always existed among the Swiss, and they have generally been too optimistic about life abroad. I believe that each emigrant comes here of his own free will; however, family affairs, reversals of fortune are often the causes which make him leave his homeland.*

F. Schaller, Swiss consul in Algiers, 1842

ON July 15, 1845, the Glarnese emigrant Mathias Dürst, on his way to southern Wisconsin, noted in his diary:

This day the captain had a search made for me all over the boat and when he found me I was on deck busy with my diary. He sat down near me with an interpreter and asked me a hundred questions. Why had we come to this country? How big was our country? What were the conditions? What products? What earnings? What kind of climate, religion, government, etc.? During and after the conversation he expressed pitying amazement. No wonder, said he, that so many thousands of people come to this country.[1]

The questions as well as the amazement of the inquisitive captain whose boat carried the Glarnese emigrants from Pittsburgh to St.

---

*Émigrations Suisses. Enquête auprès de Messieurs les Consuls de la Confédération en Europe, dans le Nord de l'Afrique, l'Amérique du Nord, l'Amérique Centrale et du Sud (Lausanne, 1845), p. 27.

1. Leo Schelbert, ed., New Glarus 1845–1970. The Making of a Swiss American Town (Glarus, 1970), pp. 101–105. The book contains a bilingual edition of the diary.

Louis have remained typical. In both the countries of origin and of destination people have wondered why emigrants have permanently left their native land and settled on foreign shores.

One persistent explanation is echoed in a recent introduction to autobiographical sketches of American immigrants: "For the America of freedom has been an America of sacrifice, and the cost of becoming an American has been high. For every freedom won, a tradition lost."[2] The implication is clear; the reason for emigration was (and has remained) a flight from oppression to freedom—to religious, political, social, or economic freedom. Thus a recent scholarly study on European emigration to the United States discusses "the sudden upsurge of emigration . . . in the late 1860's" from Norway and Sweden as accompanied by "resentment at the concentration of power in the hand of officials, at imperfect representation in the legislature, at high taxes, and at military service. . . ." In brief, the main forces that dislocated people and brought them to America were discontent at home and attractions abroad.[3] The United States in particular was "the promised land, . . . the land of the emigrants' choice."

A similar, if reverse, appraisal is often made by commentators who view emigration from the vantage point of the country of origin. In 1744, for instance, Leonhard Holzhalb (1685–1748), pastor of the parish of Henggart, Canton Zurich, commented to the antistes (i.e., presiding officer) of the Zurich Church:

Nothing seemed as grievous to me as the headlong, irresponsible emigration of those heartless parents with their many little innocent children. I was at the time dangerously ill, otherwise I would have thrown up barricades of chairs and benches to prevent it; [I] also immediately sent the magistrates to the Honorable Bailiff [to confer] in the matter, yet everything for naught. Thus my sickness was made all the more bitter for me, and these people were as if under a spell and a desperate resolution since most of them were poor and had barely gotten together enough travel money.[4]

2. Thomas C. Wheeler, ed., *The Immigrant Experience. The Anguish of Becoming an American* (Baltimore, 1972), p. 1.

3. Philip Taylor, *The Distant Magnet* (London, 1972), pp. 27, 31.

4. The originals of Holzhalb's and the other reports in "Verzeichnisse der Ausgewanderten nach Carolina und Pennsylvanien 1734–1744," Staatsarchiv Zurich, A.174; edition in English by Albert B. Faust, ed., *Lists of Swiss Emigrants in the Eighteenth Century to the*

In this man's view—echoed by most of his colleagues who reported on some twenty-two hundred people who had left—emigrants represented the restless and irresponsible fringe of the otherwise stable inhabitants of the commonwealth. A similar view is taken by Matthias Oertle (1777–1837), deputy of the Canton of Appenzell to the Federal Diet in 1817:

Now that trade and manufacture are at a complete standstill, and prices of all foodstuffs are very high after several years of crop failure, a main reason for emigration is need. Another might be found in moral corruption, the real source of increased demands and reduced prosperity, in many people's dissatisfaction with their fate. In a certain restlessness of mind which is increasingly taking hold of the people. Lastly, there can be no doubt that base self-interest has used many different enticements to lure the credulous.[5]

According to this interpreter, then, emigrants were people who left their country not only because of momentary economic distress, but because of moral decay and proneness to deception.

Even to a group of Swiss men who felt motivated by "a paternal and philanthropic interest," emigrants remained victims of seduction. Their questionnaire, elaborated in 1841 and sent to all Swiss consuls abroad, dealt with the question of causes in the following manner: "How were the Swiss," they inquired, "established in the country, pushed to this emigration? At the instigation of already established emigrants? By Swiss or by foreign publications? By American, Dutch, or other propagandists?"[6] A scholarly article published in 1885 summarized this approach succinctly: "The emigration from a country which, more than any other, is likely to arouse in its citizens the strongest feelings of attachment because of its natural beauty, its liberal institutions, and its well-ordered conditions, is one of the strangest phenomena."[7]

---

American Colonies, I, Zurich 1734–1744 (Washington, 1920; reprinted Baltimore, 1968), hereafter cited as Lists, I. Faust's edition is unfortunately marred by many errors, some ninety of them are corrected in Leo Schelbert, "Notes on 'Lists of Swiss Emigrants,' " National Genealogical Society Quarterly, 50 (March 1972), 38–42. On Holzhalb (and the other ministers) see Emmanuel Dejung and Willy Wuhrmann, Zürcher Pfarrerbuch 1519–1952 (Zurich, 1953), p. 350.

5. Abschied der . . . ordentlichen eidgenössischen Tagsatzung 1817 (Bern, 1847), pp. 163–164.

6. Émigrations Suisses. Enquête, p. 2.

7. Alfred Furrer, Volkswirtschafts-Lexikon der Schweiz (Bern, 1885), I, 104–105.

Why, one may ask, is much of the historiography dealing with emigration dominated by such generalized and impressionistic views? One reason is ideological in nature. Migration histories generally share the nationalist framework which underlies many historical studies pertaining to the era since 1500. The last five hundred years are basically viewed as the story of the growth and interaction of competing nation states. History is seen as the story of nations, with the prevalent assumption that the nation of which the historian is a member is the best or at least among the most vigorous, creative, and attractive human communities. Seen from their country of origin, emigrants are ungrateful, disturbed, and misguided people. Economic distress, occupational dislocations, political upheavals, distasteful service in wars, or ideological conflicts occurring within the boundaries of the historian's own nation are perceived as occasional trials common to all societies. Immigrants to the same nation are viewed as among the most courageous, enterprising, and enlightened members of their original communities—those who had seen a better life beckoning them elsewhere and had enough strength to respond to the call. In this manner the migratory phenomenon becomes easily embedded in national self-assertion and is offered as telling proof of the adopted nation's superior institutions and life-style.

A second reason for summary and one-sided views about the causes of migration pertains to the nature of the evidence. "Only when we examine . . . districts and townships," remarks an astute observer of migration history, "and trace the fortunes of their native sons, do we begin to understand the true anatomy of migration."[8] The historian dealing with migration is faced with an endless variation of local and regional conditions at the migrant's origin as well as destination. What may hold for an upper part of a valley may not be true for its lower region. Economic conditions may be attractive in one section of a seemingly integrated area, but

---

8. Frank Thistlethwaite, "Migration Overseas in the Nineteenth and Twentieth Centuries," Comité International des Sciences Historiques, ed., *Rapports*, V (1960), 43; similarly Taylor, *Distant Magnet*, p. 27; his work, however, follows this premise in only a limited way.

unfavorable in another. Social and political life may be highly stratified in one place, yet open and in flux in the next. To these local
variations the personal dimension has to be added. Characteristics
of individuals decisively enter the migratory process and add to
its complexity. The combination of individual modes of behavior
and motivation with regional variations makes generalizing on the
causes of migration a difficult task.

Yet, the question persists whether behind all these local and personal variations an underlying common structure can be discovered
that is operative in every case where at least a modicum of decision
making is involved. Could this structural unity, furthermore, free
the study of migration, especially of its causes, from bondage to
nationalism? The present study is an effort to achieve this result by
analyzing selected eighteenth- and nineteenth-century Swiss data.

## 1. The Process Defined

IN the diary of Niklaus Dürst (1797–1874), who served in 1845
as a scout for a Swiss emigrant group which was to settle in
southern Wisconsin, the following entry is to be found:

1845 on July 17th, we purchased for the esteemed Emigration Society of
the Canton of Glarus, at the land office in *Mineral Point, Wisconsin Territory*,
1200 (twelve hundred) acres of land, namely in *Greene County* township 4
range 7, at the government price of 1 ¼ dollars per acre which on the following days we had surveyed and divided up in 60 lots (parcels) by the surveyor
*Comfort* whom we had to pay wages of 3 dollars per day.

Sunday, 20th inst. Mr. Friedrich Streiff and myself, together with our present wagoner Mr. Friedrich Rudolf of Zurzach (Switzerland) have moved
into our colony of *New Glarus*, we have on this day done the first work on
our shelters, lit the *first fire* in this very place, took the first food, caught the
first fish in the brook [?] had the *first bread* baked by myself, slept for the *first
time* in this very place, and on this day the said Mr. Rudolf fetched for us a
load of *lumber* or *boards* at a saw mill.

Mr. Frey, our co-worker, who in the meantime [had gone] from here to
*Mineral Point* to *Como* in *Illinois* in the belief that the emigrants were there, to

welcome them and to accompany them to the colony, but returned on the 22nd inst. with the report, so disappointing to us, that he had neither met up with the emigrants nor received any letters from Mr. M. H. Blumer. In the days following his return we had the land surveyed and divided up, as mentioned above, and on the 6th of August he travelled back home.

Then on the 8th inst. in a manner most remarkable to us, two men came from the emigrants, P. Grob and M. Dürst, and brought us the welcome report that the emigrants for whom we had waited so long had arrived in St. Louis several days ago already and were waiting for us, and had sent them out to search for us (as they had heard that we were dead) until they had information about us etc.

On the morning of the 9th I travelled back with them to receive the emigrants in St. Louis; however, on the 11th inst. we already met up with them in Galena, had to wait there a few days because of the *wagon teams* so that on the 17th finally we could move into the Colony with the emigrants.

On the 20th inst. the first chickens were bought by the emigrant Fridolin Becker of Ennenda and taken to the Colony, and on the 23rd the first three cows and three calves were bought . . . and taken to the Colony.[9]

Thus began a new community in the Western hemisphere, one of the hundreds of thousands of successful settlements since the first arrival of white men in 1492. What had brought these 119 Glarnese people to the fertile woodlands of southern Wisconsin?

Niklaus Dürst, a baker and sawyer by trade who also served on the school board of his home commune and as justice of the peace of his district, had travelled over 1,530 miles since his arrival in Chicago on May 19, 1845. From there he and his companions had launched a prolonged and arduous search for a suitable place for his emigrating compatriots.[10] His joy on the day of moving to the newly acquired lands is thus easily understood. That Sunday of July 20th was for this man a truly memorable day, a day almost of creation. The "first work" on the shelters was then begun, the

---

9. Schelbert, *New Glarus*, pp. 147–149. Niklaus Dürst is not to be confused with Mathias Dürst of the emigrant group, the diarist of their journey.

10. See Dieter Brunnschweiler, *New Glarus* [*Wisconsin*]. *Gründung, Entwicklung und heutiger Zustand einer Schweizerkolonie in amerikanischen Mittelwesten* (Zurich, 1954), pp. 27–28; p. 26, a map of the route taken by N. Dürst and his collaborators which took them to St. Louis and far into Missouri and Iowa. They traveled some 370 miles on boat, 548 by horse and wagon, 279 by postal coach, and 333 on foot.

"first fire" was lit, the "first bread" baked. Before, man had been absent from that beautiful spot, now destined to serve his countrymen for generations to come. A beautiful and fertile stretch of land full of brooks and trees and rich in fish and fowl had on that Sunday become the domain of man. This consciousness, expressed by a humble man from a random settlement in Europe, points to perhaps the most basic "cause"—actually a complex web of processes—for this and many other migrations involving in all tens of millions of emigrants; the consciousness that whole continents were waiting to be occupied by white men.

The earliest map published of the new settlement had an area marked off as "Indian Village."[11] But this village was seemingly not to count; its fires were apparently non-fires; the catching of fish by its inhabitants was not the same as the white man's endeavor; their centuries- if not millennia-old residence amounted to non-occupancy. A double question arises: when and how was this particular area "cleared" of its native inhabitants and the opportunity for white settlement created? And how did this opportunity come to be known thousands of miles away and how were people induced to take advantage of it?

Only some forty-five years before the arrival of the 119 Swiss, the region within whose borders they were to settle was still in the secure possession of two nations indigenous to the Western hemisphere, the Osakiwug or "The People of the Yellow Earth," and the Meshkwakihug or "The People of the Red Earth." They numbered some five to six thousand people if white estimates are to be trusted.[12] These people had settled in the area some two hundred years earlier, pushing southward members of the Illinois nation in response to the white intrusion into the St. Lawrence and Great

11. Map at end of *Der glarnerische Auswanderungs-Verein und die Colonie Neu-Glarus. Hauptbericht des Auswanderungs-Comite*, Mit zwei Karten (Glarus, 1847).

12. These nations are commonly called in white historiography Sauk and Foxes, the first a corruption of the native name, the second a misnomer. Some basic data on them in John R. Swanton, *The Indian Tribes of North America* (Washington, 1952, reprinted 1969), pp. 250–251, 256–257.

Lakes regions which had overthrown the area's ecological and demographic balance.[13]

The two nations lived in villages scattered between the Mississippi and the Rock Rivers. The main settlement of the Osakiwug
is especially noteworthy. A visitor of 1766 gave the following
description:

> On the 8th of October 1766 we got our canoes into the Ouisconsin River,
> which at this place is more than a hundred yards wide; and the next day ar-
> rived at the Great Town of the Saukies. This is the largest and best built In-
> dian town I ever saw. It contains about ninety houses, each large enough for
> several families. These are built of hewn plank, neatly jointed and covered
> with bark so compactly as to keep out the most penetrating rains. Before the
> doors are placed comfortable sheds, in which the inhabitants sit, when the
> weather will permit, and smoke their pipes. The streets are regular and spa-
> cious, so that it appears more like a civilized town than the abode of savages.
> The land near the town is very good. In their plantations, which are adja-
> cent to their houses, and which are neatly laid out, they raise great quantities
> of Indian corn, beans, melons etc., so that this place is esteemed the best mar-
> ket for traders to furnish themselves with provisions, of any within 800 miles
> of it.

The white visitor was particularly impressed by the mineral wealth
of the area.

> Whilst I staid here, I took a view of some mountains that lie about fifteen
> miles to the southward, and abound in lead ore.... So plentiful is lead here
> that I saw large quantities of it lying about the streets in the town belonging
> to the Saukies, and it seemed to be as good as the produce of other countries.[14]

The expulsion of the Osakiwug and Meshkawkihug from their
homeland followed five well-worn paths: treaty making, divisive
tactics, demoralization, de facto occupancy, and wars of attrition.
The detailed events of the final hostilities, called the Black Hawk

13. The main recent work on these nations is William T. Hagan, *The Sac and Fox Indians* (Norman, Okla., 1958). The work is a fairly condescending portrait of "a primitive
people" (p. 7), faced with superior adversaries—conqueror's history par excellence.

14. Jonathan Carver, *Three Year Travels Throughout the Interior Parts of North America*
(Boston, 1794), pp. 23–24, although "the manuscript . . . in the British Museum . . . dif-
fers materially from the published account" (Louise P. Kellogg, "Carver," *Dictionary of
American Biography* [New York, 1929], III, 552), this particular description seems reliable.
Compare the similar account in Charles M. Gates, ed., *Five Fur Traders of the Northwest*
(Minneapolis, 1965), pp. 40–41.

War, need not be recounted here. When in 1832 the Osakiwug leader Black Hawk returned from the winter grounds to his native village with a thousand followers, men, women, and children, Governor John Reynolds declared the occurrence an invasion and called out the militia. After initial victory the Osakiwug were driven back toward the Mississippi and overpowered. Due to the lack of food and constant harassment,

the warriors were able to put up only token resistance and after the initial exchange the "battle" was little more than a massacre. The troops did not discriminate in the confusion and made most of the opportunity to retaliate against the murdering redskins. Firing at anything that moved, they slew many women and children as they cowered in the underbrush, hid behind logs, burrowed in the sand, or attempted to escape by swimming.[15]

After this defeat the fate of the Osakiwug and Meshkwakihug was sealed; the survivors were driven ever farther west until a few were put on a reservation in Oklahoma in 1867. Some scattered native families were still living relatively undisturbed in remote regions which may account for the "Indian Village" indicated on the first map of the New Glarus settlement. The removal of those remnants was relatively easy. A Swiss immigrant whose family settled only a few miles west of present-day Sauk City in 1842, reports:

An Indian village stood on the land we claimed. . . . The natives hunted and fished and their women grew corn. . . . They at times came to barter with us, but we had little to do with them on the whole. As we did not plough up the land they lived on, there was no trouble. But in due course . . . the men of the community marched against them and ordered them to clear out. They finally did so with great reluctance. A buck or two used to come back each summer to visit the old village site, and from them we gathered that the tribe had crossed the Mississippi. The graves and cornhills were, however, soon levelled and all trace of Indian occupation erased.[16]

How did the mountain farmers and artisans of the Glarus valley in Switzerland hear about the beautiful lands now cleared of their native inhabitants and available for a trifle? A full answer to this

15. Hagan, *The Sac and Fox Indians*, p. 189, the "war" is described pp. 188–190.
16. Lowell J. Ragatz, ed., "Memoirs of a Sauk Swiss. By the Rev. Oswald Ragatz," *Wisconsin Magazine of History*, 19 (1935), 207.

question is not possible since the flow of such information can rarely be fully traced. But there are at least some data that intimate how the Glarnese had gained their knowledge.

From the 1830's forward various individual Swiss seem to have settled in northern Illinois. In the late 1830's, for instance, a Swiss had settled in Galena, a "Mr. Enz, a sincere Christian who ran a hotel" and treated immigrants most kindly. He also seems to have encouraged investigating scouts to send positive reports about the region to their families. Thus Christian Ragatz, who had been sent ahead by his family to reconnoiter the area, wrote back in 1841 "that he had made the trip safely, that he was in Galena in the State of Illinois, a country not unlike parts of Switzerland, and that we should follow as soon as feasible."[17] Mathias Dürst, one of the New Glarus settlers, had already known Enz in Switzerland. He noted in his diary: "I have just learned that Captain Enz, who lived in Constance, whom I visited there in 1834 with my father, lives 19 miles from here and keeps a boarding house."[18]

The people of Glarus also heard about the region through official sources. In 1841 a group of public-minded men, members of the Federal Society for the Public Good (Société d'Utilité Publique Fédérale), formed a commission to supervise emigration by disseminating reliable knowledge and to assist its organization. To gain valid information a questionnaire was sent out via the federal government to all Swiss consuls abroad, and in 1845 the replies were duly published with detailed comments, in French and German. The questions ranged from the numbers of Swiss established in a particular country to their acculturative behavior, from the reception they had met with to the rights to acquire property. Questions pertaining to climate, prices, and legal provisions were also raised. Question 15 asked in particular: If immigration is viewed favorably, which part of the country is to be recommended?[19] De-

17. *Ibid.*, pp. 203, 189.
18. Schelbert, *New Glarus*, p. 137.
19. *Émigrations Suisses. Enquête*, pp. 1–2. The following emigration guide may also have had some influence: *Wohlgemeinte Winke für schweizerische Auswanderer nach Nordamerika. Zusammengetragen und in sieben Kapiteln herausgegeben von einem Volksfreunde* (Glarus, 1844).

tailed answers were received from Naples, St. Petersburg, Odessa, Brussels, Marseilles, Algiers, New York, Philadelphia, Madison (Illinois), Alexandria (District of Columbia), New Orleans, Rio de Janeiro, and Bahia. Consul A. Ott, living in Madison, Illinois, recommended especially the state of his residence. "It has a climate," he commented, "which calls to mind that of Switzerland and is a country especially of woods and prairies." Land prices there, he thought, were still quite reasonable—also in Wisconsin and Iowa, territories "which were soon to take the rank of States of the Union."[20]

One member of the Emigration Commission was a "Peter Jenni of Schwanden, Cantonal Counsellor."[21] It was in his village that on April 16, 1844, a meeting convened of representatives of Glarnese communes who were to discuss the task of an emigration association to be formed specifically for the valley of Glarus. It should —in this following to the letter a proposal of the Emigration Commission—organize group emigration to one of the North American states, preferably to Illinois, Missouri, Indiana, or Ohio, and send out "experts" to select a cohesive land tract and administer the necessary financial transactions in the name of the emigrants.[22] On May 17, 1844, the Glarnese Emigration Association was duly established and an executive committee selected of which Peter Jenny was made a member.[23]

The village of Schwanden had an independent contact in the United States. One of its citizens had emigrated to America in 1770 and settled in Allentown, Pennsylvania; his grandson, Wil-

20. *Émigrations Suisses. Enquête*, p. 123. The idea of such a publication had originated with Lieutenant-Colonel Huber-Saladin, a member of the Emigration Commission which presented comments on the received reports on September 18, 1844. See *ibid.*, p. 111.

21. *Ibid.*, p. iv; other members were from the cantons of Geneva, Bern, St. Gall, and Aargau.

22. *Ibid.*, p. 126: "Only a philantropic, independent, disinterested society could accomplish that goal in a fully satisfactory manner; it would purchase the land with expert knowledge and with the advantage of sufficient capital; it would organize the transport without making profit of the emigrants; it would undertake the building of homesteads, churches, schools, and take all the steps necessary for a good enterprise."

23. Brunnschweiler, *New Glarus*, p. 20, note 7.

helm Heinrich Blumer (1812–1884), was approached by the Glarnese Emigration Association for information and direct help, both of which he gladly furnished; one of his employees, Josua Frey from the Canton of Zurich, was to accompany the experts as guide and interpreter.[24]

In this manner, then, were the results of the expulsion of the Osakiwug and Meshkwakihug made known to the people of the mountainous valley of Glarus. Since the newspapers reported on the meetings which led to the formation of the Glarnese Emigration Association, many people, we may assume, became aware that fertile land could be purchased in southern Wisconsin at very low prices. This then is the first set of processes which explain why 119 immigrants had arrived on the former Osakiwug lands to found a New Glarus.

Yet why was it that these new opportunities in the American Midwest were proclaimed with such insistence? The circumstances are peculiar to the Glarus valley, especially to its remote upper villages, and must be set in their broader historical context.[25]

Since the disappearance of the epidemic known as the Black Death, which had visited the Glarus valley for the last time in 1629, the Glarnese population had been steadily increasing. Industrial crafts introduced in the early seventeenth century were unhampered by guild regulations, and their products found eager markets abroad, due to the knowledge and connections gained by Glarnese who served in foreign armies.[26] In the side valley called the Sernftal, slating was profitably undertaken for the production of tabletops, blackboards, and slate pencils. The export of these commodities led Glarnese merchants to Italy, Russia, and Scandi-

24. Compare Schelbert, *New Glarus*, p. 151, also p. 117, notes 105 and 107.

25. The following is based mainly on Jöst Hösli, *Glarner Land- und Alpwirtschaft in Vergangenheit und Gegenwart* (Glarus, 1948); Elisabeth Dürst, *Die wirtschaftlichen und sozialen Verhältnisse des Glarnerlandes an der Wende vom 18. zum 19. Jahrhundert. Der Uebergang von der Heimindustrie zum Fabriksystem*, Dissertation Zurich (Glarus, 1951); a wealth of detail also in Adolf Jenny and Otto Bartel, *Glarner Geschichte in Daten* (Glarus, 1926–1931), 3 vols.

26. Much documentation in Jenny and Bartel, *Glarner Geschichte*, for instance III, 437–439, the case of Conrad Blumer (1817–1882), whose stay in English military service in Southeast Asia later paved the way for machine-made textiles of his Glarus firm.

navia. But the main industry until 1721 was the export of hard-wood and softwood and of finished wooden products, especially tables. The latter industry had been started in 1617 by the Hessian immigrant Jakob Bellersheim. Holland was the main market for the export of wood, which proceeded along waterways down the Rhine. When the export of wood was stopped in 1721 owing to anxiety about deforestation, Glarnese merchants turned elsewhere for this coveted raw material and exported it from Scandinavia and the Mediterranean to Dutch and English cities.[27]

After 1660 the production of textiles became a major part of the Glarnese mountain peasant economy. Between 1660 and 1690 the weaving of wool and hemp into dyed textiles for export was flour-ishing. After the collapse of this market because of a change in fashion and the wars of Louis XIV, the handspinning of cotton was introduced in 1714, an occupation which spread to the most remote villages and hamlets.[28] The new industry permitted a marked in-crease of the Glarnese population from an estimated 11,500 in 1701 to over 23,000 in 1799; it also integrated the Glarnese economy into the fluctuating Atlantic market. In 1740 the mechanical appli-cation of colorful patterns to cotton textiles was introduced in the valley of Glarus and added new strength to its alpine economy.

The first two decades of the nineteenth century brought hard times. Handspinning of cotton collapsed due to automation in the form of English machines. The Napoleonic policies interfered with the import of raw materials and included the impressment of Swiss into the French armies. In addition, the years 1805, 1806, and 1814

27. A result of deforestation in the upper valley was the transformation of the lower Linth River region into a malaria infested swamp, see *ibid.*, I, 98.

28. Compare Hösli, *Glarner Land- und Alpwirtschaft*, pp. 11–13; p. 317, a table is given of the evolution of the Glarnese population from 1388 to 1941; p. 12, a contemporary description is quoted: "Young and old, women and men sit at the spinning wheel, in the valley as well as in the cottages on the summer pastures. Children from five to six years of age help their parents and earn a few pennies.... One meets everywhere whole rows of fifteen, twenty, and up to thirty spinners, boys, girls, and women sitting near the road who industriously turn the whirring spinning wheels and compete with each other in increasing their weekly income." Quoted from Johann Rudolf Steinmüller, *Beschreibung der schweizerischen Alpen- und Landwirtschaft* (Winterthur, 1802), I, 215–216.

to 1818 were marked by severe crop failures.[29] Service in foreign armies, a form of institutionalized temporary migration, and civilian emigration reduced the Glarnese population from 23,068 in 1799 to 18,000 in 1809. Not until 1824 did it reach an estimated 23,500.[30]

After 1818 handspinning had been almost completely replaced by handweaving, a craft which reached its widest expansion in the 1830's. In many particularly remote villages over one-half of the population was engaged in handweaving, which greatly supplemented small-scale subsistence farming typical of alpine regions. The numerical distribution of handweavers in 1837 shows the following structure: 369 in Linthal, 285 in Kerenzen, 188 in Nidfurn, 182 in Schwanden, 168 in Rüti, 149 in Schwändi, and 123 in Sool. In 1840 some two thousand handlooms were in operation and the population had reached the thirty thousand range.[31]

Automation led to the collapse of handweaving after 1840. In the lower part of the Glarus valley the mechanical loom was introduced with four times as much output as an expert handweaver. The effects were drastic. In 1837, 2,679 people were engaged in handweaving; in 1840, 2,500; in 1845, 1,200; in 1868, 452; in 1870, 29. At least during the initial years, the newly established factories could replace only a fraction of the jobs they had destroyed, since they produced more goods with fewer hands. They were, furthermore, located in the lower part of the valley due to the need for easy access and for water power. No immediate occupational substitute for handweaving emerged, especially for the remoter areas. In this specific form, the generally observed occupational crisis created by mechanization and automation had reached the Glarus valley at a clear-cut historical moment. Population growth, always

29. On the climatic crisis 1812 to 1817 see Jakob Keller-Höhn, "Die Hungersnot im Kanton Zürich in den Jahren 1816/17," *Zürcher Taschenbuch 1948* (Zurich, 1947), pp. 75–114; Martin Ochsner, "Einsiedeln in den Hungerjahren 1816 und 1817," *Mitteilungen des Historischen Vereins des Kantons Schwyz*, 17 (1907), 55–92; Kälin, ed., "Die Fehljahre 1812–1816 und das Not- und Hungersjahr 1817 in Schwyz und Umgebung," *ibid.*, pp. 93–102; Robert Pfaff, "Die Notjahre 1816/17 in Kanton Schaffhausen," *Schaffhauser Beiträge zur vaterländischen Geschichte*, 39 (1962), 80–105.

30. Hösli, *Glarner Land- und Alpwirtschaft*, p. 317.

31. See Brunnschweiler, *New Glarus*, pp. 13–15.

a response to the available means of livelihood and not vice versa, came almost to a standstill. In 1837 the cantonal census counted 29,348 people, the 1850 federal census, 30,213.[32]

Emigration was one response to the occupational crisis created in the hinterland by the collapse of handweaving. Between 1845 and 1848 some fourteen hundred people grasped opportunities offered in Swiss, European, or transoceanic areas. Among them were the 196 emigrants who set out on April 16, 1845, to seize the new opportunities created for white settlers in the former territory of the Osakiwug and Meshkwakihug nations.[33] But how exactly was this Glarnese emigration of the 1840's connected with the occupational crisis? A systematic analysis of the occupational characteristics has not yet been undertaken, but the New Glarus emigrants may provide a sample. The occupations of heads of families and single adult males are indicated in Table I. In comparison, the total occupational composition of the population of the valley of Glarus in 1837 is shown in Table II.

Table I

| | |
|---|---|
| 7 slaters | 1 slate pencil maker |
| 7 handymen | 1 wadding maker* |
| 4 carpenters | 1 bleacher |
| 3 printers (textile patterns) | 1 tinsmith |
| 2 farmers | 1 forester |
| 2 weavers | 1 stone mason |
| 2 cloth pattern engravers | 1 waggoner |
| 2 coopers | 1 marksman |
| 2 timbermen | 1 sap-sago laborer |
| 1 grass mower on the high alp | 9 undetermined |

TOTAL     50

SOURCE: Schelbert, *New Glarus*, pp. 200–205.
*Hösli, *Glarner Land- und Alpwirtschaft*, pp. 12–13, explains: "Waddingmakers, who produced from remnants linings, bedcovers, and also bandages, journeyed every spring to the large cities of central and eastern Europe, opened there small shops, and returned home in the fall."

32. *Ibid*. According to Hösli, *Glarner Land- und Alpwirtschaft*, p. 318, table 2, thirteen cotton goods factories were in operation between 1841–1845 which employed 1,130 workers; by 1868–1869 these establishments numbered twenty-four and employed 3,800.
33. Brunnschweiler, *New Glarus*, pp. 16–18; the term "wild emigration" is misleading, however; the 1845 group was atypical.

Table II

| | |
|---|---|
| Total population | 29,348 |
| Gainfully employed | 11,853 (40%) |
| Factory workers | 3,519 |
| Handweavers | 2,543 |
| Others in textile home industries | 136 |
| Artisans | 2,552 |
| Traders | 329 |
| Waggoners | 144 |
| Slaters | 205 |
| Farmers | 1,092 |
| Menservants | 190 |
| Day laborers | 1,143 |

SOURCE: Hösli, *Glarner Land- und Alpwirtschaft*, p. 319, table 3.

The comparison shows that there was only an indirect connection between emigration and the elimination of jobs through mechanization. Only a fraction of the emigrants bound for New Glarus were handweavers, and almost the entire range of occupations in the valley of Glarus was represented. Automation created a specific pressure on the occupational situation as a whole to which some of the people reacted by emigration.

How did the creation of specific settlement opportunities in the Osakiwug country and the dissemination of information concerning them in Glarus combine with the particular circumstances of its occupational situation and lead individuals to emigration? At this point the study of the causes of emigration enters the obscure realm of motivational processes and decision making, a complex web of partly tangible, partly intangible elements. Only a few data elucidate this aspect of New Glarus.

The two men who were chosen as "experts" and sent ahead for a suitable location are of interest. Niklaus Dürst of Diesbach, forty-eight years of age and a highly respected man in Glarus as well as among the immigrants of New Glarus, returned home some weeks after their arrival. His collaborator, Fridolin Streiff, had replaced a teacher who had unexpectedly withdrawn from the task force of "experts" only a day before their departure. After completing his assignment as a representative of the Emigration Association, Streiff did not return. The United States became his permanent home. The two men had seen the same opportunities beckoning and come from comparable circumstances. Only personal characteristics and motivations can explain their opposite decisions.[34]

The emigrants Rudolf Stauffacher (1794–1858) and Eufemia Stauffacher, born 1805, came from the village of Matt. Rudolf, a slater, had married Magdalena Stauffacher, who died in 1823; in the same year he married his second wife, Anna Beglinger, born 1781, who died on board the ship en route to New Glarus on May 28, 1845. Rudolf's sister-in-law from his first marriage was Eufemia Stauffacher, married to a Meinrad Stauffacher by whom she had a daughter Ursula, born 1831. At some point thereafter Eufemia became the mistress of Rudolf Stauffacher, by whom she had three illegitimate children while still in Switzerland: Eufemia in 1837, Verena in 1840, and Rudolf in 1842. At the time of departure in 1845, Eufemia was pregnant again; she gave birth to a fourth child by Rudolf on July 19 in Cincinnati.[35] The situation of these two emigrants had been scandalous indeed within the narrow bounds of monogamous alpine village life. Eufemia's husband stayed behind, but Anna Beglinger went with her spouse despite the presence of his pregnant mistress with her legitimate daughter and three illegitimate children. Here, too, very personal characteristics and considerations must be taken into account if the emigration decision is to be understood.

A third case is Mathias Dürst, whose diary gives an impressive account of the emigrant journey from the Glarus valley to southern Wisconsin. On the trip down the Ohio the boat's captain talked at length with Dürst, a skilled tinsmith by profession. Dürst reports the captain as saying:

---

34. See Schelbert, *New Glarus*, pp. 152, 154; on the last-minute choice of Streiff, who replaced a teacher named Marti, see *Auswanderungsverein*, p. 111.

35. Schelbert, *New Glarus*, p. 205; Beglinger's death, p. 53; the birth of Eufemia Stauffacher's fourth child, p. 111.

With such a trade, which rates among the best in America, where in St. Louis I could earn my two dollars daily, I should not wish to move to a forsaken region clearing the wilderness for which my body is too frail. I should work for a few years for wages, then I could have land if I wished, such as buying a piece of land about a mile outside of town. It would not have to be very big, only enough to plant for my own needs, then I could deliver my handiwork into town and in this way I could raise myself up and become a wealthy man within a few years.

When Dürst remained unconvinced and intent upon going on, the captain became annoyed. "Becoming more agitated he told me that if I did not want to follow his well-meant advice, I should move into the wilderness and break my back working while the other way I could live like a gentleman."[36] What was it that drove this emigrant on? What had made him leave his homeland? The occupational situation at home and the general appeal of opportunities abroad seem insufficient to explain his emigration decision. He seemed to be searching for a very special rural Swiss-like life based on land holding within a community of compatriots.

In summary, the case of the New Glarus immigrants seems to show that one has to reckon with three elements in accounting for emigration. The *preconditions* designate those processes which explain the source and distribution of information about a settlement or occupational opportunity abroad. The *circumstances* designate those factors that induce people to consider a settlement or occupational opportunity abroad. The *motivational process* designates that particular fusion of preconditions and circumstances on the basis of a particular individuality which culminates in a decision to emigrate. Each of these postulated elements, which in reality form an integrated web of total interaction, will now be examined in some detail.

36. *Ibid.*, p. 105.

## II. Elaborations

ON the basis of selected eighteenth- and nineteenth-century Swiss data—valid for continental Europe and perhaps beyond—the historically unique as well as the structurally typical in the making of emigrants may be envisaged.

### A. PRECONDITIONS

The emergence of preconditions forms the very basis for any migratory movement and includes two major facets, the emergence of preconditions in objective reality and their emergence in the consciousness of potential emigrants. An example will illustrate this double dimension. In the year 1756 about thirty Swiss entered the British military service as officers.[37] A variety of initially unconnected events explain this occupational emigration. By the middle of the eighteenth century, the whites on the seaboard of North America had reached the Allegheny Mountains; land hungry settlers tried in ever greater numbers to cross the Alleghenies and enter the Mississippi valley, nominally a French domain, but in reality still in Indian hands. The latter had recognized the deadly threat from this advance and tried to stop it.[38] An engagement occurred on July 9, 1755, some eight miles from the present city of Pittsburgh. The English contingent of fourteen hundred men, who had been sent out to break native resistance, were decisively defeated by some six hundred Indian warriors who were helped by some two hundred fifty French.[39] The defeat, in which the commanding officer Edward Braddock perished, induced the English command in London to establish a regiment especially for the

37. The list of names in Arnold Lätt, *Schweizeroffiziere als Indianerkrieger und Instruktoren der englischen leichten Infanterie* (Neujahrsblatt der Feuerwerkergesellschaft, 125 [Zurich, 1933]), pp. 6–7, based on *London Gazette*, March 16–20, 27–30, 1756.

38. See Ray A. Billington, *Westward Expansion. A History of the American Frontier* (New York, 1963), pp. 103–153, for a description of the events; he views them however mainly in the context of English and French rivalry.

39. A detailed study of the battle is Stanley Pargellis, "Braddock's Defeat," *American Historical Review*, 41 (January 1936), 253–269; Billington, *Westward Expansion*, p. 126, and Lätt, *Schweizeroffiziere*, p. 5, present partly inaccurate detail.

North American service. It was to be schooled not in classical, but in "backwoods" warfare. Each soldier was to be whatever the need of the moment might require: marksman, scout, runner, rider, or boatsman.[40] The actual formation of the regiment was put into the hands of Jacques Prévost (1725–1765) of Geneva; he as well as his friend Henri Bouquet (1715–1765) of Rolle were known as proponents of these unorthodox techniques of war. Prévost seems to have been eager to attract as many compatriots as possible; among them were his two brothers, Augustin (1723–1786) and Marcus (1736–1781), both of whom later occupied high positions in the English military service.[41]

Thus the precondition of this professional military emigration represents a confluence of disparate elements. The specific phase of Anglo-American white expansion evoked a specific attempt to resist it. The momentary defeat of the English troops led to a reassessment of military strategy in London and the employment of Swiss officers already in English service, known for their unorthodox strategic thinking. These in turn made the newly created occupational opportunity known among compatriots who were eager to avail themselves of it.

In general, what kind of opportunities abroad did the Swiss grasp, and to what extent? To answer this question a basic typology of migration may be introduced. Throughout history one observes in almost all human communities a phenomenon that may be described as *exchange migration*. Emerging and ever changing specializations in economic pursuits create fluctuating needs which are often filled either temporarily or permanently by people from the outside. Besides this form of migration a historically less frequent, but in its impact more significant, type can be observed which may be termed *expansionist migration*—the expansion of a nation's territorial or economic domain into (mostly transoceanic)

40. *Ibid.*, pp. 10, 13. Pargellis, "Braddock's Defeat," pp. 253 and 256, points out, however, that Braddock failed less because of adhering to principles of classical warfare than because of neglecting basic rules of vigilance.

41. On Bouquet's life and ideas see S. K. Stevens *et al.*, eds., *The Papers of Henry Bouquet* (Harrisburg, 1951 and 1972), 2 vols.; his "Instruction" is summarized by Lätt, *Schweizeroffiziere*, pp. 13–17. On the Prévosts see *ibid.*, pp. 6–7, 36–41.

outliers. If this migration occurs, a country becomes territorially and demographically as well as economically, socially, politically, and mentally, an "oikumene," an entity consisting of heartland and outlier. In "the age of white expansion" from 1450 to 1950, some seventy million are estimated to have left the European homeland for transoceanic areas (and Siberia) where they mingled with, pushed out, or destroyed the indigenous peoples.[42] New Spains, New Englands, New Frances, New Hollands were created, even New Switzerlands or, more narrowly, New Berns and Nova Friburgos.

The history of Swiss emigration is fully integrated into this broader context.[43] Tables III and IV suggest the size and general territorial direction of Swiss emigration. Table III shows that generally a substantial portion of Swiss people was abroad, almost balanced, however, by a significant presence of aliens within Switzerland. The geographic distribution of Swiss abroad remained concentrated in continental Europe, as shown in Table IV.

Table III

ESTIMATES OF SWISS ABROAD IN RELATION TO SWISS
RESIDENT POPULATION FOR SELECTED YEARS

| Swiss Abroad | | Swiss Resident Population | | | |
|---|---|---|---|---|---|
| Year | Estimates (in thousands) | Year | Native | Aliens | Total |
| | | | (Estimates in thousands) | | |
| 1500–1600 | 270–320 | 1600 | | | 1,000 |
| 1600–1700 | 290–340 | 1700 | | | 1,200 |
| 1700–1800 | 340–390 | 1800 | | | 1,700 |
| 1800–1850* | 100 | 1880 | 2,635 | 211 | 2,846 |
| 1850–1888* | 287 | 1888 | 2,688 | 230 | 2,918 |

42. See the survey offered by Brinley Thomas, "Migration," Encyclopedia Britannica (1971), XV, 421–427. An incisive, if colonialist, essay is A. Grenfell Price, The Western Invasions of the Pacific and Its Continents 1513–1958 (Oxford, 1963).

43. See Leo Schelbert, "Die Wanderungen der Schweizer. Ein historischer Ueberblick," Saeculum. Jahrbuch für Universalgeschichte, 18 (1967), 403–430, a fragmentary survey, but with many references to secondary sources. More complete is my forthcoming Einführung in die schweizerische Auswanderungsgeschichte der Neuzeit (Bern, 1974).

|  |  | Swiss Abroad |  | Swiss Resident Population |  |  |  |
| --- | --- | --- | --- | --- | --- | --- | --- |

| Year | Estimates (in thousands) | Year | Native | Aliens | Total |
| --- | --- | --- | --- | --- | --- |
|  |  |  | (Estimates in thousands) | | |
| 1888–1914* | 123 | 1910 | 3,201 | 552 | 3,753 |
| 1926 | 323 | 1920 | 3,478 | 402 | 3,880 |
| 1928 | 346 | 1930 | 3,711 | 356 | 4,067 |
| 1941 | 269 | 1941 | 4,042 | 224 | 4,266 |
| 1950 | 202 | 1950 | 4,432 | 283 | 4,715 |

*Estimates of emigrating Swiss.

SOURCES: The estimates for the Swiss abroad up to 1914 and for the Swiss resident population of 1600, 1700, and 1800 are taken from Wilhelm Bickel, *Bevölkerungsgeschichte und Bevölkerungspolitik der Schweiz seit dem Ausgang des Mittelalters* (Zürich, 1947), pp. 48–49, 55, 159–160. The figures for the Swiss resident population—native and alien—for the years 1880 to and including 1941 are based on Eidgenössisches Statistisches Amt, ed., *Statistisches Jahrbuch der Schweiz 1950* (Basel, 1951), p. 25, "Wohnbevölkerung der Schweiz nach Heimatklassen"; (the totals are the sum of the columns and not fully identical with the figures *ibid.*, p. 13, "Wohnbevölkerung"); also *ibid.*, p. 89 and p. 12, the figures for 1950. The figures for the Swiss living abroad for 1926 are based on *ibid.*, *1932* (Basel, 1933), p. 96; the figures for 1928 and 1941 on *ibid.*, *1941* (Basel, 1942), p. 96; the figures for the Swiss abroad for 1926 and later include those who were registered with Swiss consulates and estimates of those who did not register; double citizens, however, were not included.

## Table IV

### ESTIMATES OF THE GEOGRAPHIC DISTRIBUTION OF SWISS ABROAD FOR SELECTED YEARS

| Continent | 1850 | 1880 | 1928 | 1941 |
| --- | --- | --- | --- | --- |
| Europe | 45,954 | 119,707 | 253,484 | 183,460 |
| Americas | 20,226 | 107,780 | 83,140 | 72,230 |
| Africa | 580 | 3,456 | 7,091 | 8,506 |
| Australia | 215 | 2,300 | 1,470 | 1,700 |
| Asia | 46 | 802 | 2,470 | 3,119 |
| Unknown | 5,485 | — | — | — |
| TOTAL | 72,506 | 234,045 | 347,655 | 269,015 |

SOURCES: The figures for 1850 and 1880, probably too low, are taken from Josef Durrer, "Die Schweizer in der Fremde," *Zeitschrift für schweizerische Statistik und Volkswirtschaft*, 21 (1885), 85–88; the figures for 1928 are given in *Statistisches Jahrbuch der Schweiz 1929* (Basel, 1930), p. 92; for 1941, *ibid.*, *1941* (Basel, 1942), p. 96.

Given the size of their native population, Swiss participated substantially in the migration to the territory of the United States. Before 1790 some 25,000 are estimated to have settled in the English colonies, and about the same number emigrated to the newly established American nation between 1790 and 1860. According to the United States census there were in 1850, 13,000, in 1870, 75,000, and in 1890, 104,000, Swiss-born living in the nation. The high was reached in 1910 when 125,000 Swiss-born were counted in addition to 217,000 American-born descendants. In 1920 the Swiss stock, that is, immigrants and their American-born children, was estimated at 376,000.[44] Swiss immigrants came as soldiers, entrepreneurs, settlers, artisans, ministers, priests, and missionaries. Only a detailed micro-analytical study could precisely establish for each group the emergence of the preconditions in objective reality.

How did occupational or settlement opportunities abroad become known to the Swiss? The flow of astonishingly rich and steady information took four main forms. A first channel of news was the many letters that emigrants wrote about their journey and their first months and years abroad.[45] Terse accounts alternate with detailed descriptions, meant to help later emigrants. Reports of expectations met, or surpassed, are balanced by stories of disappointment and even despair. The impact of such letters is widely attested and involved friends and foes of emigration.

The pastor Leonhard Holzhalb (1685–1748), for instance, reported in 1744 that a Matthias Frauenfelder had sent from London a "lamentable letter in which he could not write enough about how miserably they had been deceived, warning everyone against this journey. . . . Had the above lamentable letter and this and that report not reached the country and become known, a good many

44. The estimates to 1850 from Albert B. Faust, "Swiss Emigration to the American Colonies in the Eighteenth Century," *AHR*, 22 (October 1916), 43–44; the later figures based on Bureau of the Census, *Abstract of the Fourteenth Census of the United States 1920* (Washington, 1923), pp. 16, 96, 302–303, and E. P. Hutchinson, *Immigrants and Their Children 1850–1950* (New York, 1956), p. 333.

45. A search in archives, newspapers, and libraries has yielded a valuable collection of such letters for an anthology which is in preparation. A fine example in print is Robert H. Billigmeier and Fred A. Picard, eds., *The Old Land and the New. The Journals of Two Swiss Families in America in the 1830's* (Minneapolis, 1965).

other [persons] might have decided [in favor of] this emigration."[46]
Holzhalb's colleague Johann Conrad Füssli (1704–1775) wrote similarly in 1744 that he had received letters from Hans Ulrich Frey-
hofer, a thirty year old weaver, and from his cousin Verena, twenty-
four years of age, who with two relatives had joined a well-to-do
but childless uncle now living in Germantown, Pennsylvania.

They advise, however, that no one who could help it should undertake that
journey, especially since over 200 Swiss had died on their and another ship
who could not endure the sickness at sea. They further report that, if someone
was ill on his arrival, he was not allowed to leave the ship so that many died in
the port because of bad care. They also wrote that the present war made the
trip hazardous. By this report many have been kept back who otherwise had
intended to follow them.[47]

The influence of positive letters is also widely proven. The pastor
of Wyl, a foe of emigration, referred in his 1744 report to:

Heinrich Keller, a young schoolmaster of Hüntwangen who had emigrated
with his wife, born in Eglisau, and his little son Samuel who, according to her
opinion, is to become a prophet. This young schoolmaster and the shopkeeper
of Weyach have been instigators for many years and have seduced all emigrants of the district of Eglisau, also many in the Kleggäu, with false letters
and booklets so that they finally moved away since everything was presented
to them so favorably.[48]

Another example is taken from the rich nineteenth-century materials. On August 10, 1847, the clergyman "Zimmermann Burckhardt, a candidate for the holy ministry," wrote to the town council of Basel in behalf of a Horner family.[49] In support of their emigration decision he included summaries of four letters. The first
had been sent by the butcher Johannes Rosenmund-Gysin from
Lawrenceville near Pittsburgh; his report showed how fast an immigrant "who had barely enough to start with debts, could free
himself through industrious work."[50] A second letter, dated De-

46. Lists, I, 55, list 38 (see above, note 4).
47. Ibid., p. 69, list 59; his translation is faulty.
48. Ibid., p. 99, list 77.
49. Staatsarchiv Basel-Stadt, Auswanderung A, 1819–1847.
50. Letters from the Rosenmund-Gysin family have been published by Max Bächlin,
"Briefe aus Amerika. Eine Basler Familie wandert 1845 nach den Vereinigten Staaten
aus," Basler Stadtbuch 1964 (Basel, 1963), pp. 179–216.

cember 27, 1847, had arrived from Cincinnati from a Rosina Schmied. She wrote that she and her fiance had arrived during the worst season of the year, that the trip had been very bad, and that an illness of five weeks had devoured almost all of their cash; but good pay for her service as a domestic servant and her husband's daily income of two dollars now enabled them to live very comfortably. She invited her sister to join them as soon as possible. The third letter, dated December 9, 1847, had come from the Hartmanns, then living in Milwaukee. "The report shows," commented the clergyman, "that the opportunities are spread quite evenly throughout the [Mid-] western States." The fourth letter included in the petition was written by a Wilhelmina Frei, a domestic servant in Philadelphia. After just a few months she had been able to pay back the fifty florins she had borrowed from her mother; she admonished her friend to follow her quickly and " 'not to listen to dissuading chatter since things were not half as bad as reported.' "[51] In conclusion Zimmermann Burckhardt commented: "For understandable reasons I have chosen just these letters since it is usually said that America is a country where only farmers can find a better livelihood."[52]

Letters received strong backing from returned emigrants who could speak from experience and whose credibility could be tested in personal encounters. In March 1729, for instance, a Heinrich Schneebeli, about twenty-seven years of age, had returned from Philadelphia to Knonau in the Canton of Zurich. He was neatly dressed, seemed to have much cash on hand, and had indeed made purchases in the town for over a hundred florins. This induced many to visit Schneebeli "to ask him about the nature of that land about which they had heard much already since some of their relatives also lived there from whom various letters had arrived earlier." Schneebeli informed them that the country was sparsely settled, but contained "as fertile and as good land as Switzerland"; all

51. The document says: "Nicht 'auf abmahnendes Geschwätz zu losen, denn es sei nicht halb so arg, wie man sage.' "
52. The folder Auswanderung A, 1848–1853, Staatsarchiv Basel-Stadt, contains similar petitions.

kinds of grains were grown there, but "not much wine; yet the beer was good. Wages, however, were far better than here . . . one also enjoyed there a free unhindered Exercitium Religionis, especially since there were two reformed pastors from Heidelberg." Shortly after Schneebeli's visit over thirty people presented themselves to the bailiff of Knonau to ask permission to emigrate.[53]

Throughout the eighteenth century returners were viewed suspiciously by the cantonal governments as seducers of the people; they often risked arrest, intensive questioning, and occasionally imprisonment.[54] But not all returners brought favorable news. Hans Wernhard Trachsler, for instance, a native of Elgg, Canton Zurich, who had been in the foreign service and had "felt overcome by the desire to see Carolina," had gone away on September 9, 1736. He took up residence in Charleston, South Carolina, where he worked as a butcher; he returned in the following year to Switzerland, where his rather negative report was published.[55]

Many letters as well as more general reports of emigrants, travellers, and returners were widely circulated by newspapers. In 1733, for instance, the *Hoch-Obrigkeitlich begönstigtes Frag- und Anzeigungs-Blätlein von Basel* reported in its issue of October 6 that finally trustworthy news had reached Neuchâtel. "Those who have let themselves be dissuaded from their decision to emigrate to South Carolina in America, can see from the following report how things are in the new plantations."[56] The contents of an enthusiastic emigrant's letter turned out to be a caricature of the real conditions,

53. See "Landvogtei Knonau 1706–1738," Staatsarchiv Zürich, A. 128,10, March 29, 1729; April 4, 1729.

54. Faust, "Swiss Emigration," pp. 32–40, 98–114, offers valuable detail, but interprets the material in a superficial and biased manner. See, for instance, the case of Wernhart Stohler, Staatsarchiv Basel-Stadt, Auswanderung A, 1749, nos. 101 and 105.

55. *Kurtz-verfasste Reiss-Beschreibung eines neulich auss der in West-Indien gelegenen Landschaft Carolina in sein Vatterland zurückgekommenen Lands- Angehörigen. Samt einem Bericht von disers Lands Art, Natur und Eigenschafften* (Zurich, 1738), quotations p. 3, a copy in Zentralbibliothek Zurich, Special Collections.

56. No. XL, "Allerhand Nachrichten," no. 5, copy in newspaper collection University Library Basel. The paper was published "bey Johann Burckhardt im Berichthauss."

but the same newspaper later painted an even rosier picture of the new settlement.[57]

In the nineteenth century news about emigrants and their experience was reported more frequently. Just one example may illustrate this. In 1804 the writer, educator, and publicist Heinrich Zschokke (1771–1848) started a weekly newspaper whose circulation soon fluctuated between three thousand and five thousand copies.[58] Its pages abounded with valuable and varied information about most aspects of emigration and immigrant life. The reports dealt with Swiss in the foreign military service, with artisans and professionals, and especially with settlers in transoceanic areas. News from the Crimea or St. Petersburgh alternated with reports from Sicily, Spain, or Pittsburgh.[59] The summary of a report may illustrate the astonishing detail offered to readers.

In 1804 Vinzenz Godt of Altdorf, Canton Uri, had travelled to Constance in order to investigate personally the possibilities of emigrating to the Crimea. He promptly published his findings in the *Schweizer-Bote* on May 25, 1804.[60] Godt strongly advised against the venture; the conditions offered by the Russian government seemed to him less than satisfactory. Three years later another report appeared by the same author, this time dated "Philadelphia in North America, May 1, 1807."[61] His concern for those coming

57. See below, note 88. No comprehensive research concerning eighteenth-century calendars and newspapers has been undertaken as far as these report on emigration. Some dispersed but rather general news is given, e.g., in *Verbesserter und Neuer Staats-Calender genandt der Hinkende Bott* which had appeared in Basel since 1735. In 1755 the unpaginated issue offers a report on a "rebellion in Nova Scotia," in 1756 on Braddock's defeat, in 1757 on "the horrible cruelties perpetrated by wild Indians friendly to the French," with illustration; copies in Staatsarchiv, Basel-Stadt.

58. On Zschokke see Paul Schaffroth, "Heinrich Zschokke als Politiker und Publizist während der Restauration und Regeneration," *Argovia*, 61 (1949), 5–203; Zschokke's connection with Highland, Illinois, is discussed by Rolf Zschokke, "Beitrag der Gründungsgeschichte der City of Highland, Madison County, Illinois," *Festschrift Karl Schib* (Schaffhauser Beiträge zur vaterländischen Geschichte, 45 [Thayngen, 1968]), pp. 420–458.

59. See Leo Schelbert, "Die Fünfte Schweiz in der Berichterstattung des 'Aufrichtigen und Wohlerfahrenen Schweizer-Boten' 1804–1830," *Schweizerisches Archiv für Volkskunde*, 67 (1971), 84–114, for a review of the news on emigration.

60. "Ueber Niederlassungen der Schweizer in der Krim und am caspischen Meere," *Schweizer-Bote*, I, 164–165.

61. "Anleitung zur Reise übers Meer," *Schweizer-Bote*, IV, 289–294, 297–299.

after, Godt pointed out, had induced him to present some details concerning the emigrant journey to Pennsylvania. His hints might "be of great advantage to the body as well as the pocketbook" of emigrants. In Amsterdam, he advised, one should consult a reliable lawyer who could help in drawing up the contract with the captain of the boat; various clauses as to rights and accommodations should be inserted. Emigrants should not forget to take dried fruit and cooked butter along for the prevention of scurvy; and the most desirable kinds of cooking utensils and foodstuffs for the ocean journey were recommended.

Of special interest are Godt's instructions on how to get from Amsterdam to Texel, and the actual port of embarkation. He advised emigrants to use the "Mail Boat," which was clearly marked by a triple-colored flag. This boat left every day from the Schreyerstower in Amsterdam between nine and ten in the morning. After arrival in Texel those Swiss who spoke French should lodge in the inn "The Coat of Arms of the Seven Provinces"; those who knew only German were to engage "the master tailor Kantwein, an obliging German who would serve by the hour as an interpreter for little money"; Italian-speaking Swiss should locate "the skipper Heinrich Benker, a pious man whose word they could trust."

Godt then proceeded to advise those who could afford to take merchandise along, but wanted to beat the very high customs. He further reported how emigrants could keep free from lice: "One should grind mercury with pork fat in a glass and apply the mixture weekly to one's whole body." Before leaving the boat, Godt told his readers, crew members treated their clothing with urine, "the most effective liquid for getting rid of all vermin and spots." In the same colorful and detailed manner the prospective emigrant is advised about the crossing, the formalities at landing, the procedures of purchasing land. About the people of Philadelphia, Godt had this to say: "The Philadelphians show much deference to learned inventions; each house has its lightning rod, each living room its vent for vapors of lamps and people; each house is marked with the sign of a fire company by which it is covered; and the most perfect fire houses exist here." The hospital also received praise. The *Schweizer-Bote* abounded in this kind of detailed report till about 1830 and seems to validate a historian's remark: "The image of the innocent emigrant abroad needs modification."[62]

The news spread by emigrant letters, oral reports of returners, and newspaper stories was complemented, especially in the nineteenth century, by emigrant guides, handbooks, and pamphlets published by individuals, transportation firms, or government agencies. The table of contents of a handbook written by a young emigrant from the Canton of Solothurn impressively illustrates the wide range of topics discussed.[63] Johann Hänggi pointed out that he had written his ninety-two pages "for those of [his] countrymen who plan to undertake the journey from Switzerland to America in the most secure and inexpensive way and to settle there in the most secure and inexpensive manner."

### TABLE OF CONTENTS

I The Baggage of the Emigrant and His Journey until His Landing in America
    What shall the emigrant take along?
    Cash or bills of exchange?
    Choice of route to the seaport
    The stay in the seaport
    Costs of the crossing
    Purchase of victuals for the sea [voyage]
    Conduct on the boat during the crossing
    Survey on the costs of the journey and some observations

---

62. Carlton C. Qualey, "Immigration, Emigration, Migration," in Oscar F. Ander, ed., *In the Trek of the Immigrants* (Rock Island, Ill., 1964), p. 35.

63. This literature has only partially been explored. Three titles seem especially noteworthy: A. Zwilchenbart, *Bericht und Anleitung betreffend die verschiedenen Reiserouten der Auswanderer nach allen überseeischen Landungsplätzen* (Basel, 1864); Johann Hänggi, *Der schweizerische Auswanderer nach Amerika, oder: Meine Erfahrungen in jenem Lande. Niedergeschrieben für diejenigen meiner Landsleute, welche auf die sicherste und wohlfeilste Weise die Reise aus der Schweiz nach Amerika machen und sich dort auf die sicherste und wohlfeilste Art niederlassen wollen* (Solothurn, 1852); *Ratgeber für schweizerische Auswanderer nach den Vereinigten Staaten von Nordamerika. Verfasst im Auftrag des eidgenössischen Departements des Auswärtigen, von dem eidg. Auswanderungskommissariat in Bern und schweiz. Gesandtschaft in Washington* (Bern, 1893).

II The Stay in the American Seaport and Journey to the Place of
    Settlement
        Conduct on landing in the American Seaport
        The stay in New York
        Room and board there and costs
        Situations and experiences of immigrants in the seaports
        Agencies for the inland journey
        Opportunities for the inland journey
        Costs of the inland journey
        Warning
III Settling in America
    1. The Land
        Choice of the region of settlement
        Climate
        Caution concerning land purchase
        Purchase prices of land
        Type of farming
        Planting of grains
    2. The Inhabitants
        Language
        The way Americans live, food
        Clothing
        Social conditions
        Education, schools
        Churches
        Institutions for the poor and welfare institutions
    3. Types of Professions and Income
        Day laborers, servants, and maids
        Craftsmen
        Comparison between European and American income
        Difference in the management of crafts
    4. Industrial and Agricultural Matters
        Industry and factories
        Commerce
        Sale of agricultural products
        Cattle
        Prices of victuals
    5. Legal Matters
        Personal duties
        Citizenship
        Courts and manner of trials
        Police and penal institutions
        Conclusion

The guide closes with these words about paper money: "In this as in all other respects the American motto should never be disregarded: Trust no man, help yourself, and don't be fooled."[64]

One brief excerpt from the guide will show the type of information given by Hänggi:

Clothing
Concerning this we repeat the advice already given at the beginning of the pamphlet: To dress darkly whenever possible in black; black is the customary color of clothing;—this holds for the townsman as well as the farmer, for the well-to-do as well as for the poor. One may thus imagine in what embarrassment our immigrants find themselves, if they put foot on American soil in the garb of their cantons [Landstrachten]; the bantering youths of the streets regularly appear and pursue these unfortunate people with merciless scorn. The same fate is experienced by those who wear long hair or moustaches etc. (whatever they are called). The American is usually beardless, except many who wear short side burns.[65]

These then were the main four forms by which news of opportunities abroad reached the consciousness of Swiss people and figured in their decision whether to remain in their native country or to leave. News about opportunities abroad and how to seize them combined with a wide range of circumstances to determine the outcome.

### B. CIRCUMSTANCES

When in 1744 the pastors of the Zurich church were asked to report "on those persons, who between 1734 and 1744 had left the territory of Zurich in order to travel to America,"[66] the resulting ninety-eight lists contained not only names and ages of the more than twenty-two hundred emigrants, but also valuable references concerning the particular circumstances of their leaving. Pastor Johannes Vogler of the parish of Richterswil, for instance, reported on an emigrant named Tanner who had departed with his wife and six children, "among them a newly-born of three weeks, and the

---

64. Hänggi, Der schweizerische Auswanderer, table of contents, pp. i–ii, end quotation, p. 92.
65. Ibid., p. 53.
66. See above, note 4.

oldest 12 years." Vogler had tried his best to dissuade the man, but to no avail. Tanner always answered in the same manner: "He could not ward off bankruptcy, that he wanted to sell his property, and that he would stay if he could get the best price for it; this word, however, he did not keep and said: 'He could now not do otherwise anymore.' " Tanner belonged in Vogler's view to "people who could no longer sustain themselves with their work, and nothing could be done with them; whatever you might say their reply always remained the same: they had to labor here day and night, and even then they could not earn their daily bread and were therefore forced to seek it elsewhere."[67]

A different situation is mentioned in an entry by the pastor of Fehraltorf:

Margreth Gut from [the homestead called] Sennscheür, a fief dependent on Kyburg, baptized on the 14th of October 1718, married at the selfsame place on the 23rd of May 1742 to Rudolff Brüngger, carpenter by trade, who could not get along with her husband and her father-in-law, has departed from here on the 28th of June 1743 without bidding farewell, together with those who emigrated from Dägerlen to Carolina, as far as I know, with a woman who traveled there to join her husband, a blacksmith, to help take care of her children for promised wages.[68]

Balthassar Peyer, pastor of Illnau, described yet another set of circumstances:

Barbara Schlumpf of Horben [Horgen] age 23 [left], whose husband Caspar Windsch had left in the year 1742 with her knowledge and consent for the Dutch military service and who herself had gone back to her relatives in Münch-Altorff where she had become unfaithful to her husband and had gotten pregnant by another man with whom she has departed in the year 1743 with the assistance of her father; and from the boat in Zurich she has sent her legitimate little son to his poor grandmother in Horben.[69]

Still another situation was faced by the emigrant of whom Johannes Meister, pastor of Neftenbach issued the following report:

67. *Lists*, I, 75–76, list 68; the German originals have been used throughout. Reference to Faust's partly inaccurate edition is made because of accessibility.

68. *Ibid.*, p. 91, list 85.

69. *Ibid.*, p. 61, list 47.

Hans Ulrich Hagenbucher of Hüniken, age 41, who left from here for Carolina with his wife Barbara Frauenfelder of the same age and three children, Elsbeth aged 13, Margareth aged 10, and Madgalena aged 2, on June 14, 1743, because he had been severely punished at Kyburg the previous spring due to blasphemous talk, and then had further been obliged to listen to a sermon from the pulpit directed especially at him, and was therefore ashamed to live any longer among the people here.[70]

These examples, which could easily be multiplied, show that a wide range of circumstances induced people to consider opportunities far from their homes. It seems possible, however, to group the basic circumstances under the admittedly overlapping heads of nature, economy, society, polity, and religion.

A first set of circumstances has its origin in *nature*, that is, in conditions outside the pale of human manipulatory power. Climatic conditions or the sudden growth and dispersal of plant fungi may cause crop failures and result in severe hardship.[71] Such crises occurred in Switzerland in the years 1770–1771, 1805–1806, and especially 1816–1817. The winter of 1815–1816 was especially severe.[72] Grain planted in the fall perished in the cold so that the fields had to be plowed up and reseeded in the spring. But the summer which followed was cold and wet, and the harvest reached barely half of its usual size. Winter set in very early, and even the lowlands were already covered with deep snow in November; many fields had thus remained unharvested. Lack of fodder necessitated the premature killing of pigs and cattle. Prices for bread and potatoes, the main food supply way into the nineteenth century, rose sharply. The price of bread doubled; a bushel of potatoes rose from 43 cents to 1.70 francs. Wages, however, throughout the nineteenth century near the subsistence level, showed a falling trend, especially in the textile branch due to increasing mechanization.[73] In 1812 a cotton spinner received for twelve hours of labor but 3 to 6 schillings, yet

70. *Ibid.*, pp. 67–68, list 56.
71. See, for instance, R. Dudley Edwards and T. Desmond Williams, eds., *The Great Famine. Studies in Irish History* (Dublin, 1956).
72. See above, note 29, for titles concerning this crisis.
73. See Jürg Siegenthaler, "Zur Entwicklung des schweizerischen Lebensstandards im 19. und 20. Jahrhundert," *Schweizerische Monatshefte*, 46 (1966–1967), 238.

a pound of bread cost 11 to 12 schillings and a bushel of potato peels 4 schillings.[74]

Despite valiant efforts by communes and cantonal governments, famine threatened a substantial segment of the population.[75] People began to doubt that normal climatic conditions would return, and some three thousand Swiss left their homeland in these hard times. It is important, however, not to conceive of the emigrants as a procession of starving poor; they represented fairly evenly the whole socioeconomic spectrum of the population. The emigrant Ittel of Rohrdorf, for instance, the leader of a large group of emigrants, is reported to have taken 2,400 francs along.[76] Some two thousand emigrants, who left Switzerland in 1819 to found Nova Friburgo in Brazil, were partly influenced by the prolonged climatic crisis which had culminated in 1817; but this group also represented a wide socioeconomic spectrum.[77]

Another set of circumstances conducive to emigration is rooted in particular situations within a given *economy*. Three negative situations seem prevalent: poverty, impoverishment (often leading to bankruptcy), and the collapse of a particular occupation (mostly due to automation). These are balanced by two positive possibilities: the offer of an inheritance situated abroad and entrepreneurial schemes. In these situations individual skill or incompetence seem strongly mixed with elements of chance and are embedded in events of regional, national, continental, or Atlantic dimensions.[78]

74. Keller-Höhn, "Hungersnot," p. 86, and tables, pp. 84–86; also Kälin, "Fehljahre," pp. 97–98.

75. Compare the reports in the *Schweizer-Bote*, XIII, 225–227, 289–291, 301–302, 321–322, 371–372; XIV, 97–100.

76. *Ibid.*, p. 396. Ittel was tricked out of his money in Amsterdam by an unscrupulous captain after the former had paid the passage for his emigrant group.

77. *Ibid.*, XVI, 209–210. The *Schweizer-Bote* reports widely on this emigration: in 1819 six lengthy reports, one song, eight letters; in 1820 and 1821 six letters for each year. The basic study for the early years of Nova Friburgo is Martin Nicoulin, *La Genèse de Nova Friburgo. Emigration et colonisation suisse au Bresil* (Études et recherches d'histoire contemporaine, série historique, II [Fribourg, 1973]).

78. A precise analysis of the interlocking of these dimensions is, e.g., Douglass C. North, *The Economic Growth of the United States 1790–1860* (Englewood Cliffs, N.J., 1961). A series of cases where bankruptcy led to going abroad are given by Hans Conrad Peyer, *Von Handel und Bank im alten Zürich* (Zurich, 1968), pp. 177–178; also pp. 191–192, 198–

Impoverishment is a relative concept, as a document of 1738 intimates. In that year those people who had decided to emigrate from the Canton of Basel were carefully examined by the bailiffs, who then reported their findings to the city authorities.[79] One of these reports was the "Specification of those subjects of the district of Homburg who have decided to go to Pennsylvania."[80] Besides names, the document specified the "ratio," the stated reason why a person wanted to leave, and the "status," that is a description of the petitioner's economic situation. The first entry reads as follows:

1. Martin Thommen, the saddler of Bugten [Buckten], with his wife and seven young children.

### RATIO

Since his estate was heavily mortgaged, and since he could not save enough for the [payment of the] interest because of his large household, and since his craft of a saddler was becoming overcrowded and worse every day.

### STATUS

He did not know exactly how much he owned after the payment of his debts since properties were sold at very fluctuating prices; he hoped, however, to net 900 to 1,000 pounds.

The second and third of the petitioners, from the district of Homburg, complained similarly of the great difficulty in saving enough for the payment of interest. They hoped, nevertheless, to net from the sale of their properties perhaps five hundred pounds. The last two mentioned by the bailiff were less fortunate:

---

199, the enmeshing of personal traits and broader economic developments is well portrayed.

79. The relationship between eighteenth-century ruling Swiss towns and their rural domains is analyzed by Paul Roth, *Die Organisation der Basler Landvogteien im 18. Jahrhundert* (Schweizerstudien zur Geschichtswissenschaft, 13 [Zurich, 1925]); also Klaus Sulzer, *Zürcherische Handels- und Gewerbepolitik im Zeitalter des Absolutismus* (Schweizerische Beiträge zur Wirtschafts- und Sozialwissenschaft, VIII [Aarau, 1944]). Sulzer states with precision, p. 4: "From the point of view of the countryside the Zurich polity was a pure aristocracy, in which political rights were the prerogative of a minority, namely of the urban citizens. . . . From this urban point of view, however, the democratic elements are dominant."

80. Original in Staatsarchiv Basel-Stadt, Auswanderung A, 1732–1739; published by Albert B. Faust, "Unpublished Documents on Emigration from the Archives of Switzerland," *Deutsch-Amerikanische Geschichtsblätter*, 18–19 (1920), 13–15.

4. Theodor Vögtlin of Leufelfingen with his wife and their newly-born infant.[81]

RATIO

There was nothing to earn as a day laborer, and he had nothing to lose since he could expect nothing from father and mother.

STATUS

There was not much available and it might perhaps amount to 70 pounds.

5. Hans Buser, called Ganis Hans, of Leufelfingen and his wife and five children.

RATIO

He had tried many things and had striven to make a living, but could not get anywhere; and there was not much work available for a day laborer; had already wanted to leave two years ago.

STATUS

Hoped that his debts could be paid by hook or by crook.

In the case of Martin Thommen, the first of the petitioners, it is not easy to decide whether his plan to leave had resulted from the lure of greater landholding opportunities in Pennsylvania, or whether it was the response to genuine economic distress. On January 10, 1735, the town council of Basel had indeed issued a mandate which prohibited under severe penalties the lending of money to any subject at less than five percent. This Draconian measure, which secured a higher income for the money-lending urban elite, forced the farmers to employ fewer day laborers in order to ease payment of their mortgage obligations: the latter in turn had a hard time finding work.[82] Impoverishment, a widely observed circumstance conducive to emigration, resulted in this case from the exploitative measures of an urban elite whose actions corresponded to later practices of nineteenth-century industrial employers.

The second example illustrates the rise of the entrepreneurial function in Western economies, a major if neglected circumstance

81. The text reads: "mit ihrem Kindbetteren Kindlin."

82. See Adolph Gerber, "Special Investigations" in Albert B. Faust and Gauis M. Braumbaugh, eds., *Lists of Swiss Emigrants* (Washington, 1925), II, 88. The burghers of the city seem to have been intent to buy up the best estates of the hinterland as a form of good investment, *ibid.*, pp. 87–88.

conducive to emigration.[83] Early in the eighteenth century various Swiss from the patrician elites of the towns realized the entrepreneurial opportunities which the opening up of North America for whites under English tutelage presented. In 1709, for instance, Christoph von Graffenried of Bern had set out to recover financial losses by the founding of New Bern in North Carolina. He seems to have been partly inspired by his countryman Franz Louis Michel who had explored entrepreneurial possibilities in Virginia, Maryland, and Pennsylvania between 1701 and 1704.[84]

In the 1730's Jean Pierre Purry (1675–1736), a native of Neuchâtel, followed their example.[85] Purry had originally been a wine merchant by occupation, but soon tried his luck with a variety of projects. In 1713 he went as a planter to Batavia; in 1717 he proposed a plan of settlement to the Dutch East India Company which, however, was rejected. He then invested heavily in John Law's Mississippi scheme and suffered severe losses after its collapse. Purry next turned to England and offered in 1725 to establish six hundred Swiss soldiers on the frontier of South Carolina. But this scheme also came to naught after the proprietors had withdrawn their promise to transport the settlers free of charge. After Carolina became a crown colony, Purry offered to found one of the eleven proposed border townships which were to safeguard English expansion to the South. This plan was accepted.

Purry went to South Carolina in 1730 to select a townsite about

83. For the concept see William Miller, ed., *Men in Business. Essays on the Historical Role of the Entrepreneur* (New York, 1962), especially the introductions and the essay by Robert K. Lamb, "The Entrepreneur and the Community," pp. 91–119. For the Swiss military service the entrepreneurial approach has been taken by Hermann Suter, *Innerschweizerisches Militär-Unternehmertum im 18. Jahrhundert* (Mitteilungen der Antiquarischen Gesellschaft in Zürich, 45 [Zurich, 1971]). The study, prepared under the supervision of Prof. Peyer, should be paralleled by similar investigations concerning emigration.

84. See Vincent H. Todd and Julius Goebel, eds., *Christoph von Graffenried's Account of the Founding of New Bern* (Raleigh, N.C., 1920); on Michel, J. H. Graf, "Franz Michel von Bern und seine ersten Reisen nach Amerika 1701–1704. Ein Beitrag zur Vorgeschichte der Gründung von Neu Bern," *Neues Berner Taschenbuch 1898* (Bern, 1898), pp. 59–144.

85. See Verner W. Crane, "Jean Pierre Purry," *Dictionary of American Biography* (New York, 1935), XV, 270–271; Robert L. Meriwether, *The Expansion of South Carolina 1729–1765* (Kingsport, Tenn., 1940), pp. 34–76; Eugenia Howard, "The Tale of a Legacy," *National Genealogical Society Quarterly*, 56 (June 1968), 83–116, a study that focuses on the Bourquin family.

twenty miles above present-day Savannah, Georgia. He then returned to London, where he secured a landgrant of forty-eight thousand acres and began a vigorous and perhaps unscrupulous advertising campaign. The title of the widely circulated pamphlet set its tone: "The now in the New World happily and without homesickness living Swiss. Or: Brief and pertinent description of the present state of the royal English province Carolina on the basis of recently arrived letters from Swiss who are living there, collected by J. K. L. Bern. Printed by Joh. Bondeli, 1734."[86] The tract did not fail to make a deep impression. It first offered five chapters describing Carolina, followed by answers to a series of objections people might raise to Purry's enterprise; the final part consisted of three letters which had been included "to corroborate this description." The first letter was particularly suggestive. It was entitled: "Letter to his Princely Highness, the Lord Bishop of Basel, written by Johann Baptist Bourquin, his former Secretary of Sonzaboz [Sonceboz] who had left together with his household two years ago."[87]

This inscription misled historians and contemporaries alike, who took it to mean that Bourquin was a clergyman—thus an especially trustworthy witness—and a "crypto-catholic." He was in fact neither, but had simply held the position of notary, that is of administrative official at Sonceboz, which was part of the Protestant section of the prince-bishop's secular domain.[88] The following passage of Bourquin's letter was particularly effective:

86. The title page reads in full: "Der nunmehro in der Neuen Welt vergnügt und ohne Heim-Wehe lebende Schweitzer. Oder: Kurtze und eigentliche Beschreibung des gegenwärtigen Zustands der königlichen englischen Provinz Carolina, aus den neulich angekommenen Brieffen der Alldorten sich befindenden Schweitzeren, zusammengetragen von J. K. L. Bern. Getruckt bey Joh. Bondeli, 1734."

87. *Ibid.*, p. 37.

88. See above, note 56, and corresponding text for the *Frag- und Anzeigungs-Blätlein* (1733), no. XL, "Allerhand Nachrichten," no. 5; also under the rubric "Notes and Comment," *Catholic Historical Review*, 4 (January 1919), 537–539, for the French version of the letter with English translation; p. 537 the erroneous statement: "The letter . . . is another factor in the study of what might be called the crypto-Catholicism of the Colonial period."

This is truly a country where milk and honey are overflowing. . . . It is unnecessary to make hay for the feeding of cattle, horses, etc. within the stables during the winter months, for they find plenty of pasture in the woods and fields all year round. . . . It is one of the best parts of Carolina, formerly called the great Yamasee and inhabited by Indians (of that name), but from whence the English have chased them away, which, however, does not prevent them from being at profound peace with us.[89]

Because of statements such as these Purry's pamphlet came to be known as the "Lugenbüchlein," the "booklet of lies," and various letters from emigrants were to take issue with its false and misleading claims.

Yet the enterprise had practical results. By December 1732 Purry had transported about one hundred fifty settlers to his colony, followed in 1734 by another two hundred sixty; it took some years until the bad news that started to flow back could neutralize Purry's propaganda. Purry, his sons, and especially the Bourquins became well-to-do landholders who invested in imports, slaves, and the planting of rice.[90] Positive reports seem to have been written by people who had a vested interest in the enterprise, if the report of a "Monsieur Hilti, surgeon and engineer" is to be trusted. He had visited Purrysburg in August 1735 as an investigator for the Helvetic Society of Bern and noted in his diary: "From Mr. Eberhard I received notice privately that Mr. Zuberbühler had been promised a great deal of money if he could entice 100 families to this country. I could hardly believe that such Judases exist among Christians; but he has red hair, that says enough."[91]

---

89. *Ibid.*, p. 538. The German version adds: "wie ehemals das gelobte Land Canaan," but changes the reference to the indigenous people to: "We see very little of the wild native inhabitants, and we live on very good terms with them and they with us"; see *Der nunmehro* . . . , p. 39; the term "Lugenbüchlein" in *Neu-gefundenes Eden. Oder: Ausführlicher Bericht von Sud- und Nord Carolina, Pensilphania, Mary-Land, und Virginia* (Bern, 1737), *passim*.

90. Purry's oldest son, who became the leader of the colony in 1736 after the death of his father, had married a rich widow of Charleston and resided in Port Royal. In 1754 he decided to return to Switzerland, but was killed by his slaves; see Eugene de Pradel, *La Mort de Wart* . . . (Neuchâtel et Berne, 1829), p. 9. On the holdings of the Bourquins see Howard, "Tale," pp. 92–111.

91. See *Neu-gefundenes Eden*, p. 18. Zuberbühler was the son of the clergyman Bartholomäus Zuberbühler 1678–1738) who led an emigrant group in 1736.

The founding of Purrysburg is only one example of what might be called "emigration entrepreneurship." When Purry's friend, a Mr. Jean Chambrier, had admonished Purry to imitate his example and to save at least two hundred thousand francs for his wife and children, Purry is said to have answered coldly: "One talks here only of millions; one must, therefore, risk millions, then we will profit."[92] The hundreds of Swiss settlers who went to South Carolina in the 1730's would probably not have left without Purry's entrepreneurial activity.[93] He saw it as his function to create emigrants whose transfer would bring him and his associates substantial gains. He therefore had to become a manipulator of the motivational process, a catalyst for the emigration decision, by skillfully stressing such aspects of the projected settlement as contrasted most favorably with the home situation and at the same time appealed to a wide range of human desires.[94]

A third set of circumstances affecting the decision to emigrate arises out of the fabric of a given *society*, the domain of human ties. Relations between husband and wife, parents and children, and between members of a kinship group are subject to strain. These relations are at the same time embedded in a socially fostered system of norms which are easily broken but often mercilessly vindicated by socially appointed guardians. The experience of Michael Schlatter (1716–1790) may serve as an example. When he was a young curate, he had the misfortune to fall in love with the daughter of the pastor under whom he served. When she became pregnant, he was not allowed to marry her and lost his post because of the "scandal." He subsequently went to Amsterdam, where he accepted the task of organizing the Reformed Church in Pennsylvania and New Jersey under the tutelage of the Classis of Amsterdam. He proved himself an outstanding man in every respect, but

92. Pradel, *La Mort*, pp. 5–6.
93. Compare the further notice in the *Bernische Avis-Blättlein* (1735), quoted by G. Kurz, "Special Investigations," Faust and Braumbaugh, eds., *Lists*, II, 25; "There have arrived here [London] 340 Swiss who have no money left to pay for their passage to Carolina and who are in the most dire need because of Mr. Purry's little book."
94. Howard, "Tale," p. 92, overstates perhaps: "Purry undertook a promotional scheme which would put the real estate sharks of today to shame."

the social stigma resulting from his trespass was to haunt him for years and was the main circumstance which led to his emigration.[95]

Two other examples, taken from the lists of the Zurich pastors mentioned above, illuminate relevant social realities. In the emigrant list that was handed in by the pastor of Kloten, this entry is to be found:

Jakob Brunner departed with Jacob Vetter's daughter whom he had made pregnant and by whom he had an illegitimate child. Because the honorable marriage court did not allow their marriage, he left, 44 years of age. Has left five children to the parish, two sons and three daughters, for whom the church and the commune now have to care as a heavy burden.[96]

The same harsh judgment appears also in the entry of the baptismal record, dated June 6, 1742: "Jakob; illegitimate; of Hans Jakob Brunner, scortator [adulterer], and Elsbeth Vetter of Basserstorf."[97]

Both entries are actually less than fair, nor are they fully accurate. On May 8, 1742, a month before the birth, the marriage court had declared the child legitimate, a fact the pastor must have known but chose to ignore. The situation was as follows: Jacob Brunner, a poor day laborer, had lost his wife Magdalena Altorffer (1700–1741) on May 9, 1741, only three weeks after the birth of their sixth child named Susanna; also the infant died some months later, on January 20, 1742.[98] During the summer of 1741 Jacob Brunner had apparently made the promise of marriage to Elsbeth Vetter. The children, who were between the ages of eleven and one, were certainly in need of a woman's care. The commune of Kloten, however, owing to Brunner's poverty, objected strenuously to his remarriage and brought the matter before the marriage court. The

95. See the letters of November 5 and December 17, 1751, by Heinrich Stähli, pastor in St. Gall, to the Antistes of the Zurich Church, Staatsarchiv Zurich, Sign. E II, 434. The best source on Schlatter is William J. Hinke, ed., "Diary of the Reverend Michael Schlatter," *Journal of the Presbyterian Historical Society*, 3 (1905), 105–121, 158–176.

96. *Lists*, I, 61, list 48; his translation changes the last name Vetter mistakenly to "cousin."

97. "Bassersdorf Pfarrbuch 1706–1794," p. 229, Staatsarchiv Zurich, Sign. E III, 11.2; 1742, no. 18.

98. The death dates are from the "Kloten Pfarrbuch 1734–1819," pp. 18, 20, Staatsarchiv Zurich, Sign. E III, 63.6, verso.

court honored the commune's request, but legitimized the yet unborn child. When Brunner and Vetter continued to live together, the court issued a stern warning and threatened Elsbeth Vetter with "chastisement and punishment."[99] It was under these circumstances of harsh social pressure that the couple emigrated. Their poverty probably forced them to leave the children of Brunner's first marriage behind.

The second case refers to circumstances of an entirely different sort. Johann Heinrich Holzhalb, pastor of Rafz, reported the emigration of four single young men and two girls. They left, he commented, "not exactly with the intention that they had firmly resolved to settle in Pennsylvania, but partly as journeymen of their trades. . . . They therefore entertain the hope that, if they return single and with good credentials of good behavior, this would not impair their right to citizenship."[100] These emigrants therefore left in pursuit of social mobility. Experience abroad has remained an important asset to this day in climbing the occupational ladder in Switzerland; to gain this experience has frequently been a circumstance inducing people to emigrate.

A fourth set of circumstances favoring emigration rests on *political events* of a regional or national scope. Upsets in party leadership, the overthrow of ruling families, unsuccessful revolts, or revolutions are characteristic of all political systems. Emigration offers itself as one alternative to the losers. Decisions by political authorities to further emigration positively as a solution to pressing socioeconomic problems also belong in this category.

In 1749 a group of dissatisfied Bernese citizens tried to overthrow the ruling elite, which had effectively narrowed the circle of burghers eligible to run the affairs of state. Samuel Henzi (1701–1749) was the leader of this unsuccessful attempt. He advocated broadening of the franchise and was a proponent of the French language, which was spoken in parts of the Bernese common-

99. "Ehegerichts-Protokolle 1743," p. 73, Staatsarchiv Zurich, Sign YY, 1.234, February 18, 1743.
100. *Lists*, I, 74, list 66.

wealth.[101] Among Henzi's followers was the goldsmith Gabriel Fueter who escaped to England after the attempted coup had failed. The fugitive was condemned to death in absentia, but his wife and children were allowed to follow him abroad. The family settled in Chelsea, near London, where a fifth child, named Christian, was born to the couple in 1752. Two years later the family emigrated to New York, where in 1756 a second daughter, named Catharina, was born.

The fate of the various family members, as far known, illustrates the different effect the same circumstances had on the family. The three oldest sons, Ludwig Anton, Daniel Emmanuel, and Sigmund Emmanuel, as well as the younger daughter Catharina, remained in America. Ludwig Anton, born 1742, was reportedly shipwrecked near Jamaica in 1782 and died in the West Indies in 1786. Daniel Emmanuel, born 1747, was a goldsmith and a merchant in New York City, where he died in 1824. His daughter Kitty, born 1789, returned to Switzerland and died in Bern in 1850.

The father, Gabriel Fueter, returned in 1770 to Switzerland and lived near Neuchâtel until 1779, when he was pardoned by the Bernese authorities and returned to his native city. Fueter's older daughter Maria Catharina, born 1748, also returned home, where she married the customs official Johann Rudolf Risold. The son Christian, born in England, also settled in Bern, where he worked as a noted engraver; in 1791, he advanced to the position of mint-master of the Canton.[102]

A second example shows a different dimension of the political circumstances surrounding emigration. In the 1850's the economic situation in the region of the Canton of Solothurn called the Gäu became depressed. Cold and wet weather conditions brought crop failures and rising prices. The establishment of textile factories de-

---

101. See Edgar Bonjour et al., *A Short History of Switzerland* (Oxford, 1952), p. 202; Richard Feller, *Geschichte Berns III* (Bern, 1955), pp. 447–463; G. Kurz, "Investigations," p. 32, gives the name of the father as Daniel.

102. "Aus- und Einwanderer," Staatsarchiv Bern, a two-volume manuscript which lists names alphabetically for the time span 1660 to 1830. The volumes are part of the reference materials of the supervising archivist.

stroyed the craft of handweaving in which some twelve hundred people of the canton were engaged. This resulted in an oversupply of labor and falling wages. A pound of flour cost 40 to 50 cents, a kilo of potatoes 16 to 18 cents; yet a daily wage of a laborer amounted to only 40 to 70 cents.[103]

Under these circumstances thirty-five of the approximately one hundred communes of the canton engaged in an active policy of emigration; they collectively spent a quarter million francs in subsidies to emigrants.[104] A survey for the cantonal government gave the statistics shown in Table V. According to the governmental report some communes had paid out huge sums; Hägendorf, for instance, put up 23,000 francs, Bärschwyl 20,000, Oberbuchstein 17,000, and Gunzgen 10,000. "The outlay of almost all communes consisted of the full payment of the travel costs to New York; and each person arriving there received an additional small settlement subsidy of 16 to 30 francs. The transportation contracts were almost entirely concluded by the communes themselves as the responsible contracting agents."[105] A breakdown of the subsidies given out by four communes in relation to total population and number of emigrants, shown in Table VI, provides some valuable correlations. The expenses incurred for emigrants by the commune of Gunzgen, which totalled 12,000 francs, were itemized as follows:

8750 Fr.: For transportation, paid to emigration agents (ca. 180 Fr. for adults, 130 Fr. for children).

1700 Fr.: For transportation of individual emigrants to New Orleans.

1550 Fr.: For clothing and equipment (cost for a woman's dress 1 Fr., for a man's pants and vest 1.70 Fr., for a child's dress 90 cents, for a man's pair of shoes 7 to 8 Fr.).[106]

---

103. See Ernst Häfliger, *Die Auswanderung nach Amerika in den 5oer Jahren des 19. Jahrhunderts* (Olten, 1908), p. 6.

104. *Ibid.*, pp. 13–14.

105. *Einundzwanzigster Rechenschaftsbericht der Regierung an die gesetzgebende Behörde des Kantons Solothurn* (Solothurn, 1855), pp. 171–172.

106. Häfliger, *Auswanderung*, p. 15.

## Table V

EMIGRATION SUBSIDIES OF DISTRICTS OF THE
CANTON OF SOLOTHURN FOR 1854

| District | Number of communes | Emigrants supported | Total of subsidies | Subsidies per commune | Subsidy per person |
|---|---|---|---|---|---|
| Solothurn-lebern | 1 | 1 | 100 Fr. | 100 Fr. | 100 Fr. |
| Bucheggberg-Kriegstetten | 20 | 321 | 54,622 | 2,731 | 170 |
| Balsthal-Gäu | 6 | 120 | 28,600 | 4,760 | 238 |
| Olten-Gösgen | 6 | 288 | 55,475 | 9,246 | 192 |
| Dorneck-Thierstein | 2 | 162 | 38,000 | 19,000 | 234 |
| TOTAL | 35 | 892 | 176,797 | 5,051 | 198 |

SOURCES: Häfliger, *Auswanderung*, pp. 12–13; based on *Einundzwanzigster Rechenschaftsbericht der Regierung an die gesetzgebende Behörde des Kantons Solothurn* (Solothurn, 1885), pp. 170–172.

## Table VI

EMIGRATION SUBSIDIES OF FOUR COMMUNES IN RELATION TO
NUMBER OF EMIGRANTS AND POPULATION TOTAL

| Communes | Inhabitants 1850 | Emigrants 1854 Absolute | Percent | Total Subsidies | Subsidies per person |
|---|---|---|---|---|---|
| Hägendorf | 1,113 | 120 | 10.8 | 23,600 Fr. | 191.67 Fr. |
| Gunzgen | 514 | 60 | 11.7 | 12,000 Fr. | 200.00 Fr. |
| Kappel | 550 | 76 | 13.8 | 10,000 Fr. | 131.58 Fr. |
| Boningen | 280 | 30 | 10.7 | 7,050 Fr. | 285.00 Fr. |

SOURCES: The population figures from *Uebersichten der Bevölkerung der Schweiz nach den Ergebnissen der letzten eidgenössischen Volkszählung* (Bern, 1851), pp. 148–159; the figures for emigrants are given by Häfliger, *Auswanderung*, p. 13.

The fact that many communes of the Canton of Solothurn offered people this kind of help was the result of a group decision by the respective smallest political units of the state. The emigrant transfer as a major "intervening obstacle" was practically eliminated at least in the financial sense.[107]

Still another set of circumstances conducing to emigration is embedded in the domain of *religion*, the world of mythopoeic thought and institutionalized ritual. This world is marked in the Christian West and in Islam by the tenet of ideological exclusivity. This tenet creates three historical circumstances conducive to emigration. First, new interpretations of religious perception lead within the context of exclusivity to conflict with dominant thought-forms and may drive the followers into permanent exile. This fate was experienced by the Swiss Brethren and by the separatist-minded Swiss pietists.[108] The second situation results from the missionary impulse which may be called expansionist exclusivity. Swiss missionary enterprises of the Protestant or Catholic persuasion in transoceanic lands are an expression of this drive,[109] as well as the emigration of those Swiss who were converted to the Mormon faith and then moved to Utah, the promised land of their new creed.[110] The third situation emerges as a corollary of secular emigration. Emigrants were to be preserved within the confines of their given faith; thus ministers, priests, and nuns followed their trails and often assumed leadership roles in the building up of new white societies.[111]

The migrations of the Swiss Brethren exemplify this set of circumstances. In the 1520's Switzerland like other European regions

107. The term is taken from Everett S. Lee, "A Theory of Migration," *Demography*, 3 (1966), 50. The transfer is an "obstacle" due to its cost and the risk taking it involves.

108. See especially Ernst Müller, *Geschichte der bernischen Täufer* (Frauenfeld, 1895); Delbert L. Gratz, *Bernese Anabaptists and Their American Descendants* (Scottdale, Pa., 1953).

109. A valuable survey is Johannes Beckmann, "Die katholischen Schweizermissionen in Vergangheit und Gegenwart," *Studia Missionalia*, 9 (1955–1956), 129–171; Ernst Rippmann, "Die äussere Mission," *Die evangelischen Kirchen der Schweiz* (Gotha, 1935).

110. Douglas D. Alder offers much material in "The German-speaking Immigration to Utah 1850–1950," (unpub. MA thesis, University of Utah, 1959); a returner's biased, but valuable account is Bartholome Kellenberger, *Erlebnisse eines abgefallenen Mormonen während seines siebenjährigen Aufenthaltes in Utah, dem Mormonenstaate* (Herisau, 1883).

111. Two surveys rich in detail are Ernst Stähelin, "Schweizer Theologen im Dienste der Reformierten Kirche in den Vereinigten Staaten," *Schweizerische Theologische Zeitschrift*, 36 (1918), 152–177, 196–238; and Georg Staffelbach, *Schweizer als Glaubensboten und Kulturträger in Nordamerika* (Schüpfheim, Kt. Luzern, 1940).

experienced a serious religious split. Followers of the traditional faith were faced by a mostly urban group of reformers who succeeded in translating their new vision into durable institutions. But a third group arose, incorrectly labelled by their adversaries as "anabaptists," that is "rebaptizers." This group experienced severe persecutions by Catholics and Protestants alike, not only in Switzerland but throughout Western Europe.[112] The migrations of the Swiss "Brethren," the name they themselves preferred, are thus no surprise. Some eight thousand are estimated to have emigrated directly from Switzerland or from other, mostly south German, areas, to the territory of the United States.[113]

The migrations of the Swiss Brethren were directly related to three particular tenets of their creed which were not only opposed to basic assumptions of the Swiss polity, but also to new trends in economic life after 1500.[114] First, the Brethren rejected the idea of the *Corpus Christianum*, accepted by both Catholics and Protestants, which assumed that the confines of the church were to be coextensive with those of the state. The baptism of children was a logical outcome of this view, but rigorously rejected by the Brethren. In their view the church was not a general institution, but exclusively the community of the converted, the holy people of God. Infant baptism was simply blasphemy. Neither Catholics nor Protestants were baptized, but heathens. This radical ideological assault was translated into socially visible action. Adults baptized as infants underwent this rite again and newborn children were not brought to the clergymen for baptism.

The second tenet defined the nature of the state. In the view of

---

112. Horst W. Schraepler, *Die rechtliche Behandlung der Täufer in der deutschen Schweiz, Süddeutschland und Hessen 1525–1618* (Tübingen, 1957), p. 106, estimates some 5,000 victims. Gratz, *Bernese Anabaptists*, p. 10, gives for 1534 to 1540 these figures for Bern: 158 imprisoned, 109 expelled, 20 executed.

113. Compare Harold S. Bender, "Migrations: Swiss–South German," *Mennonite Encyclopedia*, 3 (1957), 686.

114. Compare L. Schelbert, "Swiss Migration to America: The Swiss Mennonites," (PhD diss., Columbia University, 1966, Ann Arbor Microfilms, 1967), pp. 99–142; on the founder of the Swiss Brethren see Harold S. Bender, *Conrad Grebel c. 1498–1526* (Goshen, Ind., 1950); Zwingli's response to Gerbel and his father is reexamined by L. Schelbert, "Jacob Grebel's Trial Revised," *Archive for Reformation History*, 60 (1969), 32–64.

the Brethren church and state were not the twofold expression of the one divine authority among men, but antagonists. Thus the Brethren in another form of visible sociopolitical action rejected the oath, military service, and clergy who served simultaneously as civil servants, particularly within the Reformed churches. The third tenet of the Brethren affecting emigration seems to have developed no earlier than 1540. By that time it had become a firmly held view among them that farming was the only divinely ordained occupation. The creed, originally formulated by university-trained urban intellectuals or clergymen, now became ruralized not only socially but also theologically.[115]

From 1525 to about 1750 the Swiss Brethren experienced no secure peace. Imprisonment, banishment, dispossession, even sporadic executions were the weapons used against the "deviant" Brethren who adhered to their faith with impressive heroism. But emigration continued even after oppression had ceased. The need for good agricultural land for the grown sons of the mostly large families led the Brethren not only to the Rhenish Palatinate and Russia, but to Pennsylvania, and from there to Indiana, Ohio, and Illinois and on to Canada and Brazil.[116]

The creed of the Brethren was the matrix in which the circumstances of their migration arose. It must be kept in mind, however, that many Brethren never moved. They accepted periodic attacks as divinely ordained trials, or became crypto-Brethren, or gradually abandoned the rejection of the state and the strict adherence to the farming way of life.[117]

## C. THE MOTIVATIONAL PROCESS

Man's inner springs of action are seldom fully known, even to the actor himself. The decision to emigrate represents no exception, and emigrants only rarely write about what made them take their

115. Compare Harold S. Bender, "Farming and Settlement," *Mennonite Encyclopedia*, 2 (1956), 303.

116. See Bender, "Migrations," pp. 686–687.

117. An excellent case study is S. F. Pannabecker, "Nineteenth Century Swiss Mennonite Immigrants and Their Adherence to the General Conference Mennonite Church," *Mennonite Quarterly Review*, 21 (April 1947), 64–102.

momentous step. The available documents are rich in detail about the transfer and about the new world that immigrants found themselves in, yet only occasional allusions afford some insight into the motivational process. Three points are clear.

First, neither preconditions nor circumstances lead by themselves to emigration, but must coalesce into a personal motivation by a complex process which underlies the emigration decision.

Second, the emigration decision is the result of a judgment by which positive and negative elements perceived in the home country, in the transfer process, and in the receiving country are more or less carefully weighed against each other.

Third, the evaluation of those elements occurs on the basis of individual, partly inborn, partly socially conditioned traits of an emigrant.

Explanations of why people emigrated often overlook the fact that neither the sending nor receiving country, nor the process of transfer is perceived as all good or all bad. The homeland, for instance, is at least a known entity; its language, customs, institutions, climate are, at least in an immediate sense, predictable; relatives and friends, and also the dead, represent strong ties not only painful to sever but also risky. This predictability of home, and the often resulting sense of the protection that it can provide, is perceived by some as an invaluable good that keeps them at home. By others these facts are taken lightly or perceived as impediments to unfettered growth. The transfer shows a similar double face. The lure of the unknown, the experience of a wider world, the moving between a world that was and a world to come mean unbearable uprootedness and heightened vulnerability to some, but a magnificent adventure to others. One emigrant experienced the transfer as an engaging challenge, the other as a protracted nightmare to be endured.

The same holds true for the immigrant situation. The first years of reestablishing a household, an ordered rhythm of life in changed and alien natural as well as human surroundings, was experienced by some as a creative and rewarding phase of their lives, by others as a dark passage, evoking even fonder memories of the old home.

A basic principle of human experience applies also to emigration—things of existence become clarified only in the process of being acted out. The emigration decision was a step into the dark; only the actual experience enabled emigrants to assess its wisdom and its value.[118] In responding to the inherently problematical aspects of emigration the uniqueness of the individual played a decisive, if analytically elusive, role.

Some examples may intimate the part that individuality played in the emigration decision. In the lists of the Zurich pastors quoted earlier the following entry by Salomon Hirzel, pastor of Oetwyl, is baffling:

Jakob von Tobel of Willikon, baptized June 9, 1679. This man had been earlier a church warden. Finally he turned his estate over to his three sons and accepted from them for eight years annually 80 florins as a personal rent for life, besides a quarter of an acre of vines and [the amount of] hay sufficient for a cow. He was married to Elsbeth Frey of Uster, his second wife. He left without notifying his family or anybody else on Sunday morning, May 12, 1743. His family thought that he had taken along 65 florins.[119]

What inspired this sixty-four-year-old man to leave? No external situation can be discovered which made his step understandable. Was it perhaps von Tobel's way of saying no to old age, to approaching death, or just a very personal longing to get a glimpse of the wider world?

Similar questions arise in the case of Dr. Caspar Koepfli, who left Switzerland in 1831 at the head of the emigrant group which was to found Highland, Illinois.[120] He was fifty-nine years of age when he left; his children were grown and in good circumstances; he had practiced medicine for thirty years, was well-to-do and respected, though too radical a man for many circles. In a farewell note Koepfli stated why he was leaving. The document is solemnly dated "Sursee, April 22, 1831, on the day before departure, at 3 p.m." It carried the motto: "Attention you old ones, thus are the

118. Compare Lee, "A Theory of Migration," p. 50.

119. *Lists*, I, 71, list 61.

120. A general history of Highland is A. P. Spencer, *Centennial History of Highland, Illinois 1837–1937* (Highland, 1937).

new ones." He was leaving, Koepfli wrote, because he believed with Heinrich Zschokke that "the occident will soon see its sun set, and the sun setting here will be the newly rising sun in America. America or Europe! — Which man of vigor and lust for life could waver between the two?"

More precisely, Koepfli told his friends: "The feeling for religious, political, and civic freedom is the triple motivation of our decision." And again: "The learned world may preach against it as much as it likes, one can factually prove that the Old World suffers from an evil from which it can recover only by the promotion of colonisation—its name is overpopulation."[121] Koepfli had read Duden's travel account,[122] and had corresponded with him about Missouri, which Koepfli expected to be a farmer's paradise. But when he arrived in St. Louis and went out to search for a suitable place, he liked neither Missouri's soil nor the institution of slavery. He therefore turned eastward into Illinois, where his party decided to settle in the Looking Glass Prairie southeast of Edwardsville, Illinois.

After ten years in Highland, Dr. Koepfli, now sixty-nine, decided to return home. He involved himself again in public affairs and planned to publish his voluminous writings. Yet his ideas, especially on religion, were less than appreciated, and Koepfli finally decided to return to Highland, where he died in 1854.[123] Nowhere did he seem to find the type of society which his farewell note had so ardently envisioned. Was Koepfli a man who could never fully reconcile the real with the ideal? This personal trait, far more than conditions at home or abroad, seems to have accounted for his emigration decision. This decision was a way of solving a personal existential problem rather than a response to the lure of opportunities or to the pressure of circumstances.

A third example shows clearly how people who know of the same preconditions and are in the same circumstances arrive at op-

121. Zschokke, "Beitrag," pp. 422–424.
122. Gottfried Duden, *Bericht über eine Reise nach den westlichen Staaten Nordamerika's und einen mehrjährigen Aufenthalt am Missouri . . .* (St. Gallen, 1832).
123. Zschokke, "Beitrag," p. 446, note 52.

posite decisions. On March 20, 1842, the family of Bartholomäus Ragatz, consisting of the parents, eight sons, and two daughters left their native village Tamins in the Canton of Grisons, in order to settle in southern Wisconsin. The family was well-to-do, owned a good home and a profitable sawmill. The father had held the office of mayor and was well respected. Why, then, did this fifty-year-old man give up his secure economic, social, and political position and journey thousands of miles to start life anew? His son explained that his father had compared "that land of golden hope and bright prospects" with the rather depressed economic state of Switzerland. Not for his own sake, but for the sake of the children he had chosen years of insecurity during which only hard labor could establish a new foundation for the family.[124]

Ragatz's wife, a courageous and dedicated woman, did not share her husband's judgment although she bowed to his decision. At home as well as on the new farm near Sauk City, Wisconsin, she sometimes broke into tears and sobbed helplessly. "She many times said to father," reported her son: "Would that I could have your faith. Why, it will be a thousand years before this land is filled up. Our children and all that follow them, for generations to come, will be uncouth peasants!" Both parents cared for their children equally, but they judged things differently. What was for one a golden opportunity, was seen by the other as a serious worsening of conditions.

Why did Bartholomäus Ragatz see things the way he did? Perhaps the following remark by his son provides a clue. "Often at eventide, he would go before the cabin and look about him exultantly, saying: it is ours, every bit ours. We have wrested these smiling fields from the wilderness."[125] Was it a strongly developed acquisitive instinct which had driven him, or perhaps the will to prove that old age and death could not touch him for a long time still? One can never know for sure, but the case of the Ragatz family shows the force of individuality in the making of emigrants.

124. Ragatz, "Memoirs," pp. 188–189.
125. *Ibid.*, p. 219.

Both parents had the same data at hand, both loved the children with equal depth; yet one turned emigrant, the other would never have left if permitted to stay.

A last example will give a particularly detailed insight into the making of an emigrant. At the end of February 1848, Elisabeth Sommer of Basel received the following letter from her husband, then in St. Louis, Missouri:

Dear Wife,

I hope that you will read these lines in good health, the same as I am myself, thank God, and I am wishing that soon I shall not have to write anymore but will be able to talk with you and dear Arnold in person. As of now, I am married to Leonhard Musgach, tailor of Benken, which means he is my bed-fellow until you are with me again. Do write to me soon about yourself and Arnold, and tell me in detail how everything has gone since I left. You can read the report about my voyage in the letter which I wrote to Behni. If you do not have time during the day, write at night just as I am now forced to do since I have taken on work with a master.

Now get on your own feet and be a man! Put your trust in God's help; he has mercifully helped me through everything. Be prudent in whatever you do, and Behni is going to assist you with his advice. Do not lose a day so you can get here before the heat sets in, and make careful inquiries so that you will join up with trusty people. If Father could raise the travel money you would be well off in his care on your voyage. Read the letter which I wrote to Behni so you will know how to comport yourself. Do not trust anybody too much. Keep to yourself as much as possible. Be on your guard on the ship for there are rascals. Never let Arnold out of sight, for a child can quickly come to grief on board. The hatchways are mighty steep.

Your guardian must petition the orphan commission about the fare money, and if the prospects are not good have Behni compose a request for collecting. Do not be bashful; you are going to leave, after all. Mistress Eglin will also advise and help you.

You will surely like St. Louis better than Basel, and you can meet congenial people here. Even if I only work as a journeyman here, I will earn so much money that I can support my family well, and even better once I am on my own. Then you can freely dip into the butter crock. Everything is very cheap. A pound of pork cost not even one batzen according to Basel money.

It is late, I must close and see that the letter gets in the mail tomorrow. I will write again in two weeks but please answer this one right away. Remember me to all my and your family and to all who ask about me. If you still have the two books with the papers, you know the one by [?] the fishmarket and from the book shop, and the other one, take them with you, I can make good use of them.

My very best to you, your faithfully loving husband,

Melchior Sommer

[written on the margin:] You will need at least 300 fr. travel money.[126]

The woman acted with dispatch, although characterized by her guardian, Niclaus Bernoulli, as "slow in her work and unable to accomplish much." Her petition was first presented to the authorities on February 21, and finally accepted by the Citizens' Commission on March 29 for a variety of reasons. The woman was poor and "had not the least claim to her husband's property." The welfare costs for her were likely to increase in the future since her boy was growing up and the woman's health less than satisfactory. Elisabeth Sommer was therefore to receive the money for the trip, but only as a payment in advance to be repaid at a later date. She and her husband were also expected "to take immediately after arrival the necessary steps for the future acquisition of American citizenship." In the beginning of April 1848, the woman promptly left to join her husband in St. Louis.[127]

On June 6, 1848, however, the police of the city of Basel reported that it had apprehended, as instructed, the citizen Melchior Sommer, the painter, "in order to question him about his deserting his family etc."[128] The investigation had shown that Sommer "was 28 years of age, married, father of a two-year old child, married since 1842; had left from here October 17, 1847 for America and returned again last week." Concerning the charge of desertion, Sommer had this to say:

We had agreed with each other that I would have her follow me with the child if I succeeded in finding work and making a living in America. And I have always kept her informed about me. But when I considered the voyage too dangerous for my wife and child, especially from New Orleans to St. Louis where I worked last, I decided to rejoin them here. On the return voyage I was dismayed to learn in Havre that she and the child, without waiting

126. Letter and the other documents in Staatsarchiv Basel-Stadt, Auswanderung A, 1848–1853.

127. Report of the Bürger Commission, *passim*.

128. Report of police chief Landerer.

for further news from me, had departed for America last April with the help of a subsidy from here. Now I am here and waiting for her to return; but in case she wants to stay there I will again follow her and try again to make a go of it over there together with her.[129]

Sommer's friend, the baker Rudolf Stauber-Delaquis, supported this testimony. He had not preserved his friend's letter, Stauber testified.:

But I can tell you this much, that he wrote in his letter he would probably come to Basel no earlier than December because he had to earn the travel money first; therefore, I as well as many others had tried to hold his wife back . . . but to no avail. She answered me: "Once I am with him, I am sure he will be contented again."[130]

On August 10, 1848, the case was closed by the authorities. Sommer was not guilty of desertion, the final decision explained, "since he had departed [for America] with the knowledge and consent of his wife to find a new economic basis there; but he could not endure the climate there." His first letter had indeed invited his wife to come, but then various letters had advised against it and had announced his return. It was thus the fault of the woman "if she found herself in America in a sad situation."[131]

A superficial glance at Elisabeth Sommer's emigration would easily categorize her as part of a "mass migration" since she was poor and socially ill-situated. Yet a closer examination reveals that she had made a genuine decision. The first letter of her husband had persuaded her that life in St. Louis was on balance preferable to staying to Basel. The less than appealing task of begging for travel money and the risks of the trip could not deter her from acting upon that conviction. The negative letters of her husband she interpreted as resulting from homesickness and from his longing for his family. Once they were reunited, her husband would also prefer St. Louis to Basel. Elisabeth Sommer's wrong decision was not the result of irrationality. She had carefully weighed preconditions and circumstances in the light of her own personality and thus arrived at a perfectly reasonable, unlucky decision.

129. Report of the city police, June 5, 1848.
130. Letter to the city clerk, July 12, 1848.
131. Report of the Bürger Commission, August 10, 1848.

# GERMAN EMIGRATION TO THE UNITED STATES

Wolfgang Köllmann and Peter Marschalck

Translated by Thomas C. Childers

# GERMAN EMIGRATION TO
# THE UNITED STATES

## I

IN the monthly report of the Arnsberg district administration to the provincial government in Münster in February 1818, one of the earliest official references of a high Prussian civil servant to the emigration question is found:

The desire to immigrate to America which has surfaced in both Wittgenstein counties is an epidemic which has aroused our particular attention. Recently 14 heads of families with 71 dependents and 24 individuals, 109 people in all, have declared themselves ready to emigrate and have applied for permission. The wealth taken with these people is recorded at over 7,561 talers in Berlin currency. Still others are supposedly determined to follow a similar course. This same *Wandergeist* is also said to have broken out in the areas of Hesse-Darmstadt bordering the Wittgenstein counties. Although invitations from earlier emigrants with promises of better conditions in America have arrived in these regions, they are not considered the chief cause of the emigration. Instead, the poverty and the impending total lack of sustenance are expressly mentioned by district officials. Given the decline in business, we have, according to this hypothesis, very much to fear from this desire to emigrate, which is on the rise, especially if greed should intervene and take its usual toll. Therefore, we are of the opinion that the evil can be most effectively checked at the source and that, since no compulsion can be applied in this matter, the poor people lacking sustenance can perhaps best be deterred from their intention of leaving by some form of relief and provision of wage-labor.[1]

NOTE: Parts I, II, and V are by Wolfgang Köllmann, parts III and IV by Peter Marschalck.

1. State Archives, Münster; Report of the Provincial Administration no. 350, vol. 1, p. 30. The administrative levels of Prussia were: the municipality (*Bürgermeister*), the county (*Landrat*), the district (*Regierungspräsident*), and the province (*Oberpräsident* with the rank of a minister). During the reorganization of Westphalia, which was ceded to Prussia in 1815, the two counties of Wittgenstein formed a single unit. The Grand Duchy of Hesse-Darmstadt was a small sovereign state in the German Confederation.

This report is of particular interest because it not only highlights the problem of rising agrarian pauperism in the Westphalian Sauerland, the "backwoods" of the province, but also because it provides a terse but accurate analysis of the situation that led to the emigration. The immediate impetus was the agrarian and commercial crisis of 1816–1817, the effects of which were most sharply felt in these economically backward regions. A certain knowledge of the country of destination could also be assumed. At the same time, the liberal economic and social views prevailing in the Prussian state had eliminated the prohibitions upon emigration that were universal under the absolutism of the eighteenth century. Thus, those desiring to emigrate could not be restrained by force but only by providing opportunities for employment.

Certainly the small Prussian *Landrat*, from whom this report to his superior originated, had no conception of migration theories as they were later developed, but he had instinctively grasped the fundamentals. The decisive factors for the emergence of a migratory movement are the economic and social conditions in the area of departure. Furthermore, its direction and goal are determined by knowledge of better economic and social chances in another area. Every migration can therefore be defined as an effort to remove economic, social, or even cultural disparities between two areas. The capacity to provide subsistence is not, however, to be understood only quantitatively as the sum of the objectively given possibilities for existence on a particular land surface. It must also be conceived qualitatively as the sum of the possibilities for subsistence that are acceptable within the norms of the society in question. Thus, the subsistence capacity has no absolute size but can be altered by economic developments as well as by shifting social norms intimately interacting with economic and social processes. At the same time, this reciprocal relationship is the element that produces population pressure on the subsistence capacity. Absolute overpopulation beyond the objectively given possibilities for existence, as feared by Malthus and his supporters, is not the phenomenon that activates the real dialectic between economic and demographic processes. The operative factor is *relative* overpopulation or, rather, the perceived danger of relative overpopulation.

If extreme situations of this sort lead in the long run to changes in economic modes and reproductive patterns, population pressure on the capacity to provide subsistence can, in the short or fairly short run, be alleviated. The primary effect of every migration is, therefore, to reduce the surplus population in the region of departure and to fill up an underpopulated region of destination, whose subsistence capacity may be improved by the arrival of newcomers.[2] Thus for the people in the region of departure not only knowledge of the other region is presupposed but also an evaluation of it by their own social norms. The disparity between subsistence capacities therefore becomes relativized. However, this disparity is not necessarily perceived to the same extent by people from the regions of departure and of destination. When different socio-economic or even socio-cultural factors are present, the disparity is often recognized only by the newcomers. Thus, the nomadic Indians considered the prairie of the American Midwest to be completely filled up, while the peasant settlers from Europe viewed it as "empty" space for settlement and occupied it.

Since knowledge and evaluation of the area of destination are assumed, every migration is the product of conscious decision. This decision is preceded, whether consciously or not, by a relaxation of social ties in the home area, rooted in changes in living conditions. It is expressed in the motivation for the decision to emigrate, in which socio-economic, ideological-religious, political, or cultural factors are brought to bear. Thus, the available *Lebensraum* for those persecuted for their beliefs or their political convictions may be just as restricted as for the scholar who cannot find appropriate cultural or research opportunities. Since society cannot or will not provide them with the necessary latitude, they will emigrate or, in extreme cases, flee, even when the socio-economic conditions in the region of departure are characteristic of an underpopulated area. Thus, in the decision to emigrate, the evaluation of subsistence capacities is subjectively conditioned.

2. The first to point out this effect of immigration were Eugen and Alexander Kulischer, *Kriegs- und Wanderzüge, Weltgeschichte als Völkerbewegung* (Berlin, 1932), pp. 4ff.

For the emergence of migratory movements, freedom of emigration in the area of departure is not absolutely necessary, but the possibility of acceptance in a target region is. Supposing the target region to be physically capable of accommodating newcomers, their reception can be limited not only by restrictive legislation but also by social conditions which make adaptation and integration difficult. Thus, aside from economic factors, conditions in the region of destination can influence the direction, strength, and structure of emigration movements.

In contrast to free emigrations, there are forced migrations by flight and expulsion. Once again, the withdrawal of possibilities of existence in the region of departure is fundamental, but the readiness of the target region to absorb the newcomers cannot be taken for granted. Residency or occupational restrictions may strengthen the desire to return home when conditions there have taken a new turn.

As in the case of forced migration, the desire for permanent settlement in the region of destination is not necessarily present in free migrations. Such migrations with the goal of returning more often serve to improve the participants' economic and social position in the homeland than to enable them to grasp anticipated opportunities in the area of destination. However, the desire to migrate means that in both cases the existing subsistence capacity is perceived as too limited.

On these premises, a new typology of migrations[3] can be formulated which, with sufficient qualifications, permits a comprehensive classification of the individual movements. It classifies according to motivations the causes that lead directly to the decision to emigrate and relates these to the forms and goals of migration. Motivations therefore serve as the basis of the classification, because through them the process of separation from the homeland,

---

3. A summary of earlier attempts to develop typologies of migration is provided by Hans-Joachim Hoffmann-Novotny, *Migration, ein Beitrag zu einer soziologischen Erklärung* (Stuttgart, 1970), pp. 55ff. A more recent effort to establish a historical-sociological typology is found in Peter Marschalck, *Deutsche Überseewanderung im 19. Jahrhundert* (Stuttgart, 1973), p. 71.

which is short only in the case of forced migrations, can be taken into consideration.

## Table I

### TYPES OF MIGRATION

| Motivation | Impetus | Form | Goal |
|---|---|---|---|
| 1a ideological (religious) | threat | structured group (congregation) | annexation of land (closed settlement) |
| 1b | mission | individual | return |
| 2 personal-economic | speculation | individual | return |
| 3a socio-economic | relative over-population | structured group (a people or segment thereof) | annexation of land (occupation) |
| 3b | | mass | annexation of land, employment |
| 4a political | threat/expulsion | individual | return |
| 4b | expulsion/threat | mass | return |

In regard to the social structure of the region of departure, the forms of migration are not class restricted, even if class differences in the participation in various types of migration can be shown. Only ideologically or socio-economically motivated group migrations carried, or at least intended to carry, the social structure of the region of departure into the region of destination. Although members of all social classes were involved and social stratification persisted, the socio-economically motivated mass migrations were chiefly composed of the lower and middle classes. The migration of individuals for personal economic reasons consisted mainly of middle- and upper-class people. Politically motivated mass migrations also affected structured peoples or segments of them, but the established social structures and bonds in the region of departure were largely dissolved in such movements so that the old social order could not be transferred to the area of destination.

These general forms of migration are not, as such, bound to particular phases of history. However, depending on current socioeconomic conditions, the information available about other areas, and the possibilities of reaching them, each migratory form possesses a special significance at particular times. The emergence and constellation of migratory types in different periods determines the actual historical migrations, which in contrast to demographic developments cannot be regarded as a synthesis of biological and sociological ingredients. Migratory, demographic, and economic modes are interdependent insofar as they are components of an integral social process enacted in the same place. However, there is no causal relationship between forms of population or economic organization on one hand and the form of migration on the other. The socio-economically motivated mass migrations of the nineteenth century cannot be deduced from either preindustrial or industrial forms of population or economy, for given the availability of vacant areas overseas, the emigration of structured groups from the overpopulated areas of Europe would have been just as possible in one case as in the other. This example, however, also shows that new forms of economy, population, and migration did not develop in phase with one another; for the form of migration corresponding to an industrial economy, i.e., the movement of individuals for their private economic advancement, emerged later than that economy.

Migration does not, however, remain without an economic, social, and demographic effect on the areas both of departure and of destination. Economically, every emigration, as a reduction of surplus population, brings relief to the labor market of the area of departure and therefore improves the economic chances of those remaining at home. To this extent, it is capable of stabilizing the economic structure. However, the processes of economic structural change are not affected by migration until it reduces the available labor force to a point below the level of existing opportunities for employment. This is also the case in regard to consumption. Moreover, the departure of emigrants is almost always tied to an outflow of capital, for people without means are able to emigrate only when their transportation and settlement expenses are defrayed by someone else. Otherwise, migration is predicated in every case on the possession of means sufficient to meet these costs. Even in cases of flight and expulsion, some cash or property is taken along. In addition, the educational investment in the migrants accrues to the advantage of their new country. Above all, its economy gains from the growth of the labor force. The primary effect of the immigration is, therefore, to fill gaps in the labor market, thus relieving the labor shortage. In fact, this influx may alter the quality of the area by transmitting economic methods brought from the area of departure, thereby producing an expanding labor market. The settlement of farmers in areas previously controlled by nomads is an example of this development. Aside from such cases, the positions occupied by new arrivals are usually lower ones, considered less attractive by the natives of the region. They may also, however, hold new and special positions. In this sense the arrivals strengthen the dynamic forces in the development of the target region, while the inflow of capital accelerates this process. Furthermore, this influx produces changes not only in the density of settlement but also in the structure of settlement. Annexation and improvement of the land, on the one hand, and increase of employment and urbanization on the other are correlated phenomena in migration. However, the invigorating effect of the immigration for the area of destination diminishes as the limit of the region's capacity to absorb new arrivals is approached. The essential indicator for this movement is the reduction in jobs offered to newcomers. Even a partial saturation of the labor market can lead to immigration restrictions, if suitable publicity has not already produced an ebb in the flow of new arrivals. Without such restrictions, the danger exists that relative underpopulation will turn into relative overpopulation.

The social repercussions are more complicated. For the region of departure, the emigration first and foremost produces stability in the social structure, because disruptive factors have been eliminated. This applies to all forms of migration, except for the complete departure of a population as a result of flight or expulsion.

One cannot, however, exclude the possibility that precisely such relief may facilitate or even accelerate structural changes in society because social pressures are reduced or removed. In the region of destination different effects result according to the type of migration, and these effects may be derived from its motivation, form, and goals. Thus, individual immigrants with ideological-religious or personal-economic motives and with the goal of returning to the area of departure hardly appear capable of assimilation. Political immigrants, on the other hand, by continuing their activities can prove to be sources of trouble. In general, however, social structures and processes in the region of destination are scarcely influenced by such immigrants, even if they renounce the goal of returning to their homeland. Structured groups possess the least capacity for assimilation, especially if they attain their goal of closed settlement. They exist alongside the larger community as social enclaves which often persist for generations and by their deviant system of values may become objects of social and political controversy. Such segregation also occurs if an immigrating group gains dominion over a native population. However, in contrast to a social enclave, such a group, as the upper class, restructures the society of the region of destination by enforcing its own values upon the natives and redefining social positions in relation to itself. Racial and national distinctions, which can only be weakened, if at all, by long-term processes of integration, strengthen the position of the ruling class. Here the socio-economically motivated migrations of conquest and colonialism belong.

In contrast to these forms of migration, the socio-economically motivated mass migration accelerates social change in the region of destination. Geographical and social mobility are combined in this form of migration. Its social impact is strengthened by the fact that it makes possible the creation of families that could not have been formed in the homeland because holdings capable of sustaining a family according to the prevailing social standards were not available there. Social integration of immigrants is more than mere assimilation; it is metamorphosis, a forming anew. This circumstance informs Turner's celebrated thesis about the shaping of the

American people in the process of moving west,[4] the continuation of the Atlantic immigration.

This does not preclude class distinctions among various immigrant groups in the same region of destination, which can lead to ghetto-like enclaves of certain groups, especially in large cities. Thus, even in the case of socio-economically motivated mass migration, the process of integration can take several generations. Delayed integration is also characteristic of mass movements of flight and expulsion, in which the will to integrate does not grow until the hope of return has vanished. Therefore, the first generation, with its conscious special position, is burdensome to the region of destination and generates or intensifies antagonisms.

Of the demographic effects of the migration, its influence on the sex and age structures in areas both of departure and of destination is evident. Aside from the migration of closed groups and the flight or expulsion of entire groups, migration included primarily those people capable of working and holding land. It, therefore, encompassed the younger and middle-aged (15- to 45-year-old) groups of the economically and, in the cases of wives or women arriving later with a view to marriage (15- to 45-year-old women), the demographically productive forces of an area. The population of a region of departure is thereby "aged" in a relative sense by emigration, while a region of destination is relatively rejuvenated by immigration.[5] Since emigration reduces the latent population pressure upon the means of subsistence, it contributes to the stabilization of an existing population structure, that is, to retarding structural change without necessarily preventing it.[6] In the area of destination, with its underpopulation and potentially expanding

4. Frederick Jackson Turner, *The Frontier in American History* (New York, 1920), chap. I: "The Significance of the Frontier in American History."

5. It would be fruitless to attempt to compose an account of long range gains and losses resulting from such influences on the population structure, because the question of whether the emigrants would have established families and reproduced under conditions prevailing in the region of departure cannot be answered. See Marschalck, *Deutsche Überseewanderung*, pp. 87ff.

6. This conforms to the relaxing effect mentioned by Ipsen in his population doctrine. Günther Ipsen, "Bevölkerung I—Bevölkerungslehre," in Carl Petersen *et al.*, eds., *Handwörterbuch des Grenz- und Auslandsdeutschtums* (Breslau, 1933), I, 425ff.

subsistence capacities, not only are the fertile age-groups strengthened but also a corresponding change in reproductive patterns is accelerated. In extreme cases, if the economic expansion of the area of destination is dependent on an influx of people, the immigration overwhelms the established reproductive patterns of that area by preserving a population structure brought from the area of departure and aimed at growth. As a result of the differential reproductive patterns of the native and immigrant populations, a superimposition of one pattern upon the other can develop which can only be reduced by an integrated process in the course of which different class and group elements combine to form a new reproductive pattern. In this case, immigration delays the development and stabilization of a new population structure. When an immigrant population is superimposed upon the native inhabitants, with no intention or possibility of integration, a diminution in the importance of the latter, whether desired or not, is an important side effect of the penetration of settlers with a higher cultural level into a developing area. Such influences appear, however, only in socioeconomic migrations in which the necessary quantitative conditions are met. The reproductive patterns of the native population are not influenced by individual migrations, and are scarcely affected by group migrations which result in social isolation in the area of destination. In this respect, politically motivated mass migrations are relevant only when they can be deflected into areas with different reproductive patterns.

We shall now treat the German immigration to the territory of the United States within this general framework, presupposing as it does a knowledge of social, economic, and political circumstances on both sides of the Atlantic.

## II

WHEN the Westphalian official framed his report in 1818, the German migration to America already possessed a history of almost a hundred years. The first German had actually trod on North American soil much earlier, for, as the Greenland saga reports, a German by the name of Tyrkir participated in the exploratory voyage of the Viking Leif in A.D. 1000.[7] His tracks were lost in the darkness of history, and the reasons for and the manner in which he was driven into the orbit of the Vikings remain unknown. Similarly, German mercenaries followed the explorers and conquistadors, and the unsuccessful attempt of the Welser Trading House of Augsburg to secure its own colony in Venezuela in the first half of the sixteenth century[8] was an early German effort to participate in the establishment of trading settlements and colonies overseas. While the Viking voyages of exploration were forgotten, it was now recognized that lands existed beyond the sea whose riches seemed to be waiting for exploitation by European conquerors.

For Germany, however, this new knowledge had at first no consequences, because the economic and political forces of the Empire and its territorial states were tied up in the Thirty Years' War. This European war on German soil reduced the total German population by one-third and produced losses in some territories of the Empire amounting to two-thirds of the population,[9] creating an extensively devastated and underpopulated area in Central Europe. Its resettlement lasted almost an entire century. Emigration was, furthermore, hampered by the established agrarian order which bound the peasant population to the soil and by the population policy of the absolutist states which, while prohibiting emigration, encouraged immigration for the settlement of devastated areas or for

7. See C. W. Ceram, *Der erste Amerikaner* (Hamburg, 1972), p. 39f.

8. See Wilhelm Frhr. v. Schoen, *Geschichte Mittel- und Südamerikas* (Munich, 1953), pp. 129ff.; Wilhelm Mönckmeier, *Die deutsche überseeische Auswanderung* (Jena, 1912), p. 6.

9. See Ernst Wolfgang Buchholz, *Vom Mittelalter zur Neuzeit-Bevölkerungsploetz*, 3d ed. (Würzburg, 1966), III, 54f.

# GERMANY IN THE NINETEENTH CENTURY

*Scale 1:6,000,000*

*Prussia:*

Provinces (until 1865):

| | | |
|---|---|---|
| 1. East Prussia | 4. Posen | 7. Saxony |
| 2. West Prussia | 5. Silesia | 8. Westphalia |
| 3. Pomerania | 6. Brandenburg | 9. Rhineland |

10. Schleswig (until 1865 to Denmark) } (since 1866 Prussian Province Schleswig Holstein)
11. Holstein
12. Lauenburg (since 1866 Prussian Province, 1876 to Schleswig Holstein)
13. Hanover (since 1866 Prussian Province)
14. Hesse (Electorate) } (since 1866 Prussian Province Hessen)
15. Nassau
16. Hohenzollern (since 1849 Prussian Province)

| | | |
|---|---|---|
| 17. *Mecklenburg-Schwerin* | 22. *Anhalt* | 27. *Bavaria* |
| 18. *Mecklenburg-Strelitz* | 23. *Saxony (Kingdom)* | 28. *Palatinate* (to Bavaria) |
| 19. *Oldenburg* | 24. *Thuringian States* | 29. *Baden* |
| 20. *Brunswick* | 25. *Waldeck* | 30. *Württemberg* |
| 21. *Lippe* | 26. *Hesse* (Grand Duchy) | 31. *Alsace-Lorraine* |
| | | (1871–1918 to the German Reich) |

establishment and expansion of trade. The Protestant states were particularly active, receiving coreligionists (Salzburg Lutherans, Waldensians, and Huguenots) expelled from their homes by the Counter-Reformation. Thus, internal resettlement and immigration characterized the migrations of the period.

Reflecting these conditions, the migrations of the seventeenth and eighteenth centuries were group migrations with ideological-religious motives and migrations of individuals for personal-economic reasons. During the Thirty Years' War, migrations as forms of escape or flight—usually short-term movements to elude approaching mercenaries—also took place but did not lead to widespread permanent resettlement. They were not at all related to the first immigrations to North America, which occurred at the same time. The first German emigrants reached the new land in connection with the Dutch colonial ventures, and may, therefore, have been among the earliest settlers in New Amsterdam, later New York. Peter Minnewit (Minuit), its third governor, came from Wesel. This earliest German immigration to America was an outgrowth of an older seasonal migration between northwestern Germany, primarily Westphalia, and Holland. Known as the *Hollandgängerei*, it continued into the nineteenth century. Though later individual migrants from other parts of Germany also participated, the first settlers of the Dutch West Indies Company were probably recruited from elements of this migratory labor force who had found work beyond the harvest season in the Netherlands and were motivated primarily by the desire to secure additional income.[10] With few exceptions, they sprang from lower peasant, artisan, and home-industry backgrounds, although many also came to America as soldiers of the company. Jakob Leisler from Frankfurt a.M., for instance, after resigning from the service, became a capable merchant—an example of the chances for social advancement in the

---

10. Mönckmeier, *Die deutsche überseeische Auswanderung* p. 6f.; Friedrich Kapp, *Geschichte der deutschen Einwanderung in Amerika* (Leipzig, 1868), pp. 14ff. On page 15 one finds excerpts from the earliest passenger lists from 1851 to 1864 which reveal that the company's recruitment at that time transcended the scope of the *Hollandgängerei*.

new colonies—only to come a cropper as a politician in New York during the confusion of the Glorious Revolution.[11]

While these immigrants were motivated exclusively by personal and economic factors, William Penn's colonization endeavors at the close of the seventeenth century had repercussions in Germany. Above all, the ideal of religious toleration realized in Pennsylvania attracted members of denominations which, regardless of confession, were directly or indirectly threatened because of their alienation from their respective territorial churches. On a journey through western and southwestern Germany in 1677, Penn himself had established contacts with Pietist and Quaker circles and solicited for his project. The foundation of the "German Company" in Frankfurt a.M., whose shareholders were Pietists, was attributed directly to his influence. In 1683 it purchased land in Pennsylvania, and one of its shareholders, Franz Daniel Pastorius, went to Philadelphia in that same year. At his suggestion, Jakob Telner, a merchant from Krefeld who immigrated in 1684, acquired land and also encouraged others to buy. In 1683, thirteen Mennonite and Quaker families from Krefeld reached Pennsylvania and with Pastorius founded Germantown near Philadelphia, which in the following years received additional emigrants from Krefeld.[12] A Quaker congregation from Kriesheim near Worms also settled in the same area in 1685[13]—the Palatinate's first group of immigrants to America. In 1694, forty members of the *Rosenkreuzer*, a theosophic sect, reached Philadelphia, while one hundred Labadists from Friesland had founded their own settlement in Maryland a decade earlier.[14] Under the leadership of their pastors, Waldensians and Huguenots from the Palatine districts of Bretten and Mosbach, which had suffered greatly in Louis XIV's campaign of devastation, errected the first Palatine colony on the Hudson.[15] Since almost all

---

11. See *ibid.*, pp. 34ff.

12. Friedrich Nieper, *Die ersten deutschen Auswanderer von Krefeld nach Pennsylvanien* (Moers, 1940), pp. 75ff.

13. Daniel Häberle, *Auswanderungen und Koloniegründungen der Pfälzer im 18. Jahrhundert* (Kaiserslautern, 1909).

14. Mönckmeier, *Die deutsche überseeische Auswanderung*, p. 8.

15. Häberle, *Auswanderungen und Koloniegründungen*, p. 34f.

these settlements remained in contact with the old homeland, the opportunities for emigration overseas became better known. This is demonstrated by the German settlements in Pennsylvania, which more than any others continued to attract newcomers. The description of Pennsylvania, composed by Franz Daniel Pastorius and published in Frankfurt a.M. and Leipzig in 1700, was probably of considerable importance. The very fact that further editions, with supplements by other authors, were necessary in 1702 and 1704 reveals the circulation enjoyed by this work, which was aimed at advertising the settlement.[16]

Individuals migrating for personal-economic reasons and religiously motivated groups of migrants, with their centers of gravity in New York and Pennsylvania, brought basic provisions with them and at least in Pennsylvania enjoyed certain assurances for the future. However, at the beginning of the eighteenth century, emigrations began which did not meet these conditions. The German Southwest, and especially the Palatinate, was the major region of departure.[17] The reason for the great readiness to migrate lay in the region's agrarian system, which was distinguished by the predominance of the *Realteilungserbrecht*. The division of the peasant proprietor's inheritance among his children produced a splintering of peasant holdings, and because each resulting portion was considered a family plot, it also produced a particularly high rate of population growth.[18] Elsewhere in Germany, where the practice of entail provided for the inheritance of undivided holdings and therefore restricted the number of so-called family plots, there were social restraints on population growth. Thus, by the beginning of

16. *Ibid.*, p. 35f. Aside from Pastorius' pamphlet, a number of others were circulated after the turn of the century, all recruiting for the emigration. *Ibid.*, p. 40.

17. The entire immigration to America from Southwest Germany and the German areas of Switzerland is frequently referred to as the "Palatinate" emigration. This description resulted from the fact that all these emigrants reached the emigration ports via the Rhine, which was the major route of traffic from the Southwest to the North. On this route the Palatinate was the last great area of emigration. *Ibid.* Similarly, the emigrations from Southwest Germany via the Danube to southeast Europe were referred to as "Swabian migrations," although the Swabians were only the southeasternmost group in this movement.

18. Günther Ipsen, "Die atlantische und die deutsche Wanderung des 19. Jahrhunderts," *Ostdeutsche Wissenschaft, Jahrbuch des ostdeutschen Kulturrates*, 8 (1961), 50.

the eighteenth century, the Southwest had already reached a condition of relative overpopulation. Moreover, the constant danger during the wars of Louis XIV and the great devastation caused by them, especially in the Palatinate, intensified the latent readiness to migrate. When the hard winter of 1708–1709 destroyed the wine industry for years to come and also inflicted heavy damage on other agricultural endeavors, this willingness led to the first socio-economically motivated mass migration.

A group of emigrants from Landau under the direction of Pastor Josua Kocherthal were forerunners of this form of migration. Having already arrived in England with no means at all, the group was finally settled on the Indian border of New York with public support.[19] The great exodus began in early 1709 and by October at least thirteen thousand immigrants had arrived in England.[20] There they were collected in a mass camp near Greenwich similar to the refugee camps of the twentieth century and left to public and private charity. About one-quarter of them reached North America,[21] where they settled in New York and North Carolina. Although only a fraction of those who left Southwest Germany for America actually reached that destination and their start in the new land was made extremely difficult by forced settlement and work assignments, the influx of the surplus agrarian population did not let up. Emigration was facilitated by direct recruitment of labor as "indentured servants" in the region of departure. Peaks of emigration were reached in 1749–1753 (around 25,000 emigrants), 1757–1759 (around 30,000), and 1782. In this way socio-economically moti-

19. Häberle, *Auswanderungen und Koloniegründungen*, pp. 36ff; Kapp, *Geschichte der deutschen Einwanderung in Amerika*, pp. 78ff.

20. Buchholz, *Vom Mittelalter zur Neuzeit-Bevölkerungsploetz*, p. 56; also Häberle, *Auswanderungen und Koloniegründungen*, pp. 43ff.; Kapp, *Geschichte der deutschen Einwanderung in Amerika*, p. 88f; Fritz Trautz, *Die Pfälzische Auswanderung nach Nordamerika im 18. Jahrhundert* (Heidelberg, 1959), pp. 8ff.

21. According to the investigations listed above, approximately 1,000 persons died in the camp, 3,800 were sent to Ireland, while others remained in England as skilled workers or servants. Some emigrants from the Palatinate also reached Jamaica. Of the roughly 3,000 who were shipped to New York, about 770 died on the voyage or immediately after arrival. See Mönckmeier, *Die deutsche überseeische Auswanderung*, p. 9.

vated mass emigration acquired a greater significance as a form of migration in the course of the eighteenth century.[22]

However, group migration for ideological-religious motives also maintained its importance. It was partially intertwined with the socio-economically motivated mass migration when religious groups were recruited. Thus, the Swiss Christoph von Graffenried, who had already played a part in the settlement of migrants from the Palatinate in North Carolina, could win forty Mennonite miners' families for the working of mines and smelting of iron in Virginia. They emigrated as a complete congregation under the leadership of their pastor. The main destination of the religiously motivated group migrations, however, remained Pennsylvania, where Baptist Dunkers (1729), Schwenkfelders (1734), and Moravian Brethren (after 1735) settled. Salzburg Lutherans, on the other hand, founded several settlements in Georgia. In the following period all these groups received additional arrivals from their native regions.[23] In comparison, migration for personal-economic motives declined, even though the immigration of German entrepreneurs and artisans remained substantial.[24] In the War of Independence, German officers joined the American cause, the best known being Friedrich Wilhelm von Steuben, who had earlier served in the Prussian Army and later at the court of Hohenzollern-Hechingen.

After the outbreak of the War of Independence, immigration from Germany quickly diminished. This was not only because the major route of migration, which led via England, was now blocked, but primarily because the European wars, which erupted after the outbreak of the French Revolution and lasted for over two decades, interposed a *de facto* impediment. Yet the war did bring a form of forced migration, since German princes, for a suitable price, sold troops to the English. Of the roughly 30,000 soldiers bartered by these small and extravagant potentates to pay their debts, only about 17,300 returned to their homes. Approximately 7,500 fell in

22. See *ibid.*, p. 9f.
23. *Ibid.*
24. See the chapters of Kapp, *Geschichte der deutschen Einwanderung in Amerika*, dealing with the development of the individual colonies.

battle or died, while 5,000 remained in America after desertion or imprisonment.[25]

The total number of persons who came to America during this initial phase of German immigration can scarcely be calculated. Estimates of 200,000 immigrants by the end of the eighteenth century may be just as overstated[26] as the figures of the 1790 American census, according to which only 5.6 percent of the resident whites were of German descent, were understated. In Pennsylvania, above all, one-third of the inhabitants may for a time have been of German ancestry,[27] and there, with the "Pennsylvania Dutch," a German dialect peculiar to the area has partially maintained itself to the present. In the other colonies, which now formed the Confederation, the German element in the immigration played only a modest, if not entirely insignificant, role. It was, nevertheless, vital for the formation of the American economy and society and remained a major element in the development of an independent American people.


# III


ONLY the restructuring of Germany after the Napoleonic wars brought about a relaxation of the eighteenth-century prohibitions upon emigration. The Act of Confederation in 1815 allowed emigration from one state of the German Confederation to another, if the state of destination admitted emigrants and the emigrants had no undischarged military obligation. These stipulations also figured in the constitutions of the individual states; but primarily owing to the need for military recruits, emigration was made contingent upon the approval of the authorities. Yet, despite this limitation, which was disregarded by not a few secret emi-

---

25. Mönckmeier, *Die deutsche überseeische Auswanderung*, p. 11f.

26. *Ibid.*, p. 13.

27. According to Benjamin Franklin's statements, in Trautz, *Die Pfälzische Auswanderung nach Nordamerika*, p. 12.

grants, freedom of emigration was guaranteed in all of Germany. The right of immigration, however, was subject to various restrictions, above all home and settlement regulations which had developed from the responsibility for providing relief for the local poor.[28] Precisely this obligation motivated the authorities of the Southwest German states to send the village poor to America at community expense in order to reduce the strain on the public purse.[29]

In addition to freedom of emigration, information about possibilities for migrating and about the lands of destination was a crucial factor in the rise of emigration. A third major precondition for the German overseas emigration of the nineteenth century was the expansion of transportation facilities, particularly the construction of railroads and the introduction of steamships.

After 1830 immigration to America began to spread beyond the Southwest, particularly Württemberg and the Rhine Palatinate, into the remaining areas of Germany. The number of German overseas emigrants rose quickly, reaching an initial high point of 80,000 in 1847 and a second of almost 240,000 in 1854. Not until 1858 did the flow again subside. This period of increasing emigration was also the time of its greatest publicity. The emigration movement had freed itself from its traditional breeding grounds. Just as the gradual unification of Germany into a customs union involved even the remotest areas in economic fluctuations, the development of transportation facilitated and expedited the travel of emigrants to the ports. And just as political tensions began to be felt even in small rural communities, emigration in the forties and fifties became a problem of national dimensions.

28. See Alexander Müller, *Die deutschen Auswanderungs-, Freizügigkeits- und Heimaths-Verhältnisse* (Leipzig, 1841); and Friedrich Bitzer, *Das Recht auf Armenunterstützung und die Freizügigkeit* (Stuttgart, 1863).

29. Manfred Grisebach, "Auswanderung aus Württemberg auf Gemeindekosten 1846–1854," *Der Auslanddeutsche*, 10 (1927), 711–773.

## Table II

### GERMAN OVERSEAS EMIGRATION 1816–1934

| Year | Emigrants[a] 1,000 | Immigrants to USA[b] | | Average Annual Emigration rate[c] |
|---|---|---|---|---|
| | | 1,000 | percent | |
| 1816–1819 | 25.0 | | | 2.7 |
| 1820–1824 | 9.8 | 1.9 | 19.4 | 1.0 |
| 1825–1829 | 12.7 | 3.8 | 29.9 | 1.2 |
| 1830–1834 | 51.1 | 39.3 | 76.9 | 2.2 |
| 1835–1839 | 94.0 | 85.5 | 91.0 | 2.6 |
| 1840–1844 | 110.6 | 100.5 | 90.9 | 2.4 |
| 1845–1849 | 308.2 | 284.9 | 92.4 | 4.5 |
| 1850–1854 | 728.3 | 654.3 | 89.8 | 9.0 |
| 1855–1859 | 372.0 | 321.8 | 86.5 | 4.3 |
| 1860–1864 | 225.9 | 204.1 | 90.4 | 2.5 |
| 1865–1869 | 542.7 | 519.6 | 95.7 | 3.6 |
| 1870–1874 | 484.6 | 450.5 | 93.0 | 2.3 |
| 1875–1879 | 143.3 | 120.0 | 83.7 | 0.7 |
| 1880–1884 | 864.3 | 797.9 | 92.3 | 3.8 |
| 1885–1889 | 498.2 | 452.6 | 90.9 | 2.1 |
| 1890–1894 | 462.2 | 428.8 | 92.8 | 1.8 |
| 1895–1899 | 142.4 | 120.2 | 84.4 | 0.5 |
| 1900–1904 | 140.8 | 128.6 | 91.3 | 0.5 |
| 1905–1909 | 135.7 | 123.5 | 91.0 | 0.4 |
| 1910–1914 | 104.3 | 84.1 | 80.6 | 0.3 |
| 1915–1919 | 4.1 | 1.0 | 24.4 | 0.0 |
| 1920–1924 | 242.3 | 150.4 | 62.1 | 0.8 |
| 1925–1929 | 295.3 | 230.1 | 77.8 | 0.9 |
| 1930–1934 | 88.1 | 62.2 | 70.6 | 0.3 |

SOURCE: Friedrich Burgdörfer, "Die Wanderungen über die deutschen Reichsgrenzen im letzten Jahrhundert," *Allgemeines Statistisches Archive* 20 (1930), 189ff.; Mönckmeier, *Die deutsche überseeische Auswanderung*, p. 14; *Statistik des Deutschen Reichs*, 150 (Berlin, 1903), 330ff.; *Statistisches Jahrbuch für das Deutsche Reich* (1926), p. 38; *ibid.* (1935), p. 60.

a. 1816–1831: author's calculation; 1832–1870: Burgdörfer's estimate based on the immigration statistics of the United States; 1871–1934: based on the German emigration statistics.

b. 1820–1870: according to the immigration statistics of the United States; 1871–1934: according to the German emigration figures.

c. Based on the population of the areas affected by emigration: 1816–1829 Württemberg and the Palatinate; to which are added Baden 1830; Bavaria 1831–1835; the Rhineland, Westphalia, Hesse, and Nassau 1841–1846; Brunswick, Hannover, and Mecklenburg 1849–1853; the remaining German areas 1865–1869.

With the increase in emigration came a relative shift in its direction of flow. While about one-half of the overseas emigrants between 1816 and 1830 had gone to South America, North America now took the lead. Two reasons were decisive for the change. First, after concluding commercial treaties with the United States, the North German ports of Bremen and Hamburg had become emigration centers, and their trade helped to determine the direction of that emigration. Second, the expanding current of information about the new world produced in Germany a better appreciation of conditions in North America. In the first half of the nineteenth century, a great number of books and pamphlets on emigration appeared, and their reports on the countries of immigration were often taken up and circulated by the daily and weekly press. At midcentury special emigration newspapers were established,[30] and the effectiveness of their information was enhanced by emigration associations.[31] These organizations had been founded at the same time with the objective of providing sound advice for anyone considering emigration or anyone already determined on that course. If they were not simply "colonization societies" and thus tied to a particular project, usually in South or Central America, their importance lay in their potential for providing "negative" information, i.e., warnings concerning certain lands of immigration,[32] with the effect of increasing the migration of Germans to the United States.

30. *Allgemeine Auswanderungszeitung* (Rudolstadt, 1846/47–1871); *Der deutsche Auswanderer* (Darmstadt/Frankfurt, 1847–1850); *Deutsche Auswanderungszeitung* (Leipzig, 1848); *Der sächsische Auswanderer*, after 1850 *Der Auswanderer* (Schneeberg, 1848–1851); *Hansa* (Hamburg, 1852–1857); *Deutsche Auswanderer-Zeitung* (Bremen, 1852–1875).

31. Approximately thirty emigration and colonization clubs or associations had been founded in Germany before 1850, the best-known one being the "Association for the Protection of German Immigrants in Texas" or the "Mainz Association of Nobility" established in 1844. See Harald Winkel, "Der Texasverein," *Vierteljahresschrift für Sozial- und Wirtschaftsgeschichte*, 55 (1968), 348–372. The most effective, however, were the "National Association for German Emigration and Settlement" (Darmstadt, 1848) and the "Association for the Centralization of German Emigration and Colonization" (Berlin, 1849). See Marschalck, *Deutsche Überseewanderung*, pp. 21ff.

32. *Allgemeine Auswanderungszeitung*, 19 (1865), 71. The "Geography Association of Dresden, Department for Emigration Affairs" warned against the tropical climate, the political instability, and restricted freedom of religion in Yucatan. The "Frankfurt Association for the Protection of Emigrants" also warned against immigration to Mexico. *Ibid.*, p. 150.

# Table III

ORIGIN OF GERMAN OVERSEAS EMIGRANTS 1830–1869
*(in percent of the total emigration)*

|  | 1830–1834 | 1835–1839 | 1840–1844 | 1845–1849 | 1850–1854 | 1855–1859 | 1860–1864 | 1865–1869 |
|---|---|---|---|---|---|---|---|---|
| Southwest Germany[a] | 98.8 | 36.8 | 33.9 | 28.8 | 28.1 | 21.8 | 16.6 | 13.8 |
| Bavaria East of the Rhine |  | 16.4[e] | 15.7 | 11.1 | 6.8 | 5.9 | 6.3 | 3.0 |
| West Germany[b] |  |  |  | 12.5 | 6.8 | 11.5 | 12.0 | 7.9 |
| Northeast Germany[c] |  |  |  | 0.7 | 0.5 | 3.0 | 6.2 | 5.9 |
| East Germany[d] |  |  |  | 2.9 | 2.9 | 11.6 | 14.8 | 11.3 |
| Mecklenburg |  |  |  |  | 3.9[f] | 5.1 | 4.9 | 4.3 |
| Total Emigration in 1,000 |  | 51.1 | 94.0 | 110.6 | 308.2 | 728.3 | 372.0 | 225.9 | 542.7 |

SOURCES: G. Krieg, "Entwicklung und gegenwärtiger Zustand des Auswanderungswesens im Königreich Bayern," in Eugen v. Philippovich, ed., *Auswanderung und Auswanderungspolitik in Deutschland* (Leipzig, 1892), pp. 90ff.; T. Bödiker, *Die preussische Auswanderung und Einwanderung seit dem Jahre 1844* (Düsseldorf, 1879), p. 2f.; Mönckmeier, *Die deutsche überseeische Auswanderung*, p. 75; Hermann Losch, "Die Bewegung der Bevölkerung Württembergs im 19. Jahrhundert," *Württembergische Jahrbücher für Statistik und Landeskunde* (1900), II, 71; E. Hellmuth Dietzsch, *Die Bewegung der mecklenburgischen Bevölkerung von 1850 bis 1910* (Schwerin, 1918), p. 23.

a. Württemberg, Baden, and the Palatinate.
b. The Prussian Provinces—Westphalia and the Rhineland.
c. East Prussia, West Prussia, and Posen.
d. Brandenburg, Pomerania, and Silesia.
e. 1836–1839.
f. 1851–1854.

Despite the rise of emigration, no active emigration policy was initiated in any German state in the first half of the nineteenth century. However, grievances concerning various aspects of the emigration did at least provoke the regimes to issue rules for the regulation of agencies involved in the recruitment and transportation of emigrants.[33] Then, after the mid-1850's, official interest in the emigration declined appreciably, especially since the advances in

33. Eduard Friedrich Rottmann, *Die Lehre von der Aus- und Einwanderung im Königreich Bayern* (Würzburg, 1862), pp. 173ff; Rolf Engelsing, *Bremen als Auswandererhafen 1683–1880* (Bremen, 1961), pp. 45ff.

German economic development seemed to have stripped it of its "critical, foreboding appearance."[34]

The reasons for the shift in the regions of origin of German emigrants and for the sharp increase in their total numbers from the 1830's forward lay overwhelmingly in the realm of social structures, partly traditional and partly transformed, among which the rural system of authority and labor played a special role as the foundation of the economic structure.

Compared to this emigration for socio-economic reasons, the importance of emigration for religious, political, and personal-economic motives is, on the whole, quite difficult to gauge. The classification of emigrations—except for structured groups—under a particular form of migration cannot always be unequivocally accomplished owing to the insufficiency of sources for the nineteenth century. However, examination of the social and economic situation in the area of departure allows one to perceive the modest extent of migrations for personal-economic (category 2), political (category 4a), and ideological reasons (category 1a).

After the immigration of the Swabian Pietists[35] to Russia at the outset of the nineteenth century, the Old Lutherans, who had opposed the merger of Lutheran and Reformist groups in the Prussian United Church in 1817, immigrated to North America and, in smaller numbers, to Australia in the thirties and forties.[36] Their departure represented not only the last great group migration from Germany, but also the last major migration for religious reasons. The religious posture involved, recurring even later, could probably best be conveyed by the explanation "that . . . the people on the basis of traditional notions, . . . perceived the plan to emigrate

34. Hans Richter, "Hessen und die Auswanderung," *Mitteilungen des oberhessischen Geschichtsvereins*, n.s., 32 (1934), 139.

35. F. C. Huber, "Auswanderung und Auswanderungspolitik im Königreich Württemberg," in Eugen v. Philippovich, ed., *Auswanderung und Auswanderungspolitik in Deutschland* (Leipzig, 1892), pp. 243ff; and Georg Leibbrandt, *Die Auswanderung aus Schwaben nach Russland 1816–1823* (Stuttgart, 1928), p. 53.

36. Thomas Walker Page, "The Causes of Earlier European Immigration to the United States," *The Journal of Political Economy*, 19 (1911), 677; Wilhelm Iwan, *Die Altlutherische Auswanderung um die Mitte des 19. Jahrhunderts* (Ludwigsburg, 1943), vol. 1. In 1843, the peak year for this emigration, 1,600 Old Lutherans left Germany.

as something so unprecedented, that it had to be followed with the conviction befitting a commission from God."[37] However, when a group of 260 people from Lippe emigrated in 1847 because their request to use the Heidelberg Catechism was refused, the *Allgemeine Auswanderungszeitung* commented significantly: "That material improvements were also desired is self-evident."[38]

After the Revolution of 1848, the number of emigrants suddenly increased sharply. This rise has led many to attribute political motives to the emigration. In this case, the causes of emigration have unquestionably been confused with the events that precipitated it. Occupational composition and areas of origin, which were not identical with the areas of political unrest,[39] indicate that the great mass of emigrants at this time left their homes for other than political reasons. Yet, the failure of the revolution and the resulting disappointment may have supplied the final impetus to emigrate. There were certainly political fugitives from Germany in the nineteenth century. The Carlsbad Decrees of 1819 and the revolutions of 1830 and 1848 may, indeed, have driven many from their homes. The proceedings against Freiligrath, against the "Neue Rheinische Zeitung," against Rudolf Springer, E. W. Eduard Zimmermann, Martens, Ziegler, and Nees[40] enable one to form an impression of the political pressure in the midcentury, while the impact of German-Americans upon journalism, education, and, above all, politics, demonstrates the significant place that this small group had won for themselves in American life.[41]

Another small group of emigrants—numerically about the size of the religiously or politically motivated groups—was formed by those whose economic and social position at home was secure but who emigrated merely in hopes of doing still better. Their ties with

37. Joseph Scheben, "Eifeler Amerika-Auswanderung im neunzehnten Jahrhundert," *Rheinische Vierteljahresblätter*, 2 (1932), 260.

38. *Allgemeine Auswanderungszeitung*, 1 (1847), 205.

39. Marcus Lee Hansen, *The Immigrant in American History* (Cambridge, 1942), p. 80.

40. Veit Valentin, *Geschichte der deutschen Revolution von 1848–1849* (Berlin, 1931), II, 586.

41. See Rudolf Cronau, *Drei Jahrhunderte deutschen Lebens in Amerika* (Berlin, 1909), p. 303. Cronau, on the other hand, speaks of a "tidal wave" of German immigrants in intellectual professions.

their homeland were broken for personal-economic reasons. Belonging to this group are the merchants who founded settlements in the United States and rich agricultural proprietors who were tempted by the possibility of acquiring even greater holdings. German participants in the gold rush of the fifties must also be counted in this group. Only after 1900, when individual decisions to migrate became increasingly possible, did this type of personal-economic emigration become important.

A threat can be directly perceived as a reason for ideologically and politically motivated emigration, and speculation as the conscious reason for the personal-economically motivated form. Overpopulation as a cause of socio-economic migration is not, however, directly perceptible. It is felt only through some impetus, whether a poor harvest, famine, or price-rise, fear of military service, wars, or revolutionary unrest, that illuminates in experience the social situation characteristic of "overpopulation."

In preindustrial Germany, two different forms of agrarian organization had developed: on the one hand, *Grundherrschaft*, comprising areas of *Realteilungserbrecht* (equal division of estates) as well as areas of *Anerbenrecht* (with right of entail); and on the other hand, *Gutsherrschaft*. In the *Grundherrschaft* areas peasant obligations had come to consist almost entirely of dues. The peasant's position was based, therefore, on making payments rather than performing services. However, while these dues were commuted by the peasant emancipation legislation, the labor system remained untouched.[42] Moreover, the commutation achieved by the agrarian reform resulted in increasing the indebtedness of the smallholders.[43] Thus, every economic downswing (such as famines following bad harvests) affected these "dwarf farmers" to such an extent that often, even after a complete conversion to potato farming, nothing remained but for them to sell their property and emigrate.

In contrast to Southwest Germany, the *Realteilungserbrecht* was

42. Werner Conze, "Die Wirkungen der liberalen Agrarreformen auf die Volksordnung in Mitteleuropa im 19. Jahrhundert," *Vierteljahrschrift für Sozial- und Wirtschaftsgeschichte*, 38 (1948–1951), 8.

43. *Ibid.*, p. 11.

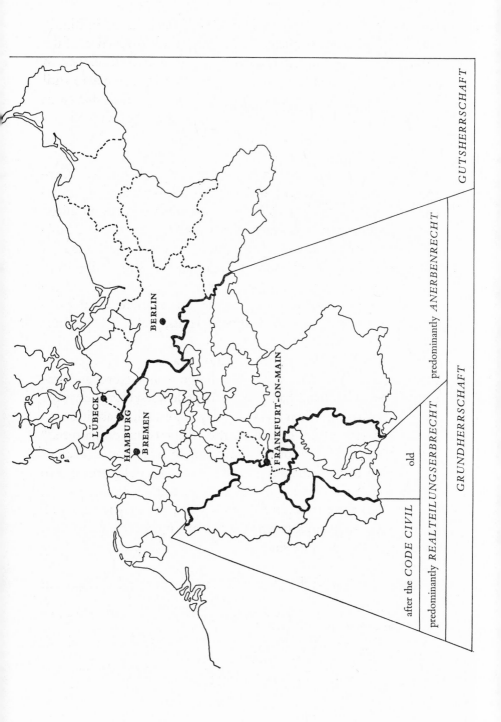

LÜBECK

HAMBURG
BREMEN

BERLIN

FRANKFURT-ON-MAIN

GUTSHERRSCHAFT

predominantly ANERBENRECHT

GRUNDHERRSCHAFT

predominantly REALTEILUNGSERBRECHT

after the CODE CIVIL

old

not initiated in the western regions of the Rhineland and in Rhine-Hesse until the Napoleonic occupation and the introduction of the Code Civil. Therefore, the conditions which had developed in Württemberg, Baden, and the Palatinate did not evolve here until later. Moreover, emigration did not reach the extent of that from the areas listed above, because the expanding industries of the Rhineland and Rhine-Hesse were able to absorb the less extensive surplus population.

In the regions with the *Anerbenrecht*, largely in Northwest Germany and in Bavaria east of the Rhine, middle- and large-size peasant holdings predominated.[44] In Bavaria trade was decentralized and without transregional importance. As the basic form of business, this limited, decentralized trade, which was also present in other territories, permitted the small agrarian proprietors, the "hirelings," an existence relatively free of crisis.[45] The number of Bavarian emigrants was small, most, aside from members of this relatively stable lower agrarian-commercial class, probably being later sons of peasants.

In Northwest Germany the situation was different. There the establishment of textiles, relying on home manufacture, and seasonal work in Holland had given a large lower-peasant class the opportunity to earn their living by day labor and, in addition, to purchase livestock that grazed on the village common pasture.[46] Aside from these occasional laborers, there was another class of propertyless tenants, the hired hands, who were obligated to give assistance to their landlord without pay. Little time, therefore, remained for them to work their own plots, and they were forced to seek additional employment. They were, moreover, confronted by perpetual uncertainty since their tenure could be revoked at any time.[47]

The emancipation legislation led to peasant indebtedness in

44. Friedrich Burgdörfer, "Die Wanderungen über die deutschen Reichsgrenzen im letzten Jahrhundert," *Allgemeines Statistisches Archiv*, 20 (1930), 396.

45. Eckart Schremmer, *Die Wirtschaft Bayerns* (Munich, 1970), p. 85f.

46. Mönckmeier, *Die deutsche überseeische Auswanderung*, p. 81.

47. Johannes Ostendorf, "Zur Geschichte der Auswanderung aus dem alten Amt Damme (Oldbg.)," *Oldenburger Jahrbuch*, 46/47 (1942–1943), 175ff.

Northwest Germany too. For those with little or no property—the tenants and occasional laborers—the first deterioration of their position came with the division of village common land. Since they had *de facto* but no *de jure* usage rights with regard to the common lands, they were rarely taken into account in its division. If they were, they received only a small portion to maintain their livestock. The necessary transition to stall feeding lay beyond their economic capabilities, so that their livestock had to be curtailed.[48]

The division of common land which provided "the precondition for intensive cultivation"[49] and helped to win new areas for "agricultural production, especially of potatoes, so important for the existence of the lower peasant class,"[50] also deprived this class of one of its basic necessities, the possibility of raising livestock.

With the division of the Netherlands in 1830, the *Hollandgängerei* of the brick workers subsided and later ceased entirely when the Dutch government prohibited the employment of foreign labor in Holland's public enterprises. As the second source of part-time work, the home production of linen, which was dependent on the cultivation of flax, had to contend with English competition and soon with German machine production and succumbed.

A fairly steady intensification of population pressure and concomitant emigration for socio-economic reasons characterized the first half of the nineteenth century. In the 1840's these manifestations of overpopulation were reinforced by the decline of home manufactures and the surplus of artisans.

The crisis in home manufactures was precipitated by the consequences of the Continental blockade. After the conclusion of peace, the pressure of cheaper English manufactured goods, especially textiles, became increasingly pronounced in European markets. Because of their technical backwardness, German home manufac-

---

48. Karl Kiel, "Gründe und Folgen der Auswanderung aus dem Osnabrücker Regierungsbezirk," *Mitteilungen des Vereins für Geschichte und Landeskunde von Osnabrück*, 61 (1941), 104f.

49. Conze, "Die Wirkungen der liberalen Agrarreformen auf die Volksordnung in Mitteleuropa," p. 13.

50. Herbert Hitzemann, *Die Auswanderung aus dem Fürstentum Lippe* (Münster, 1953), p. 26f.

tures were unable to hold their own in this competition, as older markets were lost through protectionist policies and the creation of native industries.[51]

The surplus of artisans, on the other hand, was a consequence of population growth. In Southwest Germany, handicrafts and agriculture were closely intermeshed, one often being a vital source of earnings to supplement one's "principal" occupation. With the increase of population, a surplus of artisans appeared, and together with the development of industry and the reduction in the price of factory-produced goods, a genuine occupational crisis developed. In Bavaria and Prussia, economic freedom was introduced in 1804 and 1810 respectively, thus giving each journeyman the chance, in principle if not in practice, to become a master and to have a family. However, the obligation to join a guild in order to practice a trade, which limited the number of masters, was not abolished in Baden and Württemberg until 1862. Yet even in Baden the number of masters soon exceeded that of journeymen.

While in the predominantly agrarian regions only a relatively small surplus of masters vis-à-vis journeymen and apprentices was evident, the ratio in southwestern Germany was more strongly marked in favor of the masters. This was a result of population growth which, more than elsewhere in Germany, exceeded the area of sustenance.

The preponderance of socio-economic or structurally conditioned causes for the emigration is also verified by the scanty material concerning the demographic and social composition of the emigrants. While those who emigrated for political reasons did so almost without exception as individuals, the emigrations for religious reasons were migrations of whole congregations, consisting primarily of families. However, mass migration of families was also the salient feature of the emigration for socio-economic reasons in the first half of the nineteenth century.

Family migration means that approximately as many women

---

51. See Wolfgang Köllmann, "Bevölkerung und Arbeitskräftepotential in Deutschland 1815–1865," *Jahrbuch 1968*, ed. by the minister president of Northrhine-Westphalia (Cologne, Opladen, 1968) pp. 226ff.

emigrate as men. If the number of men emigrating substantially exceeds that of women, then one must conclude that the emigration of individuals accounts for a considerable portion of the total

Table IV

PERSONS EMPLOYED IN HANDICRAFTS

|  | Year | Masters | Journeymen and Apprentices | Journeymen and Apprentices per 100 Masters |
|---|---|---|---|---|
| Kingdom of | 1840 | 410,221 | 358,660 | 87 |
| Prussia | 1849 | 535,232 | 407,141 | 76 |
|  | 1861 | 534,556 | 558,321 | 103 |
| Prussian Rhine Province | 1861 |  |  | 76* |
| Prussian Westphalia | 1861 |  |  | 92* |
| Kingdom of | 1847 | 151,006 | 149,554 | 99 |
| Bavaria | 1861 | 157,435 | 172,122 | 110 |
| Bavarian | 1847 | 17,756 | 4,717 | 27 |
| Palatinate | 1861 | 21,511 | 14,370 | 67 |
| Baden‡ | 1810 | 41,697 | 12,275† | 29 |
|  | 1829 | 46,966 | 19,563† | 42 |
|  | 1844 | 55,751 | 26,834† | 48 |

SOURCES: Fr. Eduard Keller, *Der Preussische Staat* (Minden, 1866), p. 758; Gustav Schmoller, *Zur Geschichte der deutschen Kleingewerbe im 19. Jahrhundert* (Halle, 1870), p. 358; *Die Bevölkerung und die Gewerbe des Königreichs Bayern nach der Aufnahme vom Jahre 1861*, ed. by the Royal Statistical Bureau (Munich, 1862), pp. 18ff.; Wolfram Fischer, *Der Staat und die Anfänge der Industrialisierung in Baden 1800 bis 1850* (Berlin, 1962), I, 303.

\* "Assistants" per 100 Masters.
† "Assistants."
‡ Only the most important Handicrafts.

emigration. According to American immigration statistics, nearly three-quarters of all German immigrants between 1820 and 1825 were men.[52] This indicates that at least 50 percent of the German

52. Walter F. Wilcox, ed., *International Migrations* (New York, 1929), I, 401ff.

immigrants came individually. According to the same source, individual immigrants represented at least 30 percent of the total until 1840, subsequently stabilizing at about 20 percent. If one examines the ages of the emigrants, which have partly been recorded for the period after 1850, the picture becomes clearer. About 20 percent of the Germans emigrating via Hamburg between 1855 and 1870 were children under ten years of age;[53] 26.6 percent of the emigrants from Bavaria between 1851 and 1857 were under sixteen years old,[54] while 32.8 percent of the emigrants from Brunswick in the years 1853–1872 were less than twenty years old.[55] This high percentage of children and young people indicates a high degree of family emigration which is confirmed by the average of 72 percent between 1840 and 1855 for Baden[56] and approximately 64 percent for the Osnabrück district in the years 1832–1846.[57]

The data concerning social composition, especially with regard to the occupational status of the German emigrants, are even less complete than those concerning demographic structure. In the first half of the nineteenth century, when the emigrants came primarily from Southwest Germany, one may assume that small farmers, who, despite occasional earnings from home manufacturing, could no longer support themselves and their families, provided the bulk of the emigrants. In Baden, for example, the number of peasants amounted to almost 50 percent of the emigration from 1840 to 1855, while artisans accounted for less than 30 percent.[58] Similarly, artisans represented about 40 percent of the emigration from Hesse between 1845 and 1847, while peasants and day laborers provided almost 60 percent.[59] The high percentage of emigrants from agricultural backgrounds declined in Southwest

---

53. Mönckmeier, *Die deutsche überseeische Auswanderung*, p. 139.
54. *Ibid.*, p. 137.
55. *Beiträge zur Statistik des Herzogthums Braunschweig*, I (Braunschweig, 1874), 104f.
56. *Beiträge zur Statistik der inneren Verwaltung des Grossherzogthums Baden*, V (Karlsruhe, 1857), 38f.
57. Kiel, "Gründe und Folgen der Auswanderung aus dem Osnabrücker Regierungsbezirk," pp. 165ff.
58. Eugen v. Philippovich, "Auswanderung und Auswanderungspolitik in Grossherzogthum Baden," *Auswanderung und Auswanderungspolitik in Deutschland*, p. 157.
59. Richter, "Hessen und die Auswanderung," p. 108.

Germany after about 1863, dropped in Württemberg from a previous 45 to 55 percent to about 30 percent by 1871.[60] The situation in Saxony, a region predominantly structured by trades, was different. There a mere 11 percent of the 2,750 emigrating heads of families and unmarried individuals were engaged in agriculture. An equal percentage were involved in home manufacturing, of whom almost 60 percent were masters, and more than one-third were engaged in handicrafts (40 percent masters).[61]

The sharp decline in the number of emigrants after the mid-1850's reflects a reduction of population pressure which might have been expected only for the handicrafts, and even there not to such an extent. Since about 1860, expanding industrialization had certainly produced an economic upswing expressed in high rates of growth of the social product. Yet, at the end of the 1860's hidden unemployment still remained at about 10 percent.[62] The decline of emigration, which began in 1858, must be attributed, on the one hand, to the effects of the first crises of economic expansion in Germany and, on the other, to the American Civil War. The latter not only contributed to the overall reduction of emigration from Germany but also to the lower percentage of German emigrants choosing the United States as a destination. Thus, while the high levels of emigration between 1866 and 1873 were partially caused by political crises such as the Austro-Prussian and Franco-Prussian Wars, the emigrations of the late 1860's must be viewed primarily as movements making up for opportunities lost during the American Civil War.

However, with the onset of emigration from northeastern Germany around 1865, a change in the composition of the migrating population can be demonstrated. In socio-economically motivated migrations, in contrast to movements arising out of ideological, political, or personal-economic factors, phases of migration can be shown to correspond to phases of economic and social change.

The phase characterized by family migrations of independent

60. Mönckmeier, *Die deutsche überseeische Auswanderung*, p. 156.
61. *Ibid.*, p. 156f.
62. Marschalck, *Deutsche Überseewanderung*, pp. 110ff.

small peasants and artisans, which may be considered a form of preindustrial socio-economically motivated migration, came to an end in 1865.[63] It was replaced, although with a time lag of about fifteen years in relation to the onset of industrial development in Germany, by a new phase of emigration appropriate to early industrialization and characterized by the emigration of lower-peasant and lower-middle-class elements, either as families or as individuals. In the territories east of the Elbe, the composition of the migration was different from that in Southwest or Central Germany, where independent farmers in the former and artisans and home producers in the latter played the greatest role.

In the areas where the *Gutsherrschaft* dominated (Schleswig, Holstein, Mecklenburg, and East-Elbian Prussia) and peasant dependence was expressed in labor obligations, emancipation of the peasants was found to have completely different consequences from those in *Grundherrschaft* areas.

In Schleswig-Holstein, the formation of a large lower-peasant class was prevented because the population increase after the peasants' emancipation was offset by a moderate extension of land under cultivation, thus allowing absorption of the surplus population. In Mecklenburg, however, the transition to a pure manorial economy with the exclusive employment of day laborers and domestic servants and without a free peasantry was already completed by the beginning of the nineteenth century. While Schleswig-

---

63. Preference over other possibilities is here given to classification according to the structures, motivations, and goals of the emigration. For example, the period until 1850 could be characterized as a phase of agricultural crises (1815, 1825, 1836–1839, 1847) whose repercussions provoked an increase in emigration. The period after 1850 could then be treated as a phase of financial crises (lack of capital restricting mobility), whose effects produced a reduction in emigration. However, such classifications could not explain the migrations.

The emigration in the early and mid-nineteenth century, for which there is less material concerning the composition of emigration than for any other, could be classified according to other characteristics. The period 1815–1830 could be viewed as the continuation of "traditional" eighteenth-century emigration movements from Southwest Germany, while the period 1830–1850 might be seen as a phase of the movement's extension to areas where handicrafts and home production were strongly interwined with the agricultural structure. Finally, the 1850–1865 period could be described as a phase of expansion to other agrarian regions, such as East-Elbian Prussia.

Holstein, therefore, experienced very little emigration, Mecklenburg, especially after 1850 when the constitution of 1848 was revoked, participated in the emigration by providing a contingent consisting overwhelmingly of day laborers and farmhands.[64]

Developments in East-Elbian Prussia followed an entirely different course. There the Edict of 1807 brought the abolition of peasant subservience to the manor but owing to the confusion of the war, the Edict of 1811 which regulated the commutation of compulsory labor and services was never implemented and was suspended in 1815. The matter was dropped until 1816, when a Declaration was issued to "supplement" the Edict.

The number of peasant holdings affected by the Declaration, which remained in effect until 1850, was restricted by the stipulation that in order to be released from manorial dues, a peasant's holdings had to (1) be large enough to maintain a team of draft animals, (2) be registered as peasant property, and (3) be of old tenure.[65] Accordingly, it was only middle- and large-scale peasant proprietors who could sever their obligations by ceding a portion of their property (one-third for hereditary leaseholders and one-half for those having usufruct of the land with either hereditary or nonhereditary tenure.)

On the whole, the number of peasant farms hardly changed, although their area was reduced by cessions of land. This reduction could, however, be partially offset by the distribution of common lands resulting from the legal settlement of 1821.[66] The reduced peasant holdings entailed an increase in the density of population, which was rendered feasible by the transition from the old three-field system, with one field in fallow, to the improved three-field system with its cultivation of root crops.[67]

Furthermore, the peasants were able to expand cultivation "to the limits of the old pastures" owing the transition to stall feeding.

64. Lindig, "Entwicklung und gegenwärtiger Zustand des Auswanderungswesens in Mecklenburg," in *Auswanderung und Auswanderungspolitik in Deutschland*, p. 293.

65. Holdings established between 1749 and 1774, depending on the province.

66. Günther Ipsen, "Die preussische Bauernbefreiung als Landesausbau," *Zeitschrift für Agrargeschichte und Agrarsoziologie*, 2 (1954), 33.

67. Ipsen, "Bevölkerung I—Bevölkerungslehre," p. 433.

However, stall feeding created a greater need for laborers, which in turn enabled day laborers and artisans to acquire holdings of their own. The *Gutsherr*, who had to relinquish peasant services, was now forced to occupy the vacant land with people. This he accomplished with *Insten*, "cottagers bound to the manor." In return for their labor a small parcel of land for livestock and crops was ceded to them. These cottagers, who were peasants formerly unable to maintain a team of draft animals, day laborers, and farmhands on the estate, were also given a meager cash payment, free quarters with firewood, feed for their livestock, and a share of the grain harvest. In this way, many new family holdings were created. The later-born peasant children lived as independent laborers in the village, and the farmhands, formerly never able to marry, could now have families without restraint since the rising need for labor demanded a growing population. As a result of the Prussian emancipation of the peasants and the division of common land, which involved the cultivation of new land, the intensification of agriculture, and the "possibility of acquiring independent holdings and thus establishing a family," the population grew considerably. "The population increase in the East Elbe region is, in general, to be viewed as a direct consequence of the liberal agrarian reform."[68]

Because of the greater capacity to absorb people, overpopulation and accompanying pauperism, which plagued West Germany in the thirties and forties, did not set in until the sixties and seventies in the East.[69]

With the penetration of German agriculture by the capitalist spirit, the newly created system of labor became unprofitable. The shares of the cottagers were converted into fixed allowances.[70] The result was the reduction of human relations in agricultural labor, which stood in opposition to the peasant's desire for independence and for his own land.

---

68. Conze, "Die Wirkungen der liberalen Agrarreformen auf die Volksordnung in Mitteleuropa," p. 23.

69. Wolfgang Köllmann, "Industrialisierung, Binnenwanderung und 'Sozial-Frage,'" *Vierteljahrschrift für Sozial- und Wirtschaftsgeschichte*, 46 (1959), 60.

70. Carl Jantke, *Der vierte Stand* (Freiburg, 1955), p. 148.

In the course of this development it also became apparent that permanent labor on the estates could, in part, be abandoned, and from the fifties on the great agrarian proprietors drew chiefly on Polish seasonal laborers. The pressure of cheap agricultural products from areas overseas, which had just arrived on the European market, led to an agrarian crisis which provided the inducement for emigration by the lower peasantry.

The shift of the center of emigration from Southwest Germany, which, however, always remained heavily involved, to the Northeast after about 1865 clearly reveals that the repercussions of the changes in the agrarian structure of the German East, which continued into the nineties, provided the greatest impetus to German emigration. The relatively high number of emigrants from industrial areas may be explained by the fact that German industry was not yet able to provide enough jobs capable of sustaining its workers and thus a continued migration from these areas resulted.

Table V

INVOLVEMENT OF REGIONAL GROUPS
IN THE EMIGRATION 1871–1910
(*expressed in percentages*)

| Period | NE-G.[a] | NW-G.[b] | SW-G.[c] | C-G.[d] | SE-G.[e] | W-G.[f] | Hanseatic Cities |
|---|---|---|---|---|---|---|---|
| 1871–1875 | 39.3 | 15.4 | 25.6 | 3.8 | 5.2 | 8.3 | 2.1 |
| 1876–1880 | 35.4 | 15.2 | 25.3 | 4.2 | 7.2 | 9.8 | 3.1 |
| 1881–1885 | 38.2 | 14.4 | 24.1 | 3.8 | 6.3 | 10.6 | 2.6 |
| 1886–1890 | 37.7 | 12.0 | 28.9 | 3.2 | 5.1 | 10.1 | 3.0 |
| 1891–1895 | 34.8 | 13.3 | 25.3 | 4.4 | 7.1 | 10.7 | 4.4 |
| 1896–1900 | 28.6 | 14.8 | 26.1 | 4.8 | 6.9 | 10.8 | 8.0 |
| 1901–1905 | 30.7 | 13.8 | 23.6 | 5.0 | 7.8 | 14.1 | 5.0 |
| 1906–1910 | 27.5 | 13.3 | 23.4 | 5.2 | 8.7 | 15.7 | 6.2 |

SOURCE: Mönckmeier, *Die deutsche überseeische Auswanderung*, p. 133.

a. East and West Prussia, Pomerania, Posen, Brandenburg, and Mecklenburg.
b. Schleswig-Holstein, Hannover, and Oldenburg.
c. Bavaria, Baden, Württemberg, Hesse, Alsace-Lorraine, Hohenzollern.
d. Thuringia and the Province of Saxony, Brunswick, and Anhalt.
e. Silesia, Kingdom of Saxony.
f. The Rhineland, Westphalia, Hesse-Nassau, Waldeck, Lippe.

With the emigration from the East Elbian regions of Prussia after about 1865, the composition of the emigration also underwent a change. Until approximately 1890, emigration in family units continued to predominate with roughly 60 percent of the total emigration,[71] and the number of emigrants under fifteen years of age remained relatively constant, accounting for about 25 percent until the last decade of the century.[72] However, the percen-

71. Burgdörfer, "Die Wanderungen über die deutschen Reichsgrenzen," p. 403.

72. *Ibid.*, p. 402. See also *Immigration into the United States*, ed. by the Treasury Dept., Bureau of Statistics (1903), pp. 4359 and 4361. A comparison of the German immigration to the United States with the European immigration as a whole (including Southern and Southeastern Europe) between 1873 and 1892 clearly reveals that the percentage of chil-

## Table VI

| Average for the years | Agriculture | Industry and Commerce | Trade | Workers | Free Professions | Without occupation or without declaration of such |
|---|---|---|---|---|---|---|
| **Prussia** | | | | | | |
| 1871–1874 | 35.5 | 13.4 | 5.4 | 19.5 | 6.9 | 25.4 |
| 1875–1879 | 27.8 | 15.1 | 9.9 | 20.8 | 1.4 | 25.0 |
| 1880–1884 | 20.4 | 15.4 | 5.1 | 34.4 | 0.9 | 23.7 |
| 1885–1889 | 16.7 | 13.7 | 6.5 | 30.3 | 1.3 | 34.5 |
| 1890–1892 | 14.5 | 13.2 | 6.8 | 32.3 | 1.4 | 31.6 |
| 1893–1894 | 13.3 | 14.5 | 9.8 | 24.4 | 2.5 | 35.4 |
| **Bavaria** | | | | | | |
| 1871–1874 | 24.6 | 21.3 | 5.7 | 11.3 | 0.8 | 36.4 |
| 1875–1879 | 18.9 | 23.3 | 12.6 | 11.8 | 2.6 | 30.9 |
| 1880–1884 | 16.5 | 25.8 | 5.6 | 22.6 | 1.2 | 28.4 |
| 1885–1889 | 13.2 | 23.4 | 6.2 | 17.1 | 1.5 | 38.5 |
| 1890–1892 | 11.8 | 22.4 | 7.1 | 17.7 | 4.2 | 36.7 |
| 1893–1894 | 8.3 | 22.1 | 11.5 | 15.1 | 3.9 | 39.1 |
| **Württemberg** | | | | | | |
| 1871–1874 | 12.3 | 27.1 | 5.2 | 10.3 | 1.2 | 33.9 |
| 1875–1879 | 15.9 | 30.3 | 10.8 | 7.5 | 2.1 | 33.4 |
| 1880–1884 | 19.9 | 31.5 | 5.0 | 11.9 | 1.3 | 30.4 |
| 1885–1889 | 16.2 | 26.6 | 6.8 | 8.8 | 2.4 | 39.2 |
| 1890–1892 | 14.4 | 27.4 | 7.6 | 10.1 | 1.9 | 38.5 |
| 1893–1894 | 10.6 | 23.2 | 11.8 | 11.6 | 3.1 | 39.7 |
| **Mecklenburg (both)** | | | | | | |
| 1871–1874 | 53.2 | 5.3 | 1.2 | 21.7 | 0.2 | 18.4 |
| 1875–1879 | 34.2 | 9.6 | 6.3 | 26.5 | 1.5 | 21.9 |
| 1880–1884 | 47.5 | 7.8 | 2.6 | 26.5 | 0.5 | 15.1 |
| 1885–1889 | 33.7 | 10.6 | 4.6 | 30.1 | 1.0 | 20.0 |
| 1890–1892 | 38.9 | 8.4 | 5.0 | 29.3 | 1.0 | 17.4 |
| 1983–1894 | 29.3 | 9.6 | 8.5 | 29.9 | 1.7 | 21.0 |
| **Germany** | | | | | | |
| 1871–1874 | 34.3 | 14.6 | 5.6 | 18.2 | 0.9 | 26.4 |
| 1875–1879 | 24.7 | 17.2 | 12.4 | 18.5 | 1.7 | 25.5 |
| 1880–1884 | 20.3 | 18.0 | 5.9 | 30.5 | 1.0 | 24.3 |
| 1885–1889 | 15.9 | 15.7 | 8.2 | 26.8 | 1.5 | 31.9 |
| 1890–1892 | 14.1 | 15.8 | 9.0 | 27.4 | 1.7 | 32.0 |
| 1893–1894 | 11.8 | 16.3 | 12.8 | 20.8 | 2.7 | 35.6 |

SOURCE: Mönckmeier, *Die deutsche überseeische Auswanderung*, p. 164.

tage of independent farmers and tradesmen declined, while members of the agrarian lower class increased. (See Table VI.)

Table VI shows the emigration after 1871 via Hamburg, the nearest port for Germans from the Northeast. Farmers and "workers" provide the largest number of emigrants here. While for Prussia and Mecklenburg the percentage of emigrants from agricultural backgrounds is relatively high, for Württemberg and Bavaria it is lower than that from industry and commerce. However, the number of emigrating agricultural laborers from Prussia and Mecklenburg sank sharply until 1894, while the number of workers continued to rise. Table VII permits several observations about the susceptibility of the different occupational groups to external influences. While the index figures of the very small groups of emigrants from trade and transportation change only slightly, these same figures for the group "workers and personal services" fluctuate substantially. The contention that individual emigrants were especially responsive to minor economic and political fluctuations proves false. While 55.9 percent of the farmers and 50.2 percent of the workers emigrating via Hamburg between 1871 and 1884 were family members, only 28.4 percent[73] of the emigrants from industry and commerce departed in family units. Thus, the percentage of individual emigrants was greatest in the latter group. (See Table VII.)

The picture of regionally differentiated social conditions which had loosened the ties of people to their homes and had thus become causes of emigration, must be supplemented by an analysis of the whole emigration, emphasizing the social and economic develop-

---

dren under fifteen years of age, and thus the percentage of family immigration, in the German immigration was higher than in the general European. The "new" immigration was, therefore, to a greater extent individual immigration than the "old" or German immigration.

73. Mönckmeier, Die deutsche überseeische Auswanderung, p. 169.

## Table VII

OCCUPATIONS OF GERMANS EMIGRATING VIA HAMBURG 1871–1898
*(in percentage of the total emigration; index 1877=100)*

| Year | Agriculture | Index | Industry and Commerce | Index | Trade | Index | Workers and personal service | Index |
|------|-------------|-------|------------------------|-------|-------|-------|-------------------------------|-------|
| 1871 | 27.0 | 279 | 16.2 | 266 | 7.4 | 164 | 17.7 | 280 |
| 1872 | 36.8 | 724 | 15.8 | 495 | 4.8 | 203 | 17.9 | 539 |
| 1873 | 37.3 | 656 | 12.7 | 355 | 4.5 | 169 | 19.9 | 534 |
| 1874 | 31.3 | 258 | 13.6 | 178 | 7.5 | 132 | 15.7 | 198 |
| 1875 | 26.0 | 140 | 14.1 | 121 | 9.7 | 112 | 19.4 | 160 |
| 1876 | 21.8 | 95 | 15.2 | 105 | 11.9 | 110 | 23.2 | 154 |
| 1877 | 27.3 | 100 | 17.2 | 100 | 12.8 | 100 | 17.9 | 100 |
| 1878 | 27.5 | 111 | 18.9 | 121 | 13.3 | 116 | 15.8 | 97 |
| 1879 | 21.4 | 96 | 21.4 | 153 | 14.9 | 143 | 15.8 | 108 |
| 1880 | 21.3 | 311 | 23.6 | 549 | 7.8 | 243 | 25.3 | 565 |
| 1881 | 18.3 | 528 | 17.9 | 820 | 5.1 | 313 | 36.2 | 1594 |
| 1882 | 22.3 | 541 | 17.4 | 671 | 5.5 | 284 | 28.2 | 1046 |
| 1883 | 21.2 | 403 | 16.8 | 509 | 6.0 | 243 | 31.8 | 820 |
| 1884 | 19.2 | 327 | 15.6 | 425 | 5.9 | 215 | 31.0 | 808 |
| 1885 | 18.2 | 219 | 15.1 | 290 | 7.0 | 180 | 27.3 | 503 |
| 1886 | 15.9 | 140 | 16.7 | 233 | 9.0 | 168 | 24.9 | 334 |
| 1887 | 13.4 | 103 | 16.3 | 200 | 8.6 | 141 | 27.1 | 320 |
| 1888 | 14.6 | 132 | 15.6 | 217 | 7.9 | 147 | 28.8 | 385 |
| 1889 | 16.3 | 128 | 15.1 | 189 | 9.3 | 157 | 25.8 | 310 |
| 1890 | 16.1 | 137 | 15.9 | 215 | 9.6 | 174 | 23.4 | 304 |
| 1891 | 11.8 | 128 | 15.7 | 270 | 8.7 | 202 | 30.2 | 499 |
| 1892 | 14.8 | 143 | 16.0 | 244 | 8.8 | 180 | 27.9 | 409 |
| 1893 | 11.3 | 118 | 16.7 | 278 | 12.2 | 271 | 23.5 | 374 |
| 1894 | 12.8 | 71 | 15.5 | 137 | 14.0 | 166 | 15.7 | 133 |
| 1895 | 9.7 | | 18.0 | | 16.3 | | 13.8 | |
| 1896 | 9.9 | | 19.4 | | 18.2 | | 11.6 | |
| 1897 | 9.4 | | 19.5 | | 25.3 | | 8.4 | |
| 1898 | 11.1 | | 19.4 | | 24.4 | | 3.5 | |

SOURCE: Mönckmeier, *Die deutsche überseeische Auswanderung*, pp. 163, 167.

ment of Germany. Here the material prepared by Walther G. Hoffmann will be drawn upon.[74]

In the first half of the nineteenth century, population pressure increased with relative constancy, and emigration, therefore, steadily grew. However, a graph of emigration figures for the second half of the century seems to indicate a steady reduction of this pressure if the highs of 1865–1869 and 1880–1884 are explicable as emigrations making up for the years of the American Civil War and the so-called *Gründerkrise* of 1875–1879.

The pace of economic production between 1865 and 1870 represents only a slightly reduced rate of growth over the previous five-year period, while the unchanging rate between 1875 and 1880, in contrast to the vigorous growth of the previous and subsequent five-year periods, meant an extraordinary retardation which could not be compensated for until the turn of the century. This indicates that while the emigrations of 1865–1869 can be interpreted as migrations making up for lost opportunities, the emigrations of the eighties cannot. The break in the trend during the second half of the nineteenth century becomes even clearer if one compares emigration figures with the hypothetical unemployment statistics.[75]

While unemployment declined from 1850–1854 to 1870–1874, it rose sharply in the eighties, almost reaching the high of the fifties. And while opportunities for emigration can be made up, this naturally does not apply to unemployment. The sharp drop in unemployment cannot be dismissed, even though it must be conceded that the degree to which delayed emigration can increase unemployment is not insignificant. In fact, this would explain the high rate of unemployment for the 1865–1869 period. Examination of

74. Walther G. Hoffmann, *Das Wachstum der deutschen Wirtschaft seit der Mitte des 19. Jahrhunderts* (Berlin, 1965), p. 451f. The value of economic production, expressed in millions of marks as of 1913, amounted to:

| | | | | | |
|---|---|---|---|---|---|
| 1850 | 9,449 | 1870 | 14,169 | 1890 | 23,589 |
| 1855 | 9,657 | 1875 | 17,651 | 1895 | 27,621 |
| 1860 | 11,577 | 1880 | 17,679 | 1900 | 33,169 |
| 1865 | 13,167 | 1885 | 20,417 | | |

75. For the calculation of these figures, which in absolute form have little interpretative value but are capable of describing the development of trends, see, Marschalck, *Deutsche Überseewanderung*, pp. 110ff.

Table VIII

EMIGRATION AND UNEMPLOYMENT 1850–1900
(*in five-year averages*)

| Period | Emigration in percent | Unemployment in percent |
|--------|------------------------|--------------------------|
| 1850–1854 | 8.9 | 16.0 |
| 1855–1859 | 4.3 | 17.4 |
| 1860–1864 | 2.5 | 10.0 |
| 1865–1869 | 3.8 | 10.2 |
| 1870–1874 | 2.4 | 1.4 |
| 1875–1879 | 0.7 | 5.2 |
| 1880–1884 | 3.8 | 15.1 |
| 1885–1889 | 2.1 | 11.5 |
| 1890–1894 | 1.8 | 9.5 |
| 1895–1899 | 0.5 | 4.5 |

SOURCE: Marschalck, *Deutsche Überseewanderung im 19. Jahrhundert*, pp. 113ff.

economic development between 1850 and 1900 supports the assumption that the emigrations of this era do not follow a uniform and consistent pattern. Instead, at least two phases can be distinguished in the course of the century's migrations, one lasting from 1815 to 1865, the other from 1865 to 1895. The second phase is marked by the emigration of elements of the lower peasantry from Northeast Germany and of small artisans and tradesmen on the verge of sinking into the lower middle class. It is also characterized by a slow increase in individual migration as one phase of a form of preindustrial migration for socio-economic motives.

For the small peasants and artisans migrating in families as well as for the somewhat less involved lower peasants, the goal of emigration in the phase ending in 1865 was settlement (the acquisition of land). This also applies to the emigration of lower peasant and petty bourgeois families and individuals in the 1865–1895 phase. Single males to some extent and single women to a greater extent were also looking for work. The emigration of unmarried women in quest of better marriage prospects was insignificant.

## IV

IN 1890, the end of the continuous frontier in the United States was proclaimed, and at the same time German industry was now able to absorb the bulk of the available labor supply. Emigration was no longer motivated by a desire for land but primarily by the hope for employment overseas. The flow of emigration, therefore, gradually receded and with the outbreak of war in 1914 almost dried up completely.

Not until the emigration had dwindled to insignificance did the German Empire concern itself with the matter. According to the Constitution of the German Empire of 1871, "the regulation ... of colonization and emigration to non-German countries" was to be subject to the supervision of the Empire,[76] but for the time being only an "Imperial Commissioner for Emigration Affairs" was appointed. This commissioner, however, was merely responsible for supervising conditions in the ports of emigration and had no influence on either the business practices of emigration agents and entrepreneurs or on the measures for protecting emigrants during passage.

When finally on June 9, 1897,[77] the long-awaited Imperial Emigration Law was passed, it came too late. Because of the decline in emigration, the effort to steer it in the direction of colonization was no longer practicable. Nevertheless, the Imperial authorities were determined to regulate at least the dissemination of information to emigrants on a uniform basis. While fifteen organizations had been established with this general objective since the foundation of the Empire, the "Central Information Office for Emigrants" was created to handle this task on a nation-wide level.[78]

Then in 1918 the "Imperial Office for German Immigration, Repatriation, and Emigration" was established. Its function was to advise German emigrants as well as returning "Reich Germans"

---

76. *Dokumente zur deutschen Verfassungsgeschichte*, Ernst Rudolf Huber, ed. (Stuttgart, 1964), II, no. 218.

77. *Reichsgesetzblatt 1897*, pp. 463ff.

78. A. Schulte im Hofe, *Auswanderung und Auswanderungspolitik* (Berlin, 1918), p. 10f.

and immigrants "of German descent."[79] Since immigration began to exceed emigration after the First World War, instruction about the possibilities open to immigrants and returning migrants in Germany was particularly important.

Table IX

GERMAN EMIGRATION AND IMMIGRATION 1922–1933

| Year | German emigrants (in 1,000's) | Immigrants[a] to Germany (in 1,000's) | Repatriates[b] among the immigrants (in 1,000's) |
|---|---|---|---|
| 1922 | 36.6 | 82.0 | |
| 1923 | 115.4 | 48.2 | |
| 1924 | 58.3 | 61.0 | |
| 1925 | 62.7 | 78.0 | 33.0 |
| 1926 | 65.3 | 76.4 | 29.7 |
| 1927 | 61.4 | 88.8 | 38.3 |
| 1928 | 57.2 | 103.3 | 45.1 |
| 1929 | 48.7 | 109.7 | 38.5 |
| 1930 | 37.4 | 129.2 | 43.1 |
| 1931 | 13.6 | 110.2 | 40.4 |
| 1932 | 10.3 | 106.6 | 39.7 |
| 1933 | 12.9 | 88.5 | 42.2 |

SOURCES: Burgdörfer, "Die Wanderungen über die deutschen Reichsgrenzen," p. 192; *Statistisches Jahrbuch für das Deutsche Reich*, 45 (1926), 38; *ibid.*, 49 (1930), 53; *ibid*, 53 (1934), 51.

a. Only arrivals via Hamburg and Bremen.
b. German citizens.

Although emigration in the 1920's once again assumed significant proportions, it must be viewed as a consequence of the war. By 1930 the number of returning Germans surpassed that of German emigrants, and with the depression and the gradual political and economic stabilization in the mid-thirties, German emigration once again became numerically insignificant.

The decline of family migration and the altered age and occupational structure of the emigration resulting from the increase of individual migration became the salient features of this new phase,

79. *Nachrichtenblatt des Reichsamts für deutsche Einwanderung, Rückwanderung und Auswanderung*, 1 (1919), 1.

beginning around 1895, of German emigration in the late nineteenth and early twentieth centuries.

Table X

EMIGRATION OF GERMANS IN FAMILIES
AND AS INDIVIDUALS 1891–1928

| Year | Emigration in families (in percent) | Men per 100 emigrants in families (in percent) | Men per 100 individual emigrants (in percent) | Persons under 14 years of age (per 100 emigrants) |
|---|---|---|---|---|
| 1819–1900 | 47.6 | 45.5 | 63.8 | 21.6 |
| 1901–1910 | 42.2 | 45.6 | 67.5 | 19.9 |
| 1911–1920 | 39.4 | 45.2 | 70.7 | 18.6 |
| 1921–1928 | 33.8 | 45.7 | 62.2 | 12.3 |

SOURCE: Burgdörfer, "Die Wanderungen über die deutschen Reichsgrenzen," pp. 402ff.

Despite the increase of individual migration, the proportion of men in the total emigration remained relatively constant at just under 60 percent. Thus, women assumed a greater role in the increased emigration of individuals than did their male counterparts. This greater female mobility is related to the now commencing migration for employment in American industry. The decline of German emigration in general beginning at that time had the effect of causing the number of female emigrants to drop at a slower rate than that of the male emigrants. What this means is that male emigrants were more heavily represented among the settlers on the land, who predominated until 1895, than were the women, who had found their livelihood primarily in domestic service. Individual female migrants were therefore less affected than males by the decline in agricultural settlement that had such an impact upon German emigration at large.

While in the first half of the nineteenth century the German emigration was composed primarily of independent small farmers and traders from Southwest Germany, the picture changed with the onset of the emigration from Northeast Germany in the sixties. The major contingent of German emigrants was now comprised of farm laborers, and at the beginning of the twentieth century this high percentage of agrarian workers had become even greater. In fact, less than 10 percent of the working emigrants between 1900 and 1914 were independent.

Table XI

SOCIAL POSITION OF THE EMIGRANTS 1900–1925

*Number of persons per 100 working emigrants involved in:*

| Period | Agriculture: workers and servants | Handicrafts and Industry: assistants and workers | Trade and Commerce: assistants and employees |
|---|---|---|---|
| 1900–1904 | 93.0 | 93.1 | 87.5 |
| 1905–1909 | 94.9 | 92.6 | 79.2 |
| 1910–1914 | 94.9 | 91.8 | 83.8 |
| 1921–1925 | 92.1 | 93.9 | 92.2 |

SOURCE: Burgdörfer, "Die Wanderungen über die deutschen Reichsgrenzen," p. 409.

The percentage of emigrants from agriculture declined markedly in this phase, although it did remain the second strongest group behind handicraft and industrial workers. Moreover, a decline in the percentage of nonworking dependents and, therefore, an increase in individual emigration can also be discerned in the agricultural occupations.[80] As a result of this rise in individual emigration and the corresponding decline in the percentage of female emigrants in "male" occupations, the percentage of women in the occupational category "domestic services" increased.

Table XII

NUMBER OF MALE EMIGRANTS PER 100
FEMALE EMIGRANTS EMPLOYED IN:

| Period | Agriculture and Forestry | Handicrafts and Industry | Domestic Services |
|---|---|---|---|
| 1900–1904 | 122.2 | 261.8 | 2.0 |
| 1905–1909 | 103.0 | 307.7 | 1.8 |
| 1910–1914 | 144.7 | 302.1 | 1.7 |
| 1921–1923 | 170.7 | 322.5 | 2.1 |
| 1924–1928 | 576.5 | 608.0 | 3.0 |

SOURCE: Burgdörfer, "Die Wanderungen über die deutschen Reichsgrenzen," p. 407.

80. Mönckmeier, *Die deutsche überseeische Auswanderung*, p. 170.

It is clear from the high percentage of emigrants from agriculture, that the emigrants came primarily from rural communities. Not until the onset of the emigration from the industrial working class, based in the cities, did the rural villages recede as areas of origin for German emigrants. This tendency was strengthened by the temporary arrival of agricultural workers in the cities, from which they subsequently migrated again.

The period beginning in approximately 1895 was characterized by the end of the frontier settlement in the United States, the concomitant decline of family emigration, the subsequent rise of individual emigration and thus the number of emigrants from industry, as well as by the increase of economically dependent emigrants. These developments make it imperative to distinguish between agricultural emigration (permanent emigration and family emigration) and the emigration of industrial workers with its "character of temporary, pendulum-migration conditioned by the business cycle."[81]

The phase of high industrialization in Germany, which in both an economic and social sense began around 1875, can therefore be linked, although with a time lag of approximately twenty years, to the corresponding form of migration. This phase is characterized by the predominance of individual migration by the lower peasantry and, increasingly, the industrial working class. Their goal was employment overseas.

With the decline of the percentage of Germans immigrating to the United States after 1910, with Canada, South America, and Australia becoming more important, another aspect of the emigration became clearer. Individual decisions with respect to destination, combined with high numbers of returning migrants, indicated an increase in migration for personal-economic reasons. Together with socio-economically motivated emigration, this type of migration is a class-conditioned form of emigration typical of a highly industrialized society. Although the personal-economically motivated form certainly played a subordinate role to the socio-eco-

81. Burgdörfer, "Die Wanderungen über die deutschen Reichsgrenzen," p. 409.

nomically induced variety, between them they dominated the German emigration in the first third of the twentieth century.

## V

WITH the arrival of the Depression, the economically conditioned immigration to the United States came to a temporary halt. The worldwide economic catastrophe made clear that under the current conditions of production and settlement an equilibrium between the two regions of sustenance had been reached. Furthermore, considering the two social systems and especially the national unemployment insurance available in Germany since the law of July 16, 1927, staying put now offered the best chances of surviving the crisis. For this reason, the socio-economic motive for emigration disappeared while personal-economically motivated emigration was scarcely possible. If, nevertheless, the emigration did not come to a complete standstill in the following years, this was due to political developments in Germany. In this regard, the National Socialist accession to power on January 30, 1933 constituted a turning point in the history of the German-American migration.[82]

The emigration statistics, incomplete as they are, reveal that the tendency to return to Germany, which had begun at the close of the twenties, had grown even more pronounced. While unrealized and, given the current economic situation, unrealizable hopes may be accepted as the primary motive for returning emigrants, this inclination was strengthened by the economic revival in Germany. The economic upswing had begun earlier in Germany and was more in evidence there as a result of government measures to create

---

82. While the existing body of migration research makes possible relatively firm assertions on the emigrations before 1930, a similar foundation of knowledge for the subsequent period has not yet been laid. The expositions in Part V should, therefore, be understood only as a preliminary attempt to treat the emigrations of the last forty years within a typological framework. A critique of the sources, in itself important, has been waived to a large extent in order to remain within the bounds of this work.

## Table XIII

### GERMAN IMMIGRATION TO THE UNITED STATES AND EMIGRANTS RETURNING TO GERMANY 1934–1939[a]

| Year | Emigrants | Immigrants to the United States[b] | Returning Emigrants | Surplus of repatriates |
|------|-----------|-----------------------------------|---------------------|------------------------|
| 1934 | 10,717 | 4,392 | 45,810 | 35,093 |
| 1935 | 9,104 | 5,201 | 51,954 | 42,850 |
| 1936 | 10,190 | 6,346 | 47,525 | 37,335 |
| 1937 | 9,291 | 10,895 | 44,915 | 34,624 |
| 1938 | 12,997 | 17,199 | | |
| 1939 | 7,079 | 33,515[c] | | |

SOURCES: *Statistisches Jahrbuch für das deutsche Reich*, 1937 and 1938; *Statistical Abstract of the United States*, 1935–1940.

a. The German Reich, with borders of the respective years.

b. Fiscal year. All immigrants with permanent residency in Germany (including Austria after March 1938).

c. An additional 21,520 residents were registered in fiscal year 1940 and another 4,028 in 1942.

work, especially in the early stages of rearmament.[83] Moreover, in the first years of the "Third Reich" the rising tide of returning emigrants was attracted, in part, by national enthusiasm reinforced by the *Heim-ins-Reich* propaganda of National Socialist organizations abroad. By 1935, however, the highpoint of this wave had been reached, and the more the regime revealed its true nature, the lower the number of returning emigrants sank. By 1937 the officially recorded surplus of repatriates was already less than in 1934.

While this return migration could be classified as the personal-economic form, the emigrations of this period possessed all the attributes of political flight. The rigor with which the new rulers proceeded against their opponents of every shade surpassed the measures of persecution initiated by the Carlsbad Decrees of 1819 and the actions taken against leaders of the Revolution of 1848–1849, which had produced the first politically motivated emigra-

83. See Dietmar Petzina, "Grundriss der deutschen Wirstchaftsgeschichte," *Deutsche Geschichte seit dem Ersten Weltkrieg*, ed. by the Institut für Zeitgeschichte (Stuttgart, 1973), II, 674; Eugene M. Kulischer, *Europe on the Move* (New York, 1948), pp. 192ff.

tions from Germany. But while the political refugees of those epochs represented only a numerically insignificant fringe group compared to the socio-economically motivated mass migration, the politically motivated individual fleeing in response to a direct threat dominated the emigration from the "Third Reich." Within this escape movement, two groups can be distinguished: the political and intellectual leadership of the democratic parties, unions, and other organizations banned and dissolved by the regime and, second, the German Jews who fell victims to Nazi racism. At first, they were the objects of unsystematic boycott measures, but with the "Law for the Protection of German Blood and German Honor," one of the "Nürnberg Laws" of September 1935, the systematic annihilation of their civil rights began. This action was to deprive them of "all possibility of living."[84] In 1938, pogroms, precursors of the extermination policy which reached its ghastly climax during the Second World War, took place throughout Germany. Attempts to allow the persecuted a legitimately regulated emigration failed.[85]

The emigration occurred in three waves. "The first panicky flight of refugees followed immediately after the establishment of National Socialism. The second wave came after the promulgation of the anti-Jewish laws of September 15, 1935, and the third after the pogroms of November, 1938."[86] The destination of this political escape movement was the neighboring European states where the first emigrant organizations were established. Until 1936, only offshoots of this movement reached the United States, although a comparison of German emigration and American immigration figures reveals that more emigrants gave the United States as their destination than actually arrived there.[87] This situation changed

84. Karl Dietrich Erdmann, "Die Zeit der Weltkriege," in Bruno Gebhard, *Handbuch der Deutschen Geschichte*, 8th ed., Herbert Grundmann, ed. (Stuttgart, 1959), IV, 209.

85. Göring, especially, saw the emigration of Jews as a means of improving the foreign exchange position of the *Reich*. Schacht, the president of the Reichsbank, was appointed as the minister with special responsibility for Jewish emigration in early 1939. See *ibid.*, p. 209f.

86. Kulischer, *Europe on the Move*, p. 190f.

87. The number of unrecorded emigrants from Germany may have been quite substantial in these years since those who fled illegally were not registered nor could German

only with the extension of the German sphere of influence in Europe resulting from the *Anschluss* with Austria in March 1938, and the occupation of Czechoslovakia a year later. Between July 1, 1936, and June 30, 1940, a total of 83,129 immigrants with a previous residence in Germany were registered in the United States compared to only 16,858 in the four previous years.[88] Among them, however, were only 23,147 German citizens. As late as December 1937, only a little over 15,000 of the 154,000 Jewish refugees were said to have immigrated to America.[89] The difference between the total number of German immigrants and that of German citizens received in the United States can be explained by the National Socialist practice of depriving political refugees of their citizenship. Moreover, the phenomenon of political escape unfolded in stages, and the United States was the last stop. While an additional 6,836 persons with previous residence in Germany, including 5,831 German citizens, were registered as immigrants between July 1, 1940 and June 30, 1945,[90] these may have been refugees who had earlier found haven in countries subsequently occupied by German armies. In the case of these immigrants who managed to elude the clutches of the National Socialists for a second time—often literally at the last moment[91]—escape by stages is vividly illustrated. With these exceptions, the movement came to an end at the outbreak of the war. For the opponents of the regime and, above all, for the Jews remaining in Germany, this exit was closed.

---

immigrants arriving in the United States necessarily be identified by their country of departure, since they often embarked from other European countries.

88. The difference between immigrants from Germany and immigrating German citizens cannot, however, be completely explained by expatriation measures. *Statistical Abstract of the United States*, 1933–1941.

89. According to Kulischer, *Europe on the Move*, p. 192.

90. *Statistical Abstract of the United States*, 1941–1946.

91. An example of this and at the same time an example of the possible fates of European fugitives in the twentieth century is Eugene M. Kulischer, the prominent student of migrations. In 1919 he fled the Revolution in Russia, arriving in Germany, where, after the National Socialist seizure of power, he was once again forced to flee. In 1941 he escaped from occupied Europe and traveled to America. His brother Alexander, arrested by the Pétain police, died in a concentration camp in 1942. See the introduction to *Europe on the Move*.

Many members of the intellectual and cultural elite of the Weimar Republic, of the most divergent political views, were among the refugees. These actors, directors, writers, painters, architects, and scholars of all disciplines chose emigration as the only chance to continue their creative activity in freedom, whether persecuted for political or racial reasons or not at all.[92] For Germany this meant an irretrievable loss of intellectual capacity, because for most of the refugees, emigration was a journey without return. Whether they died in exile before the fall of National Socialist tyranny, or established roots in their new homes too strong to break, or whether they loathed the idea of living again in a country in which such crimes had been committed, few returned to Germany.[93]

Table XIV

EMIGRATION FROM THE FEDERAL REPUBLIC TO THE
UNITED STATES AND RETURN MIGRATIONS 1946–1970

| Period | Emigrants | Repatriates | Surplus of emigrants |
|---|---|---|---|
| 1946–1950 | 268,000 | | |
| 1951–1955 | 260,100 | | |
| 1956–1960 | 182,772 | 25,598 | 148,709 |
| 1961–1965 | 138,798 | 45,331 | 93,467 |
| 1966–1970 | 141,978 | 44,910 | 97,068 |

SOURCE: *Statistisches Jahrbuch für die Bundesrepublik Deutschland*, 1954–1972.

After the Second World War and the defeat of Germany, emigration stood at first in the shadow of occupation. Although between 1946 and 1950 figures for immigration to the United States reached a level reminiscent of the wave of migration following the First World War, most of those involved had come to Germany during the war, whether under duress or voluntarily, from the occupied countries of eastern and southeastern Europe and could

92. Laura Fermi, *Illustrious Emigrants, The Intellectual Migration from Europe, 1930/41* (Chicago, 1968); Donald Fleming, Bernard Bailyn, eds., *The Intellectual Migration: Europe and America, 1930–1960* (Cambridge, 1969).

93. Although the question of return can only be mentioned and not discussed here, the intellectual and political impulse which emanated from these emigrants who returned (or are still returning) must be acknowledged.

Table XV

GERMAN IMMIGRANTS TO THE UNITED STATES 1946–1970

| Period[a] | Total | German citizens |
|-----------|-------|-----------------|
| 1946–1950 | 219,742 | 95,118 |
| 1951–1955 | 282,014 | 166,495 |
| 1956–1960 | 195,741 | 178,955 |
| 1961–1965 | 117,945 | 129,181 |
| 1966–1970 | 71,858 | 68,973 |

SOURCE: *Statistical Abstract of the United States, 1947–1971.*

a. Fiscal year.

not or did not want to return owing to the political changes there. These groups were repatriated only from the Soviet zone, while in the Western zones they were classified as "displaced persons" and placed under the care of the International Refugee Organization (IRO) of the United Nations. This organization made possible their emigration and settlement. By July 1, 1950, 185,935 of them had been resettled in the United States,[94] and another 39,946 arrived before June 30, 1952.[95] The immigration of German citizens was at first restricted to more or less voluntarily recruited specialists, of whom the Peenemünde rocket experts were the best known. These specialists were thus able to continue their work in the United States. Later nurses and servants were also admitted as immigrants. When the rule against fraternization was lifted for members of the Allied forces, the immigration of another special group began: the wives and children of the occupying soldiers. They were not counted as part of the contingent of German immigrants (25,814 annually) allowed by American immigration legislation nor were refugees from the German Democratic Republic, who arrived in America in the fifties. Because of such groups, the immigration quota was always exceeded until 1961. Moreover, from the beginning of the fifties, free immigration was again possible.

94. Paul Frings, *Das internationale Flüchtlingsproblem* (Frankfurt a.M., 1951), p. 82; on the organization and activities of the I.R.O., see pp. 66ff.
95. *Statistical Abstract of the United States*, 1957, p. 97.

The highpoint of immigration by German citizens was reached in 1952, when 50,283 arrived. After a temporary decline, 1957 brought another peak of 45,230. Since then the annual number has receded steadily, and since 1962 it has been lower than the quota.[96] Meanwhile, as the flow of refugees from the German Democratic Republic ended, the Federal Republic of Germany became a preferred destination of emigration for foreign workers. These workers filled gaps in the domestic labor market which could not be occupied by the German labor force. As a result of its own economic development, the Federal Republic of Germany now proved to be an underpopulated area with a high capacity for absorbing population. Under these conditions, the number of returning emigrants climbed steadily from the mid-fifties. Furthermore, approximately 14 percent of all Germans emigrating between 1956 and 1960 returned, while 33 percent of all Germans emigrating between 1961 and 1965, and 32 percent of those between 1966 and 1970, also returned. This return flow in the sixties indicates that temporary emigration for employment or education had gained a special significance.

The predominant form of migration in the present period can be recognized from such phenomena. While politically conditioned refugee migration placed its stamp on the immediate postwar years, it has declined steadily since the early fifties. Thus, despite the arrival in the United States of refugees from the German Democratic Republic, politically motivated emigration ended at the beginning of the sixties. The special group of employed experts, nurses, servants, and soldiers' wives belonged to the personal- economically motivated type of migrations, which has determined the form of migration since the early fifties. Opportunities for education and individual employment were the reasons behind the decision to emigrate. In cases where more than temporary immigration had initially been intended, the renewed weighing of opportunities

96. According to the *Statistical Abstract of the United States*, 1963ff. According to the statistics of the Federal Republic, which do not distinguish according to citizenship, the high point of the postwar wave of emigration was reached in 1949 with 120,300. A second peak with 50,792 emigrants was recorded in 1956. *Statistisches Jahrbuch der Bundesrepublik Deutschland*, 1950ff.

after a stay in the area of destination became the decisive factor in choosing whether or not to establish permanent residency.

With migration as an equilibrating agency between regions of relatively similar economic structures and standards of living, the form of migration appropriate to an industrially conditioned society emerged. It had surfaced in the first decades of the twentieth century, but declined in the period of great economic and political crises. Given the precondition of freedom of travel and settlement, this migration for personal-economic reasons proved dominant. At the same time, the three-hundred-year history of the German immigration to Britain's American colonies and to the United States came to an end, at least temporarily. Only fundamental economic and political changes could institute a new phase in this history.

# CAUSES OF MEXICAN EMIGRATION TO THE UNITED STATES: A SUMMARY VIEW

Arthur F. Corwin

# CAUSES OF MEXICAN
# EMIGRATION TO
# THE UNITED STATES:
# A SUMMARY VIEW

## 1. The Roots of Dislocation

THAT Mexico should happen to share a common land frontier with the southwestern region of the United States is a geo-social fact that readily distinguishes Mexican migration from all other currents of migration to this country. * If they could, probably half the peoples of the world would walk to the United States in search of economic improvement, but this opportunity, or temptation, or curse—"Poor Mexico," say Mexican Nationalists, "so far from God and so close to the United States"— is, in the nature of things, reserved only for the people of Mexico and Canada.

The children of the Spanish Conquest began walking to what is now the American Southwest as footsoldiers, servants, and settlers of the Spanish crown even before the founding of Jamestown in 1607. But these mestizo settlers of the Spanish and Mexican eras were a mere trickle to be numbered in the hundreds, whereas the migration of several million Mexican folk over the southwestern border is almost exclusively a twentieth-century phenomenon. Per-

* This study was made possible through the support of the National Endowment for the Humanities, the University of Connecticut Research Foundation, and the cooperation of the United States Immigration and Naturalization Service. Also, Lawrence Cardoso, Department of History, University of Wyoming, who worked in the Mexican archives under a Doherty Foundation Fellowship, and Romeo Flores of El Colegio de México, Mexico City, were only two of many individuals who gave assistance.

haps because it has been essentially a walk-in by *las clases humildes* through the nation's kitchen door, so to speak, modern Mexican emigration has received scant attention from North American or Mexican students prior to the present ethnic studies movement, with but rare exceptions such as Carey McWilliams' *North from Mexico*, first published in 1948, and the earlier works of Paul S. Taylor and Manuel Gamio.[1]

The first of two great migratory waves from Mexico lasted from approximately 1900 to 1930 when the Great Depression cut it short; the second, touched off by World War II, continues undiminished to this day. In the first wave primitive rural conditions were the principal cause of a campesino exodus that spilled into Mexican towns and cities and eventually over the United States border. *La miseria rural*, so called in Mexico, actually grew more oppressive during the regime of General Porfirio Díaz (1876–1910) when misguided colonization and land development laws allowed speculators to seize title to millions of hectares of farm and pastoral land, including the communal holdings of many peasant villages that previously had remained intact as a customary right. The land grab forced even more of the Indo-Mexican peasantry into abject peonage on the great haciendas and ranchos, or into the ranks of migratory labor.

Peonage—particularly debt peonage—was nearly universal among the landless campesinos. Because of static wages and the manipulation of accounts by hacienda owners and administrators the illiterate peon rarely could pay off a debt, and by custom debts passed from generation to generation, unless, of course, a debtor took flight. An arbitrary method of control in the hands of creole and mestizo overlords, lacking in any tradition of noblesse oblige,

1. Carey McWilliams, *North from Mexico: The Spanish-Speaking People in the United States* (1948; rpt. New York, 1968) is now considered a classic in ethnic history. Paul S. Taylor, *Mexican Labor in the United States* (Berkeley, 1928–1934), ten parts; *A Mexican-American Frontier: Nueces County, Texas* (Chapel Hill, 1934). Manuel Gamio, *Mexican Immigration to the United States: A Study of Human Adjustment* (Chicago, 1930); *The Mexican Immigrant, His Life Story* (Chicago, 1931). For other works on Mexican migration see Arthur F. Corwin, "Mexican Emigration History, 1900–1970: Literature and Research," *Latin American Research Review*, 8 (1973), 3–24.

was another good reason for stealing away in the night. Various descriptions of the evils of the Porfirian hacienda, including Molina Enríquez' celebrated indictment of 1908, depicted hacienda masters as exercising the despotic power of a feudal lord.[2]

Conditions of semistarvation were commonly reported. One account noted that at no time in the thirty years preceding the Revolution of 1910 did the average daily pay for common farm labor exceed twenty-five cents a day in United States currency, yet during the same time the cost of basic foods like corn and beans more than doubled.[3] Little wonder that the debt-ridden peons, in the words of Silva Herzog, suffered the primeval wants of food, clothing, and shelter.[4]

Moreover, with advances in public health, especially in the use of mass vaccination, and domestic peace under a paternal dictatorship, the population leaped from about nine million in 1876 to near fifteen million in 1910. At that date about eighty percent of the people lived in rural areas, and about five percent of Mexican families owned ninety percent of the land.[5] It is hardly surprising, therefore, that a rapid population increase within a semifeudal subsistence economy could only contribute to the deprivation and displacement of the peasantry.

Thus in certain areas of Mexico the combination of population growth, land shortage, and feudal conditions led to the rapid emergence of a migratory labor class, most notably in the populous states of the Central Plateau such as Guanajuato, Jalisco, and San Luis Potosí. By the 1890's increasing numbers of displaced peasants were wandering over Mexico in search of seasonal work. Many moved into cities like Guadalajara, San Luis Potosí, Monterrey, and Mexico City itself; many others headed for the thinly popu-

2. Andrés Molina Enríquez, *Los Grandes Problemas Nacionales* (Mexico, 1908). Also, a standard account of the land problem is given by George M. McBride, *The Land Systems of Mexico* (New York, 1923).

3. Fernando González Roa and José Covarrubias, *El Problema Rural de México* (Mexico, 1917), p. 180.

4. Jesús Silva Herzog, *El Agrarismo Mexicano y la Reforma Agraria*, 2d ed. (Mexico, 1959), p. 128.

5. McBride, *The Land Systems*, p. 154.

lated northern states such as Tamaulipas, Coahuila, Chihuahua, and Sonora where the development of railroads, mining, and ranching, spurred by American and other foreign investors during the permissive Porfirian era, created a rising demand for migrant labor at higher wages. By the turn of the century landless peons were gravitating northward in such numbers that hacienda owners were complaining of a labor loss.[6]

The roots of Mexico's migratory labor flow, however, are not found exclusively in peonage conditions perpetuated by the Díaz dictatorship. This is an oversimplification propagated by some postrevolutionary writers. Scattered all over Mexico there were small, semitribal groups, or extended families, who lived collectively in rude huts, still to be seen in many places, and called *rancherías* by the Spaniards. The inhabitants of these mobile villages foraged for seasonal work as their ancestors had foraged for food or game. The rancherías were, in fact, a subculture, little affected one way or another by a change in landed property, and retaining many vestigial characteristics of preagricultural tribes which had remained on the margins of the Spanish Conquest. Often rancherías became "squatter camps" near missions, mines, haciendas, plantations, railway junctions, and cities, wherever there were sources of seasonal employment.

Out of the rancherías and squatter camps of Sonora came many of the first migratory workers into the American borderlands, during the California gold rush, during the mining boom in Arizona in the 1860's and after, and during the construction of the Southern Pacific railroad in the 1880's. In railroad and mine work the ranchería migrant from Mexico mixed easily with native Indian laborers from southwestern rancherías and with native New Mexicans.[7]

6. The 1895 census showed that over ten percent of the population of the central states such as Aguascalientes, México, and San Luís Potosí had abandoned their native villages, according to Moisés González Navarro, "La Vida Social en el Porfiriato," in *Historia Moderna de México*, ed. Daniel Cosío Villegas (Mexico, 1957), IV, 26. For a fuller treatment of demographic factors in Mexican migration see a forthcoming book by González Navarro, "Historia Demográfica del México Contemporáneo."

7. On the mixed use of Coolie, Indian, and Mexican labor in mining and railway construction see Joseph F. Park, "The History of Mexican Labor in Arizona during the

In addition, there was another source of migratory labor flowing from villages where small farm properties or ranches were privately owned by creole and mestizo colonist families. Unlike the ranchería casuals or the hacienda peons, the small peasant proprietor or ranchero, or his sons, often migrated hundreds of miles seeking outside income in order to buy property near the home village (which may have been found in the Central Plateau, or in the northeastern states.)[8] From such villages in the border states of Nuevo León and Tamaulipas came migrant workers to south Texas sheep and cattle ranches as early as the 1870's. As irrigated agriculture developed there, many of these workers sought to become sharecroppers with part ownership in farm animals, equipment, and the harvest itself. Some acquired farm properties in Texas, others returned to Mexico for that purpose.[9]

Although the migratory phenomenon in Mexico has historically deep and complex origins, it was above all railroad technology that enabled the Mexican population to move en masse into the hostile desert regions of the north, and gave the so-called "Mexican casual" his remarkable mobility. Railways bridged the Great Western Desert that had separated the population centers of two countries. In 1884 the great rail center of El Paso, leading to all points including Los Angeles and Chicago, was connected with Chihuahua City which in turn was linked to Mexico City. Nogales, Arizona, leading into the Southern Pacific line, was connected with Hermosillo, Sonora, in 1882. Soon afterwards San Antonio and Corpus Christi were connected with Monterrey, Mexico, by way of Laredo, and spur lines grew like the roots of a plant. Victor S. Clark, the first to study the causes of Mexican labor migration, wrote in 1908 that railroads carried the central Mexican villager a thousand miles from his home to within sight of the border, and there American em-

Territorial Period" (unpub. Master's diss., University of Arizona, 1961); and *Reports of the Immigration Commission* (Dillingham Committee), *Immigrants in Industries*, Part 25 . . . *Diversified Industries* (Washington, 1911), pp. 11–31ff.

8. See Paul S. Taylor's study of a village where small proprietorship was common, *A Spanish-Mexican Peasant Community, Arandas in Jalisco, Mexico* (Berkeley, 1933).

9. According to Taylor's account of Mexican labor and settlement in south Texas, *A Mexican-American Frontier*.

ployers "with a gold wage, have little difficulty in attracting him across that not very formidable dividing line."[10]

Wages in the Texas border region were then $1.00 to $1.25 per day for unskilled labor on railroads, as high as $1.75 in other border states like California, and even higher further inland. Section hands who had worked on north Mexican railways deserted by the hundreds for higher wages across the border. Mexican miners did the same, and then agricultural workers. Soon Mexican pick-and-shovel gangs were found in nearly every railroad town and mining camp in the Southwest, and working down the railroads these gangs made their way to California citrus groves, Colorado beet fields, Texas cotton plantations, and railway service centers like Kansas City and Chicago, working for daily wages that ran from 50¢ to $2.00 or more, at a time when a dollar equalled two pesos.

Rural misery in Porfirian Mexico and the northward drift of migratory labor happened to coincide with the economic transformation of the American Southwest. In the broadest sense, the railroads linked this region not merely with midwestern and eastern markets but with the national economy. The sugar beet industry, much of it centered in Colorado and Kansas, quadrupled its output from 1900 to 1907. With railroads and irrigation, citrus and cotton industries flourished in the river basins of California, Arizona, and Texas after 1900. By then coal, copper, and lumber camps dotted the hills of Arizona, Colorado, and New Mexico. And everywhere it seemed that American employers and Mexican migrants were discovering each other.[11]

In many cases the employer and employee were already acquainted. American mining and railway companies in Mexico brought many of their trained gangs over the border to work with the same company in the States. For example, Mexican miners

10. Victor S. Clark, "Mexican Labor in the United States," U.S. Department of Labor *Bulletin*, 78 (September 1908), 470. This is an invaluable early account of labor recruiting practices.

11. *Ibid.*, pp. 470–475. Also, there are indications of the increasing use of Mexican labor in the voluminous findings of the Dillingham Commission; see, for example, U.S. Immigration Commission, *Abstracts of Reports of the Immigration Commission, 1907–1910* (Washington, D.C., 1911), vol. I.

were shifted from Anaconda-owned mines in northern Sonora to Anaconda mines in southern Arizona, and the Southern Pacific transferred track crews from its Mexican subsidiaries to its southwestern lines, more so after Chinese coolie labor began to dwindle following the Exclusion Act of 1882.[12]

American companies set up recruiting centers along the Mexican border before 1900. Clark noted that Mexican migrants arrived there penniless, "but with the moral certainty of securing immediate employment."[13] At the border migrants were met by company contractors, *enganchadores*, who regularly supplied an entire railroad system or its divisions; or migrants were signed up by private agents who supplied common labor for a variety of jobs. The larger contractors engaged in the business of supplying provisions and food during the worker's term of employment, "indeed, this is their main source of revenue . . . to furnish labor in return for the privilege of keeping the commissary." Clark went on to describe the commissary practice as a kind of modified debt peonage not unlike the old hacienda store.[14]

Recruiters on the Mexican side, known as *enganchistas*, or hookers, lured displaced or restless people to the border contracting offices. Most *enganchistas* were hardly a cut above the peon class, but they were familiar with company needs, and many of them were bilingual residents of the border towns. In Mexico, according to Clark, they worked "principally among the city and tramp labor population," partly because in rural areas hacienda owners were hostile to them.[15]

American employers themselves, or their foremen, often engaged in direct recruiting despite the Alien Contract Labor Law of 1885, which outlawed such activity. It was not unusual for a group of planters from Texas, Oklahoma, or Colorado to send a manager or foreman to the Rio Grande to pick up a party of one hundred or

12. Park, "The History of Mexican Labor in Arizona," and Carey McWilliams, *North from Mexico*, pp. 168–169.

13. Clark, "Mexican Labor," p. 475.

14. *Ibid.*

15. *Ibid.*, p. 476.

more men and their families.[16] Furthermore, cities near the border openly advertised for Mexican labor.[17]

Given the push and pull factors at work on both sides of the border, the mass migration of Mexican labor to the southwestern states and thence along the railroad arteries to the interior of the United States seems in retrospect to have been inevitable. Contrary to conventional interpretations, the Revolution of 1910 must be seen not as the primary cause of mass emigration but as a catalyst of an exodus already under way. Perhaps the most important impluse given by the revolution was to uproot and set in motion thousands of panic-stricken families. The semifeudal bonds between master and peon were snapped by revolutionary decrees abolishing peonage, or by conditions of anarchy and famine.[18] Each time violence broke out in the period from 1912 to 1920, refugees, including landowners and defeated troops, headed for border safety. In one instance, American border authorities granted asylum to over eight thousand persons.[19]

Here social services played an important role in attracting emigrés. Organizations such as the Red Cross and Protestant missions set up soup kitchens, gave out clothing, and arranged for lodging and employment. Many refugees were thus encouraged to stay and send for others. In the meantime, Mexican laborers and their employers had already discovered that social service agencies could help to subsidize the migrant labor cycle. Families of seasonal workers, who normally would have returned to winter in Mexico or the immediate border area, found that they could winter in cities like

16. *Ibid.*

17. Taylor, *A Mexican-American Frontier*, p. 105.

18. The agrarian revolutionaries decreed the end of debt peonage. See Manuel González Ramírez, ed., *Fuentes para la Historia de la Revolución Mexicana*, 4 vols. (Mexico, 1954–1957), I, *passim*.

19. On one occasion the whole village of Villa Acuña fled to Del Rio, Texas, as the troops of General Orozco advanced. Mexican consul, Del Rio, Texas, to secretary of foreign relations, September 23, 1912, in Archivo Histórico de la Secretaría de Relaciones Exteriores, 16-8-90. On another occasion some 5,000 defeated federal troops, plus camp followers, and hundreds of civilian refugees, crossed in a body at Presidio, Texas, according to the U.S. Department of Labor, Bureau of Immigration, *Annual Report of the Commissioner General of Immigration, 1914* (Washington, 1914), p. 34.

Los Angeles, San Antonio, and Chicago with a little help from community relief agencies, public and private. Later, the Mexican government itself contributed to this subsidy pattern.[20]

The United States entry into World War I in 1917 raised the demand for more Mexican labor. With low-cost immigrant labor from Europe shut off by the immigration act of 1917 and wartime conditions, and with millions of Americans in uniform, more American employers were discovering Mexican labor. Though the act of 1917 for the first time established general immigration restrictions on the Mexican border, employers were quick to ask the secretary of labor to exempt Mexican contract labor from literacy tests and the eight-dollar head tax.[21] Some seventy-two thousand workers came into the United States under the wartime exemptions of 1917–1921, but even more significantly the labor demands of the war and the shutoff of other sources of labor led directly to the "wetback invasions" of the 1920's. *Coyotes*, or alien smugglers, had no difficulty in guiding a migrant family past an occasional immigration inspector. Other wetbacks found their own way to border employment agencies.[22] The establishment of the Border Patrol in 1924 diverted but did not stop the wetback flow.

All the while the primary pull factor was the great disparity in wages. Anthropologist Manuel Gamio, who studied Mexican migrants in the United States in 1926 and 1927, estimated that the average wage earned was six times that for similar work in Mexico. The Mexican laborer not only earned enough to meet his elemental needs but he was able to spend money on education and luxuries. Mexican "repatriates" commonly returned home with farm animals, farm implements, radios, and even cars, and this said more

20. For example, the Mexican government provided five thousand dollars in aid to seasonal migrants stranded in Fort Worth, E. R. Cockrell, mayor of Fort Worth, Texas, to President Alvaro Obregón, May 18, 1921, Obregón Papers, Archivo General de la Nación, Ramo Obregón, 822-M-1.

21. U.S. Department of Labor, Bureau of Labor Statistics, "Results of Admission of Mexican Laborers Under Departmental Orders for Employment in Agricultural Pursuits," *Monthly Labor Review*, 11 (1920), 1095–1097.

22. See account by the Mexican consul in San Antonio, Enrique Santibañez, *Ensayo Acerca de la Inmigración Mexicana en los Estados Unidos* (San Antonio, 1930).

than a thousand words.[23] A brief comparison of wages, shown in Table I, not only suggests the commanding attraction of United States employment but also helps to explain why some migrant workers were moving from border areas saturated with Mexican labor to places as distant as Chicago, Gary, and Bethlehem, Pennsylvania, where Paul S. Taylor found them in the late 1920's.[24]

Table I

AVERAGE DAILY WAGES FOR A COMMON LABORER
IN UNITED STATES CURRENCY

| | Agriculture | | | Industry rails, mines, factories | |
| --- | --- | --- | --- | --- | --- |
| | Mexico | U. S. border | U. S. interior | Mexico | U. S. general |
| 1900 | .20–.25 | .50–.75 | .75–1.00 | .40–.50 | 1.00–2.00 |
| 1910 | .20–.25 | .50–1.00 | 1.00–1.50 | .50–.75 | 1.25–2.50 |
| 1920 | .20–.25 | 1.00–2.00 | 1.50–2.50 | .50–.75 | 3.00–4.00 |
| 1930 | .25–.40 | 1.50–2.50 | 2.00–3.00 | .50–1.00 | 3.50–5.00* |

*Before the impact of the 1929 stockmarket crash.

SOURCES: A composition of data from Clark, "Mexican Labor"; Gamio, *Mexican Immigration*; Taylor, *Mexican Labor*; Paul H. Douglas, *Real Wages in the United States 1890–1926* (Boston, 1930); U. S. consular correspondence from Mexico, National Archives, R.G. 59, file 811.111/Mexico, 1910–1929; Mexican consular correspondence from U. S. cities, in the Archivo Histórico de la Secretaría de Relaciones Exteriores, files IV/350–IV/560.

Mexican migration to the United States virtually stopped during the depression of the 1930's. Public hostility rose against alien labor and unemployed native workers eagerly grabbed for many jobs previously held only by Mexicans. In the period 1931–1934 more than 350,000 Mexicans were repatriated and during the remainder of the decade Mexican emigrant workers generally found themselves unwelcome. The depression had ended an exodus to the United States. This is shown in the United States figures, imperfect as they may be. From 1901 to 1930 about 728,000 Mexican immigrants were legally admitted to the United States, but in the

23. See Manuel Gamio's description of items taken back to Mexico by returning migrants, *Mexican Immigration to the United States*, p. 41.
24. See Taylor's series of ten studies on *Mexican Labor in the United States*.

decade 1931–1940 only some 23,000 immigrants were admitted. The number of unregistered migrants who settled on the American side during the period 1901–1930 was probably over a million, but many of these returned during the depression crisis, some attracted by the repatriation efforts of the Mexican government.[25]

World War II clearly marks the beginning of a second exodus of Mexican emigrants. Here the bracero (manual laborer) program was as important a catalyst as the Revolution of 1910 in the first exodus. Under the emergency contract labor program initiated in 1942, and prolonged until December 1964, more than 4.5 million temporary workers were admitted to the United States. Some worked on railways up to 1946, but most worked in agriculture and food processing. Some braceros were recontracted several times, but possibly 1.5 million of the total admitted were distinct persons who, for the most part, had never been in the United States before 1942, and had for the first time a taste of the high wages and adventure that old repatriates had talked about in the plazas and taverns of Mexico. Even before the first braceros had tried the program, the first recruiting center in Mexico City's National Stadium was swamped with applicants.[26]

During World War II braceros found themselves fervidly welcomed as war-workers and allies in nearly half the states of the union. The first reports of high wages and generally good treatment by gringo employers under contract agreements spread throughout Mexico erasing any memory of hostile attitudes during the depression. In a short time swarms of eager migrants began bypassing the provincial recruiting centers and making their own way to the border. A second exodus was under way.[27]

25. M. González Navarro, "Efectos Sociales de la Crisis de 1929," *Historia Mexicana*, 10 (1970), 536–558.

26. Ernesto Galarza, *Merchants of Labor: The Mexican Bracero Story* (Santa Barbara, 1964), p. 52.

27. The welcome prepared for the vanguard of the braceros by the War Food Administration and U.S. grower associations is indicated by Philip G. Bruton, director, Office of Labor, War Food Administration, to J. W. Carrigan, Division of Mexican Affairs, De-

Postwar prosperity, Cold War needs, and a growing dependence on imported Mexican labor by United States growers led not merely to perennial renewal of the so-called "emergency program" but to a rapid expansion under United States Public Law 71 in 1951.[28] By then bracero contracting had risen from some 53,000 in 1943 to over 190,000, eventually reaching a peak of over 447,000 in 1959. Many American employers who had trained braceros for certain jobs sought to keep them as permanent workers. This was often done by bringing them in as semiskilled or skilled immigrant labor. Soon these immigrant workers began sending for relatives and legal immigration from Mexico, negligible in the 1930's, began to rise. By 1955 it approached 50,000 a year, and has since remained at this level. Thus the bracero program primed a new current of legal immigration.

The contract labor program had an even more significant impact on the emergence of wetbackism. Many employers encouraged braceros to return illegally. For his part the bracero soon learned that it was an easy matter to skip a contract, or return to the United States surreptitiously. Countless thousands of other "line-jumpers" avoided an uncertain fate at the contracting centers and the usual payoffs to local Mexican officials. By 1946 the bracero-control structure was literally swept aside by hordes of wetbacks, families and all, migrating into the border states and setting up primitive rancherías and shantytowns as in the lower Rio Grande Valley.[29]

A comparison of the number of wetback apprehensions with the number of braceros legally contracted during the period 1942–1954 suggests the dimensions of the control problem: 1,329,741 braceros

partment of State, October 3, 1944. National Archives, Record Group 59, 811.504/10-344 (1940–1944).

The influence of the bracero program on the illegal alien flow is indicated by Julian Samora, *Los Mojados: The Wetback Story* (Notre Dame, 1971), pp. 43–46; Otey M. Scruggs, "The United States, Mexico and the Wetbacks, 1942–1947," *Pacific Historical Review*, 30 (1961), 149–164; and Eleanor M. Hadley, "A Critical Analysis of the Wetback Problem," *Law and Contemporary Problems*, 21 (1956), 334–357.

28. See Richard D. Craig, *The Bracero Program: Interest Groups and Foreign Policy* (Austin, 1971).

29. See Ed Idar and Andrew C. McClellan, *What Price Wetbacks?* (Austin, 1953).

were contracted and 3,371,374 "illegals" were deported.[30] Although figures for wetback deportations (like braceros contracted) include many "repeaters," on the other hand those who got away were obviously not registered. Little wonder that by 1954 a United States Border Patrol officer could denounce the wetback phenomenon as "the greatest peacetime invasion complacently suffered by a country under open, flagrant, contemptuous violation of its laws."[31]

The great deportation drives of the summer of 1954 broke the back of the so-called "wetback invasion" by herding over the border more than one million *mojados* ("wetbacks"), including women and children.[32] Thereafter apprehensions dropped to an annual average of less than 50,000 by the final years of the bracero program. In the meantime, bracero contracting averaged around 400,000 per annum in the period 1955–1964. Even so the wetback problem was by no means solved. In the bracero era perhaps two million Mexican nationals, besides legal braceros, had acquired a taste for higher wages and adventure in America, and learned the tricks of getting around. Once the bracero program ended, a latent wetbackism reasserted itself.[33] Since fiscal 1965 wetback apprehensions have risen remarkably from around 55,000 to over 576,000 in fiscal 1973. Now, however, mojados are no longer found predominantly as "stoop" labor in agriculture but in a great variety of jobs, skilled and unskilled.[34]

The second exodus was propelled by conditions similar to those that propelled the northward migration of 1890–1930. Despite some real improvements in rural life, reports and surveys of the 1940's

---

30. Galarza, *Merchants of Labor*, pp. 59, 70, 79.

31. U.S. Department of Justice, *INS Reporter*, 2 (1954), 39; quoted by Galarza, *Merchants of Labor*, p. 59.

32. Samora, *Los Mojados*, p. 46. For a gripping photographic account of the huge spillover of poverty-stricken wetback families into the Rio Grande Valley of Texas, see Idar and McClellan, *What Price Wetbacks?*

33. See Howard L. Campbell, "Bracero Migration and the Mexican Economy, 1951–1964" (unpub. PhD diss., American University, 1972), which contains interview information from former braceros and wetbacks.

34. U.S. House, Committee on the Judiciary, *Illegal Aliens. Hearings . . .* , 92 Cong., 1 and 2 Sess. (1971–1972), five parts. Hereafter cited as *Illegal Aliens, Hearings*.

found that the benefits of economic progress had scarcely touched several million farm laborers and small peasant proprietors. Typically, one study of 1945 concluded that many agrarian reform efforts had been a "lamentable waste."[35] Many peasants had, indeed, received plots of land, but without water, credit facilities, or an agricultural extension service. In many cases, the recipients reverted to pre-Columbian subsistence farming.

The National Revolutionary Party through successive administrations had struggled to improve agrarian life in a country that has been classified as more than fifty percent arid land. From 1926

---

35. Salvador Lira López et al., "La Pobreza Rural en México" (mimeographed report, Mexico, 1945), p. 34. For other critical opinions of agrarian reform see Gilberto Loyo, 3 Breves Estudios (Mexico, 1970), pp. 36–39, and Jesús Silva Herzog, Un Ensayo sobre la Revolución Mejicana (Mexico, 1946).

---

## MEXICANS EXPELLED FROM THE UNITED STATES
## FOR HAVING ENTERED ILLEGALLY ☞

| Years | Numbers | Years | Numbers | Years | Numbers |
|-------|---------|-------|---------|-------|---------|
| 1924 | 4,614 | 1941 | 6,082 | 1958 | 37,242 |
| 1925 | 2,961 | 1942 | — | 1959 | 30,190 |
| 1926 | 4,047 | 1943 | 8,189 | 1960 | 29,651 |
| 1927 | 4,495 | 1944 | 26,689 | 1961 | 29,817 |
| 1928 | 5,529 | 1945 | 63,602 | 1962 | 30,272 |
| 1929 | 8,538 | 1946 | 91,456 | 1963 | 39,124 |
| 1930 | 18,319 | 1947 | 182,986 | 1964 | 43,844 |
| 1931 | 8,400 | 1948 | 179,385 | 1965 | 55,340 |
| 1932 | 7,116 | 1949 | 278,538 | 1966 | 89,751 |
| 1933 | 15,875 | 1950 | 458,215 | 1967 | 108,327 |
| 1934 | 8,910 | 1951 | 500,000 | 1968 | 151,705 |
| 1935 | 9,139 | 1952 | 543,538 | 1969 | 201,636 |
| 1936 | 9,534 | 1953 | 865,318 | 1970 | 277,377 |
| 1937 | 9,535 | 1954 | 1,075,168 | 1971 | 348,178 |
| 1938 | 8,684 | 1955 | 242,608 | 1972 | 430,211 |
| 1939 | 9,376 | 1956 | 72,442 | 1973 | 542,934 |
| 1940 | 8,051 | 1957 | 44,451 | | |

From 1924 to 1943 only formal deportations are indicated by graph. This type would represent only about 10% of actual numbers returned to Mexico under the "voluntary departure" system. From 1943 to present graph represents both formal deportations and "voluntary departures," the former representing about 10% of the total.

SOURCES: Annual Report of the Secretary of Labor; Annual Report Immigration and Naturalization Service.

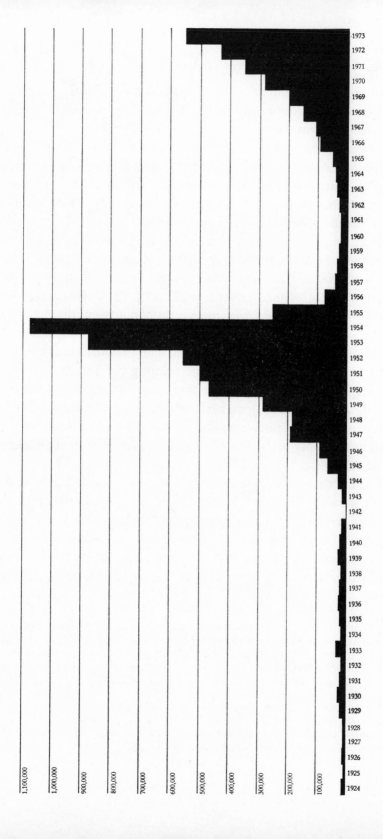

to 1940 around four to eight percent of the national budget was invested in irrigation, and from 1941 to 1960 a remarkable ten to thirteen percent. From 1917 to 1965 more than 131.6 million acres, or twenty-seven percent of the national territory, had been given to some 2.6 million families. In the Cárdenas period alone (1934–1940) more than 44 million acres were distributed to about 775,000 campesino families. Since the 1940's, relatively heavy investments have been made in developing agricultural credit, banking, education, and transportation facilities. Yet, according to one authority, the total amount of arable land in Mexico as of 1955 was less than 49.4 million acres. Of this amount about 2 million acres had a year-round supply of rainfall, and about 6.2 million acres were under irrigation (compared to 10.6 million acres in the American Southwest). The remaining acreage was classified as seasonal farmland dependent on a sometimes uncertain seasonal rainfall.[36]

The average size of a land grant during the period 1917–1965 was approximately fifty-seven acres, but in most cases this was partly arid land, or pastoral land. Where irrigated plots were given they averaged from twenty-four to forty-eight acres per family, but usually only half or less or this acreage received an allotment of water.[37]

At the same time the government's investments in public health have since the 1940's led to a population explosion of the most serious dimensions. In 1930 the population was approximately 17 million; in 1940, 19.5 million; in 1950, 25 million; in 1960, 35 million; in 1970, 48.5 million, and in 1973, 55 million, with a projection of perhaps 90 million in 1990. In January 1973 the government took

36. Adolfo Orive Alba, *La Política de Irrigación en México* (Mexico, 1960), p. 42. Other sources of data on Mexican investment in agricultural reform and productivity are: Roger D. Hansen, *The Politics of Mexican Development* (Baltimore, 1971), pp. 58–65, 77–83, 86–88; and Pablo González Casanova, *Democracy in Mexico* (New York, 1970), pp. 48, 114–115, 223; and for the period up to 1945, Nathan L. Whetten, *Rural Mexico* (Chicago, 1948).

37. Interviews with Eduardo Chávez, director of irrigation and colonization development in the lower Rio Grande Valley, 1935–1940, Mexico City, July 15, 1971; and with repatriates settled in agrarian colonies in the border states of Nuevo León and Tamaulipas, August 23, 1970, December 20, 1970, and December 24, 1970.

the first firm steps to make contraception facilities available for the lower-income groups through the public health service. Meanwhile, millions of campesinos and ranchería groups are without land, and *ejidotarios*, or communal farmers, who received plots of land have subdivided among their sons and grandsons. Small proprietors have often done the same. Thus agrarian reforms have scarcely kept pace with the population growth.[38] One critic has concluded that Mexico today suffers not so much from feudal latifundia as formerly but from minifundia for "almost 90% of agricultural holdings are minifundia."[39]

According to the 1960 census, there were 1.3 million small private proprietors whose holdings averaged less than 12.5 acres in size. Communal holdings held by 1.5 million or more *ejidotarios* were scarcely any larger.[40] As a result of the minifundia problem, the general inefficiency of agricultural cooperatives, and population pressures, many *ejidotarios* (who are forbidden to sell their land) rent their holdings to other agriculturists, and the small private owners sell or lease their property to other proprietors, or to large agricultural corporations, some of them American owned. These frustrated smallholders then seek employment in the cities as unskilled labor, or as migratory workers in Mexico or the United States.[41]

Low wages have also played an important role in the migratory phenomenon. During the war years wages had risen slightly in rural Mexico, but in 1945 common farm labor could do no better than 40¢ to 60¢ a day in most areas of Mexico, at a time of the rising cost of living. Contract labor in the United States was getting 65¢ an hour or better. In Mexico's urban areas wages averaged less than a dollar a day for unskilled labor, partly because rural migrants

38. Orive Alba, *La Política de Irrigación*, pp. 174–175. For population data and enduring poverty see González Casanova, *Democracy in Mexico*, pp. 74–79.

39. Rodolfo Stavenhagen *et al.*, *Neolatifundismo y Explotación de Emiliano Zapata a Anderson Clayton & Co.* (Mexico, 1968), p. 10.

40. Fernando Paz Sánchez, *ibid.*, *pp. 83–84.*

41. Arturo Bonilla Sánchez, *ibid.*, p. 150; and González Casanova, *Democracy in Mexico*, p. 114.

to the towns and cities depressed wages. When the same migrants poured over the United States border as wetbacks they drove farm wages down to as low as 15¢ an hour in south Texas and 25¢ an hour in California, and still they came by the tens of thousands.[42]

During the 1950's wages gradually rose in Mexico, and so did the cost of living. Real gains, however, were made in the availability of social services such as health and education. Yet the statistical story remained dismal. According to several studies carried out in the period 1958–1963, seventy-seven percent of Mexican families (representing about 27.5 million people) had incomes of $80.00 a month or less, and fifty percent of all families received less than $50.00 a month.[43] Making all allowances for the lower cost of living in Mexico such incomes still spell out the poverty of the masses. During the 1960's minimum wages for common labor in rural areas were around $1.00 to $1.25 per day in United States currency, and in urban areas from $1.50 to $1.80. But in small shops, farms, ranches, and domestic service, these minimum wages were rarely paid, and in many cases people were employed part-time only.

Presently Mexico suffers from a growing problem of subemployment in both rural and urban areas. The redundancy of employment in a semiindustrialized economy characterized by subsistence agriculture in many regions, excessive population growth, and chronic urban marginality, is suggested by Table II.

42. *Report of the President's Commission on Western Hemisphere Immigration* (Washington, 1968), pp. 71–72, 78–80; and Galarza, *Merchants of Labor*, p. 30.

43. González Casanova, *Democracy in Mexico*, pp. 104–106, 139–140. See also Ifigenia Martínez de Navarrete, *La Distribución del Ingreso y el Desarrollo Económico de México* (Mexico, 1960); Ana Maria Flores, *La Magnitud del Hambre en México* (Mexico, 1961); Hansen, *The Politics of Mexican Development*; James Wilkie, *The Mexican Revolution: Federal Expenditure and Social Change since 1940* (Berkeley, 1970); and for a study of the concentration of wealth in the hands of corporation and powerful families, Alonso Aguilar M. and Fernando Carmona, *México: Riqueza y Miseria* (Mexico, 1972).

## Table II

OCCUPATIONAL STRUCTURE OF MEXICO FOR 1940–1970

*(figures represent millions of persons)*

| Employment | 1940 | 1950 | 1960 | 1970 |
|---|---|---|---|---|
| Agriculture, livestock, and forestry | 3.8 | 4.8 | 6.3 | 8.3 |
| Services | 1.3 | 2.1 | 3.7 | 6.3 |
| Industry | .9 | 1.3 | 2.0 | 3.1 |
| Total labor force | 6.0 | 8.2 | 12.0 | 17.7 |

SOURCE: Bonilla Sánchez, in Stavenhagen *et al.*, *Neolatifundismo*, pp. 162–163. A different estimate of the occupational structure is given by the Dirección General de Estadística, Secretaría de Industria y Comercio, y Banco de México, S.A. (as reported in "Todos lo hacen, pero pocos lo comen," *Visión, Revista Internacional*, 40 (May 1972), 12–15. According to this source, there were 5.2 million persons occupied in agriculture, ranching, forestry, and mining; 2.9 million in industry; and 5.1 million in services for a total labor force of 13.2 million in 1970, compared to Bonilla Sánchez' estimated total of 17.7 million. The latter estimate seems much more realistic for purposes of explaining the persistent migrant phenomenon for it takes into account the marginal occupational structure which includes the underemployed, especially in the age group 14 to 21, and domestic service as well as casual laborers. Because nearly 60 percent of the population is under age 21 large numbers of teenagers are found in the labor force, often as *sub-ocupados*.

One student of *sub-empleo*, writing in 1965, has suggested that from two to four million agriculturists were redundant.[44] Persistent internal migration from rural areas has, in turn, created a major problem in urban underemployment. In the towns and cities of Mexico, displaced migrant families are underemployed in numerous personal service and retail activities, often consuming the energies of an entire family from dawn to dusk.[45] This bustle of marginal activities (suggestive of an Indian marketplace) includes street vendors, domestics, shoeshine boys, street hawkers, ticket sellers, beggars, prostitutes, and hustlers. Some of these types were described by Friar Sahagún over four hundred years ago.[46] Some economists maintain that most of the persons employed in the so-

44. Bonilla Sánchez, in Stavenhagen, *Neolatifundismo*, p. 129.
45. Oscar Lewis, *The Children of Sánchez* (New York, 1961); and *Pedro Martinez: A Mexican Peasant and His Family* (New York, 1964).
46. Fray Bernardino de Sahagún, *Historia General de las Cosas de la Nueva España*, ed. Angel M. Garibay, 4 vols. (Mexico, 1956), III, 130–151.

called "services sector" of the national economy—a group that swelled from 3.7 million to 6.3 from 1960 to 1970—are simply displaced rural folk performing tasks that are perhaps traditional yet unproductive and regressive from the viewpoint of a modern industrial economy.[47] In addition to the subemployed there are probably three to five million unemployed in Mexico today.[48]

In spite of the foregoing account, it would be misleading to attribute the present high level of Mexican transborder migration to poverty or subsistence living alone. This is a standard explanation that is offered to any committee in the United States or Mexico investigating the Mexican migration problem. In fact, however, some sectors of the Mexican population are emigrating more than ever before precisely because living conditions have improved along with economic opportunities. Mexico is in many ways a dual economy and a dual society. Vestigial Indian cultures may still passively resist modernization, but within "modern Mexico" general social and economic improvements have brought about a "revolution of expectations" as in many other parts of the western world. Many would-be emigrants possess industrial or managerial skills, sometimes acquired in United States subsidiaries in Mexico. They are receptive to emigration for the same reason that well-paid railroad workers and miners were before 1910. A machinist receiving the handsome wage of eighty cents an hour may well be inclined to emigrate on learning that the same work pays six dollars an hour in Los Angeles or Dallas. This suggests that even if poverty were completely abolished in Mexico it would not relieve the migration pressures on the United States border.

Among the pull factors on the American side, the difference in wage levels has remained eloquent for thirty or forty years. In Mexico, following the raises of September 1973 and January 1974,

47. Bonilla Sánchez, in Stavenhagen, *Neolatifundismo*, pp. 162–163; González Casanova, *Democracy in Mexico*, pp. 72, 84–85.

48. An estimate of five million unemployed is given by *El Universal* (Mexico City), June 2, 1972. Here again the question arises as to how many young persons, age 14 to 21, who do not pursue secondary education or technical training, and how many women who are often the sole support of the family in the lower classes, should be counted in either the unemployed or the casual labor class.

the national minimum pay for common labor ranged from $1.85 to $3.00 a day in rural areas, and from $2.50 to $4.00 a day in urban areas, with a high of $4.50 to $5.50 a day in the border zones.[49] But most of Mexico's marginal population is still not receiving a minimum wage. In the United States common labor in agricultural work usually starts at the federal minimum of $1.65 an hour (with some form of incentive plan), odd jobs are paid about the same, but common labor in construction, manufacturing, and food processing industries receives anywhere from $2.00 to $4.50 an hour, the higher wages usually found inland from the border. In skilled labor the same approximate differences hold. Moreover, in the United States overtime is paid for work shifts exceeding eight hours a day which is usually not the case in Mexico. Because of galloping inflation the outlook is that minimum wages in both countries will soon be raised again. In the meantime other pull factors are at work.

## II. Migration Control Problems since 1964

THE rapid rise in illegal migration from Mexico in recent years, aside from the push factors at work in Mexico, finds considerable encouragement in the inability of the Mexican and United States governments, singly or jointly, to stabilize and control a common economic and social frontier. Since 1964 a confluence of factors has undermined the best efforts of the United States Immigration Service to maintain effective alien control on the

49. For income distribution in Mexico today see Armando Labra, "La Concentración del Ingreso en México: Un Enfoque Sectorial," Banco Nacional de Comercio Exterior, S.A., *Cuestiones Económicas Nacionales* (Mexico, 1971); and Ifigenia M. de Navarrete, "La Distribución del ingreso en México, Tendencia y Perspectivas," David Ibarra *et al.*, *El Perfil de México en 1980* (Mexico, 1970). Minimum wages established by the Comisión Nacional de los Salarios Minimos for a variety of occupations are given in *Excelsior* (Mexico City), January 2, 1974, pp. 17A–19A.

Mexican border and in the interior of this country.[50] The abolition of the Mexican contract labor program in late 1964 had two principal effects on alien control. The braceros who were accustomed to working in the United States and could not qualify for legal immigration reverted to the customary method of illicit entry to regain access to the American labor market. Moreover, the government of Mexico, after December 1964, ceased its feeble efforts to control the movement of noncontract labor to the United States; for it no longer had a national or international obligation to protect legally contracted braceros from wetback competition. Thus on the Mexican side of the border after 1964 there was the usual accumulation of several hundred thousand "restless ex-braceros" and "deported wetbacks" and no binational labor agreement by which the Mexican government might feel obligated to make some effort to patrol its side of the border.

Officials of the Southwest region of the United States Immigration Service see no relief in sight from "wetback pressures" on the southern border, even if the Mexican government were to resume efforts to control illegal emigration. Not only has Mexico's population risen from seventeen million in 1930 to fifty-five million in 1973, but at present growth rates Mexico's population will probably double in the next twenty years. Moreover, the nature of the Mexican border region is in itself a major factor in the high level of wetback infiltration.

Today, if one counts the floating or the squatter population, Piedras Negras and Nogales would each have over 40,000, Reynosa and Nuevo Laredo over 130,000, Matamoros some 200,000, Mexicali over 400,000, Tijuana over 450,000, and Ciudad Juárez near

50. These factors are considered more at length in a paper prepared by the author for Senator Stevenson's Sub-Committee on Migratory Labor under the title "The 'New Wetback Infiltration'—A Preliminary Report" (July 1972). Many of the observations made about illegal migration in that paper and in the present study are based on firsthand information obtained from over fifty interviews with United States and Mexican immigration officials, active and retired, and from field trips along the border during a five-month period, April–August 1970; and during visits to Mexico and border region during July–August 1971, and August 10–24, 1972. See also, Samora, *Los Mojados*; and *Illegal Aliens, Hearings*.

600,000.[51] In all there is now a population approaching 4.5 million clustered tight against the "unfenced border," usually in a rather promiscuous form of "twin cities" like Ciudad Juárez and El Paso, Nuevo Laredo and Laredo, Nogales, Sonora, and Nogales, Arizona.

Aside from border-crossing opportunities, the principal reason for the rapid concentration of subemployed along Mexico's northern fringe is the so-called "free zone"—a strip of terrtory on the Mexican side about thirty kilometers wide that runsi the entire length of the common border. Within this strip the Mexican government for years made special concessions to border residents to encourage the settlement of the frontier zone and secure it against gringo expansionists. Later, commercial consideration became more important, and concessions and franchises were given to border merchants, businessmen, and residents in general to encourage trade and tourism with the United States.

In 1965 to compensate for the closing of the bracero program, and for other reasons, Mexico, in cooperation with the United States, began a Border Development Program that seeks to clean up the border, attract more tourists, and encourage both Mexican and American industries to settle there by tax exemptions, import-export concessions, and controlled labor unions.[52] As a result of new jobs created in the "free zone"—some forty to fifty thousand thus far by American subsidiary factories—the availability of jobs, legal and illegal, on the United States side, and the circulation of tourist and trade dollars, wages are definitely higher in the free zone. Moreover, the fact that border residents, unlike the rest of Mexico, can bring in American cars, household utilities, clothing, and groceries at low import duties or none at all—or maybe just a little *mordida*—is considered a powerful subsidy to wages and a ma-

51. The dynamics of border settlement are indicated by C. Daniel Dilman, "Urban Growth Along Mexico's Northern Border and the Mexican National Border Program," *Journal of Developing Areas*, 4 (1970), 487–508; and Richard L. Nostrand, "The Hispanic-American Borderlands: Delimitation of an American Culture Region," *Annals of the Association of American Geographers*, 60 (1970), 638–661.

52. Dilman, "Urban Growth along Mexico's Northern Border," pp. 501–505; and Campbell, "Bracero Migration and the Mexican Economy," pp. 293–335.

jor incentive for moving to the zone. In general, wages are twice as high in the border zone.

However, hundreds of thousands of Mexicans—many of them unattached adventurers—who are attracted to the glittering zone end up jobless or holding marginal jobs at best. For one thing, female labor is preferred in most of the new border industries. Other thousands of border-zone residents find themselves displaced by the incoming migrants who are willing to work for less at a wide variety of jobs. Today it is probable that there is a fluid population of half a million or more unemployed men and women in the zone and another million underemployed. Such people literally have their noses pushed against the border window looking into the United States, or as one immigration officer expressed it, "they have nothing to do all day but look for cracks in the border-control system."[53]

There are some interesting cracks. On border fiesta days held by twin cities like Laredo and Nuevo Laredo Mexican families and transients by the thousands are allowed to cross the bridge without inspection of papers, as during the George Washington Birthday Celebration which lasts three days. Illegal aliens from all over Mexico await this golden opportunity. Once across the bridge they lie low in rooming houses or with Mexican-American *primos* ("cousins"). Then when the Border Patrol relaxes vigilance on all roads leading out of the city, they strike out for the interior.[54] *¿Quién es Jorge Washington?*

Moreover, since approximately 1952, pregnant women on "shopping missions" are no longer stopped from passing through the port of entry, in the words of an immigrant inspector, and "leaving a little basket at Uncle Sam's doorstep," i.e., giving birth to an American "citizen" in a "gringo hospital," sometimes in a charity ward.[55] Some of the advantages of this birth-fact are that

53. Observation by U.S. immigration inspector-in-charge at El Paso port of entry, August 31, 1970.

54. Interviews with chief patrol agent and several border patrol officers, Laredo Sector, and with various Laredo citizens during period of residence in Laredo, April–June 1970.

55. Interviews with chief officer-in-charge, Eagle Pass port of entry, May 30, 1970; and with deputy chief patrol agent, Del Rio Sector, April 2, 1970; and with Wesley Stiles, retired immigration investigator, Del Rio, May 2, 1970.

the child can be placed with friends or relatives on the American side and attend public schools free. Later he or she can choose to work or live in the United States, and bring in a Mexican spouse. Furthermore, a child born on the gringo side is a preference factor in processing immigration papers for Mexican parents who may already be residing illegally in the United States. In any case, at age twenty-one the "citizen-child" is often expected to fulfill kinship obligations by bringing his parents in under the first preference category in the act of 1965 as "immediate relatives." Immediate relatives are frequently on public-assistance programs in spite of historic provisions in United States immigration law concerning the nonadmission of persons "likely to become a public charge." It should also be noted that many "American births" do not occur on the American side. For example, midwives of Mexican descent in some Texas counties register "Mexican-American births" at the local court house.[56] Whether such births occur on American soil or not is often open to question. Another practice is to bring young children across the border, have them baptized in American churches, and then offer a baptismal certificate in lieu of a birth certificate.

In the past Mexican illegals were mostly humble campesinos seeking employment in seasonal work. They were easily identified by the Border Patrol and by public-interest groups. In the "wet-back sweeps" of the 1950's conspicuous concentrations of labor gangs—men, women, and children—could be rapidly picked up by driving buses and trucks straight into the labor fields of Texas and California. But the "New Wetback Invasion" is better described as an "infiltration of new-style wetbacks." This infiltration is not only dispersive and difficult to quantify but virtually invisible. New-style wets are not the humble peons of yesteryear who in rubber-tired *huaraches* plodded over the back trails, with women folk and little *chamacos*, looking for farm and ranch work. The new-style *mojados* exemplify the increasing modernization of Mexico, the improved methodology of alien smugglers, and the grapevine

56. Observations made by officials of Fraudulent Document Center, U.S. Immigration and Naturalization Service (INS), Yuma, Arizona, September 3, 1970.

knowledge that the Border Patrol has practically closed the doors to easy agricultural employment in the border Southwest. Now more than ever wetbacks head for better wages and easier work in cities and towns far from the border regions.[57] The modern wetback usually starts out with some money in his pocket, earned often in industrial employment in Mexico. Illegals frequently pay as much as four hundred dollars to be smuggled to a distant American city, and more if the package deal includes a union job. The employed wetback now carries identification of some sort, such as a false birth certificate, a social security card, a driver's license, a draft-registration card, or a document easily obtained by any United States resident. The Mexican alien has learned that in many cases employment in the United States and even welfare subsidies for aliens require nothing more than the giving of a local address.[58]

The wetback is no longer a "wetback" in the sense that he crossed the river or desert surreptitiously. Today he prefers to walk calmly through the border port of entry flashing a false document, or he enters as a tourist, shopper, or visitor with a legal document, for example, the Border Crossing Card (Form I-186) that permits a temporary entry of seventy-two hours in a twenty-five-mile-wide zone that "leaks like a sieve." There are presently over one million such cards held by residents on the Mexican side. The new-style illegals know their way around the United States. Millions of Mexican nationals saw a good part of their northern neighbor under the bracero program, and many have now kinfolk in several states. They can find protective coloration and a birth certificate in almost any city or town that has a sizeable Mexican-American or Puerto Rican colony.

Employers are naturally inclined to prefer the "Wetback Obligato," to use Ernesto Galarza's phrase. An alien without papers is docile and works for less, and can be turned over to immigration authorities if he causes trouble. But since 1964 this standard ex-

57. Interviews, August 18–19, 1973, with several busloads of "wetbacks" at Mazatlán, a dumping spot for illegal entrants returned to Mexico's interior under the voluntary departure system of the U.S. Immigration Service.

58. *Illegal Aliens, Hearings,* Part 1, pp. 114–132; Part 2, pp. 308–309, 667–668; Part 3, pp. 692, 758, and *passim.*

planation no longer fits the full, complex pattern for alien infiltration into so many fissures of the American economy. Here one must give some weight to the universal complaints of employers that unionism in industry or agriculture makes the cost of American labor artificially high. Since the early sixties the alternatives open to businesses that face rising costs and unionized labor have included moving certain high-cost labor operations to Taiwan, Hong Kong, Puerto Rico, Mexico, or elsewhere; or "importing" low-cost or tractable labor, legal or illegal.

The War on Poverty initiated in 1964 and the relaxation of welfare rules also had a significant impact on the migration of alien labor in the United States. After 1964 many "poverty folk" apparently discovered that, considering all the benefits, cooperation with poverty-fighters and the new political patronage system was often better than working for pay, especially in physically demanding jobs. Other "poverty folk" have found that they can be much more selective about jobs. Migrant labor families, who would prefer their customary life of seasonal work, have been induced to settle down out of the labor market in order to stay on welfare programs, or to undergo training for higher-pay industrial jobs that somehow never materialize, or to keep their children in special school programs like Head Start, Upward Bound, Horizons Unlimited, Bilingual Education, and a dozen other educational, diet, and health programs for the underprivileged.[59]

The number of youths normally available for the labor market appears to have been reduced by the recruiting drives of universities and youth-opportunity programs for "underprivileged ethnics." The result of all this is that "wetback-users" complained that in the midst of mass unemployment, pseudo-employment, and massive training programs for the underprivileged, there was a na-

59. Interviews with director of County Welfare Department, Fresno, March 24, 1970; and with senior patrol agent-in-charge, U.S. Immigration Service, Sacramento, September 8, 1970; and conversations during extended period of residence in south Texas, April–August 1970, with officials and directors of Office of Economic Opportunity, Colorado Migrant Council, VISTA, and Urban Redevelopment Agency, principally in Laredo and San Antonio, both major centers of migratory labor recruitment.

tional shortage of unskilled and semiskilled labor.[60] This "labor vacuum" in its extent and its federally subsidized nature was unique in American history. Such a vacuum helped to explain the unusual number of aliens, mainly from Mexico and the Caribbean, who filtered into the American labor market. Thus in large American cities, such as New York, Chicago, and San Francisco, the casual observer saw Jamaicans, Haitians, Dominicans, Mexicans, Chinese, Filipinos, and French Canadians, among others, with or without papers, employed as bellhops, kitchen help, taxi drivers, warehouse workers, gardeners, maids, and factory hands.

The War on Poverty and the new welfare arrangements had a highly specific effect in the southwestern states. The *barrios* and *colonias* of "immigrated Mexicans" and Mexican-Americans that for fifty years or more served as "little Mexico labor pools" translated to the American side of the border, especially after the immigration law of 1917, ceased, in spite of a remarkably high fertility rate, to provide the "usual quotas" of either migratory laborers or semiskilled workers for a variety of nonagricultural jobs. The resulting labor shortage was filled, increasingly after 1965, by overflooded "labor pools" on the Mexican side of the border. This might be described as the "suction effect" of the War on Poverty.

Perhaps the best proof that Mexicans and other alien laborers were seldom taking jobs that anybody else wanted, except perhaps in the depressed, high-fertility regions bordering on Mexico, was the lack of any sustained protest on the part of unemployed native Americans. The latter—buffered by poverty agencies as they were not in the 1950's when a great cry was raised against wetbacks—were often more concerned about welfare rights, guaranteed income, and other forms of increased benefits than employment opportunities or stricter control of aliens.

In the opinion of high-ranking immigration officials the "alien invasion" from Mexico after 1964 constitutes the most difficult

60. Interviews with U.S. employers of Mexican and Puerto Rican labor, including farmers, ranchers, nurserymen, food service operators, factory managers, and auto service managers, in Texas, Colorado, California, Ohio, and Connecticut in the summers of 1970, 1972, and 1973.

enforcement problem ever faced by federal authorities in their efforts to uphold the national immigration laws and standards first generally established on United States borders in 1917. At this point the question arises: Why did the Mexican border remain an unsolved problem in immigration-law enforcement, unabated in the mid-1970's? The most forthright explanation is that the United States Immigration and Naturalization Service (INS) has never been given enough support—personnel, facilities, legislative authority, and public cooperation—to stop border leaks and return illegal aliens from interior communities.[61] Except during the depression period, 1930–1940, when Mexican migration receded, the Border Patrol since its founding in 1924 has never had enough manpower on the Mexican border. Presently the INS has about ninety percent of its entire Border Patrol strength of almost 1,800 men concentrated on or near the two-thousand-mile Mexican frontier, which must be watched day and night, seven days a week. In 1971 the INS force of 1,260 immigration inspectors was spread around the United States at some 430 ports of entry. In the same year about 250 immigration investigators out of a total force of between 750 and 800 were assigned to the Southwest region, particularly to key southwestern cities that serve as meccas for Mexican aliens, particularly Los Angeles and San Antonio. The Chicago district, with about twenty-one million people, embracing the states of Illinois, Indiana, and Wisconsin and now another principal mecca for illegal aliens, had only 60 investigators in 1971. A few hundred thousand dollars are saved each year by limiting the operational ability of the Border Patrol, yet in 1970 alone $35 million was spent principally for transporting illicit aliens back to Mexico. Many had made the trip several times and had yet to be fingerprinted and computerized for lack of funds.[62]

Apart from lack of funds and personnel, the United States Immigration and Naturalization Service and judicial authorities have

61. See testimony of high immigration officials in *Illegal Aliens, Hearings*, Part 1, pp. 3–98; and Denny Walsh, "Manpower Needs at Border Cited," *New York Times*, September 18, 1973.

62. *Illegal Aliens, Hearings*, Part 1, p. 25.

lacked legal authority to carry out certain elemental tasks. Thus immigration officers have never been authorized to confiscate vehicles used by alien smugglers. Federal law also stopped short of making it a misdemeanor or a felony for an employer knowingly to hire illegal aliens. Moreover, nearly the full burden of immigration-law enforcement has rested on the shoulders of the undermanned Immigration Service. Cooperation between the INS and other state and federal agencies that deal with aliens, such as police, welfare, social security, Office of Economic Opportunity, health and vital statistics, has often been, like cooperation with Mexico, sporadic and piecemeal. In general, there has been lacking for many years a firm legislative basis for providing interagency cooperation.[63]

In addition, public relations pressures have inhibited effective alien control. This is one reason why there is virtually no fence control along the United States–Mexico border in spite of an obvious necessity. Some high cyclone fencing was built mostly in the 1950's near Yuma and in the Tijuana–San Isidro sector and in some cities like El Paso and Nogales—no more than thirty miles in all—yet from El Paso to the mouth of the Rio Grande at Brownsville, historically the main wetback funnel into the United States, there is not one foot of alien-control fencing. For one thing border chambers of commerce have objected to such fencing usually in the name of the good-neighbor policy.[64] Presently the INS is attempting to build an invisible electronic fence along the Mexican border.[65]

The growth of ethnic militancy, fostered by the War on Poverty and the civil rights movement, has played a major role in facilitating the infiltration of illegal aliens since the early 1960's. The rapid reversal in ethnic attitudes toward this issue is closely correlated with the rise of a new Mexican-American leadership. Wet-

63. Interview with legal counsel, Southwest Regional Office, INS, San Pedro, California, September 4, 1970.

64. According to observations made by chief patrol agent, El Paso Sector, U.S. Border Patrol, April 1 and August 30, 1970; and by former Commissioner of Immigration Joseph M. Swing, San Francisco, August 1, 1971.

65. See James P. Sterba, "Electronic Vigil Fails to Stem Mexican Alien Influx," *New York Times*, July 22, 1973.

backs had long been seen by Mexican-Americans themselves as a threat to their own employment and a deterrent to the assimilation of earlier settlers from Mexico. In the 1940's and 1950's Mexican-American organizations, like the G.I. Forum and the League of United Latin American Citizens (LULACS), were conspicuous leaders in demanding wetback control. Today many Mexican-American leaders, have gone "Chicano." "Alien Mexican labor" is no longer seen as a threat, but as a welcome cultural and political reinforcement.

Mexican cultural nationalism is taking root in the southwestern states, with links to nearly every *barrio* in the country. The most sweeping expression of this Chicano nationalism is the demand for "reconquest of the Southwest by the Mexican race" and the re-creation of the mythical Aztlán, or the lost kingdom of the Aztecs. Chicano militants call for an open border with Mexico, in reparation for the unjust conquest of "Chicano territory" during the war with Mexico, and the ancient and natural, if not unalienable, right of the Indian tribes, who were in the New World first, to migrate where they please, over any "artificial boundaries," in the search for Aztlán. Chicano leaders in their concern to remove the deportation menace from the *barrios* have sponsored several workshops to discuss "Aztlán immigration policy."[66]

The implications of a Chicano militancy and Aztlán mythology for the maintenance of the existing immigration system are profound. The minority-rights movement has so changed local and national political climates that law-enforcement and immigration-enforcement officials operate under severe handicaps. The Immigration Service not only lacks the special investigators to track down hundreds of thousands of Mexican aliens in the *barrios* but it does not dare to risk a series of open confrontations with civil-rights lawyers (sponsored by other federal agencies), liberal leaders, and politicians with Mexican-American constituents. There is little

---

66. Aztlán immigration policy is reported in "Punishment by Exile," *La Raza*, I, 7 (1972), 48–53; policy statements by Chicano organizations have been printed in *Illegal Aliens, Hearings*, for example, Part 1, pp. 269–274; and for other expressions of militant attitudes toward U.S. border control, see Stan Steiner, *La Raza: The Mexican Americans* (New York, 1969).

point in an appeal to traditional Mexican-American leadership for strong public support of alien control. So many Chicano settlers, legal and illegal, have poured into the southwestern states since World War II that many established Mexican-American leaders, some of whose ancestors were in the United States before 1920 or even 1848, have been virtually overwhelmed. To retain any leadership at all among their people they must appeal to the Chicano youth wave—as in Mexico itself a very high percentage of the Mexican-American population is under twenty-one years of age.[67]

Immigration officials, certain congressional leaders, and some labor leaders have vigorously called attention to the magnitude of the illegal employment problem in the United States, and even antipoverty and welfare officials have concurred. The message however has been slow to penetrate the administration, the general body of Congress, and the American press. Since the Eisenhower administration, other problems have distracted the federal government from paying serious attention to the phenomenon of illegal aliens.

## III. The Problem of Numbers

NOTED students of Mexican migration like Paul S. Taylor, Manuel Gamio, and Leo Grebler have already wrestled with the problem of fixing definitive totals for permanent Mexican immigration and settlement.[68] As these social scientists recognized, the large flow back and forth of illegal or unregistered migrants has made the determination of Mexican migration figures a game of cautious approximations.

67. Conversations in August 1968, with the late George I. Sánchez, prominent Mexican-American educator, civic leader, and author, who for many years pressed for Mexican-American civil rights through such organizations as LULACS.

68. Taylor, *Mexican Labor in the United States: Migration Statistics*, I, 237–255, and IV, 23–50; Manuel Gamio, *Quantitative Estimate, Sources and Distribution of Mexican Immigration into the United States* (Mexico, 1936); and Leo Grebler, *Mexican Immigration to the United States: The Record and Its Implications* (Mexican American Study Project, Advance Report 2, Graduate School of Business Administration, University of California [Los Angeles, 1966]).

According to United States figures for legal immigration a mere 28,003 Mexicans moved to the United States in the period 1820–1900.[69] However, no record of Mexican immigration was kept for the years 1886–1893, nor for several thousand campesino families who moved into border regions, particularly south Texas, at a time when there were no general immigration codes or an immigration border patrol.[70] During the decade 1901–1910 more Mexicans legally migrated to the United States than during the previous eighty years. The United States figure of 49,642 reflects the remarkable rise in the use of Mexican labor, even though this number does not include thousands of unregistered migrant workers.

Probably the total number of Mexicans, registered or not, who settled in the United States in the years 1901–1910 far exceeded the total of Spanish and Mexican settlers who moved into the Southwest from early Spanish explorations to the Treaty of Guadalupe Hidalgo in 1848. By the latter date the Spanish-speaking population of the Southwest was around 75,000, distributed approximately as follows: 60,000 "Hispanos" concentrated in a northern New Mexico enclave, 8,000 Californios settled along the coastal mission belt, 5,000 Tejanos mostly in the village of San Antonio and along the lower Rio Grande, and a few hundred miners and pastoral people in southern Arizona and southern Colorado. These frontier people were mostly the result of several generations of miscegenation between the original Spanish and Mexican mestizo stock—probably not numbering more than four or five thousand in all—and the native southwestern Indians. The Indians themselves, who controlled most of the Southwest in 1848, were predominantly nomads and they may have numbered between 200,000 and 300,000.[71]

69. See Table 13 of any of the U.S. Immigration and Naturalization Service (INS) *Annual Reports*.

70. See Taylor, *A Mexican-American Frontier*.

71. Estimates based on McWilliams, *North from Mexico*, p. 52; the *Works* of Hubert H. Bancroft, particularly *History of the North Mexican States and Texas* (San Francisco, 1888); *History of Arizona and New Mexico, 1530–1888* (San Francisco, 1889); and *A History of California* (San Francisco, 1888); also D. W. Meinig, *Southwest: Three Peoples in Geographical Change, 1600–1970* (New York, 1971), pp. 31–32; and James M. Cutts, *The Conquest of California and New Mexico* (1847; rpt. Albuquerque, 1965), which contains, like Bancroft's *Works*, Mexican estimates of frontier population.

The first major wave of settlement by Mexicans in the Southwest did not occur until about 1900. This wave, consisting principally of a migratory landless peasantry, was turned into a veritable exodus by the revolutionary violence of 1910–1920, combined with rapid economic developments in the Southwest and the shutting off of "cheap-alien labor" from Europe and the Orient. According to Mexican figures 218,514 persons legally emigrated to the United States in the brief period 1910–1917.[72] Possibly a fourth of this number were, by ideological measurements, political refugees heading for border cities to wait out their political fortunes, while the remainder were mostly rural peasants and their families, either recruited to work, or driven into the United States labor market by conditions of anarchy in Mexico or fear of military conscription.[73]

World War I labor needs and the economic boom of the 1920's served to maintain the exodus. From 1918 through 1928, 550,599 legal emigrants registered their exit at Mexican border offices.[74] Except for some religious refugees from the "Cristero Revolt," most of these were laborers and their families brought in with the help of American employers.

Actually Mexican migration statistics offer little help, as Leo Grebler has found, in pinning down the actual number of illegal entrants who settled permanently, or for long periods, in the United States.[75] In 1928, Andrés Landa y Piña, then head of the Department of Migration, pointed out one of the great discrepancies: Mexican migration offices registered the loss of 769,113 nationals as legal emigrants to the United States during the years 1910–1928, but, happily, during the same period Mexico gained 1,103,044 "repatriates."[76] Gamio, with the same dry humor, observed that "con-

72. Andrés Landa y Piña, *El Servicio de Migración en México* (Mexico, D.F., 1930), pp. 19–23.
73. On the nature of Mexican emigrant settlers in the 1920's and their social and political motives, see Gamio, *The Mexican Immigrant.*
74. Landa y Piña, *El Servicio de Migración,* p. 23.
75. Letter from Dr. Leo Grebler, January 15, 1970. Dr. Grebler, director of the Mexican American Study Project, UCLA (1964–1969), visited Mexico City in search of Mexican migration data.
76. Landa y Piña, *El Servicio de Migración,* pp. 19, 23. These figures also appear in Taylor, *Mexican Labor . . . Migration Statistics,* I, 240; and in U.S. Consul George N.

trary to what pessimists have alleged, the United States far from consuming our working class serves as a marvelous incubator that actually returns more immigrants than we send there."[77]

One explanation of the incubator phenomenon is that for many years perennial migrants without legal documents reentered Mexico posing as repentant repatriates. The "perennials" cleverly exploited Mexico's longstanding repatriation policy by using Mexican consuls in American cities (as they used the United States Immigration Service) to get a free "repatriation fare" to the border.[78] By the mid-1920's the Mexican government was beginning to grasp the full extent of the abuse, but meanwhile the repatriation illusion had caused havoc with statistical control. When in 1922 the Mexican consuls were ordered to take a census of Mexican nationals in their districts, they could only throw up their hands in despair. Not only were Mexican migrants continually on the move, but for fear of detection they often refused to cooperate.[79] Since then it seems that Mexican, like American, officials have had to be content with approximations.

United States federal agencies, meanwhile, applied the general immigration law of 1917 and the visa control requirements of 1924 to the Mexican border. Counts of legal immigrants were carefully made, but countless peons and adventurers, including women and children, avoided requirements in health, literacy, head tax, visa fees, and self-support by slipping across the line without inspection, as indeed many were accustomed to do before 1917. The term "wetback," or mojado, was soon applied to those who crossed the

Winter's memorandum of 1928 on "Mexican Migratory Statistics" which was partly reproduced in 71 Cong., 2 Sess., *Congressional Record* (1930), 7117–7118.

77. Landa y Piña, *El Servicio de Migración*, p. 26; see also Gamio, *Mexican Immigration*, pp. 7–12, on inconsistencies.

78. Mercedes Carreras de Velasco, "La Repatriatión de Mexicanos, 1920–1940" (unpub. Master's diss., El Colegio de México, 1973), a study based on Mexican consular correspondence in the Archivo de Relaciones Exteriores.

79. See Gamio's explanations for illegal entrance, *Mexican Immigration*, pp. 10–11; and Taylor's account of counting variations, *Mexican Labor . . . Migration Statistics*, I, 248–251. For a brief explanation of the abortive census attempt of 1922 by the Mexican consuls see *Memoria de la Secretaría de Relaciones Exteriores de agosto de 1927 a julio de 1928* (Mexico, 1928), pp. 817–824.

Rio Grande illegally, and then loosely applied to all illegal entrants from Mexico. During the first big exodus, 1911–1930, the United States Immigration Service recorded 678,291 legal immigrants from Mexico, but how many mojados settled on the American side during this period would be a matter of conjecture, possibly a number at least equal to legal immigrants.

A comparison of the 1920 and 1930 census figures in Table III throws into relief a big shift in categories that, in turn, suggests the probable extent of illegal settlement. Daniel W. MacCormack, commissioner of immigration (1933–1936), explained the shift as apparently the result of a high birth rate: "The American-born Mexican population showed an increase between 1920 and 1930 of 562,354, or 231 percent . . . ."[80] A more likely explanation, aside from census oversights, is that the laws of 1929 providing for an alien registry and, for the first time, criminal penalties for illegal entries by individuals caused important shifts in the 1930 and subsequent census counts. Some Mexican-born who appeared in previous censuses were apparently frightened back to Mexico, some avoided census takers, but most appear to have claimed native-born status.[81] After 1929 this status became increasingly a statistical cover for illegal aliens.

Table III

|  | 1920 | 1930 |
|---|---|---|
| Mexican-born | 486,418 | 639,017 |
| Second generation and mixed immigrant and native parentage | 274,924 | 810,278 |
| Total Mexican-stock population | 761,342 | 1,449,295 |

SOURCES: INS, *Annual Reports*, Table 13; *Fifteenth Census of the United States: 1930. Population. Special Report on Foreign Families* (Washington, 1933), p. 6; and *Mexicans in California Report of Governor C. C. Young's Fact-Finding Committee* (San Francisco, 1930), pp. 28–29 and Table 8.

80. U. S. Department of Labor, *Annual Report of the Secretary of Labor 1935* (Washington, 1936), p. 79.

81. According to interviews by the author with Mexican settlers in south Texas during period May–June 1970, Mexican migrants had little fear of penalties for illicit entries and felt more at ease with census takers. See also Robert N. McLean, "Tightening the Mexican Border," *Survey Graphic*, 64 (1930), parts of which appeared in 71 Cong., 2 Sess., *Congressional Record*, 7129.

The recorded population of Mexican stock was heavily concentrated in five Southwestern states as shown in Table IV. Since United States census figures for 1930 did not include all illegal settlers, nor all descendants of native Californios, Tejanos, and Hispanos, a rough estimate of all Mexican-descent groups in the United States in that year would be over two million.[82]

82. Some estimates of Mexican population in the United States around 1930, ranging from 1.4 million to 2.5 million, are indicated *ibid.*, p. 7133. Also, McWilliams' estimate for 1930 was slightly over 2 million, *North from Mexico*, p. 56.

## POPULATION OF NORTHERN MEXICO AND THE UNITED STATES IN 1930

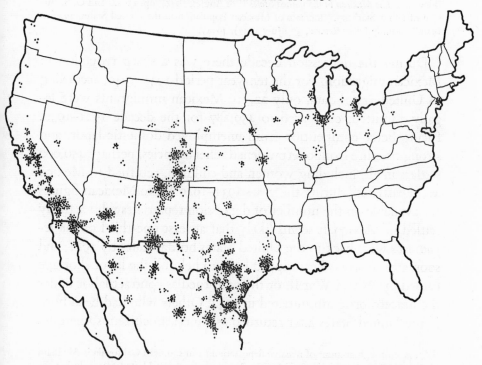

SOURCES: Mexicanos deportados. Piden informes al Visitador de Consulados Enrique González. Archivo de la Secretaría de Relaciones Exteriores, IV-574-31 (1931); U. S. Bureau of the Census, *Fifteenth Census of the United States: 1930. Population, Special Report on Foreign Families* (Washington, D.C., 1933); Mexico. Secretaría de Agricultura y Fomento. Departamento de la Estadística Nacional. *Anuario estadístico de los Estados Unidos Mexicanos* (Mexico, 1932).

Population of north Mexico states of Baja California (Norte), Sonora, Chihuahua, Nuevo León, and Tamaulipas in 1930: 1,504,000. This Mexico census figure overlooks much of floating population in border zones.

Table IV

MEXICAN POPULATION BY STATE

| | |
|---|---|
| California | 368,013 |
| Texas | 683,681 |
| Arizona | 114,173 |
| New Mexico | 59,340 |
| Colorado | 57,676 |
| Other States | 166,412 |
| TOTAL | 1,449,295 |

SOURCES: Based on Taylor, *Mexican Labor . . . Migration Statistics*, IV, 30; Emory S. Bogardus, *The Mexican in the United States* (Los Angles, 1934), pp. 13–14; and U. S. Bureau of Labor Statistics, "Increase of Mexican Population in the United States, 1920 to 1930," *Monthly Labor Review*, 37 (July 1933), 46–47.

During the depression decade there was a sharp reduction in Mexican migration. For the ten-year period 1931–1940, according to United States data, only 22,319 Mexican immigrants were legally admitted, compared to 459,287 for the decade 1921–1930. Facing fierce competition from unemployed domestic labor, and strong pressure from overburdened relief agencies, perhaps 450,000 settlers in all, including women and children, returned to Mexico as "repatriates" during the years 1931–1940.[83] No Mexican figures are available on the number of depression repatriates who actually settled in Mexico. It seems likely that at least one-third of the *repatriados* were back in the United States border states by 1941, and soon after many others slipped back to help fill the labor shortage caused by World War II, or they returned as contract labor under the bracero program initiated in 1942. Others who had been born in the United States later returned as American citizens sometimes

83. A thorough account of massive deportation from southern California is Abraham Hoffman, "The Repatriation of Mexican Nationals from the United States during the Great Depression" (unpub. PhD diss., University of California, 1970). Aside from Hoffman's study, to be printed by the University of Arizona Press, statistics on repatriation during the peak years 1930–1934 can be found in Taylor, *Mexican Labor . . . Migration Statistics*, IV, 23–25, 48; E. S. Bogardus, *Mexicans in the United States*, pp. 90–97; and in the National Archives, R.G. 59, file 811.111 Mexico. Some Mexican figures are given in Secretaría de Relaciones Exteriores, *Memoria*, 1931, 1932, 1933; and in Carreras de Velasco, "La Repatriación de Mexicanos."

with families of their own. Probably not more than one-third of the depression repatriates remained permanently in Mexico.[84]

The Mexican contract labor program (1942–1964) stimulated new waves of legal and illegal migration. According to United States figures only 60,589 legal immigrants came from Mexico during the entire decade 1941–1950, compared with 66,766 in 1927 alone.[85] Yet by 1948 thousands of Mexican laborers were settling in the Southwest and the Midwest. The deficiency in legal immigration figures may be partly explained by the tighter American visa controls inaugurated in 1929 against unskilled Mexican labor. Nevertheless, legal immigration from south of the border soon picked up remarkably. In the decade 1951–1960 this figure rose to 319,312.[86]

One factor in the upward surge of the 1950's was the McCarran-Walter Act of 1952, which liberalized certain provisions of immigration law. In addition, United States employers, uncertain of the future of bracero labor and illegal labor, especially after the "wetback sweeps" of 1953 and 1954, arranged, particularly in the years 1954–1957, for the legal immigration of Mexican workers.[87] At the same time immigrated laborers with permanent jobs began legally bringing in relatives under family preference categories. The effect was that Mexican immigration began to snowball in the 1950's, the one type of immigration feeding the other. This momentum continued into the 1970's with no end in sight.

In the 1960's legal immigration from Mexico averaged over 45,000 per year. It constituted an astounding thirteen to sixteen percent of all legal immigration to the United States. The total of 443,301 for 1961–1970 nearly equalled the 459,287 that came legally during the entire 1920's. The number of Mexican immigrants

84. Rough estimate based on U.S. consular correspondence in the 1930's in National Archives, R.G. 59, for example, file 811.504/417-423; and file 811.11/1188/1236; and on interviews with Mexican repatriates established in agrarian colonies of "18 de Marzo," Valle Harmoso, Colonia Anahuac, and other settlements in the states of Tamaulipas and Nuevo León, December 20–21, 1970, and August 23, 1971.

85. Grebler, *Mexican Immigration*, p. 106.

86. *Ibid.* and INS, *Annual Reports*, Table 14: "Immigrants Admitted by Country or Region of Birth."

87. Grebler, *Mexican Immigration*, pp. 34, 89.

admitted in fiscal 1971, 50,103 and, fiscal 1972, 64,040, plus around 70,000 in fiscal 1973, suggested that legal immigration for the decade 1971–1980 would easily surpass the total of the 1920's.[88]

None of these figures encompassed the many Mexican emigrants who had been settling in the United States illegally. In fiscal 1973 alone 576,807 deportable aliens from Mexico were located by the United States Immigration Service. No one can know for certain but it has been estimated by various observers on both sides of the border that the number of Mexican illegal aliens presently residing or working in the United States has reached two million or more.[89] Few of these aliens would show up in any category of the 1970 census. Perhaps fifty percent of the illegals would be living with relatives and not employed, and would therefore be nearly impossible to detect. The remaining fifty percent would be employed in a variety of unskilled and semiskilled jobs. A much higher percentage of the job-seekers (in contrast to kinfolk-seekers) are apprehended, and there is always some voluntary backflow to Mexico.[90] Nevertheless, reinforcements seep in and outnumber the deportees so that illegal settlers from Mexico are steadily increasing.

The census estimate of the Mexican-descent population in the United States in 1970 is shown in Table V. Every United States census since 1920 has been accused of undercounting the Mexican and the Mexican-descent groups. The 1970 census is no exception. Possibly 800,000 or more legal residents of Mexican origin did not show up in the census count.[91] A rough estimate of 2 million un-

88. Figures for 1960–1972 are from INS, *Annual Reports*, Table 14.

89. For statistics on deportable aliens located see *ibid.*, Table 27B. The rough estimate of the number of Mexican illegals presently in the United States is based on interviews with Mexican officials of the Departamento de Migración, Mexico City, August 14, 1970, and questionnaire replies, November 14, 1972, also on statements of Mexican Ambassador to the United States Juan José de Olloqui, as these appeared in *Excelsior* (Mexico City), August 31, 1973.

90. Based on interviews with immigration officers in southwestern states in summer of 1970, and in August of 1971 and 1972.

91. This conjecture is based on expected increase of Mexican-American population, which has one of the highest rates of natural increase of any ethnic group in the United States, about 2.7 percent in the 1960's, yet the expected increase did not fully show in the 1970 census count. Moreover, the Census Bureau had admitted an overall undercount of around five million in the 1970 census.

counted illegal settlers might be added to suggest a more realistic total of perhaps 7.8 million persons of Mexican descent residing permanently in the United States in 1970. Even this conjecture would not have included floating groups of "perennial repatriates" and transborder migratory workers who at any given time might have numbered 600,000 or more.

POPULATION OF NORTHERN MEXICO AND
THE UNITED STATES IN 1970

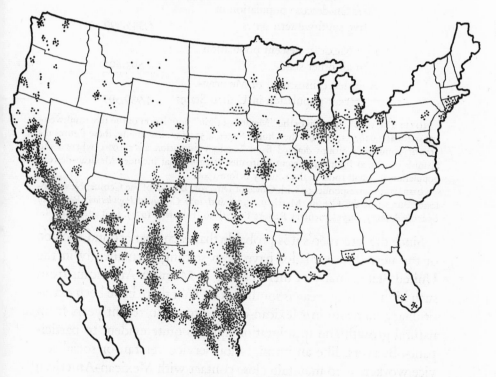

SOURCES: U. S. Bureau of the Census, *Census of the Population 1970. Supplementary Report: Persons of Spanish Ancestry*, PC(SI)-30 (Washington, D.C., February, 1972), p. II, Tables II, IV; Mexico. Secretaría de Industria y Comercio. Dirección General de Estadística. *IX Censo General de Población—1970, 28 de enero de 1970* (Mexico, 1971), Cuadro I.

Population of north Mexico states of Baja California (Norte), Sonora, Chihuahua, Nuevo Leon, and Tamaulipas in 1970: 6,733,000. This Mexico census figure overlooks much of floating population in border zones.

Table V

| | |
|---|---|
| California | 2,222,185 |
| Texas | 1,663,567 |
| Arizona | 246,390 |
| New Mexico | 324,248 |
| Colorado | 211,585 |
| Subtotal of Spanish-surnamed | 4,667,975 |
| Less Spanish-surnamed of non-Mexican descent in Southwest | 322,179 |
| Mexican-descent population in five southwestern states | 4,345,796 |
| Plus Mexican-descent population in all other states | 593,801 |
| Adjusted census total of Mexican-descent population in United States | 4,939,597 |

NOTE: The 1970 census gives the "Mexican-origin" population of the five southwestern states as 3,938,751, and for the United States, 4,532,552. Essentially, these figures represent population groups derived from Mexican migration after 1900, whereas the Spanish-surnamed figures represent a broader category that includes Mexican-descent population that had roots in the country before 1900.

SOURCES: Correspondence with Office of Director, Bureau of the Census; News Release, Bureau of the Census, March 9, 1972; and *1970 Census of Population, Persons of Spanish Ancestry*, Supplementary Report PC(SI)-30 (February 1973), p. ii and Table I.

Since the late 1960's it is probable that each year around 100,000 of the new-style mojados have been settling permanently in the United States, many of them passing as Mexican-Americans from such high fertility areas as south Texas. That there have been extraordinary increases in Mexican-origin groups in recent years from natural growth and immigration appears quite evident to participant-observers, like an immigration service veteran or social service worker, who maintain close contact with Mexican-American *colonias* and *barrios* in the Southwest and the Midwest. But, as such observers see it, much of this increase goes unreported because of its migratory nature, or because many, if not most Mexican-origin families, have members who originally entered illegally. It is hardly surprising that some Chicano militants have urged noncooperation with census takers. As Mexican-descent groups of recent origin settle down, or obtain legitimation or plausible documentation, they may allow all or most of the family (often an extended family, in sociological terms) to be counted in the next census. In the meantime, there is a widespread "invisible minority" phenomenon that has profound implications for students of ethnic acculturation and for the hapless census takers who, in a recount of March 1973, found 1.35 million more persons of Mexican origins.[92]

As for immigration totals, from 1901 through fiscal 1973 about 1.75 million Mexican immigrants have been legally admitted for permanent residence, according to United States figures. And if one were to add rough approximations of unregistered settlers then the total number of Mexicans, who, thus far in this century, have settled permanently or for long periods of time in the United States, might be close to 4 million.

## iv. Mexican Policy and Attitudes toward Labor Emigration

MEXICAN emigration to the United States has been a matter of serious concern to every Mexican government in the twentieth century. Probably no other nation has exhibited such a profound and persistent concern for a particular emigrant group in the United States. This concern is not merely the result of border proximity but of a long history of border conflict between radically different people and cultures, and the rise of a defensive nationalism

92. Some of the problems of counting the inhabitants in the Spanish-speaking *barrios* are indicated by Ralph Guzman, one of the participants in the UCLA Mexican American Study Project. The census taker, like a border patrolman, a policeman, a social worker, or truant officer, can "trigger nervousness." This is particularly true, notes Professor Guzman, "among the poor, who almost seem to have invisible antennae that warn them about 'the enemy.'" See U.S. Senate, *Hearings before the Special Committee on Aging, Availability and Usefulness of Federal Programs and Services to Elderly Mexican-Americans,* 90 Cong., 2 Sess., pt. 1 (1969), 80–81.

In the recount of Americans of Spanish descent, made in March 1973, the U.S. Census Bureau found that the Mexican-origin population had increased from 4.94 million to 6.29 million, or an increase of over twenty-seven percent in three years; *The News* (Mexico City), January 17, 1974, p. 8. However, most Chicano groups still consider this an undercount of three or four million.

in Mexico that sees the *yanqui* colossus expanding and absorbing at Mexico's expense.

The government of Porfirio Díaz (1876–1910), which was striving to increase the national population, to transform rural Mexico with European farm colonies, to import an Oriental labor force, and, in general, to overcome the national debility that had led to the territorial dismemberment of 1848, could only look on in frustration as Mexican laborers and their families began moving by the thousands into American border states and beyond.[93]

The revolutionary spirit touched off by Madero in 1910 and carried through the administration of Lázaro Cárdenas (1934–1940) not only served to accelerate the exodus of the peasantry, but, equally important, accentuated the nationalist sentiment that colored Mexican policy and attitudes toward emigration to the United States. That thousands of workers, and some political refugees, together with their families, were on their way to the United States was typically regarded as "a fatal bleeding."[94] Population facts and attitudes are important here. The ideologists of the revolution were convinced, like national leaders before them, that Mexico was underpopulated, and for that reason had lost the territories of the north. At the inception of independence in 1821, Mexico's population was less than 7 million. Nearly a century later in 1920 the census reported only 14.3 million. In the 1920's and 1930's Mexican intellectuals responded to the problem of underpopulation with what could be called a spirit of "demographic nationalism."[95] By 1920 there was an atmosphere of general alarm that Mexico would soon face a serious labor shortage and a major problem in protecting illiterate, undocumented campesinos following seasonal work

93. See unsigned memo, July 6, 1910, Archivo de la Secretaría de Relaciones Exteriores, Legajo 3050–3035, number 27; and Moisés González Navarro, *La Colonización en México, 1877–1910* (Mexico, 1960), pp. 123–139.

94. *El Universal*, August 9, 1920, p. 9; also *Excelsior*, March 2–3, 1928.

95. A. F. Corwin, *Mexican Attitudes toward Population, Poverty and Public Opinion* (Gainesville, Fla., 1963). See also works by Mexico's most influential demographer Gilberto Loyo, such as *La Política Demográfica de México* (Mexico, 1935), and *Las Deficiencias Cuantitativas de la Población de México y una Política Demográfica Nacional* (pamphlet, Rome, 1932); as well as Gustavo Durán González, *Problemas Migratorios de México* (Mexico, 1925).

in the United States. Mexican labor unions, such as the Confederación Regional de Obreros Mexicanos (CROM), joined in the cry to stop mass emigration because expatriate workers were reportedly subject to discrimination and exploitation.[96]

The Carranza government (1915–1920) beginning as early as 1917 responded to the emigration crisis by formulating and applying, as far as possible, the main outlines of nationalist emigration policies that successive governments have more or less consistently maintained to the present day. The first of these policies, which might be called a policy of discouragement, was, in fact, an alternative to demands by nationalists and employers, especially hacienda owners, that the government must stop mass migration to the United States. There were practical reasons for not attempting a migration blockade. The Carranza government, which fell in May 1920, and subsequent governments have always lacked the means for enforcing such a desperate proposal along a two-thousand-mile frontier. Moreover, the early revolutionary regimes of Carranza, De la Huerta, Obregón, and Calles frankly admitted that Mexico had little to offer miserable peons and underpaid industrial and mine workers except unfulfilled revolutionary promises. The alternative for expatriate Mexicans, in the words of a border official, was to return to "absolute misery."[97] Equally important, under the new constitution of 1917 the right of Mexican citizens to travel and migrate to any place whatever, subject only to administrative procedures, was clearly established.[98]

Another consideration was the need of shaky revolutionary governments for diplomatic recognition and support from Washington. Thus, in spite of a widespread anti-American sentiment, Presidents Carranza, De la Huerta, and Obregón permitted American employers to recruit labor during World War I and after, under

---

96. *El Universal*, March 4, 10, 16, 17, and April 6, 1920. Other examples of Mexican labor policy are given by Harvey A. Levenstein, *Labor Organizations in the United States and Mexico: A History of their Relations* (Westport, Conn., 1971).

97. *El Universal*, March 17, 1920, p. 3. See also statement by Plutarco Elías Calles, then secretary of the interior, *ibid.*, December 19, 1920, p. 9.

98. As stated in Article II of the Constitution of 1917; John T. Vance and Helen T. Clagett, *A Guide to the Law and Legal Literature of Mexico* (Washington, 1945), p. 194.

special United States exemptions for contract labor during the years 1917–1921.[99] The Mexican government did insist, however, that certain conditions be met by American employers and that contract labor be of a temporary nature with the employer obligated to pay the return passage of the worker. In addition, recruitment of labor within Mexican borders by representatives of American companies and employer interests was prohibited; checkpoints were established on railways leading north in a vain attempt to detain migrants without contracts; all would-be emigrants were ordered to register at border migration offices, and officials there were ordered to refuse passports to emigrants without work contracts or proper emigration documents.[100]

However, Mexican law did not provide for any specific penalties for illegal exits or failures to register with Mexican border officials. Then, as now, many workers and their families lacked such elementary papers as birth certificates and marriage licenses, and many were illiterate or ignorant of national law. Generally, the Mexican government has always considered the "illegal emigrants" as innocent victims of unfortunate circumstances and has felt a national obligation to help them in any way possible. Usually Mexican border officials have treated the emigrants with compassion. In other cases, they have been accused of demanding *mordidas* for arranging registration papers and border-crossing cards and for permitting labor recruiters to operate in border towns along with professional alien smugglers.[101]

As the exodus continued unabated in the 1920's the government,

99. The text of Secretary of Labor W. B. Wilson's order suspending sections of the immigration act to admit illiterate laborers is given in the U.S. Committee on Public Information, *Official U.S. Bulletin*, 2 (June 24, 1918), 10–12. Under these exemptions more than 72,000 Mexican contract workers were admitted.

100. Some of the restraining decrees are summarized in *Diario Oficial* (Mexico City), March 19, 1920, pp. 1225–1226. Throughout the 1920's other control efforts were made, and in March 1930, with the United States Congress threatening to impose a quota on Mexican immigration, the Mexican Migration Service established offices in four northern transportation centers to prevent laborers from proceeding to the border without visas. D. G. Dwyre, American consul, Mexico City, to secretary of state, May 12, 1930, National Archives, R.G. 59, 811.111/373.

101. *El Universal*, June 19, 22, 23, 1920, and March 19, 1923; also, Secretaría de Gobernación, *Memoria 1929–1930*, p. 277; *ibid., 1928–1929*, p. 147.

# PARTIAL VIEW OF RAILWAY NETWORK OF UNITED STATES AND MEXICO AROUND 1925

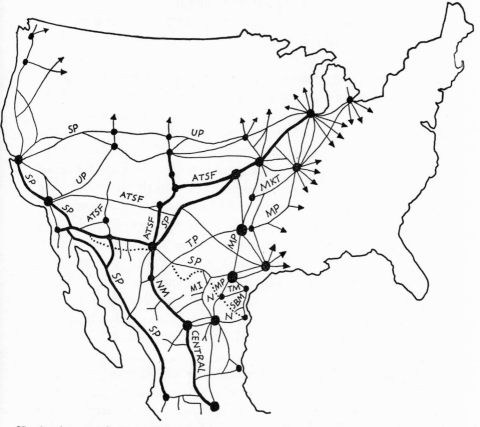

SP   Southern Pacific. Its Mexican line, via Nogales, known as Sonora or Sud-Pacifico, completed 1882–1912.

ATSF   Atchinson, Topeka and Santa Fe. To El Paso in 1884.

MP   Missouri Pacific to Laredo, 1880's.

TM   Texas Mexican. Corpus Christi to La-redo, 1880's.

SBM   St. Louis, Brownsville and Mexico, 1904.

TP   Texas Pacific.

UP   Union Pacific. Chicago to San Fran-cisco, 1869.

NM   Norte de México (Mexican Central) to El Paso, 1884.

MI   Mexican International to Eagle Pass, 1882.

N   National Railway to Laredo, 1882, and to Brownsville, 1904.

NOTE: Most transborder lines were completed between 1882 and 1910 by British, French, and American companies. On the U. S. side the network roughly coincides with the pattern of Mexican settlement from 1890 to the present. By 1930 nearly every large town or city along these routes had a colony of Mexican migratory families who, using railroads as a means of employment and mobility, often shifted from one job to another in mines, agriculture, and maintenance work on other railways, tramways, and then highways. All U. S. railroads indicated here employed Mexican labor, often pro-viding housing or boxcar apartments along company's right-of-way. Principal employers were the Southern Pacific and Santa Fe which, more than other lines, brought workers in from Mexican con-nections. Data supplied by Joseph Fichaudler.

with the patriotic collaboration of leading newspapers, resorted to a campaign of dissuasion.[102] Here the government was moved to some extent by the possibility of an unwanted quota on Mexican immigration, seriously defended then in the United States Congress, and by the pressure of American friends of the Mexican Revolution and of the Mexican labor movement, such as Samuel Gompers and William Green, who wanted the Mexican government to adopt the principle of "voluntary self-restriction," especially in the period 1923–1929. Dissuasion, rather than restriction, was as far as the Mexican government or Mexican labor leaders, like Luis Morones, would go.[103] Mexican leaders have evidently always felt that Mexican workers had a moral right to migrate to the "lost territories" with or without United States immigration papers. Nevertheless, stories of stranded families, discrimination, mistreatment, and the victimizing of mojado labor were widely circulated.[104] Works of semiofficial propaganda were sponsored, as by Alfonso Fabila, who, writing in 1928, pictured the fate that awaited Mexican settlers and their children in the United States, including forced Americanization by public schools and the inevitable erosion of La Raza, the national family.[105]

The Mexican press also informed their readers that the unscrupulous profiteering of *malos Mexicanos* was as much responsible for the exodus as poverty in Mexico or government inertia. These *enganchistas* and *coyotes*, who had infiltrated all parts of Mexico and were paid so much a head for delivering rustic campesinos to labor agents on the other side, were often characterized as scav-

102. U.S. consular communiques occasionally summarize Mexico's official propaganda efforts and noted their lack of practical effect, for example, American consul in charge, American Embassy, Mexico City, to secretary of state, November 11, 1920, National Archives, R.G. 59, 811.504/203; and David Myers, American consul, Durango, to state, March 7, 1924, R.G. 59, 150.126/141.

103. Levenstein, *Labor Organizations*, ch. viii, "An Experiment in Labor Diplomacy."

104. John R. Martínez, "Mexican Emigration to the United States, 1910–1930" (unpub. PhD diss., University of California, Berkeley, 1957), ch. x, "Emigration and Mexican Policy 1921–1930."

105. Alfonso Fabila, *El Problema de la Emigración de Obreros y Campesinos Mexicanos* (Mexico, 1928). This thirty-eight-page pamphlet was printed by the government and distributed to the consuls and Mexican newspapers.

engers living off the false hopes of their fellow countrymen. Hand in hand with this propaganda campaign, government officials appointed study groups, subsidized Manuel Gamio's field survey of Mexicans in the United States, 1926–1927, appealed to Mexican industries to raise wages, sponsored the Migration Law of 1926 fixing strict contract controls on free-lance recruiting, renewed threats to cut off all consular aid to illegal emigrants, and, in general, sought to calm hysterical nationalists.[106]

Only the depression of the 1930's really served to decrease mass Mexican emigration. After the depression decade the policy of discouragement was revived in response to a second exodus triggered by the labor needs of World War II and the binational bracero program that lasted from 1942 to 1964. The rhetoric of dissuasion, especially in the 1940's and 1950's, was again enveloped in an atmosphere of national sensitivities, political criticism, and public naiveté that could not quite comprehend the undignified scramble to cross the American border.

The Mexican government was at first embarrassed and then troubled at the rush of braceros and mojados for American wages. During the war emergency the government had hoped to ration contract workers to the North American economy as the figures for the 1940's show.[107] For one thing Mexican officials wished to avoid another repatriation problem like that of the 1930's, for another they were disturbed to see campesinos desert agrarian reform projects that had become, like Zapata, the very symbol of revolutionary rebirth.[108] And anxious to industrialize the country, Mexican leaders opposed the loan of industrial labor under the bracero

106. *El Universal*, March 11, 1920, p. 11; March 19, 1920, p. 1; March 28, 1920, p. 2. The Migration Law of 1926 made written contracts for recruited laborers mandatory. These contracts, which guaranteed hours, wages, and housing, according to Article 123 of the Constitution were to be visaed by U.S. consuls as if they were emigration documents, and American employers were required to deposit money in the Mexican Labor Bank to guarantee the return passage of the workers. According to Martínez, migrants simply ignored the law which, perhaps, was more designed to pacify public criticism, and probably the government threat of no consular aid to illegals was a more effective deterrent, "Mexican Emigration to the United States," pp. 140–141.

107. Galarza, *Merchants of Labor*, pp. 46–53, 79.

108. See Craig, *The Bracero Program*; and Otey M. Scruggs, "The United States, Mexico, and the Wetbacks, 1942–1947."

program.[109] Yet industrial workers, along with peasants, tradesmen, and assorted adventurers, dropped everything to join the labor exodus northwards.[110]

Again, the government made efforts to discourage, or redirect, noncontract workers from crossing the United States border.[111] Again, the Mexican press, and labor leaders, cooperated in a campaign to warn would-be mojados against the exploitation that awaited workers without valid papers. And, again, to judge by the huge number of wetback apprehensions, running into the millions during the bracero program, the policy of discouragement had no appreciable effects in deterring transborder migration, legal or illegal.[112]

Another historic dimension of Mexican policy toward emigration is a special emphasis on protecting Mexican colonies in the United States. As a secretary of foreign relations expressed it in 1917: "Since it is not possible for the government to prevent emigration it must take every measure to reduce the hardships of our fellow citizens while they reside in a foreign country."[113] In carrying out this policy the Mexican consuls have invariably displayed an unmatched dedication to emigrant protection. Besides serving the actual needs of expatriates, "protectionism" was designed to persuade political critics and public opinion in general that the government was actively defending Mexican nationals in the United States from exploitation, discrimination, and abandonment. Ex-

109. See correspondence on formulation of the bracero agreements during the period 1942–1943 in National Archives, R.G. 59, 811.504/Mexico.

110. Bracero motivations are indicated by Jose Lázaro Salinas, *La Emigración de Braceros, Visión Objetica de un Problema Mexicano* (Mexico, 1955); and Máximo Peón (pseudonym), *Cómo Viven los Mexicanos en los Estados Unidos* (Mexico, 1966). See also a full description of economic conditions in Mexico in the early 1940's in Whetten, *Rural Mexico*.

111. The Mexican government moved the recruiting centers to the interior of Mexico, where recruitment could be better controlled and wetback pressures on the border reduced, at the same time commercialized agriculture and industrialization were being pushed with the hope of absorbing marginal labor groups, according to interviews with officials of the Departamento de Población, August 16, 19, 1970.

112. The most complete study to date of the wetback problem is Samora, *Los Mojados*. For data on apprehensions see INS, *Annual Reports*, Table 27B.

113. *El Universal*, September 21, 1917, p. 5. See similar statement of the secretary of interior, *ibid.*, March 20, 1920, p. 1.

plaining this mission constitutes a small body of significant literature written by migration and consular officers.[114]

A remarkable facet of protectionism has been Mexico's undeviating concern for the rights of Mexican laborers across the border. Among these rights, according to the revolutionary constitution of 1917, were the fulfillment of labor contracts, unemployment compensation, disability benefits, minimum wages, and the right to unionize and strike.[115] Labor protection was promoted not merely for doctrinaire reasons and to meet the demands of Mexican labor leaders, but because of the repatriation problem. When, for example, the government found itself forced to accommodate hordes of "perennial repatriates" at the onset of the depression, the response was a further elaboration of the rights of labor. The code of 1931, which like earlier provisions foreshadowed the bracero program, sought to guarantee the return transportation of an unemployed worker at the cost of the employer, who was to place a bond with a Mexican bank.[116] Protectionism was also a reaction to the fact that Mexican workers, often illiterate, illegal, job-hungry, and underage, were easily exploited by crew leaders and employers, and often excluded, sometimes as "scabs," from American labor unions.[117] Mexican consuls vigorously intervened in their behalf most notably in agricultural labor strikes.[118] But, in fact, the consuls were insisting on rights not clearly conceded to American farm labor even after the New Deal era of the 1930's and the recent Huelga! movement of César Chávez.[119]

During the bracero program, 1942–1964, labor protectionism

114. One example is Landa y Piña, "La Migración y Protección de Mexicanos en el Extranjero" (Mexico, 1928), later published as El Servicio de Migración. Another example is Santibañez, Ensayo Acerca de la Inmigración Mexicana en los Estados Unidos, then Mexican consul in San Antonio.

115. Vance and Clagett, A Guide to the Law of Mexico, pp. 227–235.

116. Campbell, "Bracero Migration and the Mexican Economy," pp. 39–40.

117. See Levenstein, Labor Organizations.

118. See, for example, Charles Wollenberg, "Race and Class in Rural California: El Monte Berry Strike of 1933," California Historical Society Quarterly, 51 (1972), 155–164; and Ronald W. Lopez, "The El Monte Berry Strike of 1933," Aztlán, 1 (1970), 101–114.

119. President's Commission on Migratory Labor in American Agriculture (Washington, 1951), pp. 52–53; and President's Commission on Immigration and Naturalization, Hearings (Washington, 1952), pp. 1630–1632.

was carried to the level of a binational accord whereby both the Mexican and the United States governments agreed to uphold an elaborate listing of guarantees. Students of these accords, and of U. S. Public Law 71, protecting braceros, have made ironic comments that during the bracero period alien workers were better protected than native American labor or, for that matter, labor in Mexico, where many constitutional guarantees were a dead letter. Mexico's protectionist policy, to point out another irony, was also a major factor in encouraging United States employers to prefer wetbacks rather than contract laborers.[120] This, in turn, led to futile Mexican demands that American employers of illegal braceros be punished.

Another remarkable dimension of protectionism as carried out by Mexican consuls in the United States has been the defense of Mexican nationals, and even Mexican-Americans, against discrimination and segregation in schooling, housing, and social services, their exemption from military conscription during World War I and World War II, and their protection from arbitrary deportation or arrest.[121] This accorded with the official view that under Mexican law Mexican emigrants, including children born abroad, were still Mexican citizens (unless they expressly renounced this status.)[122] Protectionist ardor was also in accord with a national folk consciousness that regards all Mexican-origin peoples in the United States as members of La Raza.

After World War II the Mexican consuls continued to play the role of zealous defenders of the Mexican colonies in the United States, but not on such a large scale. Beginning in the 1920's organizations began to emerge such as LULACS, the American G.I. Forum after World War II, and more recently PASO and La Raza Unida, which seek to defend the Mexican colonies through sociopolitical action. Furthermore, since the depression the federal gov-

120. *Ibid.*

121. Many examples of this protectionist activity can be found in National Archives, R.G. 59, file 311.12/(1910–1929).

122. For the concept of Mexican nationality at home and abroad, see S. A. Bayitch and José L. Siqueiros, *Conflict of Laws: Mexico and the United States* (Coral Gables, Fla., 1968), pp. 30–34.

ernment in the United States has increasingly provided for welfare benefits, school desegregation, legal protection, and the like, for both native and alien residents. Moreover, since the 1930's the consuls have become more selective by giving first attention to those Mexican emigrants and visitors who have legal authorization to be in the United States.[123]

Still, protection of La Raza in the United States has always been characterized by an intensive Mexicanization program that has no exact counterpart in United States immigration history. The purpose of *Mexicanidad* simply stated was, and is, to prevent Mexican emigrant groups from being absorbed or assimilated by American culture. From the Carranza administration until World War II, the Mexican consuls, assisted by the citizen-committees, carried out this mission with a devotion little short of religious.[124] This devotion reflected a popular feeling that the revolution must do everything possible to restore *la patria* and the *indomestizo* culture to the *hermanos de la raza* who through no fault of their own had been driven into an alien land.

Until *la restauración* the Mexican consuls and patriotic committees were charged with guarding against insidious forms of *pochismo* or de-Mexicanization, for it was felt that *pochos*—Mexicans who had adopted American customs or standards of materialism—would not easily fit again into Mexican society.[125] On *fiestas patrias*, such as Mexican independence day, and other holidays, the Mexican consuls, particularly in the border states, rarely missed an opportunity to harangue assemblies of Mexican emigrants and their families on the virtues of Raza loyalty and patriotism, the glorious figures of revolutionary history like Juárez and Zapata, and the disgrace of *pochismo* in a land that once belonged to Mexico.

123. Interviews with personnel of Mexican Consulate General, San Antonio, May 21, 1970, and January 4, 1973.

124. According to Gamio, "There is hardly an immigrant home in the United States where the Mexican flag is not found in a place of honor, often altars are made for saints and flags . . . giving patriotism thus an almost religious quality," *Mexican Immigration*, p. 128.

125. See Fabila, *El Problema de la Emigración*; and a theatrical work that portrays the anguish of Mexican emigrant parents who look on helplessly as their children reject their Mexican heritage, Humberto Robles, *Los Desarraigados* (Mexico, 1962).

Robert N. McLean, for many years a missionary and social worker among Mexican emigrants, and a man who struggled to understand the Mexican's outstanding resistance to Americanization or naturalization, reported a speech characteristic of those delivered by the Mexican consul to La Raza brotherhood: "When I say 'Mexican' I do not mean that nameless hybrid creature who proves false to the mother who bore him by taking out American citizenship." And noted McLean, "the chorus of 'Viva Mexico!' drowned the speaker's voice." The American bystander added: "These strangers have not really crossed the boundary line; they have pushed it ahead of them."[126]

That the migratory experience itself—a constant flux back and forth across the border—also played a major role in the development of a Raza consciousness or subculture in the United States can hardly be doubted. As Gamio observed, the migratory experience, together with feelings of social discrimination, transformed what was formerly a tribal sense of village identity—*la pequeña patria*—to a larger and deeper sense of nationality.[127] This new sense of identity was reinforced by the protectionist mission of the consuls. In this respect, it is probably no exaggeration to say that until World War II, and even later in many instances, Mexican migratory groups of the campesino class were more in contact with the Mexican Revolution's message of nationalization, political indoctrination, and modernization than the isolated rural population of Mexico that still clung to ancient folkways.

Aside from patriotic sentiment, the *Mexicanidad* mission readily perceived Raza workers in the United States as an important source of national income for Mexico. The first full taste of the dollar flow occurred during World War I and after, when contract workers averaged around $1,500 per year in United States employment, and some up to $5.00 a day, a fabulous sum compared to Mexican

---

126. Robert N. McLean, *That Mexican! As He Really Is, North and South of the Rio Grande* (New York, 1928). Note also the patriotic songs of the immigrants in Gamio, *Mexican Immigration*, pp. 84–107.

127. *Ibid.*, pp. 74–75, 128–130.

wages at that time.[128] The Mexican government was advised to follow the example of Italy and Poland, and through the consular service, teach emigrant workers how to organize saving accounts and credit unions, and how to send money back to relatives. A branch system of Mexican banks in the United States was also proposed.[129] That the consul succeeded in teaching some of the lessons seems substantiated by Gamio's study of postal money orders sent to Mexico in the 1920's.[130]

The bracero program was regarded as an opportunity to establish through binational accords not only fair wages and fair treatment for Mexican contract labor but also a better flow of income back to Mexico then seeking to industrialize.[131] If the bracero program were to be revived, there seems little doubt that these same economic considerations would again be incorporated into a binational agreement.[132]

All the while Mexican governments have consistently promoted the repatriation of Mexican-origin groups in the United States. Here we touch on one of the most sacred obligations of defensive nationalism. The roots of the *repatriado* policy lie much deeper than 1910. From time to time after the Treaty of Guadalupe Hidalgo various Mexican governments tried with little success to repatriate at least some of the seventy to eighty thousand *hermanos* who remained in the lost territories. The new spirit of mestizo nationalism aroused by the Revolution of 1910 rejected foreign colonization and embraced the historic repatriation mission with a new fervor. The governments of Carranza (1915–1920) and Obregón (1920–1924), although desperately short of pesos, made heroic efforts to

128. Memorandum of June 10, 1922, exped. 711–M–30, in Archivo General de la Nación, Ramo Obregón-Calles.

129. *Ibid.*

130. Gamio, *Mexican Immigration*, pp. 13–30.

131. Craig, *The Bracero Program*, pp. 17–18. See also Frank Brandenburg, *The Making of Modern Mexico* (Englewood Cliffs, N.J., 1964).

132. Interviews with personnel of the Departamento de Población, August 20, 1970; and with U.S. immigration officials attached to the U.S. Embassy, Mexico City, August 14, 1970.

subsidize the return of Mexican nationals and their families.[133] But according to Mexican consuls, repatriation aid was frequently exploited by the "perennial repatriates" in seeking free transportation home during the off-season, only to return again in the spring.[134] Nevertheless, from time to time, the government encouraged repatriation through free travel on Mexican railroads, exemption of custom duties on nonluxury goods, farm implements, or animals, and occasional offers of land.[135] These concessions were given in the belief, commonly professed by Mexican leaders, that emigrant families were learning useful agricultural and industrial skills while residing in the United States. This thinking, which conceived of the United States as a kind of "free technical training school" for temporarily displaced Mexicans, was described by Manuel Gamio in 1933.

During the last thirty years the United States has played the part of a giant university in which more than a million Mexicans, for the most part poor and unschooled, have gained a free practical education of great importance, consisting not of reading and writing but of learning to live on a higher scale. In food standards, they eat meat and milk; they have better furniture and clothing. They have learned to operate machinery and use modern tools. They have become acquainted with sports and hygienic practices. Returning to their homeland many of them have contributed a great deal to the progress the country has made in recent times.[136]

How much useful knowledge was actually acquired by migratory workers is open to question, let alone how much of their acquired knowledge or mannerisms survived when they returned to rustic villages in Mexico.[137] Yet this same rationale was again used by Mexican writers to justify the "temporary migration" of con-

133. *El Universal*, May 11, 1921, p. 1; September 2, 1921, p. 3. See also, Martínez, "Mexican Emigration to the United States," pp. 131–132.

134. Frequent complaints of abuses of repatriation aid are found in consular correspondence in the Archivo de la Secretaría de Relaciones Exteriores, files IV/350 to IV/560.

135. *Ibid.*; in these same consular files are many references to exemptions and subsidies for repatriates during the 1920's.

136. Manuel Gamio, "Migration and Planning," *Survey*, 66 (1933), 1.

137. See Gamio, *Mexican Immigration*; Taylor, *A Spanish-Mexican Peasant Community*; James Gilbert, "A Field Study in Mexico of the Mexican Repatriation Movement," (unpub. Master's diss., University of Southern California, 1934); and Carreras de Velasco, "La Repatriación de Mexicanos."

tract workers, and even "wetbacks," during the bracero program. In this respect, one American researcher has found that Mexico, which had reached an incipient stage of industrialization and agricultural planning by World War II, could then make better use of returning workers.[138] Meanwhile, the depression was at first regarded as an opportunity to retrieve Mexican emigrés. The Mexican government readily cooperated via its consuls with United States welfare agencies and Immigration Service in transporting unemployed Mexicans and their families to Mexico. But Mexico, still struggling with economic underdevelopment and a regressive agrarian structure, soon found that it could not begin to meet the expectations of some four hundred thousand repatriates who returned in the period 1930-1935. Most of these returnees, disillusioned, sought ways of returning to the United States.[139]

Under Cárdenas, 1934-1940, the Mexican government, which had accumulated its own feelings of disillusionment with so many *ingratos*, initiated a more cautious policy of "selective repatriation" tied in with major agrarian reforms.[140] Only those Mexicans in the United States who had actually acquired useful skills, or farming experience, or were willing to work hard, and had not been spoiled by relief agencies—as a consul in San Antonio put it—were to receive transportation aid and an opportunity to settle in a planned agrarian community with irrigation facilities.[141] In essence, the Cárdenas government followed a policy that an old repatriate described as "bringing the good ones home."[142] During the Cárdenas years possibly forty thousand or more Mexicans received repatriation aid.

138. Campbell, "Bracero Migration and the Mexican Economy," ch. vi, "The Impact of the Bracero Program."

139. See U.S. consular correspondence from Mexico for the 1930's in the National Archives, R.G. 59, 811.504/440 and 811.111/1188-1236.

140. Carreras de Velasco, "La Repatriación de Mexicanos."

141. On the mission of Ramon Beteta in 1919 to select agricultural repatriates see files in Archivo de la Secretaría de Relaciones Exteriores, IV/524.5(72:73)/1; IV-744-49; and Archivo General de la Nación, Ramo Cárdenas, exped. 503.11/3-1, Leg. 2, #05827; and exped. 503.11/3, Leg. 1.

142. Memorandum sobre repatriación, Rafael de la Colina, consul general in San Antonio, September 7, 1935, ASRE, B/525.5(73)/91. Quotation is from an interview with a repatriate in the colony "18 de Marzo" in the state of Tamaulipas, December 18, 1969.

After the depression and the decline of agrarian reform in the post-Cárdenas years no more missions were sent to the United States to recruit repatriates for agrarian colonies. On an individual basis the Mexican government still follows a selective repatriation policy, but the emphasis since World War II has been on industrial skills.[143]

During the past fifty or sixty years other purposes have been served by the rhetoric of discouragement and protectionism. A responsible government has expressed proper political and humanitarian concern about an unsolved national problem, and the problem, in turn, has become a powerful rationale for pushing economic and social development. For the leaders of the National Revolutionary Party that rules Mexico have not been content with efforts to discourage or protect emigration, they have also sought, since the growing political stability of the 1920's, to provide as far as possible a better livelihood for the laboring classes. Until World War II this effort mainly took the form of agrarian reform. Since then, however, the emphasis has been on social security programs and industrialization as the only long-range solutions to poverty and underdevelopment and the runaway population growth that clearly manifested itself in the 1940's.[144]

At present there is no vigorous official effort to discourage Mexicans of the unskilled labor or campesino class from emigrating. More than ever Mexico is blessed, or burdened, with a vast reservoir of unemployed or subemployed people in both urban and rural areas. Agrarian reform has run its course, and industrialization cannot absorb the population increase.[145] Massive illegal emigration is now tacitly regarded not only as a form of income compensation for the closing of the bracero program but as an outlet for a restive, potentially explosive labor force that could be ex-

143. Interview in Mexico City, July 15, 1971, with Eduardo Chávez, director of irrigation and colonization development in the lower Rio Grande Valley, 1936–1940.

144. For example, Manuel Germán Parra, *La Industrialización de México* (Mexico, 1954).

145. For hard and enduring facts of poverty, subemployment, and grossly uneven income distribution, see Hansen, *The Politics of Mexican Development*; González Casanova, *Democracy in Mexico*; Stavenhagen, *Neolatifundismo*; and Campbell, "Bracero Migration and the Mexican Economy."

ploited by leftist demagogues. In any event, the government cannot build a "Berlin wall" on the border.[146] One consideration here is the failure of the border industrialization program, started in 1965, to absorb the rapidly growing ranks of unemployed braceros.

Presently Mexican illegals working in the United States on a yearly or part-time basis are probably three times more numerous than bracero contract labor at its height in 1959, when 447,000 were legally admitted. In addition there are probably over one million Mexican family members illegally in the United States. As a matter of long-established policy the Mexican government is concerned with protecting all Mexican nationals in the United States, but obviously cannot do so if perhaps two million or more of them lack immigration documents or valid work contracts. High Mexican officials now see this as the number one problem in United States–Mexican relations.[147]

In the meantime, some government spokesmen still practice the rhetoric of discouragement, and they still feel obliged to say, as President Luís Echeverría has said on several occasions, that there is no need to migrate over the border since remunerative employment is now more available in Mexico than ever before. Yet the Echeverría administration, sensitive to rising concern about the unprecedented size of the present illegal exodus, and the explosive growth of Mexico's marginal population, has recently taken some

146. Interviews with Mexican migration officials, Ciudad Juarez, August 25, 1972; and questionnaire replies from Mexican officials, Oficina de Población y Departamento de Migración, prepared by Professor Romeo Flores, El Colegio de México, November 14, 1972.

The regulations of the General Population Law of Mexico (1962) state that a national leaving the country must meet all the requisites needed to enter the country of destination (Art. 84, I); and, "The necessary vigilance shall be established along the borders and sea coast to prevent clandestine emigration, for which purpose the federal and local authorities shall cooperate" (Art. 79, II). But Mexican migration officials say that since the suspension of the bracero contract program there is no serious effort to enforce vigilance against illegal emigration.

147. According to officials of the Mexican Consulate General, San Antonio, January 4, 1973; and the statements of Mario Moya Palencia, secretary of the interior (Gobernación), as reported in El Porvenir (Monterrey), June 13, 1973; and José Juan de Olloqui, Mexico's ambassador in Washington, Excelsior, September 1, 1973.

significant steps that may affect future transborder migration. Through Mexican initiative both governments established in the fall of 1972 high-level committees to study and exchange views on what can be done to control illegal emigration to the United States. Renewal of the bracero program was one of the most important points under consideration.[148] Another step was taken in January 1973 when, for the first time, the Mexican government inaugurated a national campaign to promote and implement fertility control through the public health service. Furthermore, the government has undertaken a campaign to punish unauthorized labor contractors (*enganchadores*) on the Mexican side, as well as persons engaged in smuggling Mexican, Latin American, or other nationals into the United States or Mexico. Provisions for demographic planning and smuggler control appear in a new population law which went into effect on February 6, 1974.[149]

That the present Mexican government has not neglected, in the interim, the Mexican colonies in the United States is indicated by President Echeverría's visit of "renewal" in June 1972 and his vigorous sponsorship of the traditional programs of *Mexicanidad* and selective repatriation. Like the Cárdenas government, the Echeverría administration has expanded cultural missions in American cities where there are major concentrations of Mexican-origin peoples, cities such as San Antonio, Los Angeles, and Chicago. Meanwhile, through "La Hora Nacional," a radio program that for years has been sponsored by the Secretariat of Foreign Relations, the mother country reminds Mexicans and the children of Mexicans "on the other side" that they have not been forgotten.

148. According to conversations with the minister of the Mexican Embassy, Washington, January 6, 1973; and with three members of the United States study group appointed by the President to report on the illegal migration problem, Washington, January 5–7, 1973.

149. *Tiempo*, Seminario de la Vida y la Verdad (Mexico City), February 12, 1973, pp. 19–28; and interviews with public health personnel (Seguro Social), Monterrey, Mexico, January 2, 1973. Aside from establishing the basis for national population planning the new population law in Article 118 provides for a penalty of two to ten years in prison and a fine of 10,000 to 50,000 pesos for unauthorized labor contracting and alien smuggling. See *Diario Nacional* (Mexico City), January 7, 1974, and February 6, 1974. It remains to be seen, of course, whether or not the provisions of the law can be carried out consistently.

## v. United States Attitude toward Mexican
## Transborder Migration

THERE are some officials of the United States government, particularly in the consular service, who maintain that the federal government has no special immigration policy toward Mexico, that there is no law, nor body of laws, that specifically defines such a policy, and that if there is such a policy it would be contained in the traditional Pan-American or western hemisphere preferences of the United States, such as good neighbor reciprocity, which would be essentially the same for Canada and other Latin American republics.[150] Obviously, this is not a fully satisfactory answer to anyone seeking to explain the special relationships between certain federal agencies and border migration and this migration and immigration-law enforcement. It is the purpose of this section to suggest that there is indeed a special United States policy toward Mexican migration, but that it is to be found not so much in the principles of immigration law or Pan-Americanism *per se* as in a series of *ad hoc* exemptions and administrative adjustments to those principles—exemptions that have in a cumulative fashion over the years served not merely to stimulate Mexican transborder crossings but to give Mexican immigration the *de facto* status of the most-favored nation.

Virtually none of the restrictionist principles contained in federal immigration acts from 1875 through 1924, nor the civic concern behind them, were aimed specifically at transborder migration from Canada and Mexico. Until World War I, if we except some efforts to check clandestine European and Oriental immigration by way of Mexico and Canada, there is scarcely any evidence of federal concern over unskilled native labor moving in from contiguous countries without inspection, in spite of the prohibitions against alien contract labor contained in the act of 1885.[151]

150. Interviews with officials of the U.S. Consulate, Ciudad Juárez, August 24, 1972, and Visa Office, Department of State, January 5, 1973.

151. Based on examination of the *Annual Reports of the Commissioner General of Immigration to the Secretary of Labor*, 1895–1917; congressional hearings; and U.S. Immigration Commission, *Reports of the Immigration Commission*, 42 vols. (Washington, 1911).

Furthermore, there is little or no published evidence that the Mexican Revolution which erupted in 1910 had any influence on the qualitative restrictions codified in the law of 1917, nor on the quota system first established, in principle, by the law of May 19, 1921. On the contrary, it was during the Mexican upheaval that the federal government first applied to transborder migration its *ad hoc* policy of exemptions as thousands of panic-driven refugees crowded against the gateways to border cities. Following the advice of the State Department, and with the approval of the secretary of labor who was then responsible for immigration affairs at the cabinet level, United States immigration officials quietly dropped qualitative restrictions or gave them such a flexible interpretation that they were, in effect, suspended.[152]

Border immigration authorities were also inclined to be permissive because North American missionaries and social workers, who saw forced Mexican migration as an evangelical opportunity, were more than willing to give temporary aid to indigent refugees, thus obviating to some extent the need to apply the "likely to become a public charge" restriction of immigration law.[153] Similarly, immigrant-aid societies adopted the Mexican as a plausible substitute for the masses of Europe cut off by the immigration act of 1917.[154]

Before the end of the 1920's another type of exemption, the border commuter, a special status that has deep roots in land-border customs, was established in American immigration policy. Years before the general immigration act of 1917 several thousand Mexican and Canadian nationals were daily commuting across the border to work without a passport or immigration document. The Department of Labor in 1927 classified the commuter as an "immigrant" and provided that future applications for commuter-immigrant status would have to follow standard immigration proce-

152. Thousands of refugees were paroled, it was believed, temporarily, into the border states. *Annual Report of the Commissioner General of Immigration, 1912*, pp. 224–225.

153. For the evangelical viewpoint see Robert J. Lipshultz, "American Attitudes toward Mexican Immigration, 1924–1952" (unpub. Master's diss., University of Chicago, 1962); and Vernon McCombs, *From Over the Border: A Study of the Mexican in the United States* (New York, 1926).

154. McWilliams, *North from Mexico*, pp. 206–207.

dures. It seemed to the federal government that this arrangement was somehow in harmony with nonquota exemptions for Pan-American countries and with the need for reciprocal border relations, as well as the need to prevent job dislocations or personal hardships.[155]

Commuters, in the broadest sense, are today a fluctuating group in Mexican border towns. Most are nonresident aliens who work in the United States, but some are United States citizens of Mexican origin living in Mexico. At a given time probably half of all Mexican commuters, so-called, cross the line to work at permanent, seasonal, or part-time jobs. Presently Mexicans holding legal commuter documents—"greencards"—number about forty-five thousand, and Canadians about eighty-five hundred. Greencarders are eligible to move to the United States as permanent resident aliens.[156] The special character of this border migration policy has, in fact, been aptly described in a 1954 decision of the Board of Immigration Appeals as a form of good neighbor favoritism: "The commuter situation manifestly does not fit into any precise category found in immigrant statutes. The status is an artificial one, predicated upon international relations maintained and cherished between friendly neighbors."[157]

The commuter "greencard" as used on the Mexican border serves as a license to hunt for a permanent job. Once secured, such a job can give the commuter and his immediate relatives the incentive and the means to immigrate permanently. Over the years thousands of commuter-immigrants have moved into the United States from Mexico and their place has been taken by new commuters. An American consular officer of Irish extraction made this pointed remark about the border commuter: "He would not exist

155. Karnuth *v.* Albro, 279 U.S. 231, 1929, cited in U.S. Senate, *Hearings . . . Committee on Labor and Public Welfare, Migrant and Seasonal Labor Powerlessness*, 91 Cong., 1 and 2 Sess. (1970), 2017.

156. *Ibid.*, pp. 2016–2018.

157. *Ibid.*, p. 2020. The U.S. Court of Appeals for the District of Columbia in a recent opinion again has maintained the legality of the daily border commuter but denied the legality of the seasonal commuter, a post-1964 phenomenon, in Robert Bustos *et al.*, United Farm Organizing Committee, Appellant *v.* John Mitchell, Attorney General of the United States, *et al.*, No. 72–1178, April 16, 1973.

if the border area involved was the Atlantic Ocean which effectively prevented my own ancestors from becoming 'commuters.' "[158]

Another facet of border reciprocity that has facilitated migration from Mexico since the general act of 1917 is the issuance in good faith of permanent visiting cards to presumed residents of Mexican and Canadian border towns. Through the years these cards, now issued as form I-186, have served to admit countless thousands of Mexican workers and settlers, under the guise of shoppers and visitors, into the United States, where they simply disappear into Mexican-American communities.[159] Many obtain false birth certificates and if undetected, they have, in fact, "immigrated." Since the visa requirements first established in 1924 many applicants denied commuter or immigrant status by United States consular officers in Mexico have discovered that the smart way to cross "without getting one's feet wet" is to move to a Mexican border city and obtain a visitor's card under the border reciprocity policy. For a small fee Mexican border officials have always been ready to vouch for the long-time residence of the applicant and to issue the needed identity documents for obtaining the border-crossing card.[160]

Another instance of the relaxation of immigration controls or standards toward border peoples is the admission of temporary labor in times of national emergency. An early but instructive example of this policy is the period of "departmental exceptions." As a reaction to the labor shortage of World War I the secretary of labor authorized immigration officials to exempt illiterate temporary laborers from the restrictionist clauses and head tax pro-

158. Statement of John Killea, U.S. consul general, Tijuana, February 9, 1968, in U.S. Congress, Select Commission, *Hearings before the Select Commission on Western Hemisphere Immigration* (Washington, 1968), II, 16.

159. Before 1969 one could travel 150 miles inland with a border-crossing card, which, in effect, permitted many holders to live and work in such cities as Los Angeles and San Antonio. After 1969 this card was limited to 25 miles. See David S. North, *The Border Crossers, People Who Live in Mexico and Work in the United States* (Washington, 1970), pp. 134–135; Lamar B. Jones, "Alien Commuters in the United States Labor Markets," *International Migration Review*, 4 (1970), 65–86; and testimony of George K. Rosenberg, District Director, INS, Los Angeles, in *Hearings before the Select Commission*, II, 13.

160. Interviews with U.S. immigration officers along the Mexican border, June–August 1970, and August 1972.

visions of the 1917 law.[161] These exceptions, which ran from May 23, 1917, to March 2, 1921, are significant as the first time the federal government practiced its *ad hoc* policy of regarding neighboring nonquota countries like Canada, overpopulated islands like Jamaica, Bahamas, Haiti, the free state of Puerto Rico, but above all Mexico, as handy pools of emergency labor to be turned on and off according to national needs.

One might have thought that the Alien Contract Labor Act of 1885 had prohibited once and for all the importation of unskilled alien workers, but the 1917 act contained an emergency clause known as the Ninth Proviso which authorized the commissioner of immigration to admit temporary contract labor on approval by the secretary of labor.[162] This proviso was not intended to favor the use of Mexican labor. Mexican labor was simply the most available.

In the fundamental recasting of American immigration policy in the 1920's, Mexico and other western hemisphere countries were exempted from the quota system despite the common knowledge that Mexican immigrants by the tens of thousands were being sponsored by southwestern employers seeking to import low-cost labor. Of greater concern to certain congressional leaders was the rising current of Mexican settlers coming in illegally as "wetbacks" without meeting any of the inspection standards embodied in immigration law.[163] Senator Frank B. Willis of Ohio, one of the sponsors of a Mexican quota and an outspoken opponent of special exemptions for transborder laborers, pointed out in the quota de-

161. U.S. Committee on Public Information, *Official U.S. Bulletin*, 2 (June 24, 1918), 10–12.

162. See U.S. House, Committee on Immigration and Naturalization, *Admission of Mexican and Other Alien Laborers into Texas and Other States, Hearings . . .* , 66 Cong., 2 Sess. (1920), 3–7, for the statement of John C. Box questioning the legality of their admission. Authority under the Ninth Proviso is explained by Grebler, *Mexican Immigration to the United States*, D-13, D-14.

163. Otey M. Scruggs, "The First Mexican Farm Labor Program, 1917–1921," *Arizona and the West*, 2 (1960), 319–326; and 71 Cong., 2 Sess., *Congressional Record*, 7115. See also statement by James J. Davis, secretary of labor, made on April 15, 1924, in *Mexicans in California. Report to Governor C. C. Young's Fact-Finding Committee* (San Francisco, 1930), p. 18.

bate of 1924 that unrestricted backdoor migration was a ridiculous contradiction.

The senate yesterday very definitely adopted the policy of restricted selected immigration. . . . Now what does it amount to if we shut and padlock the front door . . . yet leave the back door open?

Mr. President, upon what theory shall it be said that applied to Englishmen, for example, only two per cent on the basis of the census of 1890 can come in, and yet as to Mexicans . . . practically without education and largely without experience in self-government, and in most cases not at all qualified for present citizenship or for assimilation . . . say in effect, "As many as you please . . ."?[164]

A decisive factor that worked against quotas for New World countries was the administration's concern with safeguarding special relations with Pan-American governments, but particularly Mexico and Canada. At the time the federal government was deeply concerned about the sensitive state of United States relations with revolutionary Mexico, where North American investments in oil, mining, and ranching were threatened with expropriation. In the 1920's nearly all American foreign investments were concentrated in Mexico, Canada, and Cuba.[165]

Pan-American considerations are exemplified by Senator David A. Reed of Pennsylvania, who spoke in the quota debate of 1924 as one deeply concerned about excluding illiterate and unskilled immigrants yet unwilling to offend Mexico, or any part of Latin America, chiefly because this might adversely affect United States commercial expansion under the aegis of Pan-Americanism and the Monroe Doctrine.

If we want to hold them to us—and I think we do so long as we maintain the Monroe Doctrine—we have to treat them differently from the rest of the world, and we ought to treat them differently in the measure now pending,

---

164. 68 Cong., 1 Sess., *Congressional Record* (1924), 6621.
165. Joe W. Neal's pioneer study presents a full coverage of the arguments, pro and con, and the reasons for the defeat of the Mexican quota movement, "The Policy of the United States toward Immigration from Mexico" (unpub. Master's diss., University of Texas, 1941), pp. 108–121; another relevant work is Lipshultz, "American Attitudes toward Mexican Immigration."

because there is no occasion for singling them out and slapping a quota down upon them.[166]

Such sentiments, no matter how naive, had the effect of placing Mexican transborder migration (and Canadian) under the protective umbrella of Pan-American rhetoric where it remained.

Another consideration that influenced those legislators not familiar with the Southwest was the fervid affirmation by spokesmen for employer interests that Mexican laborers were not really immigrants at all but merely migrant workers, who returned to the mother country at the end of the harvest season.[167] This explanation, especially fostered by Texas employers like John Nance Garner, was partly true for seasonal farm and ranch labor along the Rio Grande frontier, but it is not supported by census data.[168]

It was hoped by the administration that higher fees and visa controls established by the act of 1924, and a modern Border Patrol, also established in 1924, would sharply curtail Mexican migration, both legal and illegal. These expectations were unfulfilled. In 1926 Representative John C. Box of Texas introduced a bill, not merely an amendment, specifically designed to place Mexico and other western hemisphere countries under a quota. Box, who believed that legal and illegal migration from Mexico made a farce of the quota system, provided the rationale for the measure when he attacked the migratory labor system.

These gentlemen have their eyes on the floating Mexican peons . . . sometimes stolen and carried away by the carloads in the night. They are to be imported in trainloads and delivered to farmers who have contracted to grow beets for the sugar companies . . . and to do menial work. . . . People of that type, whatever their nationality, are not desirable as immigrants.[169]

From 1926 until the full onset of the depression in 1931 Congress debated the Box Bill and compromise proposals such as the

166. 68 Cong., 1 Sess., *Congressional Record*, 6623.

167. U.S. House, Committee on Immigration and Naturalization, *Temporary Admission of Illiterate Mexican Laborers, Hearings . . .* , 66 Cong., 2 Sess. (1920), 3–19.

168. *Mexicans in California, Report*, pp. 17–39.

169. U. S. House, Committee on Immigration, *Seasonal Agricultural Laborers from Mexico, Hearings . . .* , 69 Cong., 1 Sess. (1926), 325. See also Neal, "The Policy of the United States," p. 146.

Johnson and Harris Bills, presented in 1930, which would have placed low quotas on Mexico and other Latin American countries, but would have allowed a higher quota for Canada (which was a way station for many European immigrants).[170]

The State Department, acutely aware of official Mexican resentment at the quota movement and fearful of possible retaliations against United States investments, sought desperately to devise an alternative method of immigration control less offensive to Mexican nationalists. Again, the preferred expedient was a special administrative control policy reflecting the State Department's position, shared by a number of knowledgeable men in Congress, that enforcement of the immigration standards of 1917 could reduce legal immigration from Mexico radically without recourse to a quota. It was not the responsibility of the Immigration Service, according to the immigration act of 1924, but of the State Department to enforce visa standards, and according to a department memorandum of 1928 a comparative study revealed the embarrassing fact that visa standards were decidedly lower in the United States consular offices in Mexico than in Europe.[171]

Tighter administrative controls were followed by a sudden drop in legal Mexican immigration from 40,154 in 1929 to 12,703 in 1930, and to a mere trickle of 3,333 in 1931; but the depression was simultaneously paralyzing the national economy. Yet the State Department by presenting such figures to Congress struck a decisive blow against the Mexican quota movement[172] and established a visa-control policy that at least sharply reduced the legal migration of unskilled laborers.

Meanwhile, during the quota debate Congress passed a law which promised to establish better immigration control. The act of March 4, 1929 for the first time made illegal entry by an individual a misdemeanor punishable by imprisonment for not more than one

---

170. Robert A. Divine, *American Immigration Policy, 1924–1952* (New Haven, 1957), ch. iii.

171. Memorandum is reprinted in 71 Cong., 2 Sess., *Congressional Record* (1930), 7114–7116. See also Consul Thomas McEnelly, "Confidential Memorandum. Immigration Work in Mexico," November 9, 1928, National Archives, R.G. 59, 811.111/113 1/2.

172. *Annual Report of the Commissioner General of Immigration 1931*, pp. 15–16.

year, and a fine of not more than one thousand dollars, or both.[173] The 1917 act, which had not contemplated overland migration, had made illegal entry a misdemeanor but only for carriers or smugglers who brought in illegal aliens. The penalties provided by the 1917 act did not apply to individuals who entered the country by their own efforts, such as Europeans, Orientals, and wetbacks who walked over Mexican and Canadian borders.

The penalties of the 1929 act have never been applied to the great mass of Mexican illegals not merely because Mexican nationals easily become "invisible" in previously established Spanish-speaking colonies, but because by that date an administrative expedient called "voluntary departures" was almost uniformly being applied to illegal aliens from contiguous countries. Since the general immigration act of 1917 it has been an established practice to exempt Mexican illegals from the penalty of formal deportation. As in other immigration matters this policy was not originally designed to favor Mexican illegals, nor American employers of wetback labor, for the privilege of voluntary departure has always been available to any noncriminal alien agreeing to pay his or her transportation back to the country of origin.[174] The significance of the voluntary departure policy for the Mexican border can hardly be overemphasized for it is one of the more remarkable examples of *ad hoc* exemptions from the regular procedures and penalties established by immigration laws.

There are several reasons underlying the development of this lenient policy. Until the act of March 4, 1929, the penalties for illegal entry by an individual were not clearly established in law; and aliens seeking to enter the United States illegally but in search of more remunerative employment or to join relatives have never been considered guilty of criminal intent by United States judges or immi-

173. Act of March 2, 1929, in U.S. Department of Labor, Bureau of Naturalization, *Naturalization, Citizenship and Expatriation Laws July 1, 1929* (Washington, 1929), pp. 35–39; and Act of March 4, 1929 in *U.S. Statutes at Large*, XLV, pt. 1 (1927–1929), 1551–1552.

174. Interviews with U.S. immigration officials, Central Office, INS, December 10, 1970, and December 8, 1971.

gration officials.[175] Moreover, aliens from contiguous countries were hardly considered a deportation problem. Since even the poorest Mexican (or Canadian) could walk back to his country of origin he was as a matter of course encouraged to do so.[176] Later, during the bracero period, 1942–1964, and after, the voluntary departure practice would be expanded to include shipping wetbacks to the interior of Mexico at American expense, but without penalty to the "deportee." Another reason for this enforcement practice is that after the 1917 act Congress failed to provide the Immigration Service with sufficient detention facilities for formal deportations, or funds to return every illegal entrant to the country of origin. In many cases for lack of funds the illegal entrant was not even escorted to a port city or the border but was released on his own recognizance to make his or her way, supposedly, back to the country of origin. This practice is still commonly used today. In other cases, as on the Mexican border, it has always been a common custom since 1917 to "shoo wetbacks" across the border.[177]

In the contract labor era that followed, 1942–1964, there are other illustrations of *ad hoc* decisions. The federal government would again tap the Mexican surplus labor reservoir but this time, or so it was believed, there would be adequate supervisory controls over recruiting and return of temporary laborers. Both the United States and Mexican governments thought that they had learned a lesson from the exemption period of 1917–1921. This time not employers but Mexican and American officials would supervise the programs, and now there would be a well-developed and mechanized Border Patrol to enforce control.[178] The authorization for the contract labor program was again found in the emergency labor proviso of the 1917 act, and later in the H-2 nonimmigrant

175. *Ibid.*
176. Interviews with Border Patrol officers, active and retired, in California, Arizona, and Texas, April–August 1970; and U.S. Senate, *Report of the Committee on the Judiciary* . . . , *The Immigration and Naturalization Systems of the United States*, 80 Cong., 1 Sess. (1950), 634.
177. Interviews with Border Patrol officers, in California, Arizona, and Texas, April–August 1970.
178. According to correspondence between United States and Mexican officials for 1942–1943, in R.G. 59, file 811.504/Mexico.

category established in the current Immigration and Nationality Act of 1952.

As it turned out, the bracero program, more so than the revolutionary violence in Mexico, 1910–1920, or the special exemptions of 1917–1921, became a great catalyst for Mexican migration, legal and illegal. As a spokesman for the National Agricultural Workers Union expressed it in 1952:

Agreements with the Republic of Mexico for the legal entry of 45,000 to 200,000 contract workers each year since 1942 . . . acted as a magnet drawing hundreds of thousands to the border from deep in the interior of Mexico. When the Mexican worker arrives at the border and finds that he cannot be accepted as a legal contract worker . . . it is a relatively easy matter to cross the 1,600 miles of practically unguarded boundary. Once in the United States there are always employers who will hire them at wages so low that few native Americans will accept. Thus legal importation of Mexicans has created the vicious situation now prevailing.[179]

Here Mexico's insistence that braceros be protected by labor standards that were actually better than those American farm laborers enjoyed and, for that matter, far better than labor standards in rural Mexico, had an unfortunate backfire effect. Employers simply preferred free-lance wetbacks.[180] There followed certain administrative exemptions that made a parody of immigration laws and solemn international agreements. At Mexico's request thousands of wetbacks already in the United States and at work were "dried out" or legalized as contract labor. During the three years 1947–1949, when this practice was most prevalent, only 74,600 braceros were contracted in Mexico whereas 142,000 wetbacks already in the United States were put under legal contract.[181] To save appearances a charade was worked out whereby wetbacks were brought to the border and "deported" by momentarily stepping over the boundary line. The "dried out" wetback was then "paroled" to an employer as a legitimate contract worker.[182] In other cases braceros and wetbacks were "immigrated" by their

179. President's Commission on Immigration, *Hearings* (Washington, 1952), pp. 41–42.
180. See Galarza, *Merchants of Labor*; and Samora, *Los Mojados*.
181. *President's Commission on Migratory Labor* (1951), pp. 40, 52–53.
182. *Ibid.*; Samora, *Los Mojados*, pp. 46–48; Galarza, *Merchants of Labor*, pp. 63–64.

employers to meet an alleged shortage of unskilled or semiskilled labor in agriculture.

Meanwhile, so many citizen groups were protesting the "wetback invasion" and new forms of wage-peonage, vagrancy, child labor, and displacement of native labor that Congress was forced to take special action. Public Law No. 283, signed by President Truman on March 20, 1952, made it not a mere misdemeanor but a felonious offense to recruit, transport, conceal, or harbor illegal aliens.[183] This law was apparently the first designed expressly for the purpose of controlling illegal Mexican migration. It also tightened border control by authorizing immigration officers to enter suspected premises within twenty-five miles of the border without a search warrant.

The foregoing law, which ended a remarkable period of congressional laxity, helped to close one loophole, but it left another wide open. No penalty was provided for the employment of illegal aliens, and it was clearly understood that providing illegal laborers and their families with living quarters and other such employment facilities was not to be considered "harboring illegal aliens." An employer could be subject to prosecution only if he were caught wet-handed in the act of assisting illegal aliens to enter the country. Since the vast majority of illegals make their own way to places of employment, or are brought in by Spanish-speaking contractors and crew leaders, the employer was virtually exempted from any responsibility for upholding immigration laws. This exemption was appropriately called the "Texas proviso," for it was a concession to powerful agricultural interests in the southwestern states, but especially those in Texas, who had influential spokesmen in Congress.[184]

The wetback invasion also influenced the penalty provisions of the Immigration and Nationality Act of 1952. This law reaffirmed in section 275 that illegal entry is a criminal offense and then reaffirmed the law of March 4, 1929, by making the second and sub-

183. U.S. Statutes at Large, LXVI (1952), 26.

184. Information provided by office of general counsel, Central Office, INS, December 8, 1970.

sequent offenses not a misdemeanor but a felony punishable by imprisonment up to two years, or a fine of not more than one thousand dollars, or both.[185] However, this penalty against "wetback repeaters," as well as Public Law 282 against alien smugglers, would both be interpreted with remarkable leniency by United States District Court judges. Rarely would a wetback repeater be imprisoned or fined for a first, second, or even third offense. This same leniency applied to alien smugglers who were rarely prosecuted for a first offense.[186] Nevertheless, such legislation marked a step forward in congressional concern for stopping illegal migration.

In 1954, a new commissioner of immigration, Joseph M. Swing, with the full support of the Eisenhower administration, launched a massive deportation drive. More than a million men, women, and children were given speedy "voluntary departures" under "Operation Wetback."[187] This roundup, and Swing's stern and efficient policy of enforcement along the border, ended a long era of easy access by American employers to illegal rustic labor and forced most of them to use legal braceros. By 1964, the year the bracero program ended, the number of wetback apprehensions had dropped to fewer than forty-five thousand. Since then, however, the number of Mexican illegals apprehended each year has steadily risen to a point where immigration officials now speak of an invasion of "new-style wetbacks."

In the meantime, legal immigration from Mexico has been favored by new directions in immigration laws that seek to liberalize requirements for admission of certain immigrant groups. The Immigration and Nationality Act of June 27, 1952, which replaced the general act of 1917, retained basic restrictionist principles and a modified quota system, but it also contained three important pol-

185. U.S. Statutes at Large, LXVI, 229; 8 U.S. Code § 1325 (1952), text in U.S. Statutes at Large, LXVI, 229–230.

186. Interviews with immigration officers and apprehended aliens in border region, April–August 1970, and August 1972.

187. INS, Annual Report 1954; ibid., 1955; and "Report of the American Section of Joint Commission on Mexican Migrant Labor," submitted by Joseph M. Swing, commissioner, INS, September 3, 1954 (mimeographed).

icy changes that have served to favor immigration from underdeveloped countries like Mexico. First, Congress sought in this law to allow a greater representation of non-Nordic immigration and to eliminate "Oriental exclusions." Second, Latin America was again exempted from quotas because of a "traditional Pan-American policy," and because it was believed that nonquota status, like foreign aid, would help to keep Latin American governments aligned with the United States against communist powers. Third, and most important, the law inaugurated the present era of giving preference to relatives of United States citizens and resident aliens.[188] Mexican laborers who immigrated to the United States after World War II found it easier to bring in family members.

Liberalization in national immigration policy was reaffirmed and radically expanded in the act of October 3, 1965. This law, mainly because of foreign policy considerations, abolished the historic quota system in favor of hemispheric visa allotments intended to favor no special nation but rather to favor the admission of any qualified immigrant and the uniting of families. Under this system, in force since July 1, 1968, the eastern hemisphere was given a ceiling of 170,000 and the western hemisphere countries a ceiling of 120,000. But no ceiling was placed on the number of immediate relatives joining kinfolk in the United States, and immigration from western hemisphere countries was established on a first-come, first-served basis with no maximum per country.[189]

The full consequences of the 1965 amendments were apparently not foreseen by federal legislators. Placing immediate relatives in the no-limit category quite unintentionally favored those poverty-stricken countries where kinship migration is most common, such as Jamaica, Haiti, the Philippines, Hong Kong, Taiwan, but most of all

188. Divine, *American Immigration Policy*, pp. 175–176; and Frank Auerbach, *Immigration Laws of the United States*, 2d ed. (Indianapolis, 1961), pp. 14–17. Immigration policy and precedents that helped shape the law of 1952 are presented in U. S. Senate, *Report of the Committee on the Judiciary . . . , The Immigration and Naturalization Systems of the United States*. See also compendium by Charles Gordon and Harry N. Rosenfield, *Immigration Law and Procedure* (Albany, 1959), with looseleaf supplement.

189. Immigration law and policy is discussed by several congressmen, the commissioner of immigration, and other specialists, in "U.S. Immigration, 1970: Policies, Procedures, Problems," special issue of *The International Migration Review*, 4 (Spring 1970).

Mexico because there were already several million Mexican-Americans and Mexican immigrants in the United States living in close border proximity with the mother country. These groups have strong cultural and extended-family obligations to send for relatives. Moreover, all along the border region it is common for Mexican-Americans and resident aliens to marry Mexican nationals and bring them in as immediate relatives. In addition, the great backlog of prior visa applications gave immigration from that country an obvious advantage on a first-come, first-served basis.[190]

In fiscal 1972, for example, over sixty-four thousand legal immigrants entered from Mexico. This was over fifteen percent of the total immigration from all countries, and over thirty percent of the total admitted from the western hemisphere. In addition, it is probable that since 1970 over one hundred thousand Mexican illegals, not counting "perennial repatriates," have been permanently settling each year in the United States.[191]

The radical shift in national origins of immigrants to the United States in recent fiscal years, not counting illegals, may be illustrated by the comparisons in Table VI. These figures would differ if "country of last permanent residence" were the criterion. For example, the Canadian figure for 1961–1970 would rise to 413,310, and for fiscal 1972 to 18,776. These increases would represent reimmigrated Europeans for the most part. Nevertheless, it is a notable fact that since 1956 immigration from Canada has tended increasingly to lag behind immigration from Mexico. One reason is that a much higher percentage of Canadian applicants, many originally from Europe, seek to immigrate as individuals and are thus subject to rigid labor certifications, especially since 1965.[192] In 1972, 43,358 persons with no occupation reported immigrated from Mexico. The comparable figure for Canada was 7,274.[193]

190. Interviews with U.S. immigration officers, U.S. Embassy, Mexico City, August 14, 15, 18, 1970; and with U.S. consul, Ciudad Juárez, August 25, 1972.
191. This conjecture is based on a broad range of tours and interviews since April 1970 to the present, and on the rough calculation that probably twenty-five percent to fifty percent of illegal settlers from Mexico escape detection.
192. William G. Hartley, "United States Immigration Policy: The Case of the Western Hemisphere," World Affairs, 135 (Summer 1972), 67.
193. INS, Annual Report, 1972, Table 8.

Table VI

LEGAL IMMIGRATION FROM SELECTED COUNTRIES
*according to country of birth*

|  | 1961–1970 | 1972 |
|---|---|---|
| Mexico | 443,301 | 64,040 |
| Canada | 286,667 | 10,776 |
| West Indies (less Cuba) | 262,730 | 41,327 |
| Cuba (excludes parolees) | 256,769 | 20,045 |
| British Isles | 230,452 | 10,078 |
| Italy | 206,650 | 21,427 |
| Germany | 199,980 | 6,848 |
| China and Hong Kong (1962–1971) | 136,065 | 21,730 |
| Philippines (1962–1971) | 127,298 | 29,376 |
| Poland | 73,286 | 4,784 |
| France | 34,300 | 1,966 |
| Ireland | 42,395 | 1,780 |

SOURCES: Figures provided by the office of general counsel, INS, July 23, 1973. See also INS, *Annual Reports*, Table 14.

Immigration from Mexico is encouraged in other ways. If an alien—any alien—can just manage to cross the border and successfully join kinfolk or find a potentially permanent job then it seems that he has liberalized immigration law and social-rescue agencies pulling for him. In the parlance of immigration lawyers and counselors this type of illegal is considered to be "building up equity." The Immigration Service in fact has a special Mexican Equity Visa program (MEV) which gives *de facto* priority to "hardship cases," many of which arise from illegal entry. With help from such organizations as the International Institute of Los Angeles and the Legal Aid Society of Denver several hundred Mexican illegals are legitimatized each year.[194] The number is not large in itself but since the equity system is from one point of view a reward for taking a shortcut to the United States it serves to encourage more illegal aliens to seek out jobs and kinfolk in the United States. Moreover, the equity system raises many false and

194. *Illegal Aliens, Hearings*, pt. 1, pp. 227–230.

costly hopes which are exploited by a whole species of immigrant counselors and shyster lawyers in Mexico and in Mexican-American communities. Little wonder that Chicano militants are today demanding blanket validation for Mexicans who feel they have some equity.

The huge dimension of migration, legal and illegal, from Mexico, compared with that of traditional migration currents from the British Isles and Europe, has recently become a matter of some concern to the federal government. Undermanned federal agencies have sought to plug the holes in the Mexican border sieve. The Immigration and Customs Services have imposed closer checks on commuter-aliens, border-crossers, tourists, and anyone from Mexico seeking to enter the United States. The Border Patrol has improved its detection methods and increased the number of apprehensions in a dramatic manner since 1969. In the past three years more "repeaters" have been denied voluntary departures and held over for prosecution. Under a new magistrate system that speeds up hearings more immigration-law violaters have been receiving sentences. Also, judges in the past three years have been handing out somewhat stiffer sentences to alien smugglers. In September 1972 the chief executives of Mexico and the United States appointed special, high-level study groups to explore ways to obtain binational cooperation in control of transborder migration and to consider the revival of a modified bracero program as a possible control measure.[195] Thus far, however, nothing seems to be an effective deterrent against smuggler organizations, fraudulent documents, kinship migration, and new-style wetbacks who now head for cities and nonagricultural jobs.

Exhaustive hearings on illegal aliens held in 1971–1972 by Congressman Peter W. Rodino, Jr., and others have made quite clear the historic need for a law holding employers responsible. Several bills were introduced in Congress that would revive Senator Paul Douglas' proposal of 1951–1952 and the recommendations of the President's Commission on Migratory Labor of 1951, and carry

195. See note 148; and *El Porvenir*, June 13, 1973.

forward the intent of a California law of 1971 ruled unconstitutional by the courts, to make it a felony, or at least a misdemeanor, knowingly to employ illegal aliens. The "Rodino Bill"—an omnibus bill—would provide a fine of five hundred dollars for each illegal alien employed, and would authorize the confiscation of smugglers' vehicles. This bill (H.R. 982), which passed the House by a large majority on May 3, 1973, is now before the Senate. Meanwhile, it has been causing consternation among employers and Chicano militants.[196]

At present there are other proposals to resolve the inequities, real or imagined, of Mexican migration. On the one hand, organizations of Chicano militants, who claim to be the original settlers of the Southwest, have presented demands that range from an "open border," through "blanket legalization" for all Mexican illegal aliens presently in the United States, to special preferences for Mexican immigrants.[197] On the other hand, there are a series of congressional proposals that seek to limit yet favor legal immigration from contiguous countries. House Resolution 2328, the so-called "Administration Bill" introduced on January 26, 1971, would remove Canada and Mexico from the western hemisphere allotment and give each a separate ceiling of thirty-five thousand annually for all categories of immigrants, including immediate relatives. All other countries would be limited to the same twenty thousand ceiling provided by the law of 1965.[198] In a companion bill, H.R. 981, introduced in 1973, Rodino, the chairman of the House Judiciary Committee, proposed just such an arrangement. The reasoning here seems to be that close neighbors deserve preference. And yet so far as the principles of immigration policy are concerned this thinking seems to reduce Pan-American favoritism to contiguous countries only. That most congressmen object to

196. Letter from legal counsel, Southwest Regional Office, INS, June 1, 1973; and "Racismo Legalizado? Proyecto de Ley Rodino," *La Raza,* I, 11 (1973), 20–23.
197. Chicano attitudes are expressed, for example, in *Bert Corona Speaks on La Raza and the 'Illegal Alien' Scare,* pamphlet (New York, 1972); and in the magazine *La Raza.*
198. Donald G. Hohl and Michael G. Wenk, "Current U. S. Immigration Legislation: Analysis and Comment," *International Migration,* X, 3 (1972), 91–94. This article appeared originally in the *International Migration Review,* 5 (1971), 339–356.

spelling out a "special relationship" for Mexico and Canada in United States immigration law, such as the British Isles once enjoyed under quota preferences, seems abundantly clear in the amendments to H.R. 981 made by a large majority of the House. Among other things a twenty thousand limit was placed on all countries including Mexico and Canada, but this limit would not apply to immediate relatives who presently constitute about forty percent of Mexican immigrants. In other words, had amended H.R. 981 been in force in fiscal 1973 Mexican immigration would have included 26,650 immediate relatives plus 20,000 others, for a total nearly twice as high as the next largest immigrant group.[199]

Thus the status of "immediate relative" is still an open door that particularly favors Mexican kinfolk seeking to join relatives over the border. Immigration authorities, who generally favor a fixed ceiling for Mexico, now fear that otherwise there would be a sharp rise in fraudulent marriages, birth certificates, and naturalization papers. In the meantime, H.R. 981 faces long debates in the Senate where it remains to be seen to what extent United States immigration policy will continue to make Mexico, in *de facto* fashion, the most-favored nation.

199. For recent accounts of immigration legislation in Congress see: David S. North, "Pulling in the Welcome Mat, U. S. Government Moving to Cut Back Immigration from Mexico," *Agenda*, 2 (Winter 1973), 12–14; and U. S. House, Committee on the Judiciary, *Immigration and Nationality Act Amendments of 1973, Report No. 93–461 on H.R. 981, with additional views*, 93 Cong., 1 Sess. (1973), 1–49.